More Praise for
Liberation, Imagination, and the Black Panther Party

"I was the national organizer and chairman of the Black Panther Party when it catapulted into a dynamic resistance movement that drew thousands of members into
forty-five chapters across the country in less than four years, a time Huey Newton
mostly spent as a political prisoner. The essays collected here help clarify the way
we seized the time with revolutionary grass roots programs, broad coalition politics, and empowerment strategies. However, I think the work is incomplete since it
neglects to include our electoral campaigns, coalitions, and service programs in
the vision for revolutionary change. Understanding this legacy is significant—we
must continue the struggle for human liberation in this fast-paced, computerized,
globalizing, scientific social order and we need to create a broader paradigm of
revolutionary humanism."

—Bobby Seale, co-founder and former chairman,
Black Panther Party

More New Political Science Readers

After the Fall
1989 and the Future of Freedom
Edited by George Katsiaficas

Explorations in African Political Thought
Identity, Community, Ethics
Edited by Teodros Kiros
With a Preface by K. Anthony Appiah

Latino Social Movements
Edited by Rodolfo D. Torres and George Katsiaficas

The Politics of Cyberspace
Edited by Chris Toulouse and Timothy W. Luke

The Promise of Multiculturalism
Education and Autonomy in the 21st Century
Edited by George Katsiaficas and Teodros Kiros

Liberation, Imagination, and the Black Panther Party

A New Look at the Panthers and Their Legacy

*Edited by Kathleen Cleaver
and George Katsiaficas*

Routledge
New York • London

Published in 2001 by
Routledge
29 West 35th Street
New York, NY 10001

Published in Great Britain by
Routledge
11 New Fetter Lane
London EC4P 4EE

10 9 8 7 6 5 4 3

Library of Congress Cataloging-in-Publication Data

Liberation, imagination, and the Black Panther Party: a new look at the Panthers
and their legacy / edited by Kathleen Cleaver and George Katsiaficas.
     p. cm.
  Includes bibliographical references and index.
  ISBN 0-415-92783-8 — ISBN 0-415-92784-6 (pbk.)
     1. Black Panther Party. 2. Afro-Americans—Politics and government. 3. Black
power—United States. 4. United States—Race relations. I. Cleaver, Kathleen. II.
Katsiaficas, George N. [date]

E185.615.L4777 2001
322.4′2′0973—dc21

00-056026

Contents

Introduction

George Katsiaficas

Although we like to think in linear terms, history has its own cunning that carries us along strange and mysterious paths. Long-forgotten, "defeated" movements and their ideals sometimes emerge with a renewed popularity unpredictable only the blink of an eye before. Victors may define the history of an era in large type, but between the lines of the boldface script of textbooks or news programs, a better sense of the future may be gleaned from the margins.

This book gathers writings from the margins of the present to reconsider the historical impact of the Black Panther Party (BPP), the most significant revolutionary organization in the United States during the latter half of the twentieth century. Following in the footsteps of Charles Jones's pioneering work, *The Black Panther Party Reconsidered,*[1] our book also brings together scholars and activists to probe the history of the BPP. Silenced voices reach across the caverns of imprisonment or exile and speak with an eloquence forged by years of reflection, tempered by thousands of sacrifices. Some famous movement martyrs are known: Fred Hampton, Mark Clark, Bobby Hutton, John Huggins, Bunchy Carter (to name only a handful). For every one of them, dozens more whose names are forgotten also lost their lives while fighting for liberation during the 1960s and 1970s.

Compared with the Congress of Racial Equality (CORE) or the National Association for the Advancement of Colored People (NAACP), the sixteen-year existence of the Black Panther Party seems brief indeed. While its revolutionary period lasted for less than half its life, the Black Panther Party gave organizational expression to a tendency in the movement that long pre-dated the BPP: the idea that the entire system is corrupt and needs to be reconstructed. Dozens of groups dedicated to revolutionary change appeared in the United States during the 1960s, but the BPP was the only one able to develop a massive following and appeal to a broad constituency.

The Panthers' notoriety initially turned on their overt practice and explicit advocacy of armed self-defense. This dimension of the larger movement has systematically been deleted from history books and recollections of past struggles. Mississippi Freedom Summer of 1964, mythologized by sociologists and screenwriters alike for its nonviolent resistance to racist terrorism, contained a militant theme of quiet self-defense woven throughout its history. Our meticulously researched essay by Akinyele Umoja touches on that in his examination of the development of the Black Liberation Army. That dozens of films, award-winning books, and Hollywood scripts and intense media coverage could universally ignore, overlook, and distort this aspect of the resistance movement in Mississippi is itself worthy of study. No doubt such an analysis would reveal a great deal

---

[1]Charles Jones, *The Black Panther Party Reconsidered* (Baltimore: Black Classic Press, 1998).

about the ways that prevailing ideologies deform accounts of social movements, emphasizing superficial characteristics and ignoring deeper connections to broader historical currents, suppressing in fact movements' appeals, ideals, and actions. In portrayals of the Panthers trickling through the media gatekeepers and exhibited before millions of us in Hollywood accounts of the 1960s, militant actions are treated as episodic, whereby the fundamental break with the legitimacy and power of the established system that the Panthers represented is hidden from view.

As the Panthers' influence spread far beyond U.S. borders, they affected the entire global movement of the 1960s. A global awakening to the need for freedom shook the planet, and in at least six countries, organizations formed that modeled themselves on the BPP. For its part, the BPP drew inspiration from several African, Latin American, and Asian revolutions, particularly through the work of Frantz Fanon, Che Guevara, and Kwame Nkrumah. In their groundbreaking essay on the Black Panther Party's international impact, Michael Clemons and Charles Jones (chapter 2) joyfully recount many of the places where the BPP resonated with indigenous activists. In nearly every country in the world in 1968, movements pressed for revolution. From Vietnam and China in the east to India, Czechoslovakia, Senegal, Syria, Mexico, Brazil, and France, a globally united upsurge suddenly emerged—and everywhere the Panthers were intuitively (if not actually) tied into the fabric of feelings, images, and actions. Once again, most histories of this period neglect a critical dimension of the movements: the international bonds and global imagination—how we inspired each other and went far beyond the patriotism propagandized by every government. Love for each other as human beings was a palpable wave that rolled over the whole planet.[2] Nonetheless, the vast majority of histories in every country describe the 1960s as a *national* phenomenon.

In the United States, the archives of research libraries and availability of information surpass the intellectual resources of any country in history, yet studies here consistently ignore the movement's global character and our fundamental break in the late 1960s with the entire system. Written out of history books and largely ignored in most participants' narratives is the fact that from May to September 1970, the United States was in a prerevolutionary situation in which emergent revolutionary forces led by the BPP organized to transform totally the existing system. During this period, the largest strike in U.S. history occurred. Over 4 million students and half a million faculty on the campuses demanded an end to the war in Indochina as well as freedom and peace for imprisoned Panthers. The events in the United States from May to September 1970 were similar to the now-legendary French *événements* of 1968 in which a student revolt precipitated a strike of 10 million workers—creating a revolutionary situation. When the spiral of militant actions and massive resistance in the United States reached its apex in 1970, the consciousness-in-action of millions of people called for the abolition of the existing system and the creation of one based on justice and peace. In place of patriotism, millions of Americans acted according to norms of international solidarity; they rejected hierarchy and competition for equality and cooperation; racial division for solidarity; conformity and acquisition for free experimentation and altruism. People not only thought about revolution, they acted on their beliefs and convictions.

Recognizing this dynamic, the BPP called for a gathering of representatives of all radical constituencies in Philadelphia in September 1970 for a Revolutionary People's

---

[2]I develop the concept of the "eros effect" to describe the rapid spread and spontaneous emergence of social movements. See my book *The Imagination of the New Left: A Global Analysis of 1968* (Boston: South End Press, new printing 1998).

Constitutional Convention (RPCC), and the vision produced there by the popular movement went a long way toward reconceptualizing America. Although the police terrorized the Philadelphia Panthers and threatened to stop the convention, nearly 15,000 of us assembled to rewrite the Constitution. Led by the Panthers, an extraordinary alliance was forged, including the American Indian Movement (AIM), the Brown Berets, the Young Lords, I Wor Keun (an Asian-American revolutionary organization), women's liberation groups, former members of Students for a Democratic Society (SDS, which had a membership of well over 70,000 at its high point), and the newly formed Gay Liberation Front. As I discuss in chapter 10, "Organization and Movement: The Case of the Black Panther Party and the Revolutionary People's Constitutional Convention," the outline of a freer society is visible in the proposals from the workshops, and the energy and enthusiasm of the popular movement made the Panther program of 1966 appear to be quite modest.[3]

These were times when history accomplished more in days than in other years. In this volatile period Huey Newton was released from a three-year imprisonment; eighteen-year-olds were granted the right to vote; the Chicano moratorium was viciously attacked in Los Angeles; women called for a national strike, and the symbol for feminism was born; troops in Vietnam mutinied and sometimes killed their officers; and millions of Americans viewed themselves as revolutionaries and acted accordingly. The Army Math Research Center in Madison, Wisconsin where research used to capture and kill Che Guevara was conducted, was gutted by an explosion, and in California, Jonathan Jackson took over a courtroom, kidnapped a judge, and demanded the liberation of his brother before a volley of gunfire killed him and two prisoners who had joined him.[4]

The Panthers were intricately connected to all the events of this period. When a group of us who had been arrested at Boston University (and savagely beaten inside a Boston police station) were arraigned in court, my most vivid memory is of Eric Mann, a leader of the local Weathermen, grimly informing us during a break in court proceedings that Fred Hampton had been murdered earlier that morning. By April 1970, after Bobby Seale had been severed from the Chicago 8 conspiracy trial and taken to New Haven, where he faced murder charges and the death penalty, many of us felt nothing was more important in our lives than banding together with those whose lives were also dedicated to the movement.

These were extraordinary times. Hundreds, sometimes thousands, of Vietnamese were killed every day, and police repression in the United States, already murderous, threatened to become sanctioned by the judicial system. Something had to be done to save Bobby Seale. When a few of the Panthers asked two of us they knew from the Rosa Luxemburg chapter of Students for a Democratic Society (SDS) at MIT to speak for them at a movement meeting (since they rightfully felt that if they said what we were prepared to say, they would simply be arrested), we agreed. The April 15 antiwar moratorium, an event sure to draw tens of thousands of people, was nearly upon us, and we thought that a "white riot" for Bobby Seale was our best shot at saving his life. When my friend Peter Bohmer and I were introduced by the Panthers as brothers who had important things to say, we had everyone's rapt attention. Over the next few weeks, as a small group of us worked day and night to bring our project to fruition, the treatment we received at the hands of movement activists changed radically. As the date approached, some people became openly hostile to our project—to the point of throwing us out of the movement offices and effectively ostracizing us from any gatherings. The

---

[3]These documents and others are included at the end of this book.

[4]As Russell Shoats reminds us in chapter 9 in this book, Ruchell Magee, the only survivor, has spent nearly all of the intervening thirty years in the hole.

night before the action, a delegation arrived at our Cambridge apartment in a final attempt to forestall any violence. I alone refused to agree to call off the event, motivated among other things by my commitment to free Bobby Seale and my conviction that radical street actions were one of our few avenues to have an impact.

The next day, at least 100,000 people gathered on the Boston Common for the antiwar moratorium. The radical contingent there, noted by their red, yellow, and blue National Liberation Front (NLF) flags, began to gather as Abbie Hoffman's time to speak approached. I had spoken with Abbie hours earlier, and he agreed to help form the Bobby Seale Brigade out of the diverse participants in the rally. When his turn finally came, he gave a magnificent speech, probably enhanced by his being high on LSD. Pointing at the John Hancock Building, he screamed at the top of his lungs, "John Hancock wasn't a life insurance salesman. He was a revolutionary! Here we are in the cradle of liberty. Are you going to rock that cradle or are you going to cradle that rock?" The thunderous response left me assured that our action would succeed.

As the rally broke up, the Bobby Seale Brigade assembled on Beacon Street. First hundreds, then thousands of us made ready to march across the river to Cambridge, and "do more than march and shout." We had made elaborate preparations to march across the Longfellow Bridge and made sure the Cambridge police caught wind of them. As we began to march, rather than heading down Charles Street, however, we directed everyone to march down Beacon. I rode ahead on a motorcycle, checking for police roadblocks and activity. I rode back and forth, communicating with only two or three other people. As we turned the crowd over the Harvard bridge, it became apparent we were a huge gathering, since we completely filled the bridge where the Charles River Basin was at its widest. Busloads of Cambridge police dressed in riot gear were moving from the foot of the Longfellow Bridge to Central Square, where they were setting up a blockade. Quickly driving to the various projects and informing people there of the march and impending action at Harvard Square (to which they responded with boundless enthusiasm), I rode back to the march and roared through the crowd until I located a friendly attorney. With him on the back of my motorcycle, waving the permit gotten a week before, we rode ahead to the police line and convinced them we were a legal march and had no desire for a riot in Central Square. Miraculously, the police lines parted as the march approached, and we had made it to Harvard Square. The rest is history—the largest riot in the history of Cambridge, one that unfortunately resulted in many injuries and arrests, but one that also changed the fate of Bobby Seale. Before the end of the month, Kingman Brewster (president of Yale University, where protests were scheduled for May 1) offered his most famous opinion, one with far-reaching implications and effects: he was skeptical that a black revolutionary could get a fair trial in America.

Today, three decades later, ample grounds remain for such skepticism—as can personally be verified by Mumia Abu-Jamal, currently locked up on death row in Pennsylvania. As a seasoned member of the Black Panther Party in 1970, Abu-Jamal was one of the hosts and organizers of the RPCC. Unlike many 1960s activists, he continued to organize well into the 1980s, despite being continually targeted by the police. Convicted under highly dubious conditions in 1982 of killing a Philadelphia policeman, Abu-Jamal appealed for a new trial. The appeal was rejected by Albert Sabo, the same judge who had so arbitrarily presided over his trial. Sabo has sentenced more people to death (thirty-two—all but two of whom are racial minorities) than any other judge in the United States. From death row, Abu-Jamal has continued his work as an award-winning journalist and completed his master's degree. He has received so much support from around the world that all his mail cannot fit into the cell in which he lives. In chapter 3 we include a small portion of rich text he produced when he wrote his dissertation, "A Life in the Party: An Historical and Retrospective Examination of Projections and Legacies of the Black Panther Party." Abu-Jamal's firsthand account of Panther meetings and his humorous recollection of the times provide an invaluable sense of what it meant to be a Panther. Responding to author Hugh Pearson's one-sided attacks on the Panthers, he relates the experiences of female party members to illustrate the vacuous character of Pearson's position.[5] Using the examples of new Panther-style groups that have formed in the 1990s in Dallas, New York, and Los Angeles, Abu-Jamal traces a direct line from the original BPP to contemporary activism.

For decades, Kathleen Cleaver's remarkable life of courageous actions and intelligent choices has involved being on the defensive against government agencies. From the Free Huey campaign in 1967 to her life in exile with her former husband Eldridge Cleaver and her years working for the release of Geronimo ji Jaga, she has spoken countless times on behalf of imprisoned revolutionaries. She continues to intervene energetically on behalf of those victimized by police and judicial violence, as she relates in chapter 4, "Mobilizing for Mumia Abu-Jamal in Paris." Melding personal reminiscences and political history in a manner in which she is uniquely capable, Cleaver discusses the Mumia support movement in Paris, weaving into her narrative personal observations of contemporary dynamics among French activists.

The former defense minister of the Los Angeles Panthers, Geronimo ji Jaga, in chapter 5 presents his thoughts on the nature of the struggle. Imprisoned for twenty-seven years in California for a murder he did not commit, ji Jaga was offered parole if he would admit his involvement; he refused to submit and finally won a habeas petition that released him in 1997. The office of the Los Angeles district attorney has appealed the order releasing ji Jaga, and for his part ji Jaga has brought a civil action against the Los Angeles Police Department and the DA's office. Like Abu-Jamal, ji Jaga emphasizes the important roles played by female participants in the Panthers. Touching on a wide range of issues, ji Jaga argues strongly for the continuing importance of the BPP's demand for a UN plebiscite to determine the destiny of African Americans. True to Panther positions, he believes that "our enemy cannot be defined by race." For ji Jaga, "revolutionary love" should be the basis of the movement.

The hope and optimism of ji Jaga, Cleaver, and Abu-Jamal is a tribute to their humanity, which they sustained and enhanced despite the murderous repression meted out by the U.S. government. In an essay that gives for the first time a comprehensive overview of the brutality inflicted on the BPP by the FBI, Ward Churchill demonstrates in chapter 6 that the BPP was so massively assaulted that by the end of 1971, it was "effectively destroyed." With mammoth documentation, Churchill provides details of the assassination of Fred Hampton and the murder of twenty-seven other Panthers; the arbitrary arrest and persecution of hundreds of other BPP members; the FBI media campaign against the Party; the use of dozens of infiltrators; the neutralization of the Black Panther newspaper; the shutting down of Breakfast for Children programs; and the generation of negative publicity through circulation of rumors that Party leaders were anti-Semitic, embezzlers, or extortionists (depending on the audience). FBI counterintelligence programs undermined coalitions (as between the Panther and SNCC); exacerbated interorganizational tensions to the point of gunfire (as with the US organization); defamed and incapacitated key Panther supporters; coordinated military assaults on Panther headquarters around the country; and maliciously and falsely prosecuted leaders like Geronimo ji

---

[5]Hugh Pearson, *The Shadow of the Panther: Huey Newton and the Price of Black Power in America* (Reading, Mass.: Addison-Wesley, 1994).

Jaga, Bobby Seale, the New York 21, the Los Angeles 13, and so on. By the end of 1969, some thirty Panthers were in jail facing the death penalty; another forty were looking at life imprisonment; fifty-five were up on charges punishable by thirty years or more; and over 150 others have been forced underground. To complete the destruction of the BPP, the FBI fomented an internal split that tore the organization apart. Churchill's article is essential reading if we are to learn from history how to counter and offset government repression.

If not for the carefully orchestrated disintegration of the leadership of the Panthers, who knows where the revolutionary impetus they led could have taken us? Although it occurred some thirty years ago, little has been written about the split in the Panthers. For too long, the Newton-led Oakland Panthers, who used intimidation tactics when the abject flunkyism of Newton's followers failed to silence criticism, were assumed to be the "real" Panthers. Their version of the split—that Eldridge Cleaver's wackiness abetted the mindless advocates of armed struggle—was largely accepted without question. Don Cox, former BPP Field Marshal, now living in exile in France, in chapter 7 sets out some of his own observations of the split based upon his firsthand knowledge of this tragic chapter in the movement. Cox recounts for us murder and mayhem, not as grist for right-wing propaganda but as an appeal for sane and humane treatment of each other—and as a way of understanding how he, too, has been left alone to deal with the historical consequences of being part of a revolutionary movement. Anyone who has participated in such movements knows how quickly and loudly established voices are raised to denounce us, and how heavily we are called upon to struggle with the agony of defeats, recriminations, betrayals, and acts of sabotage. In the glare of media spotlight and police surveillance, it is nearly impossible to find a space where free discussions of our failures can occur.

This book attempts to unlock some of the doors that have concealed an accurate comprehension of history, as well as to respond to malicious critics. None of us sees the Black Panther Party as error-free. We acknowledge the need for a broader discussion of many of the issues raised here. Patronizing outsiders, looking at the history of the Panthers as concerned radicals, often paint the picture of female involvement in the Party as one of subservient members seeking to gain equality. Based upon her own experiences and unique insights, our coeditor Kathleen Cleaver offers a different reading in chapter 8, "Women, Power, and Revolution." She reveals for us a glimpse of the power of women in the Black movement. From Gloria Richardson to Assata Shakur, we can see a generation of women whose leading role is difficult to conceal—unless one falls victim to the mass media's portrayal of male spokesmen as indicative of substantive power.

Like ji Jaga, Russell Shoats has served decades in prison as a survivor of the often-overlooked wave of repression that rolled back the revolutionary tide sweeping the country (and the world) in 1970. Today he finds himself encased within the same prison as Mumia Abu-Jamal, serving a life sentence for a murder of a policeman at which he was not even present. Shoats's essay "Black Fighting Formations: Their Strengths, Weaknesses, and Potentialities" (chapter 9) is remarkable for its reconstruction of details from the past as well as for Shoats's ability to show how even the Panther leadership in Oakland refused to acknowledge and take responsible leadership of the revolutionary upsurge. As a result of the sea change that so rapidly eviscerated the movement, Shoats—as well as hundreds of others like him—was left hanging out to dry as the revolutionary momentum was arrested, fractured, and finally collapsed.

John McCartney's incisive essay (chapter 11) on the impact of the BPP on the radical movement of the Bahamas provides an empirical case study that validates Clemons and Jones's general analysis of the global importance of the Panthers. McCartney was himself involved in the Vanguard Party of the Bahamas. From his vantage point of participant and using his own keen analytical powers, he presents for us an example of how acting locally can be a global event.

Eldridge Cleaver sought refuge in Cuba in 1968, and Huey Newton spent years exiled there during the 1970s. In her well-researched analysis of the relationship between Cuba and the Black movement, Ruth Reitan furnishes us in chapter 12 with previously unrecounted details of the intricacies of the ebb and flows of Cuban hospitality and solidarity. From the outside, Cuba and the BPP are two sides of the same coin, but Reitan shows us how internal developments in the BPP and Cuban responses to changing international dynamics led to periods of more and less collaboration.

Anyone who remembers the Panthers and their weekly newspaper has images penned by Emory Douglas sketched somewhere in their cranial walls. We are pleased to present an analysis of Emory's art by Erika Doss (chapter 13). She is able to provide us with an understanding of the significance of art to the BPP as well as to demonstrate conclusively how much Emory's images were structured according to the precise beliefs of the Party.

Eternal Yippie Stew Albert graces our book with his Panther reminiscences from the San Francisco Bay Area (chapter 14). Identifying himself as the "official best white friend of the BPP," Albert pens fascinating accounts of his interactions with Eldridge, Huey, and Bobby. Framing the Panthers within the context of white radicals' own liberation movements, Albert draws the Peace and Freedom Party into the picture, and in so doing offers hilarious remembrances of inner movement antics as well as of bringing Huey to meet John Lennon and Yoko Ono in New York. Albert presents a very different side of Newton than the one generally seen.

As the BPP disintegrated, Newton became addicted to cocaine. Having long been vilified by both mainstream and movement writers. Newton's character was assassinated in Hugh Pearson's unbalanced and poorly researched book *Shadow of the Panther.* Understanding a man as complex and dynamic as Newton is no easy task, but Pearson glibly recasts Newton's bravery as thuggery and his genius as little more than enlightened criminality. In a thoughtful response to Pearson, Errol Henderson (chapter 15) patiently dissects his work and carefully notes the superficialities and inadequacies of his analysis. After taking Pearson to task for reducing Huey—and through him the entire BPP—to a caricature of reality, Henderson calls on us to understand better the character of Newton and the BPP in order to carry on the struggle.

In 1996, former Panther Lee Lew-Lee released a documentary about the destruction of the BPP entitled *All Power to the People.* Lew-Lee presents a great deal of previously undisclosed material on the use of infiltrators and the ultimate demise of the Party. His film grew out of his own experiences as a cameraman during the 1992 Los Angeles uprising, and after viewing it, Victor Wallis was inspired to assess the Panthers, as someone rediscovering them today (chapter 16).

Decades ago, local police departments and the FBI amassed huge files on the BPP, using them to fabricate charges against thousands of suspected Panthers and their supporters. While these materials are part of the public's repository of knowledge, accessing them is no easy task. Claudia Dahlerus and Christian Davenport in chapter 17 recount some of the firsthand difficulties they have encountered in doing empirical research on the BPP. Judging from the experiences of Dahlerus and Davenport, police willingness to provide access to information is sadly constrained by some of the same unjust and prejudicial attitudes that pervaded these same agencies years ago.

Although society today celebrates Malcolm X and Martin Luther King, Jr., dozens of activists from the movement remain unjustly imprisoned. In chapter 18,

"Remembering King's Assassination," written on January 17, 2000—when the holiday for King's birthday was observed and also the anniversary of the date when Bunchy Carter and John Huggins were gunned down by the Stiner brothers (FBI informants in the US organization)—Kathleen Cleaver demands a "full-scale, impartial investigation of all federal and state counterintelligence operations." Nothing less will do justice to those arbitrarily imprisoned, assassinated, and otherwise victimized by the forces of law and order. We call on our readers to heed her call (for which the Human Rights Research fund has been newly formed to implement).

In our concluding article, we include Scott Fleming's synopsis of the cases of Albert Woodfox, Robert King Wilkerson, and Herman Wallace (chapter 19). Known as the Angola 3, Woodfox, Wilkerson, and Wallace founded a chapter of the Black Panther Party at the Louisiana State Penitentiary at Angola in 1971. For their efforts, they have been punished with nearly twenty-seven years of continuous solitary confinement, convicted (and framed, the evidence suggests) of the 1972 killing of a prison guard. Building awareness of this case may be a small step in winning justice for the Angola 3 (and others like them), but we hope it—and this book—will become part of a renewed collective commitment to continue on the journey we all depend on for our freedom.

The previous publication of many of the articles in this book as a special issue of *New Political Science* gave Kathleen Cleaver and me a tremendous sense of accomplishment. Celebrating the appearance in print of long-suppressed voices, she remarked that she "hadn't ever expected to see this material in print." Over the past five years, it has been enormously edifying to work with her on this project. Her political acumen and patient ability to clarify even the most difficult issues are extraordinary gifts. For years I felt isolated when I contemplated many of the issues we discuss. As I have gotten to know many of our authors, new friendships and a renewed hope for the future have come into my life. Recent protests in Seattle against the World Trade Organization (at which I am happy to have been present) are one indication that history is shifting once again in the direction of a global upsurge against world structures of domination.

In its day, the BPP improvised and innovated, rapidly developing a new organization that inspired revolution globally. In the face of overwhelming force wielded by armed government agents, the Panthers struck back. A challenge of the next phase of struggles is to reveal those painfully learned lessons of the past to future activists who will attempt to transform existing social orders, neither unduly glorifying our accomplishments nor falsely deprecating them. History's rapid pace and humanity's density ensure that future insurgencies will experience wide fluctuations in popular support and activism. This book anticipates the future emergence of organizations with the temerity and vision of the BPP that will inspire and activate millions of people—and it is to their success that we dedicate it.

PART ONE

Revisiting the
Liberation Struggle

1

Repression Breeds Resistance

The Black Liberation Army
and the Radical Legacy of the
Black Panther Party

Akinyele Omowale Umoja

The Black Panther Party (BPP) was one of the most significant radical movements in American history. As an organized political organization, the BPP existed from 1966 to 1982. Many activists and scholars argue that the BPP only existed as a revolutionary organization from 1966 until 1971, in the initial period of its existence. In these years the BPP emphasized armed resistance as a primary means of achieving social change. After 1971, historians of the BPP argue, the organization dropped its revolutionary, pro-armed resistance agenda to pursue reformist politics.[1] For example, Charles Hopkins's study "The Deradicalization of the Black Panther Party" argues that governmental repression was a central factor in transforming of the organization from radicalism to reformism: "The result of the interaction between the Panthers and the government from 1966 through 1973, was the transformation of the Black Panther Party (BPP) from a black radical organization to a deradicalized social protest group."[2] While governmental repression led to the ascendancy of a reformist agenda for one faction of the BPP, this was not the only organizational response. Some BPP members committed themselves to involvement in or support of clandestine military resistance, which accelerated the development of the armed movement called the Black Liberation Army (BLA).

Some accounts of the Black Liberation Army argue that "the BLA grew out of the B.P.P. and its original founders were members of the Party."[3] The BLA is often presented as a result of the repression of the BPP and the split within the Panthers.[4] Other participants in the Black revolutionary movement give a different perspective to the BLA and its relationship to the Panthers. For example, former political prisoner and Black revolutionary Geronimo ji Jaga suggests that the BLA as a movement concept pre-dated and was broader than the BPP. Ji Jaga's perspective is that several Black revolutionary organizations contributed to the ranks of the Black underground collectively known as the Black Liberation Army.[5] Consistent with the view of ji Jaga, BPP and BLA member

The author would like to thank Kathleen Neal Cleaver, Nandi S. Crosby, Geronimo ji Jaga, Charles E. Jones, and George Katsiaficas for their helpful and supportive comments. He would also like to thank Che McGrath, Christopher Norman, and Shakeena Lowe for their assistance.

Assata Shakur asserts in her autobiography that "the Black Liberation Army was not a centralized, organized group with a common leadership and chain of command. Instead there were various organizations and collectives working together out of various cities, and in some larger cities there were often several groups working independently of each other."[6] Given the character of the BLA as a movement of autonomous clandestine units, one can understand the different interpretations of its origins and composition. While acknowledging the positions of ji Jaga and Shakur, this paper argues that the intense repression of the BPP did replenish the ranks of the Black Liberation Army. Since the BPP was the largest revolutionary nationalist organization of the Black liberation movement of the 1960s and '70s, its membership contributed greatly to the BLA. Panther participation in the BLA represented a continuation of the radical legacy of the BPP and was a response to the counterinsurgency strategy to destroy the Party and the Black liberation movement.

The role of the underground and the armed struggle was a critical issue in the split that occurred within the BPP in 1971. In the split, BPP chapters in Los Angeles and New York, the International Section of the Party, and other members were expelled by the national hierarchy led by Huey P. Newton. These factions of the BPP all supported armed resistance and viewed themselves, not the national hierarchy, as the sustainers of the revolutionary legacy of the BPP.

This study focuses on the influence of BPP members and supporters on the revolutionary armed movement, the Black Liberation Army. This aspect of the legacy of the BPP has not been emphasized in previous scholarly studies, an omission that reflects the willingness of scholars and popular accounts of the BPP to narrow its existence to the national leadership in Oakland. In the introduction to his recently published book *The Black Panther Party Reconsidered*, Charles E. Jones argues that the Oakland-based BPP existed sixteen years (1966–1982).[7] This study asserts that the activity of the radical faction of the BPP, in the guise of the BLA, lasted just as long as that of the Oakland-based Panthers, perhaps even longer, since it has current manifestations.

Scholarly research on the BLA is a challenging endeavor. Most books that focus on this organization have been journalistic or biographical.[8] The journalistic texts have primarily relied on police or prosecution records. American newspapers have also reported on BLA activities based upon information offered to the media to support police investigations and prosecutions of Black radicals.[9] The journalistic literature on the BLA is usually written from a perspective that is uncritical of American law enforcement and its counterinsurgency tactics. Since the BLA is a radical clandestine movement, its activities by their very nature are illegal, making it difficult for scholars to interview its members. Facts are often omitted from biographies and BLA statements to protect incarcerated or indicted members of the movement. The nature of the organization also does not provide the researcher with organizational archives. This study will utilize public documents of the BLA and other movement literature and statements and autobiographies from incarcerated BLA members, as well as from former BLA militants and supporters, as a balance to police and prosecutor-oriented literature and records.

The Black Underground and the Black Freedom Movement

A clandestine insurgent military force has existed in different periods of the Black freedom struggle in North America. The insurrections and attempted uprisings of enslaved Africans utilized secret, conspiratorial organizations. Insurgent Africans certainly could have brought with them a tradition of secret societies (e.g., Egungun, Oro, and Ogboni among the Yoruba peoples, Zangbeto in Dahomey, Poro in Sierra Leone). Conspiratorial networks were established to connect African fugitive communities with those on the plantation with the objective of creating a general uprising. Northern Blacks also created secret societies to aid the escape of fugitives and to plan for general insurrection.

In 1919, the African Blood Brotherhood (ABB) emerged as a radical Black secret society in American urban centers. The ABB advocated that Black people "organize in trade unions, build cooperatively owned businesses, and create paramilitary self-defense units."[10] The ABB dissolved as an organization in the late 1920s as its members decided to become the Black cadre of the American Communist Party.

In the 1950s and '60s, in several southern towns and rural locations, armed clandestine networks protected civil rights activists and activities, retaliated in response to acts of white supremacist violence, and served as an accountability force within the Black community during economic boycotts of white-owned business districts.[11] The secretive, paramilitary Deacons for Defense and Justice, considered by many to be the armed wing of the southern civil rights movement from 1965 through 1969, never identified the majority of its membership or revealed the size of its organization. Deacons selectively recruited, and its members understood that revealing organizational secrets could result in death.[12] In 1969 activists in the southern movement formed a clandestine paramilitary organization to retaliate against white supremacists who committed heinous acts of violence on southern Blacks.

The early 1960s saw the emergence of the Revolutionary Action Movement (RAM) as a radical clandestine organization within the Black liberation movement. RAM was initiated in 1962 by northern Black radicals who defined themselves as "revolutionary Black nationalists" seeking to organize an armed struggle to win national liberation for the "colonized Black nation" in the United States.[13] In 1963, due to political repression, the RAM cadre decided to "go underground." In 1964 RAM members involved in Student Nonviolent Coordinating Committee (SNCC) projects in the Mississippi Delta worked with SNCC field staff to develop armed self-defense units to defend the project. In the spring of 1964 RAM chairman Robert Williams, a political exile in Cuba, published an article titled "The USA: The Potential for a Minority Revolt." Williams stated that in order to be free, Black people "must prepare to wage an urban guerrilla war."[14] During the fall of the same year, RAM organizers presented a twelve-point program to Black youth at the National Afro-American Student Conference in Nashville, Tennessee, including "development of Liberation Army (Guerrilla Youth Force)."[15] The RAM cadre were active in urban guerrilla warfare during the urban uprisings occurring from 1965 through 1968.[16] In his work *Black Activism*, Black political scientist Robert Brisbane stated that RAM's objective was "to build a black liberation army consisting of local and regional groups held together under a tight chain of command."[17] In 1967 RAM began to organize Black urban youth into a paramilitary force called the Black Guards. A RAM document, titled "On Organization of Ghetto Youth" projected developing the Black Liberation Army: " In the early stages of the mobilization of Black ghetto youth we must prepare for the ultimate stage, a protracted war of national liberation; therefore the type of organization that must be established is a paramilitary organization."[18] This document referred to the paramilitary organization as the Black Liberation Army or BLA.[19] Due to intensive federal and state counterinsurgency campaigns, in 1968 RAM decided to disband the organization and function under other names, including the Black Liberation Party, Afrikan Peoples Party, and the House of Umoja.

The above-mentioned efforts preceded the 1971 split within the Black Panther Party and the subsequent identification of the BLA by state and federal police. While often omitted from the historiography of the Black freedom movement, the concept of armed struggle and a Black underground has a long history and is a legacy that would influence the early development of the Black Panther Party.

The Black Panther Party and the Black Underground

The question of the underground was a principal issue for the Black Panther Party from its inception. Prior to founding the Black Panther Party for Self-Defense with Huey Newton, Bobby Seale was a member of the Revolutionary Action Movement, but Seale did not share RAM's insistence on the revolutionary vanguard being clandestine. RAM preferred primarily to interact with the public through mass front organizations; RAM structure, membership, meetings, and other activities were secret.

While Seale and Newton disagreed with RAM's clandestine posture, the BPP organized an underground from its earliest days. By developing an underground wing, the BPP leadership prepared for the possibility that its political activities would not be allowed to function in the public arena. In this context, the BPP envisioned a clandestine guerrilla force that would serve as the vanguard of the revolution. In 1968 Newton stated, "When the people learn that it is no longer advantageous for them to resist by going into the streets in large numbers, and when they see the advantage in the activities of the guerrilla warfare method, they will quickly follow this example. . . . When the vanguard group destroys the machinery of the oppressor by dealing with him in small groups of three and four, and then escapes the might of the oppressor, the masses will be overjoyed and will adhere to this correct strategy."[20]

The Panther underground was not openly referred to or publicly acknowledged; it was decentralized, with autonomous cells in different cities that were referred to by different names at different times. Some large cities contained several autonomous units. These underground units were all part of a movement concept called the Black Liberation Army (BLA). The BLA was broader than the BPP, representing the underground military forces of the revolutionary nationalist Black movement.[21] By 1968 the official rules of the BPP stated "No party member can join any other army force other than the Black Liberation Army."[22] Besides serving as an urban guerrilla force, the Panther underground included an underground railroad to conceal comrades being sought by federal and state police. Clandestine medical units were also developed to provide care to BLA soldiers or Panther cadre wounded in combat.[23]

The Southern California chapter of the BPP had an underground almost from its inception. Former Los Angeles gang leader Alprentrice "Bunchy" Carter virtually brought a military force into the BPP when he joined in 1967. Carter was the leader of the Renegades, the hard core of the Slausons. In the early 1960s, the 5,000-strong Slausons were the largest street force in Los Angeles. The same social forces (the desegregation struggle in the South, African independence, other anticolonial struggles, and so on) that were politicizing tens of thousands in their generation began to radicalize members of the Slausons, including Carter. Many of the Slausons and other street force organizations engaged in guerrilla attacks on police and national guard during the Watts uprising of 1965. While incarcerated in the 1960s, Carter joined the Nation of Islam and was deeply influenced by former prisoner turned revolutionary Malcolm X. In Soledad State Prison in California, Carter met the radical intellectual inmate Eldridge Cleaver, who taught Soledad's African-American history and culture class. His associations and the changing political and cultural climate motivated Carter to adopt a revolutionary nationalist ideology. In Soledad, Cleaver and Carter made plans to form a revolutionary nationalist organization, including an underground military wing. Upon leaving prison, Bunchy Carter worked to transform loyal members of his street organizations, ex-inmates, and other Los Angeles street gangs from the gangster mentality to revolutionary consciousness. In late 1967, when Carter joined the BPP, he was also able to contribute an autonomous collective of radicalized street forces organized after leaving incarceration.[24]

In his role as southern California minister of defense, Carter made it his responsibility to organize an underground Panther cadre. Carter's most trusted comrades formed the southern California Panther underground, often referred to as the "Wolves." The true identities and activities of the Wolves were not revealed to aboveground rank-and-file Panthers. Carter's Wolves carried out secret operations to support the work of the BPP in Los Angeles.[25]

Probably the most significant recruit Bunchy Carter made to the BPP underground was Geronimo ji Jaga (then known as Geronimo Pratt). Ji Jaga, an ex-U.S. military special forces commando and Vietnam War veteran, was sent to Los Angeles to work with Bunchy Carter by a relative who had become acquainted with Carter's effort to build a Black freedom organization in Los Angeles. While he did not become an official BPP member, ji Jaga's military skills became a valuable asset in assisting Carter to develop the L.A. BPP underground. After Carter was murdered in an FBI-provoked clash between the BPP and the U.S. organization on the campus of UCLA in 1969, ji Jaga assumed Carter's position as southern California minister of defense. With national minister of defense Huey Newton incarcerated at this time, the national responsibility of organizing the military wing of the BPP also fell upon the shoulders of ji Jaga. Ji jaga saw it as his responsibility to utilize his military skills to develop the Panther underground and to build a cooperative relationship with other clandestine military forces in the Black liberation movement under the banner of the Black Liberation Army.[26]

After the assassination of Martin Luther King Jr. in 1968, the BPP grew rapidly, transforming itself from a California-based organization to a national movement with chapters in most American urban centers with a significant number of Black people. By 1969 the BPP had "approximately five thousand members in forty chapters."[27] In his role as acting minister of defense, ji Jaga helped to develop new chapters of the organization in places like Atlanta, Dallas, New Orleans, Memphis, and Winston Salem, North Carolina, among others. Along with aboveground units of the organization, ji Jaga played a significant role in developing the underground apparatus of the BPP nationally. Besides initiating new chapters, he visited existing party chapters to offer his expertise in establishing their clandestine cadre.[28]

One of the most significant chapters of the BPP to join after the rapid expansion of the BPP in 1968 was in New York City. As in Los Angeles, a clandestine force was established in the New York BPP virtually from its inception. By 1969 a New York police officer reported at federal congressional hearings that "members of the Black Panthers are not secret, with the exception of those who have been designated as 'underground.' This group are secret revolutionaries, and their identities are kept secret."[29]

One influence on the development of the Panther underground in New York was the Revolutionary Action Movement. After the assassination of Malcolm X, RAM played a significant role in promoting a revolutionary nationalist program in New York City. New York Panthers had a cooperative relationship with RAM, in contrast to the competitive and even antagonistic relations between RAM and Newton and Seale's BPP in northern California. Some New York City BPP recruits were affiliated with RAM or RAM front organizations prior to becoming Panthers, and many in the New York BPP cadre were influenced by RAM and Republic of New Afrika leader Herman Ferguson. Ferguson, a New York City educator, served as an inspirational leader and mentor to several New York City youth who eventually joined the BPP and became leaders in the New York chapter. RAM's perspectives on guerrilla warfare and underground organization may have influenced the development of a clandestine wing of the New York BPP.

On September 8, 1968, FBI Director J. Edgar Hoover designated the BPP as "the greatest threat to the internal security of the country."[30] Hoover's pronouncement signaled an intensified counterinsurgency campaign to destroy the BPP. In his study on police repression, Frank Donner classified 1969 as the "year of the Panther." That year alone, police conducted over thirteen raids on BPP offices across the United States.[31] Due to the counterinsurgency campaign waged by the U.S. government on the BPP, Donner states that by the end of 1969, "it was estimated 30 Panthers were facing capital punishment, 40 faced life in prison, 55 faced terms up to thirty years, and another 155 were in jail or being sought."[32] In December of 1969 predawn police raids on the BPP in Los Angeles and in Chicago (in which Fred Hampton and Mark Clark were murdered) are distinguished in terms of their impact on the national Black liberation movement.

The increased repression enhanced the importance of ji Jaga in the BPP. First, the increased repression made underground organization more necessary. Panthers who faced charges needed refuge in the clandestine network. Those wounded in battles with police often needed care from the underground medical cadre. Geronimo's status as a nationally known BPP leader was also well established after the vigilant defense of the primary office of BPP in Los Angeles. The Los Angeles BPP office, mainly staffed by teenagers, was able to survive a five-hour predawn police attack that included the use of SWAT forces and the detonation of a bomb on the Los Angeles Panther headquarters. While ji Jaga was not present during the raid, the preparations and militarily training provided by him were decisive to the survival of his comrades.[33] After the defense of the Los Angeles Panther headquarters, the *Black Panther* hailed ji Jaga as the "essence of a Panther."[34]

Upon his release from prison in 1970, Huey Newton inherited a national military force that had been primarily developed during his imprisonment. The military development of the BPP paralleled the tremendous increase in the size of the membership, the transition from a local organization to a national movement, and the recent national and international status of the BPP since the arrest and incarceration of Newton in October of 1967. While the BPP always envisioned an underground military wing to complement its underground activities, Newton was uncomfortable with the military development of the BPP. The rapidly expanded clandestine military wing of the BPP had been primarily organized by ji Jaga. While ji Jaga was trusted by other BPP leaders and rank-and-file cadres throughout North America, Newton became very insecure about his presence. Newton did not trust and did not include in his circle key Panther members he did not know prior to his incarceration in 1967.[35] In due time, government operatives and ambitious BPP members convinced Newton that ji Jaga was a threat to his leadership and the party. While the overwhelming repression of the BPP contributed to Newton's decision to move away from his original positions on armed struggle, his fear of ji Jaga and the developing BPP military apparatus must also be taken into consideration. Significantly, the cleavage between Newton and the BPP military played a central role in what has come to be known as the split in the Black Panther Party.[36]

The Panther Split and the Black Liberation Army

The question of armed struggle and the role of the underground were critical in the BPP split of 1971. It is an acknowledged fact that the divide-and-conquer tactics of the FBI were central to the division within the leadership and rank and file of the Party. The FBI and other government counterinsurgency forces played on internal tensions and developing ideological differences to encourage the BPP split. The influence of counterinsurgency efforts must be taken into account when examining the ideological tensions in the BPP. Operatives were instructed to manipulate ideological differences and exploit insecurities within the organization. These counterinsurgency efforts created an environment that made resolving internal contradictions within the BPP virtually impossible.

The major ideological conflict was over the question of armed struggle. Newton and Party Chief of Staff David Hilliard were perceived by radical forces in the Party as moving away from their original support for the development of an armed clandestine vanguard at the very moment when repression was forcing members of the Party underground. As early as 1969, the national leadership had initiated a policy to expel those members involved in "unauthorized" military and clandestine activity.[37] Simultaneously, the increased political repression of the Black liberation movement, and particularly the BPP, convinced many it was time to develop the underground vanguard. In the face of intense counterinsurgency campaign and court cases, many Panthers concluded it was better to struggle in clandestinity than spend years incarcerated. Panthers' lack of trust in receiving justice in American courts was well founded. In 1970, even Yale University president Kingman Brewster publicly questioned "the ability of Black revolutionaries to achieve a fair trial anywhere in the United States."[38] Due to the new policy of the BPP national hierarchy against clandestine activity, Panthers going underground to avoid state repression were placed in a precarious position.

The BPP split was the result of a series of "purges" of collectives and groups within the BPP, culminating with the expulsion of leading Central Committee members by Huey Newton. The turning point was the expulsion of Geronimo ji Jaga. In August of 1970, ji Jaga had gone underground to further develop the BLA. Based upon his assessment of the counterinsurgency assault on the Black liberation movement, ji Jaga concluded that the "establishment of guerrilla bases" was "an integral necessary part of the overall freedom movement." His strategy was to strengthen the revolutionary nationalist clandestine network in urban and rural areas throughout the United States, particularly in the historic Black belt in the Southeast.[39] Ji Jaga and his comrades Will Stanford, Will "Crutch" Holiday, and George Lloyd were arrested in Dallas, Texas on December 8, 1970. At another location in Dallas later the same day, BPP member Melvin "Cotton" Smith (later identified as a police informant) was also arrested. Smith had been sent to Dallas by Huey Newton and Elaine Brown to meet with ji Jaga. After the arrests, Newton was encouraged by members of his inner circle who were opposed to ji Jaga's influence and by secret operatives of governmental counterinsurgency campaigns to expel ji Jaga. In January of 1971 Newton publicly denounced ji Jaga, his wife Nsondi ji Jaga (Sandra Pratt), and their comrades and codefendants Stanford, Holiday, and Lloyd for exhibiting "counterrevolutionary behavior." A directive carrying Newton's name but written by Brown (at that time part of Newton's inner circle) stated, "Any Party member who attempts to aid them or communicate with them in any form or manner shall help to undermine and destroy the Black Panther Party." Newton's directive also implied ji Jaga was a government operative loyal to the CIA. Referring to ji Jaga's involvement in the U.S. Army's Special Forces prior to joining the Panthers, the Oakland BPP's leader concluded,"He is as dedicated to that Pig Agency as he was in Vietnam."[40] Needless to say, this attack caused major division and confusion in the BPP.

During the weeks following the suspension of ji Jaga, tensions increased between the New York chapter of the BPP and Newton and his followers, in part because of an intensive counterinsurgency campaign by the FBI. The tensions became public after an open letter from incarcerated leaders and members of the New York chapter (aka the Panther 21) to the Weather Underground, a white American left clandestine organization. The

"Weathermen" had engaged in bombing of political targets primarily concerning the Vietnam War and had officially recognized the BPP as the vanguard of the revolution in North America. The Panther 21 letter proclaimed the Weathermen as part of the vanguard of the revolutionary movement inside the United States while criticizing the national leadership of the BPP. In their letter of support to the Weather Underground, the Panther 21 stated, "We feel an unrighteous act has been done to you by the self proclaimed 'vanguard' parties by their obvious neglect in not openly supporting you. . . . But they have ignored us also. . . . these 'omnipotent' parties are throwing seeds of confusion, escapism, and have lost much of their momentum by bad tactics."[41] The Panther 21 sentiments reflected the views of many members who believed it was necessary to respond to state repression by strengthening the armed clandestine capacity of the BPP, not abandoning it. The incarcerated New York Panthers called for an underground guerrilla offensive because "racism, colonialism, sexism and all other pig 'isms' . . . can only be ended by revolution. . . . ARMED STRUGGLE."[42] They believed the Weather Underground was going in the direction that the BPP should take. For their open letter, the Panther 21 were expelled by the national leadership.[43] Remaining Panthers struggled to maintain peace in the BPP and negotiate between the national leadership in Oakland and the New York 21. Recognizing the confusion created by the expulsions of ji Jaga and the New York 21, the FBI determined to "more fully exploit" the ideological and factional differences in the BPP. On January 28, 1971, FBI offices in Boston, New York, San Francisco, and Los Angeles received the following message from headquarters: "The present chaotic situation within the BPP must be exploited and receipts must maintain a high level of counter-intelligence activity. You should each give this matter high priority attention and immediately furnish the Bureau recommendations . . . designated to further aggravate the dissension within BPP leadership."[44] It is important to note that the inability of BPP leadership to transcend their ideological differences was magnified through the divide-and-conquer tactics of a counterinsurgency campaign that manipulated the insecurities of key Panther leaders.

On February 13, 1971, New York Panthers Michael Tabor and Dhoruba Bin Wahad (aka Richard Moore) and Newton's personal secretary Connie Matthews were expelled after they went underground. Later that month, Panthers from northeastern chapters called a press conference in Harlem calling for the expulsion of Newton and Hilliard. The East Coast Panthers recognized BPP national leaders Eldridge Cleaver, Kathleen Cleaver, Donald Cox, and Bobby Seale as the legitimate national leadership of the BPP. At the time, the Cleavers and Cox were political exiles in Algeria, and Seale was incarcerated in Connecticut. New York would become the headquarters for this faction of the BPP.[45] After the split, the East Coast Black Panther Party became the aboveground apparatus of BPP members who joined the BLA. From their New York headquarters the East Coast BPP put out their newspaper *Right On!*, which became a public organ of the armed movement. Through the *Right On!* newspaper, instructions on guerrilla warfare, news about airline hijackings and other military actions were disseminated.

After the expulsions of ji Jaga and key members of the Los Angeles and New York Panthers, exiled BPP members in Algeria entered the fray. One critical objective of the U.S. government's counterinsurgency program was to create a split between Newton and Eldridge Cleaver, head of the International Section of the BPP.[46] The members of the International Section were deeply concerned about the expulsions of ji Jaga and the Panthers in Los Angeles and New York, believing these actions represented the ascendancy of authoritarian rule by Newton and Hilliard. Particularly after the expulsion of ji Jaga, Cleaver appealed to Newton and Hilliard from Algiers to no avail. The International Section was also concerned with the lack of support for BPP members and supporters engaged in acts of armed resistance.[47] On February 26, 1971, Newton arranged a telephone conversation with Cleaver on a San Francisco television show, intending to demonstrate the unity of the two most visible BPP leaders, in spite of the expulsions of Los Angeles and New York Panthers. At the end of the televised conversation, Cleaver called for the reinstatement of the expelled Panthers in New York and Los Angeles and the resignation of BPP Chief of Staff David Hilliard. After the television program, Newton called the BPP international office in Algiers and expelled the entire International Section. Supporting the sentiment of expelled Panthers in Los Angeles and New York, the International Section saw the radical elements of the organization as the "true" Black Panther Party, and criticized Hilliard and Newton because they had "consciously set about to destroy the underground." Given the repression of the BPP and the Black liberation movement, the exiled Panthers centered in Algeria believed it was "necessary . . . to advance the armed struggle. . . . We need a people's army and the Black Panther vanguard will bring that about."[48] The International Section and the BPP factions centered in New York and Los Angeles all aligned around a more radical pro-armed struggle position than did Newton and the Oakland-based BPP. The radical BPP no longer recognized Newton and the Oakland-based Panthers as a revolutionary organization but considered it an opportunist right-wing clique, the "Peralta street gang" (after the street where the Newton-led BPP was located in Oakland).[49]

Ignoring his previous position, Newton would blame the influence of Cleaver for the development of pro-armed struggle currents in the BPP. Newton argued that Cleaver's influence overemphasized the "gun" and moved the BPP into military action without the support of the community.[50] As Newton's Oakland-based leadership moved in a more reformist direction, some forces supporting the development of an underground military presence maintained loyalty to the Oakland-based BPP. Within the California prison system, BPP Field Marshal George Jackson attempted to transform incarcerated Black men into revolutionary soldiers. Jackson's published prison letters reveal his desire to develop a clandestine army to defend and complement the activity of the aboveground Black Panther Party under Newton's leadership. The murder of Jackson on August 21, 1971, and the disruption of his recruits by government forces would eliminate this potential clandestine army for the BPP.[51]

While they did not engage in revolutionary violence, Newton and his cohorts did see the need for a military group. In 1972 the Oakland-based BPP created a security force (aka "the squad") to protect its leadership. In time Newton would use the security force as his personal "goon squad" to maintain internal discipline and to pressure local enterprises to contribute to the BPP. Newton envisioned controlling legal and illegal activity in Oakland. While the BPP became involved in local electoral campaigns, the military elements loyal to Newton struggled for control of drugs and prostitution in Oakland. Increasingly, Newton's squad would be used for intimidation and criminal activity.[52]

In response to the development of the split within the BPP, U.S. government counterinsurgency operatives employed a carrot-and-stick strategy in dealing with both factions of the BPP. As the Oakland-based BPP moved in a more reformist direction, the harassment, government-sponsored military raids, and political internment subsided. Within four years the Oakland-based BPP, then under the leadership of Elaine Brown, would receive federal and foundation funding. In 1976 Brown served as a delegate to the National Democratic Convention.[53] Panther members and supporters associated with the radical BPP factions, however, found themselves under greater surveillance and harassment by federal and local police. As a result, the aboveground radical BPP factions were generally reduced to being defense committees for captured BLA comrades or as a support and propaganda mechanism for the underground. By 1975, within four years of the split, the radical factions had no visible aboveground presence.

Repression of the East Coast Panthers and the Black Panther Party

The BLA saw its purpose as to "defend Black people, to fight for Black people, and to organize Black people militarily, so they can defend themselves through a people's army and people's war."[54] Within the context of the Black community, the BLA waged a campaign to eliminate and sanction internal enemies, including thieves and drug peddlers.[55] In New York, the BLA initiated a campaign called "Deal with the Dealer" to make it "difficult" and "unhealthy" for drug peddlers to traffic in Black communities. BLA units would identify the "hangouts" of prominent drug merchants and drug-processing facilities and raid them. In some cases, drug dealers were physically attacked and even killed. Both Assata Shakur and H. Rap Brown (aka Jamil Al-Amin) were involved in trials related to Black underground attacks on drug activity in the Black community.[56]

BLA members also waged a "defensive/offensive" campaign against police. Between 1971 and 1973, nearly 1,000 Black people were killed by American police.[57] Of particular concern to the BLA were the murders of Black teenagers and children at the hands of police officers. These killings included sixteen-year-old Rita Lloyd in New Jersey as well as eleven-year-old Rickie Bolden and ten-year-old Clifford Glover in New York City. BLA members saw themselves coming to the defense of an oppressed and colonized people that were victims of a genocidal war. American police were seen as the occupation army of the colonized Black nation and the primary agents of Black genocide. So the BLA believed it had to "defend" Black people and the Black liberation movement in an offensive manner by using retaliatory violence against the agents of genocide in the Black community. In the two years after the BPP split, the U.S. government attributed the deaths of twenty police officers to the Black Liberation Army.[58]

In 1971 the BLA response to police repression and violence was bold and intense. On May 19, 1971 (the forty-sixth birthday of Malcolm X), the BLA claimed responsibility for the shooting of two New York police guarding the home of Frank Hogan, the New York district attorney in charge of prosecuting the New York Panther 21.[59] Two days later, two New York police officers were killed in an ambush by BLA members. BLA activity was not confined to New York. In August 1971 BLA soldiers carried out several actions in San Francisco, including an attack on two San Francisco police stations and one police car that resulted in the death of one police officer and the wounding of several others. These actions and others were in retaliation for the shooting death of incarcerated Black revolutionary and BPP Field Marshal George Jackson on August 21, 1971, and the FBI and Mississippi police raid on the headquarters of the Provisional Government of the Republic of New Afrika on August 18, 1971.[60] On November 3, 1971, police also suspected the BLA of shooting a police officer in Atlanta, Georgia. On December 21 of the same year, police accused BLA combatants of participation in a grenade attack on a police car in Atlanta, resulting in injuries to two police officers.[61]

In response to these and other actions claimed by the Black Liberation Army, the FBI initiated new counterinsurgency campaigns. One campaign in particular was "NEWKILL," organized to investigate New York police killings for which the BLA claimed responsibility or were suspected. NEWKILL would signal greater repression of East Coast Panthers and their associates, allies, and supporters. In an FBI memorandum concerning NEWKILL, J. Edgar Hoover stated, "The Newkill cases and others terrorist acts have demonstrated that in many instances those involved in these acts are individuals who cannot be identified as members of an extremist group. . . . They are frequently supporters, community workers, or people who hang around the headquarters of the extremist group or associate with members of the group."[62] As part of its campaign against the BLA, the FBI's domestic intelligence division (aka Division Five) ordered its field officers to detain East Coast Panthers and other Black revolutionaries and to document the identities of "supporters and affiliates of these groups with your file numbers on each. . . . If you have no file, open files."[63] The selected targeting of East Coast Panthers and affiliated radical organizations and supporters forced even more Black revolutionaries underground.

The FBI and local police also initiated a national search-and-destroy mission for suspected BLA members, collaborating in stakeouts that were the products of intensive political repression and counterintelligence campaigns like NEWKILL. On May 3, 1973, BLA members Zayd Shakur, Sundiata Acoli (Clark Squire), and Assata Shakur (Joanne Chesimard) were stopped by New Jersey police on the New Jersey Turnpike. A shootout ensued, and when the smoke cleared, one of the police officers and Zayd Shakur were dead, and Assata Shakur was severely wounded. After a "massive manhunt," Acoli was captured days later in New Brunswick, New Jersey.[64] Police hailed the capture of Assata Shakur, calling her the "black Joan of Arc" and the "high priestess" and "the soul" of the "cop-hating BLA." The FBI and the New York and New Jersey police attempted to tie Assata to every suspected action of the BLA involving a woman.[65] Shakur and her legal defense were able to win acquittals on all charges for incidents prior to the shootout on the New Jersey Turnpike. Shakur and Acoli were both convicted by all-white juries (in separate trials) for the murder of the New Jersey state trooper and of Zayd Shakur, and sentenced by New Jersey judges to life plus thirty years. No evidence was ever presented to confirm that Assata ever fired or handled a weapon during the 1973 shootout. Indeed, evidence was presented proving she was shot twice in the back while her hands were up in the air in a position of surrender.[66]

On November 14, 1973, BLA member Twyman Meyers was ambushed by a joint force of FBI agents and New York police in the Bronx. As Meyers was leaving a Bronx apartment, he was surrounded by dozens of police. Meyers responded with gunfire, and a firefight ensued between the twenty-three-year-old Black revolutionary and the New York police and FBI. According to witnesses, Meyers ran out of ammunition and was then killed by police.[67] With the death of Meyers, New York Police Commissioner Donald Cawley announced that the campaign of the FBI and local police had "broken the back" of the Black Liberation Army. Between 1971 and 1973, police claimed responsibility for the deaths of seven suspected BLA members and the capture of eighteen others believed to be "key figures in the movement."[68]

Ideology and Consolidation

In the face of the capture and murder of its comrades, the BLA had to reevaluate its position. A BLA communiqué issued in 1975 details the deaths and capture of BLA combatants from 1971 to 1975.

> *With the deaths of Woody and Kimu we launched assaults against the police that set them on edge; their counter-attack saw us at the end of 1973 with four dead, over twenty comrades imprisoned in New York alone. In New Orleans, Los Angeles, and Georgia, B.L.A. members were taken prisoner by Federal agents working with local police to crush the B.L.A. 1974 found the guns of the B.L.A. quiet until April, when with so many comrades imprisoned we assaulted the Tombs in an effort to liberate some comrades; the attempt was unsuccessful; and two weeks later found three more comrades captured in*

Connecticut. While our ranks outside were being diminished, our ranks inside started to grow. Within the prisons themselves comrades launched numerous assaults and attempt escapes on a regular basis. Before 74 was over, another comrade was shot and captured, victim of an informant. Now in the third month of 1975 we have one dead, two captured in Virginia, and another escape attempt in New York.[69]

The above quote was part of an assessment done in 1975 by captured BLA militants, titled "Looking Back," in which the BLA reviewed its successes and defeats. Part of their assessment was that "we [the BLA] lacked a strong ideological base and political base." In spite of its losses, BLA members decided to assert themselves as a political force. In the same year, incarcerated BLA members and some of their supporters on the streets attempted to consolidate the ranks of the movement under a central command, the BLA Coordinating Committee (BLA-CC). "Get Organized and Consolidate to Liberate" was among the primary slogans of the BLA-CC, which published and distributed the political document "A Message to the Black Movement" to win support for the concept of armed struggle and expand its political base.[70] The BLA-CC also began to circulate a newsletter within the penitentiaries and movement circles to create dialogue and ideological unity within the BLA.[71]

Some BLA members began to unite with the political objective of the Provisional Government of the Republic of New Afrika (PGRNA). (The RNA was a movement initiated by 500 Black nationalists at the Black Government Conference in Detroit in March 1968. The participants in this conference declared their independence from the U.S. government and called for a Black nation-state to be formed in the southern states of Mississippi, Louisiana, Alabama, Georgia, and South Carolina. This new nation state would be called New Afrika.)[72] The New York branch of the PGRNA and the radical New York chapter of the BPP developed a close working relationship that included selling each other's newspapers and jointly organizing forums and rallies, particularly around the issue of political prisoners.[73] Some New York Panthers began to identify themselves as citizens of the Republic of New Afrika and pledged their loyalty to the PGRNA. Captured Black Liberation Army members also began to support the New Afrikan independence movement. In January 1975, two captured BLA members declared they were citizens of the RNA and that American courts had no jurisdiction over them. Their positions and the statements of others represented a clear ideological trend developing within the ranks of BLA fighters.[74]

The adoption of a nationalist perspective by BPP members who joined the BLA should not come as a surprise. Besides the role of the underground and armed struggle, another underlying ideological issue in the BPP split was the issue of nationalism. At its inception, the BPP described its ideology as revolutionary nationalism. The BPP saw people of African descent in the United States as a colonized nation. In 1968, the BPP demanded a United Nations supervised plebiscite to determine the political destiny of the colonized Black nation. One cause of tension between the New York BPP chapter and the national leadership based in Oakland was the issue of nationalism. As noted earlier, the Oakland-based leadership had a history of conflict with nationalist organizations, like RAM, while the New York BPP enjoyed cooperative working relationships with Black nationalists. After leaving prison in 1970, Newton began to distance himself from the plebiscite demand. In his philosophy of intercommunalism, articulated in early 1971, Newton argued that nations and struggles for national self-determination were no longer relevant.[75] Many Panthers in New York disagreed with Newton's ideological shift away from Black nationalism.[76] New York Panther Assata Shakur commented, "Politically, I was not at all happy with the direction of the Party. Huey went on a nationwide tour advocating his new theory of intercommunality. The essence of his theory was that imperialism had reached a degree that sovereign borders were no longer recognized and the oppressed nations no longer existed, only oppressed communities. The only problem was that somebody forgot to tell oppressed communities that they were no longer nations. Even worse, almost no one understood Huey's long speeches on intercommunalism."[77] After the split, New York Panthers and Panthers in the BLA maintained their radical nationalist viewpoints. For many BPP and BLA members, support for the objective of an independent Republic of New Afrika was a logical conclusion.

The BLA Is Not Dead: The Liberation of Assata

On November 2, 1979, members of the BLA conducted an armed action at Clinton Correctional Institution for Women in New Jersey, resulting in the escape of Assata Shakur. Prison authorities described the action as "well planned and arranged."[78] Three days later on Black Solidarity Day in New York, a demonstration of 5,000 marched from Harlem to the United Nations Building under the slogan of "Human Rights and Self-Determination for the Black Nation." Hundreds of the marchers carried signs stating,"Assata Shakur Is Welcome Here." At the rally that day, blocks away from the United Nations Building, a statement was read from the BLA: "Comrade-Sister Assata Shakur was freed from racist captivity in anticipation of Black Solidarity Day, November 5th, . . . in order to express to the world the need to Free All Black Prisoners is of fundamental importance to protection of Black Human Rights in general. . . . In freeing Comrade-Sister Assata we have made it clear that such treatment and the criminal 'guilt' or innocence of a Black freedom fighter is irrelevant when measured by our people's history of struggle against racist domination."[79]

A statement written by Assata a few days prior to her liberation from the Clinton state prison was also circulated at the rally. Assata's statement condemned U.S. prison conditions and called for freedom for political prisoners, support for human rights and an independent New Afrikan nation-state.[80] Despite the boasts of the FBI and police of "breaking the back" of the BLA six years prior, the BLA had certainly achieved a victory; one of its most sought after and well known members had escaped captivity through the actions of her comrades. Despite the casualties suffered from 1971 to 1975, the BLA was not dead.

Assata's liberation was hailed by the activist and progressive elements in the national Black community as a heroic event. In December of 1979 the *Amsterdam News*, a New York–based, Black-owned newspaper, published an article,"Run Hard Sister, Run Hard," by the Reverend Herbert Daughtry, the leader of the National Black United Front. Daughtry applauded the BLA soldiers who participated in the freeing of their sister comrade, stating, "They say three brave brothers and a sister went to fetch Assata from the cold confines . . . where she had been held fast against her will. . . . Who the four were, I do know not. But, every Black person knows them and have met them in the collective unconscious mind of the race. Their heroic deed will be told and retold around a million years to come . . .where Black people gather to reminisce about heroes and heroines, great acts of courage and daring deeds, their exploits will be remembered."[81] In January 1980, supporters of Shakur also placed a half-page advertisement in the *Amsterdam News* proclaiming support for the fugitive Black revolutionary. The ad, entitled "Peace to Assata Shakur (aka Joanne Chesimard)," urged Shakur to "stay strong and free" and offered her moral support.[82]

The liberation of Assata also led to a renewed campaign of repression by federal and state police agencies. One week after the liberation of Assata, a joint FBI and New York police force raided the home of New York Panther Sekou Hill, a friend of Shakur, who was arrested and held without bond for three weeks. Evidence produced at Hill's bail hearing proved that he was in Brooklyn at the time of Assata's escape. Hill was released, and eventually charges were dropped.[83]

On April 19, 1980, fifty armed federal agents engaged in a predawn raid of a Harlem apartment complex. Police ransacked the homes of residents in an apparent search for Shakur. Without warrants, police forced their way into residences, breaking down doors, detaining residents, and searching through personal items. One resident, Ebun Adelona, a doctoral student at Columbia University, was awakened by police, with guns pointing in her face, and forced into the hallway of the complex. The police "suspected" that Adelona was Shakur. In the hallway, federal agents demanded she raise up her nightgown so they could search her body for gun shot wounds.[84] In the summer of 1980, federal agents and local police maintained intense surveillance of a Brooklyn community center called "the Armory," which housed several grassroots programs including Uhuru Sasa (Kiswahili for Freedom Now) school, one of the premier black nationalist freedom schools in the United States. Due to its long history and community support, police officials were hesitant about raiding the Armory.[85] To collaborate more efficiently, the FBI and New York police decided to form the Joint Terrorist Task Force (JTTF), which would serve as the coordinating body in the search for Assata and the renewed campaign to smash the BLA.[86]

In the midst of the JTTF campaign to capture Assata, during November 1980, the hunted BLA soldier herself released a taped message from clandestinity. This message was played at community programs and grassroots public affairs radio shows across the United States. Titled "From Somewhere in the World," it detailed acts of white supremacist violence that had occurred in the United States in 1979 and 1980. Due to those acts of violence, Assata concluded, Our backs are up against the wall and more than any time of our history . . . of being captives in America, we need an army . . . to defend ourselves and to fight for our liberation."[87] She also thanked "the many sisters and brothers who have opened their doors" to her after her liberation from captivity. She described those who offered refuge to her as part of the "underground railroad."[88]

In response to the new wave of repression, Black activists organized a campaign to challenge the JTTF's counterinsurgency efforts and win support for the Black underground, particularly for Assata Shakur. On July 18, 1981, the National Committee to Honor New Afrikan Freedom Fighters mobilized 1,000 people for the first New Afrikan Freedom Fighters Day, to honor Assata Shakur and the Black Liberation Army.[89] Throughout Black sections of New York, "Assata Shakur is Welcome Here" posters were plastered in visible outdoor spaces and hung in homes.[90]

The Revitalization of the Armed Struggle

On October 20, 1981, an incident occurred that would eventually reveal that there had been a significant resurgence of BLA activity within four years of police claims of the revolutionary organization's demise. Three white revolutionaries—Judy Clark, David Gilbert, and Kathy Boudin—and one Black man with radical associations, Solomon Brown, were arrested in the aftermath of an attempted holdup of a Brinks armored truck and a subsequent shootout at a police roadblock in Rockland County, New York. Several Black men escaped the scene of the shootout. The holdup and shootout resulted in the death of one Brinks guard and two police officers.[91] The JTTF immediately followed a trail of physical evidence that led them to members of the Black underground. On October 23, 1981, in the Queens section of New York City, police pursued two Black men they suspected of being involved in the Rockland holdup. A shootout between the police and the Black men ensued, resulting in the death of one of the men, Mtayari Shabaka Sundiata, and the capture of the other, Sekou Odinga. Odinga, the former Bronx BPP section leader, had been a fugitive since January 1969 on charges related to the New York Panther 21 case. After his capture, Odinga was taken to a police precinct where he was tortured to extract information from him concerning the Black underground and the whereabouts of Assata Shakur. Police beat and kicked Odinga, burned his body with cigars, removed toenails from his body, and forced his head into a toilet bowl full of urine, repeatedly flushing the toilet. Throughout the torture, Odinga defiantly remained silent. As a result of this brutality, Odinga's pancreas was severely damaged, and the Black revolutionary had to be fed intravenously for three months.[92]

In the days, weeks, and months following Odinga's capture several others, including many former members of Panther chapters, were arrested by the JTTF, and others were forced underground. By the end of November 1982, several members of the New York Panther chapters, including Kuwasi Balagoon, Abdul Majid, Jamal Joseph, Bilal Sunni Ali, and New Jersey Panther Basheer Hameed, were all captured and charged with acts linked either to the events on October 20, 1981, in Rockland County or to other expropriations and suspected BLA activity. Members of the Provisional Government of the Republic of New Afrika, including Mutulu Shakur, Nehanda Abiodun, and Fulani Sunni Ali were also charged with acts related to BLA activity.[93] Abiodun was forced underground and surfaced in Cuba in 1994. The Cuban government granted Abiodun political asylum. Criminal charges were dropped against Fulani Sunni Ali when it was proved she was in New Orleans during the October 20, 1981, incident in Rockland. Even after being cleared of criminal charges, Sunni Ali and several others were interned in a federal prison for refusing to testify to a federal grand jury investigating their friends and comrades in the movement.[94] Besides Clark, Gilbert, and Boudin, other whites were subsequently arrested and charged, including Silvia Baraldini and Marilyn Buck. Baraldini, an Italian national, was active in solidarity efforts among white anti-imperialists with the New Afrikan and Puerto Rican movements.[95] Buck had been underground since 1977, and she was charged and convicted of purchasing ammunition for BLA members.[96] Many other white anti-imperialists were also interned by the federal grand jury for refusing to testify against the BLA and the New Afrikan and anti-imperialist movement.

On November 5, 1981, members of the Black Liberation Army issued a communiqué to put into political context the events in Rockland County and the subsequent arrests. The October 20, 1981, holdup was described as an "expropriation," the seizure of property by political or military forces.[97] One BLA member defined expropriation as "when an oppressed person or political person moves to take back some of the wealth that's been exploited from him or taken from them."[98] The BLA communiqué stated that the attempted expropriation was the responsibility of the Revolutionary Armed Task Force (RATF), a "strategic alliance . . . under the leadership of the Black Liberation Army" of "Black Freedom Fighters and North American [white] Anti-Imperialists."[99] The whites in the RATF not only participated in armed actions but infiltrated right-wing and white supremacist organizations to gain information for the BLA.[100] This alliance was racially diverse and politically diverse; the RATF included underground fighters who identified themselves as revolutionary nationalist, Muslim, anarchist, or communist under the leadership of clandestine forces from the New Afrikan Independence Movement (NAIM).[101] This ideologically diverse alliance came together in response to an escalation of acts of white supremacist violence in the United States during the late 1970s and early 1980s, including the murders of Black children in Atlanta and of Black women in Boston, the shooting of four Black women in Alabama, and the acceleration of paramilitary activity by the Ku Klux Klan and other white supremacist organizations. According to the communiqué, the RATF initiated a "decentralized intelligence strategy" to establish the strength and capability of white supremacist paramilitary forces and their networks, which extended into the U.S. military as well as federal, state, and local police forces. The RATF believed this white supremacist upsurge was connected to right-wing and profascist financial and political elites. Through expropriations from American capitalist financial institutions, the RATF hoped to acquire the resources needed to support a resistance movement to oppose the right-wing, white supremacist upsurge; they planned to "accumulate millions of dollars under the political control of . . . revolutionary elements" to establish self-defense units and community cultural, health, and educational institutions in Black communities throughout the United States. Due to the political character of the actions of the RATF, the communiqué stated, "the comrades who are in jail are not criminals. They are Prisoners of War. . . . They are heroes struggling against RACISM, FASCISM, AND IMPERIALISM."[102] Supporters of the defendants in these cases argued that proceeds from the expropriations were being used for "the maintenance of the Army and certain other causes." These causes included grassroots youth and, community health programs and political mobilizations. Movement literature also stated that proceeds were contributed to African liberation movements, particularly the struggle against settler colonial rule in Zimbabwe.[103]

The JTTF and federal prosecutors determined that the Rockland County incident was one of several expropriations by the BLA and its white allies from 1976 until December 1981. Besides bringing New York State criminal charges related to the RATF expropriation in Rockland County, federal prosecutors charged several captured revolutionaries and political activists with RICO (Racketeer-Influenced Corrupt Organization) act conspiracy charges originally designed for the Mafia and other criminal organizations. Charges related to the liberation of Assata Shakur and the providing of refuge to BLA and the RATF were also linked to RICO conspiracy charges.

While not pleading guilty to participation in any particular act, in their legal defense, Sekou Odinga and Mutulu Shakur (in two separate trials) argued that the acts of the BLA and RATF, including expropriations and the liberating of Assata Shakur, were political acts, not criminal offenses. Since the BLA units involved in the RATF were committed to fighting for an independent New Afrikan nation, Odinga and Shakur argued these acts were actions of a national liberation movement. The two New Afrikan liberation fighters and their legal defense teams argued that under international law, these actions of combatants of a national liberation movement should be tried by an international tribunal, not by domestic criminal courts.[104]

The investigations of the JTTF led to three separate trials. Balagoon, Clark, Boudin, and Gilbert were convicted by a Rockland County jury on murder and armed robbery charges for the October 20, 1981, expropriation by the RATF. Federal prosecutors held two federal RICO conspiracy trials. In the first, the defendants were charged with twenty-eight counts of criminal conduct. After a five-month trial, a jury of eight Blacks and four whites returned not guilty verdicts on twenty-two of the twenty-eight counts. Bilal Sunni Ali was acquitted of all charges in the RICO conspiracy case. In the same case, Joseph and former PGRNA worker Chui Ferguson were acquitted of racketeering conspiracy, murder, and robbery charges but convicted of acting as assessories, and Odinga and Baraldini were acquitted of robbery and murder but convicted of racketeering and racketeering conspiracy. Federal judge Kevin Duffy sentenced Odinga and Baraldini to forty-year terms.[105] In the second RICO trial, Marilyn Buck and Mutulu Shakur, captured in 1985 and 1986 respectively, were convicted of federal racketeering conspiracy, murder, and armed robbery. New York federal judge Charles Haight sentenced Buck and Shakur to fifty and sixty years respectively.[106]

While federal prosecutors acknowledged Odinga was not a part of the events in Rockland County, they viewed the Black revolutionary as the leader of the BLA units responsible for organizing the RATF. Odinga, who escaped a police raid attempting to capture him in 1969, was granted political asylum by the Algerian government in 1970 and served as a member of the International Section of the BPP. Federal investigators estimate Odinga reentered the United States around 1973. A profile on Odinga in movement literature asserts, "In the mid-1970's, Sekou returned to the U.S. to organize . . . and help to build the Black Liberation Army."[107] During the period when federal and local police believed they had destroyed the BLA, Odinga and other Black revolutionaries rebuilt the organization's capacity as an effective radical underground network. The focus of the "revitalized" BLA units during this period (from 1976 until 1981) was different from that during the post-BPP split period (1971 to 1975); in the first period, it seemed to be on retaliation against police, the occupying army of the colonized nation, while in the second period, it seemed to be the development of the infrastructure of the armed clandestine movement and support for aboveground institutions, organizing, and mobilization.

The BLA and the Legacy of the Black Panther Party: The Struggle Continues

The BPP participation in the BLA clearly shows multiple responses to repression by Party leaders and rank-and-file membership. The Oakland-based BPP led by Huey Newton determined that it was necessary to subordinate BPP's association with armed struggle and emphasize community service programs and participation in the electoral arena. Other BPP factions believed that due to the intense repression against the BPP and the Black liberation movement, it was necessary to go underground and resist from clandestinity through the vehicle of the BLA. Possibly the most important issue was not whether the BPP emphasized a reformist or radical agenda in response to counterinsurgency, but its inability to maintain its organizational unity and cohesiveness in the face of repression.

After the split in the BPP, several BPP members joined the ranks of the BLA. While the BLA may have pre-dated the BPP, the influence of the BPP on its ranks cannot be denied. Party members who went underground saw themselves continuing the revolutionary agenda of the BPP from clandestinity. The radical expression of the BPP through the BLA has a history as long as the Oakland-based BPP, if not longer. Scholars of the BPP argue that its organizational expression continued until June 1982, the year its last program in Oakland, the Oakland Community School, closed. According to the JTTF, the last *known* action of Panthers involved in the BLA was in December 1981, six months prior to the closing of the Oakland Community School. Even in captivity, captured BLA members continue to forward political agendas consistent with their involvement in the BPP. For example, in November 1993, former BPP members and associates, including Jalil Muntaqim, Sekou Odinga, Sundiata Acoli, Geronimo ji Jaga, and Mutulu Shakur made a call to revolutionary nationalist organizations, collectives, and individuals to form a New Afrikan Liberation Front.[108] After months of dialogue and debate, inspired by the call of the prisoners, seven revolutionary organizations united to form the New Afrikan Liberation Front (NALF).[109] In 1997, from prison, former Panther and BLA member Jalil Muntaqim made a call for "Jericho 98," a march and rally demanding amnesty for political prisoners in the United States.[110] On March 27, 1998, the NALF and the PGRNA sponsored Jericho 98, mobilizing 5,000 people, the largest demonstration in the United States for the freedom of political prisoners. Despite incarceration, death, and exile, the revolutionary legacy of the Black Panther Party and Black Liberation Army continues.

2

Global Solidarity

The Black Panther Party in the International Arena

Michael L. Clemons and Charles E. Jones

The centrality of eradicating legal racial discrimination in the African-American freedom struggle partially accounts for a decidedly domestic focus in the systematic examination of African-American politics. As Hanes Walton has noted, "Few words by political behavioralists on international politics have ever included, in any fashion, black groups and individuals as forces and actors."[1] Unfortunately, students of politics tend to equate the lack of African Americans in formal positions of authority in the foreign affairs apparatus with apathy by the Black community toward global issues, an oversight further compounded by concentration on the nation-state in the study of international relations. Therefore, the full extent of African-American participation in global affairs is often overlooked. The emigrationist societies formed during the late 1700s to return to Africa reflect early Black interest in international affairs. Emigrationist ventures undertaken by Paul Cuffee, Martin Delany, and Bishop Henry Turner continued throughout the 1800s. Also during this century, the propaganda techniques employed in England by Frederick Douglass and Ida B. Wells-Barnett attest to the historical importance that African-American leaders placed on the international arena. The activities of early Pan-Africanists such as W. E. B. Du Bois, Anna Julia Cooper, and Marcus Garvey, echoed by latter-day Black Power advocates (1965–1975), allude to the continuity of African-American global interest. Similarly, Malcolm X placed the African-American freedom movement in an international context as evidenced by his meeting with the Organization of African Unity (OAU). In addition, Student Nonviolent Coordinating Committee (SNCC) activists' opposition to the Vietnam War and their various global forays reflected a concern about international politics that pervaded the Black Power movement.[2]

During the post-civil-rights era, Congressional Black Caucus (CBC) members utilized the formal levers of legislative power to address Black foreign policy interests. The CBC proved to be instrumental in mobilizing congressional opposition to apartheid in South Africa. Outside the corridors of Congress in 1978, Randall Robinson formed TransAfrica, the premier African-American foreign affairs interest group. At the individual level, Black activists have exercised citizen diplomacy. Jesse Jackson's successful negotiations with the Syrian government in 1984, resulting in the release of Lieutenant Robert Goodman, represents one prominent example of African-American citizen involvement in foreign affairs.[3] In short, African-American internationalism has been an integral aspect of the struggle for Black equality. Consequently, to restrict Black political participation to the confines of the American borders limits an understanding of the global initiatives, linkages, and accomplishments of African-American actors. This shortcoming is particularly apparent in the case of the Black Panther Party (BPP). An important, yet often ignored, aspect of the legacy of the Black Panther Party has been its international dimensions and global role in the New Left activism of the late 1960s.

As one of the prominent organizations of the Black Power era, the BPP distinguished itself by galvanizing progressive activists throughout the world. The Black Panther Party enjoyed immense international stature. In a mere four-year span, the Panthers grew from a local Oakland-based self-defense group to a global organization with an international section in Algiers, Algeria. International Panther solidarity committees mobilized financial support and public opinion on behalf of the BPP. Party members were treated as foreign dignitaries by the world's socialist nations. On several occasions, Black Panthers received political asylum from sympathetic foreign governments. Moreover, "Panther activism served as a revolutionary exemplar for various oppressed indigenous groups in several foreign countries."[4]

This essay seeks to illuminate the international character of the Black Panther Party. We examine the BPP's international ideological influence, global network, and impact on international left-wing activism. The following section introduces the prism that guides our examination of the international dimensions of the BPP. We then assess the global emulators of the Panther model of political activism and analyze the revolutionary ideologies and experiences that shaped Panther praxis. Finally, a discussion of the linkages that sustained the BPP's international solidarity concludes our analysis.

Through the Prism of World-Historical Movements

The analytic lens of this essay is drawn from George Katsiaficas's study *The Imagination of the New Left: A Global Analysis of 1968.* In this theoretically rich assessment of the global impact of leftist politics, Katsiaficas developed the world-historical movement construct. He delineated five historical periods (1776–1789, 1848–49, 1905–7, 1917–19, and 1967–70) in which political turmoil erupted on a worldwide scale and culminated in new conceptions of power and authority. According to Katsiaficas, these rare occasions constituted world-historical movements, which broadened the conception of freedom for millions of people around the globe. For example, the expansion of individual democratic rights established by the victories of the American and French revolutions was a by-product of the 1776–89 world-historical movement. World-historical movements democratize societal hierarchical power and are "rooted in the popular need to transform power structures in everyday life."[5] Katsiaficas notes, "In each of these periods, global upheavals were spontaneously generated. In a chain reaction of insurrections and revolts, new forms of power emerged in opposition to the established order, and new visions of the meaning of freedom were formulated in the actions of millions of people."[6]

It is the proliferation of social upheavals across the international arena that undergirds the world-historical movement construct: "The globalization of conflict in these periods and the massive proliferation of the movement's ideas and aspirations is a crucial aspect of their world-historical character."[7] Critical to the globalization of political protest is both the dissemination and the universal adoption of insurgent goals and aspirations. Key to this process is a global network that develops the international consciousness and interconnectedness that sustain the unified world-historical movement. Activists in one part of the international arena draw upon the ideas of protestors from other global locations. Ultimately, the cross-fertilization of goals and tactics that challenge existing power relationships culminates in "activation of whole strata of previously passive spectators, the millions of people who decide to participate in the conscious re-creation of their economic and political institutions and social life."[8] Katsiaficas offered the Vietnamese struggle for national liberation as a case in point: "During the 1960s, it was the resistance of the Vietnamese people to foreign domination which catalyzed the entire global movement. The prolonged intensity of their independence movement shattered the illusion of the democratic content of *pax Americana,* giving rise to movements in the industrialized societies aimed at transforming the structures of the world system. At the same time, their battlefield victories inspired anti-imperialist movements throughout the third world. As a global wave of new social movements occurred, even Eastern Europe was affected."[9]

These political crises generated what Katsiaficas labeled the "eros effect," defined as "the massive awakening of the instinctual human need for justice and for freedom."[10] The salient ideas that undergird the thought and practice of a particular world-historical movement are disseminated in both a direct and an indirect fashion. Movement ideas and tactics that catalyze the "eroticization of politics" are transmitted via the media, political symbols and propaganda, and acts of political solidarity and collaboration.

In his assessment of world history, Katsiaficas designated only five historical epochs that satisfied the criteria of the world-historical movement construct. These rare historical moments include the successful expansion of individual democratic rights as a result of the American and French revolutions (1776–1789); the introduction of workers' insurgency and rights (1848–49); the ascendancy of the proletarian strike and the victories of various national liberation movements, such as Japan's 1905 defeat of Russia (1905–7); the seizure of state power (1917–19); and the commitment to the self-determination of all people (1967–70). Each world-historical movement has four major components. Fundamental features of the world-historical movement construct include the dominant class of the insurgency; the nature of the organization responsible for implementing the new vision; the particular aspirations and goals of the social movement; and the protest tactics of the insurgents.[11] While these fundamental dimensions vary among the different world-historical movements, commitment to the reconfiguration of power remains an underlying principle of each historical epoch. Although the activists of one world-historical movement may fail to capture state power, their contestation and opposition lay the groundwork for subsequent advances. As Katsiaficas explains, "Even when these movements were unsuccessful in seizing power, immense adjustments were necessitated both within and between nation-states, and the defeated movements offered revealing glimpses of the newly developed nature of society and the new kinds of class struggles which were to follow."[12]

The New Left world-historical movement (1967–70) offers great utility for our analysis of the international character of the Black Panther Party. The examination of Panther politics within the contours of this particular world-historical movement illuminates the international role and impact of the BPP. During this pivotal period insurgent movements engulfed the global landscape, activists in industrialized and third-world nations challenged imperialism, racism, patriarchy, and the monopoly of power. An extensive international network characterized the New Left world-historical movement, which was marked by a "fusion of the various national, ethnic, and gender movements into a world-historical movement that produced a new vision of freedom."[13] The broad cross-section of global activists of the New Left world-historical movement transcended the primacy of a singular insurgent actor. Whereas the proletariat dominated the political insurgency of earlier world-historical movements, the New Left historical epoch of

1967–70 was comprised of a multitude of diverse participants, who collectively constituted a broader notion of class antagonists. The heterogeneity of New Left activists resulted in the adoption of varied protest tactics in different arenas of contestation that moved beyond the sole preoccupation of capturing state power. Katsiaficas notes that, "despite their tactical differences, all these groups articulated similar goals, a decentralized world with genuine human self-determination, and they increasingly acted in unison."[14]

Political collectives served as the primary emergent organization of the New Left world-historical movement. Activists of this historical epoch tended to rely on the collective mechanism rather than a vanguard party or representative assembly to implement the proposed vision of the world-historical movement. Similar to the four preceding world-historical movements, an extensive international network characterized the New Left historical epoch. The multitude of New Left social movements throughout the global arena often inspired and provided one another with organizational (symbolic and material) support that advanced their shared goals. In short, the New Left world-historical movement construct elucidates the manner in which Panther activism fused with and impacted international New Left activism. The conceptual framework permits one to ascertain the convergence of Panther politics—ideas, tactics, and goals—with those of the global insurgency of the 1960s. The Black Panther Party's presence and stature in the New Left global network profoundly impacted the process that universalized the tactics and goals of New Left activism.

Global Emulators of the Black Panther Party

The Black Panther Party catalyzed indigenous insurgent organizations in at least five nations other than the United States. Both Black Britons and White activists in England, respectively, formed organizations patterned on the BPP. The Black Panther Movement and the White Panthers of the United Kingdom represented British manifestations of the Panther phenomenon. The BPP also inspired Oriental Jews in Israel, Aborigines in Australia, and members of the "untouchable" caste of India to form insurgent organizations modeled on the Black Panther Party. Finally, colonized subjects in Bermuda drew from the BPP in America to combat racial oppression in the Caribbean Islands (see table 1).[15]

Table 1 *Global Emulators of the Black Panther Party*

Organization	Country	Year Founded
Black Panther Movement	England	1968
Black Beret Cadre	Bermuda	1969
White Panther Party (U.K.)	England	1970
Black Panther Party of Israel	Israel	1971
Black Panther Party of Australia	Australia	1972
Dalit Panthers	India	1987

The formation of these Panther global emulators revealed the prominent role of the Party in the global network of the New Left world-historical movement. The Party's international stature was evident by the literal adoption of its official name and symbol.[16]

Panther politics in the United States served as a source of political inspiration for the world's dispossessed. The Panther model of activism particularly resonated for ethnic minorities across the global landscape; people of color comprised five of the six global Panther-style organizations. Activists from the lowest stratum of India's caste system, known as the "untouchables," formed the Dalit Panthers to oppose the discriminatory features of India's society.[17] Runoko Rashidi, founder of the National Coordinator of the African/Dalits Support Group, proclaimed that "the Black Panther Party is absolutely revered by members of the Dalit community."[18]

Political actions taken by Oriental Jews in Israel also illustrated the Panthers' appeal to marginalized ethnic minorities across the globe. Jews of African and Asian descent, known as Orientals, are expected to "learn and adopt" the existing mores, values, and customs of the Ashkenazim.[19] Individuals in the Ashkenazim group of Jews are of European descent and enjoy privileged status in Israel's society, while Oriental Jews have confronted second-class treatment in an Ashkenazim-dominated society. In late 1970, young Oriental Jews in the slums of Jerusalem formed the Black Panther Party of Israel to combat ethnic discrimination.

Aborigine protestors in Australia also emulated America's Black Panther Party. According to one observer, living conditions for Aborigine people have been "a litany of physical, political and cultural brutality which has continued, uninterrupted, since January 26, 1788."[20] On January 18, 1972, the Australia Black Panther Party was founded by Dennis Walker, a twenty-five-year-old militant from a family with a long tradition of activism. Upon founding the Australian version of the BPP, Walker declared his organization "the vanguard for all depressed people, and in Australia the Aboriginals are the most depressed of all."[21]

Reflecting upon the BPP's international appeal among global activists, a member of England's Black Panther Movement recalled that the "Panthers in the United States moved from talking to initiating programs vital and necessary for Black people. They embodied self-help. The Panthers expressed a militancy which moved the fight against oppression to a level of confrontation."[22] Black activists in England formed the Black Panther Movement during the summer of 1968. Shortly afterward, protestors in Bermuda established the Black Beret Cadre in 1969. Outside the United States, the lone exception to the pattern of nonwhites emulating Panther activism was the White Panther Party of the United Kingdom, the geographical distribution and heterogeneous ethnic composition of which represented a microcosm of the diversity of actors in the New Left world-historical movement. The BPP capsuled the global character of New Left activism by its influence on local opposition in five nations across four continents.[23]

Panther global emulators mirrored the goals, ideological orientation, and tactics of the Party. An organization committed to revolutionary politics, the BPP opposed all forms of oppression. Its ten-point platform addressed the concrete material needs of the people. Striking parallels existed between the BPP's ten-point program and the goals of the Israeli Panthers:

1. the elimination of slums;
2. free education for those in need;
3. free housing for those in need;
4. the elimination of juvenile delinquency institutions;
5. increased wages for those supporting families; and
6. full representation of Orientals in all institutions.[24]

In both cases, the respective Panthers sought to address the basic needs of people. Both organizations targeted police abuse. Members of the Panther Party in Israel called for the elimination of the juvenile judicial system, while Panthers in the United States demanded an immediate end to police brutality and the release of all Black men from jails and prisons. The platforms of the two organizations underscored the role of the police in maintaining racial subordination in their respective nations.

Tactical congruence of the BPP and its global emulators signified the generalization of strategies within the New Left world-historical movement. However, the tactics and strategies of the preceding historical epochs predominated. Katsiaficas argued that the collective rather than the vanguard party constituted the defining tactical feature of the New Left world-historical movement. Instead, the BPP and its global emulators preferred the Lenin vanguard party model. A Black Beret Cadre communiqué declared that "the Black Revolution in Bermuda must have a well-supported vanguard party! The party must be able to instill faith in the people and constantly show them by example the line of demarcation between us and the enemy and . . . in many respects the Black Beret Cadre has definite potential to be a successful vanguard party."[25] England's Black Panther Movement and the Black Panther Party in Australia shared similar views on the vanguard party.

These global social movements also assumed the BPP's confrontational style and stance on political violence. Executive Mandate No. 1, authored by Newton and read at the California State Legislature in Sacramento by Bobby Seale on May 2, 1967, noted, "The Black Panther Party for Self-Defense believes that the time has come for Black people to arm themselves against the terror before it is too late."[26] Several Panther global emulators adopted similar positions on political violence. Comrades of the Black Beret Cadre argued that "the only way to total freedom in Bermuda is through armed struggle."[27] In a statement reminiscent of Executive Mandate No. 3, in which Newton ordered all BPP members to acquire weapons, Dennis Walker, leader of Australia's Black Panther Party, said that "members must learn to use and service weapons correctly."[28] In the tradition of the BPP's militant style, S. Maricano, a leader of the Israeli Panthers, warned, "We want a share of the cake, if not—there won't be a cake."[29]

International offshoots of the BPP developed programs and initiated activities patterned on Panther activism in the United States. The Black Panther Movement in England conducted political education classes and sponsored workshops on self-defense. Members of the Black Panther Movement, like their American counterparts, mobilized against police brutality in the Black community. Darcus Howe, a former member of England's Black Panther Movement, recalled, "When I came here [England] police harassed black people. They got promotions by arrests. In the Black Panthers we hit back so violently that they learnt. Now if you are policing out here you have to be diplomatic."[30]

The Black Panther Movement sponsored the historic National Conference on the Rights of Black People, held May 22–23, 1971. Panthers in England initiated the conference to mobilize opposition to the passage of pernicious legislation by members of Parliament. The first day the conference featured the play entitled *The Black Experience* and held sessions on legal rights, organizing for self-defense, and black political prisoners. On the second day of the conference, the activists focused on education, employment, immigration, and other local issues. However, these issues were viewed in a global context, as evidenced by the scheduled reports given on worldwide struggles including the United States, the Caribbean, the Middle East, southern Africa, India, and Pakistan. Althea Jones of the Black Panther Party Movement explained, "We believe such resistance is not simply confined to the British National Borders, but is expressing itself internationally among all oppressed people."[31]

Many of the survival programs popularized by the BPP in the United States were also implemented by international Panther offshoots. Bermuda's Black Beret Cadre sponsored liberation schools and political education classes on revolutionary principles and tactics. Members of the Abbey Wood chapter of the White Panther Party of the United Kingdom organized free food programs, liberation schools, free transportation, and plumbing assistance. These international activists, like their BPP comrades in America, also boldly confronted all manifestations of racial oppression in their respective local communities. Shortly after the founding of the organization, the Israeli Panthers held a series of militant demonstrations opposing the government's reduction of food subsidies, discrimination in housing policies, and police brutality.[32] In short, the participants of Panther global emulators exemplified the spirit of community service and resistance that defined the political persona of the Black Panther Party. Despite the success of these Panther emulators, our limited assessment of their organizational effectiveness indicates that they failed to realize many of their stated objectives. Both internal and external factors undermined the effectiveness of the Panther global emulators. Internally, these groups were beset by a small core membership. Consequently, they lacked a sufficient base to wield meaningful political influence. The Israeli Panthers, members of the Black Beret, and the Black Panther Movement in England all shared this organizational liability. As Deborah Bernstein reported, the Israeli Panthers "were a small informal neighborhood core-based group with an active periphery that helped keep things going."[33] She estimated that the core of the organization consisted of approximately twenty to thirty young males. Intra-organizational strife hampered the effectiveness of the Panther emulators, including the derailing of the political activism of the Israeli Panthers and the Black Panther Movement in England. Tactical disagreements and organizational expulsions also adversely impacted the fortunes of the international offshoots of the BPP.[34]

As did the BPP, the global Panther-style social movements experienced government repression. The external factor of political repression targeting the leadership of the various Panther global emulators often mirrored the pattern of government harassment endured by the BPP. In England, three members of the Black Panther Movement were arrested on the charge of conspiracy to incite the murder of a police officer as a result of an inflammatory flyer authored and distributed by the movement at a Hyde Park rally. On another occasion, Black Panther Movement leader Benedict Obi Egbuna, a Biafran author, was arrested for obstructing the police. Members of the White Panther Party also experienced frequent arrests on minor charges. Four White Panther Party activists were charged with posting flyers without the consent of the owner of the property, although the magistrate dropped the charges. In a preemptive strike reminiscent of a tactic frequently utilized against the BPP, Israeli government officials arrested the ten leaders of the Israeli Panther Party on the eve of a major demonstration. As support for the Israeli Black Panther Party increased, one observer noted, "police brutality intensified, as did the campaign to buy them off, penetrate the organization with provocateurs, bring about splits in the organization and slander them in their media."[35]

In short, regardless of geographical locale, each of the international social movements emulating the Panther model of insurgency suffered political repression. While much of the government harassment experienced by these Panther-style groups paralleled that of the BPP, the severity of that repression never reached the proportion lodged against the Black Panther Party. None of the Panther global emulators suffered fatalities, nor did their members become longtime political prisoners. Ironically, the same boldness and commitment to leftist ideas that the BPP dared to display within the "Belly of the Beast," which inspired global imitators, also accounted for the brutal repression of the organization.

Global Influences on the Panther Ideology

The Black Panther Party for Self-Defense represented, arguably, the premier Black left organization in the African-American freedom struggle. Throughout its sixteen-year history (October 1966 through June 1982) the BPP situated Black protest within a global framework. Kathleen Cleaver, an early prominent Panther leader, explained, "From its inception the Black Panther Party saw the condition of blacks within an international context, for it was the same racist imperialism that people in Africa, Asia, and Latin America were fighting against that was victimizing blacks in the United States, according to their analysis."[36]

Initially a Black nationalist organization, the BPP underwent four major ideological orientations. During his historic speech delivered at Boston College three months after being released from prison in 1970, Newton noted that the Party evolved from Black nationalism to a revolutionary Black nationalist organization, and subsequently saw themselves as internationalists. Ultimately, the BPP moved to what Newton referred to as revolutionary intercommunalism, "the time when the people seize the means of production and distribute the wealth and the technology in an egalitarian way to many communities of the world."[37] During its Black nationalist stage the BPP, nonetheless, conceptualized the African-American freedom struggle as a manifestation of international dynamics. This international perspective was apparent in the BPP's advocacy for a Black plebiscite to be supervised by the United Nations. The colonial model of racial oppression undergirded the Party's demand for a referendum vote on the political fate of African Americans.

One of the first efforts to expand the global focus of the BPP was related to Eldridge Cleaver's strategy to internationalize the "Free Huey" campaign. After an October 27, 1967 shooting incident that left one Oakland police officer dead and Huey P. Newton and another law enforcement officer seriously wounded, a massive legal campaign launched by the Panthers soon popularized the "Free Huey" slogan worldwide. Newton recalled, "All across the country, Black people were relating to my imprisonment." He continued, "We were also gaining international attention. Soon groups in other countries began to ask us to send speakers. At that time we still considered ourselves revolutionary nationalists that is, Black nationalists who took a revolutionary position in the United States. We had not as yet, developed an international policy."[38]

In the process of constructing an international policy, the BPP drew from a wide array of revolutionary theorists from Africa, Europe, Asia, and Latin America (see table 2). The Party's ideological orientation and practice were inextricably linked to the ideas, aspirations, and strategies of the New Left world-historical movement. Moreover, the Panthers, like other New Left activists, were influenced by the tactics and goals of prior world-historical movements. Each member of the BPP's leadership triumvirate (Huey P. Newton, Bobby Seale, and Eldridge Cleaver) was well versed in the classics of revolutionary thought and practice. Newton recalled in his autobiography, *Revolutionary Suicide,* "The literature of oppressed people and their struggle for liberation in other countries is very large, and we pored over these books to see how their experiences might help us understand our plight. We read the work of Frantz Fanon, particularly *The Wretched of the Earth,* the four volumes of Chairman Tse-tung, and Che Guevara's *Guerrilla Warfare."*[39]

The successful drive for independence by many African states from the 1950s through the 1970s reified the dual objectives of civil rights and human dignity for African Americans. Especially significant in this regard were the rise of Ghanaian independence under Kwame Nkrumah, Kenya's Mau Mau rebellion, the resistance of Patrice Lumumba

Table 2   *Global Influences on the Ideological Praxis of the Black Panther Party*

Individual	Concept	Major Texts
Mikhail Bakunin	Conspiratorial revolutionary action by small groups	*The Catechism of Revolutionist*
Fidel Castro, Regis Debray, Che Guevara	*Foco* theory and guerrilla warfare tactics	*Revolution in the Revolution?* *Guerrilla Warfare*
Frantz Fanon	Revolutionary violence and colonial analogy; revolutionary potential of the lumpen proletariat	*The Wretched of the Earth*
V. I. Lenin	Vanguard Party and anti-imperialist struggle	*What is to be Done?*
Karl Marx, Friedrich Engels	class struggle; dialectical materialism; proletarian internationalism	*Communist Manifesto*
Kwame Nkrumah	Neocolonialism and guerrilla warfare tactics	*Neo-Colonialism;* *Class Struggle in Africa*
Kim Il Sung	*juche*	
Mao Tse-Tung	Revolutionary organizing principles (internal and external); Serving the People programs	*Quotations from Chairman MaoTse-Tung* *(The Little Red Book)*

in the Congo, and the violent Algerian revolution against the colonial power of France. The political thought and practice of these indigenous African movements had a decisive impact on the international orientation of the Panthers. Foremost among the African revolutionaries that profoundly impacted Panther praxis was Frantz Fanon, the Algerian psychiatrist who was born in Martinique. Fanon's seminal work, *The Wretched of the Earth,* introduced BPP theorists to three major concepts: the colonial analogy; revolutionary violence; and the revolutionary potential of the lumpen proletariat (see table 2). As Bobby Seale remembered, "We would sit down with *Wretched of the Earth* and talk go, over another section or chapter of Fanon, and Huey would explain it in depth."[40] Fanon's colonial analysis had significant relevance for Newton and other Panther theoreticians who adopted the view that the experience of Black people in America paralleled that of colonialized people under the traditional colonialism. Party leaders maintained that the Black community in America constituted an internal colony that suffered from cultural destruction, White economic exploitation, and racial oppression by an occupying White police force.

In the decolonization process, Fanon viewed revolutionary violence as an essential component of the struggle for independence. He unapologetically declared that "the naked truth of decolonization evokes for us the searing bullets and bloodstained knives, which emanate from it. For if the last shall be first, this will only come to pass after a murderous and decisive struggle between the two protagonists."[41] Newton and Seale were convinced that Fanon's theory of the centrality of revolutionary violence in transforming the oppressed had direct relevance to the process of liberation for African Americans. Fanon's prescription for revolutionary violence offered the Panthers an additional rationale for the organization's stance on armed self-defense. Moreover, BPP theorists relied heavily upon Fanon's insight on the role of the lumpen proletariat in the African liberation movement. According to Fanon, "It is within this mass of humanity, this people of the shanty towns; at the core of the *lumpen proletariat* that the rebellion will find its urban spearhead. For the *lumpen proletariat,* the horde of starving men, uprooted from their tribe and from their clan, constitutes one of the most spontaneous and the most radically revolutionary forces of a colonized people."[42] Fanon provided Panther leaders with a revolutionary justification for organizing the "Brothers off the block." Seale explained, "Huey understood the meaning of what Fanon was saying about organizing the lumpen proletariat first, because Fanon explicitly pointed out that if you didn't organize the lumpen proletariat and give a base for organizing the brother who's pimping, the brother who's hustling, the unemployed, the downtrodden, the brother who's robbing banks, who's not politically conscious—that's what lumpen proletariat means—that if you didn't relate to these cats, the power structure would organize these cats against you."[43]

Ironically, the revolutionary premium that Panther leaders placed on the lumpen proletariat contrasted sharply with Marxist doctrine; Karl Marx had expressed serious reservations about the revolutionary viability of the lumpen class. Notwithstanding this departure from orthodox Marxist thought, the BPP embraced several important aspects of Marxism-Leninism. Principal among these ideas were the notions of class struggle, the vanguard party concept, and dialectical materialism. Huey Newton declared, "The Black Panthers grew out of the Black Power movement, but the Party transformed the ideology of Black Power, into a socialist ideology, a Marxist-Leninist ideology."[44] In its ideological transformation, the BPP subscribed to a Marxist class analysis of society. Panther theoreticians now incorporated race and class in their assessment of the African-American predicament. BPP leaders accepted the Marxist viewpoint that capitalism produced a maldistribution of societal resources due to an inherently exploitative system in which the ruling class exploited the labor of the working class. As Marxist-Leninists, the BPP advocated revolutionary struggle to establish a socialist society. Eldridge Cleaver argued that the "great definition by Marx and Engels became the mightiest weapon in the hands of oppressed people in the history of ideology. It marks a gigantic advance for all mankind."[45]

Panther leaders turned to Marxism-Leninism for guidance in the BPP's opposition to racism, sexism, and capitalism. For example, scientific socialist principles dictated gender equality among Party members as well as interracial and international solidarity. Bobby Seale explained, "The fight against male chauvinism is a class struggle—that's hard for people to understand."[46] These principles also directed the BPP to Lenin's vanguard party notion. BPP members clearly viewed themselves as disciplined, full-time revolutionaries committed to mobilizing support for a socialist revolution. The Richmond, California branch of the Party proclaimed, "The Black Panther Party or the Vanguard Party's main function at this stage of revolution is to educate the Black community to the absurdity of their complacent situation within this racist decadent society, and to instill in them a correct political revolutionary ideology."[47] Eldridge Cleaver voiced similar views: "The Black Panther movement was never a mass activity. We were a vanguard organization with rigid entry standards, rules and regulations."[48]

Also of great importance to BPP theoreticians was the method of dialectical materialism—a cornerstone of Marxism-Leninism. According to BPP leaders, Marx provided a revolutionary framework that could be applied to many different political settings. Newton stressed that "The Black Panther Party is a Marxist-Leninist party because we follow the dialectical method and we also integrate theory with practice."[49] For Party theoreticians, adherence to the method of dialetical materialism precluded a static, mechanical application of Marxism-Leninism. Newton argued, "If we are using the method of dialectical materialism we don't expect to find anything the same even one minute later because one minute later is history."[50] This approach led to a flexible, adaptive application of Marxism-Leninism by BPP leaders. Eldridge Cleaver noted, "When we say that we are Marxist-Leninists, we mean that we have studied and understand the classical principles of scientific socialism and that we have adapted these principles to our own situation for ourselves. However, we do not move with a closed mind to new ideas or information. At the same time, we know that we must rely upon our own brains in solving ideological problems as they relate to us."[51] The BPP's propensity for making such adaptations was particularly evident in the revolutionary role BPP theoreticians assigned to the lumpen proletariat.[52] The Party's position on the lumpen engendered criticism and many misconceptions concerning the class origins at the organization.[53]

Arguably the most influential revolutionary thinker impacting Panther doctrine was Mao Tse-Tung, the former leader of the People's Republic of China. According to a July 18, 1973, inner BPP memorandum, 50 percent of the morning political education classes concentrated on the "little red book." Indeed, from the inception of the BPP, the *Quotations from Chairman Mao Tse-Tung* featured prominently in Panther praxis. The organization's first cache of weapons was purchased with proceeds from the sale of the "little red book" to Berkeley college students. Subsequently, Party leaders incorporated verbatim Mao's eight points of attention and three main rules of discipline—both found in the "little red book." Chairman Mao's quotations were frequently published in the organization's newspaper. Eldridge Cleaver, the first editor of the voice of the BPP, recalled that "by 1969 *The Black Panther* paper was saturated with Mao slogans."[54] The thought and practice of Mao Tse-Tung served as a revolutionary guide to action for BPP leaders. Eldridge Cleaver recalled that "there were some aspects of Chairman Mao's thought that had helpful and sensitive application for the life of the Panthers in the ghetto."[55] Mao's dictums fashioned BPP strategies, mobilization tactics, and organizational discipline. Paramount among these principles of Maoism was his discussion of "war and peace," which fostered the BPP's call for "picking up the gun." Mao's insights on organizational discipline in his discussion of criticism and self-criticism were central to discipline among BPP comrades. Chairman Mao's adaptation of Marxism-Leninism to specific unique conditions of Chinese people had great appeal to Panther leaders. His application of socialist principles to the experience of Chinese peasants coincided with the party's adherence to the self-determination of all people.

Similarly, the Party's disdain for a mechanical application of Marxism-Leninism buttressed its attraction to the writings of Kim Il Sung, the "Great Leader" of North Korea. BPP theoreticians were particularly drawn to Kim Il Sung's *juche* concept, which they considered a major contribution to Marxism-Leninism. In a June 1970 issue of the *Black Panther,* Eldridge Cleaver wrote that *juche* was "a major breakthrough, it is a concept of self-reliance that justified the independent existence of each party."[56] The *juche* concept exemplified the BPP's commitment to self-determination of revolutionary parties. As in the case of Mao Tse-Tung, the writings of Kim Il Sung regularly appeared in the *Black Panther.*

The Fidel Castro and Ernesto Che Guevara–led Cuban revolution in the veritable backyard of the United States captured the imagination of the Black Panther Party. Castro and Guevara were frequently referenced in BPP propaganda—speeches, political education classes, literature, and strategy. At a 1969 BPP rally in San Francisco, Field Marshal Don Cox told the audience the Party "dig on all the people that held the light before . . . revolutionaries like Fidel [and] Che," while Newton commented in his autobiography that he "supported Castro all the way." Che Guevara's photo also adorned the masthead of the international news section of the *Black Panther.* Furthermore, the leadership of the BPP mandated Guevara's *Guerrilla Warfare* as required reading in BPP political education classes.[57]

Tactically, the Cuban model of revolutionary struggle demonstrated the viability of guerrilla warfare to BPP strategists. Since the inception of the organization, Party leaders had disavowed the spontaneous riots that engulfed the nation in the late 1960s. Instead, Party leaders drew upon the lessons of Third World movements that utilized guerrilla warfare and deemed the strategy to be most effective because "guerrilla tactics attempt to make a virtue out of relative weakness."[58] Peter Sederber explains, "Guerrilla warfare offers the weaker side a third option to either stand-up, conventional combat leading to probable defeat or outright surrender. The guerrillas—if blessed with sufficient power, skill and luck—may delay defeat, raise the cost of victory to a discouraging level, or even transform themselves into a more equal adversary to their opponents. They also may lose."[59]

In the case of Cuba, the outmanned revolutionaries won, leading Che Guevara and Regis Debray to advocate the *foco* theory of revolution for others to emulate. According to the *foco* model, small cells of dedicated revolutionaries can generate the necessary conditions for a successful revolution. Guevara argued that the conclusions of *foco* theory "refute those who feel the need to wait until, in some perfect way, all the required objective and subjective conditions are at hand, instead of hastening to bring these conditions about through their own efforts."[60]

Other global guerrilla movements also contributed to the development of the Party's strategy on armed struggle. Newton was inspired by "all the guerrilla bands that have been operating in Mozambique and Angola, and the Palestinian guerrillas who are fighting for a socialist world. I think they all have been great inspirations for the Black Panther Party. As I've said before, they're examples of all these guerrilla bands. The guerrillas who are operating in South Africa and numerous other countries all have had great influence on us. We study and follow their example."[61]

Chief among the other guerrilla movements which impacted the BPP was the Vietnamese liberation struggle. Members of the BPP greatly admired the heroic struggle of the Vietnamese people against powerful adversaries. Connie Matthews, the international coordinator of the BPP, told demonstrators at an antiwar rally that "the Vietnamese are a good example of the people being victorious. Because with all of America's technology and her greatness she has been unable to defeat the Vietnamese. Every man, woman and child has resisted."[62]

The Panthers' admiration of the courage of the Vietnamese people in their fight against imperialism prompted Huey Newton to offer troops to the National Liberation Front and Provisional Revolutionary Government of South Vietnam. However, Deputy Commander Nguyen Thi Dinh graciously declined the Party's offer.[63] On another occasion, Eldridge Cleaver authored an open letter entitled "To My Black Brothers in Vietnam," imploring Black soldiers not to fight against the Vietnamese people.[64] While many BPP leaders viewed guerrilla warfare tactics as a viable strategy, the use of this tactic did cause dissension within the organization and stimulated intense external criticisms of the BPP. The failure to implement a full guerrilla assault contributed significantly to the 1971 organizational split between members committed to guerrilla warfare against the power structure of the United States, and those who favored Newton's reemphasis on community service.[65] In short, Panther praxis largely reflected a synthesis of the writings and activism of international revolutionaries. The interrelationship between the BPP and other international social movements leading to the BPP's amalgamation of revolutionary thought did not appear by happenstance. Rather, the Party's adoption of international revolutionary ideas and tactics stemmed from its linkages to global leftist opposition.

BPP and the New Left Global Network

Katsiaficas underscored the extraordinary global consciousness and interconnectedness of myriad New Left actors sustained by an extensive global network. During the period of the New Left world-historical movement (the late 1960s through the early 1970s) a multitude of insurgent organizations—workers, radicalized students, politicized soldiers, ethnic minorities, feminist formations, gay liberation fronts, and national liberation movements—provided mutual assistance. This expansive global network provided a conduit for the symbiotic relationship of international support that characterized the New Left world-historical movement.

The BPP's ideological affinity with New Left actors and its contestation within the borders of the world's most industrialized nation prominently situated the Panthers in the international network of New Left activism. The dominant presence of the BPP in the New Left global network was also largely based on the international movement's solidarity with the BPP, which suffered horrific political repression, particularly during its revolutionary phase (October 1966 to May 1971). Indeed, by the end of 1969 the FBI's COINTELPRO campaign had decimated both the national and local leadership of the organization. Huey Newton remained in prison as a result of the October 27, 1967, shooting incident. In 1968 Eldridge Cleaver fled the country, while another four Panthers died in gun battles with local police officers. Many of the BPP branches sprouting up across the country met with persistent police resistance. National headquarters in Oakland and affiliates throughout the nation were frequently raided by the police. The political repression of the BPP intensified in 1969. The Party's other cofounder and chairman, Bobby Seale, spent mid-1969 through mid-1971 imprisoned on conspiracy charges of inciting a riot at the Democratic Convention and murder charges in conjunction with the New Haven 14 murder case. On the local level the BPP office in Des Moines, Iowa, was bombed, while other Panther national units continued to face police raids on a regular basis. The leadership of the New York chapter was arrested on an assortment of conspiracy charges in the Panther 21 case.[66]

The arrest of key Panther leaders necessitated the development of legal mobilization campaigns to secure their freedom. Many of these defense campaigns extended across the global landscape. For instance, a "Free Huey" rally was held in Tanzania, while "Free Bobby Seale" mobilization activities occurred on the European continent.[67] International media (establishment and dissident) coverage of the BPP enhanced its stature among global activists. The global visibility of the BPP within the international network of the New Left world-historical movement was manifested in the foreign travels of Party members; in BPP solidarity committees; in the formation of the International Section of the Black Panther Party in Algiers, Algeria; and in Panther expatriate communities.

Within a year of Newton's initial arrest on October 27, 1967, Panther representatives personally interacted with international activists and sympathizers. Members of the Black Panther Party traveled throughout Europe, Asia, Latin America, and Africa, mobilizing organizational support and in turn providing Party assistance to the international struggle of New Left activism. The Party's first foreign travel occurred in August 1968, when BPP leaders Eldridge and Kathleen Cleaver were invited by Japanese activists to give a series of speeches in Japan. Earl Anthony, who substituted for Eldridge Cleaver on the speaking tour, noted that the lecture engagement coincided "with a month of conferences in protest of the Vietnamese war and nuclear weapons."[68] Opposition to the Vietnam War served as a major linkage issue among New Left activists.

Another international venture headed by David Hilliard in August 1968 was aborted en route to Cuba when Mexican officials halted the Panther contingent. The Hilliard-led delegation attempted to follow up on prior discussions with Cuban officials at the United Nations concerning the establishment of a Panther base of operations in Cuba. Later that year, however, Eldridge Cleaver fled underground to Cuba to escape charges associated with the Panther-police shootout on April 6, 1968, in Oakland. In July 1971 Erika Huggins represented the BPP at the annual celebration of the Cuban Revolution. Throughout the existence of the BPP, the socialist Cuban nation remained an important external ally of the organization. Even after the formal demise of the BPP in 1982, Cuban officials continued to express global solidarity by permitting Panther expatriates to reside in the country.

Besides Cuba, BPP international forays established personal contact with global New Left activists and the leaders of socialist nations. During the winter of 1969, Bobby Seale traveled extensively on a speaking tour through the Scandinavian countries of Finland, Sweden, and Denmark to mobilize support for Newton and other imprisoned Party members. Another Panther delegation visited Japan in September to meet with members of the Sanya Liberation League, economically impoverished Japanese residing in the Sanya district of Tokyo. In an expression of political solidarity among global New Left actors, BPP members Roberta Alexander and Elbert "Big Man" Howard, the deputy minister of information, spoke at a Sanrizuka political rally in Japan.[69]

On the eve of the First Pan-African Cultural Festival in July 1969, exiled Panther leader Eldridge Cleaver publicly resurfaced in Algiers, Algeria. The North African nation would become a valuable political sanctuary for Panther expatriates. Party members interacted with a constellation of global revolutionaries, including representatives from the Yasir Arafat–led Al Fatah, the leading Palestinian liberation movement; the National Liberation Front of North Vietnam; PAIGC (African Party for the Independence of Guinea-Bissau and the Cape Verde Islands); and South African and Zimbabwean liberation movements. Panther presence in Algiers also gave BPP members direct access to the diplomatic officials of socialist nations. This interaction resulted in several formal invitations extended to BPP members by various revolutionary countries.[70]

One such invitation extended in 1969 by the ambassador of the Democratic Peoples' Republic of Korea led to Eldridge Cleaver's attendance at the International Conference of Revolutionary Journalists in Pyongyang, North Korea. Kathleen Cleaver reported that "for nearly a month [Eldridge Cleaver and Bayon Booth] traveled across the country, receiving lessons in Marxism-Leninism and Korea's history."[71] Eldridge Cleaver returned to North Korea in July 1970 with a delegation of progressive American activists at the behest of the North Korean government. The American Peoples Anti-Imperialist Delegation headed by Eldridge Cleaver included a broad cross-section of radicals. The only other BPP member among the delegation was Elaine Brown; the remainder included two Asian activists and seven white radicals (five women and two men). Members of the

Anti-Imperialist Delegation toured the country, attended cultural events, and met with Korean political activists. An unexpected by-product of the delegation's tour in North Korea was an invitation to visit Hanoi, extended by the Vietnamese ambassador. On route to North Vietnam, the delegation of American New Left activists were hosted by the Committee for Friendship with the American People during a five-day stay in Peking.[72] The Committee of Solidarity with the American People of North Vietnam hosted the Eldridge Cleaver–led delegation during a twenty-day stint in the country. Vietnamese government officials in Hanoi honored the radical American activists on August 18, 1970, by celebrating International Day of Solidarity with Black People of the United States. An editorial entitled "An Inevitably Victorious Cause," published in *Nhan Dan*, the official newspaper of the Communist Party of North Vietnam, declared that "the Vietnamese people who are now opposing the American imperialist aggressors with arms, considered the black people of the United States in the struggle for their emancipation as their natural companions in arms and allies."[73]

Eldridge Cleaver also spearheaded the BPP's primary international venture in sub-Saharan Africa. While still in Algeria, Cleaver received an invitation from the Congolese Socialist Youth Union to attend the International Conference of Solidarity with the People under Portuguese Domination held in the People's Republic of the Congo. Members of the Panther delegation, including Kathleen Cleaver, met with representatives from Africa's national liberation movements, such as the PAIGC (Partido Africano para a Independência da Guinéa e Cabo Verde), the MPLA (Movimento Popular de Libertacão de Angola), and FRELIMO (Frente de Libertacão de Mocambique). The visiting Panthers remained in the Congo after the conclusion of the conference, toured the country, and attended meetings with representatives of the Congolese Workers' Party and the People's Republic Army. The Cleaver-led Panther delegation to Congo-Brazzaville had two major objectives: to document the historic visit to the African socialist country, and to acquire governmental approval to establish a BPP international unit in the People's Republic of Congo. Kathleen Cleaver reported that with the support of French radicals, the Panthers produced a film entitled *We Have Come Back*. However, the group was unsuccessful in relocating to the Congo due to an overthrow of the sympathetic socialist Congolese government.[74]

In the early 1970s the BPP strengthened its linkages to the People's Republic of China with two Party ventures to the country. First, in September 1971, a Huey Newton–led Panther contingent including Elaine Brown and Robert Bay went to China for a ten-day visit. The Peking government first extended the official invitation to Newton upon his release from prison in August 1970. However, the Party's legal defense efforts in the case of the New Haven 14 delayed his acceptance of the invitation. Ironically, the visit by the cofounder and minister of defense of the BPP preceded President Richard M. Nixon's historic diplomatic meeting with Chinese government officials in Peking. Newton recalled, "While there, I achieved a psychological liberation I had never experienced before. It was not simply that I felt at home in China; the reaction was deeper than that. What I experienced was the sensation of freedom—as if a great weight had been lifted from my soul, and I was able to be myself, without defense or pretense or the need for explanation. I felt absolutely free for the first time in my life—completely free among my fellow man."[75]

Newton's international foray to China laid the groundwork for a larger 1972 Panther delegation to visit the country to observe the concrete application of Marxism-Leninism to the Chinese experience. Members of the delegation were assigned to subcommittees representing five major societal categories of the People's Republic of China: Culture, Education, Industry, Medicine, and Historical Background of China. For example,

Emory Douglas, the Party's Minister of Culture, along with two other people, was assigned to the Culture Committee, which interacted with the Revolutionary Ballet and Revolutionary Opera. A five-member medicine committee, which included Dr. Bert Small and Audrea Jones, who headed the BPP's George Jackson Free Health Clinic in Berkeley, toured the Shanghai People's Hospital and the Peking Hospital, a communal medicine center, and held discussions with various health medicine workers.[76]

While in many instances sympathetic socialist governments hosted visiting Panther delegations, various international leftist support committees also contributed to the mobilization efforts of the Party. Black Panther Party solidarity committees proliferated in Europe, appearing in Germany, England, Sweden, Italy, Finland, France, Belgium, Denmark, Norway, and the Netherlands. Japanese activists formed the Committee to Support the Black Panther Party. Panther solidarity committees consisted of international leftist formations forming united fronts to assist the Back Panther Party. For example, the Japan Committee in Support of the Black Panther included four Japanese leftist organizations; the International Revolutionist League, the South Osaka Liberation Front, the Young Chinese Organization, and the Isolated Island. Panther support committees were critical linchpins in the Party's internationalized approach to combating political repression. First and foremost, BPP solidarity committees assisted in publicizing Panther activism. These left-wing formations sponsored speaking engagements by Panther representatives, distributed BPP literature, organized protest rallies, and raised money on behalf of the BPP. The Panther leadership created the position of international coordinator of the Black Panther Party in 1969 to organize the activities of the Panther support committees. In Kathleen Cleaver's assessment, "the Scandinavian and the West German committees were the most dynamic and the best organized as they were tied to strong student movements in countries where socialist parties were well-represented in the national government."[77]

International Panther solidarity committees also sponsored numerous demonstrations on behalf of BPP political prisoners. "Free Huey" rallies, Panther 21 demonstrations, and mass meetings protesting the imprisonment of Bobby Seale, Erika Huggins, and their New Haven comrades were held throughout Europe. The Black Panther Party Solidarity Committee in Scandinavia organized a protest rally in support of Bobby Seale in Stockholm on September 21, 1969. Members of the Danish BPP Solidarity Committee clashed with police officers in June 1970 during a demonstration against the Danish government's refusal to guarantee exiled Panther leader Eldridge Cleaver's safe passage through the country. The "Intercommunal Solidarity Day" sponsored by the BPP indicated extensive coordination between actors of the New Left world-historical movement. On March 5, 1971, global leftist activists in eight nations in conjunction with the BPP held political rallies in observance of global solidarity among leftist actors.[78]

In turn, the BPP reciprocated in this international support, which reflected the symbiotic nature of the relationship undergirding the New Left global network. Members of the BPP were frequent speakers at anti–Vietnam War demonstrations. Bobby Seale was the featured speaker at Montreal's Hemispheric Conference to End the War in Vietnam. David Hilliard, the Party's Chief of Staff, spoke at the San Francisco Moratorium Demonstration, one of the largest antiwar protest rallies of the period, and Connie Matthews, the international coordinator of the organization, delivered a speech at the Vietnam Moratorium Demonstration held at San Jose State College in 1969. The Black Panther Party expressed international solidarity with global activists on other issues as well. The Seattle chapter of the BPP demonstrated against a French law prohibiting left-wing political organizations in a cosponsored rally with the Socialist Workers Party and the Vietnam Committee of the University of Washington. On other occasions, the BPP donated medical supplies to African revolutionary movements in Mozambique, Angola, and Guinea-Bissau. Panthers disseminated the literature of other leftist global social movements and frequently published articles on international activism in the pages of the *Black Panther.* [79]

Eldridge Cleaver's strategic decision to internationalize BPP opposition to governmental repression proved fruitful. His foresight garnered the BPP international solidarity from a host of revolutionary leaders, leftist activists, and foreign dignitaries. The much admired Kwame Nkrumah of Ghana and socialist leader President Sekou Toure of Guinea issued public statements supporting the freedom of Huey P. Newton. International leftist celebrities, such as the French intellectual Jean Genet, aided the BPP. Genet's political empathy and solidarity with the Panthers prompted his clandestine visit to the United States in 1970. Although Genet entered the country illegally, he maintained a public profile on behalf of Bobby Seale and other Panther political prisoners. Genet spoke at several elite educational institutions imploring white college students to support BPP legal defense activities. In another gesture of international solidarity, Bernadette Devlin, an Irish political activist of the Derry Labor Party, gave to the Black Panther Party the key to the city of New York, previously given to her by Mayor John Lindsey. According to Devlin, giving the key to the Panthers was "a gesture of solidarity with the black liberation and revolutionary socialist movements in America."[80]

The BPP's international stature among leftist global actors partially accounts for the Party's revolutionary welcome in Algeria, which subsequently led to the formation of an international Panther unit. The Panthers' visibility and role in the New Left global network was enhanced by the formal establishment of the International Section of the Black Panther Party in Algeria. The genesis of the BPP's international chapter originated with Eldridge Cleaver's public appearance in Algiers shortly before the First Pan-African Cultural Festival in July 1969. At the conclusion of the historic festival, the Panther contingent led by Eldridge Cleaver lost its guest status with the Algerian government. During the festival an assortment of American fugitives from Cuba also joined the Cleavers in Algeria. Eldridge Cleaver subsidized the living expenses of the Panther delegation in Algeria with his publishing royalties until the Algerian government accorded the BPP accredited movement status. The intervention of Elaine Klein, a former associate of Frantz Fanon and friend of *Front de la Libération Nationale* (FLN), and Mohammed Yazid, an influential Algerian politician, eventually gained the BPP the status of a national accredited movement. This governmental accordance "placed the BPP in Algeria on the same level as the Afrikan National Congress (A.N.C.) of South Afrika and the Palestine Liberation Organization (P.L.O.). With the status the BPP was given a large chateau and a budget to operate its office."[81] Under the leadership of the exiled Minister of Information, Eldridge Cleaver, the BPP formally opened its international headquarters in a ten-room, two-story villa formerly occupied by the National Liberation Front of South Vietnam in September 1970.

The objectives of the International Section of the BPP included publicizing BPP activism in the global arena; developing united fronts with other international social movements; mobilizing organizational resources for the BPP; and developing and delivering Party initiatives to the United Nations. Contrary to Michael Newton's assessment that the Party's international section was of minor significance, the Panther global outpost greatly enhanced organizational fortunes.[82] First, the international Panther affiliate in Algeria provided Eldridge Cleaver with a venue to resume his influential leadership role in the BPP. President Houari Boumedienne's commitment to anticolonial struggle in Africa and the country's severed diplomatic relations with the United States offered Cleaver a political setting conducive to continuing his revolutionary activism. He now regularly communicated with fellow BPP members, since his residency in the North African country granted him access to other Panthers. Shortly after his arrival in Algeria, Cleaver had the opportunity to strategize with members of the BPP's Central Committee when a three-member Panther delegation attended the historic First Pan-African Cultural Festival in Algiers. David Hilliard, the Party's Chief of Staff, and Raymond "Masai" Hewitt, Minister of Education, joined Eldridge along with his wife, Kathleen, who held the position of Communications Secretary, and Emory Douglas, the Party's Minister of Culture. During the twelve-day festival, nearly half (five out of eleven members) of the Central Committee was in one place at the same time. Intense political repression against the BPP, particularly the leadership, made such an occasion rare. Moreover, while in Algiers Cleaver had access to telex communications, which facilitated contact with national headquarters in Oakland. The BPP's international office in Algeria served as a safe haven for exiled Panthers. Donald Cox (Field Marshal), Sekou Odinga (a New York Panther leader), and Larry Mack (also of the New York chapter) resurfaced in the North African nation after going underground. Another member of the Panther 21, expatriate Michael "Cetewayo" Tabor, also appeared in Algiers. In addition, Cleaver frequently published his writings in the organization's newspaper. In contrast, "while in Cuba, Cleaver published nothing; officially his location was unknown, and so the Black Panther Party could not print any new items."[83] Finally, Party members' travel to the countries of sympathetic allies was facilitated by the location of its international section. As previously discussed, several BPP international ventures were initiated in Algeria.

Notwithstanding the positive benefits of the BPP's international outpost, the Panther office in Algiers was a short-lived experiment; in less than three years, the Panther affiliate ceased operations. Cordial relations between the BPP and the Algerian government officials quickly deteriorated, and the Panther delegation in Algeria became a political liability when the government signed a billion-dollar liquefied gas deal with an American oil corporation. Tensions also arose over the Algerian government's confiscation of ransoms secured by American hijackers. Finally, Eldridge Cleaver embarrassed President Boumedienne when he authored an open letter criticizing the government's policy of returning ransom monies to the United States. This action resulted in the house arrest of the Panthers by the Algerian government.[84]

The final manifestation of the BPP international presence lies in the Panther global colonies created by political asylum. Sympathetic foreign governments provided the BPP with political sanctuaries to which Party members fled to avoid political persecution. In some instances, the government formally granted political asylum to the exiled Party members, official recognition that entitled a Panther expatriate to subsidized living assistance. On other occasions, Party refugees benefited from the goodwill of socialist governments, which permitted Panthers to live in the country but without government subsidies.

In the case of Algeria, the BPP was the eventual beneficiary of national accredited movement support, which superseded that of political asylum. After the close of the International Section in Algiers, several of the remaining Panthers in Algeria relocated across the African continent. Michael Tabor and his wife, Connie Matthews, resettled in Zambia. Pete O'Neal, the former founder of the Kansas City, Missouri, branch of the BPP, and his wife, Charlotte, went to Tanzania. Sekou Odinga and Larry Mack also traveled to this African socialist nation led by Julius Nyerere.

Pete O'Neal fled the United States to escape imprisonment for a felony weapons conviction of illegally transporting a gun across state lines. He maintains that the four-year sentence was politically inspired: "I am convinced that there is a particular reason why they came down so hard on us. With our programs, we started making serious inroads into the heart of the people."[85] In 1972 Pete and Charlotte O'Neal resettled in Arusha, Tanzania. Since 1979 the former Panther couple has owned a farm thirteen miles outside of Arusha, where they continue the practice of community service honed during their tenure in the BPP. This activism led the Wameru people to select Pete O'Neal as one of the elders of their ethnic group. The couple built the United African-American Community Center, which recruits foreign student volunteers, and in 1994 organized an exchange program for delinquent black youth from their former home of Kansas City. Although Pete O'Neal found a safe haven in Tanzania, he never enjoyed the benefits of official political asylum.

From August 1974 through June 1977, Cuba was a political sanctuary for Huey Newton. The Party's cofounder fled the United States to avoid prosecution for murder and assault charges involving two separate incidents. Newton's wife Gwen and his two children joined him in Cuba during his near-three-year exile. Initially, Newton requested work in the sugar fields as a sugarcane cutter, but officials refused due to Newton's inexperience, which they maintained would have adversely affected sugarcane production. Instead, Newton worked in a cement truck repair factory in the Santa Clara province. Later, he was an instructor at the University of Havana, where he taught a course entitled "Social Movements in the United States." In late June 1977 Newton left Cuba and voluntarily returned to Oakland to face his pending criminal charges. Upon returning to the United States, Newton expressed his appreciation for the international solidarity extended by Cuba: "And I'd also like to thank the courageous Cuban people for giving me refuge when I was in need. The Cuban people made what would have been a difficult experience, a rewarding, beautiful experience, learning socialism—that socialists' way of brotherly and sisterly love."[86]

Cuba's international assistance continued in 1988 when Assata Shakur, BPP activist and alleged member of the Black Liberation Army, resurfaced on the socialist island after living ten years underground. On November 2, 1979, Shakur was liberated from a prison in Clinton, New Jersey, by members of the Black Liberation Army. During her exile in Cuba, Shakur, the recipient of official political asylum, earned a Ph.D. in social history from the University of Havana. She regularly gives interviews to the dissident press and frequently participates in academic and political conferences held in Cuba. Recently, the Cuban government failed to yield to intense pressure from American officials to have Assata Shakur deported to the United States. In 1997 the New Jersey State Highway Patrolmen's Association petitioned Pope John Paul to lobby Fidel Castro to extradite Assata Shakur to the United States during the Papal visit to Cuba; Governor Christine Whitman of New Jersey offered a $100,000 reward for the return of Shakur to the state of New Jersey; and members of the House of Representatives passed a near-unanimous resolution making the 1998 deportation of Shakur to the United States a stipulation for improved diplomatic relations between the two nations. Cuba's unwavering support of Shakur and other Black Power activists in the midst of American political and economic pressure continues to demonstrate the nation's commitment to international solidarity.[87]

Astonishingly, a small black nationalist organization from the slums of west Oakland, California, with fewer than fifty members, developed into one of the most significant actors of the global insurgency of the late 1960s. The Panthers benefited from the international solidarity of sympathetic foreign allies—nation-states, political organizations, and influential leftist activists. Concomitantly, the BPP reciprocated by providing invaluable assistance to the political efforts of international leftists. The ideological trajectory and political activism of the BPP situated the Panthers firmly within the New Left world-historical movement. In their search for optimal political strategy, BPP theoreticians gleaned lessons from a host of revolutionary thinkers and guerrilla movements spanning Africa, Europe, Asia, and Latin America, incorporating the ideas, strategies, and goals of past world-historical social movements, particularly those of the New Left historical epoch. Panther doctrine, undergirded by Marxist-Leninist thought, advocated the self-determination of all people and the transformation of the U.S. political system. The BPP, like other New Left global actors, opposed all forms of oppression; the Party's slogan, "All Power to the People," resonated with oppressed people across the globe. Notwithstanding accusations that its philosophy reflected sloganeering rather than ideological coherence, BPP leaders adamantly reserved the right to make any necessary adaptation of revolutionary principles to the unique experience of African Americans. Hence, BPP doctrine was a synthesis of many political ideas, ranging from the Declaration of Independence to the revolutionary thought of the New Left. While the Panthers failed to capture state power, an improbable objective from the onset, the BPP did advance the interests of the oppressed regardless of race, gender, nationality, or sexual orientation. Furthermore, the Black Panther Party inspired and activated scores of individuals throughout the world to fight for a new vision of freedom.

3

A Life in the Party

An Historical and Retrospective Examination of the Projections and Legacies of the Black Panther Party

Mumia Abu-Jamal

Malcolm X, seen as "one of the great prophets of black liberation" at the time of his 1965 assassination, so deeply inspired Huey P. Newton (hereafter HPN) that he would refer to the Black Panther Party as the "heirs of Malcolm."[1] In such a context, then, imprisonment, rather than a social stigma, became a mark of honor. With Malcolm gone HPN, one of Malcolm's "heirs," was seen by many Party faithful as the man most able to realize his radical Black Nationalist vision.

How then was HPN perceived by those inside the BPP?

Summer 1969 was a hot time in Philadelphia and a time the local branch spent spreading the party message of rebellion and resistance. One internal highlight of the season was a visit to Philadelphia by the respected BPP field marshal, D.C., a member of the Party's leading Central Committee. His visit to the city served to provide an invaluable opportunity for an authentic party elder to teach and guide younger Panthers.

This, D.C. did with sensitivity and alacrity. Wednesday evenings at 7:30, the Party held p.e. (political education) classes for Party members, community workers, and supporters. Usually, more advanced members would read passages from Marxist or radical texts, and then "break them down," or analyze and explain them.

D.C., with his calm reassuring manner, didn't read from the stodgy, hoary texts but talked informally about his history in the Party, and of conflicts with the state.

"Huey is the baddest muthafucka in Black America. His love for Black folks is so strong, you can walk on it; you can feel it, man!

Editors' note: This essay consists of fragments extracted from Mumia Abu-Jamal's master's thesis of the same title, which he completed in 1999 at California State University, Dominguez Hills. We selected these particular passages because they give a sense of Mumia's involvement in the BPP, his understanding of the significant roles women played in the Party, and his analysis of the BPP's programs and impact. Woven into the narrative is also his response to Hugh Pearson's defamation of Huey P. Newton.

"And Huey built the Black Panther Party to be the vanguard party, the revolutionary party; the mule for our people to ride to get to Revolution!

"Now, what is the objective of the Black Panther Party? Can anybody answer that?"

A smattering of hands go up.

"You, sister" D.C. points to Candy, a beautiful, dimpled seventeen-year-old Panther.

"Um—to defend black folks from the racist-dog-pig cops!" she announced, proud of herself.

Nervous laughter raced around the room, a linoleum-tiled, wood-paneled meeting area that less than ten hours later would serve as the place where over sixty neighborhood kids would gather to eat their breakfasts.

D.C. smiled gently and joked, "Damn, sister! Did you call 'em enough names?"

The nervous laughter became genuine, and exploded from thirty young mouths.

"That's a good answer, Candy, but I want all of y'all to understand this: the Black Panther Party's objective is to establish revolutionary black political power for Black people in America; and also, to achieve self-determination for our people though a UN-supervised plebiscite where our people can freely determine our destiny."

"Brother D.C.?"

"Yeah, brother?"

"Uh . . Umm—What's a pleeb . . uh—pleeb-o-site?"

More nervous titters are heard, by many who, no doubt, hadn't the faintest idea of what the term meant.

"Well, Brother Jeff, that word only means vote. You see, Black folks never chose American citizenship; it was imposed onto us. And over one hundred years after slavery 'sposed to end, Blacks still treated like aliens in this country. That's why we need the plebiscite (laughter)—uh, vote (more laughter)—to have our people determine, once and for all, whether we want to be American citizens, or if we want our own separate, socialist nation; that's for the people to decide."

"Well, D.C.—uh, can I ask you something, Brother?"

"Sure, Brother—who is that, Brother Tick?"

"Right on—O.K. Now if pleebo?—uh—

"Pleba-uh—"

"Plebiscite"—

"Yeah—However you say it (laughter)—If that word mean 'vote,' why not just say, 'vote'?" (laughter, again).

"Well, Brotha Tick, lemme put it to ya this way: When our brother, Huey P. Newton, founded the Black Panther Party, with brother Bobby Seale, the Minister of Defense wrote our Ten Point Program and Platform. Point 10 of that program talks about a 'plebiscite', a 'UN-supervised plebiscite' to determine the destiny of our people in the Black Colony; you, dig me, Tick?"

"Right on."

"Well, is you gonna tell Huey P. Newton, the Minister of Defense of the Black Panther Party—our leader, one of the baddest niggas ever to walk the earth—how and what to write?"

Tick, nervous now, begins to stutter, "Uh—uh—No, sir! Field Marshal D.C.! Uh—"

"Well, I ain't either!"

The room erupts in gales of laughter, as the tension is released by D.C.'s humorous manner. When it subsides, he continues in a serious tone:

"Brothers and Sisters: When y'all joined the Black Panther Party, y'all joined the revolution to free our people from this racist, capitalist power structure. Now, being a revolutionary in an oppressive system is hard work, ain't it?"

"Yup!"

"Un—huh"

"Right on, Brother!"

"Well, then—we can't let a little word like 'plebiscite' get in our way. As revolutionaries, we gotta study the revolutions in other countries, like Cuba, or Mozambique, or China. If you ain't scared of this racist, fascist white power structure, of the most powerful empire on earth, how we gonna be scared of words?

"In our party, Huey P. Newton says, 'Each one, teach one.' That means when a Panther learns something, he teaches it to his fellow Panther. That way, we all learn, right?"

"Right on!"

"Huey P. Newton is the greatest, boldest, most righteous black man to lead Black people this nation's ever seen!"

"Right on!"

"Huey P. Newton faced down this fascist pig and said, 'If you shoot me, pig, I'ma shoot ya back!' and when he did this, he stood up for Black folks all over this country! Am I right, y'all?"

"Right on, Brother D.C.!" "Right on, Field Marshal!" "That's right!"

"Huey P. Newton is the only Black leader who could walk across this country, and millions of our people would follow him!"

"Right on!"

"So that mean's we gotta Free Huey!"

"Free Huey!" "Right on!"

"Now, study the Ten Point Program—"

"Right on!"

"Memorize it—"

"Right on!"

"And also memorize the Party's Three Main Rules of Discipline—

1. Obey orders in all your actions;
2. Do not take a single needle or piece of thread from the poor and oppressed masses; and
3. Turn in everything captured from the attacking enemy."

Winding up now, D.C. launched into the party motto, memorized by most with ease, and therefore joined by all who composed this secular chorus:

> "All Power to the People!
> Black Power to Black People!
> Brown Power to Brown People!
> White Power to the White People!
> Panther Power to the Black Panther Party!"

"Right on!" D.C. chanted, his voice echoed in two dozen youthful throats, and the group had a palpable sense of release, an open, psychic suffusion of commonality that gave the p.e. class the special elatedness that one feels after church.

For D.C., with his warm, open manner, and as one who walked with the beloved Minister of Defense, seemed more like a priest than a Field Marshal, and his patient presence was a blessing to the assembled young, who would go out on Columbia Ave. and work harder than ever to bring Huey home, to build the Party, and to make revolution.

For most Panthers who sat through the summer night's heat for D.C.'s political education class, if he was a priest then HPN was like a god; or perhaps more aptly, a man-god akin to Prometheus who, instead of stealing fire, unleashed the raging fire of Black millions at a system that spat on them and their ancestors for centuries. HPN, although a young man of barely twenty-five, unlike Martin Luther King Jr. called himself and his party revolutionary.

For most Panthers, "making the revolution" meant selling newspapers, managing the various party programs, feeding children in the breakfast program, passing out leaflets, giving speeches, arranging meetings with area community groups, and the like.

This kind of hard, consistent, and unpaid labor bespeaks a deeply felt idealism that is the very antithesis of the cynical criminality projected by Hugh Pearson.[2] It also reflects a highly ideologically driven motivation that is either absent from Pearson's account or seriously misrepresented by his textual manipulation of the documentary and evidentiary data in order to fit his preexisting bias.

While it is undeniable that HPN played a seminal role in BPP history, one cannot discount nor diminish the powerful forces of radical change and revolutionary transformation that permeated this period; the forces, in fact, that motivated a HPN to seize the moment, to coalesce, to build, and to dare.

HPN was part of an historical continuum, of which Malcolm's militant martyrdom, Robert Williams's armed defiance, and Frantz Fanon's cutting anticolonial analysis and critique were constituent parts and accessible historical referents. That said, it is simply ahistorical to decontextualize the life experience of HPN, as if he were the very movement itself.

No man is a movement.

To suggest otherwise is to adhere to the "Great Man theory" of historical interpretation, which has been largely supplanted and discredited by more comprehensive ways of examination.[3]

Seen in this light Pearson's work, albeit ambitious, seems deeply flawed.

Women in the Party

One cannot read Pearson's portrayal of the role of women in the BPP without coming to the conclusion that male abuse of women was flagrant, wide-ranging, and routine.[4] While Pearson seeks to present several cases as reflective of national practice, his conclusions are again found wanting because of the narrowness and the paucity of his evidence. Just as his fundamental analysis suffers from a parsimoniousness of perspective, his presentation of the life and experiences of female Panthers is severely flawed.

While it is undeniable that the BPP was primarily a male organization, it was forced of necessity to promote bright, capable women to positions of power, like section leader Afeni Shakur, who, although claiming she was neither "brilliant" nor had any "leadership ability," simply had to do the job.

When two leading Panthers were busted on old bench warrants from old, pre-BPP membership offenses, they appointed her to this key party organizing post, despite her objections, "and every time I'd tell them that I shouldn't be in any position like that, they would just look at me and tell me there's nobody else to do it. That's how they justified it."

As an angry, alienated, desperately poor girl from North Carolina, living in the cold, hellish city, how did she interact with the BPP? After hearing a "cute little nigger" (cofounder Bobby Seale) making a street-corner soapbox speech on 125th Street and

Seventh Avenue, she learned of the BPP. Shortly after hearing Bobby speak, she made her way to the BPP Harlem office, attended a political education meeting, and joined. How was this young female treated? "When I met Sekou [Odinga] and Lumumba [Shakur] it was the first time in my life that I ever met men who didn't abuse women. As simple as that. It had nothing to do with anything about political movements. It was just that never in my life had I met men who didn't abuse women, and who loved women because they were women and because they were people."

Afeni hailed from the Harlem office. From the Brooklyn office, former Panther Frankye Malika Adams challenged the very notion of the BPP as a "male's party": "Women ran the BPP pretty much. I don't know how it got to be a male's party or thought of as being a male's party. Because those things, when you really look at it in terms of society, these things are looked on as being women things, you know, feeding children, taking care of the sick and uh, so. Yeah, we did that. We actually ran the BPP's programs."[5] Indeed, if a more balanced account of the Oakland office was written, it would've significantly undermined Pearson's central thesis that the sexual abuse of Party women was flagrant, wide-ranging and routine.[6] Further, a systematic review of the treatment of women in Oakland would have, at bare minimum, examined the fate of the first woman to join the Party, Oakland native Tarika Lewis, as she lived, struggled and worked as one of the few females in an all-male milieu.

Lewis received no special treatment and was subject to the same organizational regulations as her male counterparts. In addition to regular attendance in political education classes, she trained in the usage, cleaning, disassembly, and reassembly of small arms. In her first year of service she made rapid advancements in rank, was appointed a section leader, ran drills, and taught political education. That said, she was still challenged: "When the guys came up to me and said 'I ain't gonna do what you tell me to do 'cause you a sister,' I invited 'em to come on out to the weapons range and I could outshoot 'em."[7] Such a Panther, woman or no, would earn the respect of her comrades with her undeniable abilities and demonstrated performance. The omission of Lewis—an Oakland native, and indeed one of the first female Panthers—from Pearson's narrative is troubling.

Our other examples, gleaned from the public record, were equally accessible to the principled researcher, and their glaring lack of reference in Pearson's work denotes either a demonstrable denial of the positive role women played in the Party, or a willing ignorance. While our examples do not, and could not, discount the specific example of the sexual abuse of women cited by Pearson, they call into question his premise that such treatment was flagrant, wide-ranging, or routine. Moreover, by balancing the picture, the foregoing examples surely mitigate Pearson's portrayal of "the better half" of the BPP.

This is not to suggest, however, that sexism was not a serious problem in the party; that it hampered Party growth, development, and maturation cannot be gainsaid. What is clear, however, is that sexism did not, and could not, exist in a vacuum. As a prominent feature of the dominant social order, how could it not exist in a social formation drawn from that order, albeit from that order's subaltern regions?

And for men who, often for the first time in their lives, exercised enormous power, sexism became a tool for the exercise of sexual dominance over a subordinate, as noted by a young Panther, and now scholar, Regina Jennings:

> *All I wanted was to be a soldier. I did not want to be romantically linked with any of my comrades, and even though I gave my entire life to the Party—my time, my energy, my will, any clothes, and my skills; yet my captain wanted more. My captain wanted me. . . . I lacked maturity and the skill necessary to challenge authoritarian men, so I searched for ways to circumvent the sexism of my captain. I was determined not to leave the Party*

because I felt there was no other place in America where I could fully be my Black revolutionary self. . . . After a year of transforming myself into a young woman who cared deeply for my people and becoming a fixture within Oakland and enjoying all of its rights and privileges, I found that my captain searched for greater ways to push me out of the Party. . . . There were women who came through the Party and would immediately leave because of the vulgar male behavior. There were women in the Party like me who tried to hold on because we understood the power, the significance, and the need for our organization. Black men, who had been too long without some form of power, lacked the background to understand and rework their double standard toward the female cadre. Perhaps, if the Party had external observers—community elders who respected our platform—such unfair practices against women may not have occurred.[8]

As a precocious sixteen-year-old, Jennings, a Philadelphia native, took a plane to Oakland with the express intention of joining the BPP; when asked why she wanted to join, she would answer with youthful brio, "I wanna kill all the white people; that's why."

The Officer of the Day, a mature Panther who had heard it all, calmly took down her information and, after a suitable investigation, accepted her for membership, even though she was a drug addict who had a somewhat simplistic view of the Party's role. They cured her of her addiction and filled the drugless void "with a pure and noble love for my people." That such bright, energetic, and idealistic women such as she were subjected to the debilitating effects of sexism was a tragedy, but Jennings reminds us this was not an all-encompassing feature of BPP life: "All men in the Party were not sexist. In fact, many fought with me against the foolishness of our captain. These men were also ostracized by the leadership." Jennings' experience teaches us that while sexism certainly existed in the Party, and poisoned some interactions between male and female comrades, it most often had at its roots imbalanced power relations between the higher and lower ranks—an imbalance reflected in contemporary bourgeois life in the army, air force, and other male-dominated institutions of society. Indeed, former Party chief Elaine Brown's account of her life on the "throne" is a tale of gender politics, power relations, and the sexual dominance she exhibited when she was appointed to the top post by HPN as he left for exile.[9]

Angela D. LeBlanc-Ernest, director of the Black Panther Party Research Project at Stanford University, writes of a period in the Party marked by intense state repression, a time when the organization of necessity turned inward and relied on its women literally to save the group:

During this state of organizational flux, women in the Party emerged as national and local Party leaders. Some assumed the rank and duties left unoccupied by the departure of their male comrades, while other women filled prominent local positions from the outset. Under both patterns of leadership succession, the individual's talents, skills, and performance formed the selection criteria for advancement in the BPP. Both Kathleen Cleaver and Patricia Hilliard held influential positions at the national level, Communications Secretary and Finance Secretary respectively. In Panther affiliates throughout the nation, Elaine Brown, Ericka Huggins, Barbara Sankey, Ann Campbell, Afeni Shakur, Yvonne King, and Audrea Jones were among many women who became influential leaders in their respective chapters during the revolutionary phase of the BPP.[10]

Pearson's broad-brush attack on the Party quite obviously misses these salient features of the role of women in the Party life. It does not serve the thesis he advances, so it is apparently ignored.

Similarly, one would never guess nor learn that the late Eldridge Cleaver, BPP Minister of Information, gave the most unambiguous and principled directive in Party history on the necessity for gender quality in BPP ranks, in a letter from exile published in the *Black Panther* of July 5,1969. In what Cleaver termed a "stinging rebuke to all manifestations of male chauvinism within our ranks," he praised the commitment and tenacity of imprisoned Panther Ericka Huggins, and all Panther women: "Let it be a lesson and an example to all of the sisters, particularly to all the brothers, that we must understand that our women are suffering strongly and enthusiastically as we are participating in the struggle."[11]

The BPP, like other groups of the period, had sexism within its ranks, and this tendency caused serious damage to group cohesion and morale. It is also fair to say that the BPP openly acknowledged its deficits on this score, and fought against it, with varying degrees of success. Yet, as we have seen, a man does not a movement make. Nor can the events of one chapter be transposed to the events of over forty separate chapters and branches situated across America. As different cities have different tempos, rhythms, and feels, so too did different branches of the BPP; northern Party branches were far more assertive than their southern compatriots; southern chapters moved at a more restrained pace.

Former BPP Chief of Staff David Hilliard, who ran the Party for several years during the incarcerations of the cofounders HPN and Bobby Seale, and the exile of Minister of Information, Eldridge Cleaver, has been criticized by some for his "harshly authoritarian" stewardship of the organization (ca. 1969–70).[12] As a southern-born, California-reared boyhood friend of HPN, Hilliard found several of the eastern chapters quite disconcerting. Indeed, years later, he would condemn the New York chapter by using one of the most damning epithets imaginable—"cultural nationalists."[13]

While such a charge is absurd on its face (it might be accurate to call them "culturally informed," however), it reflects Hilliard's honest perception of Panthers who had names like Dhoruba, Afeni, Oba, and the like. This was exacerbated by the high percentage of New York Panthers who were Muslims, because of the powerful influence of Hajj Malik Shabazz (Malcolm X). Of the New York 21, at least two (Dr. Curtis Powell and Richard Harris) either talked to Minister Malcolm X or heard and saw him preach in the Mosque. Malcolm X spent some of his most productive years as head of Temple 7 in Harlem. It is only fitting that many New York Panthers would be deeply influenced by Malcolm X, politically as well as religiously.

Although HPN heard Malcolm X speak in person and was deeply "impressed" by his ministry, he rejected religion, as did most West Coast Panthers.[14] In a party as ideologically hostile as the BPP became to any smattering of cultural nationalism, the New York chapter, with its Muslims, Yorubas, and Puerto Ricans (and probably a few Santerios), while thoroughly New Yorkers, were seen as somehow suspect. This reveals the very real, visceral differences between members of the same radical formation, who happened to grow to adulthood in a differing sector of the same Black colony.

As noted elsewhere, there was no single BPP; there were many, unified in one national organization, to be sure, but separated by the various regional and cultural influences that form and inform consciousness. That said, it is important to say here that statements of negation provide some insight into what the party wasn't, while this writer hasn't overtly stated what the party stood for.

Former BPP chairman Bobby Seale introduced HPN to the potent political analyses of the brilliant Martinique-born psychiatrist and Algerian revolutionary Frantz Fanon, from which arose the position that African Americans, like most of the 1960s-era Third World, were "colonial subjects." Fanon's *Wretched of the Earth* was an important learning tool for all Panthers, and was assigned as a required study.[15] Works such as this, the speeches of Malcolm X, the *Red Book* of Mao Tse-Tung, and the like, once intertwined with the BPP Ten Point Program and Platform, served to develop a united, revolutionary nationalist consciousness, and joined BPP people from coast to coast, or from Winston-Salem, North Carolina, to Boston, Massachusetts.

In this sense, then, clearly, the BPP was one party; yet, it was several parties as we have noted above, divided by region and culture. A broader perspective would have taught Pearson this valuable lesson: the macrocosm cannot truly be found in the microcosm.

Political Education of the Masses

The BPP took its responsibilities to educate the black and working-class masses quite seriously, and expressed this commitment through several of its programs, among them the establishment of liberation schools, the regular publication of a radical and independent newspaper, and the erection of its Intercommunal Youth Institute, later renamed the Oakland Community School. The BPP-operated school was so remarkable that it garnered a special award from the California legislature in September 1977 for "having set the standard for the highest level of elementary education in the state."[16] The school operated for over a decade.

As we have noted above, the political education program was an important party vehicle for the dissemination of the BPP message, ideology, and outlook. The P.E. classes, as they were called, were the adult equivalents to liberation schools, and although their quality, regularity, and program content might differ from city to city, in most instances they would feature a reading from a central text from a leading member, and an explanation asked for from, or by, a community person. From such readings would arise discussions about contemporary life as it related to the cited passage. P.E. classes also served as important recruitment devices.

In a broader sense, these classes also gave the BPP an opportunity to interact with the community, and to develop channels of communication separate and apart from those mediated through and via the establishment press. In furtherance of this latter goal, the BPP established the *Black Panther: Intercommunal News Service,* a weekly newspaper that was a regional, national, and international journal of radical and black revolutionary news, analysis, and opinion. Although the BPP was under relentless government repression for years, the Party organ met its deadline every week for over a decade, and incidentally produced a product that, in the words of archconservative critic E. D. Hirsch Jr., was clearly first-rate: "The writers for *The Black Panther* had clearly received a rigorous traditional education in American history, in the Declaration of Independence, the Pledge of Allegiance to the flag, the Gettysburg Address, and the Bible, to mention only some of the direct quotations and allusions in these passages. [And] they also received rigorous traditional instruction in reading, writing and spelling. I have not found a single misspelled word in many pages of radical sentiment I have examined in that newspaper."[17] The paper sold well over 100,000 copies per week, more than many "mainstream" papers. To the extent Hirsch's critique was correct, it was due to the editorships of Raymond Lewis, Frank Jones, Elbert "Big Man" Howard, Bobby Heron, Judy Douglass, David DuBois, JoNina Abron, and Elaine Brown, among others. This writer, who functioned as writer, graphic artist, typist, proofreader, and assistant to editor Judy Douglass during her period of production of the *Black Panther,* was also a high school dropout who, given his ghetto upbringing, hardly received "a rigorous traditional education."[18]

That said, the newspaper, which was spectacularly successful, was produced by a highly motivated, and nonprofessionally trained cadre of young people who were taught to perform the skills needed to produce the paper.

The paper was a major target of the state, and a number of FBI reports made this clear: "The Black Panther Party newspaper is one of the most effective propaganda operations of the BPP. Distribution of this newspaper is increasing at a regular rate thereby influencing a greater number of individuals in the United States along the black extremist lines. Each recipient is requested to submit by 6/5/70 proposed counterintelligence measures that will hinder the vicious propaganda being spread by the BPP. The BPP newspaper has a circulation in excess of 139,000. It is the voice of the BPP *and if it could be effectively hindered it would result in helping cripple the BPP"* (emphasis added).[19]

The response from the field was not long in coming. Former editor JoNina Abron notes that less than a week after the above memo was issued, "the San Diego FBI office proposed to spray a foul-smelling chemical on copies of the *Black Panther."*[20] In fact, such actions did happen in several cities across the country, from "foul-smelling chemicals" to urine, all designed to make the product unsellable. Indeed, there was a rather painstaking investigation of the paper by members of the U.S. Congress, a source, no doubt, of much unfriendly attention from U.S. intelligence agencies.

Much has been written by scholars and ex-Panthers alike that notes or is critical of the FBI's infamous COINTELPRO (counterintelligence program) operation. Even the doctoral thesis of HPN concentrated on this facet of government surveillance, to the exclusion of much else.[21] From the very earliest days of party organizing efforts, the FBI surveilled BPP activists and sent copies of their reports to other agencies of government, including Military Intelligence (MI), Naval Intelligence (NISO), and the Secret Service, among others, under the rubric RM—"Racial Matters."

Because the BPP and its voice, the *Black Panther,* were addressed to the needs, concerns, and rebellious spirits of the repressed lumpen proletariat and working-class sectors of the black colony, it attracted the class antipathy of the bourgeois and petit-bourgeois elements who traditionally constituted Black leadership. Implicit in such a stance is the rejection of the previously projected notions of the Black bourgeoisie. It was the institutionalization of the broad or deep wave of discontent that swelled through Black America, and remained unmet by the passivity of Martin Luther King's movement. This voice called not for integration but for liberation through revolution, and for the establishment of black revolutionary political power.

A feature, therefore, of BPP existence can be seen in the authentication of an antiestablishment point of view that contrasted sharply with the state's. This dissenting position interjected a new language and a new consciousness that devalued "bougie" behavior, and valued political activism against the U.S. empire.

International Impact and Inspirations

When the BPP emerged in the working-class and ghetto neighborhoods of Oakland, California, and particularly after the May 1967 "invasion" of the California General Assembly, it burst through into the world's press with remarkable and unexpected results. The Party's unabashedly militant and audacious political stance attracted and inspired young militants of other oppressed national minorities, who, as political scientists Charles E. Jones and Judson L. Jeffries note, formed similar radical configurations:

> *The impact of the BPP transcended the borders of the United States. Panther activism served as a revolutionary exemplar for various oppressed indigenous groups in several*

foreign countries. Left-wing political formations in England (Black Panther Movement),
Israel (Black Panther Party of Israel), Bermuda (Black Beret Cadre), Australia (Black
Panther Party), and India (Dalit Panthers) drew from the organization founded by Huey
P. Newton and Bobby Seale in the United States. Members of the Black Beret Cadre
formed in Bermuda in 1969 adopted the Panthers' signature black beret and sponsored
liberation schools and political education classes. Similarly, the Black Panther Party of
Israel created by Jews of Moroccan descent in 1971 implemented community services for
the children in the slums of West Jerusalem.[22]

That so many radical and revolutionary groups could borrow the imagery, name,
and format of the BPP bespeaks the power and potency of the original organization's
performance in the realm of politics and radical resistance. While few of the overseas
groups had any organizational link to the BPP headquarters in Oakland, California, by
their very existence they helped project the party's image and message of militant self-
defense and community service to the poor and oppressed deep into an international
popular consciousness.

They also served to validate, if only implicitly, HPN's Fanonist insight that, in an
imperial and anticolonialist context, nations were essentially illusions: "We found that
because everything is in a constant state of transformation, because of the development of
technology, because of the development of the mass media, because of the fire power of
the imperialist, *and because of the fact that the United States is no longer a nation but an*
empire, nations could not exist, for they did not have the criteria for nationhood." (emphasis added).[23]

HPN's "intercommunalism" theory (discussed elsewhere at length) is based upon the
notion that the imperialist and capitalist penetration of the so-called undeveloped countries
is so great that nations acting in imperialist as opposed to national interests cease to be, in
fact, nations. They remain nations in name, but as international capital directs its internal,
external, and military policies, they are functionally colonies, at best, and geographically
spaced communities at worst.[24] Hence the term intercommunalism. The revolutionary formations in Bermuda, England, and other places were expressions of a degree of "revolutionary intercommunalism," as they saw the importance of a struggle that, like empire, permeated national boundaries.[25]

The BPP, therefore, had global impact that moved radicals and revolutionaries
worldwide to emulate some of its more positive attributes, perhaps proving the old adage,
"Imitation is the sincerest form of flattery."

National Radical and Revolutionary Formations

As the emergence of the BPP stimulated the emergence of similar groups in the international sphere, so too did the decline and fall of the BPP give rise to several local and regional radical and revolutionary formations that borrowed much from the BPP.
Especially following the rancorous East-West split of the BPP, ex-Panthers organized
coastal, regional, or local groups that served to continue radical and grassroots work
without reliance on the Oakland center.

In Philadelphia, ex-BPP cadre formed the Black United Liberation Front (BULF),
which, through declining membership and resources, was largely defunct after six years
of operation.[26] In Kansas City, Missouri, a militant and aggressive cadre of ex-BPP
personnel transformed their chapter into a group named the Sons of Malcolm. They, too,
ceased to exist.

While the African People's Socialist Party (APSP) was more a contemporary competitor than a successor formation, the St. Petersburg, Florida–based nationalist organization utilized ex-BPP talent like Akua Njeri (née Deborah Johnson) to preside over the APSP-led National People's Democratic Uhuru Movement. Njeri was the fiancée of the martyred Fred Hampton, the popular and extremely able Chairman of the Illinois chapter of the BPP, and was herself seriously wounded in the deadly police fusillade that ended the lives of Hampton and Peoria, Illinois, BPP branch captain Mark Clark on December 4, 1969. In addition to using key ex-Panthers in the APSP apparatus, organizational propaganda depicted the close relationship between APSP and BPP theory and ideology. Njeri, in her current work, calls it a "continuation of the Panther legacy."[27]

In 1991 a talk-show assistant, Aaron Michaels, formed a group calling itself the New Black Panther Party, headquartered in Dallas, Texas. In clear imitation of its namesake, the New BPP sponsored breakfast programs, made food donations, and attracted a cadre of some 150 persons.[28] Most recently the New BPP, led by the former Nation of Islam official Dr. Khalid Abdul Muhammad, led an armed group to the Jasper, Texas, courthouse where avowed white supremacist John King was being charged in the torture-dragging death of James Byrd Jr. Although there were no incidents, their appearance caused considerable controversy. This was the second major armed demonstration by the New BPP, the first being an attendance by armed members at a Dallas school board meeting in the summer of 1996, where Michaels and two others were arrested.[29]

In 1994 the New African Vanguard Movement (NAVM) emerged in Los Angeles, California. The organization was led by, and its collective leadership partly composed of, former members of the original BPP formation. The group has formulated an Eight Point Platform and Program, updated and developed from the original Ten Point Program set forth by HPN.[30] The L.A. formation shows continuous development and maturation, reflected by its subsequent name change and reformulation of its program to ten points. It is now known as the New Panther Vanguard Movement (NPVM), and its newspaper bears a similar masthead and typeface to that of the original party organ. Its title is virtually identical: the *Black Panther International News Service*. According to the fall 1998 edition of the quarterly, NPVM collectives are established in Indianapolis, Indiana, and Decatur, Georgia.

Interestingly, the L.A.-based NPVM was cofounded by a former Panther, B. Kwaku Duren who is now an attorney, which puts one in mind of the ultralegalist tendencies of the original BPP founder, HPN, who dared to cite to armed cops California statutory law, chapter and verse, while himself legally armed. Here we see, in the original formulations as in the successor groupings, a strong orientation toward legal forms, if not ends (recognizing, as we must, that all revolutionary movements are inherently antagonistic to the established legal norms, seek their dissolution, and therefore are seen as criminal in nature, even as they claim a higher moral basis).

In New York City, a group partly composed of former BPP members organized the Black Panther Collective (BPC) in 1994. They describe their objectives as follows:

1. To continue the revolutionary legacy of the Black Panther Party
2 To put forth a vision of a new and just society
3. To build a revolutionary infrastructure
4. To engage in protracted revolutionary struggle

As we have seen, the BPP stimulated, sparked, and inspired a number of successive, imitative, and strikingly similar radical formations, some of which continue their work, drawing on models over three decades old.

That in itself is a remarkable legacy.

4

Mobilizing for
Mumia Abu-Jamal in Paris

Kathleen Neal Cleaver

Returning to the City of Light

The strike halted all railways, subways, and buses. Bumper-to-bumper traffic flooded the narrow streets of Paris, and walking became the fastest way to travel. The gray beauty of the Seine felt soothing that December morning as I walked by the river looking for number 19 Quai Bourbon, the law office of Roland Dumas. It was only Friday, but so much had happened that week, my head was spinning. It felt like the time I first met Dumas, back in the seventies.

Eldridge Cleaver and I, among hundreds of other revolutionaries, lived clandestinely in Paris then, and Dumas was our lawyer. A deputy in the French assembly at the time, he petitioned the government to legalize Eldridge's presence when he was a fugitive Black Panther leader facing imprisonment in the United States.[1]

Cities were still going up in flames after King's assassination that night Eldridge was arrested with eight other Panthers following a gun battle with the Oakland police in 1968. Once his parole was revoked, it looked like he would spend his next four years in prison regardless of how the shoot-out trial ended. But to everyone's astonishment, he won a habeas corpus petition that June, and was out on bail a week after Bobby Kennedy was killed in Los Angeles. Eldridge was the presidential candidate of the Peace and Freedom Party and the author of the best-selling *Soul on Ice,* and thousands of people turned out to hear him speak. He claimed over and over that the San Quentin guards would murder him if he ever returned to prison, and I believed it. When the appellate court ordered him back to prison, Eldridge fled to Cuba, and later to Algeria, where I joined him in 1969. Four years later we reached France, where Dumas's legal effort failed to win asylum, but our friendship with him remained alive for years.

Over twenty years later, life circled me back to the City of Light with my friend St. Clair Bourne, the black filmmaker. We arrived in late November 1995 to join radical lawyer Leonard Weinglass at several events sponsored by a collective of French organizations opposed to Mumia Abu-Jamal's execution.[2] Uncertainty marked our departure—

This essay was first published in the *Yale Journal of Law and Humanities* (Vol. 10, No. 2, 1998) while the author was a visiting professor at Benjamin N. Cardozo School of Law. The author is indebted to Maud Maron, Cardozo Law Class of 1998, for her excellent research assistance on this article.

up to the day we left New York, we didn't know whether the transportation workers' walkout in France would shut down the airport. But our flight arrived in Paris just in time for us to join the throngs that packed the sidewalks along the route of the national protest march for women's rights.[3]

On Sunday morning, the day after we arrived, all transportation unions went on strike. The national student strike took off a few days later and caught me in its turbulence. I felt like the seventies had sprung back to life.[4] Before I left Paris, I wanted to see Roland Dumas again. I valued his friendship immensely; I drew from it a sense of stability that came from reconnecting with people who in some real way helped save my life when I lived underground.

I reached his elegant law office fifteen minutes early. The enormous wooden doors opened onto a spacious courtyard where horsedrawn carriages used to enter. His office occupied one of the four suites whose tall, painted shutters faced each other. Dumas was still walking to his office from home, his secretary explained, and showed me into a wood-paneled sitting room where I glimpsed morning sunlight sparkling on the river flowing past the windows.

Roland Dumas had served as minister of foreign affairs while François Mitterand was France's president. Framed photographs of Dumas standing beside world leaders were clustered on the mantel above the fireplace. I skimmed past the color photograph of him greeting President Ronald Reagan and the one showing him standing with British prime minister Margaret Thatcher, but an older, black-and-white photograph caught my attention. Its silvery tones portrayed a younger, dark-haired Dumas sitting on a sofa next to Pierre Mendes-France, the famous French socialist leader. Behind them an exquisite Chinese lacquer screen shimmering in the background enhanced the picture's aura of intrigue. Leaning toward them from a stiff-backed chair was Chou En-lai, Communist China's austerely aristocratic foreign minister.

While I was absorbed by the photograph, Dumas, an elegant and energetic man with thick white hair, swept into the room. We embraced, and I congratulated him on his appointment to the highest court in France. Then I asked when that picture was taken in China.

"It was in 1968," he answered cheerfully.

Ironically, I was hearing the words "sixty-eight" repeated all over Paris, as demonstrators swarmed into the capital to mark the start of the nationwide student strike. "Sixty-eight" served as shorthand for an incredible year of brilliant expectations and violent defeats that still provoked excitement. Those were the days when French students fought pitched battles with the police in the streets of Paris protesting restrictive government policies.[5] They were joining the uprisings of revolutionary students in Mexico, Germany, Japan, and the United States, where the Black Power revolt inspired French demands for "student power." Striking workers who challenged the authority of the de Gaulle government joined the radical students. That same year saw the Soviet invasion of Czechoslovakia to overthrow a liberal regime,[6] the stinging defeat of U.S. troops during the Tet offensive in Vietnam,[7] the bloody battles of protestors outside the Democratic presidential convention in Chicago, and the longest American student strike in history at San Francisco State—as well as the Black Panther Party's sudden spread across the United States in the wake of King's assassination.

Dumas and I crossed the hall into his office. It had been during the summer of 1994 that I saw Dumas for the first time in nineteen years. He told me then about the memoir he was writing, and asked me to help him locate several items published in English about Eldridge. I was continuing my research about my life in Paris for the memoir I was writing, and that week I'd interviewed Ellen Wright, the widow of the great writer Richard Wright. Ellen, a literary agent, had been tremendously helpful to me and Eldridge from the day I first met her back in 1969. I handed Dumas copies of old clippings from the *International Herald Tribune* about Eldridge's departure from Paris I'd received from Ellen a few days earlier.

Dumas's manuscript, a thick stack of pages easily a foot high, each chapter separated by a colored paper folder, rested on his lap. He gave me quick synopses of the chapters as he pulled them from the stack. One was called "Lawyer for the People," another "The Death of Jean Genet."

"The Cleaver Case," Dumas recited. He paused, then smiled, saying, "You're sitting in the same chair that Eldridge Cleaver sat when he first came to my office."

How odd—to pick up that fleck of information, to feel it on the walls of the room, to sit where my presence flashed a vision from 1973 into the immediate moment.

"The War Years," the title across a blue folder, provoked my curiosity. "Were you an adult during the war?" I asked incredulously.

"No, but I fought," he replied with perfect self-assurance.

I was impressed. "You were in the Resistance?" I asked.

"Yes," he replied.

"And how old were you then?"

"Nineteen."

He was younger than I had been when I joined the Afro-American resistance movement called the Black Panther Party in 1967,[8] but older than Mumia Abu-Jamal was when he signed up with the Philadelphia Black Panther chapter as a fifteen-year-old high school student.[9] Years later the judge presiding over Mumia's murder trial in 1982 insisted that his having been in the Black Panther Party established his motive for killing a policeman, and then Mumia was sentenced to death.[10]

In France the increasingly critical scrutiny by intellectuals and activists opposed to Mumia's death was fueling protests, petition drives, forums, and other demonstrations of support for his case. The campaign called "Vie Sauve Pour Mumia" ("Save Mumia's Life") escalated when Pennsylvania governor Thomas Ridge signed the death warrant in June 1995, only days before Mumia's lawyers filed an appeal to reverse his conviction.[11] The French collective was confident their protests had helped win the unprecedented stay of execution the judge had granted during Mumia's hearing that August.[12]

As I strolled across the Ile Saint Louis after leaving Dumas's office, I felt sad that it was my last day in Paris. The red letters on a small, engraved plaque mounted by a doorway caught my eye, proclaiming that in 1941 one hundred and twelve people had been deported to the German camps from that building, among them forty children who died. Gazing at that plaque made me wonder if the Nazi occupation of France played some part in creating the sensitivity to racial persecution I'd observed in the energetic campaign to save Mumia's life. That stark phrase—"forty children who died"—burned my consciousness and jerked my thoughts back to the death penalty, the gruesome words I heard every time Mumia's case was discussed.

French Support for Mumia Rooted in Political Struggles

Julia Wright, who had asked me to come to Paris, was the spokesperson for the Support Committee for Political Prisoners in the United States, one of the Collective members. Julia's father, Richard Wright, had brought his family to live in France at the end of World War II to escape the McCarthyite persecution in America.[13] The radical Parisian political world that nurtured Wright became Julia's home.

I first met her during the summer of 1969. I'd arrived in Paris in late May, the same day that all the members of the New Haven chapter of the Black Panther Party were arrested on charges of conspiracy to commit murder. Ericka Huggins, the widow of John Huggins, who had been murdered that January on the UCLA campus along with the Los Angeles Panther leader Alprentice "Bunchy" Carter, Eldridge's best friend, had started the chapter. She had returned to her husband's hometown to fulfill his intention of starting a Panther branch, and within months she was behind bars herself. Remembering how several New York party members—those few who hadn't been swooped up in the mass arrest that April—tried to entice me to visit New Haven made me shudder. At the time, my schedule was so full it left no room for a New Haven trip. When I reached Paris, it hit me that those people insisting I visit New Haven were probably police infiltrators trying to ensnare me in the conspiracy they were setting up! I was one of the few remaining Central Committee members not under arrest, in exile, or imprisoned. The dragnet was tightening; I felt like I'd barely escaped.

Julia actively supported the black revolution, in Africa, the Caribbean, and the United States. She and her husband had sponsored a Black Power rally in Paris a few months before we met, and they were energetically assisting the independence movement on the island of Guadalupe when I first met her. I was seven months pregnant at the time, and Julia became essential in navigating my trip to Algeria, where I was determined to join my husband in time for the birth of our first child. Her combination of indomitable fierceness, appealing delicacy, and political savvy made me like her immediately. The way she merged French and African-American culture made her an invaluable ally. We became friends that summer, and have remained close ever since.

Julia had attended the hearing in Philadelphia on Mumia's motion for a new trial during the summer of 1995.[14] I was delighted at the chance to see her again, and we met for dinner at her hotel in New York. That's when I first learned the details of the French campaign against Mumia's execution, which had been barely covered, if at all, by the American press. As a member of one of the defense committees, Julia needed to find out what was happening with the competing fundraising efforts supporting Mumia's appeal. In the years after I had returned to the United States, I had finished college and had become a lawyer. Julia was certain that I could help her unravel the complexities of Mumia's support network, and I put her in touch with three women who could explain it all, people whose judgment I trusted. She also asked to interview me about the case, which dominated our conversation.

As she talked about the presiding judge, Albert Sabo, her face squinched up as if she smelled a putrid odor.[15] "He has a little thin mustache, a bald head, he looks like—a Nazi." I knew what she meant, but the unfortunate part was that hearing about a judge who looked like a Nazi—or who even made decisions as if he were part of a police state apparatus—no longer shocked me. But Julia's enthusiasm about blocking Mumia's execution was contagious, and ultimately drew me into the French campaign.

A special exhibition of *Art against the Death Penalty* had been shipped to Paris and hung at the Donguy gallery, where the drawings, paintings, and photographs were being sold to benefit Mumia's defense.[16] On Sunday my friend St. Clair accompanied me to the gallery. Above the entrance, posters with black and red block letters denouncing Mumia's execution hung from the ceiling, and on the table below the posters, stacks of petitions, postcards, compact discs, pamphlets and other literature were spread out. Collective members sat there taking donations, soliciting signatures on petitions, and selling everything displayed on the table. I was one of the speakers for the event the Support Committee was sponsoring at the gallery in conjunction with the show.

Julia introduced the program by reading the statement from political prisoners about the genesis of this art show, which she had translated into French.

"Most of us," she read, "have had quite enough of being the objects of campaigns, victims cited on petitions, defendants in legal cases or the topic of an occasional conference or panel discussion." Men locked inside Lewisburg federal prison conceived the project of *Art against the Death Penalty,* the statement continued, "as a prisoner directed collaboration because we want to break with the dynamic of people doing things about us while asserting ourselves anew as creative political people."[17] They asked the viewers to act creatively and reach out to the art communities, to actors, dancers, rappers, and painters, to explore how their work can be used to support Mumia.

Speaking in French, I welcomed the audience to the benefit and thanked them for their invaluable support in winning a stay of execution. Then I said a few words about how National Public Radio's refusal to air its planned broadcast of Mumia's program *Live from Death Row* had sparked the idea for the art show.[18]

Expatriate African-American musicians and poets performed as people continued to flock into the gallery, and after all the chairs were filled, pillows were lined along the wall to seat the overflow. After Jo Ann Pickens, the opera singer, led the audience in singing "Give Me That Old-Time Religion," Julia again stepped up to face the audience so she could translate while Leonard Weinglass spoke.

His clear voice slowly pronouncing each word, Weinglass began by saying how delighted he was to speak on the same platform with me, evoking the decades over which our lives intertwined. Then he launched into a detailed report on the domestic and international efforts that had successfully blocked Mumia's execution.[19] The simple way he spoke as he patiently listed the barriers remaining to a new trial underlined the gravity of the events. Weinglass told the assembled supporters that Judge Albert Sabo, a member of the Philadelphia Sheriff's Department for fourteen years before ascending to the bench, still retained close ties to the Fraternal Order of Police.[20] He has publicly stated that he'd never seen an innocent man in his court. Sabo, he said, has sent more people to death row than any other judge in the United States.[21]

It was Sabo who presided over Mumia's original trial, then came out of retirement to rule on the new trial motion.[22] Only four days after a lengthy hearing ended, Sabo issued a 154-page opinion refusing to grant a new trial.[23] On the fifth day a meeting of the Fraternal Order of Police took place in Philadelphia, and Judge Sabo's opinion denying Mumia a new trial turned the meeting into a victory celebration.[24]

At least the corruption Mumia faces is being publicized, I thought while Weinglass spoke. I wondered how many other nameless prisoners remained trapped by legalized injustice without anyone hearing about their cases.[25] I myself could immediately think of twelve prisoners in that situation, and I knew that represented only a fraction.

Julia mounted the raised platform at the front of the gallery and talked about Jean Genet, who strongly supported the Black Panthers, and who, years earlier, had asked the French playwright and actor André Benedetto to write a play about the prisoner George Jackson, one of the Soledad Brothers whose cause the Black Panther Party advocated.[26] But before Benedetto could complete the play, San Quentin guards murdered Jackson in the prison yard, just before his trial, claiming that he was trying to escape.[27]

Julia's comments spun my thoughts back to my old life in Paris: it had been through Genet's insistence that Roland Dumas agreed to represent Eldridge back in 1973 when we first arrived in Paris.

Benedetto was a stocky man with wavy gray hair whose dark shirt and dark suit gave him an aura of intensity. That Sunday would be the first performance of his one-act play about Mumia.[28] "Since people traditionally come to the theater to see plays in which you know the ending" Benedetto explained, "what I will present is really not theater because this drama has no ending."

In a one-man improvisational presentation, Benedetto brilliantly elaborated the web of events that caught Mumia—first on the streets of Philadelphia moonlighting as a cabdriver, then when he was wounded by a police bullet, then when the witnesses in his favor never managed to testify, then on death row. Even though my French was not fluent enough to understand every word, I was captivated by Benedetto's spellbinding performance, which the Parisian audience loved.

That following Monday morning MRAP[29] (Popular Movement against Racism), another of the organizations active in the collective, arranged for Weinglass to meet the widow of Pierre Mendès-France, an influential public figure.[30] Outspoken in the campaign to save Sarah Balabagan, a young Filipina condemned to death in the United Arab Emirates for killing the employer who raped her, Marie-Claire Mendès-France was a well-known advocate for abolishing the death penalty. Her support carried considerable weight, and after talking to Weinglass, she issued a statement condemning the death sentence imposed against Mumia Abu-Jamal, saying that "the fate of Mumia Abu-Jamal upsets me because it appears to me that his trial was conducted hastily and carelessly, that his guilt was not proven, and that he was condemned to death in part because he is Black."[31]

I waited at a nearby café with Michel Muller, the journalist who had covered Mumia's hearing in Philadelphia for the Communist newspaper *L'Humanité,* while Weinglass met with Mme. Mendes-France. A slender French woman walked over to my table, introduced herself to me as Monique, and said that she was responsible for the logistics of the meeting sponsored by the Collective to Save Mumia, at which Weinglass and I were speaking that evening. She was the first person I'd met from MRAP who gave me details about the meeting. Each speaker was allotted ten minutes—except for Weinglass, she said, whose time was unlimited.

I had drafted notes for my talk several days earlier, and I asked Julia to translate them into French for me. My speech explained how Mumia's situation grew from the past, and what his predicament revealed about the current political development in the United States. That day Julia and I had met at a cafe near Weinglass's hotel to go over the speech, a solitary man sat near us. All he did was roll cigarettes, smoke, and drink coffee. We couldn't tell whether he was watching us or not.

I boldly assured Monique that I would speak in French. In Algiers I had done some translation for the Black Panther Party, while I lived in Paris I spoke French daily for years, and for three weeks prior to my departure I'd been tutored in French. I felt certain that I could deliver the statement, and was particularly relieved to dispense with both inadvertent and deliberate mistakes involved in simultaneous translation—especially since my speech could only be five minutes if I had a translator.

Muller drove Weinglass and me to the headquarters of the French Communist Party, where a formal meeting with George Marchais was scheduled. For years Marchais had been the general secretary of the French Communist Party, and currently, he served as chairman of the Committee for the Defense of Liberty and Human Rights, an organization spearheading opposition to Mumia's execution.[32]

A huge poster of Mumia's smiling face framed by long dreadlocks hung in the ultramodern lobby where Marchais's assistants met us, then escorted us upstairs to a spacious office. I never imagined I'd meet Marchais. When I shook his hand, I felt that sudden shock of recognition that came from encountering the real person whose photograph I'd seen countless times in French newspapers years ago. We all sat on leather sofas surrounding a glass-topped table where a pot of coffee and a tray of soft drinks were neatly arranged.

Marchais began speaking to us slowly, to allow time for his words to be translated, in that assured tone of voice men accustomed to being listened to possess. "We've been in this campaign for Mumia's freedom for six years," he said. "From the beginning, our demands were clear. First, Mumia's life must be saved. Then we demanded that he receive a new trial in a different place before a different judge." He spoke about the petition campaign his committee had mounted, which he described as bigger than the start of the campaign to win Nelson Mandela's release. "Our support came from working people, from intellectuals, and reached to the highest levels of society."

Resting on the table in front of him was a letter. Marchais, proudly picking up the letter, said, "I wrote to the president of the Republic, Jacques Chirac. I received an answer from him. He told me that he has instructed our ambassador in the United States to take whatever steps are necessary to save Mumia's life. It's not often," Marchais remarked, "that the French president gets involved in this way."[33]

Marchais's blue eyes twinkled as he talked about the stack of petitions he had delivered to the American embassy. "We are part of a Collective," he stated, "but we like to preserve our freedom of action. We took thousands of petitions demanding that Mumia's life be saved to the embassy. They said that they were very aware of our efforts. That day the ambassador, Pamela Harriman, was not there, but she left a message that she would be glad to meet me if I came again." Then he pointed to two cardboard boxes stacked one on top of the other, to the right of where I sat. "We have collected over 40,000 signatures on petitions since then, and we want to deliver them to you, Mr. Weinglass.

"The next area on which we need to focus is the question of funds. But let me thank you for your visit, and ask you, how is Mumia feeling?"

The way Georges Marchais and Leonard Weinglass spoke to each other through interpreters reminded me of those stilted conversations I'd heard years ago when I was part of Black Panther Party delegations visiting the Korean or Vietnamese embassies in Algiers.[34] That stylized dialogue expressed specific agreement over goals we shared, transcending whatever vast differences marked our worlds, and helped each of us fulfill our distinct missions.

Weinglass, his remarks translated by Muller, conveyed Mumia's gratitude for the mobilization of French support, then brought Marchais up to date on the legal actions taken. Then he outlined the obstacles facing his effort to win a new trial for Mumia.

"His next appeal is to the Supreme Court of Pennsylvania, where the justices are all elected. And the Fraternal Order of Police, a right-wing police union, is one of the biggest contributors to their political campaigns. On that court a vote for Mumia is considered a vote against the police.

"We are worried, but we should get a decision in 1996. If we lose at this level, we can go before the federal court. There, judges are appointed for life, which is better for us. But there we face another obstacle.

"The new crime bill that President Clinton has indicated he will sign[35] will diminish Mumia's rights, so by the time his appeal reaches the federal court, there may be little the judges can do.

"Then, the state of Pennsylvania, which has the third largest death row in the United States, has the highest percentage of African Americans on death row.[36] The percentage is higher than in Georgia, Alabama, or Texas.

"Despite all that," Weinglass said, "Mumia remains very strong. His whole life has been devoted to political action. He always says that he hopes his case can shine a small light on the darkest corner of American society—death row."[37]

Marchais asked, "How long will the process of appeal take?"

"Approximately two years," Weinglass answered, "but the new federal legislation may speed it up."

"And what do you expect it to cost?"

Weinglass smiled and said, "Mumia's supporters tell me that I'm a very good lawyer, but a terrible fund-raiser. I forget to talk about the cost.

"We spent over $71,000 to prepare for his hearing. We hired investigators, a pathologist, a ballistics expert, and a polygraph expert. For the next appeal we'll need to raise at least $150,000."

I flicked the tape of my memory back to the countless times I'd spoken at or participated in events to raise legal defense funds for revolutionaries—Huey Newton, Eldridge Cleaver, Bobby Seale—everyone I was intimately connected with. My very presence here in Paris was indirectly tied to my association over the decades with Geronimo Pratt, the former leader of the Los Angeles Black Panther Party.[38] During the creation of a citizens commission to pressure Los Angeles district attorney Gil Garcetti for a hearing on Pratt's case, Geronimo insisted all his supporters do what they could to keep Mumia from being executed. Always being on the defensive, attempting to rescue ourselves from the abyss of prison, raising money for lawyers—it seemed to be the drumbeat of my life.

At the Bourse de Travail, white posters showing Mumia's face with American flag bars behind him and "Sauvons Mumia Abu-Jamal" in huge letters were tacked across the walls and the low table where the speakers sat facing the audience. MRAP's chairman, Mouloud Aounit, briefly introduced each speaker, who then mounted an elevated podium in back of our table. The chairman of France's section of Amnesty International began the meeting. In his speech he acknowledged—for the first time, I was told—that Mumia was a political prisoner.[39] A gentle woman named Christine Serfaty representing the International Prison Observers followed him. Sounding like a librarian, she softly contrasted prison conditions in various nations. She denounced the death penalty and concluded with a quotation from a poem by John Donne, "...never send to know for whom the bell tolls; it tolls for thee."[40]

Then Marie-Agnès Combesque, a youthful journalist who chaired the American Commission of MRAP, vividly described her visit to a black political prisoner in a remote upstate New York prison.[41] The disruption of the train strike had delayed the start of the program, but by the time she started talking, the auditorium was nearly full. In a way, that was fortuitous, because her voice was the first to express any energy. What struck me was how much the crowd looked like an Upper West Side meeting of old labor organizers and socialists in New York City. Only a handful of students sat in the audience, and of the three hundred people gathered in the hall, perhaps eight were black.

I began talking about the late sixties, when the confrontations between black liberation fighters and the state had produced hundreds of political trials and political prisoners. Back then, Mumia was a Philadelphia high school student attracted to the revolutionary Panther program, and I was a member of the Black Panther Party's Central Committee. Mumia, then known as Wesley Cook, was designated for the FBI's Security index because he "made public speeches and has written several articles expounding the ultra militant revolutionary views of the Black Panther Party."[42]

Mumia also was part of another category that the FBI targeted in its counterintelligence program (COINTELPRO) to undermine the black struggle. A March 1968 memorandum from the San Francisco special agent in charge (SAC) to Director J. Edgar Hoover stated that the Negro youth wanted something to be proud of, but he must be made to understand that if he turned to revolutionary views, he would become a "dead revolutionary."

I was a candidate for the California State Assembly on the Peace and Freedom Party ticket in 1968.[43] My campaign platform included freedom for all political prisoners. Bobby Seale, then Black Panther Party Chairman, gave this definition of a political prisoner: "To be a revolutionary is to be an enemy of the state. To be arrested for the struggle is to be a political prisoner."[44]

Mumia, had not been arrested on any serious charges before being picked up for selling Black Panther newspapers in Oakland.[45] He subsequently left the Panthers and aligned himself with other black organizations, but before he enrolled in college, Mumia briefly became the Philadelphia correspondent for the newspaper *Babylon*[46] a short-lived enterprise published by the International Section of the Black Panther Party in the wake of the COINTELPRO-provoked "split" in the party.[47] At that point the FBI reopened Mumia's file because he was identified with what they called "the Cleaver faction" of the Black Panthers—those who rebelled against Newton's authoritarian and reformist program.[48]

Years later, I said, Mumia became an award-winning journalist.[49] In radio broadcasts and articles, he remained vigilant in opposing police brutality, openly supporting the MOVE members convicted of killing a Philadelphia policeman in the late 1970s.[50] At the time of his arrest for murder, Mumia, president of the Philadelphia chapter of the National Association of Black Journalists, continually spoke out and condemned the abuse of state power, especially by the Philadelphia police.[51]

I connected the specific predicament Mumia faced with general social conditions within the United States. I spoke of how the gap between rich and poor had grown exponentially since the end of the Vietnam War,[52] explaining how our government has rushed to offer tax benefits and corporate subsidies to the wealthy, while generating more homelessness, unemployment, and despair for the poor.[53] As the average American's standard of living was declining, politicians were laying the blame at the doorstep of black criminals and welfare mothers.[54] And in this era of reaction, racism, and class warfare against the poor, the death penalty has been turned into a political weapon.[55]

I ended by saying how the mobilization around Mumia's case was reuniting many of those who had fought in the radical struggles during the sixties. Our success in winning a stay of execution demonstrated once again the power of the people!

Enthusiastic applause erupted from the audience.

Then Weinglass, flanked by his interpreter, mounted the podium. He gracefully thanked the audience for their invaluable support in winning the stay of execution, then traced the botched trial that led to Mumia's conviction. Mumia had been unable to hire any ballistics or medical experts to testify on his behalf, since only $150 was allowed for expert witness fees.[56] No forensic testimony about how Mumia's injury from Officer Faulkner's gun may have affected his ability to place a bullet between the policeman's eyes was offered.[57] The bullet that killed Faulkner, Weinglass said, was never identified as having been shot from Mumia's pistol, a .38, nor was it determined on the night of the murder whether or not that gun had even been fired.[58] The court-appointed attorney was ill equipped to handle the trial, and Mumia instead represented himself.[59] But during much of the trial Judge Sabo excluded him from the courtroom because of his protests at the conduct of the trial.[60]

Four witnesses who did not know each other each told the police they saw a black man running away from the scene after the shooting.[61] For various reasons, not one of these people was available at the trial.[62] One was a white woman who flatly refused to testify because she said she didn't like black people.[63] The witnesses who did testify that they saw Mumia shoot Faulkner were each facing criminal charges, which left them highly vulnerable to police manipulation.[64]

Weinglass pointed out that the policeman who filled out the arrest report that night wrote that "the male Negro made no statement."[65] Months later, other police officers claimed that they heard Mumia brag about killing Faulkner in his hospital bed that night.[66] During the trial, the police department claimed that the officer who filled out the original arrest report was away on vacation, and he was never called to testify.[67] But our investigation found out, Weinglass explained, that he was actually at home, not far from the courthouse, at the time of the trial.[68]

Weinglass also spoke of the personal hostility to Mumia that his reporting had evoked. Back when former chief of police Rizzo was Philadelphia's mayor, he told Mumia at a public meeting that people believed what he said and wrote about the police, and that he had better stop it. Rizzo said, "One day—and I hope it's in my career—you're going to be held responsible and accountable for what you do."[69]

Weinglass then spoke briefly about how the Philadelphia police had become so blatantly abusive that in 1979 the U.S. Department of Justice sued the entire police department.[70] The indictment echoed observations that Mumia's writing and radio broadcasts made, charging the police with a pervasive practice of brutality and intimidation in the minority community.[71] Weinglass spoke of another investigation into the corruption of the Philadelphia police that led to indictments against many officers in the Sixth District, where Mumia had been arrested.[72] Captain Giordano, the officer who first arrived on the scene where Mumia and Faulkner were shot, pled guilty to corruption charges brought by the U.S. attorney's office in Philadelphia in 1983, a year after Mumia's conviction.[73]

After explaining the obstacles he faced at every stage of the appeal process, Weinglass then talked of the amazing outpouring of international support. He announced that the Italian parliament was passing a resolution about his case, and so was the parliament in Denmark.[74] For the first time in an American legal proceeding, observers from the Japanese parliament were sent to Mumia's hearing. Former political prisoners Václav Havel and Nelson Mandela,[75] who are now presidents of their countries, expressed their opposition to his execution. Even the pope issued a statement condemning Mumia's death sentence.[76]

Of course Mumia wants to live, Weinglass concluded. But even if he loses his life, Weinglass said, he will be pleased if it has shed a little light on the darkest corner of American society—death row.

The audience gave him sustained applause.

Following the speech, Mouloud Aounit stood up and presented Weinglass with checks totaling $4,500 raised during the Collective's campaign to block Mumia's execution. The audience applauded again, and as people started to stand up and leave, Weinglass and I answered a few questions from the audience. Afterward, people crowded around our table. Most of them wanted to speak to Weinglass, but a few, mostly Africans, ventured over to me.

A tall young man wearing a suit and trench coat shook my hand. "I just want to thank you for coming to Paris," he said pleasantly. He told me that he was a student—from Mali, I believe. Next, a light-skinned woman with long dreadlocks introduced herself to me as an African journalist. "I write for a black news magazine here," she said and informed me it was "something new." Then she asked why so few Africans were at the meeting, given how many lived in Paris.

"Do you think these people want to organize Africans?" I said to her, almost by reflex. "That would be dangerous."

I didn't say what I knew so well—that any major political prisoner campaign has a way of falling prey to political schisms, rivalries, and pre-existing agendas, and this one was no different. Julia felt insulted that she had not been personally invited to the mass meeting, but she kept Weinglass ignorant of her distress at the way MRAP treated the Support Committee, the only part of the Collective with black members.

I merely said to the woman, "They didn't even bother to announce the benefit being held tomorrow by African Americans in the Collective—did they?" I showed her my copy of *L'Humanité* with the story about the event and the address of the gallery, and suggested that she come.

A rail-thin, dark-skinned young man with a fierce gleam in his eyes stood away from the table, staring at me. He was wearing a knitted cap and an army surplus jacket, and carrying a worn cotton backpack across his shoulder. He approached the table haltingly, then mumbled something. I asked him his name, which he told me, and then I asked where he was from. I noticed that his face had hardened, and he radiated anger.

He spit out, "Burkina Faso," the name of a small West African nation that used to be a French colony.[77] His hands clutched a shiny, hardcover book about the recent assassination of Burkino Faso's president. "Why do they talk about the prisoner in America?" he growled. "The same things happen here!"

"Yes, I know."

But that was not why I was invited to speak in Paris. Mumia's credentials as an imprisoned writer helped galvanize French supporters, who were energized by a simmering resentment of America's cultural imperialism. French radicals were far less interested in exposing the struggle of Africans subjected to French colonial domination. Although the descendants of Africans enslaved in America evoked hostility and fear among white Americans comparable to that Africans faced in France, African Americans were not treated like Africans in Paris. No African or Algerian prisoner could generate the attention Mumia attracted, especially because his blackness served as evidence of America's racist backwardness to which the French could feel superior.

The young African drew himself up straight, raised his voice, and said, "I get stopped by the police all the time, they always ask me for identity. They harass me. Even here," he said, his voice becoming louder as he pointed emphatically toward the floor. "Even here in this meeting!" As he trembled with anger, I saw the same smoldering rage in his face that was consuming young black people in America's ghettos, a rage that one generation earlier had catapulted the Black Panther Party onto the political stage.

Something to Do with the Color of Our Skin

A friend of Julia's who belonged to MRAP had given St. Clair and me her Latin Quarter apartment during our stay in Paris, and she invited us to lunch the day after the event at the Bourse de Travail. The massive demonstration planned for Tuesday was to march along rue Gay Lussac right directly in front of Point du Jour, the Marxist bookstore where she was working that day.[78] She asked us to meet her there.

Prime Minister Juppé had announced reforms of the national social insurance that had been the cornerstone of French society since the end of the war.[79] Popular reaction was swift and hostile, rejecting the new taxes, limitations on retirement benefits, and cutbacks. Newspapers had widely quoted Juppé's remark that "if two million French take to the streets, the government will fall." His opponents, particularly the train unions, who adamantly rejected government efforts to shut down thousands of miles of rural routes, were mobilizing actively to bring that many people into the streets.[80]

As St. Clair and I mounted the hill leading to the bookstore, tow trucks were pulling the parked cars away, uniformed police were placing red traffic cones by the curb in the street, and traffic dwindled to nothing. Later we learned that not only was the street being cleared, but plainclothes police were asking businesses along the demonstration route to close.

Across the street from the bookstore our hostess took us and her friend Steve, a unemployed British journalist, to an Indian restaurant. Once we were seated, she inquired whether the police had asked the restaurant to close.

"No, no one asked," the waiter replied.

"Ah, discrimination against foreigners," she complained. "They asked the French businesses to close. They're treating you differently."

The brown-skinned waiter shrugged.

Steve, a thin, tired-looking, blue eyed fellow, chattered on and on about his gaffes with language when he first emmigrated to the United States with his parents and started high school in Hayward, California. At the time, I barely noticed how determined he seemed to keep the conversation going regardless of whether he had anything to say.

After lunch the four of us took up a position along the sidewalk in front of the bookstore to watch the demonstration. St. Clair focused his Nikon on the arriving marchers waving square red flags with "FO" (Force Ouvrière) in large letters.[81] Marchers chanted rhythmically "Retirez, retirez, retirez le plan Juppé"—insisting that Juppe's austerity measures be rescinded. As I looked at the workers filing past us along rue Gay Lussac, I was struck by how much they resembled what we call the rank and file, ordinary working people with jobs in the public sector as well as private industry. The reactionary Republicans were legislating far more drastic changes than Prime Minister Juppé was promoting, yet organized opposition to American cutbacks was much weaker. I wished the Contract with America had provoked such spirited resistance—but France's long history of labor organization, which made such demonstrations possible, could not be easily duplicated in the United States.

Some of the marchers held large banners identifying themselves as employees of the Treasury Department, or hospitals, or Kodak, but hundreds of the demonstrators had no banners. Waves and waves of Force Ouvrière union members marched past us. Several times passersby informed me of the origins of FO.

It was created with CIA money after the war, I was told at least twice; originally the Communist labor federation, the General Trade Confederation (CGT) was known as CGT-FO, but the American intervention split the FO away from the CGT and made it more like an American union—and anticommunist. How familiar it all sounded, after surviving the COINTELPRO-induced split in the Black Panther Party. Many years later I found out that the CIA had a hand in that as well.

"Look at their flags," one collective member who had joined us remarked. "They're brand-new. You can tell they're not used to striking. In fact, they're so busy signing agreements with management we call them 'force-stylo' [force ballpoint pen]." Unions from around France marched past, some from Bretagne to the north and a cheerful band of mechanics from Catalan. The singsong chants, "Retirez, retirez, retirez le plan Juppé," continued. The flow of demonstrators seemed unending.

St. Clair and I decided to go back to the apartment to rest before the evening's program at the gallery. On the way, we looked for a place to change our dollars into French francs, but every post office and bank we passed had closed in response to the demonstration. At the foot of the hill where avenue Gobelins and rue Claude Bernard met, we saw a cloud of smoke rising above a slowly moving mass of marchers holding a white banner. Drumbeats accompanied their motion. A flare thrown into the street hissed and gave off white smoke. The CGT segment of the demonstration was heading toward us.

Their banners were worn; their members included the train workers, adamant in their opposition to the government. I heard a young demonstrator shout, "Juppé salaud, payez votre loyer" ("Bastard Juppé, pay your own rent")—referring to a scandal a month earlier that exposed how Juppé had obtained a reduced-rent apartment for his family at government expense.[82] Once the story broke, Juppé resigned, but President Chirac had asked him to form a new government. He returned to his position as prime minister and then proposed radical cutbacks to reduce France's deficit in its social insurance program. Thousands upon thousands of union demonstrators marched past us, closely observed by three different police units—the national police, the special riot squad called CRS, and the gendarmes.

That evening Weinglass and I were scheduled to speak at a cultural program similar to the previous event at the gallery. St. Clair and I hoped we'd be able to get a taxi to the Right Bank, but every one that passed was flashing the yellow busy light. We walked toward the Seine, but still didn't see a taxi that wasn't occupied. I felt certain we'd catch one before we reached the Pont d'Austerlitz, but there we found throngs of pedestrians patiently walking across the bridge, and we joined them. We ended up walking all the way to the gallery on rue de la Roquette, the first time I'd ever walked an hour to reach a speaking engagement.

"Where's Len?" Julia asked nervously as we came in the door, nearly ten minutes after the program was set to start.

I'd glanced at his itinerary last night, and remembered seeing back-to-back appointments. "I haven't seen him all day," I told her.

Julia's telephone calls failed to locate him. After we'd decided to start the program, even though none of the musicians we'd expected to perform had arrived, Weinglass showed up. He too had walked all the way from the Left Bank.

Attendance was lighter than the previous evening, but the students, artists, and professionals who came showed deep interest in Mumia's case. First, Benedetto gave another brilliant performance of his play. I delivered the same speech I'd given at the Bourse de Travail. Then Weinglass spoke. An intense question-and-answer session concluded the event.

It was past 11:00 P.M. by the time St. Clair and I left the gallery, and we hadn't eaten dinner. The first three restaurants we walked past were closed, but when St. Clair and I saw a rather expensive restaurant that was still open, we rushed inside. After our dinner, we walked back outside to the rue de la Roquette, certain that by this time of night we would find a taxi. Two empty cabs passed us by.

"I wonder why they won't stop," I mumbled.

"Maybe it has something to do with the color of our skin," St. Clair answered, half joking.

A skinny French teenager standing near us on the sidewalk piped up in English, "The taxi drivers are very racist. You should take out your gun and shoot them."

The remark had a wry irony, given that I'd just left a meeting protesting the death penalty being given a black man for shooting a white policeman. Maybe, I thought for a moment, he'd heard a line like that in a rap song —but I knew there was more to it. Such sensitivity to racial violence would not have been so openly stated twenty years earlier. When I lived in Paris during the seventies, probably before the kid was born, the evidence I saw of the simmering French hostility to Africans was racist graffiti scrawled on the walls of the subway stations, but now an openly racist political party elected delegates to the government.[83]

The Dragnet of Surveillance Grows Tighter

Every Wednesday, Mumia's supporters demonstrated outside the American consulate, and they held a demonstration in front of the American embassy once a month.[84] By Wednesday, however, exhaustion from planning the recent programs, added to the disruption of the metro strike, kept most people away.

Every day since our arrival, to St. Clair's dismay, Steve had manufactured some reason to stop by the apartment where we were staying. He'd been house-sitting there until we showed up, and had left some luggage in a back closet. When he stopped by on Wednesday, Steve asked me if I planned to go to the demonstration, and I told him it was unlikely. "There's a plainclothes policeman who comes, always the same guy," he said. "He asks how many people are coming, and I like to push up the numbers."

Not even the person responsible for bringing the banners managed to get to the consulate that Wednesday. Only Steve, who walked all the way from the Left Bank, showed up.

Wednesday afternoon I finally managed to find a money exchange office that was open. Singing students were filing down the street, some pulling papier-mâché dinosaurs, as I walked toward the exchange office on boulevard St. Michel. At the intersection of boulevard St. Michel and boulevard St. Germain a spontaneous demonstration of students was assembling, a sort of pep rally for Thursday's big march. The anticipation building toward the nationwide student strike starting Thursday was palpable. Newspapers were evoking comparisons with the demonstrations of '68, and so was everyone I heard talking about the strike.[85] The train strike made it impossible for most students to travel across France, so instead of the national demonstration originally planned, there were going to be regional demonstrations at each campus, and mainly students from the twelve Paris campuses would march in the upcoming demonstration.

On Thursday morning, as usual, Steve came into the apartment carrying his copy of *L'Humanité,* made himself coffee, smoked a cigarette, and informed me that the student demonstration was starting at Place d'Italie around 2:30 P.M. I thanked him, and said I was looking forward to seeing it. That afternoon, as I walked toward the post office on rue de la Reine Blanche, I saw a row of blue CRS vans parked on avenue Gobelins. I knew I was in the right place. By the time I left the post office, striking student protestors flooded the streets. I perched on the base of a streetlamp to get a better view of the students walking twenty abreast down avenue Gobelins.

Long banners representing the campuses, such as Nanterre or Censier, identified the throngs of protestors. Some students held up tall posters showing a caricature of François Bayrou, the minister of education. The atmosphere seemed serious and peaceful, although I saw a couple of young people guzzling beer from green bottles as they walked past me. The overwhelming majority of students appeared to be European, but I saw a few black faces scattered among the crowd. I took a copy of every leaflet being passed out, one of which called for equality between foreign and French students. A huge mass of protestors, including professors, high school teachers, a cluster of demonstrators from a lycée identifying themselves as "future students on strike," and throngs of university students, proceeded past me. In the very last segment of the demonstration I saw a band of striking train workers marching in solidarity with the student strikers, holding a white banner and shouting "Retirez, retirez, retirez le plan Juppé." The energy emanating from all the demonstrations against French government policies felt exhilarating. The catchy phrase, "retirez le plan Juppé" rang in my head, and I sensed a rekindling of that optimistic spirit of resistance I'd felt decades ago.

While I watched the demonstration, St. Clair was meeting several French television executives whose offices were on the Right Bank. We planned to meet for dinner later that evening, but we couldn't set a definite time—not knowing whether he would have to walk all the way back to the Left Bank. I ate lunch at the Café Kanon, where the plate-glass windows gave me a clear view of avenue Gobelins. There I watched the CRS squad marching in formation after the last of the demonstration had passed. They projected a threat, a cold show of force in response to the onset of the student strike.

From a phone booth on the sidewalk I called the office where St. Clair was expected at 4:00 P.M. I left a voice mail message for him to call me, then returned to the apartment. The phone rang, and I answered, expecting to hear St. Clair's voice. Instead, it was Steve.

"This is urgent," he said excitedly. "I'm calling from a phone booth. The student delegates from all the campuses are having a meeting tonight, and they'd like to have you come to talk about Mumia's case."

"I'm not sure that I'm the best person to do that." I hesitated, then said, "Perhaps it would be better if someone who lives here in France went to that meeting."

"No, they want to hear from you," he said. "The novelty of having you speak appeals to them."

His answer put me on guard— clearly, he wanted me to participate in some way in the student action. I asked where they were meeting.

"At Jussieu; it's not far from where you are."

"Well, I'm not sure whether I'll be available, I'm still waiting to hear from St. Clair. But give me the information just in case."

"Ampitheatre 44 in Jussieu at 8:00 p.m.," he answered. "The students will stay in the building all night. I've just got an assignment to cover the occupation, so I'm going to spend the night there too."

"Congratulations on getting work," I told him.

The Scars of Psychological Warfare Remain Unhealed

While Steve was speaking, I calculated whether going to the student delegates' meeting could be interpreted as interference with the internal affairs of France—which might be viewed as grounds for expulsion. That wasn't idle speculation on my part: I'd been expelled from France before, back in 1970.[86] The expulsion came about after I'd been forbidden to enter the Federal Republic of Germany,[87] where the German equivalent of SDS (Students for a Democratic Society) had invited me to speak at a Thanksgiving rally being held at the university in Frankfurt. I'd flown from Algiers to Paris, and at Orly airport I changed to a Lufthansa plane for Frankfurt.

It was dark by the time the flight landed, and heavyset uniformed border guards greeted me and escorted me off the airplane. They drove me in a jeep along back roads, which was a terrifying experience—being whisked away by beefy, uniformed Germans to an unknown destination. After about ten minutes, it seemed, we pulled up to the airport, where I caught a glimpse of camouflage-clad riot police and a paddy wagon full of longhaired demonstrators. I was escorted to the airport police station, where they stamped "verboten" on my passport and ordered my return to Paris on the next flight out. The German government declared my presence to be against the best interests of the Federal Republic.[88]

Shortly after I was invited to Germany, two young black men, one a U.S. Army deserter, had been arrested after they shot and killed a guard at Ramstein Air Force Base.[89] In the trunk of the car they were driving the German police found Black Panther Party newspapers and flyers announcing the rally that I had come to attend. The impact the Ramstein incident had on the ongoing turmoil black soldiers felt over the Vietnam War and the Black freedom movement in the United States was the real reason that I was being banned from Germany, but the government issued its official reason in bland diplomatic code words.

Germany sent me back to Orly airport, but I arrived so late that no flights were scheduled to leave for Algiers until the next morning. All night I was held under police guard in a hotel room at the airport, and the next morning police escorted me through underground tunnels directly onto the runway and into an Air Algérie plane back to Algiers.

I was forbidden to enter France again. For years, if I came to France I sneaked across the border from Switzerland using fake passports. That ban was not lifted until after Eldridge and I were granted French residence permits in 1974.[90]

Could going to Jussieu get me expelled again? I wondered. Could Steve be a provocateur—or an informant?

I called Julia. When I told her about the invitation to attend the student delegates' meeting, it struck me that I had no way of determining whether or not it actually came from the students. While I was talking on the phone to Julia, the doorbell rang. I put the phone down, opened the door, and saw Steve standing there. "I'm running from the police," he gasped, out of breath. "Students were smashing windows after the march, the police were blocking off the crowds, and I just managed to slip out, but I got hit on the hand by a broken bottle being thrown at the police."

I stared at him in surprise.

"I need to change my jacket," he volunteered, by way of explanation, I suppose, and walked back toward the closet where he kept his suitcase.

I resumed my conversation on the phone with Julia, telling her exactly what was happening and, how uneasy I felt, and insisted that she stay on the line with me until Steve left. I didn't know who he was, really, nor why he had come to Paris two months ago, but his "urgent" phone call and sudden arrival at the apartment set off my danger alert.

St. Clair, whose massive girth and height would be intimidating if he weren't so gentle, walked in the apartment door about fifteen minutes after Steve popped up. I felt overwhelmed with relief, even though Steve continued to rummage in the back closet. Those minutes when I'd been alone with Steve shook me. I felt threatened. I asked Julia to tell St. Clair some of our suspicions. I wanted him to know what was actually going on at the apartment, but I didn't want the conversation overheard. Steve walked into the living room area wearing an entirely different outfit. I wished he would leave, but he sat down at the table and lit a cigarette.

"The Anarchists were out there fighting the police," he announced.

"Where I come from, it's usually the police that form such groups," I replied, recognizing the agent-provocateur style of disruption.

He looked confused for a moment, then made some innocuous remark.

Just then, our hostess and two friends breezed in the front door. Steve continued to chat for a while with them. As he stood up to leave, he turned and asked me, "So I guess it's certain that you're not coming to Jussieu?"

"That's right," I said, staring straight at him. "I'm not coming."

"Well, I'll just tell them I wasn't able to reach you," he mumbled, and then walked out of the door.

Later that evening, I learned, rioting at Jussieu caused thousands and thousands of dollars' worth of damage. The police had turned out in force.

That's all we need, I thought to myself, to have someone identified with Mumia's campaign connected to the riot during the start of the student strike. That certainly would discredit us, just when the international level of support for stopping his execution has reached as far as the pope.

I couldn't shake my suspicion that Steve had deliberately tried to set me up. Julia had warned me about spies when I saw her over the summer in New York: "Our old friends have taken an interest in what we're doing for Mumia," she said. Of course, it was possible he merely had very poor judgment, but that explanation somehow didn't ring right. All along, he'd shown too much interest in finding out who was calling us, who we were talking to, where we were going. Possibly that curiosity came from training as a journalist, or possibly from some other training for which journalism served as a cover. I'd spent too many years of my life being followed, chased, stalked, or otherwise spied upon by police and intelligence agents. It gave me a sixth sense, an alertness to their methods, and I instinctively recognized the source.

Fighting for the Future

That night St. Clair found out that Ken Loach's new film, *Land and Freedom,* set during the Spanish Civil War, was being shown nearby.[91] "I missed it at the New York Film Festival, but I hear it's really good," he said. After dinner we saw a cab waiting at the stand outside the restaurant, climbed in, and arrived right in front of the tiny Europa Pantheon theater where the film was playing with time to spare.

Land and Freedom was adapted from George Orwell's account in *Homage to Catalonia* of his own participation in the antifascist campaign. The opening scene shows David, a young Englishman, enthusiastically joining the antifascist forces fighting in Spain. We soon see him in a uniform on a train, and despite being a member of the British Communist Party, he lands in a militia being trained by Spanish anarchists and Trotskyites. His unit stakes out in Catalonia, and the dramatic political shifts that marked the Spanish Civil War unfold in his village encampment.

Orwell wrote that what "happened in Spain was, in fact, not merely a civil war, but the beginning of a revolution"—something, he explained, "that the anti-Fascist press outside of Spain made its special business to obscure." "Outside of Spain," according to Orwell, "few people grasped that there was a revolution. Inside Spain nobody doubted it."[92] The revolution was crushed; the Fascists won.

David, the English newcomer, meets Blanca, a passionate Spanish revolutionary who is in love with an Irish Republican Army volunteer. She explains what was at stake in her terms: "We are fighting for our future. If we don't win this war, we have no future."

Those lines reverberated in my heart; they captured the essence of what we felt during the 1960s black revolutionary movement. We fought to destroy once and for all the legacy of slavery and create a new future for America. Those commitments seem so distant now to most people. Nothing dims their power more than the erasure of that past—now buried by a triumphant white supremacist political rhetoric.

I vividly identified with the film—its theme was the betrayal of the antifascist struggle by Stalinist troops. Although the scale was different, the stakes more global, I experienced that same betrayal in our movement—the inconceivable betrayal by people who you believe are "on your side."

When the Soviet-backed Popular Army disbands the militias, David's unit included, he tears up his Communist Party membership card in disgust. As I watched *Land and Freedom,* I clearly understood how the imperialist democracies' failure to wage all-out war against the Spanish Fascists, whom they found more compatible than the revolutionaries, continues to haunt us. By aligning with Franco's authoritarian terrorist regime to crush the revolutionaries in Spain, they stacked the deck against popular democracy. Then, these powerful imperialists fought to suppress the independence struggles percolating in their colonial territories in Asia, Africa, and Latin America, exposing the racist core of their domination. No longer able to hide behind anticommunism, the European and American "democracies" now display a resurgence of the authoritarian right.

Today, on both sides of the Atlantic, virulent eruptions of racist violence accompany reactionary social policies that are ravaging working and poor people. Nazi uniforms, parties, and political statements are back in plain view. Encouraging signs are rare for those of us who fought for a revolutionary change in the distribution of power. I was forced to ask, Do we have a future, or will an American fascism destroy us?

The pace at which our state and federal governments pursue the draconian use of the death penalty indicates part of the answer. But in France, where the death penalty has been abolished, revulsion at the barbaric punishment galvanizes the massive effort to save Mumia's life. When Pennsylvania governor Thomas Ridge signed the death warrant merely days before Mumia's new trial appeal was filed in June 1995, he provoked an astonishing outpouring of protest. The European Parliament passed a resolution condemning the general use of the death penalty in the United States and its specific use against Mumia Abu-Jamal. Dramatic popular opposition to Mumia's execution was expressed in Germany, England, Italy, Japan, and France, as well as in the United States. Finally, Judge Sabo granted a stay of execution—the first in his career.[93] While that stay indefinitely postponed the execution, it did not rescind the death warrant.

From his bleak death row cell, Mumia's fight to live has captured the imagination of people all over the world and inspired them to act. Among the thousands demanding justice for Mumia in Paris, I met people who had marched and signed petitions demanding freedom for Angela Davis, Bobby Seale, and other political prisoners. I met people who had fought for Algeria's independence, and people who had fought in the anti-Nazi Resistance. I met former political prisoners, professors, lawyers, doctors, schoolteachers, students, and working people. I felt energized by the hope surging through the campaign to save Mumia, and tried to understand its power.

Mumia's predicament continues to provide his supporters with an opportunity to speak truth to an awesome power—and they are escalating their calls for justice. Mumia's book *Live from Death Row* sold over 70,000 copies.[94] He received so much mail it could not all fit into his cell. But it must be remembered that when Mumia spoke out against the abuse of power by Philadelphia's police, they set their sights on silencing him forever. Even though the letter of the law is on Mumia's side, that is no guarantee that the police will not ultimately succeed.

PART TWO

Understanding the Fight for Freedom

5

Every Nation Struggling to Be Free Has a Right to Struggle, a Duty to Struggle

Geronimo ji Jaga

Like I tell everyone, my role in the movement was not behind the microphone, and I make no bones about it. I'm trying to do the best I can to bring a message to you, as I was asked to do by those who I left behind the walls. It's hard to come after twenty-seven years and make you understand, because you have been told a lot of stories, like we say down home, a lot of lies, a lot of untruths. But I have always dealt with truth.

I could have left prison a long time ago. They offered me big money, they would have let me escape. But they charged me with a murder I didn't do, and I was not going nowhere until I cleared it up. I wanted the truth to come out. They put me in the hole for the first eight years, and they attacked me, but I wanted to expose the truth that my mother did not raise a murderer. Don't put that on me.

 I didn't know about COINTELPRO then, but I knew something was amiss. I knew there was something more going on than those little peons, more than the LAPD (Los Angeles Police Department) and the FBI playing their little games. I was in Folsom Prison, facing sadistic guards who were shooting us with guns and all kinds of manipulating prisoners who were trying to kill us with knives, when it was revealed that Richard Nixon and his girlfriend, J. Edgar Hoover, had plotted to destroy one of the most beautiful movements that history had ever seen. And these sick individuals were allowed to get away with it. In prison, we couldn't have TVs and radios back then, we hardly got any mail, we hardly got any visits. At the time, I wondered what was happening. President Nixon was exposed as one of the worst criminals that ever sat in the White House. It was all revealed: the details of the Pentagon papers, the corruption around Vietnam, and the attacks against the Black Liberation Movement, the Asian Liberation Movement, the Mexican Liberation Movement, the Native Liberation Movement. No one was left untouched. Oh, he got kicked out of office, but it was strange that we went to San Quentin, and he went to San Clemente. It didn't add up.

We are faced with a very vicious enemy. Now how to define that enemy, that's another question. You have to define your enemy accurately, or else you are going to be

This article was excerpted from a speech given at Pasadena City College, in Pasadena, California, October 1997.

defeated time and time again. When anyone sends their killer dogs after you, are you going to spend the rest of your life plotting to kill the killer dogs, or are you going to get the people that trained them? It's as simple as that.

You hear a lot of people, especially in what we now call the New Afrikan communities or the Black community, saying, "The White folks this, them White folks that." That's a big mistake. Our enemies cannot be defined by race. Now, you got to be careful with that. In a lot of cases, you'd better watch that brother next to you. It is true of every ethnic group, every liberation movement, not only in this country but throughout the world, that it gets heavily infiltrated with people who like to play cops, people who like to operate from the premise of what Che Guevara called mechanical discipline. They go for the big bucks, go and do what Massa tells them to do. So stay cautious about these things and be cognizant of the fact that the enemy has to be understood. Sun Tzu says, "Know your enemy and know yourself, in a thousand battles you will never be defeated."

I always try to encourage people to wake up. Now they have you believing when you see me twenty-seven years later that you should come up and ask me for an autograph. I love you for your sentiment, but I have to tell you that you don't know who I am. I am not a movie star. It's natural for people in the movie business to promote themselves, to give out their autographs. But I did not join a movement to sign autographs. I did not join a movement for fortune or fame. I joined a movement to win. And that's the bottom line. But I have to explain to you that we are under collective discipline not to promote ourselves. We cannot promote individuals, we can only promote the revolution, the struggle. When you confront the level of commitment of someone like Ruchell Magee, or Hugo Pinell, Leonard Peltier, Sundiata Acoli, Dr. Mutulu Shakur, Marilyn Buck, Susan Rosenberg, on and on and on, understand that we don't care if you form committees out here and say free this person, free that person, or put our names on posters. We didn't join the movement for that. We understood that we were making a sacrifice, and we did not expect this. With Mumia sitting up there on death row, he understood when he joined, like we all did, that we might go to prison, that we might get killed, that we might end up exiled—because we knew the nature of our enemy.

As I try to bring forth the truth after twenty-seven years, I see all these misconceptions, "Oh, he's a movie star." I don't blame you. Now, when I see brothers and sisters who were with us in the sixties, sometimes I don't even recognize them. I just left Dallas a few days ago, where this brother went to court to get an injunction. He was down there, claiming nobody else could use the name of the Black Panther Party! I mean, it blows my mind. Especially after Bunchy has died, George has died, Fred Hampton, Mark Clark, Fred Bennett, I mean so many have died, so many are still in prison. And these people, what we call Black Power pimps, are out here doing this. It's wrong! When they see me coming, they hide. By the time this dude got involved in '74, the Black Panthers had been infiltrated, and they were promoting Democratic Party principles, which was not the original intent. And when you study history, you will learn that.

I try to explain the truth as we know it. We didn't join the liberation struggle to be a part of the Democratic Party. We joined because we believed, as we still do today, that Africans in this country constitute the second largest African nation in the world, next to Nigeria. The second largest in the world! We have the wherewithal to feed an entire nation. We have brainpower and skills equal to any in the world. We have a common culture, common language, common everything, and we still turn around and call Clinton "our" president. We have a right to elect our own leadership, to govern our own selves, and this is what we fought for.

Read the Panthers' Ten Point Program from the sixties. It states very clearly that we called for a United Nations–supervised plebiscite to let it be known what we want. We did not want some handpicked leaders imposed upon us who'd tell us, "Oh, black people want this." They do not speak for us, we can speak for ourselves. This country prides itself on democratic principles, but for us, the plebiscite is the epitome of democracy. We don't want the government of the United States involved in it, we want the United Nations to supervise it. Because we do not trust the United States. And it is as clear as that.

"Oh, you talking about a separate nation, where is it going to be?" You hear about the thirteen states. Don't go for that. Every nation in the world is struggling to determine its own destiny. We are a big old nation, a rich, powerful, intelligent nation. We tell them that wherever the nation is going to be will be decided by that plebiscite. I can't answer it, only the people collectively can answer that! Put it on the plebiscite! You understand? A lot of people feel confused, they can't see us all moving to Georgia, Louisiana, the thirteen states. That was a good ideological framework for understanding the struggle back during the day, but it by no means represents the ultimate solution. What the people's vote says determines the solution; it's not what I say, but what the people say. That's the epitome of democracy. And if we are denied that, then it is they who are being anti-democratic. We have a right to fight against that!

You have to go this route. Because this gives everybody in the nation the right to express what he or she so desires, for the first time since our ancestors were so-called emancipated after slavery. In the sixties, if you remember, the opinion polls and surveys, even *Newsweek* did one, I think in 1969, and it showed overwhelming support not only for the Black Panther Party, but for nationhood, national independence. Around that same time the government escalated their COINTELPRO. It's a shame to be so huge, so capable, so qualified, that we still turn around and let Ol' Massa patrol our community. Our children are dying from dope, our children are sent to these schools where they miseducate them and confuse them. It is a shame we haven't called a state of emergency over the rate at which our young men and women are going to prison. And you going off to the White House or Capitol Hill, asking "Ol' Massa, can I do this," "May I start this program?" Oh yes, he'll give you a few million, then turn around and build fifty prisons behind your back, hire your nieces and nephews to work in the prisons to kill us.

I just left them. I just left a little brother, a little Crip standing up arguing with another Crip, didn't throw no blows. Before he knew it, a bullet blew the whole back of his head off. Right there in Tehachipi Prison. I was there. The guard that killed him was blacker than midnight. It's the same in Soledad, the same way in Folsom. You got Mexican guards, killing young beautiful promising Mexican prisoners. These prisons are carrying out genocide. These prisons are nothing but tools to further this war of genocide against people of color especially.

You should see what they are doing to the Black and Brown prisoners in those prisons today—it was a shame when I went in, but it ain't nothing like it is today. I have looked into the souls of brothers of all nationalities, who were manipulated, who were more or less put into that prison situation. It's the brother who didn't have money, who didn't have advantages, that gets condemned to death. He lands on these prison yards, where these sadistic guards, who don't even have a GED, are over them, armed with 30-30s, and manipulate them into arguments so that they can shoot them. That's murder. It's sickening. You ought to see their bodies when they get through shooting them. And don't let another one be stabbing him. It is one of the ugliest things you are going to see, and it is more prevalent in California than anywhere else in the country.

They put all this propaganda out, and you go for it and vote for all these resolutions and initiatives to build more prisons. That's not the solution. You are creating a monster so large that you will not be able to control it. It is already out of control, and guess who it is going to come back on? Like the old saying goes, "If they come for me in the morning, they coming for you that night."

I can't stress enough the importance of letting us speak for ourselves. And when you get questions about, "Oh, he's preaching separation," study our history. We were the first to coalesce with my kinfolks the Native American Movement, American Indian Movement. We were the first to coalesce with the Asian Liberation Movement, the Chicano/Mexicano Liberation Movement—I want to salute MECHA. I also want to say to the young Chicano brothers and sisters that I was very surprised to learn that you did not know about the Brown Berets! Those were champions! Corky Gonzalez, the Brown Berets, they worked very closely with the Black Panthers. When the racist pigs were going to the Mexican communities, into the barrios, like they did in the African communities, we would come together, we would patrol together. We had beautiful coalitions with our sisters and brothers from the Chicano and Mexicano communities. You should read your history, learn everything you can about the Brown Berets, it was very important. I always encourage my Brown brothers to learn about that so you can teach the younger brothers. The Brown Berets, those brothers sacrificed so much and they were so targeted by COINTELPRO, the acronym of the counterintelligence program the FBI launched against our Movement. Operation Chaos was the CIA's operation against the Movement. So when you study your history, don't forget to study Operation Chaos. And you will have a clearer understanding of the lengths that Nixon and his operatives went to destabilize, neutralize, and kill our various movements. I like to point out they spent more money trying to overthrow us than they did in trying to overthrow Salvador Allende in Chile. And they boast about that. This is all in books, you can read the Church Committee report, the report of the Senate Select Committee on Intelligence Operations, particularly book 3, and you can read *Agents of Repression* by Ward Churchill and Jim Vander Wall.

You have to take everything you hear about those days, and about today, with a grain of salt. Be careful when you hear rumors and gossip about someone who is on your side of the fence; it's one of the ways they cause those divisions. We have to struggle to keep our unity, that unity we solidified during the sixties. You've heard about the Weather Underground. Did you know that some of those people are still in prison? You've heard of Assata Shakur, but you probably never heard about Marilyn Buck. You don't read about Marilyn Buck or Dr. Mutulu Shakur, who were both convicted for breaking Assata out of prison. I can't talk enough about Marilyn, she's one of my heroes. She's doing seventy-seven to life in prison right now. You know about Angela Davis, but have you heard of Ruchell Magee? If it hadn't been for his case, when Jonathan Jackson came to break him out of the Marin County Courthouse, you may never have heard of Angela Davis. I'm not trying to take anything from anyone, but I am just trying to let you know. There's always more to it than what you see. So you should struggle to see what is beneath the surface.

I was born into a tradition of resistance. I grew up in lower Louisiana, the Atchafalaya swampland. It's a part of the Mississippi Delta. Before I was born, my uncle was a part of Marcus Garvey's Universal Negro Improvement Association. He was a Legionnaire. He organized largely in the South. Back then, the older members of the community were usually deacons. A lot of life was centered around the church. The deacons were the ones who would protect the church from the Klan violence. You may have heard of the Deacons for Defense and Justice, and other groups came about because of that.

When I finished our little segregated high school across the track, there were only seventeen of us who graduated. I wanted to go to Grambling or to Southern to play football and chase the girls and what not. But the Elders, they counseled us and said,

"You are the young soldiers now. We have been in Korea and World War II, but we are getting old. So you have to fill our ranks." They advised us to join the army, and we always followed the Elders' advice. That's how I ended up in the army.

I want to make that clear, because I am not a hypocrite. I'm a Vietnam vet, I have a lot of comrades who are Vietnam vets, but I didn't join the army out of any sense of patriotism to the United States. I joined because my Elders advised me to join. Me, Frank Francis, Tony Delco, and Jesse Bradford—out of that little swamp town in lower Louisiana. We meant nobody no ill-will. We did what the Elders told us to do because they never told us wrong.

In a few months I'm in Santo Domingo, in a few more months I'm in Vietnam. As soon as I got in, there was constant warfare. Martin Luther King was like the god of the older people, and Malcolm X was like our god. We were the young crazy people. But we respected the Elders, and we loved Martin Luther King through the wisdom of the Elders. But when Martin Luther King was killed April 4, 1968, the Elders, of Louisiana, Mississippi, Texas, Alabama, Georgia, Florida, sent out a call. We can talk about this now. We were told to come home. And we came home. They used to sing "We Shall Study War No More." That wasn't the hymn they was singing. They told us, we have to defend these communities. They have killed our King, our hope is lost. So, now we got the backing of the Elders.

I did what I was told. I went throughout every ghetto, every swamp, every one-horse town that they sent me to, teaching people how to defend themselves, what I had learned in the military. I went to Philadelphia, New York, Chicago. When I came out here to California, I worked with a young group called the Black Panther Party. The police were killing them at random. They were standing up and shooting back with half-loaded guns, with bullets that they got from the army surplus store! So I took them and we had classes on how to defend themselves. And for that, I was attacked. A lot of people say that I shouldn't say that. But that was my role. I had to help build the Ministry of Defense, not only for the Black Panther Party. I also had to help build it for the Republic of New Afrika, for the Mau Mau, for the Texas Black Liberation Front, for the Alabama Black Liberation Front, and many other groups in the sixties. And though I wasn't behind a microphone doing it, I didn't hide it.

Under international law we have a right to defend ourselves. And we knew international law back then real well. And we know it more so today. In the process of teaching them, there were shootouts here in Los Angeles, in New Orleans, and Seattle. I went there and I told them, "I take responsibility for those brothers and sisters doing that because they were following my orders. And every court in the land, everything we did, I'll take responsibility for it. Don't give me no credit, but I'm the one who put them out there, trained them to do that. Don't put them in jail. If you think there is a law being violated, attack me." O.K., they came at me, I went to trial. We were acquitted. The jury said, "No, the police were wrong." So what do they do?

After that, the police came after me with the Tate-LaBianca murders. You all know about Charles Manson. Well, Charlie wasn't arrested for that at first, I was. When the police took me down to Newton Street and tried to scare me, I did not know what they were talking about, they would do it so often. But someone had written "Off the Pigs" in the blood of the victims on the wall. Automatically they believed the Panthers did it; they came and arrested me for the Tate-LaBianca murders. A few weeks later, they arrested Charlie. Then the police tried to come at me with another murder. That didn't stick either. The criminalization process.

Next comes the Olsen murder. If I had Johnnie Cochran here, he's more eloquent than I am, or Stuart Hanlon, who was with me all those years, they'd really tell you about that case. But even at that murder trial, with the FBI putting an informant agent in the jail with me, an informant agent in Johnnie Cochran's office, and an informant agent who said I did the murder on the stand, they still almost lost the case. They spent a lot of money doing these things, all throughout the country, targeting certain individuals who they wanted to kill. I got bullet holes all up in me, but that didn't work either.

After that comes the denigration part. The slander, you know, the lies and deceit that people usually go for. Because they got high-powered media machines that tell you that I was the quintessence of evil, out for the destruction of all white people, that I wanted to kill all the Indians—people began to believe it all. They say when war begins, truth is the first casualty. And that's correct. We have to write our own history. We have to bring forth the truth of these things.

We had some problems with male supremacist attitudes, this decadent culture that puts these kinds of things in our head. We didn't know no better. In the sixties, we were organizing and oppressing these sisters in the movement. We were running into sisters like Red, who is not famous, she's dead now, but many of you may have heard of Tupac's mother, Afeni Shakur, Kathleen Cleaver, we ran into some of the most beautiful sisters in the world. That made us look at our male supremacist attitudes, our chauvinistic ways toward them. And they transformed a whole generation of Black male attitudes to loving and understanding the importance of the woman.

I have to say that everywhere I go the youth culture seems to have a tendency to put the woman down, to disrespect the woman. It's crazy. Until you understand that not only do you have to uphold her, but sometimes put her on a pedestal, you are not going to get anywhere. After years of study, I came to the conclusion that none of us would have survived slavery if it were not for the Black woman. I really believe that. So it hurts me deep in my heart when I hear you brothers call them sisters names. I'm talking about Mexican sisters, Asian sisters, Native sisters, not just African sisters, because they're all beautiful.

What we really are fighting to build is a matriarchal system. I say that everywhere I go, because I believe that the backbone of the Black woman enabled us to survive the holocaust of slavery. Our nation has to be led by a woman. And that's what I fight for. I'm a man, I don't think right now that men have the full capacity to love. We've been twisted and wrenched under this white male supremacist system for too long. We need a civilized, loving nation; women seem to have that capacity for love to build the nation that we want. I don't see a lot of men clapping. You ain't got to clap. I've studied this for years, and you have a right to disagree with me, but I challenge you on this.

When I first went to prison, if you came in because you had raped somebody, you would get a knife stuck in you. Nowadays, damn near every other prisoner has raped some kid. We've got to address that. Women are suffering. As long as women are suffering, especially from our hands, we ain't going nowhere. You men have got to face the fact that to a large extent the reason why our movement is so retarded is because our enemy plays on those sexual concepts that have twisted your mind. We've got to bring these women back up. We've got to protect them. We've got to get our families back together. And if we don't, we are not going anywhere.

Before I close, I want to make you understand that I am highly trained, and that there are a lot of others like me, all the way from Ranger school. We used to teach the Green Berets. We could have caused all kinds of havoc across this country. But we listened to our Elders. I just said that all we were doing was based on love, it comes from that principle. Che used to say, "We can only hate our enemies with revolutionary love."

We are not trying to overthrow the United States government. All we're trying to do is build our own. Let's get serious about the plebiscite, so we can move forward to the twenty-first century as a free and independent nation governed by ourselves. Let's refer back to the voter registration drives of the early sixties, when we had to get educated about the ballot. But this time we'll do it on an international scale, like Quebec just recently did, like Puerto Rico has been trying to do for years, like Hawaii is doing. Vote for where we are at. Let's be declared a nation where we are, then go for dual citizenship. That's what they don't want you to know about. You go for dual citizenship next. Then all kinds of doors are going to open to you, the International Monetary Fund, banking allowances, these are the things we have to study. We got to get this first referendum down as soon as possible.

If we don't, all these crazy, buck wild fools, I love them, throughout these communities are going to get crazier, and you are going to have more innocent people dead. You are going to have more of these beautiful young sisters and brothers dead in these prisons. And I'm talking about all communities, all the poor and oppressed communities, if we don't start moving on this. Let the people speak for themselves. And if you think I'm crazy, I want to see you after that first referendum comes back. And then we can stand proud.

Every nation struggling to be free has a right to struggle, a duty to struggle. Study your international law. Under the Geneva Accords, under the later Helsinki Accords of '77, what we call the Protocols of '77, we not only have a right to fight for our self-determination, but we are not the only ones. We always supported the national liberation struggles of the Mexicano people, of the Native people, of all people who are struggling to be free. And I encourage you to continue. If we don't come together, we are not going to win right now. We have to come together! Before you have internationalism, you have to first have nationalism. We have to organize ourselves first, and then we can interact as a nation, with national dignity.

6

"To Disrupt, Discredit and Destroy"

The FBI's Secret War against the Black Panther Party

Ward Churchill

The record of the FBI speaks for itself (J. Edgar Hoover, Introduction to The FBI Story, *1965).*

The Black Panther Party was savaged by a campaign of political repression that in terms of its sheer viciousness has few parallels in American history. Beginning in August 1967 and coordinated by the Federal Bureau of Investigation as part of its then-ongoing domestic counterintelligence program (COINTELPRO), which enlisted dozens of local police departments around the country, the assault left at least twenty-eight Panthers dead,[1] scores of others imprisoned after dubious convictions,[2] and hundreds more suffering permanent physical or psychological damage.[3] The Party was simultaneously infiltrated at every level by agents provocateurs, all of them harnessed to the task of disrupting its internal functioning.[4] Completing the package was a torrent of disinformation planted in the media to discredit the Panthers before the public, both personally and organizationally, thus isolating them from potential support.[5]

Although an entity bearing its name remained in Oakland, California, for another decade, as did several offshoots situated elsewhere, the Black Panther Party in the sense that it was originally conceived was effectively destroyed by the end of 1971.[6] During the 1960s, similar if less lethal campaigns were mounted against an array of dissident groups, including the Socialist Workers Party, the Student Nonviolent Coordinating Committee (SNCC), the Revolutionary Action Movement, Students for a Democratic Society, the Republic of New Afrika, and the Southern Christian Leadership Conference (SCLC). The list goes on and on, and the results were more or less the same.[7]

The FBI's politically repressive activities did not commence during the 1960s, nor did they end with the formal termination of COINTELPRO on April 28, 1971.[8] On the contrary, such operations have been sustained for nearly a century, becoming ever more refined, comprehensive, and efficient. This in itself demonstrates a marked degradation of whatever genuinely democratic possibilities once imbued "the American experiment," an effect amplified significantly by the fact that the bureau's targets consistently were groups that, whatever their imperfections, have been most clearly committed to the realization of egalitarian ideals.[9] The FBI is and has always been a frankly *anti*democratic institution, as are the social, political, and economic elements it was created to protect.[10]

Predictably, the consequences of this systematic suppression of the democratic impulse in American life, and the equally methodical reinforcement of its opposite, have now engulfed us. Not only does the ever greater concentration of wealth among increasingly narrow and corporatized sectors of society reflect this, but so does the explosive growth of police and penal "services" over the past thirty years, accompanied by the erosion of constitutional safeguards for the basic rights of average citizens, and a veritable avalanche of regulatory encroachments reaching ever more deeply into the most intimate spheres of existence.[11] The United States has been a police state for some time now. The only real issue is what to do about it now that it's occurred.

Understanding history, therefore, is in many ways paramount. Without that we can neither fix our present position nor hope to move forward. There are a multiplicity of lenses through which we might fruitfully examine this tumultuous past, but few offer the explanatory power embodied in the experience of the Black Panther Party. This essay probing the repression of the Panthers uncovers the ugly history of their destruction in hopes of gleaning valuable lessons embedded in their exemplary struggle for liberation.

A History of Racist Repression

Despite its carefully contrived image as the country's premier crime-fighting agency, the FBI has always functioned primarily as a political police force.[12] The depth of John Edgar Hoover's antipathy toward political leftists was by no means his only ideological qualification for his new position as director of the FBI. As a middle-class Virginian, the intensity of his belief in white supremacy dovetailed quite well with the need of U.S. elites to maintain African Americans in a perpetually subordinate economic position.[13] His personal perspective made any sort of activity that might disturb the rigid race/class hierarchy of American life a "threat" that would be subject to targeting by the bureau. Several examples illustrate this point, beginning with the BoI's criminalization of world heavyweight boxing champion Jack Johnson in 1910,[14] but the best is probably the treatment meted out to Marcus Garvey, head of the Universal Negro Improvement Association (UNIA).

Although Hoover considered the Jamaica-born Garvey a "radical" and "the most prominent Negro agitator in the world," the sorts of programs Garvey advocated during the 1920s were not especially different from those the right wing of the Republican Party currently espouses.[15] Under his leadership, UNIA, which to this day remains the largest organization of African Americans ever assembled, devoted itself mainly to the realization of various "bootstrapping" strategies (i.e., undertaking business ventures as a means of attaining its twin goals of black pride and self-sufficiency). Nonetheless, despite UNIA's explicitly capitalist orientation, or maybe because of it, Hoover launched an inquiry into Garvey's activities in August 1919.[16]

When this initial probe revealed no illegalities, Hoover, railing against Garvey's "pro-Negroism," ordered that the investigation be not only continued but intensified.[17] UNIA was quickly infiltrated by operatives recruited specifically for the purpose, and a number of informants developed within it.[18] Still, it was another two years before the GID was able to find a pretext—Garvey's technical violation of the laws governing offerings of corporate stock—upon which to bring charges of "mail fraud." Convicted in July 1923 by an all-white jury, the UNIA leader was first incarcerated in the federal prison at Atlanta, then deported as an undesirable alien in 1927. By then, the organization he'd founded had disintegrated.[19]

Hoover, in the interim, had vowed to prevent anyone from ever again assuming the standing of what he called a "Negro Moses."[20] More than forty years later, he was repeating the same refrain, secretly instructing his COINTELPRO operatives to "prevent the rise of a 'messiah' who could unify and electrify . . . a well-concerted movement" of African Americans to improve their socioeconomic and political situations. In 1968 his targets were Martin Luther King Jr., Elijah Muhammed, and Stokely Carmichael, but along the way an untold number of others—Chandler Owen, for example, and A. Philip Randolph—had been subjected to the attentions of the FBI simply because they were deemed "defiantly assertive [about] the Negro's fitness for self-governance."[21]

> *Bureau agents investigated all black-owned newspapers, recruited paid black infor-*
> *mants, and tapped the telephones and bugged the offices of racial advancement groups,*
> *ranging from the procommunist National Negro Congress to the anticommunist NAACP.*
> *Investigative fallout included a mail cover on Rev. Archibald J. Carey, Jr.'s, Woodlawn*
> *African Methodist Episcopal Church in Chicago, where the Congress of Racial Equality*
> *had an office; a file check on Olympic track and field champion Jesse Owens (an agent*
> *compared the date of Owens's marriage with the birthday of his first child); and the*
> *transmittal of derogatory information on the NAACP and the National Urban League to*
> *prospective financial contributors.*[22]

In effect, Hoover was committed to "the repression of any black dissident who challenged second-class citizenship," irrespective of their ideological posture or the mode by which their politics were manifested.[23] In this he sometimes displayed a surprising degree of public candor, at one point actually going so far as to insist that investigation of black activists was justified insofar as their collective threats of "retaliatory measures in connection with lynching" represented a challenge to "the established rule of law and order."[24] In private, he was often more forthright, employing crude racial epithets such as "burrhead" when referring to Martin Luther King and others.[25]

COINTELPRO

Both surveillance of and counterintelligence directed against "subversives" had become standard FBI procedure by the end of World War II, and were increasingly regularized and refined during the ensuing spy cases and show trials of 1946–54.[26] The initial COINTELPRO, aimed at the U.S. Communist Party, was ordered on August 28, 1956. Although this was the first instance in which the Internal Security Branch was instructed to employ the full range of extralegal techniques developed by the bureau's counterintelligence specialists against a domestic target in a centrally coordinated and programmatic way, the FBI had conducted such operations against the CP and to a lesser extent the Socialist Workers Party (SWP) on a more ad hoc basis at least as early as 1941.[27] In this, the bureau was helped along immensely by passage of the Smith Act, a statute making "sedition" a peacetime as well as a wartime offense, in 1940. Instructively, Hoover began at the same time to include a section on "Negro Organizations" in reports otherwise dedicated to "Communist Organizations" and "Axis Fifth Columnists."[28] In 1954 there was also the Communist Control Act, a statute outlawing the CP and prohibiting its members from holding certain types of employment.[29]

Viewed against this backdrop, it has become a commonplace that, however misguided, COINTELPRO-CPUSA, as the 1956 initiative was captioned, was in some ways well intended, undertaken out of a genuine concern that the CP was engaged in spying for the Soviet Union. Declassified FBI documents, however, reveal quite the opposite. While espionage and sabotage "potentials" are mentioned almost as afterthoughts in the predicating memoranda, unabashedly political motives take center stage. The objective of the COINTELPRO was, as Internal Security Branch chief Alan Belmont put it at the time, to block the CP's "penetration of specific channels of American life where public opinion is molded" and to prevent thereby its attaining "influence over the masses."[30]

Expanded in March 1960, and again in October 1963 to include non-party members considered sympathetic to the CP, COINTELPRO served as a sort of laboratory in which the bureau's agents perfected the skills necessary to conducting a quietly comprehensive program of domestic repression.[31] From the outset, considerable emphasis was placed on intensifying the bureau's long-standing campaign to promote factional disputes within the Party. To this end, the CP was infiltrated more heavily than ever before—it has been estimated that by 1965 approximately one-third of the CP's nominal membership consisted of FBI infiltrators and paid informants—while bona fide activists were systematically "bad-jacketed" (that is, set up by infiltrators to make it appear that they themselves were government operatives).[32] A formal "Mass Media Program" was also created, "wherein derogatory information on prominent radicals was leaked to the news media."[33]

Still more ominously, beginning in 1966, an effort dubbed "Operation Hoodwink" was begun in which undercover agents were used to convince the leadership of New York's five Mafia families that CP organizing activities on the city's waterfront constituted a threat to the profits deriving from their union racketeering, smuggling, and related enterprises. Although it never materialized, the intended result was the murder of key organizers by the mob's contract killers.[34] Thus, under COINTELPRO, not only the methods but the objectives of operations directed against U.S. citizens were rendered indistinguishable from those involving foreign agents. All pretense that those targeted possessed constitutional or even human rights was simply abandoned. As one anonymous but veteran COINTELPRO operative reflected in 1974, "You don't measure success in this area by apprehensions, but in terms of neutralization."[35]

In April 1965, Hoover ordered the beginnings of what would become COINTELPRO–New Left, an operation intended to destroy the effectiveness of predominately white leftist organizations like Students for a Democratic Society and the Student Mobilization to End the War in Vietnam. On August 25, 1967, twenty-three field offices were instructed to commence another "hard-hitting and imaginative program," this one "to expose, disrupt, misdirect, discredit, or otherwise neutralize the activities of [civil rights and black liberation organizations], their leadership, spokesmen, membership, and supporters."[36] On March 4, 1968, "COINTELPRO–Black Nationalist Hate Groups" was expanded to include all forty-one FBI field offices.[37] Specifically targeted were SCLC, SNCC, the Philadelphia-based Revolutionary Action Movement (RAM),[38] and the Nation of Islam (NoI).[39] As has been noted, SCLC's Martin Luther King Jr., SNCC's Stokely Carmichael, and NoI head Elijah Muhammad were targeted by name. Scores, perhaps hundreds, of individuals were shortly added to the various lists of those selected for personal "neutralization," as were organizations like the Republic of New Afrika (RNA) and Los Angeles–centered US (United Slaves).[40]

During the spate of post-Watergate congressional hearings on domestic intelligence operations, the FBI eventually acknowledged having conducted 2,218 separate COINTELPRO actions from mid-1956 through mid-1971.[41] These, the bureau conceded, were undertaken in conjunction with other significant illegalities: 2,305 warrantless telephone taps, 697 buggings, and the opening of 57,846 pieces of mail.[42] This itemization, although an indicator of the magnitude and extent of FBI criminality, was far from complete. The counterintelligence campaign against the Puerto Rican independence movement was not mentioned at all, while whole categories of operational technique—assassinations, for example, and obtaining false convictions against key activists—were not divulged with respect to the rest. There is solid evidence that the other sorts of illegality were downplayed as well.[43]

It is true that Hoover was less than detailed in these and other reports. It is equally true, however, that he was never asked to provide further information. His superiors were told more than enough to know that there was much more to be learned about the FBI's domestic counterintelligence program. Indeed, they were sufficiently apprised to know that it smacked of political policing in its most illegitimate form. That none of them ever inquired further is indicative only of their mutual desire to retain a veneer of "plausible deniability" against their own potential incrimination if the program were ever to be exposed.[44] And since none of them elected to avoid jeopardy by simply ordering a halt to such operations, we can only assume they viewed COINTELPRO as a useful and acceptable expedient to maintaining the status quo.

COINTELPRO–BPP

Every dissident group in the United States was targeted by COINTELPRO during the late 1960s, but the Black Panther Party was literally sledgehammered. Of the 295 counterintelligence operations the bureau has admitted conducting against black activists and organizations during the period, a staggering 233, the majority of them in 1969, were aimed at the Panthers.[45] And this was by no means all. "Counterintelligence was far more pervasive than the readily available record indicates," one researcher has observed. "It is impossible to say how many COINTELPRO actions the FBI implemented against the Panthers and other targets simply by counting the incidents listed in the COINTELPRO–Black Hate Group file. The Bureau recorded COINTELPRO-type actions in thousands of other files."[46]

During the late 1960s the United States was in the process of losing a major neocolonial war in Southeast Asia. It was also facing a rising tide of guerrilla insurgencies throughout the Third World. The U.S. elites were beset by a substantial lack of consensus among themselves about how to restore global order. Simultaneously, they confronted a highly dynamic "New Left" opposition, not only on the home front but in western Europe.[47] By May 1968 they had witnessed the near overthrow of the Gaullist government in France, and a huge student movement was offering something of the same prospect in West Germany. Even within the Soviet bloc, a massive antiauthoritarian revolt had also challenged prevailing structures in Czechoslovakia, further threatening the balance of Cold War business as usual.[48]

At home, the liberal, egalitarian civil rights movement of the early 1960s had been transcended by a far more demanding movement demanding "Black Power."[49] By 1967 this had evolved into an effort to secure the outright liberation of African Americans from what was quite accurately described as "the system of internal colonial oppression." These shifts were marked by an increasing willingness on the part of black activists to engage in armed self-defense against the various forms of state repression and to develop a capacity to pursue the liberatory struggle by force, if necessary. Shortly, groups emerging within other communities of color—the Puerto Rican Young Lords Organization (YLO), for example, as well as the Chicano Brown Berets and the American Indian Movement (AIM)—had entered into more or less the same trajectory.[50]

A fresh generation of white radicals had simultaneously developed their own movement and, for a while, their own agenda. Students for a Democratic Society (SDS), probably the preeminent organization of Euro-American New Leftists in the United States during the 1960s, had been founded early in the decade to pursue visions of "participatory democracy" among the poor and disenfranchised.[51] With the 1965 buildup of U.S. troop strength in Vietnam, however, it adopted an increasingly pronounced anti-imperialist outlook. By mid-1968 SDS could claim 80,000 members and was in the process of birthing an armed component of its own.[52] A year later, in combination with a broad array of other activist groups, it was able to bring approximately one million people to the streets of Washington, D.C., to protest the war in Southeast Asia. Even combat veterans showed up in force.[53]

A burgeoning counterculture composed primarily of white youth, including a not insignificant segment drawn from the country's more privileged circles, added to the volatile mix. Not especially politicized in a conventional sense, they nonetheless manifested a marked disinclination to participate in American society as they encountered it, and seriously attempted to fashion an "alternative lifestyle" predicated on peace, love, and cooperation.[54] All told, from elite and dissident perspectives alike, it appeared that America was on the verge of "coming apart at the seams."[55]

It began to seem as if the Black Panther Party, a smallish but rapidly growing organization founded in 1966 by Huey P. Newton and Bobby Seale in Oakland,[56] might hold the key to forging a relatively unified movement from the New Left's many disparate elements. In part, this was because of the centrality the black liberation struggle already occupied in the radical American consciousness.[57] In part, it was likely because the Panthers, almost alone among organizations of color, had from the outset advanced a concrete program and were pursuing it with considerable discipline.[58] It was also undoubtedly due in no small measure to the obvious courage with which they'd faced off against the armed forces of the state, a matter personified by Defense Minister Newton's dubious conviction in the killing of a white cop, and the skill with which Minister of Information Eldridge Cleaver was able to publicize it.[59]

In any event, "by 1968–69 the Panthers were considered by many to be the exemplary revolutionary organization in the country and the one most explicitly identified with anti-imperialism and internationalism."[60] As such, the Party had become far and away "the most influential" such group in the United States, an assessment confirmed by J. Edgar Hoover when, in September 1969, he publicly declared the Panthers to be "the greatest threat to internal security of the country."[61] Meanwhile, on November 25, 1968, he had ordered the initiation of "imaginative and hard-hitting [counter]intelligence measures designed to cripple the BPP," and on January 30, 1969, a considerable expansion and intensification of the effort to "destroy what the BPP stands for."[62]

Several of the operations targeting other African-American organizations—SNCC, for example—were explicitly designed to impair the Panthers' ability to develop coalitions.[63] The same can be said with respect to approximately half the 290 COINTELPRO actions recorded as having been carried against SDS and other white New Left organizations from May 1968 through May 1971, and at least some of those conducted against Latino groups like the Young Lords and the Brown Berets served the same purpose.[64] There were also myriad operations to neutralize specific individuals, and another host that have never been admitted at all.[65] What Party founder Huey P. Newton aptly described as the "war against the Panthers" entailed every known variant of counterintelligence activity on the part of the FBI and collaborating police departments, and thus constitutes a sort of textbook model of political repression.[66]

The FBI's Media Offensive

From the outset, the FBI made "containment" of the Black Panther Party a top counterintelligence priority, setting out to bar potential recruits from joining it and blocking alliances with/absorption of other groups.[67] More broadly, the FBI sought to create "opposition to the BPP on the part of the majority of ghetto residents," an astonishing 62 percent of whom professed admiration for what the Panthers were doing by 1969.[68] In pursuit of both objectives, COINTELPRO operatives sought to discredit the Party by orchestrating false and derogatory stories that appeared in the news media.

Agents had at their disposal an already developed network of some 300 "cooperating journalists," many of them nationally syndicated and all of them prepared to pump out the bureau line on virtually any topic, including in some cases a willingness to simply sign their names to "news" stories and opinion pieces written by FBI propaganda specialists.[69] They included such then-big names as "labor columnist" Victor Riesel, who has been more accurately described as "a human funnel for the FBI."[70] Another was Gordon Hall, "freelance exposé specialist for radio station WMEX and television station WBZ" in Boston.[71] Ron Koziol, a mainstay reporter for the *Chicago Tribune*, was yet another.[72] The Chicago field office alone listed twenty-five such "friendly area sources," the New Haven office twenty-eight, and there were many others.[73]

On July 7, 1968, station WCKT-TV in Miami actually went so far as to air as its own "special report" on the Panthers a program, *Black Nationalists and the New Left*, which had in large part been prepared for it by FBI personnel. "This exposé ended with quotations from the Director, with excellent results," reported the special agent in charge (SAC) of the Miami field office.[74] The program was later packaged together with a second, this one on the NoI, and distributed to more than a hundred television stations around the country.[75] "Each and every film segment produced by the station was submitted for our scrutiny to insure that we were satisfied and that nothing was included that was in any way contrary to our interests," the Miami SAC crowed to headquarters.[76]

The primary themes pursued through the media in the FBI's campaign to cast a negative light upon the Party were that it was extraordinarily violent or at least "violence-prone," that it was devoted mainly to criminal rather than political activities, and that those associated with it were of a uniformly "low moral caliber."[77] Vice President Spiro T. Agnew's denunciation of the Panthers as a "completely irresponsible, anarchistic group of criminals" was quoted frequently in FBI-prepared materials, as was Assistant Attorney General Jerris Leonard's description of them as "nothing but hoodlums."[78] By late 1969 drumbeat repetition of the pat phrase "violence-prone Black Panthers" in both the press and electronic media had reached such saturation proportions that many people seem to have believed it was all one word.

A classic example was the *Chicago Tribune*'s Ron Koziol. At the specific request of Chicago SAC Marlin Johnson, who provided much of the (dis)information upon which the stories were based, Koziol "produced a whole series of articles portraying the Panthers as 'highly violent.'"[79] The stories, replete with factual errors, "were [intended] to support and lend credibility to [other] stepped up COINTELPRO operations" undertaken by Johnson's agents against the Chicago BPP chapter from January 1969 onward.[80] When these operations culminated in the murders by a special police unit of Illinois Panther leaders Fred Hampton and Mark Clark on December 4, an event sparking an outpouring of local support for the Party, Hoover personally expressed to several of the bureau's ranking Chicago media collaborators an "immediate need for concise compilation[s] of all the violent acts that will surely portray the Black Panther Party . . . as an aggregate of violence-prone individuals who foment and initiate violence."[81]

[In response] the media let loose with a deluge of literally hundreds of articles over the next few weeks, justifying the police shooting and saying basically that the Panthers deserved whatever they got. The message driven home again and again was put out by a Tribune *columnist—those who want to "rule by force and terror [speaking of the Panthers, of course, not the pigs who murdered them] can expect nothing less than disaster. . . ." "Violence-prone," "schooled in hate," a "threat to our democratic society" was the continuous refrain employed to justify the killings.*[82]

Koziol was again a star performer, cranking out seven such articles in just three weeks.[83] Probably the worst press coverage, however, was provided by *Tribune* reporters Robert Wiedrich and Edward Lee, who produced an exclusive front-page interview with State's Attorney Edward V. Hanrahan and participating police on December 11.[84] Therein, under a banner headline proclaiming "Hanrahan, Police Tell Panther Story," they presented an unchallenged regurgitation of virtually every official untruth uttered up to that point in the Hampton/Clark case and added a raft of new ones. Prominently displayed were a pair of photographs of purported bullet holes in the door and doorframe of Hampton's apartment, by which participating the killers claimed to have "proven" that the Panthers fired first, and had thus been shot in "self-defense."[85] Chicago's CBS television affiliate WBBM followed up the same evening with a "reenactment" of events told entirely in terms of the police account.[86] A day later, presumably inspired by such "analysis," the FBI-affiliated Fraternal Order of Police released a statement to the press calling for the Party as a whole to be "wiped out."[87]

The charade finally began to unravel when a few independent reporters finally managed to demonstrate that the "bullet holes" in the police photos published by the *Tribune* were actually nail heads standing out in bold relief against the Hampton's white woodwork.[88] As it turned out, the Panthers had fired only one shot—and that by Mark Clark during his death spasm—while the police had fired ninety-nine, including two rounds point-blank into Fred Hampton's head after he'd been badly wounded.[89] Charges of attempting to murder the police raiders were subsequently dropped against seven Party members who'd survived the assault, all but one of whom had been shot by their supposed "victims," but no criminal action was ever taken against the killers or their superiors.

Nor did Koziol, the *Tribune,* WBBM, or any of their mainstream media cohorts ever recant the grotesque defamation to which they'd subjected the Party, much less launch a campaign to portray the police as being "schooled in hate" or a "violence-prone threat to democracy." On the contrary, six months later the editors of the *New York Times,* while forced to concede that Chicago officials had "engaged in a deliberate publicity campaign to depict the Panthers as the aggressors [the FBI's involvement was not yet public information]," as well as "doctored evidence . . . coached police witnesses," and falsely arrested the surviving victims, still felt it appropriate to "balance" such findings by reciting the usual litany of unsubstantiated allegations about the character of the Party itself.[90]

Silencing the Black Panther Newspaper

Attending the bureau's carefully crafted manipulation of the Panthers' image in the mass media were its efforts to prevent the Party from speaking for itself. Although it was not until May 5, 1970, that the BPP newspaper, the *Black Panther,* was formally targeted for neutralization, counterintelligence operations had commenced against it as early as July 1968.[91] Early on, while the newspaper's circulation was still quite limited, the approach seems to have hinged mainly on prompting reporters and public officials to grossly misrepresent the BPP's positions, then arrange for local police to arrest Panthers attempting to distribute the Party's published response, impounding as many copies of the paper as possible in the process.[92]

A prime example of this occurred in February 1969, when San Francisco mayor Joseph Alioto, on the basis of a "briefing sheet" provided by the local SAC Charles Bates, made a widely publicized assertion that "the Black Panthers encourage violence [and that] the ten commandments of the Black Panther Party [include a] section on robbing and raping."[93] The mayor had been led to confuse the Party's Ten Point Program, which made no mention of either robbery or rape, with its Eight Points of Attention, which did. Far from encouraging such crimes, however, the Eight Points plainly stated that any Panther found to have engaged in them would be summarily expelled from the Party.[94] Since both the program and the Points of Attention appeared every week in the *Panther,* Alioto's remarks were quickly followed by a surge in arrests of individuals trying to distribute it in the Bay Area.

As the paper's circulation grew to an estimated 139,000 copies per week,[95] the counterintelligence initiatives undertaken against it became more sophisticated, or, in some cases, bizarre. In August 1970, for instance, the SAC of the San Diego field office proposed an operation to contaminate the *Panther* printing facility with Skatol, a chemical powder he believed would duplicate the stench of "the foulest smelling feces imaginable," in hopes of rendering the building "uninhabitable" and thereby halting the paper's publication.[96] San Diego also proposed using infiltrators within the Minutemen, a right-wing paramilitary group, to convince that organization to "disrupt publication of this newspaper." In the alternative, it was suggested that COINTELPRO operatives should simply forge threatening letters on Minutemen stationery in hopes of frightening *Panther* staff members into quitting.[97]

The New York field office came up with the idea of convincing the management of United Airlines, through which the paper was usually shipped, to cancel the Party's bulk rate discounts, standard in the business, increasing fees to "the full legal rate allowable for shipping newspapers." It was estimated that the maneuver would cost the BPP in excess of $10,000 per week in New York alone.[98] In 1970 the Internal Revenue Service was also asked to conduct an entirely arbitrary investigation of the *Panther*'s finances, in hopes that a tax case could be developed that might result in impoundment of its assets.[99]

In November 1970 Hoover prevailed upon Victor Riesel to write a column reiterating the standard allegations of Panther "violence" before calling upon the Teamsters and other unions "to refuse to handle shipments of BPP newspapers." A memo to thirty-nine field offices then instructed each of them to "anonymously mail copies of the [column] to officials of appropriate unions, police organizations and other individuals within [your] territory to encourage such a boycott."[100] Another headquarters recommendation was to use the bureau's "racial informants" to foster antagonism between the Panthers and the Nation of Islam in Chicago, mainly in the belief that this would provoke Elijah Muhammad "to take positive steps to counteract the sale of BPP newspapers in the Negro community" there.[101]

A January 1970 directive went still further, calling upon nine field offices to develop plans "to counteract *any* favorable support in publicity to the Black Panther Party [emphasis added]."[102] Methods used to achieve these results varied considerably, but centered in large part on the issuance of anonymous threats to the physical safety either of a Panther speaker or the sponsoring institution. As illustration, an appearance by Party Chairman Bobby Seale at the University of Oregon was canceled in May 1969 after a COINTELPRO operative in the San Francisco office, impersonating "a concerned black brother," telephoned Seale's mother to warn that her son might "be assassinated, like Malcolm X" during his speech.[103] Other sorts of disinformation were also employed, as when agents in the San Francisco office provided copies of FBI-produced articles describing Panther Chief of Staff David Hilliard as "anti-Semitic" to members of a Jewish organization shortly before Hilliard was to address it. The engagement was of course canceled.[104]

A different approach was taken with respect to the Party's Deputy Chairman, Fred Hampton, in Chicago. On January 24, 1969, shortly before Hampton was to appear live on a television talk show, Robert Stoetzal, supervisor of the FBI's Racial Matters Squad in that city, called a contact among the local police and requested that Hampton be intercepted in the studio and arrested on an outstanding warrant for "mob action" before he could go on the air.[105] Afterward, Hoover personally commended Mitchell for timing the arrest so that it would occur "under circumstances which proved highly embarrassing to the BPP."[106]

The FBI's No Breakfast for Children Program

A major reason for the Party's extraordinary popularity among urban blacks during the late 1960s was its "serve the people programs" (redesignated "survival programs" in 1971). There were several of these, ranging from liberation schools to free clinics, but the first and in many ways most important was the Free Breakfast for Children Program, begun in 1969.[107] Hoover was quite aware that it would be impossible to cast the party as merely "a group of thugs" so long as it was meeting the daily nutritional requirements of an estimated 50,000 grade-schoolers in forty-five inner cities across the country. Rather than arguing that the government itself should deliver such a program, however, he targeted the Panthers' efforts for destruction.[108]

When San Francisco SAC Charles Bates objected that this might serve "to convey the impression that . . . the FBI is working against the aspirations of the Negro people,"[109] Domestic Intelligence chief William C. Sullivan offered a sharp rejoinder in Hoover's name.

> *Your reasoning is not in line with Bureau objectives. . . . You state that the Bureau . . . should not attack programs of community interest such as the BPP "Breakfast for Children." You state that this is because many prominent "humanitarians," both white and black, are interested in the program as well as churches that are actively supporting it. You have obviously missed the point. The BPP is not engaged in the "Breakfast for Children" program for humanitarian reasons, including their efforts to create an image of civility, assume community control of Negroes, and to fill adolescent children with their insidious poison.[110]*

Bates was then given two weeks to initiate COINTELPRO actions designed to "eradicate the [Panthers'] 'serve the people' programs."[111] In short order, agents were visiting businesses in Oakland, trying to convince them not to contribute either foodstuffs or money to feed hungry children. Panther Captain Robert Bay, who was simultaneously soliciting such support, was arrested on five counts of "robbery" and held for a month in jail before charges were dropped.[112] Sullivan, meanwhile, suggested that efforts be made to misrepresent the breakfast program as a medium through which children were being indoctrinated with "violent . . . anti-white propaganda" such as the idea that they should "hate police."[113]

Conveniently, Bates's agents were able, almost immediately, to come up with what appeared to be conclusive physical evidence supporting Sullivan's thesis. This took the form of a coloring book depicting "policemen as pigs, and filled with pictures . . . showing black children stabbing, shooting and otherwise assaulting policemen."[114] The item had supposedly been discovered by local police after it was distributed to youngsters being fed each morning in the basement of San Francisco's Sacred Heart Church, and was quickly circulated by the FBI to Safeway, Mayfare Markets, the Jack-in-the-Box Corp., and other retailers, expressly to "impede their contributions to the BPP 'Breakfast Program.'"[115]

The coloring book has a rather interesting history. Rendered in the highly characteristic style of Panther Minister of Culture Emory Douglas, illustrator for the *Black Panther*, it was created in late 1968 by James Teemer, an aspiring recruit in the Panthers' Sacramento chapter eager to impress the BPP leadership with his graphic talents (see chapter 13 in this volume).[116] Upon review of a twenty-five-copy pilot edition, the Party's Central Committee determined that the book's content was inappropriate for young people. Bobby Seale thereupon instructed that the book not be produced, and that the original proof copies be destroyed.[117]

Nonetheless, a print run of 1,000 copies was quietly ordered and paid for by Larry Clayton Powell, a member of the Los Angeles chapter who'd been promoted to work among the Party's Oakland-based national cadre. There is no evidence as to how many of these unauthorized publications were distributed to children before the remainder found their way into the hands of the San Francisco police and, thence, the FBI.[118] The mystery of how all this might have happened was dispelled in June 1969 when Larry Powell and his wife, Jean, also a former L.A. Panther cum national cadre member, appeared before Senator John McClellan's Permanent Subcommittee on Investigations to testify that the Panthers were an "organized criminal enterprise" along the lines of the Mafia.[119] Both of them, along with another national office staffer, Tommy Jones, were thereupon revealed to have infiltrated the Party in 1967, first as informers for local police, later for the FBI as well (at which point Larry Powell, at least, had begun to function as an outright agent provocateur).[120]

Decked out in the full Party uniform of black berets, jackets, trousers, and boots, with offsetting powder blue shirts, the Powells offered a perfect photo opportunity for the bureau's host of "friendly media sources," as they sat before the senators and solemnly recounted how the Panthers were garnering "$50,000–100,000 per month" from armed robberies and the "extortion" of businesses in the black community. Much of the money, they claimed, was being embezzled by David Hilliard and other Party leaders. Objections by legitimate activists—such as themselves, they implied—were regularly silenced by a "Panther hit squad."[121]

None of this has ever been supported by anything resembling evidence. Indeed, in 1974, after a further *five years* of intensive investigation, the FBI's San Francisco field office was forced to admit that it had "failed to develop information that [the BPP] is or has been extorting funds from legitimate businesses."[122] Nor had it been able to establish that the Panthers raised money via "the old communist technique of political robberies."[123] Moreover, for all the official rhetoric about the Panthers' defensive stance against police brutality equating to their being "cop killers," there were only two police fatalities attributable to Party members by the end of 1969.[124]

Nonetheless, the Powells' FBI-orchestrated performance provided a veritable bonanza of negative publicity, which was then used in COINTELPRO operations to discredit the Panthers overall. By October 1969 the former were beginning to bear discernible fruit as the bishop of the San Diego Diocese, deluged for over a month with anonymous calls from agents[125] as well as their equally anonymous mailings of "relevant" press clippings,[126] abruptly transferred Frank Curran, a "Panther-friendly" local priest, to "somewhere in the State of New Mexico for permanent assignment." The Party's permission to use the basement of what had been Curran's church to feed children was simultaneously revoked.[127] Similar scenarios unfolded over the next few months in New Haven and elsewhere.[128]

Where such tactics failed to have the desired effect, other approaches were taken. One of the more "innovative and hard-hitting" was that taken by Charles Gain and William Cohendet of the San Francisco office's "Panther Squad" (a subpart of its COIN-TELPRO section). During the fall of 1969 they effectively obliterated a breakfast program that had been thriving in the city's Haight-Ashbury district by "surreptitiously" convincing parents that the Panthers serving food to their children were mostly "infected with venereal disease."[129] In Chicago, Philadelphia, Cleveland, Baltimore, and several other cities the method was cruder: riot-equipped tactical units were repeatedly dispatched by cooperating local police to the sites where children were being fed, stormed in, terrified everyone, ruined food, and wrecked the premises while claiming to look for nonexistent "contraband" or "fugitives."[130]

Preventing Coalitions

Preventing the establishment of viable coalitions between the BPP and other radical organizations was, for obvious reasons, considered a key to containing its growth potential and political effectiveness. The first of the COINTELPRO initiatives undertaken in this connection relates to the announced "merger" of the Student Nonviolent Coordinating Committee with the Panthers in early 1968, and appears to have been more a part of the bureau's ongoing campaign against SNCC than a new operation focusing on the BPP.[131] Still, given that several prominent SNCC leaders publicly accepted positions in the Party on February 18—Stokely Carmichael was named Prime Minister, H. Rap Brown became Minister of Justice, and James Forman was named Minister for Foreign Affairs—the point is somewhat academic.[132]

In any event, utilizing the services of infiltrators already in place within both organizations, agents set out to exacerbate ideological disputes and questions of personal hegemony between the two groups for purposes of driving them apart once again.[133] Such conflicts were largely brought to a head in mid-July, when, according to a subsequent *New York Times* article, a group of Panthers headed by Eldridge Cleaver "asserted their authority" over James Forman by torturing him. The story, which both Forman and SNCC leader Cleveland Sellers have insisted is false, appears to have originated with Earl Anthony, an FBI operative posing as a captain in the BPP's Los Angeles chapter, who participated in the supposed "torture session."[134] With media depictions of the alliance becoming increasingly demeaning, SNCC formally withdrew from its relationship with the Panthers in early August, while Forman, already reduced to a state of "paranoia" by FBI operations targeting him, checked into a hospital for psychiatric treatment.[135]

Carmichael, who was playing a substantial role in building the BPP into a fully national organization, remained with the Panthers and was consequently expelled from SNCC.[136] He had long been a priority target for COINTELPRO neutralization, and now efforts against him were quickly intensified. In July, an effort had been made to bad-jacket him by way of having an infiltrator, probably a bodyguard named Peter Cardoza, plant a forged document making it appear that Carmichael was a CIA informant:[137]

> *One method of accomplishing [this] would be to have a carbon copy of [an] informant report reportedly written by CARMICHAEL to the CIA carefully deposited in the automobile of a close Black Nationalist friend. The report should be placed so that it will be readily seen. . . . It is hoped that when the report is read it will help promote distrust between CARMICHAEL and the Black Community. . . . It is also suggested that we inform*

a percentage of reliable criminal and racial informants that "we heard from reliable sources that CARMICHAEL was a CIA agent." It is hoped that these informants would spread the rumor in various large Negro communities across the land.[138]

On September 4, an agent in the New York office followed up by telephoning Carmichael's mother, claiming to be an anonymous friend whose purpose was to warn her that the rumor had been believed and that a Panther "hit squad" had been dispatched from Oakland to kill her son.[139] Whether or not this was the cause, Carmichael himself quickly relocated to the African country of Guinea, took the name Kwame Turé, and announced his resignation from the BPP a few months later.[140]

By then, the bureau would be putting the finishing touches on its drive to split SNCC and the BPP, surfacing accounts in the media to the effect that the former had begun to refer to the latter as "pinheads," since "the difference between a panther and other large cats is that the panther has the smallest head."[141] In response, a number of SNCC personnel severed their relations with the organization, several of them assuming even more prominent roles as Panthers. Kathleen Neal (Cleaver), for example, became the Party's Communications Secretary, while Don Cox ("D.C."), was named Panther Field Marshal for the eastern United States, Carver "Chico" Neblett and Landon Williams were appointed to the same rank in the West, and Bobby Rush became Deputy Minister of Defense in Chicago.[142]

SNCC itself continued to be eroded from within, as two unidentified infiltrators played a role in Forman's December 1968 expulsion of veteran organizers Willie Ricks and Cleveland Sellers for their refusal to sever ties with either Carmichael or the Panthers.[143] In June 1969 Forman in turn was forced to resign as H. Rap Brown, desperate to reverse the organization's decline, attempted to reorganize in a more Panther-like manner.[144] This, too, was forestalled when Brown went underground to avoid prosecution on a battery of pending charges, and on March 9, 1970, two of his closest remaining associates, Ralph Featherstone and William "Ché" Payne, were murdered by a car bomb during an apparent assassination attempt on Brown himself.[145] Although SNCC was in total eclipse thereafter, it would be another three and a half years before the FBI finally closed its file on the group.[146]

In the interim, the bureau repeated its maneuvers to block BPP alliances with other organizations, most notably a number of inner-city street gangs the Party was seeking to politicize and absorb into itself.[147] While there were variations on the theme in every locality where the Panthers attempted such mergers, the clearest record pertains to Chicago. There, by December 1968, Fred Hampton and Bobby Rush had made considerable progress toward bringing such lesser groups as the Black Disciples, the Mau Maus, and the Conservative Vice Lords into the Party, and were conducting potentially fruitful negotiations with Jeff Fort, head of the 5,000-strong Black P. Stone Nation (formerly the Blackstone Rangers).[148] Given that the BPP as a whole had at that time reached its peak of somewhere between 3,000 and 5,000 members, consummation of the Hampton/Rush initiative would have served to double the size of the Party almost overnight.[149]

To counter this "threat," the FBI's infiltrators of the Chicago BPP chapter as well as informants within the larger black community were instructed to begin circulating rumors that the Panthers were making disparaging remarks about Fort and other P. Stone leaders.[150] Counterintelligence specialist Roy Mitchell, a member of Robert Stoetzal's Racial Matters Squad, then proposed sending an anonymous letter to Fort: "Chicago . . . recommends that Fort be made aware that [Hampton] and [Rush] together with other BPP members locally, are responsible for circulating these remarks concerning him. It is felt that if Fort were to be aware that the BPP were responsible, it would lend impetus to his refusal to accept any BPP overtures to the Rangers and additionally *might result in Fort having active steps to exact some form of retribution toward the leadership of the BPP"* (emphasis added).[151]

The letter was sent and, by January 10, 1969, Stoetzal was able to report that the P. Stones and the Panthers had "not only not been able to form any alliance, but enmity and distrust have arisen."[152] He also spelled out exactly what was meant by Mitchell's earlier use of the phrase "exact some form of retribution" in a January 13 memo in which he explained his view that, for Fort and other P. Stone members, "violent type activity—shooting and the like—is second nature."[153] Instructively, he also noted in the latter document that proposals to send anonymous letters to the BPP had been discussed but rejected because, contrary to what was even then being fed to Ron Koziol and other "cooperating journalists," the "BPP is at present *not* believed [to be] violence-prone" (emphasis added).[154]

With this said, Stoetzal proposed to send a second Mitchell-composed letter to Fort, this one purporting to be from "a black brother you don't know," and warning the P. Stone leader that "there's supposed to be a hit out on you" (contracted by Fred Hampton). The intent of this second mailing was laid out quite clearly: "It is believed that the [letter] may intensify the degree of animosity between the two groups and may occasion Forte [*sic*] *to take retaliatory action* which would disrupt the BPP or *lead to reprisals against its leadership"* (emphasis added).[155] Authorization to send the "hit letter" to Fort was made by J. Edgar Hoover, personally, on January 30, 1969.[156]

As was later observed by Arthur Jefferson, staff counsel to the Senate Select Committee on Intelligence Activities and the Rights of Americans and author of a committee special report entitled *The FBI's Covert Action Program to Destroy the Black Panther Party,* there is no evidence that Jeff Fort responded to such provocations by ordering the executions of BPP members.[157] This seems, however, to have been more a matter of restraint on Fort's part than anything else. As Jefferson also concluded, "the Bureau's intent was clear," and certainly not of the "nonviolent" sort Chicago SAC Marlin Johnson would later claim under oath.[158]

As it was, the possibility of a Panther/P. Stone merger or working coalition dissolved into a public announcement by Fort that he would "blow [Hampton's] head off" if he or any other BPP member were to venture into P. Stone territory in the future.[159] Thus freed from the "danger" of politicization and engagement in constructive community activities such as the Panthers' Breakfast for Children and antidrug programs, the Black P. Stone Nation was virtually assured of continuing to evolve along its traditional line of social criminality. Unhindered by significant FBI interference, it had by the mid-1980s become known as "El Rukn," reputedly the largest and most efficient distributor of illicit drugs in all of Chicago.[160]

Neutralization of Panther Supporters

While working to prevent what Stokely Carmichael termed a "Black United Front," with the BPP at its center, the bureau's COINTELPRO operatives also set out to destroy organizations composed mostly of whites and established for the express purpose of providing support to the BPP. Although a certain amount of effort was put into creating breaches between the Panthers and the Peace and Freedom Party (PFP), a national electoral organization fielding racially mixed slates of candidates and featuring Eldridge Cleaver for president in 1968,[161] the main weight seems to have fallen on a Los Angeles–based group calling itself "Friends of the Panthers" (FoP).

Donald Freed, a college professor and award-winning playwright with numerous contacts in the entertainment industry, organized the group. Its primary purpose was to generate funds and favorable publicity for the BPP, objectives plainly antithetical to the bureau's desires.[162] Hence, agents were assigned to neutralize those considered key functionaries within it, beginning with Freed himself, the idea being to make examples of those targeted to deter other "liberal and naive individuals" from becoming involved in Panther support work:[163] "It is felt that any prosecution or exposure of Freed or [name deleted] will severely hurt the BPP. Any exposure will not only cost the Panthers money, but additionally, would cause other white supporters of the BPP to withdraw their support. It is felt that the Los Angeles chapter of the BPP [in particular] could not function without the financial support of white sympathizers."[164]

The operations against Freed personally included mailing bogus memoranda in his name designed to "cause a rift" between him and the Panthers.[165] When that failed, infiltrators spread rumors that he was a police informant.[166] When that too failed to have the desired effect, efforts were made to have the LAPD raid his residence in search of "fugitives . . . illegal firearms [and] explosives."[167] This fell through as well. Finally, Phil Denny, an agent assigned to the COINTELPRO section of the Los Angeles field office, managed to get Freed fired from San Fernando Valley College and then to prevent his obtaining a new position on the faculty of Cal State/Fullerton.[168]

In a related if somewhat inept action, an attempt was made to discredit Academy Award–winning actress Jane Fonda by surfacing a story through *Los Angeles Times* gossip columnist Amy Archerd that the FoP member had joined Panthers during a public rally in threatening to murder "Richard Nixon and any other motherfucker who stands in our way."[169] Unlike many of her supposedly more reputable colleagues, Archerd declined to write the desired column.[170] Agents compensated for this setback, however, by quickly "furnish[ing] information to a Los Angeles TV news commentator who agreed to air a series of shows against the BPP, 'especially in the area of white liberals contributing to the BPP.'"[171]

Subsequently Shirley Sutherland, a Canadian citizen and former wife of actor Donald Sutherland, was charged in 1971 with providing illegal weapons to the Panthers. Although the case was dismissed—it was demonstrated that Sutherland had been set up by a Los Angeles police provocateur named James Jarrett, and that Sam Bluth, another police operative, had infiltrated her defense team—the charges ultimately precipitated her deportation as an "undesirable alien."[172] Senate investigators later discovered several comparable cases of the bureau's having manipulated the media, the judicial process, or both to dissuade "famous entertainers" from contributing money or making favorable comments about the BPP.[173]

Among the ugliest such initiatives was that undertaken in April 1970 by COINTEL-PRO specialist Richard Wallace Held to "cheapen the image" of the talented but psychologically unstable actress Jean Seberg, one of the FoP's more committed members.[174] Upon learning that Seberg was pregnant, Held requested and received authorization to provide disinformation that the father was BPP education minister Raymond "Masai" Hewitt rather than Seberg's husband, novelist Romain Gary.[175] On May 19, gossip columnist Joyce Haber published a thinly veiled recapitulation of Held's proposed text in the *Los Angeles Times*.[176] It was then picked up by the *Hollywood Reporter* on June 8, and by another hundred papers before it was repeated in great detail by *Newsweek* on August 24.[177]

Traumatized by this tidal wave of publicity concerning the details of her private life, Seberg attempted suicide on August 7. On August 23, having received her subscription copy a day before the offending issue of *Newsweek* appeared on the stands, she went into premature labor. Born at the beginning of its third trimester, the baby had little possibility of survival and died two days later. Seberg never recovered from the ordeal, repeatedly attempting to take her own life on the anniversary of the infant's death until, in 1979, she finally succeeded. Romain Gary followed a year later.[178]

Exacerbating Intergroup Tensions

Some organizations, for ideological reasons of their own, were openly hostile to the Panthers from the outset. In such cases, especially where a high potential for violence was discerned among the groups in question, the deliberate exacerbation of intergroup tensions became a standard COINTELPRO method of isolating and weakening the Party itself. The earlier-mentioned operation to prevent a merger of the P. Stone Nation with the Chicago BPP chapter plainly falls within this mold. A better example, however, is that of US, a cultural nationalist organization based in southern California, for whom the Panthers' brand of revolutionary nationalist agenda was anathema.[179]

Although no specific illustrations were provided, agents in both San Diego and Los Angeles began to report as early as November 1968 that "an aura of gang warfare" attended BPP efforts to build chapters in those cities, long considered by US leader Maulana Karenga (Ronald Everett) to be his group's exclusive political turf.[180] Initial efforts to "capitalize" on this situation included the use of provocateurs in both organizations to "raise the level of paranoia" among leaders and members alike; rumors were spread within their ranks that US members intended to assassinate Panther Information Minister Eldridge Cleaver while the Party had its sights set on Karenga himself.[181] On at least one occasion, Darthard Perry, a onetime Military Intelligence specialist who had infiltrated the BPP's Los Angeles chapter for the FBI, physically assaulted an US member in order to facilitate "the promoting [of] discord between members of US and the Party in Los Angeles."[182]

Things were apparently not moving fast enough to suit the FBI. According to Perry, known as "Ed Riggs" to the Panthers but codenamed "Othello" by Brendon Cleary, Will Heaton, and Michael Quinn, the agents to whom he reported in the COINTELPRO section of the Los Angeles field office, the next step was to arrange the outright assassinations of L.A. Panther leaders Alprentice "Bunchy" Carter and John Huggins.[183] On January 17, 1969, the two men were duly shot to death by a team of five ostensible US members after a student meeting in UCLA's Campbell Hall. Perry, who was present, subsequently identified the shooter as Claude Hubert, whom he claimed to know as an FBI operative within Karenga's organization; Hubert's two primary "back-ups" were identified as the brothers George and Larry Stiner, whom Perry also named as infiltrators.[184] In 1995 M. Wesley Swearingen, an agent assigned to the Panther Squad of the Los Angeles COINTELPRO section from 1970 to 1973, confirmed much of Perry's account.

> *Soon after I had been assigned to the Los Angeles racial squad, I was told by a fellow agent,* Joel Ash, *that another agent on the squad,* Nick Galt, *had arranged for Galt's informers in the United Slaves to assassinate Alprentice Carter, the Panthers' Los Angeles [deputy] minister of defense, and John Huggins, the deputy minister of information. Following Galt's instructions, informants George Stiner and Larry Stiner shot them to death on the UCLA campus. . . . I later reviewed the Los Angeles files and verified that the Stiner brothers were FBI informants. (emphasis original)*[185]

The bureau moved quickly to escalate the situation into a full-fledged "shooting war." On February 20, 1969, Robert L. Baker, who headed up the COINTELPRO section of the San Diego field office, proposed to prepare and distribute throughout the local black community a set of cartoons, composed to look like a product of the Us organization, which depicted the BPP as being "ineffectual, inadequate, and riddled with graft and corruption";[186] "One of the caricatures was 'designed to attack' the Los Angeles Panther leader [Elmer 'Geronimo' Pratt, who had replaced the slain Carter] as a bully toward women and children in the black community. Another accused the BPP of 'actually instigating' a recent Los Angeles police raid on US headquarters. A third cartoon depicted Karenga as an overpowering individual 'who has the BPP completely at its mercy.'"[187]

FBI headquarters ordered that the forgeries be distributed by COINTELPRO operatives working out of the San Diego, Los Angeles, and San Francisco field offices for the express purpose of intensifying what already appeared to be a lethal level of "feuding" between the two organizations.[188] A major problem emerged, however, when the supposedly "violence-prone" Panthers declined to respond in the desired manner. Indeed, by late March, despite the critical wounding of yet another L.A. Panther by an unidentified US gunman, agents were reporting "a lessening of tensions," as the Party had set upon a course of attempting to "talk out their differences" with US.[189]

To break the logjam, the Los Angeles office's Richard W. Held instructed Julius Carl Butler, one of his operatives within the Los Angeles BPP chapter, to shoot up the home of US member James Doss on the night of March 17.[190] Although Geronimo Pratt quickly expelled Butler as "a loose cannon and possible provocateur," Karenga was apparently convinced by the incident that the Panthers' intentions were the opposite of what they claimed. The initial response from US nonetheless came not from a legitimate member of the organization but from John Stark, still another FBI infiltrator. Ironically enough, the "Panther" Stark shot and killed turned out to be Al Holt, a bureau operative only recently insinuated into the San Diego BPP chapter.[191] It was not until May 23 that Tambuzi (Jerry Horne), a legitimate member of US, finally gunned down a bona fide LA Panther named John Savage.[192]

By the time Savage was killed, the San Diego office had already released a second batch of cartoons that it credited with having shattered any possibility that there might be a peaceful resolution to the US/Panther conflict. Noting in a June 13 memo to headquarters that the pattern of violence between the two groups had escalated dramatically over the preceding sixty days, agents observed with evident glee that Karenga's "Simbas," an armed security formation, had accelerated their program of weapons training and begun to stockpile ammunition.[193] In its reply, the headquarters staff concurred that the situation was developing well, but expressed frustration that the operation had still failed to elicit a violent response from the BPP.[194]

In another attempt to "correct" the situation, Baker requested authorization from FBI headquarters to send a forged letter from the BPP San Diego chapter to the Party's national office in Oakland vociferously protesting this "inaction" and demanding permission to retaliate in kind.[195] Although national BPP leaders at first declined to approve any such response, their position may have shifted to some extent when, on August 14, two San Diego Panthers were wounded in an ambush by US gunmen.[196] A day later Sylvester Bell, another genuine Party member, was killed in a drive-by shooting Wesley Swearingen attributes to "FBI informers" lodged within US.[197] On August 30 the United Slaves' San Diego office was bombed, an apparent Panther retaliation at long last, although according to Darthard Perry that too may have been the work of a bureau operative.[198]

Whether or not Swearingen and Perry are accurate in their assessments of who did what during the August events, Baker and his colleagues were shortly crowing that "shootings, beatings and a high degree of unrest continues to prevail in the ghetto area of San Diego," a matter they claimed was substantially and "directly attributable to this program [COINTELPRO]."[199] Given such "success," argued San Diego SAC Robert Evans, the operation should be renewed: "In view of the recent killing of BPP member Sylvester Bell, a new cartoon is being considered in the hopes that it will assist in the continuance of the rift between BPP and US."[200]

Nor was this all. On September 3 the same agents, alluding to a recent article in the *Black Panther* critical of US leader Ron Karenga's political positions, sent a bogus letter to Karenga in hopes of provoking him to undertake "some sort of retaliatory action . . . against the BPP."[201] By October, agents as far away as Newark had gotten into the act, attempting to whip up the same kind of violence between the East Coast US organization headed by Amiri Baraka (LeRoi Jones) and regional Panther chapters.[202] In that operation, not only was a publicly distributed cartoon issued—the Party was depicted as a pig, its program as "dung"—but a "box score" bearing the caption "Watch out, Karenga's coming!" and a tally: "US–6, Panthers–0."[203]

On January 29, 1970, a final round of cartoons was approved for dissemination in San Diego, San Francisco, and Los Angeles,[204] and as late as May of that year agents in the Los Angeles COINTELPRO section were still plotting ways and means of "maximiz[ing] opportunities to capitalize on the situation."[205] In the end, they seem to have decided that their best course of action would be simply to keep US "appropriately and discreetly advised of the time and location of BPP activities in order that the two organizations might be brought together and thus grant nature the opportunity to take her due course."[206]

Infiltration

As the Party was cut off ever more effectively from constructive interaction with broader society, the FBI made increasingly determined efforts to place "informants" within it, instigating an accelerating spiral of internal turmoil and decay. This was of course an old bureau procedure, dating back to 1919 or earlier,[207] and carried out with great intensity against the Communist Party from the 1940s onward. But with respect to the Black Liberation Movement and the Panthers in particular, it entailed an unparalleled degree of virulence in operational intent.

In a counterintelligence context, the word *informant* is itself deliberately innocuous and misleading, implying as it does that the task assigned those individuals inserted or "developed" within target organizations consists merely of information-gathering. In actuality, while each of them undoubtedly reported regularly to their handlers on internal Party matters, the jobs of the operatives installed under the rubric of COINTELPRO invariably involved much more. As is evidenced by the actions already attributed to several such "informants" within the BPP—Larry Powell, Darthard Perry, and Julius Butler, as examples—they routinely functioned as outright agents provocateurs.[208]

When the FBI first initiated COINTELPRO-BPP in 1968, it maintained approximately 3,300 "racial ghetto-type informants." By the time the acronym was officially discontinued in 1971, the number had climbed to nearly 7,500.[209] From this mass, the bureau's counterintelligence specialists had set out to cull those imbued with "above average imagination and initiative . . . unique knowledge or ability . . . leadership ability [and] a willingness to expand his current affairs." Their purpose was "to create an elite informant squad and send it around the country and the world in pursuit of 'domestic subversive, black militant, or New Left movements.'"[210] Of these, at least sixty-seven, upon whom the FBI lavished $7.4 million in payouts, were active within the Black Panther Party in 1969.[211]

Nor was this by any means the extent of it. Each local police department that collaborated in the bureau's counterintelligence campaign against the Panthers fielded its own informants, infiltrators, and provocateurs. Some of these, like Larry and Jean Powell, who reported to both the FBI and the Oakland Police Panther Squad, were "shared assets." Julius Butler and another provocateur, Louis Tackwood, both of whom were simultaneously on the informant rosters of the Los Angeles field office's COIN-TELPRO section and the LAPD's Criminal Conspiracy Section (CCS), also fall into this category.[212] Such operatives have typically been included within the number employed by the FBI. Others, however, like New York police undercover operatives Leslie Eggleston and Wilbert Thomas, were local personnel pure and simple:[213] "Undercover police officers from the New York City police department's Bureau of Special Services (BOSS) had a history of infiltrating Black political organizations. Ray Wood had successfully infiltrated the Revolutionary Action Movement and the more moderate Congress for Racial Equality. Eugene Roberts was a bodyguard for Malcolm X before joining the Panthers. Wood and Roberts, along with undercover cop Ralph White, provided the bulk of state testimony during the eight-month Panther 21 conspiracy trial [of 1969–70]."[214]

It is impossible to establish with any precision the overall number of police operatives infesting the Party's forty-three chapters, since the records of local departments have generally proven even less accessible than those of the FBI. Extrapolating from the fact that a half-dozen BOSS undercover men are known to have infiltrated the BPP in New York alone,[215] however, it may be reasonably assumed that there were at least one hundred. Taken in combination with their federal counterparts, a working estimate might be that about 10 percent of the BPP's total membership consisted of "law enforcement personnel" by the end of 1969.[216]

Bobby Seale and other Panther leaders had become acutely aware of this problem by November 1968, and set out to purge suspected infiltrators.[217] A significant difficulty with this procedure was that the task of identifying those to be expelled fell mainly upon security units formed within each chapter, a number of which were themselves headed by FBI or police operatives. Examples include the FBI's William O'Neal, who not only ran the Panther security team but served as Fred Hampton's personal bodyguard in Chicago; BOSS detective Ralph White, who, along with a civilian operative called Shaun Dubonnet (William Fletcher), established "spy hunting" units within the New York chapter; and Melvin "Cotton" Smith, who was in charge of security for the L.A. chapter.[218] The result was that a number of legitimate Panthers were bad-jacketed as "snitches and provocateurs" and summarily ejected, while the infiltrators themselves became even more entrenched.

Worse, as repression of the Party intensified on all fronts over the next year, such operatives were perfectly positioned to advocate, and in some cases to implement, ever more draconian means of combating infiltration. O'Neal, for instance, is known to have employed a bullwhip in conducting interrogations of "suspected informers," and built an electric chair with which to intimidate his victims. To all appearances, only the intervention of Fred Hampton, who had been incarcerated while most of the brutality was going on, prevented O'Neal from setting one or more "deterrent examples" with his device.[219]

Where all this led became obvious in May 1969 when George Sams, a self-styled "Party security expert," showed up in New Haven, Connecticut, to assist the local BPP chapter in "ridding itself of spies." Sams proceeded to interrogate a young recruit named Alex Rackley at great length and under severe torture—the victim was chained to a bed for a week, and repeatedly scalded with boiling water—before killing him and enlisting several chapter members to help dispose of the body.[220] Then, on August 21, a dozen Panthers, including not only Sams but Bobby Seale, Ericka Huggins (widow of slain L.A. Panther leader John Huggins), western regional Field Marshal Landon Williams, and New Haven chapter head Warren Kimbro, were indicted for conspiring to murder Rackley.[221]

It turned out that Sams, previously institutionalized as a psychotic, had been retained by the FBI as early as 1967, first to infiltrate Stokely Carmichael's faction of SNCC and thence the BPP.[222] Once apprehended, the killer quickly entered a guilty plea (he was *pardoned* after serving four years of his resulting life sentence) and became the state's star witness against Seale, Huggins, and Kimbro, a matter that led to the latter's also being sentenced to a life behind bars.[223] Seale and Huggins were acquitted,[224] although another New Haven Panther leader, Lonnie McLucas, was tried separately, found guilty of complicity in Rackley's death, and sentenced to fifteen years.[225] Charges against Williams and the others of the "New Haven 14" were eventually dropped, but not until May 1971, after they'd spent nearly three years in jail.[226]

Meanwhile, in April 1970, seventeen Baltimore Panthers, along with Arthur Turco, a white lawyer, were accused of murder conspiracy in the death of a suspected police infiltrator named Eugene Anderson. Among those arrested were virtually the entire Baltimore leadership cadre.[227] Also charged was Don Cox, the Party's East Coast Field Marshal, who evaded arrest by joining exiled Minister of Information Eldridge Cleaver's International Section in Algeria.[228]

Although there were serious questions as to whether the remains upon which the case was based were even Anderson's, local authorities took the "Baltimore 18" to trial after meeting with Attorney General John Mitchell and his Civil Rights Division head, Jerris Leonard, as well as FBI officials.[229] The case finally dissolved when it was revealed that the state's key "participant witnesses"—Mahoney Kebe, Donald Vaughn, and Arnold Loney—were not only the likely killers but FBI operatives inserted into the Baltimore BPP chapter. Indeed, Kebe, the supposed "star" of the group, was so obviously lying under oath that the trial judge ordered him removed from the witness stand and his testimony stricken from the record.[230]

Charges were then withdrawn, with the district attorney publicly admitting that there had never been a genuine evidentiary basis for the case and that his own office had indulged in what he called "improper prosecution tactics." Nevertheless, those accused, like several of those accused in the Rackley case, had already been held for months in jail without bond while their chapter disintegrated. And, as in the Rackley case, the FBI's media manipulators had in the interim availed themselves enthusiastically of yet another bureau-created opportunity to paint the Panthers as little more than a "gang of vicious thugs."[231]

There are several other instances, notably those involving the deaths of Fred Bennett and Jimmy Carr in California during the early 1970s, in which bona fide party members may have been killed because they were suspected of being FBI operatives. Given the otherwise lethal nature of Party factionalism fostered and fueled by COINTELPRO during those years, however, it is difficult to determine whether such suspicions really constituted the motive underlying their murders. If so, the questions remain open as to whether the victims were bad-jacketed by the bureau for purposes of bringing about their physical elimination and, in Bennett's case, whether the killer or killers were not themselves federal operatives.[232]

Whatever the answers, such killings, taken in combination with the waves of expulsions, interrogations, and otherwise increasingly pervasive climate of paranoia engendered within the Party because of its infiltration—"The BPP in San Diego [is] so completely disrupted and so much suspicion, fear and distrust has been interjected into the party that the members have taken to running surveillances on one another in an attempt to determine who the police agents are," as Robert Baker put it[233]—in large part account for the oft-remarked exodus of Party members that was occurring by early 1970. Bobby

Seale has estimated that 30 to 40 percent of all Panthers had quit by the end of that year, and the actual proportion may be even higher.[234]

Raids and Pretext Arrests

There is no way to adequately assess the extent to which pretext arrests were employed as a means of slicing into the ranks of bona fide members during the FBI's drive to neutralize the BPP. As Party attorney Charles Garry reported in early 1970, between "May 2, 1967 and December 25, 1969 charges were dropped against 87 Panthers arrested for so-called violations of the law" in Los Angeles County alone, and this was before the cases ever went to trial. Another dozen were dismissed for lack of evidence once they arrived in court.[235] "[Even] incomplete records tell a story of systematic arrest and harassment. . . . A man or a woman or a group of men and women would be charged with murder, be held in jail . . . and all at once the charges against them would be dropped. . . . Yet these men and women were kept in [jail] for days, weeks, and months even though there was no evidence against them."[236]

In Baltimore, for example, six Panthers were arrested on February 25, 1969, for "interfering with the arrest" of another. The case actually went to trial before an investigative reporter disclosed that the seventh "Panther" was actually an undercover police operative. At that point, State's Attorney Hillary Kaplan had no alternative but to withdraw the charges. Although he admitted that eight police officers had lied in their sworn statements, and that these comprised the entire body of evidence upon which he'd based his case, Kaplan declined to bring charges against the cops for their obvious conspiracy to pursue a false prosecution.[237]

In Chicago, arrests of Panthers were effected on 111 occasions during the summer of 1969, with only a handful of charges, most of them minor, ever taken to trial. Many of these had to do with a series of raids conducted by Chicago police on the Party's West Madison Street headquarters. During the first of these, conducted on June 9 and later admitted by Chicago SAC Marlin Johnson to have been part of his office's COINTELPRO operations, the raiders claimed to be looking for provocateur George Sams, then a "fugitive" on the Alex Rackley murder charge.[238] Although Sams was nowhere to be found, the police, personally supervised by Johnson, impounded "posters, literature, money, financial records and voluminous lists of members and contributors, as well as numerous [legal] weapons."[239] All eleven people at the office were hauled away to jail.

Chicago was by no means the only chapter to experience such treatment at the hands of the FBI and police units supposedly in hot pursuit of the elusive Mr. Sams. Before he was finally "apprehended" in Toronto toward the end of July, combinations of agents and police had "stormed into [Party] headquarters in Washington, Denver, Indianapolis, Salt Lake City, Des Moines, Detroit, San Diego, [Sacramento and Los Angeles,] and in every case they smashed or confiscated office equipment, literature, supplies and money, and arrested whoever was there on charges that were often dropped later."[240] There were, moreover, fatalities such as Larry Roberson, shot to death during a raid on the Chicago office conducted on July 16.[241]

On July 31 the police were back yet again at the Chicago office, this time on the basis of a tip, probably provided by O'Neal, that illegal weapons were being stored therein. When no such weapons were found, the police went quite literally berserk: "typewriters were smashed, the office set on fire, newspapers and food for the breakfast for children program and supplies for the health clinic destroyed, and the arrestees beaten." On October 3, the whole process was repeated yet again. In the aftermath of each raid, agent Roy Mitchell of the Racial Matters Squad saw to it that they were "widely sensationalized by the news media."[242]

The Los Angeles chapter, too, was racked by repeated raids. On the evening of January 17, 1969, a few hours after John Huggins and Bunchy Carter were murdered, a large force of heavily armed police swooped down on the home of Huggins's widow, Ericka, "detaining" several of the Panthers who had gathered to console her. Although the official pretext was that such measures were necessary to "avert further violence"—an utterly implausible contention, given the nature of the ongoing COINTELPRO operation that had claimed the two men's lives—it did nothing to explain why one of the raiders placed the muzzle of a gun to the head of John and Ericka Huggins's six-month-old baby, Mai, and laughingly proclaimed, "You're next."[243]

Another raid occurred at the Los Angeles chapter headquarters on May 1, during which police "seized weapons, arrested eleven people and subsequently released all of them without bringing charges."[244] Then, at 5:30 A.M. on December 8, the LAPD's newly formed SWAT units launched simultaneous assaults on three of the four BPP facilities in South Central L.A. In view of the execution-style murders of Fred Hampton and Mark Clark during a similar raid in Chicago only four days previously, those inside the Party's Central Avenue office opted to defend themselves by shooting it out with the police for nearly five hours, refusing to surrender until their arrests could be effected in broad daylight and before hundreds of spectators.[245] Charged with a variety of serious offenses and held against extremely high bail, L.A. chapter leader Geronimo ji Jaga Pratt and a dozen other Panthers involved in the standoff, known collectively as the "LA 13," were sweepingly exonerated on December 24, 1971.[246]

A similar situation prevailed in Philadelphia, where a special anti-Panther police squad headed by Lieutenant George Frencl, together with FBI personnel ostensibly searching for another fugitive (not Sams), hit the local BPP headquarters on September 23, 1969. Although no one was there, they "smashed in a back door [and] looted the office of its daily activities log book, personnel files, photographs, and signed petitions gathered by the party in its campaign for community control of the police. In addition, office equipment was destroyed or removed."[247] Another such foray was conducted on March 12, 1970, with the result that seven people were arrested on charges—later dropped—of burglary and violation of the Uniform Firearms Act.[248] "The final confrontation came at 6:00 A.M. Monday, August 31, 1970, when three separate teams of about forty-five heavily armed police stake-out men, each team accompanied by eight to ten detectives . . . simultaneouly raided Black Panther Party offices on Wallace Street in West Philadelphia, Columbia Avenue in North Philadelphia, and Queen Lane in Germantown. As in all of the major Philadelphia raids, police commissioner Frank Rizzo mobilized a corps of newsmen and photographers to record and photograph the action."[249]

The August 31 raids were rationalized in the press as having to do with the deaths of three cops a few days earlier, although no evidence linked the Party to these killings, and no related charges were ever filed.[250] As was reported in the *Philadelphia Bulletin* the same evening, the fourteen Panthers arrested in the raids had been "ordered against [a] wall and the men were ordered to strip naked"; a photo of six Panthers with bare buttocks appeared on the front page of the *New York Daily News* and was then placed in Associated Press distribution nationwide. As if this degradation were not enough, Commissioner Rizzo, who was on the scene, was widely quoted as taunting the handcuffed Panthers with having been "too yellow" to have shot it out with his SWAT-equipped police, and later about having caught "the big, bad Panthers with their pants down."[251]

Analyst Frank Donner, among others, has concluded that the whole affair was designed much more to provoke the sort of confrontation in which Panthers might be killed than to apprehend people genuinely suspected of being "cop-killers."[252] Failing that, the idea was to publicly humiliate the Party and wreck its local infrastructure immediately prior to a much-publicized national conference, the "Revolutionary People's Constitutional Convention," to be held in Philadelphia the following week.[253] Not only the well-orchestrated barrage of negative publicity but the magnitude of damage inflicted on local BPP offices lend credence to Donner's thesis:

> *The raiders . . . cleaned out all three search sites—furniture, bedding, clothing, file cabinets, party records, and even, in some cases, refrigerators and stoves. In a rampage of destruction, they demolished [walls and] even ripped out pipes in some of the bathrooms. They also made off with typewriters, tape recorders, cameras, and a duplicating machine, as well as a sum of money—estimated by the police at $1,067, and by the Panthers at between $1,500 and $1,700.*[254]

Elsewhere there were still more raids, beginning in 1968: in Denver on September 12–13, when police attempts to force entry resulted in a sensational firefight and siege; in Denver again on December 7, resulting in $9,000 in damages when the raiders ripped out walls while looking for a fictitious weapons cache;[255] in Indianapolis on December 18, when "federal agents and local police stormed Panther offices . . . firing teargas and ransacking the premises in their search for a nonexistent submachine gun";[256] in Des Moines on December 27, when a "combined force of local police and FBI stormed Panther headquarters to serve . . . arson warrants";[257] at the San Francisco office on April 28, 1969, during which police "arrested sixteen people, booked four for illegal use of sound equipment and released twelve."[258]

The pace did not slacken in 1970. In New Bedford, an August raid left twenty Panthers jailed against $2 million bond before charges of "conspiring to riot" were quietly dropped for lack of evidence.[259] And the beat went on: in Toledo, Party headquarters was riddled by police gunfire twice on the evening of September 18, 1970;[260] in New Orleans, there were three police assaults on the local office between September and November, two of them involving gunfire;[261] in Detroit, police harassment of a Panther for selling papers outside the local office led to a firefight that left one cop dead and three Panthers wounded on October 24, 1970.[262]

As all this was going on, other avenues were also being taken in reaching the same end. Many arrests were petty, as when the inimitable Robert Baker requested that the San Diego Police Intelligence Unit run warrant checks on local Panthers for routine traffic violations,[263] but they are indicative of the extent to which Party members were being arrested on virtually any excuse by mid-1969. It should be noted, moreover, that violation of Motor Vehicle Code laws was also the pretext used by San Diego police in mounting a raid on November 20, which resulted in the arrest and release of six people on weapons charges.[264]

Probably the most ridiculous of all pretext arrests was that of Panther Chief of Staff David Hilliard, who was indicted for "threatening the life of the President of the United States" after asserting that the Panthers would "kill Richard Nixon [and] any other motherfucker who stands in the way of our freedom" during a speech before an estimated 250,000 people on November 15, 1969.[265] The charge was shortly dropped when it became clear that the FBI would be forced to disclose its electronic surveillance of the Party's Oakland headquarters if the case went to trial, but by then the BPP had been forced into posting an entirely exorbitant bond, including a nonrefundable $30,000 premium, to get Hilliard out of jail.[266]

Other efforts to bring about arrests carried even more serious implications. In Chicago, William O'Neal, responding to instructions from his handlers to "impel" such behavior, was working hard to interest other members of the chapter in a variety of criminal activities.[267] At one point, he tried to entice a pair of bona fide Panthers, Robert Bruce and Nathaniel Junior, into "bombing city hall" with a mortar he planned to acquire.[268] At another, he "attempted to get Bruce to participate in robberies and offered to train him in the art of burglary."[269] At another, he unsuccessfully attempted to convince a Panther named Jewel Cook, recently released from prison on parole, to carry a gun.[270] At still another, fully aware that it was tapped, O'Neil openly conducted a drug transaction over the Party's office telephone.[271]

Wilbert Thomas, the BOSS detective who infiltrated the New York Panthers' Brooklyn branch, went much further, concocting a scheme to rob a hotel and then ambush police as they arrived on the scene. The gambit culminated in the arrest of Brooklyn Party leader Alfred Cain and two other legitimate Panthers as they rode in a car driven by Thomas on August 21, 1969, supposedly en route to perpetrate the crime. The state's case collapsed during the ensuing trial of the "Panther 3" when it was demonstrated that the only tangible acts associated with the supposed "cop-killer conspiracy" had been committed by Thomas himself, and electronic surveillance tapes revealed that none of the accused had been especially interested in his plan.[272]

Nor was being falsely arrested and prosecuted necessarily the worst of the fates awaiting those against whom such tactics were used. This was abundantly illustrated in the early morning hours of May 15, 1970, when Seattle police ambushed and killed Larry Ward, a young, unemployed Vietnam veteran, during what they thought was a "Black Panther bombing attempt." The bomb proved to have been made by Alfred Burnett, an FBI plant in the BPP's local chapter, who had been trying to convince a Panther named Jimmy Davis to use it. When Davis refused, Burnett paid Ward, apparently desperate for cash but never a member of the Party, to do so. Burnett then tipped off the police before driving Ward to the location at which a veritable firing squad was waiting.[273]

It was this climate that caused Seattle mayor Wesley Uhlman to finally cast the whole strategy of pretext raids and arrests into official disrepute by disclosing to the media that he'd been approached by federal agents with a proposition to arrange exactly such an assault on the local Party headquarters. Noting that the agents had offered no evidence at all that the Panthers were storing illegal weapons in their office—or anywhere else, for that matter—Uhlman announced that "we don't want these kinds of Gestapo tactics used in Seattle."[274]

The mayor's public pronouncements finally forced J. Edgar Hoover to lift at least one corner of the veil of subterfuge and disinformation with which the bureau had shrouded its collaborative raids and arrests. Going before the House Subcommittee on Appropriations in March 1970 to argue for the FBI's annual budget increase, the director defended his policy, asserting that in the course of the hundred-odd collaborative raids conducted to that point, "authorities uncovered a hundred and twenty-five machine guns, sawed-off shotguns, rifles and hand grenades, together with thousands of rounds of ammunition, forty-seven Molotov cocktails plus homemade bombs, gunpowder, and an accumulation of bayonets, swords, and machetes."[275]

Even this meager list, suggesting a seizure rate of fewer than five items per raid, was grossly misleading. By lumping the category of machine guns in with rifles and shotguns, Hoover made it seem as if agents were finding automatic weapons on a regular basis (actually, they'd come up with one M-14 rifle at that point, and an M-14 is not a "machine gun"). Nor did he mention that the great bulk of the firearms at issue were illegal only in the narrowest technical sense—local permit issues, for example—or that there was nothing in the least unlawful about possessing "ammunition . . . bayonets, swords, and machetes." Still less did he remark upon the proportion of actual contraband, especially incendiaries and explosives, attributable to the scores of FBI and police provocateurs operating within the Party rather than to the BPP itself.

Malicious Prosecutions

As has undoubtedly been apparent in the sections above, the cobbling together of fraudulent prosecutions was an integral aspect of the FBI's COINTELPRO against the Panthers. Even as he was being dragged into the Rackley case, Bobby Seale was slapped with an indictment for "conspiring" with seven white activists, only one of whom he'd so much as met, to incite riots during the 1968 Democratic Convention in Chicago.[276] Although Seale's being in Chicago at all had been dictated by a last-minute need to replace Eldridge Cleaver in delivering a speech, and despite the facts that he'd stayed only twenty-four hours, that a federal commission had found that it was the police rather than the demonstrators who'd "rioted," and that the Panthers had not participated either way, Seale was taken to trial along with his "co-conspirators."[277]

In court, the travesty became even more grotesque. The judge, Julius Hoffman, declined to grant a continuance when Charles Garry, Seale's attorney, was forced to undergo emergency surgery, and followed up by refusing to allow Seale the exercise of his constitutional right to defend himself pro se. Hoffman then handed down contempt citations, eventually totaling four years in penalties, each time the defendant attempted to do so anyway. The whole spectacle culminated with the judge ordering Seale bound to his chair and gagged as a means of "maintaining courtroom order." The trial of the "Chicago 8" then became that of the "Chicago 7" when Hoffman finally severed Seale's case from the others and scheduled him for a retrial that never occurred.[278]

More absurd still were the charges brought against the "Panther 21" in New York, a bill of particulars that included conspiring to use aerosol spray cans to blow up department stores, subway and police stations, and the Bronx Botanical Gardens. The moment the indictment was handed down on the morning of April 2, 1969, BOSS detectives launched a citywide sweep, gathering up or otherwise accounting for sixteen of the accused and what they claimed was "substantial evidence" of the plan.[279] Simultaneously, there was a veritable blizzard of police- and FBI-generated publicity:

> *Most newspaper stories concentrated on the [alleged] coordinated acts of terror and the Black Panther Party. Banner headlines on the Daily News of April 3 read "Smash Plot to Bomb Stores," and the story was titled "Indict 21 Panthers in Store Bomb Plot." Bold print above the front-page New York Times story read "Bomb Plot Is Laid to 21 Panthers; Black Extremists Accused of Planning Explosions at Macy's and Elsewhere." On the afternoon of April 3, the New York Post reported the arrest of another one of the defendants—"Nab One More in Panther Bomb Plot." On April 4, the lead editorial in the Daily News congratulated the authorities for "superior police work" which, the News said, "went into Wednesday's cracking of an alleged Black Panther plot to dynamite five midtown Manhattan department stores during the Easter buying rush, plus, for good measure we suppose, the Morrisania Police Station and the Penn Central tracks above 148th Street."[280]*

With the defendants thus convicted in the press, Judge Charles Marks set bail for each of them at the uniform and impossibly high level of $100,000, a ruling plainly intended to ensure that virtually the entire leadership cadre of the New York Panthers would remain behind bars for the duration.[281] The maneuver worked quite well: it was not until January 1970 that sufficient funds could be raised to obtain release of a single defendant, Afeni Shakur; a second, Richard Moore (Dhoruba Bin Wahad), followed in March; and finally another two, Michael Tabor (Cetewayo) and Joan Bird, in July, after the bond requirement was reduced to $50,000.[282] The other Panthers remained in lockup until the proceedings ended on May 13, 1971. And, of course, during the entire twenty-six months of their collective incarceration, the FBI was able to use the prisoners' situation in combination with those of the New Haven 14, Baltimore 18, and L.A. 13 as fodder in its anti-Panther propaganda campaign.

At trial, however, things proceeded along a rather different axis. Even Ralph White and Eugene Roberts, the most professional and highly placed of the several BOSS infiltrators, could provide no credible testimony that the "Easter Plot" had ever existed. White, whose recollections of events consistently and often sharply contradicted his own field reports, ended up professing to know nothing about it.[283] Roberts, who was intended to be the real star of the show, did little better, conceding that the only aspect of the "plot" that had ever materialized was reconnaissance of the alleged targets, and that he himself had performed it. When he tried to report his findings at a meeting of the chapter security group, coordinators "forgot" to put him on the agenda; on March 4, just a week before the bombings were to occur, only four people attended a meeting he'd called to discuss the plan; a day later, he was the only person who'd shown up.[284]

> *In a lengthy cross-examination, he made the following admissions: [the Panthers] had never had any dynamite to his knowledge and never gave Roberts orders to do anything but community work; Roberts himself was never given orders to bomb anything; there was never any agreement that he knew of to place explosives at any particular department store; no one had ever agreed to place any explosives at the railroad sites; he did not recall anyone being assigned to bomb anything.[285]*

Although it was at that point the longest criminal trial in New York history, generating more than 13,000 pages of testimony and attended by scores of exhibits—at one point prosecutors even showed a film entitled *The Battle of Algiers* to demonstrate how the Panthers were "influenced by African terrorism"—it took the jury just ninety minutes to reach "not guilty" verdicts in all 156 of the charges against the thirteen defendants who ultimately stood trial.[286]

The government's resounding defeat in the Panther 21 case, coming as it did almost simultaneously with the failure to convict Seale and Huggins in New Haven, and followed by another round of acquittals in the L.A. Panther case a few months later, signaled the end of attempts to eradicate the Party leadership through the contrivance of mass conspiracy prosecutions.[287] From then on, the approach would involve a much more surgical selection of targets and the advancement of less obviously political sets of charges. While the propaganda value of individual prosecutions was considerably less than that attending multidefendant show trials, it proved to be a far more effective method of obtaining wrongful convictions.

Among the first examples of the new strategy at work were the cases of Dhoruba Bin Wahad and Geronimo ji Jaga (Pratt), key leaders of the New York and Los Angeles BPP chapters respectively. One of the Panther 21 defendants who had gone underground when his bond was posted in November 1970, and had been acquitted in absentia, Bin Wahad was arrested shortly after the verdict in the process of accosting neighborhood drug dealers in a Bronx after-hours club. He was then charged with having attempted to murder a pair of police officers on May 19, 1971. After two mistrials, he was finally convicted in 1973 and sentenced to life imprisonment.[288]

The conviction was finally overturned, and Bin Wahad released on bond pending possible retrial in March 1990, after it was proven that the FBI and BOSS had collaborated to suborn perjury from the state's major witness, and had jointly suppressed ballistics test re- sults indicating that the strongest piece of physical evidence, a gun found in Bin Wahad's possession at the time of his arrest, was *not* the weapon used in shooting the police.[289] Although the government ultimately declined to retry the case, Bin Wahad had already spent seventeen years behind bars—more than twenty, when preconviction jail time is in- cluded—eight of it in solitary confinement, for crimes there'd never been the least evi- dence he'd actually committed.[290]

For Pratt, the situation was even worse. Having failed to neutralize him by other means, agents Richard W. Held, Richard Bloesser and Brendan Cleary of the Los Angeles COINTELPRO section apparently caucused with CCS detectives Daniel P. Mahoney and Ray Callahan, sifting through a pile of the LAPD's unsolved case files to find a murder with which they might plausibly charge him. Eventually they settled upon the December 1968 "Tennis Court Murder" of a white schoolteacher named Caroline Olson, illegally extradited their quarry from Texas, and went to trial.[291]

In court, the crucial evidence presented against Pratt was the testimony of infiltrator Julius C. Butler, who claimed the defendant had "confessed" the crime to him. Butler also solved a major problem with the state's physical evidence—as in the Bin Wahad case, ballistics tests indicated that a gun attributed to Pratt had not been used to commit the murder—by testifying that he'd witnessed the defendant changing barrels on the weapon. Finally, Butler asserted in response to direct questions on the matter posed by Pratt's defense counsel, Johnnie Cochran, that he was not and had never been an under- cover operative for either the FBI or the police.[292]

Pratt's main line of defense was that he could not possibly have killed Mrs. Olson because at the time of her death in Santa Monica he was more than 350 miles away, in Oakland, attending a meeting of the BPP Central Committee. This could be verified, he contended, through the FBI's records of its electronic surveillances of Party facilities in both Oakland and Los Angeles. In rebuttal, prosecutors called to the stand a bureau offi- cial who denied under oath that any such surveillance had been conducted. Pratt was then convicted and sentenced to a term of life in prison, the first eight years of which were spent in solitary confinement.[293]

Although the average time served in California for persons convicted of first-degree murder is 14.5 years, Pratt was repeatedly denied parole, not for reasons related to his supposed crime but because, as Assistant Los Angeles DA Diane Visani put it during a 1987 hearing, he was "still a revolutionary man."[294] It was not until June 10, 1997, that California Superior Court judge Everett W. Dickey finally reversed Pratt's 1972 convic- tion on the grounds of Butler's by-then-undeniable perjury and the FBI's suppression of its wiretap evidence.[295] Although Los Angeles District Attorney Gil Garcetti initially an- nounced he would retry the case, all charges were dropped in 1998. Meanwhile, the for- mer Panther had served fully twenty-seven years in prison for a murder authorities knew all along he'd had absolutely nothing to do with.

Worse still are the situations Ed Rice and David Poindexter, leaders of the Panthers' National Committee to Combat Fascism chapter in Omaha. In April 1971 they were con- victed of ordering the August 17, 1970, bombing that resulted in the death of police offi- cer Larry Minard. The main witness against them was the bomber, a teenager named Duane Peak, who mentioned neither of the accused in his confession—indeed, he named six other men as accomplices, none of whom were prosecuted—changing his story only after he was offered an immunity deal in exchange for testimony against the two "key ag- itators."[296] In 1974, federal district judge Warren Urbom found sufficient irregularity with the case to order a retrial, a ruling upheld by the Eighth Circuit Court, but in 1976 the Supreme Court reversed the reversal itself on a post hoc jurisdictional technicality.[297]

While the bipartisan Nebraska Parole Board has voted unanimously and repeatedly since 1993 to commute the men's sentences to time served—and Amnesty International, the NAACP, the Congressional Black Caucus, and other entirely reputable groups have strongly endorsed the idea—the state's Republican-controlled Board of Pardons has adamantly refused to so much as entertain the possibility (one member has been quoted in the press as stating that there are "no circumstances" under which he'd consider a commutation).[298] Thus Rice and Poindexter (Mondo we Langa) remain in prison after twenty-eight years, with no immediate prospect for release.

The reasons underlying this circumstance are not difficult to discern. A 1970 memo from the local FBI office, which had a fine collaborative relationship with local police, then and now, explicitly targets the two men for COINTELPRO neutralization.[299] In an interview conducted twenty years after the fact, Jack Swanson, the Omaha detective who headed up the local police effort against Rice and Poindexter, opined that he believed he'd "done the right thing at the time, [since] the Black Panther Party . . . completely disappeared from Omaha [after] we got the two main players."[300] Former governor Frank Morrison has been even more candid, acknowledging that the pair "were convicted for their rhetoric, not for any crime they committed."[301]

Even a cursory examination of Panther cases reveals a similar pattern in a number of instances. L.A. Panther Romaine "Chip" Fitzgerald, for example, was convicted in 1969 in "the senseless murder of a Von's security guard shot seven times in a Los Angeles shopping center on September 29" despite the fact several witnesses confirmed that he'd been halfway across the city, "wounded [by police] and scarcely able to move" at the time the shooting occurred.[302] Originally sentenced to death, Fitzgerald had his sentence commuted to life imprisonment when California's capital punishment statute was declared unconstitutional in 1971. He remains in maximum-security lockup after thirty years.

Then there is Baltimore Panther leader Marshall "Eddie" Conway, convicted in 1971 of the 1970 slaying of a Baltimore patrolman, largely on the strength of testimony provided by a jailhouse informant who, in exchange for preferential treatment and a reduced sentence on his own charges, claimed the accused had "confessed his crime" while they were cellmates. Conveniently for the state, this sensational "evidence" emerged at more or less the moment its contrived charges against Conway and other defendants in the above-mentioned Arthur Turco case had to be abandoned.[303] In any event, Conway too remains behind bars after approximately three decades, the possibility of parole at best a forlorn hope.

Obviously, as in the New Haven 14, L.A. 13, Panther 21, and Chicago conspiracy cases, Party members were often successful in defending themselves against malicious prosecutions. Nonetheless, the fact that by the end of 1969 at least 30 Panthers were in custody and facing the death penalty, another 40 facing life imprisonment, 55 facing sentences of thirty years or more, and still another 155 forced underground or into exile as a means of avoiding prosecution on bogus charges of comparable magnitude had a plainly devastating effect on the morale, cohesion, and overall effectiveness of the BPP.[304]

Combined with the permanent loss of leaders like Pratt, Bin Wahad, Rice, Poindexter, and Conway to the government's extralegal utilization of the judicial system for purposes of political repression,[305] such factors left the Party in an utterly deformed state as it entered the new decade. Nor would it be allowed anything resembling a respite in which to step back and regroup itself in coming months. Veteran defense attorney Charles Garry observed in January 1970 that "in over thirty years of practicing law, [he had] never experienced the type of persecution faced by the Black Panther Party."[306] Even in financial terms, the impact is obvious. By then, the Party's central office alone had been forced to expend more than $200,000 in nonrefundable bail premiums by that point in an effort to keep its personnel on the street.[307] If anything, the onslaught against the BPP in some ways intensified during 1970 and 1971. Thereafter, the repression seems to have abated to a considerable extent, but at that point there was precious little of the party left to repress.

Assassinations

As the FBI's role in the so-called "Panther/US conflict" abundantly reveals, assassination was also used to eliminate genuine Party activists. In the case of John Huggins and Bunchy Carter, the approach was quite selective; in others, it seems, as with Sylvester Bell and John Savage, a more random kind of targeting was apparent. Whether random or selective, the bureau invariably retained a veneer of "plausible deniability" about its involvement in the murders by using contract personnel like Claude Hubert and the Stiner brothers or Party infiltrators like George Sams, and sometimes police surrogates, for the actual killings.

The classic example of a COINTELPRO selective assassination was that of Illinois Panther leader Fred Hampton. Although the special fourteen-man unit that assaulted Hampton's apartment in the predawn hours of December 4, 1969, was composed entirely of police, it was later proven in court that the raid had been arranged by FBI counterintelligence specialists Robert Piper and Roy Mitchell.[308] Mitchell, in fact, provided the raiders with a floor plan of the apartment, drawn by infiltrator William O'Neal. Despite a report from O'Neal specifically stating that no illegal weapons were kept there, Mitchell passed along information to police that the opposite was true.[309]

While a search for illegal weapons thus served as a pretext for the raid, it is impossible to avoid the conclusion that participating police were as aware of their real mission as Mitchell and Piper. The map prepared by O'Neal clearly indicated the location of Hampton's bed, and during the action itself two of the raiders, Joseph Gorman and James "Gloves" Davis, blind-fired forty-two rounds, from a Thompson submachine gun and an M-1 carbine respectively, through a wall and into the bed where their FBI-provided information led them to expect their target would be sleeping.[310] Incredibly, Hampton was hit only once during the volley and, though badly wounded, was still alive. The situation was quickly corrected by another raider, Edward Carmody, who fired two rounds at close range into the victim's head.[311]

One reason Gorman and Davis had been confident Hampton would be in his bed when they fired was that they were aware O'Neal had slipped their target a dose of secobarbital earlier in the evening. The victim was thus comatose even before the raid began.[312] For their part Piper and Mitchell, who, along with Chicago SAC Marlin Johnson, had notified FBI headquarters on December 3 that the upcoming raid should be viewed as a COINTELPRO initiative against the BPP, proclaimed it "successful" in a teletype sent to headquarters at 9:26 A.M. on December 4.[313] On the eleventh, Piper followed up with a request, approved by headquarters on December 17, that O'Neal be paid a $300 bonus because of the "tremendous value" of his services to the raiders.[314]

In the immediate aftermath of the attack, which left Peoria Defense Captain Mark Clark as well as Hampton dead, and four of the seven other apartment occupants badly wounded, the surviving Panthers were charged with attempting to murder their attackers.[315] Although it was shortly demonstrated that none of the accused had fired a weapon at police, charges against them were not dropped until May 8, 1970, after Assistant U.S. Attorney General Jerris Leonard had brokered a quid pro quo in which neither the police raiders nor their superiors in the Chicago State's Attorney's Office would be criminally prosecuted.[316]

Meanwhile, as has been discussed, SAC Johnson was a major player in orchestrating the disinformation campaign designed to cover up what had actually occurred during the raid. More formally, he arranged for the convening of a federal grand jury investigation of the matter, with regard to which he himself coordinated the extensive suppression of evidence, before going on the stand in February 1970 to testify that the FBI's role had been "extremely peripheral."[317] Thereafter, Johnson availed himself of an early retirement, returning periodically to commit additional perjuries in response to subpoenas issued pursuant to a civil suit filed by the surviving Panthers and families of Hampton and Clark in 1973.[318]

Johnson was quickly replaced as SAC by Richard G. Held, father of the Los Angeles office's Richard W. Held and widely considered to have been the "dean of domestic counterintelligence operations." Held the elder presided over the cover-up for several years, at one point straightfacedly denying under oath that the Chicago office had compiled *any* investigative paperwork on the Black Panther Party in Illinois (117,000 pages were eventually released), and ended up promoted to the rank of FBI associate director for his trouble.[319] Under such conditions, it was not until November 1982 that Federal District Judge John F. Grady finally ruled that the bureau and its police collaborators had in fact violated the civil rights of Fred Hampton, Mark Clark, and the others, ordering payment of some $1.85 million in damages.[320]

It does not appear that the Hampton assassination was the only such "surgical elimination" envisioned as part of COINTELPRO-BPP in Chicago. The raiders expected that Bobby Rush, the Party's second in command in Illinois, would also be in Hampton's apartment at the fatal moment. When O'Neal's information proved erroneous in that respect, a predawn raid of Rush's apartment was arranged for the morning of December 5. Forewarned by Hampton's fate, however, the target had taken refuge at another location. A day later, he presented himself for arrest in the highly public—and therefore relatively safe—setting of Jesse Jackson's Operation Breadbasket.[321]

Similarly, the predawn raids conducted in Los Angeles on December 8 were designed, at least in part, to "neutralize" Geronimo Pratt in the same manner as Fred Hampton. It has been established that, prior to the assault on the Party's Los Angeles facilities, infiltrator Melvin Cotton Smith provided detailed floor plans on which Pratt's bed was clearly marked. As in Chicago, this information was passed along to the police raiders, who fired bursts of automatic weapons fire through a wall and riddled the area where the Panther leader was supposed to have been sleeping.[322] Infiltrator Louis Tackwood has also confirmed that Pratt was the "main target" of the attack. Hence, it is clear that only the Panthers' spirited defense of the office, in combination with the fact that Pratt was not in his bed when the attack began, averted another selective assassination.[323]

Random assassinations are harder to tie down. A likely candidate is Frank Diggs, known as "Captain Franko," an L.A. Panther whose bullet-riddled body was found in a vacant lot in the San Pedro area of South Compton on December 30, 1968. While Diggs may have been yet another casualty of the FBI-sponsored "war" between the Panthers and US—in which case he may well have been killed by Claude Hubert, the Stiners, or any of several other federal provocateurs known to have been active in Karenga's organization at the time—it is equally likely that he was simply picked up by police and executed. Either way, the least likely of all scenarios, that Diggs was murdered by the BPP itself, was the only one ever explored by LAPD homicide detectives in this still-unsolved case.[324]

Other Panthers were murdered under mysterious circumstances, beginning with Arthur Morris, older half-brother of L.A. chapter leader Bunchy Carter, whose body turned up in March 1968.[325] There followed Nathaniel Clark, a member of the L.A. chapter shot to death in his sleep by "party or parties unknown" on September 12, 1969, and Sterling Jones, a Chicago Panther similarly dispatched by a point-blank shot to the face when he answered a knock on the door of his family's apartment on Christmas night, 1969.[326]

Then there are cases like that of the seventeen-year-old Welton Armstead, who was shot to death by a Seattle patrolman claiming to be in pursuit of a car thief on October 5, 1968. The shooter was subsequently exonerated by an internal review board—surprise, surprise—after he contended variously that Armstead had been armed with a rifle and that the young Panther had made a grab for the patrolman's own service revolver. As analyst Michael Newton has pointed out, however, there are a few "nagging questions" imbedded in this obviously convoluted explanation: "If young Armstead had truly been armed with a rifle, why had he grabbed for the officer's gun in the first place? And if he was *not* armed, why had the officer approached him with gun drawn, ready to fire?"[327]

And so it went: on August 25, 1968, L.A. Panthers Steve Bartholomew, Robert Lawrence, and Tommy Lewis were gunned down by police who rousted them as they stood next to their car in a service station lot; on October 10, 1969, L.A. Panther Walter Touré Pope was shot and killed by police while preparing to order food at a Jack-in-the-Box restaurant ("Thought he was trying to rob the place," police said);[328] on July 27, 1970, Babatunde X Omarwali, founder of the southern Illinois chapter of the Party's National Committee to Combat Fascism (NCCF), was killed by Chicago police;[329] on July 28 Carl Hampton, founder of People's Party II, a local BPP offshoot, was shot to death by Houston police during an assault smelling suspiciously like that launched against the Central Avenue office in L.A. in December 1969.[330]

Overall, it seems hardly exaggeration to observe that the police were very nearly as busy coming up with pretexts upon which to kill Panthers as they were finding excuses to arrest them. By early 1970 the mounting fatalities had produced a decisive "chilling effect" in terms of the Party's ability to sustain its existing membership base, much less its ability to gain new recruits. As Dhoruba Bin Wahad would recall nearly a quarter-century later, "The Party was at the peak of its popularity in 1969. We'd achieved a genuine mass base of support for our program. But people were scared. Nobody wanted to go to prison for a million years or become just another pop-up target for the death squads. And so, just at the moment when it had become possible for us to accomplish what we'd set out to do, a lot of people began to distance themselves from us. They saw it as a matter of self-preservation."[331]

Exacerbating Intraparty Tensions

While the scale and intensity of repression against the Panthers mounted, the question of how best to respond became ever more acute. Simultaneously, the Party's ability to formulate anything resembling a unified position in this regard was greatly constrained by the fact that its leadership had been scattered to the winds, the energy, attention, and dwindling resources of its experienced cadres increasingly riveted upon the tactical demands of assembling legal defense efforts in behalf of the scores of "key activists" targeted for prosecution. Under such conditions, even the rapid growth of the BPP from mid-1968 to mid-1969 became something of a liability as the influx of new members quickly outstripped the Party's capacity to provide proper screening, training, and political orientation.[332]

Out of this confused welter, an environment ideal for the functioning of opportunists and provocateurs of every variety, two rather different lines of strategic thinking, both of them finding a firm footing in the Panthers' original theoretical posture, had begun to crystallize by 1970. The first of these, generally associated with the national office in Oakland and such outposts as Fred Hampton's Chicago chapter, called for a deemphasis

Table 1 *The Panther Dead: Police-Induced Fatalities, 1968–1971*

1968	
March 14:	Arthur Morris, age 28, Los Angeles
April 6:	Bobby Hutton, age 17, Oakland
August 25:	Steven Bartholomew, age 21, Los Angeles
August 25:	Robert Lawrence, age 22, Los Angeles
August 25:	Tommy Lewis, age 18, Los Angeles
October 15:	Welton Armstead, age 17, Seattle
December 30:	Frank Diggs, age 40, Los Angeles
1969	
January 17:	Alprentice Carter, age 26, Los Angeles
January 17:	John Huggins, age 23, Los Angeles
May 21:	Alex Rackley, age 24, New Haven
May 23:	John Savage, age 21, Los Angeles
August 15:	Sylvester Bell, age 34, San Diego
September 4:	Larry Roberson, age 20, Chicago
September 12:	Nathaniel Clark, age 19, Los Angeles
October 10:	Walter Touré Pope, age 20, Los Angeles
November 13:	Spurgeon Winters, age 19, Chicago
December 4:	Fred Hampton, age 21, Chicago
December 4:	Mark Clark, age 22, Chicago
December 25:	Sterling Jones, age 17, Chicago
December ?:	Eugene Anderson, age 20, Baltimore
1970	
July 27:	Babatunde X Omarwali, age 26, Chicago
July 28:	Carl Hampton, age 23, Houston
August 7:	Jonathan Jackson, age 17, San Raphael, Calif.
1971	
January ?:	Fred Bennett, age 29, Santa Cruz, Calif.
January 13:	Sandra Lane Pratt, age 23, Los Angeles
March 8:	Robert Webb, age 22, New York
April 17:	Samuel Napier, age 30, New York
April 17:	Harold Russell, age 23, New York
August 21:	George Jackson, age 29, San Quentin

of the military dimension of Panther activity, with increasing weight placed upon the Party's service programs, community organizing, coalition building, and electoral politics.[333]

The second, associated mainly with Eldridge Cleaver's International Section in Algeria, as well as the Los Angeles and New York chapters, pointed out that these were precisely the kinds of activities that had been targeted for eradication by "the military forces of the state," and that they were by definition vulnerable to such repression. Correspondingly, the "Cleaverites" called for a deemphasis of aboveground organizing in favor of creating a genuine "Afro-American Liberation Army" of urban guerrillas capable of meeting the state on its own terms.[334]

Things were never quite so clear-cut as a "military versus nonmilitary dichotomy," of course. The latter tendency, which consolidated itself under the leadership of Party founder Huey P. Newton after his release from prison in August 1970, always retained a military dimension, both literally and symbolically.[335] And the operations of what would shortly become the Black Liberation Army (BLA) would always be devoted in substantial part to sustaining community service programs such as a heroin treatment component of the Lincoln Detox Center in the Bronx.[336] Nonetheless, ideological disagreements between the emerging Party factions were quite real.

As early as September 1969, the FBI's infiltrators had made it aware of the growing differences of opinion within the BPP, and several field offices were instructed to devise plans to exacerbate them to the point of outright disputes.[337] By January 1970 this resulted in the first of a series of bogus letters sent to the exiled Cleaver, many of them written over the forged signature of International Section liaison Connie Matthews, informing him that David Hilliard and other "BPP leaders in California were seeking to undercut his influence."[338] Cleaver, as was noted by the bureau, responded by expelling three Panthers he believed had been sent to Algeria by the "Hilliard clique" to disrupt the functioning of his group.[339] "Encouraged by the apparent success of this letter, FBI headquarters instructed its Paris Legal Attaché to mail a follow-up letter, again written to appear as if Matthews were the author, to Black Panther Chief-of-Staff David Hilliard, in Oakland, California. The letter alleged that Cleaver 'has tripped out. Perhaps he has been working too hard,' and suggested that Hilliard 'take some immediate action before this becomes more serious.'"[340]

By May, those aligned with Cleaver and Hilliard alike had become aware that the "Matthews" letters were forgeries, and efforts were made to reconstitute a viable working relationship.[341] Prospects for success in this regard were, however, severely impaired by a combination of Cleaver's distance from day-to-day events and the fact that Hilliard himself had been thrust by circumstance into a position of responsibility well beyond his capabilities:[342] "David Hilliard had implemented a harshly authoritarian policy that engendered intense resentment. Purges of rebellious Panthers were disrupting entire chapters, and the rank and file across the country were furious at the heavy-handed treatment meted out from Oakland. Transfers of Panthers from chapter to chapter and cultivation of loyalty to the central staff in Oakland kept decision making tightly centralized. Faced with mushrooming trials and arrests, Hilliard had attempted to keep order at the expense of continuing revolutionary activity."[343]

All sides appear to have counted upon Huey Newton, soon to be released from prison, to put the Party back in order and on track. These hopes were in vain. Three years behind bars, several months of which were spent in one of Alameda County's notorious "soul breaker" cells,[344] had left the high-strung Panther founder seriously out of touch with the new personalities who had joined the BPP during his absence, and also, seen in retrospect, in a dangerously degenerate state of psychological imbalance. When he did appear, it was to (re)assert his authority over the Party with such megalomaniac zeal as to make Hilliard's regime seem both benevolent and enlightened by comparison.[345]

Whatever possibility may have existed that the "Supreme Commander," as Newton became titled, might regain his equilibrium was quickly preempted by a blizzard of phony missives pumped out by counterintelligence specialists around the country.[346] The Philadelphia field office, for example, produced and distributed a "directive," attributed to the local BPP chapter, stressing "the leadership and strength of David Hilliard and Eldridge Cleaver while intimating Huey Newton is useful only as a drawing card."[347] A copy of the document, along with a note purporting to be from a Philadelphia Panther "incensed" at what was said therein, was then mailed to Newton.[348]

By mid-December 1970, playing upon the "counterintelligence opportunity [offered by the] distance and [lack of] personal contact between Newton and Cleaver," the Los Angeles field office was sending bogus letters to Algiers "designed to provoke Cleaver to openly question Newton's leadership."[349] San Francisco, meanwhile, was sending similar letters to Newton, complaining about the "incompetence" of leaders in the Party's Philadelphia chapter,[350] while the San Francisco and Boston field offices shortly posted missives of their own to Algiers.[351]

Within a month, Newton responded to the torrent of rumors by expelling the incarcerated but Cleaver-aligned Los Angeles Panther leader Geronimo Pratt and several of his closest colleagues, whom Newton claimed were plotting to kill him.[352] At about the same time the body of Pratt's wife, Sandra Lane (Nsondi ji Jaga), was found, riddled with bullets and stuffed into a sleeping bag, alongside an L.A. freeway. The killers were never identified, but it was suspected that she'd been killed on Newton's orders as a means of "sending a message" to Pratt, Cleaver, and anyone else inclined to challenge his authority.[353] For its part, the FBI observed that "Newton has recently exhibited paranoid-like reactions to anyone who questions his orders, actions, policies, or otherwise displeases him. His . . . hysterical reaction . . . has very likely been aggravated by our present counter-intelligence activity. . . . *It appears Newton may be on the brink of mental collapse and we must [therefore] intensify our counter-intelligence*" (emphasis added).[354]

In New York, several of the Panther 21 defendants, frustrated by their inability to gain a hearing on their differences with Newton, published an open letter in an underground newspaper in which they denounced the Oakland leadership as not only authoritarian but financially corrupt, proclaimed the Weathermen faction of SDS to comprise the new "revolutionary vanguard" of struggle in the United States, and aligned themselves explicitly with Pratt and Cleaver.[355] Newton replied by expelling them as "enemies of the people."[356] The FBI was exultant, calling for intensified efforts to "further aggravate the dissension within the BPP leadership," in view of "the present chaotic situation within the BPP [and] apparent distrust by Newton of anyone who questions his wishes."[357]

> On February 2, 1971, FBI headquarters directed each of twenty-nine field offices to submit within eight days a proposal to disrupt local Black Panther Party chapters and the Party's national headquarters in Oakland. . . . For three solid weeks, a barrage of anonymous letters flowed from FBI field offices in response to the urging from FBI headquarters. The messages had become more and more vicious. On February 19, 1971, a false letter, allegedly from a Black Panther Party member in the Bay Area, was mailed to Don Cox, Cleaver's companion in Algiers. The letter intimated that the recent disappearance and presumed death of Black Panther leader Fred Bennett was the result of Party factionalism.[358]

On February 10, an anonymous letter was sent by the San Francisco office to Newton's brother, Melvin, "warning" him that "Eldridge Cleaver and the New York BPP chapter were planning to have [Huey Newton] killed."[359] Two weeks later, a teletype purporting to be from BPP Central Committee member Elbert "Big Man" Howard to Cleaver complained that Newton was skimming Party funds to pay the rent on an extravagant Oakland penthouse.[360] Cleaver was also warned not to allow his wife, Kathleen, herself a member of the Party's Central Committee, to go to Oakland for purposes of attempting to straighten things out because of a distinct "possibility of violence" against her.[361]

In what was perhaps a last effort at restoring some semblance of Party unity, Newton arranged for himself and Cleaver to appear together on a San Francisco television program on February 26 (Cleaver via satellite feed from Algiers). Cleaver seized the opportunity to demand the reinstatement of the Pratt group and the Panther 21, as well as the expulsion of Hilliard and others of the national office staff.[362] Newton retaliated during an FBI-monitored postprogram telephone call, expelling Cleaver and the entire International Section. Cleaver replied that, to the contrary, it was the International Section that was expelling Newton's entire following, and that it would henceforth function as "the *real* Black Panther Party."[363]

The entire New York chapter thereupon declared its alignment with Cleaver and issued a public demand for a "people's tribunal" to assess Newton's reputed abuse of Party funds.[364] On March 8, in what was/is generally believed to have been another of Newton's attempts to "send a message" to Party dissidents, New York Panther Robert "Spider" Webb was shot to death in broad daylight on 125th Street, in Harlem.[365] Then, on March 18, Bill Seidler, a sixty-two-year-old white Panther supporter in Philadelphia who had been providing invaluable service to the International Section in its efforts to maintain open communication links with the U.S., met a similar fate.[366]

At this point, the bureau declared that "the differences between Newton and Cleaver now appear to be irreconcilable," but nonetheless undertook to inflame the passions of participants even further.[367] On March 25, for example, a message was sent—in Newton's name and over David Hilliard's forged signature—to all Panther "embassies" and support groups abroad. The bogus communiqué not only declared the International Section's expulsion but asserted that "Eldridge Leroy Cleaver is a murderer and a punk without genitals. D.C. Cox is no better." It closed by announcing, in a transparent reference to the slain Webb, that "Leroy's running dogs in New York have been righteously dealt with. Anyone giving any aid or comfort to Cleaver and his jackanapes will be similarly dealt with no matter where they might be located."[368]

As intended by the agents who penned it, the document was accepted as genuine by the New York Panthers. Their response, rather predictable under the circumstances, was to settle the score for Robert Webb while answering "Newton's" threat with a message of their own. On the night of April 17, 1971, the New York distribution office for the *Black Panther* was put to the torch. When the smoke cleared, firefighters discovered the charred body of Newton loyalist Sam Napier, who had been executed by six gunshots fired at close range.[369]

While the murders of Fred Bennett, Sandra Pratt, and Robert Webb had elicited little more than yawns on the part of police "investigators" and their FBI counterparts, the Napier killing sparked a frenzy of law enforcement activity and the arrests of Cleaver-aligned Panthers in several states. This disparity in effect "confirmed the rampant suspicion among New York Panthers that Newton's clique was collaborating with the police in some fashion."[370]

> *The Panthers in Algiers [and] the New York Panthers [made] a desperate effort to salvage the crumbling Party. Lengthy long-distance phone conversations between New York, Algiers and San Francisco took place in hopes of pulling together a new Central Committee. The New York chapter began publishing its own newspaper,* Right On, *to counteract* The Black Panther—*now totally under Newton's control. Although the New York Panthers were able to rally a few dedicated people to their side, the attempt to reorganize the entire Party failed. Panthers who aligned themselves with the more radical New York faction were being arrested across the country and faced threats on their lives from Newton's supporters, while those connected with the Newton faction seemed immune from police attention no matter what they did.*[371]

By the time the New York Panthers finally threw in the towel, there was very little left of the BPP. Regardless of who'd actually pulled the triggers, the mounting toll of Panthers apparently killed by Panthers, the Webb and Napier murders in particular, precipitated the exodus of up to 40 percent of all remaining Party members during the last half of 1971.[372] Expulsions claimed well over a thousand others.[373] Having facilitated the eviction of the International Section from its station in Algeria in 1972, Newton effectively abolished the Party as a national organization as well, ordering the closure of local chapters and "recalling" the thousand or so remaining cadres to Oakland.[374] A year later, total membership had shrunk to less than 500, and, by 1974, to only about 200.[375]

The War at Home Continues

In retrospect, it seems that the revolutionary Black Panther Party never had a chance. Both the relative inexperience of its leadership and the obvious youthfulness of the great majority of its members helped prevent the Party from mounting a mature response to the situation it confronted. The scale and intensity of the repression to which it was subjected, moreover, especially given the sheer speed with which the onslaught materialized and the intensity with which it was maintained from 1968 to 1971, make it doubtful that even the most seasoned group of activists would have done better.

"Given the level of sophistication, unlimited man-power and resources available" to the FBI and its local police collaborators, it should come as no surprise that the Panthers were destroyed. Instead, as imprisoned former Panther Herman Bell has observed, we should find it "remarkable . . . that the Party lasted as long as it did."[376] And, as Dhoruba Bin Wahad points out, "What's most amazing is how much was accomplished in so short a time. The growth of the Party, its programs and resiliency, the support it was able to command from the community, all that was put together in just two years, really. Had it not been for COINTELPRO, one can readily imagine what might have been achieved."[377]

Both Bell and Bin Wahad believe there are significant lessons to be learned from the experience of the BPP. One of the most important must be that, despite the highly publicized conclusions of the Church Committee and other official bodies during the mid-1970s that COINTELPRO was an inherently criminal enterprise,[378] and despite a raft of more localized findings over the years that the criminality at issue extended even to murder, not one cop nor intelligence agent has spent a minute of time in prison as a result. Although two of the only four FBI men ever charged with COINTELPRO-related offenses were duly convicted in 1980, they were pardoned by President Ronald Reagan before setting foot inside a cell.[379]

With all due sanctimony, Reagan intoned that the pardons were appropriate because the early 1980s were "a time to put all this behind us" and begin a "long overdue process of national healing and reconciliation."[380] Such generously forgiving views toward official perpetrators of COINTELPRO-era offenses did not, of course, extend to their victims. Former Panthers like Bin Wahad and Geronimo ji Jaga (Pratt) continued to languish in prison without so much as a sidelong glance from the president, no matter how blatantly fraudulent the charges that had landed them there.

Nor does the fact that the convictions of Bin Wahad and ji Jaga were eventually overturned prove the old saw that "in the end, whatever its deficiencies, the system works." To quote ji Jaga, "If the system worked the way they'd have you believe, I'd never have gone to prison in the first place, much less spent 27 years there. Dhoruba wouldn't have gone to prison for nineteen years. Rice and Poindexter would not still be sitting in prison out in Nebraska, and Mumia wouldn't be on death row. If the system worked the way they say it does, the agents and the cops and the prosecutors who perjured themselves and fabricated evidence when they framed us would themselves be in prison, right alongside those who murdered Fred Hampton, Mark Clark and Bunchy Carter. But those things didn't happen, did they?"[381]

To the contrary, many of those involved in making COINTELPRO a "success" tangibly benefited by their activities. Richard Wallace Held, arguably the agent most responsible for fabricating the case against ji Jaga, is a prime example.[382] So valuable to the FBI were his peculiar skills that, in 1975, he was detached from his slot in Los Angeles and sent to South Dakota, where he assisted in assembling an equally fraudulent case against American Indian Movement (AIM) leader Leonard Peltier.[383] Then, in 1981, while still a relatively junior agent, he was promoted to the position of SAC, San Juan. In this role, he presided over a plethora of legally dubious operations against the Puerto Rican independence movement, including islandwide raids conducted on August 30, 1985.[384] For this coup he was rewarded again, this time by being promoted to the more prestigious position of SAC, San Francisco. There, his major achievement appears to have been the attempted neutralization by car bombing of Earth First! activists Judi Bari and Darryl Cherney on May 24, 1990.[385]

Still more to the point, the Reagan administration's response to the idea that FBI officials might be held to some extent accountable for their more egregious violation of civil and human rights was simply to legalize much of what had been deemed criminal about COINTELPRO only a few years earlier.[386] This was undertaken through a series of congressional hearings designed to demonstrate the need for the bureau to "combat terrorism" by being given the "flexibility" to neutralize "organizations and individuals that cannot be shown to be controlled by a foreign power, and have not yet committed a terrorist act but which nonetheless may represent a substantial threat . . . to the security of our country."[387]

Although legislation affording specific statutory authorization for the bureau to engage in COINTELPRO-style activities has accrued piecemeal during the years since 1985, and is still in some respects being formulated, Reagan cut to the chase on December 4, 1981, by signing Executive Order 12333, for the first time openly authorizing the CIA to conduct domestic counterintelligence operations.[388] On May 7, 1983, Attorney General William French Smith confirmed the obvious by announcing a new set of FBI guidelines allowing agents to resume full-scale "investigative activity" vis-à-vis any individual or organization they wished to designate, on whatever basis, as "advocat[ing] criminal activity or indicat[ing] an apparent intent to engage in crime."[389]

At the local level, the proportionate deployment of police, both in terms of personnel and as measured by the budget allocations necessary to acquire more sophisticated weaponry, computerization, and so on, has swelled by approximately 500 percent since 1970.[390] Simultaneously, there has been a distinct militarization of law enforcement, a matter evidenced most readily in the proliferation of SWAT units across the country, first created by the LAPD for purposes of assaulting Panther offices in 1969. By 1990 "every police department worth its salary had a SWAT team, a special weapons and tactics squad. Every one."[391]

Since 1980, the entire apparatus has been increasingly tied together in an unprecedented fashion.[392] In large part, this was accomplished by the Federal Emergency Management Agency (FEMA), headed during the early Reagan years by California-based counterinsurgency specialist Louis O. Giuffrida. This corresponded with consolidation of the FBI database, inaugurated by J. Edgar Hoover during World War I and expanded steadily thereafter, in a form including files on virtually *every* American citizen.

During Giuffrida's tenure, FEMA ran a series of exercises—dubbed "Proud Saber/Rex 82," "Rex 84/Nighttrain," and so on—by which the procedures through which rapid deployments of federal, state, and local police could be integrated with those of the National Guard, the military, and selected civilian organizations in times of civil unrest.[393]

Although there have been several major exceptions—the Philadelphia police bombing of MOVE headquarters in 1985, for example, as well as the Committee in Solidarity with the People of El Salvador (CISPES) investigation and operations against several right-wing organizations—the still evolving U.S. police/intelligence/military complex does not appear to be devoted extensively to direct political repression.[394] Rather, its purpose seems primarily to have been to intensify the condition of pacification to which COINTELPRO had reduced oppressed communities, especially communities of color, by the early 1970s.

Most prominently, this has taken the form of the so-called War on Drugs declared by the Reagan administration during the mid-1980s and continued by both Republican and Democratic successors through the present date.[395] Leaving aside the fact that U.S. intelligence agencies have been heavily involved in the importation of heroin and cocaine since at least as early as the late 1960s—and that if the government were really averse to narcotics distribution in the inner cities, the FBI would have assisted rather than destroyed the BPP's antidrug programs and attempts to politicize street gangs like the P. Stone Nation—the "war" has been used as a pretext by which to criminalize virtually the entire male population of young African Americans and Latinos.[396] By 1990 the United States had imprisoned a greater proportion of its population than any other country on the planet.[397]

One in three men of color between the ages of eighteen and twenty-five is, has been, or will shortly be incarcerated, a rate making an American black four times as likely to do prison time as was his South African counterpart at the height of apartheid.[398] Physically, the U.S. penal system has expanded by more than 300 percent since 1969 to absorb this vast influx of "fresh meat," an expense that, like spiraling police appropriations, has been underwritten with tax dollars once allocated to education and social services. Even at that, the construction of private prisons has become one of the fastest-growing sectors of the U.S. economy, while the approximately 2 million prisoners have themselves been increasingly integrated into the system as a ready source of veritable slave labor fueling transnational corporate profits.[399]

While the "crime of black imprisonment" has reached epidemic proportions, the situation of the African-American community has, according to every statistical indicator, steadily deteriorated.[400] The repression of the black liberation movement can be correlated with a decline in living standards below the 1959 level, a trend that has continued without interruption.[401] In many ways, not only resurgent racism but the increasing marginalization of the American workforce as a whole is responsible, a condition due more to the genuine world dominance presently enjoyed by the U.S. corporate elites and their consequent policies of economic globalization than to domestic polices in themselves.[402]

A Legacy of Lessons

In sum, the conditions of poor and racially oppressed people in the United States today are objectively worse than those that gave rise to the Black Panther Party and affiliated groups a third of a century ago. It requires no great leap of intellect or understanding to appreciate that it was the destruction of the BPP and its allies that allowed this degenerative process of socioeconomic decay to set in, or that the best and perhaps only antidote resides in a reconstitution of something very Pantherlike in its essence. By this, I mean an organization or movement that is truly multinational/multiracial in both orientation and composition, committed to the attainment of practical self-determination on the part of the subjugated, and willing to defend its achievements by *every* necessary means.

For much too long, the history of the Party has been the preserve of poseurs and opportunists, deployed mainly as a "moral lesson" on why the ideals of liberation are inherently "unrealistic," the consequences of serious struggle toward such goals much too severe to be undertaken by "reasonable" people. The latter, such purveyors of "political pragmatism" habitually insist, are devoted exclusively to modes of activism centering in a "nonviolent" and an at best incrementally "progressive" vision rather than one of revolutionary transformation, their strategies devoted exclusively to situational "renegotiations of the social contract" through such state-sanctioned tactical expedients as voting, lobbying and litigation, boycotts, and more symbolic protest.[403]

Nowhere in such "alternative" prescriptions is there a place for development of the popular capacity to physically confront, much less defeat, the increasingly vast repressive apparatus with which the status quo has elected to defend itself against precisely the sorts of meaningful socioeconomic and political change progressivism purports to pursue. Indeed, anyone suggesting that such concepts as armed self-defense are both useful and appropriate tools within the present context are automatically, and usually vituperatively, consigned ipso facto to the realm of "counterproductivity."[404]

It is high time such postulations were interrogated, challenged, and discarded. The legacy of the Panthers must be mined not for its supposed negative lessons but for the positive values, ideals, and analyses that propelled the BPP so rapidly to a position of prominence, and which lent its members their astonishing valor and tenacity. To excavate the understandings embodied in the party's programmatic successes, no matter how abbreviated the interval in which these were evident, is to reclaim the potentials that attended them. Such a project is worthy if for no other reason than that nobody, of *any* oppositional orientation, has been able to equal the Party's record and appeal in the post-Panther context.

Only in this way, moreover, can we arrive at a proper apprehension of the Party's theoretical/organizational defects, appreciate and correct them in their own terms, and thus avoid replication of the emic contradictions that beset the BPP in its original form. For instance, such investigations should offer insights as to how groups might best retain internal discipline without being afflicted with the sort of despotism and stratification exemplified by Huey Newton's "personality cult."[405] Other questions demanding clarification concern the proportionate blend of lumpen and nonlumpen members best suited to organizational functioning under particular circumstances,[406] the most appropriate balance to be drawn between overt service/survival programs and often covert armed components, the manner and extent to which these should be rendered interactive, and the relative degree of emphasis/pace of development most productively accorded to each under given conditions or phases of struggle.[407]

In many ways the most important lesson to be gleaned from the Panther experience has to do with the nature of the enemy with which all domestic oppositionists, regardless of the ideological and other distinctions that divide us, are mutually faced. No elite willing to assemble an apparatus of repression comparable to that evident in the United States, or to wield it with the savagery evident in the Panther example, displays the least likelihood of being susceptible to the powers of logic, moral suasion, or other such nonviolent manifestations of popular will. On the contrary, to the extent that these approaches might at some point demonstrate a capacity to compel fundamental alterations in the bedrock of social order, they will be suppressed with essentially the same systematic and sustained resort to lethal force that was once visited upon the BPP.[408]

Those committed to achieving fundamental change rather than cosmetic tweakings of the existing system are thus left with no viable alternative but to include the realities of state violence as an integral part of our political calculus.[409] We are in a war, whether we wish to be or not, and the only question before us is how to go about winning it. Here too, the legacy bequeathed by the Black Panther Party provides invaluable lessons. By studying the techniques with which the counterinsurgency war against the Party was waged, we can, collectively, begin to devise the ways and means by which to counter them, offsetting and eventually neutralizing their effectiveness.[410]

The current prospects for liberatory struggle in the United States are exceedingly harsh, even more than was the case a generation ago. Far harsher, however, is the prospect that the presently ascendant system of elite predation might be allowed to perpetuate itself indefinitely into the future, exploiting and oppressing the preponderance of the population in the midst of every moment along the way. We owe it to ourselves to abolish the predators, here and now, or as rapidly as possible, enduring whatever short-run sacrifice is required to get the job done, reaping the longer-term rewards of our success. We owe it to those who sacrificed before us to fulfill the destiny they embraced. Most of all, we owe it to our coming generations to free them from that against which we must struggle. Thankfully, the fallen warriors of the Black Panther Party have left us many tools with which we may at last complete their task.

7

The Split in the Party

Donald Cox

My name is Donald Lee Cox. I was born in Appleton City, Missouri, on April 16, 1936. After graduating from high school I went to live with an uncle in San Mateo, California, where I spent two years at the University of San Mateo, studying general science, thinking of eventually entering medical or dental school.

To make a long story short, after a marriage, a child, and one year at the University of California in Berkeley, I ended up working at a small graphic arts firm in San Francisco. I became the manager and was a member of the San Francisco Chamber of Commerce, the California State Chamber of Commerce, the Christian Businessmen's Association, the Negro Historical and Cultural Society, and other things forgotten. I stayed there ten years until I resigned to become an open member of the Black Panther Party in May 1968. I was asked by Bobby Seale to become a member of the Central Committee of the Black Panther Party in November 1967. I became the Panther Field Marshal.

Most party titles were of a military nature because of the military climate that reigned at that time. In the summer of 1967, Airborne troops were fighting in the jungles of Vietnam and in the ghetto streets of Detroit.

In the spring of 1970 the repression that had been unleashed by J. Edgar Hoover and Richard Nixon to destroy the Panthers caught up with me, and I went into exile in Algeria. In Algiers I participated in the creation of the International Section of the Black Panther Party and served on its staff until I resigned at the end of 1971.

I spent my first seven years of exile in Algiers and the last twenty-one in France. I am now growing perfume plants and distilling their essential oils. I specialize in lavender.

I am convinced that it is more beneficial to analyze mistakes and errors than to glorify and inculcate only successes. It is in this spirit that I share the epilogue of a book project, *Maiden Voyage,* a history of the Black Panther Party.

The International Section of the Black Panther Party in Algiers, Algeria, in February 1971 used a live TV hookup between Huey Newton in the United States and Eldridge Cleaver in Algiers to announce our disagreement with the direction the BPP had taken. That Cleaver made this announcement on live TV, talking directly to the founder and leader of the BPP, was devastating, in light of consequences, to Huey Newton's ego. After the television program ended and Huey could get to a telephone, he called me in Algiers. The epilogue of the *Maiden Voyage* project begins with that phone call.

As soon as the TV show ended, Huey called me in Algiers, wanting to know my position. When I said that I was against him, he laughed in a high-pitched, excited manner and said that he was going to "crush" me.

Nothing in my previous life experience, nor my experience in the Black Panther Party, nor what I thought I knew about Huey Newton prepared me for the panic-stricken telephone call I received a few days later from Zayd Shakur in the Harlem Panther office, hysterically shouting that Robert "Spider" Webb had just been ambushed and killed at the crossroads of Harlem, 125th Street and Seventh Avenue![1]

I stared at the telephone. When I tried to talk, there was no coordination in my thoughts or speech, so Eldridge took the phone out of my hands. I sat on the couch in the hall the next three or four days without talking. I couldn't even think. Apparently the shock had put my brain into neutral. It was like abruptly losing my Missouri country-boy moral virginity after being sucked into a black hole and perceiving the real world for the first time in all its naked callousness, producing a sentiment of absolute impotency and simultaneously plunging me into bottomless despair.

I was just not strong enough to cope with the magnitude of Huey's desire for revenge. He lashed out with megalomaniac, perverted rage and ordered the assassination of Spider just to hurt me, to avenge his injured, bloated ego.[2] Even Huey was incapable of fathoming how successfully he had crushed me.

Neither the understanding of the human psyche that I've acquired through the years, nor learning that history is a succession of MEN imposing themselves by bloodshed and terror, could ever make me forgive, therefore accept, what Huey did. Given the appalling circumstances, it seemed inconceivable that things could get worse.

But get worse they did! The filming of videos became the means for bridging the distance between the International Section and comrades in particular and the rest of the American public in general. Thanks to friends in Algiers, the personnel of Air France, and people that received and distributed them in the states, like William and Miriam Seidler in Philadelphia, we would film a video and it would be showing inside the United States within twenty-four hours.

The Seidlers lived, and had a women's and children's clothing store, across the street from the Philadelphia BPP office. They were the only whites in the North Philly neighborhood. The Panthers and Seidlers mutually adopted each other, and they were called Moms and Pops.[3] When asked, What is a nice Jewish mother doing with folks like that? Miriam replied that, for one thing, she had introduced them to "Jewish penicillin"— chicken soup—"because they go out in all kinds of weather." The Seidlers were very active in the defense of the Rosenbergs, and all worthy causes brought to their attention. Concerning blacks, Miriam said, "Unless we have black liberation, we won't get anywhere. . . . Until the tokenism stops, until the fences stop being built higher and higher, until we stop speaking in terms of 'they' and 'them' and start saying 'I' and 'we,' oppression will continue."

Barbara Easley, whom I had assigned to Philadelphia to work with Reggie Schell and Jamal (Mumia Abu—who must be set free!) to bring the chapter into conformity, was offered hospitality by the Seidlers and given a room. Since Barbara and I had lived together before the necessities of the struggle scattered us all to the four corners of the country, whenever I had the occasion to pass through Philly I stayed with Barbara and the Seidlers, whom I truly came to respect and love for their commitment.

The nightmare continued. Bill Seidler, sixty-two years old, was assassinated on March 18, 1971, at 4:40 P.M. Philadelphia newspapers unanimously declared that Bill Seidler was slain in a holdup. Miriam, his wife of thirty-nine years, was present. Why did they not quote her?

"They say that my husband was murdered but I say he was assassinated. They say he was killed during a robbery, but I was in the store when it happened and there was no holdup. This man came in and he walked by two cash registers and pulled out a gun. My husband said, "Put that thing down," and the man just shot him . . . seconds later Bill Seidler lay dying, dying for the things he believed in, dying among the people with whom he chose to live and whose lot he worked constantly to improve. . . . Although Bill Seidler died at the hands of a black man, he would certainly have been the last person to condemn blacks for his . . . murder. . . . It takes more than guns to kill a man."

Speaking of the assassin, Miriam said, "I have no vindictive feelings toward him. I would only like to meet him one day and ask him, 'Why?' If he only knew who my husband was . . ."

The assassination of William Seidler was one of the only times in the history of the United States of America that a black man killed a white man and no one was arrested for the crime.

When making an analysis, one should assemble all possible evidence to put objectivity on one's side. Believing that, consideration should be given to the fact that arrangements for the shipment and reception of the videos were made by telephone. It is true that the phones of the International Section were monitored by the National Security Agency (NSA), amongst others. Therefore, it could be within the realm of possibility that the U.S. Secret Service organized the assassination of William Seidler to disrupt the flow of information coming out of Algeria and also to sustain hostilities between headquarters and the International Section.

Nevertheless, because of all our contacts, the flow of videos was never interrupted. The Secret Service knew about the other contacts. And after what was done to "Spider," antagonisms could not have been deepened further. So personally, I rule out the possibility.

And when I die and meet Huey Newton in hell, I will duel with him for eternity.

Since the sacrifice of "Spider" on the altar of the bloated ego of the "Supreme," I had been in a state that can best be described as anesthetized—a defense against being utterly destroyed.

Retrospectively, it's curious how my mind defended itself by plunging over the line into denial and treating Bill Seidler's assassination almost like an anonymous event heard on the news. A vague souvenir subliminally passed through my consciousness at the speed of light, but my mind would not let me entertain the thought that Bill's assassination could have been a continuation of Huey's dementia. That would have been too heavy to bear. Carry the deaths of Spider and Bill on my shoulders just because I told Huey that I opposed him? No way! No one should be forced to accept such pain. In that new world, dreamed of since time immemorial, where everyone's needs are provided for and where each individual has the possibility of developing into his or her fullest genetic potential without hindrance, that world we so often discussed, and that we were even willing to kill or die in order to achieve, there is absolutely no place on the agenda for malicious assassinations.

The demise of the Black Panther Party, as of many organizations, was and is the result of disorders of competitiveness and aggressiveness, inherited from prehistoric times and manifested in the perverse, cutthroat comportment of males in our species. Even though exceptions can be cited of some women manifesting disorders that they had acquired by osmosis, and in some instances even exaggerating, like Elaine Brown[4] and Margaret Thatcher, nature had bestowed upon women a life-nurturing maternity that has created a completely different mindset.

In ancient Egypt, the pharaohs were considered to be gods. Five thousand years later, in the Black Panther Party, Huey Newton was successively the Supreme Commander and the Supreme Servant of the People. There are no qualities of difference between the two phenomena, precisely because the cult of the personality and the ensuing megalomania underlying the two phenomena are the same.

At a decisive moment, Huey Newton directed his competitivity and his agression toward what many of us considered to be the enemy and became a hero. For some of us, Huey represented the equivalent of the Messiah. Since we didn't want to see any more of our leaders eliminated, we launched a massive campaign to assure that Huey would not be condemned to the death penalty. A cult of his personality was created. Huey was elevated to the status of the gods, and his every word became gospel.

When Huey was wounded and captured, there were between five and ten people who could be called Panthers. After a two-year campaign, when the prison gates were opened and he was freed, there was a multitude waiting to welcome and acclaim him. Thousands of people. Huey was smothered with love, adulation, money, penthouse, Cadillac, swagger stick; Hollywood was at his feet, and the progressive movement saw in Huey's liberation the freedom of the pharaoh.

We loved Huey to death. He succumbed and accepted to become the all-powerful, the Supreme, with power over life and death for Fred Bennett, Robert Webb, and Bill Seidler—and without compassion.

The nightmare could not be allowed to continue. An action was decided upon to oppose Huey's barbaric behavior, and the principal distribution office of the Panther newspaper on Fillmore Street in San Francisco was blown up.

Newton and Hilliard had used the paper as an arm against any that fell from their favor—the slander against Geronimo at the time of his expulsion being an eloquent example.[5] In appearances, the decision to destroy the distribution office was politically correct.

Shortly afterward on April 17, 1971, the East Coast distribution office was also destroyed, by fire. Momentarily, the distribution of the paper would definitely be disorganized; Newton should have received the message. However, the arsonists had worked overtime. Inside the burned office they found the charred remains of Sam "What Is to Be Done" Napier.[6]

Sam had plunged into organizing the distribution of the Panther paper with zealousness and selflessness. When circulation reached 250,000 a week, organization was such that when the newspapers arrived from the printer, by dawn all subscriptions and deliveries, to sales points throughout the country and abroad, were dealt with. A solid, dedicated, anonymous team were on hand every week to sort, bundle, wrap, and mail, under the direction of Sam. The paper was Sam. Sam was the paper.

It was an ignominious, cowardly act to kill Sam in response to the assassinations of Fred, Spider, and Bill, an act on the same level as Huey's madness.[7] The criterion for judging the merits of a given action should be based upon whether or not there is justice. It would have been justified if it had been someone that deserved it. But Sam Napier?

Marty Kenner said, "It was so unjust. Sam had never been involved in the military aspect of the party. He only worked on distribution. He was defenseless and his murder was unspeakably brutal: he was caught unarmed and unprotected in the . . . distribution office in Queens, tied to a bed, tortured, shot to death, then burned. . . . The assassins grabbed the two-year-old child that Sam was taking care of in the office and literally threw him out the door, giving him lasting injuries. . . . Not long after, two members of the N.Y. 21, Dhoruba Bin-Wahad and Jamal Joseph, a teenager himself, were arrested and convicted for being part of the gang that killed Sam."[8]

As a result of the split in the Black Panther Party in February 1971, four close comrades, dedicated to the struggle for a better life for everyone, were assassinated. Four more sacrifices in the continuing, prehistoric pastime of men. Three of them were from San Francisco—a heavy tribute for such a small city.

The cutthroat comportment of men must be marked with the onus of infamy and condemned to the pillory of history.

8

Women, Power, and Revolution

Kathleen Neal Cleaver

When Black Classic Press director Paul Coates invited me to speak at the Howard University symposium featuring the book he'd published, *The Black Panther Party Reconsidered,* he asked me to be on the panel discussing the party's legacy. I dislike the term "legacy", to me it signifies what has been left after death. Since I am not dead, and a lot of other former Panthers aren't dead, I told him I'd rather speak on a different panel. The afternoon panel, he said, would focus on gender. I suggested that it be called "Women, Power, and Revolution," because I think what we have to say about gender transcends the experience of being involved with the Black Panther Party. The organizers, however, followed the conventional thinking, and entitled my panel "Gender Dynamics within the Black Panther Party."

Regardless of what name was chosen, I think the relevant question to discuss is this: How could a young black woman raised during the 1950s find someplace to take collective action against the repressive social conditions she faced, and bring about revolutionary change? While I was growing up, I saw black women who inspired me to ask that question, and showed me where I could find that place. I saw Gloria Richardson standing face to face with National Guard soldiers, bayonets sticking from the guns they pointed at the demonstrators she led in Cambridge, Maryland. I saw Diane Nash speaking at Fisk University, leading black and white Freedom Riders onto Greyhound buses that got set on fire when they reached Alabama. I saw Ruby Doris Robinson holding a walkie-talkie, dispatching the fleet of cars that transported civil rights workers across the state of Mississippi during the 1964 Freedom Summer. These women were unfurling a social revolution in the Deep South. Gloria Richardson, Diane Nash, and Ruby Doris Robinson all worked with the Student Nonviolent Coordinating Committee (SNCC). That's where I was determined to go.

About two weeks before I joined SNCC, "Black Power" replaced "Freedom Now" as the battle cry. We, young women and young men who flocked to the front lines of the war against segregation, were contesting the remaining legacy of racial slavery. What we sought to eliminate were the legal, social, psychological, economic, and political limitations still being imposed on our human rights, and on our rights as citizens. That was the context in which we fought to remove limitations imposed by gender, clearly aware that it could not be fought as a stand-alone issue.

This is a revised version of a speech given at Howard University's Mooreland-Springarn Library on October 16, 1998 during a symposium for the book *The Black Panther Party Reconsidered,* ed. Charles Jones (Baltimore: Black Classic Press, 1998).

During that era, we hadn't developed much language to talk about the elimination of gender discrimination. Racism and poverty, imposed by bloody terrorists backed by state power, seemed so overwhelming then, and the ghastly backdrop of the war in Vietnam kept us alert as to what was at stake. It was not that gender discrimination wasn't apparent. It was evident in the most intimate matters—separate bathrooms marked "colored women" or "white ladies"; it was obvious in the facts that so many schools did not allow women to attend, and that so many jobs were not available if you were a woman. But from the early to mid-1960s, the first order of business was not how to advance our cause as women but how to empower the community of which we were a part, and how to protect our lives in the process.

Being in the Movement gave me and everyone who joined it a tremendous education. That experience taught us how to understand the world around us, how to think through the issues of what we could do on our own to advance our people's cause, how to organize our own people to change the world around us, and how to stand up to terrorism. Everything I learned in SNCC I took with me into the fledgling Black Panther Party. I started working there in November 1967, three or four weeks after Huey Newton was jailed on charges of killing an Oakland policeman in a predawn shoot-out. I organized demonstrations. I wrote leaflets. I held press conferences. I attended court hearings. I designed posters. I appeared on television programs, I spoke at rallies. I even ran for political office in order to organize the community around the program of the Black Panther Party and mobilize support to free Huey Newton.

At times, during the question-and-answer session following a speech I'd given, someone would ask, "What is the woman's role in the Black Panther Party?" I never liked that question. I'd give a short answer: "It's the same as men." We are revolutionaries, I'd explain. Back then, I didn't understand why they wanted to think of what men were doing and what women were doing as separate. It's taken me years, literally about twenty-five years, to understand that what I really didn't like was the underlying assumption motivating the question. The assumption held that being part of a revolutionary movement was in conflict with what the questioner had been socialized to believe was appropriate conduct for a woman. That convoluted concept never entered my head, although I am certain it was far more widely accepted than I ever realized.

Nowadays, the questions are more sophisticated: "What were the gender issues in the Black Panther Party?" "Wasn't the Black Panther Party a bastion of sexism?" Etc., etc., etc. But nobody seems to pose the question that I had: Where can I go to get involved in the revolutionary struggle? It seems to me that part of the genesis of the gender question, and this is only an opinion, lies in the way it deflects attention from confronting the revolutionary critique our organization made of the larger society, and turns it inward to look at what type of dynamics and social conflicts characterized the organization. To me, this discussion holds far less appeal than that which engages the means we devised to struggle against the oppressive dynamics and social conflicts the larger society imposed on us. Not many answers to the "gender questions" take into consideration what I've experienced. What I've read or heard as answers generally seem to respond to a particular model of academic inquiry that leaves out what I believe is central: How do you empower an oppressed and impoverished people who are struggling against racism, militarism, terrorism, and sexism too? I mean, how do you do that? That's the real question.

My generation became conscious during a period of profound world turmoil, when the Vietnam War and countless insurgencies in Africa, Asia, and in Latin America challenged the control of the resources of the world by the capitalist powers. They were facing a major assault. Those of us who were drawn to the early Black Panther Party were just one more insurgent band of young men and women who refused to tolerate the systematic violence and abuse being meted out to poor blacks, to middle-class blacks, and to any old ordinary blacks. When we looked at our situation, when we saw violence, bad housing, unemployment, rotten education, unfair treatment in the courts, as well as direct attacks from the police, our response was to defend ourselves. We became part of that assault against the capitalist powers.

In a world of racist polarization, we sought solidarity. We called for Black power for Black people, Red power for Red people, Brown power for Brown people, Yellow power for Yellow people, and, as Eldridge Cleaver used to say, White power for White people, because all they'd known was "Pig power." We organized the Rainbow Coalition, pulled together our allies, including not only the Puerto Rican Young Lords, the youth gang called the Black P. Stone Rangers, the Chicano Brown Berets, and the Asian I Wor Keun (Red Guards), but also the predominantly white Peace and Freedom Party and the Appalachian Young Patriots Party. We posed not only a theoretical but a practical challenge to the way our world was organized. And we were men and women working together.

The women who filled the ranks of our organization did not have specifically designated sex roles. Some women worked with the newspaper, like Shelley Bursey, who became a grand jury resister when she was jailed because she refused to respond to one of the investigations into the Black Panther Party newspaper. Some of us, like Ericka Huggins, saw their husbands murdered, then were arrested themselves. In Ericka's case, she was jailed along with Bobby Seale and most of the New Haven chapter on charges of conspiracy to commit murder. She was later acquitted, but imagine what happens to an organization when fourteen people at once get arrested on capital charges. That doesn't leave much time to organize, or to have a family life. Maybe that was the kind of pressure that they hoped would force us to give up.

I created the position of Communications Secretary, based on what I had seen Julian Bond do in SNCC. I sent out press releases, I got photographers and journalists to publish stories about us, I wrote articles for our newspaper. I ran for political office on the Peace and Freedom Party ticket, against the incumbent Democratic state representative—who, by the way, was Willie Brown (now mayor of San Francisco). We ran a campaign poster in the *Black Panther* newspaper, which was a drawing of Willie Brown with his mouth sewed up, his body tied up in rope. The caption read: Willie Brown's position on the Vietnam War, political prisoners, and racism, you get the idea. We were imaginative in our approach to political organizing. Matilaba, one of the earliest women members of the Black Panther Party, published drawings in the newspaper along with Emory Douglas. Connie Matthews, a young Jamaican who was working for the United Nations in Copenhagen, met Bobby Seale when he came over there on a tour, joined the Black Panther Party, and became our International Coordinator. Assata Shakur, who joined the New York chapter of the Black Panther Party, later became convicted of murdering a state trooper after a shoot-out on the New Jersey Turnpike in which she was wounded and another Panther, Zayd Shakur, was killed. Fearing that she would be killed, she escaped from prison, lived underground for a while, and eventually received asylum in Cuba.

In fact, according to a survey Bobby Seale did in 1969, two-thirds of the members of the Black Panther Party were women. I am sure you are wondering, why isn't this the picture that you have of the Black Panther Party? Well, ask yourself, where did the image of the Black Panthers that you have in your head come from? Did you read those articles planted by the FBI in the newspaper? Did you listen to the newscasters who announced what they decided was significant, usually, how many Panthers got arrested or killed? How many photographs of women Panthers have you seen? Think about this: how many newspaper photographers were women? How many newspaper editors were women? How many newscasters were women? How many television producers were women? How many magazine, book, newspaper publishers? Who was making the decisions about what information gets circulated, and when that decision gets made, who do you think they decide to present? Is it possible, and this is just a question, is it possible that the reality of what was actually going on day to day in the Black Panther Party was far less newsworthy, and provided no justification for the campaign of destruction that the intelligence agencies and the police were waging against us? Could it be that the images and stories of the Black Panthers that you've seen and heard were geared to something other than conveying what was actually going on?

What I think is distinctive about gender relations within the Black Panther Party is not how those gender relations duplicated what was going on in the world around us. In fact, that world was extremely misogynist and authoritarian. That's part of what inspired us to fight against it. When women suffered hostility, abuse, neglect, and assault—this was not something arising from the policies or structure of the Black Panther Party, something absent from the world—that's what *was* going on in the world. The difference that being in the Black Panther Party made was that it put a woman in a position when such treatment occurred to contest it. I'll always remember a particular mini-trial that took place at one of our meetings. A member of the Party was accused of raping a young sister, who was visiting from the Los Angeles chapter of the Black Panther Party, and he got voted out of the Party on the spot. Right there in the meeting. In 1970 the Black Panther Party took a formal position on the liberation of women. Did the U.S. Congress make any statement on the liberation of women? Did the Congress enable the Equal Rights Amendment to become part of the Constitution? Did the Oakland police issue a position against gender discrimination? It is in this context that gender relations—a term that we didn't have back then—in the Black Panther Party should be examined.

I think it is important to place the women who fought oppression as Black Panthers within the longer tradition of freedom fighters like Sojourner Truth, Harriet Tubman, Ida Wells Barnett, who took on an entirely oppressive world and insisted that their race, their gender, and their humanity be respected all at the same time. Not singled out, each one separate, but all at the same time. You cannot segregate out one aspect of our reality and expect to get a clear picture of what this struggle is about. In some cases, those who raise issues about gender are responding to what they think is the one-sided portrayal of the Black Panther Party as some all-male, macho revolutionary group. But look at where the picture is coming from before concluding that the appropriate response is to investigate gender dynamics within the Black Panther Party. I am not criticizing the project, but I am criticizing the angle.

The way Black women have sustained our community is phenomenal. Historically, we did not live within the isolation of a patriarchal world, we were thrust into that brutal equality slavery imposed. Our foremothers knew we would have to face the world on our own, and they tried to prepare us for that. What I think need to be examined and explained more fully are the powerful contributions women have made to our resistance against slavery, to our resistance against segregation, to our resistance against racism. Placing the participation of women in the Black Panther Party within that context illuminates a long tradition of fighting women. But that tends not to be what scholars asking these gender questions seem to have in mind.

To conclude, I refer to W. E. B. Du Bois, who pointed out that until emancipation, blacks faced two alternatives: we could either revolt and resist, or assimilate and submit. Emancipation provided a third alternative that Du Bois called "separate development." It could be seen as the ground of nationalism, or some might prefer to call it pan-Africanism. What I think is unique about the Black Panther Party is that as an organization, it combined all these possibilities in one. It provided the chance to revolt, to assimilate, and to have separate development at different aspects and at different times. I think that needs to be understood. I think the Black Panther Party's leadership structure, organizational structure, and military structure all need to be better understood. I think the way the organization furthered the main currents of African-American resistance from slavery to the present needs to be better understood, and that is the context within which gender dynamics should be placed.

Look at the demands raised by the Colored Peoples' Conventions at the end of the Civil War: they asked for the right to education, the right to be treated in law the same as white people, for equal treatment under the law. When you look at the Appeal to Human Rights issued by the student movement in Atlanta when they launched the campaign of sit-ins, what did they demand? Jobs, housing, education, and an end to police brutality. When you look at the Charter of the Kenya Land and Freedom Army, the African liberation movement that we called the Mau Mau, what did they ask for? They wanted self-government. They wanted to get rid of foreigners. They wanted an end to the trial of criminal and murder cases by the Europeans. Things like that. All these demands were similar to what we asked for in the Black Panther Party's Ten Point Platform and Program. We insisted on power to determine our destiny, full employment, decent education, and an end to police brutality. These have been our peoples' demands for over a century. The Black Panther Party continued to fight for what our people demanded in those Colored Peoples' Conventions, in those civil rights protests, and in those African liberation struggles, and this is what the black women who joined the organization were fighting to bring about.

I am part of a group of women, former Black Panthers, who have been meeting for the past few years. We hold retreats to come together and discuss what has happened to us, to restore our health, and to recover from the injuries and traumatic experiences that we have endured. A few days ago, I was at the Newark airport to catch a 5:00 A.M. flight to Atlanta, on my way to one of these retreats, and I ran into the actor Danny Glover, who was also taking that 5:00 A.M. flight to Atlanta, where he was going to visit his family.

We talked, and of course, I asked him about his work in the film *Beloved,* and told him that I was going to a Black Panther women's retreat. Danny Glover lived down the street from me in San Francisco. He told me, "I came to San Francisco in 1967 to go to San Francisco State." I said, "I came to San Francisco in 1967, but I went to Eldridge Cleaver's apartment." We all lived on Oak Street, only a few houses apart. He was involved with the BSU (Black Student Union). Many students who belonged to the BSU were active in the Black Panther Party; our organizations were very close. In fact, one of the demands made when the students at San Francisco State initiated their strike concerned George Murray, a professor who was fired and was then on the Central Committee of the Black Panther Party. So I told him about our Black Panther women's retreat.

Danny was sitting beside me at the gate. He tilted his head back and looked up as if he were remembering something that happened a long time ago. Then he said, "Oh, those women. . . . Those women in the Black Panther Party, you all held it together. The men—there was a lot of chaos going on. Things were wild. But it was the women who held it all together."

9

Black Fighting Formations
Their Strengths, Weaknesses, and Potentialities

Russell Shoats

A study of the various Black political organizations in the United States between the years 1960 and 1994 will reveal a number of "fighting formations." These formations were usually offshoots of larger organizations that had been further divided. As such, they were not primarily envisioned as fighting groups. This lack of original dedication to a "fighting mission" will help elucidate organizational strengths, weaknesses, and potentials (or loss of same). Not included in this study are the nonpolitical Black fighting formations found among the street gangs, or those dedicated to criminal activity. However, they will be mentioned as they relate to the lost potential amongst Black political fighting formations.

For the most concise writings on the philosophy of warfare (ultimate contributing factors, and the many and varied dynamics), we must look to Sun Tzu (ca. fifth century B.C.) and Karl von Clausewitz (nineteenth century A.D.). Sun Tzu's *Art of War* and von Clausewitz's *On War* are widely recognized by military practitioners of all countries and races as two of the best volumes available.[1]

There have been many outstanding military practitioners of African descent: Thutmose III (the first imperial conqueror); Ramses II and Ramses III (consistent subduers of the barbarian and savage hordes of Europe and Asia); the queens Ann Nzinga and (the) Candace(s) (Ethiopia and Angola); Hannibal Barca (of known fame); Shaka Zulu (warrior par excellence); Toussaint Louverture and Antonio Maceo (who outwitted and outfought vastly superior European armies in Haiti and Cuba). Also included among these are the outstanding guerrilla leaders among the Maroons and the African anticolonial fighters (it should, however, be remembered that guerrilla warfare is only a subdivision [sometimes a forerunner] of total war, although this form of warfare is sometimes all that is required). Unfortunately, the superlative accomplishments of these African practitioners of the art of war are not available to us.

Sun Tzu's *Art of War* instructs, "War is a matter of vital importance to the state: The province of life and death; the road to survival or ruin. It is mandatory that it be thoroughly studied." Similarly, *On War* asserts, "War is an extension of politics; politics by different means." Both authors point out the connection between politics and warfare, and the relative importance of each. For the purposes of this discussion we shall define politics as the science and art of governing people. It must follow then that those involved in political affairs must recognize that they will very likely be required to pursue their political objectives by different means in order that the journey along the road to survival not detour along the road of ruin. Warfare!

This cannot be a haphazard or belated consideration; rather, strict attention to these principles is required to avoid total destruction (the result of nonviolence). Therefore, all of our Black political organizations should have been designed to include a military component from the outset. The primary mission of this component would have been thorough study and preparation for war—from the very beginning! This presupposes political and military leadership sagacious enough to discern the long-range interests of their people, and the conflicts they might potentially encounter in pursuing these interests. In other words, our Black political organizations should have known to build a military component capable of defending our people from attack as they struggled to free themselves from all forms of domination and oppression. Sadly, this was never done; let us now examine what has been accomplished.

With the exception of the paramilitary "Fruit of Islam," due primarily to the tireless efforts of the Nation of Islam's Malcolm X, there was no Black fighting formation in 1960. Unfortunately, the Fruit of Islam's efforts were centered primarily around internal security and static defense of organizational leadership and property. They were further hobbled (in qualitative development) by their unwillingness to become actively involved in the struggle for civil rights, where all the action was! Subsequent events would expose their weaknesses. To their credit, they had perfected a method of recruiting, organizing, and training (although little training was provided) that was unparalleled until the present. The secret of their success was in recruiting efforts that targeted the most downtrodden members of the Black community. Among these were drug addicts, prison inmates, prostitutes, and the destitute poor. It took a great effort to recruit and organize these people; however, once they were brought firmly into "the midst," they became loyal and devoted members of their new (psychological) family. By the time the Nation of Islam had fished them in out of the mud, their biological families had for the most part turned their backs on them in despair. They were kept under close supervision and provided with the means to acquire such necessities as food, clothing, shelter, security, and entertainment— usually social fellowship guised in religious trappings. The Nation provided for them everything that a well-functioning family would provide.

The Nation itself was nationalist in tone; however, no strategy was implemented toward achieving nationalist goals. The first dictum —"War is a matter of vital importance to the state . . . it is mandatory that it be thoroughly studied"— was clearly not observed. This is not merely an arbitrary opinion, but an assertion supported by an examination of activities during their early days in the 1930s until the present. It simply does not take sixty years to build military capability, particularly if it is a priority! To be fair, they had hardly been idle. Ongoing battles against government infiltration and manipulation, along with petty jealousies and rivalries among their leaders, fragmented energies that could have been more productively directed.

The civil rights movement was launched in 1955 with the Montgomery, Alabama, bus boycott. It quickly took off and spread throughout the South. In addition to the local groupings, who in some cases had already been active in their communities, a number of other organizations began to emerge on the national scene by 1960: the Southern Christian Leadership Conference (SCLC), the Congress of Racial Equality (CORE), the Urban League,and the Student Nonviolent Coordinating Committee (SNCC). The National Association for the Advancement of Colored People (NAACP) had been around since the early 1900s. Between 1955 and 1965 all of the major action in the Black freedom struggle took place in the South, led by the aforementioned organizations. It should be noted here that all of these organizations professed nonviolence as their strategy; however, each ultimately relied on someone's armed forces to protect it. In most cases, reliance upon the U.S. government met with disastrous results. Calls to the FBI for protection would result in calls from the FBI to local police contacts—(card carrying Ku Klux Klansmen)—or undercover agents/operatives in the Klan, who would subsequently organize a violent episode, e.g., shooting, burning, or bombing. In their lack of preparedness and in their dependency these organizations violated every rule in the art of war. Instead of observing the dictum, "Destroy your enemy and preserve yourself," they were assisting their foe in their own destruction! This pattern was carried out, to some degree, when the U.S. government provided marshals or federal troops. However, the heroic sacrifices that were heaped on the rank and file, mostly Black men, women, and children because of this cowardly, ignorant strategy did force a number of social changes. During this period these same groups did engage in a few noteworthy incidents of fighting involving (armed) subdivisions and offshoots.

The Monroe County, North Carolina, NAACP branch was headed by a Black man named Robert F. Williams. This brother saw early on that his NAACP chapter could not survive without significant casualties unless they were willing to abandon the nonviolent approach and adopt an armed self-defense posture. Williams believed strongly that all Blacks in the United States should adopt armed self-defense. His work mirrored these beliefs, and the Monroe County NAACP chapter was armed and trained. This preparation is undoubtedly responsible for their survival in a number of shoot-outs with the local Ku Klux Klan (citizens and police).

Williams could not, however, gain widespread acceptance or adoption of his methods. His chapter was therefore isolated, and after a so-called kidnapping of some white people he was forced to leave the country. Williams continued his work in exile by traveling throughout Africa and China in an attempt to garner support for the struggle in the United States. He became a nationalist and published a paper called the Crusader. In this paper, Williams advocated the overthrow of the United States through guerrilla warfare. A number of years later he returned to the United States as head of the revolutionary Republic of New Afrika (RNA). Williams was able to stay out of prison because the RNA successfully exposed and defused the trumped-up kidnapping charge.

In the meantime the Deacons for Defense and Justice organized in Louisiana and Mississippi. The Deacons were not a subdivision like the Monroe County group; instead, they were an offshoot, and consequently free to act independently of the nonviolent leadership. Their mission was armed self-defense; they were recruited, organized, and trained solely for that purpose. Accordingly, the Deacons were much more advanced, militarily speaking, than any other (part-time) gun-toting Blacks in the civil rights struggle. For example, while civil rights groups posted marshals with armbands, the Deacons employed roving patrols armed with automatic rifles. The Deacons were responsible for the sophisticated security and communications net around some of the most important marches. After Klan members and Night Riders (part-time Klansmen afraid to show their colors during daylight) got into a few skirmishes and firefights with the Deacons, the racists had no choice other than to allow the Deacons a great deal of latitude. Unfortunately, the Deacons had relatively limited potential for growth because of the civil rights movement's overall strategy of reliance on the U.S. government for protection.

Rural Mississippi also made believers of the young SNCC cadre. SNCC started its Mississippi Freedom Summer campaign in 1964 as nonviolent activists. Reeling from the deaths of comrades and supporters like James Chaney, Andrew Goodman, and Michael Schwerner, and the raw terror of the police and Klan/Night Rider attacks, all of SNCC's cadre had taken up arms by the time they left Mississippi. H. Rap Brown, SNCC leader, was arrested when a rifle and banana clips were found in his luggage after a flight from

Mississippi. SNCC even changed its name to the Student National Coordinating Committee—dropping the "nonviolent." Unfortunately, it was too little too late. The momentum was beginning to shift to the cities of the North and West. One last effort by SNCC in 1965 centered around the Lowndes County Freedom Organization, whose emblem was "The Black Panther" (no real association with the later Black Panthers). The Lowndes County group subscribed to armed self-defense from the beginning. However, despite experimentation with the Black Power slogan, they were unable to make any real progress because their political goal was still civil rights.

The Watts, California, rebellion of 1965 signaled a significant shift in the momentum of the Black struggle, toward the cities. Within two years there would be a number of major rebellions in the big cities, and many lesser rebellions in smaller towns. This was a qualitatively different situation, no longer marked by peaceful demonstrators seeking to acquire their civil rights. These rebellions were massive and widespread: in New York, Philadelphia, Birmingham, Newark (thirty-four dead), Detroit (forty-three dead), and Watts (twenty-six dead) hundreds were wounded, with massive property damage. The keen political observer could not miss the parallels between these rebellions and those that had preceded revolutions and armed struggles in other countries.

It may be obvious to the reader that this equation was not complete; no urban-based Black political groups had armed components.[2] There were no Black fighting formations that could organize, control, and direct these rebellions. The Fruit of Islam was clearly not up to the task; they had been unable to respond adequately to the killing and shootings of their members by local police. Nor could rural-based groups lend any support; they were still in a life-and-death battle to keep the Klan and southern police at bay. SNCC made a half-hearted attempt to transfer their operations to the urban areas, but apart from H. Rap Brown and a few others, it seemed their southern experiences rendered them ineffectual.

The urban rebellions brought forth scores of new political formations. These formations generally adhered to the idea of armed self-defense, at least in theory. This shift in tactics was accompanied by new nationalist-sounding politics, usually with a separatist tone, although a rediscovery of the Pan-African concept was also becoming apparent. Unfortunately, the formations adopted the high-profile operation characteristic of the civil rights struggle, which relied too heavily on television, radio, and print media. In reality this was no longer the civil rights struggle; it had become the Black liberation struggle. The civil rights leaders needed this type of exposure to get their message across and to help protect themselves from the most flagrant abuses. This strategy was maladaptive in its application to the Black liberation struggle, which necessarily demanded more clandestine ways of operating. Preparation for guerrilla warfare is most successfully carried out surreptitiously. This patently obvious fact was lost on the new (younger) organizations, who were impressed by Malcolm X and the fiery orators but failed to recognize Malcolm's specific role as stimulator/educator. Clearly, they were now embarking on a new phase that demanded quiet, patient organizing and training of those tens of thousands already sufficiently stimulated—as evidenced by the massive rebellions—and waiting for someone to show them how to get the job done. "Rattling a sword makes a lot of noise—drawing one is silent."

A great deal of agitation, propagandizing, and educating still needed to be done, but not by those who, according to their mission, were concerned with creating Black fighting formations. Lack of focus and prioritization usually led to this mistake as groups tried to combine the activities of the military and political workers in each cadre. They failed to realize that each situation demanded specialization: political workers (stimulators, educators, marchers, and so on) and military workers (armed self-defense and assault units). The Deacons had it right!

An outstanding practitioner of this new form was the Revolutionary Action Movement (RAM), which began an intensive organizing drive in the northeast states around 1967; much of their activity centered around Philadelphia. Militant, nationalist, and high profile, RAM even had their cadre spray-paint their slogan, "Join the Black Guard," on walls throughout the community ("The Black Guard" was their [out front] military arm). RAM's leaders were in front of cameras on all important issues. Their "Black Guard" cadre could be seen at their cultural centers in their fatigues and black berets. They even had a youth group called "The Liberators." This contributed to a feeling of hopefulness among Black people, who began to believe the revolution was right around the corner (few in Philadelphia had yet heard of a similar group that had cropped up in California, the Black Panther Party for Self-Defense). The effects of their activities were not quite so positive among whites, who felt threatened and afraid (some people went out of their way to frighten the white folks; it made them feel better about the injustices they had suffered). Around 1967 the white folks began to strike back. Over a period of several months, all known RAM leaders and key cadre were arrested. Although RAM advocated armed self-defense and owned weapons, they did not carry them in public. Consequently, they were arrested for everything from "J-walking, to conspiring to put cyanide in the police department rations at the next major holiday celebration."[3] RAM had not (essentially) fired a shot. (However, some alleged members and supporters were arrested bringing dynamite from Canada, allegedly to blow up the Statue of Liberty.)

These arrests crippled RAM, and they never regained their former vitality. Their leaders and cadre were forced to fight these trumped-up charges for years afterward. This treatment was not reserved only for RAM; similar scenarios played out in Black communities throughout the country. In fact, the attacks on RAM and other militant groups were spearheaded by police forces throughout the country, including the FBI. The success of law enforcement officers in carrying out these plans was almost certainly related to the inexperience of RAM and other organizations, which were never able to get grounded after they showed their hand through their supermilitancy, their dress, and so on. Black fighting formations of this era never even had a chance to fight. Many of the activists became discouraged after these experiences and turned to drugs or crime.

When it came to the Black Panther Party for Self-Defense (BPP), circumstances were a little different. Founded in 1966 in Oakland, California, BPP followed the same pattern as RAM. However, because of a clause in the California state law, any citizen was allowed to carry arms in public as long as they were not loaded. The BPP took advantage of this clause in order to brandish weapons wherever they went. At the time, this seemed the height of militancy, and they received more attention than any other group from the community, media, and police. Despite this attention they could not be put down as easily as RAM because they always had their guns with them—and they were loaded. After a few confrontations with the police it became apparent that these young Blacks could not be intimidated. Before long, BPP members were being provoked into gun battles with the police. Within a year, one of the cofounders, Huey Newton, had been shot and imprisoned for killing the police officer who shot him. Bobby Seale, another cofounder, had been jailed for marching into the state capitol with other armed Panthers to protest the law passed to ban the carrying of guns in public. "Little" Bobby Hutton was the first BPP member to be killed during a Panther/police shoot-out, in which several members of the Party were wounded and jailed when two carloads of Panthers were ambushed by the police. Eldridge Cleaver would later flee the country to avoid incarceration for charges associated with the shoot-out. Shortly after the inception of the BPP, its top three leaders (Newton, Seale, and Cleaver) were either in prison or in exile, a fate that also confronted several key local leaders and cadre members.

On the positive side, membership skyrocketed! Chapters were formed throughout the West Coast, in the Midwest, Northeast, and South. The BPP became a magnet for most of the smaller local organizations who were of a similar mind. And with the assassination of Martin Luther King Jr. in 1968, even more people were eager to join the BPP. By this time no Panthers were carrying guns in public, but this did nothing to stop the onslaught. BPP offices and homes were raided from coast to coast. Police agents who had infiltrated the ranks were provoking deadly confrontations with the police and other Black organizations. BPP members were even hunting and killing each other, goaded by agents provocateurs. The Panthers, potentially a strong Black fighting formation, were forced to take to the field before they were ready. As a result, "the field of battle [was] a land of standing corpses." Panthers were dying in the streets; they were dying in raids and in prison (Soledad, San Quentin, Attica, Atmore-Holman)—it was "war to the knife!"[4]

The Panthers were not the only Black fighting formation; other revolutionaries and "free shooters" were just as committed, armed, and involved. For example, Fred "Ahmad" Evans and a squad of Black guerrillas trapped the Cleveland, Ohio, police in a deadly ambush. A number of officers were killed and wounded, some guerrillas were also killed or wounded, and Ahmad Evans was put in prison (where he died). Mark Essex, free shooter, held off an army of police officers atop a high hotel in New Orleans. Officials had to call in a helicopter gunship to kill him, but not before he had inflicted casualties on them. Jonathan Jackson walked into a courtroom in San Rafael, California, and pulled a submachine gun from his duffel bag. After disarming all of the sheriffs, he gave pistols and a shotgun to James McClain, William Christmas, and Ruchell "Cinque" Magee, three Black prisoner comrades of his brother, George Jackson. They rounded up the white judge, the district attorney, and a number of jurors as hostages and forced their way past the rest of the sheriffs and police officers, but their getaway van was riddled with bullets, killing Jackson, McClain, and Christmas. Magee was wounded but survived. Before they died, they blew the judge's head off with the shotgun they had taped under his chin. The district attorney and jurors were also shot, but survived. George Jackson, a Field Marshal in the BPP, was killed the following year in San Quentin, but not before three prison guards and two "inmate snitches" were knifed to death. It was later learned that all of those brothers were set up by an agent provocateur who had infiltrated their inner circle. The agent, Louis Tackwood, had married one of their sisters.[5]

The revolutionary Republic of New Afrika (RNA), once headed by Robert F. Williams, gunned a number of Detroit police down after they tried to storm a meeting their leaders were holding at a church. A few years later they killed a sheriff after their headquarters were raided in Jackson, Mississippi. That raid sent their entire leadership to prison.[6] Free shooters were killing police officers in sniper attacks in Philadelphia, Chicago, St. Louis, and New Orleans housing projects. H. Rap Brown became a fugitive after a bomb went off outside a court building in his comrades' car. A year or so later he was wounded and captured after a running gun battle between his Liberators (from East St. Louis) and the New York City police. A number of Liberators were also captured. Police officers were killed while they sat in their cars or directed traffic; this was war. There were brothers and sisters hijacking passenger jets to Cuba and Algeria, where the BPP had a branch of fugitives headed by Cleaver (he had left the country to avoid going back to prison for his participation in the shoot-out that left "Little" Bobby dead).

This was very sobering for BPP members. All of the early flash and high profile began to dissipate even as the Panthers searched desperately for ways to regain the initiative and plug the security gaps. Finally, it was decided that an autonomous strike force that could handle all armed actions was needed. Other BPP members would continue with and expand community programs such as free breakfast, educational and sickle cell testing, clothing donations, and so on. Unfortunately, it was again too little, too late. The seeds of mistrust sown by the agents and their handlers (the police/FBI) were cultivated in an environment of youthful and inexperienced leadership, which demonstrated little understanding of intelligence and counterintelligence activities, or how to combat them. More importantly, they had only a fleeting grasp of "the art of war," which as a critical component of their growth and survival could not have been overemphasized. Still, they pressed on. Orders went out to the field marshals to begin organizing (separating) guerrilla groups, a Black Liberation Army.

A very important opportunity was missed at this point; the BPP had made some halfhearted attempts to recruit street gangs, but these were unsuccessful. They overlooked the fact that street gangs were typically responsive only to programs focused primarily on fighting. As we've seen, the old BPP party wanted cadres who were political and military workers. Almost invariably gang members responded to recruitment efforts with, "Get back when it's time to fight." When the time to fight did arrive, in their haste to go into the new phase, they pushed that knowledge out of their minds. Of course it would not have been easy to slow down at this point, but a little foresight would have indicated the strategic benefits of doing so.

Growing unrest among the rank and file proved to be a major stumbling block to launching the new phase. Further, leadership was less than swift in developing a response to the problem. Nevertheless, the new phase was launched with the BPP cadre studying texts on guerrilla warfare, refusing to be arrested for any reason, and launching planned attacks on various targets. In New York City a gun battle erupted between the police and BPP members when officers tried to arrest members for carrying concealed weapons. When the smoke cleared, a cop and BPP member Harold Russell were dead, and two other BPP members, Robert "Ra'uf" Vickers and Anthony "Kimu" White, were wounded. Kimu was arrested, but Ra'uf escaped to the underground, where doctors eventually healed his wounds and allowed him to go back into the field. In California, Geronimo ji Jaga Pratt, who was out on bail in connection with the 1969 gun battle that ensued after a police raid of the Los Angeles headquarters, went underground and formed a guerrilla group. In Philadelphia, a guerrilla group raided a police station, killing one cop and wounding another. BPP guerrilla groups were raiding banks for funds, hijacking food to give to the community, and acquiring sophisticated military weapons.

This intensified activity put pressure on the BPP political workers. After the raid on the Philadelphia police station, every BPP office in the city was raided by the police. Fortunately, Party members anticipated these raids. After gun battles at two of the offices, however, the Panthers were forced to surrender. This activity also provoked gun battles between the police and other Blacks. In forty-eight hours the score was: six cops in the hospital with gunshot wounds, one cop at the morgue, and Panthers and guerrillas in prison, while other guerrillas were on the run. All of the Panthers were released after massive protests by the Black community, and because the police could not fully justify the raids. These episodes clearly demonstrated that they should have been operating this way all the time, but this new appreciation of how to attack the problem was not universally shared, and division grew around the disagreement. There was a split between those who advocated this new phase and (surprisingly!) other leadership elements who favored removing guns from the strategy entirely. Such a reversal would cause an about-face that seems ludicrous in view of the Philadelphia lesson, where police officers were killed and wounded, Panthers sustained no casualties, and all detained Panthers were shortly released from prison. The community support and participation engendered by the Philadelphia episodes was also a positive result of the new phase. BPP members held a major convention in Philadelphia within weeks of these events without any police interference. It was enough for the Black community to see that the roles of those participating in planned assaults (the guerrillas) and the BPP political workers were strictly dichotomized. There was absolutely no reason, therefore, to suspend all armed actions. Besides, it was too late!

There were other complaints about the opulent lifestyle that various leaders had adopted (on release from prison in 1970, Huey Newton began to hang out with Hollywood stars and rent expensive apartments). But the real beef was the poor strategy that killed members and sent others to prison. Huey Newton, the top leader, advocated no guns in the program. For those who wanted to fight, or who were underground, he sent an open communiqué to the North Vietnamese government that he would make BPP members available to fight in Vietnam against the U.S. forces. This was strange, to say the least! Not that the Panthers weren't sympathetic to the Viet Cong's fight, but very few could see any reason that we should not show our sympathy by stepping up our armed actions inside the United States. The Vietnamese government was of a similar mind, and they openly declined the offer, suggesting that the BPP could better help by supporting them from within the United States. Eldridge Cleaver, who had been feuding with Huey from Algeria countered that it was time to stop the bullshit and lend full support to the armed struggle. He had made arrangements with the Algerian government whereby Panthers, and others, could go to Algeria to be trained. Another clear voice was that of Field Marshal George Jackson, who had been advocating and writing about the necessity for a shift in strategy, and how it could be carried out. Highly regarded by many and a master theoretician, he would have unquestionably been the most effective leader to implement this new phase. These traits were complemented by his desire to implement theory—and by his desperation; at the time, he was preparing to go on trial for killing a prison guard. It would not have been difficult to liberate him from prison, provided the BPP put their full resources behind the effort. There was no lack of BPP members, male or female, who would have volunteered for such an honorable mission. Sadly, the West Coast leadership (Huey Newton and co.), and the police/prison officials had him cut off from direct contact with those who were ready, willing, and able to carry out such a plan. Consequently, the police/prison officials set Jackson up and assassinated him. Nevertheless, George and his prison "Black Guerrilla Family" killed five of the enemy. Ruchell "Cinque" Magee, who had recovered from his courthouse wounds, was in this battle also.[7]

August 21, 1971, the date of Jackson's death, was a sad day. Shortly afterward, "Attica Prison" blew up after a memorial for him; forty-three guards and prisoners died. Black guerrillas walked into a California police station, killed a police sergeant, and riddled the station with bullets—the "George L. Jackson Assault Team" of the Black Liberation Army claimed responsibility.

The question of the split on strategy was solved after enforcers dispatched by Huey Newton shot and killed a Panther who had given unfavorable details of the inner workings of the West Coast leadership clique. Robert "Spider" Webb was a top Panther leader and bodyguard of Huey Newton. At a New York meeting attended by disgruntled Panthers from all over, Webb reported opulence, pimping BPP female members, and cocaine addiction. The following day, Webb was assassinated by Newton enforcers. Afterward the primary West Coast representative, Central Committee member Samuel Napier, was found in an office destroyed by fire, his bound body had been riddled with bullets. Shortly afterward, the West Coast delegation placed themselves under police protection until they could make arrangements to return to California. The word went out that the police were looking for a number of people in connection with the shooting and preceding meeting. This forced many people to go underground. Again we see a fatal disregard for the dictums of the art of war; preparations for this chain of events were made only haphazardly or belatedly. All the same, these preparations swelled the ranks of the guerrillas considerably. Intensive training for these new guerrillas included bank raids for funds and gun stores for arms and ammunition. This could have been a new beginning; however, because it was forced on them, and unplanned, their hasty actions all but destroyed any aboveground political activity. They were making the same mistake in reverse that the civil rights organizations had made: the civil rights organizations were all political workers with no military component, while guerrilla groups such as the Black Liberation Army were all military with no political workers.

Revolutions must be led by professionals if success is the goal. One may not start as a professional, but must certainly become one if destruction is to be avoided. The hallmark of the professional is being able to proceed from point A to point B without wasted energy. This means learning from the mistakes of others—as well as your own—and not repeating them. It also means learning the best practices from others and adapting and emulating their successes, wherever applicable.

This new phase was now solidly being launched, but on an unprofessional basis. The past, present, and future were not adequately evaluated. After finally adopting the right style, the guerilla groups lost contact with the substance of what this was all about. They forgot—most had not yet learned—that "war is an extension of politics; politics by different means." It follows, then, that they should have taken their cue from whatever was happening in the political arena, as the Deacons used to do. But that did not happen, at least not initially.

The BLA guerrilla groups were busy acquiring and consolidating their logistical base (raiding banks and gun stores, acquiring transportation and safe houses, and so on). This is understandable and proper. But at the same time they were launching deadly attacks on the police. Since these were planned assaults, they were considerably more successful than the past shoot-outs to which the BPP had been subjected. Usually these attacks were carried out so swiftly that when the smoke cleared, the cops were dead or wounded, and the guerrillas had disappeared. They had learned how to reverse the ratio of killed and wounded in their favor. The success of these attacks clearly indicates the benefits of operating this way and more than suggests that this should have been the mode of operation from the beginning.

However, BLA members still suffered casualties from the rare operation that resulted in a running gunfight, or when they were sometimes subjected to car stops or forced into confrontations because the local police were looking to hassle some Blacks. These casualties were by and large irreplaceable. This was so because the BLA did not have an adequate political apparatus from which to replenish their forces, nor did they see the necessity of developing a way to integrate the street gangs into their activities.

The BLA had also become the top priority of special FBI/local police joint task forces. The title is more impressive than what they were able to accomplish; the BLA guerrilla groups did not fall victim to police infiltration in any significant way. So, aside from being caught off balance (as indicated), their demise must be attributed to some other mistake that gave these task forces an opening, (such as their frequenting places under surveillance, or "attrition.")

The BLA fielded the most effective Black assault units since the Maroons! Their primary weakness, and the thing that caused the most harm, was their failure properly to integrate themselves with the Black masses, through their inability to interact with a revolutionary, aboveground political group.

The BLA did attempt to reintegrate with political workers who had left or been expelled from the BPP. Since most of these workers were located on the East Coast, they were known as the "East Coast Panthers." They did not have any of the vitality, stature, resources, or connections they had previously enjoyed, but the BLA did have the know-how to put together a new political organization that could eclipse even the BPP, using aboveground cadres recruited from former Panthers and other political Blacks. In order to do this, they would have to channel their energies and resources away from their armed activities, but before they could come to this conclusion, they had all been imprisoned, killed, or exiled.

The BLA continued their revolutionary commitment after being imprisoned. Some of them escaped or attempted to escape. In 1976 BLA member John "Andaliwa" Clark was killed in a New Jersey state prison after BLA members, armed with homemade weapons, fought against armed guards. One BLA member was killed in a fall from a high-rise prison in New York after another prisoner had descended on the same rope. BLA member Herman Bell was overpowered after holding a guard hostage in an escape attempt from Rikers Island in New York; A rubber raft and other gear were discovered outside his building. BLA members Anthony "Kimu" White and Woody "Olugbala" Green were ambushed and killed after escaping from a prison in New York City. In 1977, Russell "Maroon" Shoats and three other BLA members escaped from the state prison at Huntington, Pennsylvania. Two of these brothers were recaptured, and BLA member Wayne "Musa" Henderson was killed. Maroon was recaptured after a twenty-seven-day hunt. In 1979 a BLA task force walked into the Clinton Prison in New Jersey, and after commandeering the visiting area, liberated BLA member Assata Shakur, who later surfaced in Cuba. Kuwasi Balagoon, a BLA member who had escaped from a New Jersey state prison, was part of the BLA task force that liberated Assata Shakur. In 1979 Arthur "Cetewayo" Johnson and Robert "Saeed" Joyner, two BLA members, took over a cell block at the state prison in Pittsburgh in an attempt to escape. They and a few other brothers who had helped were overpowered.

In 1980 BLA members Russell "Maroon" Shoats and Cliff "Lumumba" Futch escaped from a maximum-security state mental hospital in Pennsylvania. They and Phyllis "Oshun" Hill, who had smuggled them the escape weapons, were captured three days later after a gun battle with police and FBI. In 1980–81, BLA member Sundiata Acoli and a number of other prisoners were almost killed when guards at the federal prison at Marion, Illinois, opened fire after they were discovered trying to cut through the security fence. In 1981 BLA member Joseph "Joe Joe" Bowen and three other brothers held guards at gunpoint for six days after a failed escape attempt at the state prison at Graterford, Pennsylvania. (Joe Joe and BLA member Fred "Muhammad Kafi" Burton had assassinated the warden and deputy warden at the Holmesburgh, Philadelphia, prison in 1973.)

There was much more. . . .

The prison authorities came to grips with this by keeping BLA members in the hole for five, ten, fifteen years and even longer. BLA member Ruchell Magee has spent most of his thirty years in prison in the hole! The prison authorities have them cut off just like they did Field Marshal George. Most of them have sentences that make release back into society unlikely. A campaign for amnesty or deportation to a foreign (African) country holds real possibilities that can serve as an organizing tool. There is much more that can be said about what lessons the fighting formations learned on a tactical level. However, that's another paper.

As it stands, in 1994, we're essentially back to square one. There are no Black fighting formations active in the African communities in the United States. The Nation of Islam's Fruit of Islam have potential (they always did, for that matter), and the street gangs also still hold great potential. Outside of that, there are tens of thousands of young

African men and women ready to become fighters for their survival, but as of now, those who are capable of recruiting, organizing, and training them are either "cut off" or "scared straight."

>Long live the spirit of Alprentice "Bunchy" Carter (BPP)
>Long live the spirit of John Huggins (BPP)
>Long live the spirit of Sandra Pratt (BPP)
>Long live the spirit of Zayd Malik Shakur (BLA)
>Long live the spirit of Twymon Ford Myers (BLA)
>Long live the spirit of Frank "Heavy" Fields (BLA)
>Long live the spirit of Wayne "Musa" Henderson (BLA)
>Long live the spirit of Fred Hampton (BPP)
>Long live the spirit of Lumumba Shakur (BPP)
>Long live the spirit of Captain, Richard S. (BLA)
>Long live the spirit of Woody "Olugbala" Green (BLA)
>Long live the spirit of Anthony "Kimu" White (BLA)
>Long live the spirit of Spurgeon Jake Winters (BPP)
>Heroes and martyrs all !!!
>The struggle continues!!!

PART THREE

Envisioning the Imagination
of the Movement

10

Organization and Movement
The Case of the Black Panther Party
and the Revolutionary People's
Constitutional Convention of 1970

George Katsiaficas

Millions of "ordinary" people pay with their lives for the decisive events that determine the outcome of world events. Their actions and thoughts enter into most histories, how-ever, only as *objects* affected by momentous decisions leaders make, not as *subjects* of the social world upon which decision-makers depend. Historians typically study the writings of world leaders and construct meticulously researched biographies of such figures in order to shed light on momentous events, such as the creation of constitutions. Yet the notion that "people make history," long ago incorporated into the language of social scientists, seldom informs accounts of World War II, the Civil War, or even many cases of social movements—grassroots attempts to change outmoded patterns of everyday life. Take the case of the civil rights movement, for example. Biographies of Martin Luther King Jr. or Malcolm X are the norm, not accounts of the millions who changed their lives and revolutionized society through sacrifice and struggle, transforming even Martin's and Malcolm's worldviews. Every child knows King's name, but how many Americans have ever heard of Fred Hampton's assassination or know what COINTELPRO stands for? How many of us could say even one knowledgeable sentence about the massacres of students at Orangeburg, Jackson State, or North Carolina A&T?

Even the movement tends to regard the ideas of its leaders, political parties and orga-nized groups as most significant. No less than conventional historians, radical analysts often seem unable to comprehend the intelligence of crowds that embody the popular imagination. There are many reasons for this blind spot, including the ease with which ac-counts of leaders and organizations can be constructed compared with the difficulties one encounters when seeking to comprehend single events in the ebb and flow of sporadic gatherings of nebulous groups—precisely those incidents thought to be little more than ac-tions by random collections of people. Sometimes pivotal events are so shrouded in mys-tery that historians do not even agree as to whether the events in question even took place.[1]

The author wishes to acknowledge the helpful comments on earlier versions of this article given to him by Kathleen Cleaver, Russell Shoats, Stew Albert, David Gullette, Billy Nessen, and Victor Wallis.

History seldom cooperates by providing us with clear indications of participants' thinking during instances of "spontaneously conscious" crowds.[2] One such exceptional case is the Revolutionary People's Constitutional Convention (RPCC), a multicultural public gathering of between 10,000 and 15,000 people who answered the call by the Black Panther Party (BPP) and assembled in Philadelphia on the weekend of September 5, 1970. Arriving in the midst of police terror directed against the BPP, thousands of activists from around the country were determined to defend the Panthers. They also intended to redo what had been done in 1787 by this nation's founding fathers in the City of Brotherly Love—to draft a new constitution providing authentic liberty and justice for all. Although seldom even mentioned in mainstream accounts, this self-understood revolutionary event came at the high point of the 1960s movement in the United States and was arguably the most momentous event in the movement during this critical period in American history.[3]

This essay seeks to develop an understanding of the hearts and minds of the diverse community drawn to the convention. By examining primary documents produced by the RPCC, I hope to shed light on the popular movement's aspirations. By comparing these written statements with the original platform and program of the BPP, drafted four long years earlier, I seek to illustrate how the intelligence of popular movements sometimes outpaces even the most visionary statements of its leading individuals and organizations. (All these documents are appended at the end of this book.) In the tradition of using primary documents to probe the essential character of historical events, to negate more historically superficial analyses like those relying primarily upon individual biographies of Great Men and Women, I will first discuss the BPP platform (formulated by Huey Newton and Bobby Seale in October 1966) and then analyze the proposed new constitution drafted at the RPCC. Besides the primary documents of the RPCC and fragmentary accounts by a few historians and activists, I draw from my own personal experiences as a participant in the RPCC. For thirty years I have kept a copy of the original proposals generated by the workshops that formed when the large plenary session broke down into at least ten smaller working groups. These documents convey unambiguous statements of the movement's self-defined goals and provide an outline of a freer society. Although it has been practically forgotten by historians, the RPCC is a key to unlocking the mystery of the aspirations of the 1960s movement. The majority of my essay deals with the RPCC because so little has been written about it.[4] I hope this article encourages future work on the RPCC.

Many writers have examined the early history of the 1960s, but far fewer look at the time when the movement spread beyond the upper-middle-class constituencies and elite universities that gave rise to both the civil rights and student movements. Popular stereotypes of the 1960s often end with Martin Luther King's assassination, yet by late 1969 the movement had become so massive and radical that its early proponents did not recognize (or sometimes even support) it. In 1970, when the movement reached its apex, working-class students, countercultural youth, and the urban lumpen proletariat (unemployed street people and those who supported themselves through criminal endeavors) transformed its tactics and goals. Shortly before their murders, both Martin Luther King Jr. and Malcolm X were coming to much the same radical conclusion as that shared by the participants at the RPCC: the entire world system needs to be revolutionized in order to realize liberty and justice for all.

Part of the problem involved with historical accounts of the 1960s concerns the profound character of the rupture of social tranquillity and social cohesion that occurred in the United States. Consistently uncovered in Harris polls and Yankelovich surveys, the revolutionary aspirations of millions of people in the United States in 1970 constitute a significant set of data for understanding how rapidly revolutionary upsurges can emerge—and how quickly they can be dissipated. In 1970, immediately after the national student strike, polls found that more than 1 million students considered themselves revolutionaries.[5] The next year, a *New York Times* investigation found that 4 out of 10 college students (more than three million people) thought that a revolution was needed in the United States.[6] While these are substantial numbers, they do not count millions more outside American universities in the ghettos and barrios, the factories, offices, and suburbs. For a brief historical moment, the movement in the United States accomplished a decisive break with the established system. Unlike similar events in France in May 1968, whose discontinuity from the established society is common knowledge, the "break" in U.S. history has been hidden. Neither revolutionary activists nor mainstream historians want to acknowledge the revolutionary stridency of that period, both preferring to promulgate more socially acceptable ideas like those of the young Martin Luther King Jr. or the still-not-mature Malcolm X. Under these circumstances, it is understandable that the revolutionary upsurge of 1970 is quite difficult to recall thirty years later.

Elsewhere I have written that the popular imagination can best be comprehended in the actions and aspirations of millions of people during moments of crisis—general strikes, insurrections, episodes of the eros effect, and other forms of mass struggle.[7] The RPCC was one such episode, and even in apparent failure, the convention inaugurated many ideas that subsequently have become so significant that millions of people were actively involved in pursuing them. For revolutionary movements, the dialectic of defeat often means that aspects of their aspirations are implemented by the very system they opposed.

Writing the Panther Platform and Program

No doubt individuals are products of their times, but that is not all we are, particularly when we set out to change the world and, like Newton and Seale, have an impact far beyond what we imagined. Within a few short years of their fateful decision to organize the BPP around the platform and program they drafted in 1966, Newton and Seale were both locked in prison facing murder charges, and the organization they had founded exploded from a handful of members to more than 5,000. By the end of 1968 their newspaper (the *Black Panther*) sold over 100,000 copies weekly.

For fifteen days Seale and Newton worked collaboratively to produce the platform and the program.[8] With typical self-effacing modesty, Seale insists Newton "articulated it word for word. All I made were suggestions." After they finished distilling the wisdom of years of Africans' yearnings for freedom, putting into the language of the young and rising baby-boom generation their innermost dreams and the basic needs of African Americans, they established the party. As Seale recounts,

> When we got through writing the program, Huey said, "We've got to have some kind of structure. What do you want to be," he asked me, "Chairman or Minister of Defense?"
>
> "I'll be the Minister of Defense," Huey said, "and you'll be the Chairman." "That's fine with me," I said. . . . With the ten-point platform and program and the two of us, the Party was officially launched on October 15, 1966, in a poverty program office in the black community in Oakland, California.[9]

At the center of their vision stood two dimensions of the legacy of Malcolm X: armed self-defense and the United Nations' attention to the plight of African Americans. But

Newton and Seale were not simply the heirs of Malcolm X's vision; they went further, demanding "power to determine the destiny of our Black community." They insisted that the federal government should provide "full employment for our people," decent housing "fit for the shelter of human beings," and an "end to the robbery by the white man of our Black community." The program demanded that Black men be exempt from military service, that Black prisoners be retried by a jury of their peers, that the education system teach the "true nature of this decadent American society." What attracted the most attention was their call for "an immediate end to POLICE BRUTALITY and MURDER of black people." Point 7 called for "organizing black self-defense groups" and maintained that "all black people should arm themselves for self-defense." Continuing from the exemption of all black men from military service, point 6 stated, "We will protect ourselves from the force and violence of the racist police and the racist military, by whatever means necessary." True to their words, Newton and Seale immediately began organizing groups of Panthers to patrol the police, and Newton's stubborn insistence on his right to observe and criticize the police—even at the point of a gun—became legendary (or notorious, depending on one's perspective).

Remarkable in its ability to grasp the past and make it part of the present, the Black Panther Party program resurrected neglected promises like forty acres and a mule. Nonetheless it still bears the birthmarks of the society from which it emerged. The words "man" or "men" appear no fewer than fifteen times in the ten points. Even with regard to Black prisoners, point 8 reads: "We want freedom for all black men held in federal, state, county and city prisons and jails." The next sentence, not italicized and omitted from public summations of the ten points in speeches, extends the demand: "We believe that all black people should be released from the many jails and prisons because they have not received a fair and impartial trial." When composing a jury of peers that would presumably rehear the cases of these prisoners, however, reference is made to the "average reasoning man" of the black community. Similarly point 2 maintains that "the federal government is responsible and obligated to give every man employment or a guaranteed income." No mention is made of women's rights to jobs.

While language indicates assumptions being made, I believe that neither the content of the program nor the actions of the BPP should be obscured or twisted by a rigid linguistic analysis. At the time the platform was written, usage of "man" for "human" was commonplace and unquestioned. Martin Luther King's call for a "society not of the white man, not of the black man, but of man as man" and Herbert Marcuse's book *One Dimensional Man* are examples with which one could begin. Even as Huey Newton wrote his public endorsement of women's liberation and after sexism in the BPP was officially condemned, he continued to use "man" rather than "human."[10] On balance, the BPP opposed sexism within its own ranks and in the larger society. That is part of what makes it so important historically. Four years after the program was written, the party took a formal position in support of women's liberation, but even before then, as the feminist movement developed in the society at large, the BPP was transformed in its internal affairs, public statements, and practical actions.[11]

The platform and program were written during the party's black nationalist phase. Still to come were three more phases in the ideological evolution of the BPP: revolutionary nationalist, revolutionary internationalist, and intercommunalist. In the four years beginning in October 1966, history accomplished more than in the preceding forty years, at least in terms of the self-understanding and status of young urban, African Americans. It is difficult to overestimate how much the Panthers transformed young African Americans. Under Panther influence, hardened criminals rose before 6:00 A.M. to serve free breakfasts to thousands of schoolchildren; drug addicts kicked their habits and worked to expel dealers from the neighborhoods; and men used to having their way with women learned to listen to and respect their female counterparts.

A keen, insightful document, the program's third point contained an often overlooked analogy between African Americans and Jewish victims of the Nazis. Using the case of German reparations being paid to Israel for genocide of the Jewish people, Newton and Seale argued for reparations for African Americans. Claiming the "Germans killed six million Jews. The American racist has taken part in the slaughter of over 50 million black people; therefore, we feel that this is a modest demand [forty acres and two mules] that we make." No lawyer in a court of international law could make a better case based on historical precedent.

The final point both summarized the problems and offered a solution: "We want land, bread, housing, education, clothing, justice and peace. And as our major political objective, a United Nations–supervised plebiscite to be held throughout the black colony in which only black colonial subjects will be allowed to participate, for the purpose of determining the will of black people as to their national destiny." The program concluded by rephrasing the declaration of independence's insistence in 1776 on the right of revolution. Governments, it was remembered, are created to serve people, and "whenever any form of government becomes destructive of these ends, it is the right of the people to alter or abolish it, and to institute new government, laying its foundation on such principles, and organizing its powers in such form, as to them shall seem most likely to affect their safety and happiness." With these words, Huey and Bobby had unwittingly laid the groundwork for the RPCC four years later.

Writing a New Constitution the Panther Way

Before we discuss the specific documents produced by the RPCC, a few words about its context are needed. In the week before people gathered in Philadelphia, police bloodily assaulted all three Panther offices in the city, arresting every member of the Party they could find. The Panthers had not accepted their fate without a gunfight—as was their practice across the country—and three police were wounded in the shooting. Afterward, the police forced captured Panther men to walk naked through the street while being photographed by the press. Police Chief Rizzo gloated he had caught the "big, bad Black Panthers with their pants down."[12] Publicized widely, the atmosphere created by these events was an important part of the aura of the RPCC. Philadelphia Panther member Russell Shoats recounts that in the weeks before the RPCC the Panther Central Office in Oakland made it clear to Philadelphia party members that even Huey Newton was "afraid to come to Philadelphia." Shoats remembers that they "went on to express their opinion that the racist Philadelphia police would feel comfortable in attempting to assassinate him during the planned Revolutionary People's Constitutional Convention Planning Session"[13]

Tension and anxiety were the companions of everyone contemplating the trip to Philadelphia, particularly for Newton. Since 1967, the "Free Huey" campaign had mobilized and amalgamated diverse constituencies from around the country (and the world). Within a few years of its founding in 1966 (during most of which Newton sat in prison), the BPP became the "most influential revolutionary organization in the US."[14] More ominously, J. Edgar Hoover labeled them the greatest threat to the internal security of the country. The FBI and local police departments massively assaulted Panther offices across the country. As police murdered Panthers, destroyed their offices, and arrested hundreds of them, a reaction against the FBI set in not only in the black community but among all minority groups, millions of college students, and the radicalized counterculture—all of whom descended on Philadelphia to support the Panthers. As a global uprising in 1968 swept the planet, the Panthers were best positioned (as the most oppressed in what Che Guevara called "the belly of the beast") to embody global aspirations to transform the entire world system. Delegates from local black groups and from an array of organizations—the American Indian Movement, the Brown Berets, the Young Lords, I Wor Keun (an Asian-American group), Students for a Democratic Society (the national student organization, with a membership of at least 30,000), the newly formed Gay Liberation Front, and many feminist groups—all regarded the BPP as their inspiration and vanguard. This extraordinary alliance constituted the RPCC, and they were able to unify and develop their future direction. Most remarkable of all, this diverse assembly was able to write down their vision for a free society.

Despite the massive police actions designed to scare people away from Philadelphia, thousands came. Various estimates of the numbers exist, none of which claims to be definitive. Hilliard says there were 15,000;[15] the Panther paper used numbers ranging from 12,000 to 15,000;[16] social scientist G. Louis Heath states that the plenary sessions on September 5 and 6 attracted 5,000 to 6,000 people (of whom 25 to 40 percent were white) but doesn't count thousands more who were outside and could not get in.[17] The *New York Times* declared there were 6,000 people inside with another 2,000 outside (about half of whom were white);[18] and the *Washington Post*, probably parroting the *Times*, later claimed 8,000.[19] People came from around the country, as spontaneously assembled groups rented buses. In at least two cities, people reported that these buses were suddenly canceled without explanation, compelling people to improvise rides. Twenty-two persons from East St. Louis in a three-car caravan were arrested and charged with firearms violations, and at least one New York Panther was arrested en route to Philadelphia.[20] Organizations and delegates from Florida and North Carolina made a notable impression, as did representatives from African liberation movements, Palestine, Germany, Colombia, and Brazil.[21]

When we arrived, rather than face police terror as we expected, we found the homes of African Americans opened to us, their churches hospitable refuges, and the streets alive with an erotic solidarity of a high order.[22] Signs in storefronts read "WELCOME PANTHERS," and five flags flew outside the convention center: in descending order, they were the Panther flag; the flag of the National Liberation Front of South Vietnam; the green, black, and red flag of black nationalism; the Yippie flag (green marijuana leaf on black flag); and a flag of Che Guevara. Evidently the Panthers had done a huge amount of planning for the event, as food was also provided for many people. Contrary to some accounts, armed expropriation was one tactic the BPP employed to feed everyone. Russell Shoats recounts how a fifteen-ton refrigerated truck with tons of frozen meats was commandeered and unloaded on the same day Panther squads robbed a bank.[23]

Some Party members were preparing and implementing the armed struggle, while others were organizing the planning session for the RPCC. On August 8 and 9, the planning group met at Howard University. Present were representatives of welfare mothers, doctors, lawyers, journalists, students, tenant farmers, greasers from Chicago, Latin Americans, high school students, gays, and concerned individuals.[24] Simultaneously, the Philadelphia black community unified in support of the convention. After the police raids Panther offices had been sealed, but people opened them back up on their own initiative. The Panther paper reported, "In North Philly, two rival gangs had made a truce. . . . They emerged 200–300 strong and when 15 carloads of pigs drove up and asked them who gave them permission to open up the people's office, their reply was 'the people,' and the police had to eat mud rather than face the wrath of an angry armed people.[25]

Registration on Friday and Saturday morning went off without police problems, and later on Saturday, people gathered for the plenary. Inside McGonigle Hall at Temple University, where the plenary sessions took place, a vibrant and festive atmosphere prevailed. We had won. The police had been unable to stop us. As waves of people accumulated, the hall swelled to its capacity, and anticipation grew. Panther security people indicated the speakers were about to begin. Suddenly, hundreds of gay people entered the upper balcony, chanting and clapping rhythmically: "Gay, gay power to the gay, gay people! Power to the People! Black, black power to the black, black people! Gay, gay power to the gay, gay people! Power to the People!" Everyone rose to their feet and joined in, repeating the refrain and using other appropriate adjectives: Red, Brown, Women, Youth, and Student. (Although the BPP officially supported "white power for white people" alongside all other powers to the people, the crowd in the gym didn't go there.)

The first speech was given by Michael Tabor, a young member of the Party who had written a pamphlet entitled "Capitalism plus Dope Equals Genocide" and was one of the twenty-one defendants in a New York conspiracy trial. Like Newton, Tabor had only recently been released on bail. At times brilliant and always charismatic, Tabor spoke for over two hours. He laid out how the present constitution was inadequate and had historically functioned to exclude and oppress "240,000 indentured servants, 800,000 black slaves, 300,000 Indians, and all women, to say nothing of the sexual minorities."[26] Tabor's keen analytical mind also took apart other illusions. At one point he listed the policies and actions of the U.S. government and reminded us that then-president Richard Nixon, fresh from invading Cambodia and daily bombing people in Vietnam, "made Adolph Hitler look like a peace candidate." His eloquent oration suddenly broke off as he gestured in the air and demonstrated how the fist—symbol of the radical movement—should be replaced with the thumb and forefinger in the shape of a gun. Following Tabor, speakers included Audrea Jones, leader of the Boston Panthers, and attorney Charles Garry, legal counsel for Newton and Seale (then in prison). In some ways, the break between sessions was more soberly focused, yet simultaneously more exhilarating. In the streets surrounding McGonigle Hall, Muhammad Ali, an "ordinary" participant, shook hands, signed autographs, and offered words of encouragement while other people talked with old friends or made new ones as they looked for a place to stay. All the while, hundreds discussed their coming task: to draft a new constitution for the United States. Jubilation alongside criticism, but nowhere fear or resignation.

That evening, Huey Newton finally appeared. Only released from prison on August 5 (exactly one month before the RPCC), he was a complete stranger to practically everyone present. We had demonstrated for his freedom, read his essays, and followed his trial, but few of us had heard him speak. So many of us had put energy into organizing for his release from jail that his ability to attend was itself regarded as the fruit of our labor, as a victory for the movement. Even for "much of the [Black Panther] Party membership on the East Coast, this was an opportunity to hear and see the man for whose freedom they had been endlessly working. For much of the rank and file attending the plenary session it was a sort of celebration of their victory."[27] Elated with our newfound power in the charged political atmosphere, our expectations of the eloquence of Newton's speech were stratospheric. In the month he was out, he had been a busy man, offering the National Liberation Front and Provisional Revolutionary Government of South Vietnam troops to "assist" them in their "fight against American imperialism"[28] and authoring a strident article in the Panther paper fully supporting gay liberation.[29] He warned men that if they had a problem relating to homosexuals as equals, it was a sign of their own male insecurity. In another public statement, he stressed the importance of an alliance with women's liberation. He was the Supreme Commander of the Panthers, a title later changed to

Supreme Servant of the People, and his orders to respect gays and feminists were essential to our unity. Newton's presence electrified the overflow crowd. Even though the hall was completely full, thousands more were outside trying to get in. Only the firm action of Panther marshals and a promise that Huey would speak twice kept the situation under control.[30] (His second venue, the Church of the Advocate, had 2,500 people inside and more outside.) When Newton finally arrived in McGonigle Hall, he strode onto the stage surrounded by a phalanx of security people, and the capacity crowd quieted without being asked.

Huey was everyone's hero, but once he took the microphone, we were stunned to discover he was not a charismatic speaker. In a high-pitched, almost whiney, voice he went on at length about U.S. history, using abstract analytic arguments:

> *The history of the United Sates as distinguished from the promise of the United States leads us to the conclusion that our sufferance is basic to the functioning of the government of the United States. We see this when we note the basic contradictions found in the history of this nation. The government, the social conditions and the legal documents which brought freedom from oppression, which brought human dignity and human rights to one portion of the people of this nation had entirely opposite consequences from [for] another portion of the people.*[31]

By the time he was done, our disappointment in him was already palpable, and in turn, he said that we were not ready for analytical thinking. "They're hung up on Eldridge's slogans and revolutionary talk," Huey told Hilliard immediately after his speech.[32] Unbeknownst to thousands of participants, Newton and Hilliard were totally alienated from what they called the "bogus Constitutional Convention." Unable to connect even with Huey's security people after his speech, the two top Panther leaders simply left the proceedings and partied at a stranger's house.[33] Newton never appeared at the Church of the Advocate.

The next day, people broke down into working groups to formulate and discuss proposals for a new constitution. If only for a few hours, representatives of all major constituencies of the revolutionary popular movement huddled together to brainstorm and discuss ideas for achieving our goals of a freer society. The form of the gatherings was slightly different than in 1787. Each workshop was led by Panther members, who also coordinated security contingents that ensured a trouble-free working environment. Panthers had also prevented the media from attending, fearing their presence would only make a circus of the proceedings. While many journalists complained about being barred from the plenary and workshops, the space created by the absence of media was too valuable to sacrifice to publicity. Here was the movement's time to speak to itself. Seldom do groups communicate with such a combination of passion and reason. Person after person rose and spoke of heartfelt needs and desire, of pain and oppression. As if the roof had been taken off the ceiling, imaginations soared as we flew off to our new society. The synergistic effect compelled each of us to articulate our thoughts with eloquence and simplicity, and the "Right on!" refrain that ended each person's contribution also signaled that the time had arrived for someone else to speak. An unidentified Panther later described how even the children had not been boisterous: "The children were to be for the three days like adults, infected with a kind of mad sobriety." The same author promised, "There is going to be a revolution in America. It is going to begin in earnest in our time. . . . To have believed in a second American revolution before Philadelphia was an act of historical and existential faith: not to believe in a new world after Philadelphia is a dereliction of the human spirit."[34] In describing the workshops, she/he went on:

*The pre-literate black masses and some few saved post-literate students were going to, fi-
nally write the new constitution. . . . The aristocratic students led by the women, and the
street bloods, they were going to do the writing. So there were the first tentative meetings,
led brilliantly by "armed intellectuals" from the Panthers. . . . In the schools and
churches—the rational structures of the past—the subversive workshops of the future met
to ventilate the private obsessions of the intellectual aristocrats and the mad hopes of the
damned.*[35]

As the time allotted for the workshops drew to an end, each group chose spokespersons
entrusted to write down what had been said and to present our ideas to the entire plenary's second session.

As is clear in the documents, differences of viewpoint were sometimes simply left
intact rather than flattened out in an attempt to impose a Party line.[36] Under more "normal" circumstances involving such a diverse collection of people in groups as large as
500 persons, screaming fights (or worse) might have been expected, yet these workshops
generated documents that offer a compelling vision of a more just and free society than
has ever existed. Alongside an international bill of rights and redistribution of the world's
wealth, there were calls for a ban on the manufacture and use of genocidal weapons, as
well as an end to a standing army and its replacement by "a system of people's militia,
trained in guerrilla warfare, on a voluntary basis and consisting of both men and women."
Police were to consist of "a rotating volunteer non-professional body coordinated by the
Police Control Board from a (weekly) list of volunteers from each community section.
The Police Control Board, its policies, as well as the police leadership, shall be chosen by
direct popular majority vote of the community." The delegates called for an end to the
draft; for prohibition on spending more than 10 percent of the national budget for military and police—a provision that could be overridden by a majority vote in a national referendum—and for proportional representation for minorities and women (two forms of
greater democracy missing from the U.S. Constitution). Universities' resources were to
be turned over to people's needs all over the world, not to military and corporate needs;
the billions of dollars of organized crime wealth was to be confiscated; there was to be
free decentralized medical care, sharing of housework by men and women, encouragement of alternatives to the nuclear family, "the right to be gay, anytime, anyplace," increased rights and respect for children, community control of schools, and student power,
including freedom of dress, speech, and assembly. Although there is one paragraph in
which *man* and *he* are used, the very first report of the workshops contained a mandate always to replace the word *man* with *people* in order to "express solidarity with the self-
determination of women and to do away with all remnants of male supremacy, once and
for all." As summarized by the BPP a week later:

*Taken as a whole, these reports provided the basis for one of the most progressive
Constitutions in the history of humankind. All the people would control the means of production and social institutions. Black and third world people were guaranteed proportional representation in the administration of these institutions as were women. The right
of national self-determination was guaranteed to all oppressed minorities. Sexual self-
determination for women and homosexuals was affirmed. A standing army is to be replaced by a people's militia, and the Constitution is to include an international bill of
rights prohibiting U.S. aggression and interference in the internal affairs of other nations. . . . The present racist legal system would be replaced by a system of people's
courts where one would be tried by a jury of one's peers. Jails would be replaced by community rehabilitation programs. . . . Adequate housing, health care, and day care would*

> *be considered Constitutional Rights, not privileges. Mind expanding drugs would be legalized. These are just some of the provisions of the new Constitution.*[37]

In the society at large, racism, patriarchal chauvinism, and homophobia; at the RPCC, solidarity, liberation, and celebration of difference. From this vantage point, the RPCC provides a glimpse of the break from "normal" life. It prefigured the kind of international system that was thought to best replace the current one composed of militarized nation-states and profit-hungry transnational corporations. Scholar Nikhil Pal Singh has noted that the RPCC "was an astonishing attempt to imagine alternative forms of kinship and community. . . . Liberation politics, as inaugurated and exemplified by the Panthers, in other words, was based less upon the defense of reified notions of identity than upon the desire to fracture a singular, hegemonic space by imagining the liberation of manifold symbolic spaces within the (national) territory, from the body, to the streets, a section of the city, the mind itself."[38]

The Philadelphia constitution's international bill of rights was one indication of just how much the legitimacy of patriotism was transcended. Structurally situated in the center of the world system, the popular movement's imagination expounded the contours of a new world—not simply a new nation. The twin aspirations of the global movement of 1968—internationalism and self-management—were embodied throughout the documents. The term *self-management* may not have been used in the documents, but its American version, *community control* was used in reference to schools, police, women's control of their own bodies, more autonomy for children, students, and youth. We did not attempt to create paradise, but rather to mitigate the structures of repression (police, racism, patriarchal authoritarianism, the military) that were the source of our unfreedom. We sought at least to go halfway to paradise, fully conscious that we will never be absolutely free. If we continually jump halfway to paradise, never reaching it, we nonetheless approach it.

Thirty years later, the RPCC could be thought of as the first national gathering of the Rainbow Coalition, originated by Fred Hampton in Chicago and popularized by Jesse Jackson's presidential campaigns. But it should not be confused with electoral politics, even though within that limited sphere, the idea of proportional representation, introduced by the Philadelphia convention, has since become part of many groups' understanding of how to better organize the United States.[39] In addition, the concept of a national referendum, part of the spontaneously generated constitution, also seems like an excellent innovation whose provision in the constitution would have meant that the war in Vietnam would certainly have come to a faster end.

Some of the demands today appear outlandish, particularly those related to drugs. After calling for "eradication" of hard drugs "by any means necessary" and help for addicts, the workshop on Self-Determination of Street People came to the conclusion: "We recognize that psychedelic drugs (acid, mescaline, grass) are important in developing the revolutionary consciousness of the people. However, after the revolutionary consciousness has been achieved, these drugs may become a burden. No revolutionary action should be attempted while under the influence of any drug. We urge these drugs be made legal. Or rather they should not be illegal, that is, there should be no law made against them."

Significantly, the RPCC position on drugs displays graphically that more individual freedom was part of the aspirations of the Panther-led bloc; that this impetus, while appearing to some as only concerned with minorities, actually formulated universal interests. No one should discount or trivialize the importance of the drug issue. As the primary symbolic vehicle used for the imposition of class rule and cultural hegemony, it affects hundreds of thousands of people daily. One in three male prisoners in New York was serving a drug sentence in 1997; nationally, that figure is six of ten women; and in

California, one in four male state prisoners (and four out of ten females) is doing time for drugs.[40] According to the FBI, there were 682,885 arrests for drugs in 1998, 88 percent for possession not for sale or manufacture, and since Clinton has been president, more than 3.5 million people have been arrested for drugs.[41] Given the existing system's abysmal failure to wage an effective "war on drugs," its continual enrichment of organized crime syndicates and CIA-connected covert operatives while thousands of users languish in jails, and the irrationality of alcohol's and cigarettes' legal status compared with the illegal status of marijuana, history's judgment may yet prove that the RPCC policies are more sane and prudent than those now in place.[42] In two European venues apparently unaware of the RPCC, the Panther position on drugs essentially appeared unchanged: in the 1970s, among Italian youth known as the Metropolitan Indians, and for over thirty years in Christiania, a countercultural community in Copenhagen.[43]

Panthers went on the attack against heroin dealers, confiscating cash and flushing their stash after giving them plenty of public warnings. In one of the more daring actions undertaken by movement activists, H. Rap Brown was captured by police after he was cornered on the rooftop of an after-hours club frequented by big dealers—a hangout he and others had sought to close. Ron Brazao, underground from a 1970 bust of the Panther Defense Committee in Cambridge, Massachusetts, was killed in a shoot-out with a dealer in Marin, California, in 1972. Other similar accounts lead to the inescapable conclusion that the movement's war on hard drugs cost too many casualties.

Comparing the Platform and the Constitution

Comparing the words of two men with those of thousands of people four years later could be thought of as unfair to either side. I must admit that Newton and Seale are heroes to me and always will be. Yet I want to emphasize (and I think Bobby Seale would agree) that the capability of "ordinary" people to organize and speak for themselves, to run their own institutions and manage all of their own affairs, can be astonishing. Within the constraints of the existing system, it takes moments of exhilarating confrontation with the established powers to lift the veil concerning people's capacities. In these moments of the "eros effect" everyday life in the hoped-for society of the future is prefigured. Unleashed from institutional masters and political bosses, spontaneous actions of millions of people become a potent force in national and local politics. Even when they fail to accomplish their immediate objectives, they can have far-reaching international effects as well.[44]

To be fair to Seale and Newton as well as to appreciate properly their individual historical roles means to place their program and platform at the beginning of a turbulent and rapidly changing historical epoch. Between the Oakland launch of the Party and the RPCC, four years of rapid change occurred, transforming the nation and the BPP as part of it. In the months after Philadelphia, Huey had a change of heart about the direction of the party, and he enunciated a new orientation, one he called intercommunalist.[45]

When held up against the RPCC documents, the 1966 program is timid, its vision limited. The program and platform contain no mention of international solidarity. While there is an understanding of "people of color in the world who, like black people, are being victimized by the white racist government of America," Third World people were coequal objects of repression; they had yet to become subjects of revolution. Nowhere in the platform is there a hint, for example, of Huey Newton's subsequent offer to send troops to the National Liberation Front of South Vietnam to assist them in expelling the United States. Nor are gay people's rights, the liberation of women, and proportional representation of minorities and women anywhere to be found in the 1966 documents. Not only is women's liberation conspicuously absent, but the idea of Panther women fighting as soldiers alongside the National Liberation Front, an idea insisted upon by Huey, was inconceivable in 1966.

Instead of exempting black men from military service, the RPCC calls for an end to a standing army. Rather than black prisoners receiving new trials within the existing system, all prisoners were to be judged afresh by decentralized revolutionary tribunals. The modest national reparations of forty acres and two mules for African Americans was superseded by international reparations and the redistribution of the planet's wealth. Table 1 summarizes the positions adopted in the two sets of historic documents.

As should be apparent, comparison of the political program of the BPP with the vision of the popular movement at the RPCC calls attention to the ways in which the movement itself surpassed the visionary capacity of its most heroic and historically prescient leaders and organizations (all of whom, despite their centrality to the movement, remain partial and fragmentary). I want simultaneously to emphasize, however, that unlike the amorphous RPCC gathering that produced no concrete organization or ongoing program, Newton and Seale were ready to act *and did act* immediately after they wrote the pro-

Table 1 *What the Black Panther Party Wanted, 1966–1970*

October 1966 Black Panther Party Platform (Black Nationalist phase of the BPP)	September 1970 Revolutionary People's Constitutional Convention (Revolutionary Internationalist phase of the popular movement)
Rights of Black people	International Bill of Rights
UN plebiscite to determine the destiny of the Black community	United States not a nation; no genocidal weapons; end to NATO, SEATO
Black men exempt from military service	No standing army; no draft; people's militia; return of all U.S. troops from around the world
End to robbery of the Black community	Abolish capitalism
Freedom for Black prisoners; new trials by peers	Freedom for all prisoners; decentralized revolutionary tribunals
Fifteen mentions of *man* in ten points	Replace *men* with *people*; encourage alternatives to nuclear family; support for women's and gay liberation
Forty acres and two mules	Inernational reparations
Education teaching the "true nature of this decadent American society"; student power	Community control of education; Proportional representation; national referenda

gram. Even in comparison to the previous year's conference against repression that the Panthers had pulled together, RPCC participants were never asked (nor were some able) to make a long-term commitment.

The BPP was steel, standing firmly up to police barbarity, and the popular movement was water, rapidly flowing with the currents of popular consciousness and actions. More than any other U.S. organization in the latter half of the twentieth century, the BPP pushed ahead the revolutionary process, and this dialectical synchronicity of popular movement and revolutionary party, the interplay between the two, their dependence on each other and mutual amplification, accelerated and reached its climax at the RPCC. Even the purest steel will explode as water contained within it turns to steam. As the movement spontaneously surged in militant and unforeseen directions, the Panthers, unable to hold the disparate forces together, burst asunder from the pressure of the popular impetus from which it originated—and whose development it had accelerated. In many cities, Panthers and others responded to police repression by taking up arms and meeting the enemy with gun in hand. In 1970, the popular impetus from below involved millions of people, but as historical events turned into war against the police, the space for popular mobilizations and political engagement collapsed. Simultaneously the dynamic tension among the various tendencies contained within the BPP proved too much, and the organization exploded from within. Inside one vanguard party, there had been many conflicting directions: formation of armed groups or consolidation of a legal political party; autonomy for African Americans or leadership of an emergent rainbow; a black nation plebiscite or an international bill of rights. As long as it was tied to a vibrant popular movement, the Party's various tendencies had been able to coexist.

All movements experience rises and declines. The Philadelphia convention expressed the apex of the popular insurgency we call the 1960s movement. For thousands of us who participated, it became the pivot around which mutual synergy, celebration of difference, and most importantly, unity in the struggle turned into their opposites: mutual self-destruction, internecine warfare, and standardization in the ranks. When Newton and Hilliard left the plenary after Huey's speech, no one knew it at the time, but the high point of the movement had passed. The stage was set for the subsequent split that tore the BPP (and the movement) apart. Although Huey would later disclaim any responsibility for the "crazy Constitutional Convention" and would see it as part of Eldridge's misdirection of the party, the Panther program Huey wrote had pointed toward the RPCC. Although Newton could not understand it, Cleaver's implementation of the Panther program was part of his desire to follow the leadership of Newton[46]—not, as subsequently maintained, an attempt to overthrow him. In his memoirs, Hilliard tells us that Huey thought his original vision ran completely counter to "Eldridge's plan to create a national popular front with this crazy Constitutional Convention.[47] The division of opinion on the RPCC was used by the FBI as a means to initiate the split between Huey and Eldridge. The Los Angeles bureau wrote a memo recommending that "each division which had individuals attend [the RPCC] write numerous letters to Cleaver criticizing Newton for his lack of leadership . . . [in order to] create dissension that later could be more fully exploited."[48]

The Fate of the Philadelphia Constitution

The idea behind the RPCC was that there would be a two-step process, first drafting and later ratifying the new constitution. After being warmly accepted by the 5,000 to 6,000 at Sunday's plenary, the documents produced in Philadelphia were supposed to be circulated by a "continuance committee" that formed on Monday. Then discussions at the local level (as well as among the party cadre and leadership) were to lead to a second gathering, originally scheduled for November 4 in Washington, D.C. This second convention was to consider ratification and implementation of the final document. The date of the second convention was changed to Thanksgiving weekend (November 27, 1970). When thousands of people (7,500 according to one estimate)[49] arrived in D.C., however, they were sadly disappointed when the convention failed to materialize. Apparently the Panthers refused to pay the full rent for use of several buildings at Howard University, where the plenary was to have transpired.[50] No meeting occurred on the first night, and Newton told those who attended his speech the following evening that they had a "raincheck" for another convention to be held after the revolution. He subsequently made clear that he had had a change of mind about the wisdom of continuing with the new constitution as well as with the entire idea of building the broad alliance into a hegemonic bloc capable of leading the whole society forward.

Rather than allow the insurrectionary impulse to continue, Newton systematically undermined and blunted the revolutionary initiative and aborted the multicultural alliance the Panthers had built as part of the Free Huey campaign. In a manner reminiscent of Stalin's treatment of Trotsky, every form of political deviation from Huey's new line was blamed on Cleaver. Huey closed down nearly all chapters of the BPP and concentrated cadres in Oakland, where he could personally supervise them. He claimed ownership of the Party, copyrighted the newspaper, and even had Bobby Seale whipped to assert his autocratic control.[51] Insisting it go "back to the black community," he also confined the Party's public actions to maintenance of Oakland's survival programs and electoral politics. With these revisions underway, Newton secretly tried to control Oakland's drug trade and fell into drug addiction. All that was left was for time to take its toll before the Panthers as an organized force were history.

There were many reasons why the BPP leadership changed their goals and distanced themselves from the movement's publicly formulated aspirations at the RPCC. Under murderous attack across the country, the Party was on the defensive, its leaders scattered in jails or in exile. From these isolated positions, key leaders were far away from the rapidly transforming popular initiatives that accomplished more in weeks than history usually accomplishes in decades (throwing off the shackles of sexism and homophobia, racism and authoritarianism, forging a new popular space for action). The centralized Leninist organizational form of the Panthers also made the Party's leadership more vulnerable to disruption by the police, not less. Locking up, murdering, and sending into exile a dozen or so individuals incapacitated the central committee and the Party. When the BPP's centralized structure fell into the hands of David Hilliard, the only member of the top leadership left in Oakland, authoritarian tendencies multiplied. Even though the popular movement and most cadres initially supported him, many in the Party bitterly resented his heavyhanded imposition of order. Along with his brother June, he forced implementation of directives that were never discussed, and the primacy of Oakland enervated emergent leadership around the country. When Huey came out of jail, the Supreme Commander intensified central control and became the chief enforcer of party discipline.

The RPCC's amorphous fluidity contradicted the rigid structure of Panthers. Its constituencies were so diverse and scattered, however, that while the Panthers were able to unite and inspire us, their organizational form was insufficient to hold us together—even if they had been able to formulate a collective will to do so. Soon after the D.C. fiasco, the Panthers bloodily split apart along much the same lines as SDS and most other movements in the world in the same period (strident insurrectionism vs. a more sedate community-based orientation). As the movement split, the system simultaneously destroyed the most radical advocates of revolution (George Jackson, the Attica inmates, the Black Liberation Army) while reforming itself to prevent in advance the conditions for further popular mobilization. While individuals from the broad array of constituencies at the RPCC continued to work with the Panthers, the popular movement never regained its amazing unity and synergy.

As the movement disintegrated, the Philadelphia constitution was apparently tossed on the dustbin of history—or was it? United in Philadelphia, the popular movement's vision continues to animate action. In the three decades since the RPCC, millions of people have acted to implement various portions of the Philadelphia constitution. In the 1970s the feminist movement initiated a campaign for one of its provisions—equal rights for women and men. In the 1980s, the disarmament movement sought another: a ban on the manufacture and use of genocidal weapons. But the most impressive actions in response to Philadelphia were undertaken by the prisoners' movement that swept the United States in the months after the Philadelphia convention. From California to New York, imprisoned Americans like no other constituency were activated by the movement's call for justice. As inmates demanded decent, humane treatment, a wave of rebellions swept through the nation's prisons, culminating in the uprising at Attica State Prison in New York in which forty-three people were killed almost exactly one year after the RPCC.

Many of the RPCC's ideas have already stimulated subsequent social movements, and they will probably do so again in the future. If just two RPCC provisions were enacted—proportional representation and a provision for national referenda—the current political structure would be far more representative of the entire population. As the "rationality" of the existing world system as a whole becomes increasingly unreasonable, the reasonability of the decentralized, self-managed forms of governance advocated by the RPCC will receive renewed attention.

If not for the split in the party and the disintegration of the movement, who can gauge in what direction this hegemonic bloc might have led? Who can be certain where the 1960s upsurge might have ended? Like a baby learning to speak, the revolutionary movement of 1970 was immature—unprepared to provide long-term responsible leadership capable of leading the whole society forward. Unable to reach the second stage of struggle—consolidation of the revolutionary impetus—it split into thousands of pieces.

Three decades later, the RPCC remains unexplored, a unique event that sparkles with insight from the hearts and minds of thousands of participants who represented millions more in 1970. At the beginning of the twenty-first century, the phenomenal pace of change accelerates, and shifting group identities, changing affiliations, atomization, and detachment characterize the daily life of many nations. Since these postmodern elements make it problematic to focus on groups that provide universalistic vision, we might be led to the conclusion that the RPCC represented the last of the great public gatherings of modernity—instead of a precursor to our multicultural future. It was both—and in so being, became the hinge around which this entire historical period moved.

11

The Influences of the Black Panther Party (USA) on the Vanguard Party of the Bahamas, 1972–1987

John T. McCartney

Most scholars of the modern civil rights movement date its existence from the Montgomery bus boycott of December 1955, started by Ms. Rosa Parks, to the death of Dr. Martin Luther King Jr. in 1968. King was selected to direct the boycott that followed Ms. Parks's action, and subsequently a nationwide antisegregationist movement developed in which King played a prominent role until his death. After King's assassination, the movement declined. There is much debate as to why this is so, but most analysts see the passage of the Civil Rights Act of 1964, "creating the Equal Opportunity Commission and ending discrimination in public accommodation," and the Voting Rights Act of 1965, which ensured the protection of Black voting rights, as fulfilling two fundamental goals of the movement and as such contributing to its demise.[1] In any case, even before King's assassination, it was clear that the movement had lost much of its momentum. Another reason advanced for the decline of the civil rights movement was the realization by many Blacks by the late 1960s that their ability to participate fully in the political process did not translate into earthshaking social and economic gains. Despite a decade and a half of vigorous protest, in 1965 the problems of inferior schooling, unequal criminal justice application, bad housing, and de facto segregation, especially in the northern urban centers, had intensified.[2] The frustrations in the North resulted in a series of urban riots that started in the Watts area of Los Angeles in 1965, continued sporadically over the next few years, and reached their height in the wake of Dr. King's murder on April 4, 1968. King's assassination set off disturbances in more than 100 cities throughout the United States. It was in the context of the deteriorating urban centers of the mid-1960s that the Black Panther Party for Self-Defense was founded in the fall of 1966 by two black youths, Huey P. Newton and Bobby G. Seale, in Oakland, California. Newton and Seale were named Chairman and Minister of Defense of the Party, respectively.

The Vanguard Party

The decade of the 1960s was also one of change in the Bahamas, America's closest offshore neighbor, situated less than thirty miles off the Florida coast at their closest point. In 1966, in this British colony of 250,000, where a White minority of 10 percent dominated political and economic affairs for nearly 300 years over the Black majority, the

Progressive Liberal Party (PLP), a political party that had campaigned for majority rule since its formation in 1953, won a tenuous majority in the local assembly through the support of two independent legislators, one Black and the other White. The shift to majority rule was consolidated in 1967 when in the new general election, the PLP won a convincing majority over the opposition United Bahamian Party (UBP), which represented White minority interests. The Bahamas went on to gain independence from Britain in 1973. Ironically, the Vanguard Nationalist and Socialist Party (VNSP) was formed in 1972, six years after the attainment of Black majority rule, to combat the deteriorating social and economic conditions that were occurring in the Bahamas, especially in the urban areas. (The Black Panthers faced a reverse demography in the United States.)[3] In this article, I will compare the Vanguard and Black Panther Parties' ideologies and programs and illustrate how the latter influenced the former.

Landmarks in the Social, Economic, and Political Development of the Bahamas

Bahamian economic history shows that as a result of remaining a British colony for over 300 years, the Bahamas developed an economy that is not only dependent but often parasitic, relying on the misfortunes of others just to function. The parasitism is exemplified by the important roles played by piracy and the scavenging of ships in the economy in the seventeenth and eighteenth centuries, by smuggling resources into the Confederate states during the American Civil War, by hauling illegal liquor into the United States during Prohibition, and by the transshipment of illegal drugs into the United States in the 1980s. From the turn of the twentieth century until the 1960s, the White mercantile elite minority, through their control of the economy, profited enormously from both parasitic and nonparasitic activities like tourism. When the Vanguard Party was formed in 1972, it vowed to alter this economic dependency and parasitism.

Because of their control of the Bahamian economy, the White minority controlled Bahamian politics until 1967 and dominated public life. Their political supremacy was maintained by methods such as gerrymandering parliamentary seats, retaining a "property vote" in which a man could vote not just once, but for every piece of property owned by himself, and by withholding the vote from women until 1962.[4] Their political power enabled the white merchant minority dubbed the "Bay Street Boys"—so called because their businesses were located on the nation's business center, Bay Street—to own the Bahamian economy almost literally. They controlled banks, food stores, major construction companies, shipping, docks, and major law firms, and what they did not control, they owned. Their economic and political power was buttressed by racist educational and social policies designed to assure the continuance of white supremacy. However, as popular opposition to the Bay Street Boys increased, the British government, which had overall control of the Bahamas, sometimes intervened to correct the worst abuses.[5]

Party politics started in the Bahamas in 1953 with the formation of the multiracial but mostly Black PLP, and in response the White minority created the UBP in 1956. The PLP was founded by a group of middle-class Bahamians that included accountant Henry Milton Taylor, journalist Cyril Stevenson, real estate broker William Cartwright, businessman Samuel Carey, and farmer-teacher Felix Russell, among others. Originally led by Taylor, by 1956 the PLP was headed by a British-trained lawyer, Lynden Pindling, who the party's founding fathers felt could relate to the masses more effectively than themselves.[6] The UBP was controlled by a white lawyer, Stafford Sands, who represented its extreme right wing and who was staunchly committed to the racist status quo. After the introduction of party politics, the UBP continued to win elections until the PLP-led coalition government of 1966 ended their control of the legislature. As stated earlier, in 1967 the PLP won an outright majority and became the government.

The Promise and Contradictions of Black Majority Rule

In 1967 a minority of Whites and Blacks feared majority rule, but the Bahamian masses felt that a golden age was in the offing, especially since the transformation was achieved through the ballot and by nonviolent means. When the PLP won, the average Bahamian believed that in the future there would be an end to indignities like racism, a restrictive secondary educational system that accommodated only 2 percent of the pupils, limited access to bank loans for Blacks, a regressive tax system based on the collection of customs duties, and difficulty in acquiring and purchasing government land. The mood of optimism engendered by the PLP's victory was comparable to that felt by African Americans on Emancipation Day, January 1, 1863. In fact, Frederick Douglass's description of the way the African Americans of Boston and their supporters welcomed emancipation captures perfectly the mood of expectation that struck the Bahamian masses in 1967: "The effect of the announcement was startling beyond description, and the scene was wild and grand. Joy and gladness exhausted all forms of expression, from shouts of praise, to sobs and tears. My old friend Rue, a colored preacher, a man of wonderful vocal power, expressed the heart-felt emotion of the hour, when he led all voices in the anthem, 'Sound the loud trimbrel o'er Egypt's dark sea, Jehovah hath triumphed, his people are free!'"[7] Unfortunately, as in the United States, so too in the Bahamas, future events were to write a different script.

PLP Government in the Bahamas from 1967 to 1992

At first, it seemed as if the PLP government would fulfill the people's expectations, for in the first three years of its first five-year term it upped the school-leaving age, built scores of secondary schools, integrated the top levels of the civil service and government, and widened access to financial institutions and so on. However, after this promising start, the policies of the government became so regressive that by 1970 critics began to describe it as a Black version of the UBP. Despite the growing criticism, the PLP soundly defeated its major opposition, the Free National Movement (FNM), in the elections of 1972. (The FNM was made up of PLP dissidents who opposed Prime Minister Lynden Pindling's increasingly authoritarian control of the party and UBP interests).

In what ways had the PLP transformed itself from a mass democratic party in 1967 to an authoritarian patronage machine by 1970 and beyond? The party squandered public funds on prestige projects that mainly benefited their supporters, filled the public service with party hacks, struck deals with shady foreign investors and casino operators, and made peace with members of the white minority who allied with them but tried to crush those members of the minority who did not. Even worse, the Pindling regime continued the white minority's hateful practice of victimizing and ostracizing Bahamians who spoke out against its policies. In fact, some argued that the repression of the PLP was more totalitarian than the white minority's.

Furthermore, social and economic indicators documented the continued subjugation of the Bahamian masses. For example, the Bahamas had an income distribution far worse than the U.S. and most developing countries. As one study put it, "Of every $100 earned in the Bahamas, the poorest fifth received only $2.90, while the richest fifth received $50.00. This means that over half of all income goes to the richest 20% of the people." Also, the study revealed that in the World Bank's category of high income developing countries, in which it places the Bahamas, "The highest 5% receive 16.1% of income (compared to 20.8% in the Bahamas) and the lowest 20% received 6.6% of the income compared to 2.9% in the Bahamas. And the Bahamas also fares badly when compared with many Caribbean countries, including Barbados, the Dominican Republic and Guyana."[8]

In spite of the deteriorating conditions, the Pindling regime, especially because of its skillful use of the race card, remained in power until 1992. When challenged, Pindling, now the maximum leader, would constantly warn his supporters that if he were defeated there would be a return to white minority rule. The blatant appeal to race resonated with the Black masses, who did not see a trustworthy nonracist alternative to the PLP until the Vanguard Party was founded in 1972. In effect, by 1972, the Bahamas had moved from white minority colonialism to the neocolonialism of Black majority rule under the PLP. It was in this atmosphere of authoritarianism and social paralysis that the Vanguard Party was formed.

The Vanguard Party: Origins, Program, Development, and General Influences of the Black Panther Party

In the PLP's first term the chief group outside of Parliament that expressed opposition to the government was an organization called "One Community" (UNICOM), made up largely of Bahamian college students and graduates. UNICOM was an important organ of criticism, but by 1971 it became clear that not just a civic organization but a political organ that could challenge for state control was necessary to defeat Pindling and transform the nation into a genuine democracy. Most UNICOM members were reluctant to form a political party, but a wing of the organization that included Dr. John McCartney (professor at Purdue University, USA), Wallis Carey (businesswoman), Lionel Carey (businessman and economist), and Charles Fawkes (journalist) decided to form such a party. Subsequently, a significant number of youths, intellectuals, community activists, and workers joined them in forming the Vanguard Party.

Philosophically, the organizers of the Vanguard viewed the Party as a new type in Bahamian society, since its ultimate goal was not just the attainment of state power but to use the latter to empower the Bahamian people in such a way that competitive parties based on class interests, including the Vanguard, would become unnecessary eventually. In other words, the Vanguard's measure of final victory would be its own negation! Black Panther leader Huey P. Newton expressed the notion of party negation well when comparing the spiritual mission of the Christian church and the secular vision of the Panthers. According to Newton, in Christian teachings, "as humans develop and understand more, they will approach God, and finally reach heaven and merge with the universe. I've never heard one preacher say that there is a need for the church in heaven; the church would negate itself!"[9] He went on to say that, as Panther programs empowered the people to gain control of their communities and the nation, like the church, "We [the Black Panther Party] will negate our own necessity for existing!"[10] In short, the Vanguard Party saw as its mission the creation of a new Bahamas, not the re-creation of a version of the old.

Programmatically, the founders envisioned the party serving the nation in a variety of ways. First, it aimed to be an organization led by courageous, principled, and disciplined

Bahamians who would openly oppose the neocolonial practices of the Pindling government. In the Bahamas, the average citizen was fearful of speaking out, and the Vanguard would serve as their voice until they lost that fear. Second, it would establish branches in every community to assess the needs of the grassroots and establish a party newspaper called the *Vanguard* to articulate those needs. Third, the party would serve as a forum for the political education of the people and establish a school to train leaders regardless of their literacy levels. In this regard, the party emphasized the training of women leaders, for it was committed to bringing women and their concerns to the forefront of national life. Fourth, the Vanguard would establish programs and propagate teachings to instill cultural pride and patriotism in all citizens, but especially the Black masses who had been super-suppressed. However, party membership was open to every race because the problems afflicting Blacks affected citizens of every creed, color, or ethnic group in the nation. It is because of the latter condition that the Vanguard declared itself a nonracial party committed to fighting all exploitation of human by human. It should be noted that Black Panther leader Newton, in defending the willingness of his party to forge multiracial alliances, expresses a nonracialism that is roughly similar "We [the Black Panthers] do not suffer in the hang-up of skin color. We don't hate white people, we hate the oppressor, and if the oppressor happens to be white then we hate him. When he stops oppressing us then we no longer hate him!"[11] Fifth, the party advocated a mixed economy in which an activist state could assure mass economic gains and ensure that economic opportunity was open to all. Furthermore, the Vanguard's planners were convinced that a mixed economy was needed to lay the groundwork of a self-reliant and nonparasitic economy. Sixth, the party advocated the introduction of a graduated income tax, both to give the state access to enough resources to modernize the country and to help instill a sense of patriotism and fairness in the people. Seventh, the party pledged to change the Westminster model of parliamentary democracy that had produced one-party despotism in the Bahamas. Under this system, governments must be elected every five years, but the system lacks real checks on the party that governs between elections. The Vanguard advocated a federal model of government, in which strong local government would check the central government, and where initiative, referendum and recall would be used as tools to advance democracy. Eighth, the Vanguard pledged to create a system of quality mass education from primary school through college, that would not only expand the skill and information base of the community, but also teach models of democratic living. Such people orientated instruction would instill in the masses the psychological strength to empower themselves and run the nation. Ninth, the party was dedicated to upholding civil rights like religious freedom, free speech, and so on, for empowerment is impossible where rights are repressed. Tenth, having witnessed the Bahamas suffer from colonialism and neo-colonialism, the party pledged to combat these evils and the imperialism that spawned them, worldwide. In fact, the planners stressed that only in a world free of imperialism could the empowerment of the Bahamian people be assured. After months of consultations, the Vanguard Party was launched officially in the summer of 1972.

Concrete Influences of the Black Panther Party on the Vanguard Party

The Context

When the Vanguard Party was formed in 1972, three alternate paths to development had emerged in the Caribbean: Michael Manley and his experiment in democratic socialism in Jamaica, 1972–80; Forbes Burnham and his Cooperative Socialism in Guyana, 1966–85; and the socialist model of Fidel Castro that had existed since the 1959 Cuban revolution. The Vanguard's planners examined these experiments to see if they had useful lessons for the struggle in the Bahamas, and simultaneously analyzed the ideology, program, and practice of the Black Panther Party.[12]

A study of Fidel Castro's Soviet-influenced path to socialist development revealed that Cuba had made significant gains in health, education, employment, and so on, but the model had limited relevance to the Bahamas, where governmental change had come through the electoral process and not by violent revolution as in Cuba. Furthermore, in the Bahamas there was still a strong loyalty to Anglo-American social and economic forms, despite their limits, so the Vanguard's mode of struggle had to reflect a different reality.[13] In 1972 Michael Manley and his Peoples National Party (PNP) came to power in Jamaica, and for the next five years advocated a nonaligned foreign policy and internal development through democratic socialism. Elements of the Manley model, particularly its commitment to an activist state, triggered the Vanguard's interest, but the practice of the PNP was not as relevant. For example, the PNP was a mass party that had been in existence since 1938,[14] while the Vanguard hoped to develop into a mass party in the future. Finally, there was Forbes Burnham's attempt to create the Cooperative Socialist Republic in Guyana in which the state sector, popular mobilizations, and a private sector, working jointly with the state, would establish an economy based mainly on cooperatives in the future. However, Burnham's alleged racist politics, the alleged charges of human rights violations for which he was frequently cited, and the widespread belief that his 1977 declaration of the "state paramountcy" of his party, the Peoples National Congress (PNC), was "a thinly disguised proclamation of dictatorship" made the model unattractive in most aspects.[15] As the deliberations deepened, the Vanguard's planners concluded that the Black Panther Party—because of its base in the U.S. urban centers, its focus on the problems of the Black underclass, its having to function in a capitalist democracy with a notion of rights, its commitment to develop black pride in a multiracial context, and the fact that it was *seeking power* and not a party *already in power* like the others—was the most attractive pedagogical source.

An examination of the Vanguard's theory and practice as it developed over the years shows that it was influenced by the Black Panther Party in six concrete ways. First, the Black Panther Party's requirement that members be uniformed and abide by rules of conduct impressed the Vanguard's planners. Especially when an organization is attempting to deal with the problems of the underclass, whose members often lack social skills, uniforms and rules of conduct are excellent means to foster discipline and a sense of pride, and provide an egalitarian spirit. As a result, in the initial four years of the Vanguard's existence, uniforms were worn at public party functions. By 1976, after the party had become a recognized force, the practice was deemed unnecessary and stopped, but the Vanguard retained the rules of conduct throughout its existence. In this connection, the Black Panther Party's wearing of uniforms was also used to signal to the police authorities that a visible force would shadow their behavior in Black communities. However, the Vanguard Party functioned in a nation where guns were not carried even by policemen, so the police brutality and law enforcement issues that were major concerns of the Black Panther Party were not pressing issues in the Bahamas at the time.

Second, the Vanguard saw as insightful the Black Panther Party's Ten Point Program, which encapsulated the aspirations of the community in short and understandable forms. The Vanguard Party emulated this system, and its Ten Point Program proved an effective means of educating both members of the party and the public at large about the party's goals. A comparison of the Ten Point Programs of both parties shows that points 1, 2, 4, 5, and 10 of the Black Panther Party's program, which call for full employment, quality education, decent housing, and an end to racism, are reflected in the Vanguard's. However, points 3, 6, 7, 8, and 9, which focus on police brutality, the draft, and the criminal justice system, were mostly irrelevant to the Bahamian situation.[16] (In 1979, the Vanguard Party expanded its Ten Point Program into a party text, *The Struggle for Freedom in the Bahamas,* a text that is still viewed by many citizens as the most comprehensive analysis of the challenges facing the nation.)

Third, the members of the Vanguard were impressed by the quality, scope, and effectiveness of the Black Panther Party's newspaper, the *Black Panther,* as a source of information, education, and humor, especially for the youth of the underclass. In 1975 the Vanguard Party commenced publication of its newspaper, the *Vanguard,* and by 1979 it had become a popular source of news and inspiration for many Bahamians. Closely connected to the newspaper was the Vanguard Party's cadre school for training officers, which was started in 1977 as a local adaptation of the Black Panther Party's "liberation school" concept. As with the Black Panther Party, the Vanguard Party's officer trainees were required to sell the newspaper as a demonstration of commitment.

Fourth, the Black Panther Party advocated constitutional changes in America to further empower the average citizen, and the Vanguard called for similar changes in the Bahamas. For example, when the Black Panther leader Huey Newton spoke at the Revolutionary People's Constitutional Convention in Philadelphia in 1970, and called for constitutional change because the American masses were "waiting for a foundation of their own life, liberty and pursuit of happiness,"[17] he was articulating the disappointment of many Bahamians in the Westminster model of parliamentary democracy also.

Fifth, the Vanguard Party was dedicated to empowering the women of the Bahamas, and if it was to succeed in this goal, the party itself had to be a model for society. In 1975 the party opened its Women's Section, and the courageous voices of talented Black Panther women leaders, like Kathleen Cleaver, energized the women members of the Vanguard into asserting their rights both in the party and society at large.

Sixth, the Vanguard Party saw its fight against racism, colonialism, neocolonialism, and imperialism as an international struggle just like the Black Panther Party. Thus, when Huey Newton stated that the Black Panther Party's "struggle for liberation is based upon justice and equality of all men," he was articulating the exact sentiment expressed in point 10 of the Vanguard Party's program that deals with its international obligations.[18] It would be erroneous to conclude that the Vanguard Party was a mere clone of the Black Panther Party, for the Bahamian people's long history of struggle brought forth heroes and organizations that inspired the Vanguard Party in the first place. Furthermore, the Bahamas is linked to a Caribbean region that has produced many political leaders and intellectuals who have sought to initiate social change. The list includes Michael Manley (Jamaica), Eric Williams (Trinidad), C. L. R. James (Trinidad), George Weekes (Trinidad), Fidel Castro (Cuba), Juan Bosch (Dominican Republic), and Cheddi Jagan (Guyana), to name a few. These leaders and what they represent provided the Vanguard planners with comparative experiences from the region itself. However, despite its debt to the aforementioned, it is indisputable that the Vanguard Party's theory, program, and practice echoed those of the Black Panther Party more than any other organ seeking social change during this period. Marcus Garvey teaches that "one's nationality has nothing to do with great ideals and great principles"[19] and although the Black Panther Party's theory and practice were grounded in the experiences of urban America, they provided valuable lessons for the Vanguard Party in its struggle against neocolonialism in the Bahamas.[20]

The Demise of the Black Panther and Vanguard Parties

By the mid-1980s, a combination of internal splits, contradictions, and state repression had so enfeebled the Black Panther Party that by the late 1980s it had ceased to exist. However, its legacy of fearless confrontation against unjust authority, its politicization of the underclass, and its instilling of pride in so many of the oppressed still serve as inspirations to the downtrodden in present neo-liberal America. Similarly by 1986, the Vanguard's fourteen years of battling the neocolonial Pindling government in the press, elections, grassroots campaigns, demonstrations, and so on, in the face of continuing victimization and ostracism, led to a call from party leaders to recess, rethink strategies, and regroup. The regrouping failed to occur, and by 1987 the party was a memory. At the same time, although the Vanguard Party is defunct, its spirit is very much alive, for its efforts to mobilize the youth, its program for progressive change, and its open stand for justice in a society paralyzed by fear and caution continue to inspire Bahamians in dark times.

Table 1 *Abbreviated Version of the Ten Point Program of the Vanguard Nationalist and Socialist Party* (June 1972)

1. We believe in independence, but it must involve the restructuring of the society along democratic lines.
2. We believe in religious toleration, by which we mean the right of every individual to worship as they please.
3. We encourage the Bahamianization of religion, by which we mean (a) Bahamians control the churches and (b) a church that reflects the Bahamian way of life.
4. We believe in socialization of the means of production, by which we mean an economy controlled by Bahamians.
5. We believe in meaningful checks and balances in our political system.
6. We believe in effective local government.
7. We believe in mass education at all levels in a Bahamian context. Until such an educational system is devised, talk of nationalism is meaningless.
8. We believe that the educational system to prepare the citizens for their responsibilities should include social training, academics, vocational training, and the need for Bahamian self-help.
9. We believe in a culture that recognizes and promotes the experience of all groups in society.
10. We believe in and *support the struggles of oppressed people* throughout the world, especially the people who are struggling against colonialism and imperialism.

Source: The Vanguard Party, *The Struggle for Freedom in the Bahamas* (Nassau: The Vanguard, 1980), 44–45.

12

Cuba, the Black Panther Party, and the U.S. Black Movement in the 1960s
Issues of Security

Ruth Reitan

During the decade of the 1960s, racial and class tensions exploded in the United States. Revolutionary Black leaders gained international recognition and notoriety as the pacifist civil rights leadership of the 1950s and early 1960s yielded to the proponents of Black Power and militant nationalism. The Vietnam conflict and its progeny, the antiwar movement, were heating up, anticolonial guerrilla warfare was being waged around the globe, and Cuba became a lightning rod for both conflict between geopolitical rivals—the United States and the Soviet Union—and inspiration to those in struggle for radical change.

From the raucous inception of the regime, Cuban revolutionary leaders—Fidel Castro, Ernesto "Che" Guevara, and others—had an interest in exploring and then strengthening relations with the emerging militant leaders of the U.S. Black movement. Key players in forging this alliance were members of the Black Panther Party for Self-Defense. "The Black Panther Party was very present in the early years of relations with the Cuban Revolution," remembered Eldridge Cleaver, the Party's Minister of Information. "The Castro regime certainly believed there could be a U.S. revolution. The Panthers believed we were the vanguard action group that would lead by setting examples. And the Cubans never argued with us about our vanguard role. There was no *time* for arguments."[1]

Cuba was perceived as a natural ally by many within the burgeoning militant wing of the U.S. Black movement for a number of reasons: the revolution exemplified a successful eradication of "yanqui" imperialist control from an oppressed nation; Cuba bravely fought for the liberation from colonialism in Africa; the regime offered solidarity and support to both the civil rights leadership and urban revolutionaries; through its media, it internationally spotlighted racism in the United States; the regime promised to train U.S. militants in insurrectional tactics and weaponry; and it provided a haven for exiles. Perhaps most importantly for U.S. Blacks, Cuba claimed to have purged the scourge of racism from its society.

Yet conflict and confusion shook the alliance. An important element in the deepening of these relations and the conflicts these ties engendered is the issue of security—both individual Black leaders' safety concerns as well as the broader, national security issues facing the Cuban regime. In the final analysis, a complex interplay of factors both drew these leaders together and at times drove them apart. The most critical factor in dictating the parameters for these relations was the struggle within the Cuban leadership for ideological dominance and for the power to set security policy.

Two opposing factions emerged, centered around Che Guevara's revolutionary vision and active promotion of armed insurrection at one extreme, and those who were part of the more conservative, pro-Moscow leadership of the prerevolutionary Cuban Communist Party, called the Popular Socialist Party (PSP), at the other. This latter faction included PSP chief theoretician and lawyer Carlos Rafael Rodríguez, Secretary General Blás Roca, Director of Information Aníbal Escalante, Fidel's brother Raúl Castro, and the Minister of Interior under the Castro regime, Ramiro Valdés. These men took a more cautious approach to the Black nationalists and toward security policy in general.

Cuba's growing economic and military dependence on the USSR severely impeded the ideological development and autonomy of the Cuban government in establishing foreign policy and strengthened the hand of the pro-Soviet faction. This in turn led to an increasingly tepid view throughout the 1960s of the radicalizing U.S. movement. Despite deviations in policy decisions and propaganda throughout the decade, a definite trend emerged toward an orthodox Moscow-oriented ideology and national security position, antithetical to the original views of Guevara and Castro.

Guevara maintained his purist position and was thus forced from power by mid-decade, while Castro eventually either yielded to, in order to maintain power, or accepted the wisdom of the Soviet ideology and security dictates. This polarization into factions—with Castro taking up the middle ground only by passing through on his way to and from the extremes—made for erratic shifts in policy toward the U.S. movement.

Briefly, it will be argued that national security concerns placed limits on the solidarity and support that the Cubans were willing to provide, particularly as the pro-Moscow faction gained prominence around mid-decade. Relations with the United States, or rather survival tactics in the face of a powerful and hostile neighbor, were the source of these concerns throughout the 1960s. Overt threats from the U.S. military compounded with covert meddling and sabotage by the FBI and CIA added strain and an element of distrust to the relationship.

Intense debate within the regime centered around the best way to safeguard Cuba's national security: through active support for socialist revolution throughout the hemisphere (the Guevarist approach) or by closer ties with the Soviet Union and thus cooperating with agreements made between the superpowers (the traditional Cuban Communist Party approach). At the root of this debate were fundamental differences in revolutionary ideals.

The shifts in power and thus policy toward the Black movement affected the regime's willingness to grant asylum to U.S. exiles. The Cubans had to perform a dangerous political balancing act between their national security and their sympathy for oppressed Blacks when making these decisions. The most notorious, and thus politically dangerous, exiles for the Cubans to harbor—namely Eldridge Cleaver in 1968, party founder and minister of Defense Huey P. Newton in 1974, and East Coast party activist Assata Shakur in 1979—came from the Black Panther Party. All were escaping arrest and imprisonment in the United States and feared for their lives, and all were taken in by the Cubans. A forerunner of these fugitives was Robert Williams, who fled the United States in 1961 for the island. The exile experiences of Williams and Cleaver during the decade of the 1960s will be examined below.

The nature of relations with the U.S. Black movement, then, depended on which faction was influencing Castro directly and which held positions of power with the ability to set policy independently. Throughout the decade, policy toward the U.S.

movement was inconsistent and thus confusing for African Americans. A useful way to view these fluctuations is by examining the rise and decline of the influence of the two camps. By the second half of the decade, Castro was increasingly either seduced by or unable to halt the conservative pro-Moscow influence over security policy in Cuba.

Safeguarding Cuban national security—both economic stability and preventing or withstanding outside attack or internal counterrevolution—necessitated choosing one of the following: searching for rapprochement with the United States, bargaining with the USSR and China for the best comprehensive security pledges that would still allow a degree of independence, or embarking on a totally new path. The two opposing camps, outlined below, clashed over the best route to take to protect the regime and ensure the viability of the revolution.

The Guevarist Faction

Based on his experience in Cuba, his travels in Latin America, and his extensive theoretical studies, Guevara concluded that Cuba's national security would best be protected when all the nations of Latin America achieved economic and political independence. He therefore encouraged the forceful overthrow of the current capitalist and neocolonial governments throughout the hemisphere. A revolution in a country with a large economy, such as Venezuela, Argentina, or Brazil, was desperately needed to ensure the survival of socialist Cuba, which was becoming increasingly isolated. This isolation was due mainly to direct and indirect maneuverings by the United States and to policies of the Castro government, which antagonized the United States and Cuba's former allies in Latin America and elsewhere.

Guevara made no distinction between the Third and the First World (namely the United States) when supporting insurrection; Cuban security would be ensured by promoting revolution in every part of the world. Ultimately, his strict adherence to this security policy was the primary reason for his forced departure from power in Cuba.[2] Although the idea of a revolution in the United States in the early 1960s seemed remote, Guevara did not rule it out, and rather—at least theoretically—held it as a possibility as long as U.S. Blacks united in violent protest and the working class mobilized in support.[3] In Guevara's view, if revolution ought to be fueled anywhere it springs up, then flames of unrest in the "belly of the beast" should surely be fanned, since U.S. intervention was Cuba's primary security concern.

It is reasonable to conclude that Castro also supported Guevara's approach to Cuban security policy. Being the consummate politician that he is, Castro seemed to cast Guevara (possibly with Che's initial approval) as a formidable "extremist." This gave Castro some maneuvering room with the Soviets and the pro-Moscow forces within the regime and allowed him to portray himself as the accomodationist among all parties involved. As U.S. and Soviet pressure grew and constricted maneuvering space throughout the decade, Castro could then blame Guevara and his faction when violence failed and Che's (*not* Castro's) security policy yielded disappointing results. The death blow to this policy, and perhaps Castro's final step away from the Guevarist faction, was dealt in Che's failed insurrectional attempt and ultimate execution in Bolivia in 1967.

Guevara grew disenchanted with the USSR as he came to understand that true international solidarity and support for insurrection did not figure heavily into the Soviets' perceived national interests. Particularly after the 1962 Cuban missile crisis, Guevara became more and more wary of yielding to Soviet advice. As his frustration mounted, however, the influence of Cuba's pro-Soviet Communists increased over security policy.

Traditional Communist Party Faction

The pro-Moscow faction followed the Soviet lead and largely deferred policy decisions about relations with the United States and support for insurrectional struggles to the Kremlin. This was during the era of "peaceful coexistence" with the West, the Soviet view of the correct road to ensuring national security. Therefore, with regard to the U.S. movement, during the civil rights phase only general, verbal support was given to the pacifist leadership, since this stance would not threaten to jeopardize Soviet and Cuban attempts at rapprochement with Washington and could not be misconstrued as an attempt to meddle internally, which would surely risk retaliation.[4]

But late in the 1960s, when groups such as the Black Panthers began advocating armed self-defense and insurrection, the traditional Communists recoiled. This emerging radical stage of the U.S. movement posed a much greater threat to the facade of "revolutionary internationalism" behind which the conservative leaders hid. Robert Williams, and later Eldridge Cleaver, discovered that the "Bourgeois Communists," as Williams branded them, benefited from maintaining revolutionary rhetoric and official support of insurrection. This official stance was necessary lest their own people either demand truly progressive leadership that would remain faithful to the precepts on which the revolution was based, or call for a return to a consumerist society under which a decent standard of living could be afforded, since building the enlightened, socialist man would be exposed as having failed.[5] Revolutionary slogans pervaded the official Cuban media, encouraging Third World insurgents to wage armed struggle, during the middle and late 1960s. However, the pro-Soviet-dominated government tried hard to avoid acts that would in any way suggest to the U.S. government that the regime sponsored violence on the part of the Black revolutionaries.[6]

Nevertheless, Fidel—in a state of defiant nostalgia or frustration against the increasingly bureaucratized and conservative government—would fire off revolutionary proclamations in support of U.S. Black insurrection. The combination of the official radical propaganda and Castro's passionate pleas led many to believe that Cuba would still take risks to support the U.S. Black revolution; but from the perspective of the traditional pro-Moscow faction to which Castro increasingly subscribed, national security issues took precedence over the rhetorical revolutionary posture in the regime's actual decision making.

Two Divergent Policies Toward the U.S. Movement

The Black Panther Party platform represented the closest ideological fit of any U.S. militant organization with the Cuban rhetoric of class warfare and solidarity with the oppressed poor and people of color the world over. The Panthers were vocally supportive of the Cuban revolution, propagated a Marxist-Leninist ideology, and forged alliances with white progressives. Their Ten Point Program, "What We Want, What We Believe," called for land redistribution, community control of resources and police, decent housing, proper education, freedom, and self-determination. They opposed the Vietnam War as racist and pointed out the right of the people to end a government that has become destructive to the liberties of its citizens.[7] It appeared as though Havana could not have asked for a more willing ally within the U.S. movement.

Yet upon closer observation, the view of the role that the Black revolutionaries could play within the growing antiwar movement, as well as the hoped-for outcome of the entire U.S. struggle, was quite different between the two Cuban factions. The traditional

Communists determined that the objective conditions in the United States did not exist—nor could they be brought about by a small group of militants such as a vanguard Black Panther Party—to begin an insurrection. Therefore, since struggle based on ethnicity was seen as divisive and illegitimate, the best that the Black "proletariat" could do was be absorbed into the larger antiwar and workers' struggle.[8] In this way, the pro-Soviets hoped to force Washington's hand not to interfere in Cuban affairs.

The opposing belief was held by those within the regime who subscribed to Guevara's guerrilla *foco* theory.[9] The exile experiences of Williams and Cleaver revealed that the Guevarists were in fact hopeful that a Black vanguard would ignite the antiwar movement and push for radical change in the United States. The most idealistic hope was that an insurrection could take hold in the United States, led by the country's most oppressed people, the African Americans.[10]

The factional struggle to set security policy in the early years was evident throughout the many changes, challenges, and upheavals faced by the new regime. In June 1959, five government ministers resigned. Castro temporarily distanced himself from Guevara, who was considered too far to the left, by sending Che on his first tour of Africa and Asia.[11] After Castro consolidated his power, Che was appointed head of the Ministry of Industry within the National Institute for Agrarian Reform (INRA) and, soon after, president of the National Bank of Cuba.[12] Another governmental shake-up in early 1962 took place when hundreds of "Stalinist" Communist Party members were replaced in their government positions by "revolutionaries" from Castro's and Guevara's camp; two weeks later, the Soviet news organ *Pravda* finally acknowledged Cuba as a socialist country. In the aftermath of the 1962 missile crisis, pro-Moscow party members again lost credibility within the regime, but by 1964 it was apparent that Guevara's 1961 four-year plan of industrialization was failing, and thus a closer involvement with the Soviets would have to be pursued if the Cuban economy and revolution as a whole were to survive.[13]

Castro, caught in the middle of this factional debate, instinctually agreed with Guevara, yet he viewed the pro-Soviet path as the most pragmatic approach for resolving Cuba's immediate security crisis. "For Castro himself," asserted the author Carlos Moore, "the dependent relationship posed the problem of how Cuba could enjoy Soviet military protection and economic aid without becoming a mere Caribbean satellite of the USSR."[14] Therefore, a compromise between the two camps was apparently reached around mid-decade, most likely brokered by Castro, once again playing the role of accomodationist bridging the two "extremes": the traditional Communist Party's approach to security would be adopted toward the U.S. movement, but the Guevarist approach would still be attempted in the Third World. This two-tiered policy of insurrectional support allowed for a revolutionary stance toward those countries from which the Cubans did not fear retaliation, and a more cautious approach toward the First World, namely the U.S. revolutionary movement.

The pro-Soviets had effectively defeated the Guevarist approach to security with regard to the U.S. movement by 1965, before the birth of the Black Panther Party and the surge of revolutionary elements within the U.S. Black movement. That year Che disappeared and could not push for a more militant policy toward the United States. To seal the fate of the Guevarist faction, those closest to Che were either demoted, transferred to the provinces, or sent to Africa on international missions. But despite the triumph of pro-Soviet security policies, with respect to the U.S. movement, Cuba's official rhetoric did not change. Therefore, U.S. Black nationalists did not learn of the change in policy and priorities until they came face to face with revisionism in exile.

Black Leaders' Personal Safety Concerns amid Fluctuating Cuban Security Policy

Throughout the 1960s every U.S. Black leader was faced with issues of personal security. The FBI began its surveillance of the Southern Christian Leadership Conference (SCLC), its president, Martin Luther King Jr., and the Nation of Islam in the late 1950s; the Student Nonviolent Coordinating Committee (SNCC), a southern civil rights group that was later taken in a more militant direction by Black Power leader Kwame Turé (formerly Stokely Carmichael), was targeted for surveillance in 1960.[15] Efforts were stepped up in the first part of the 1960s against King, Malcolm X, Turé, and the Black Panther Party and escalated throughout the decade.[16] These leaders' cries against U.S. racism and imperialism were met with intensified surveillance as well as harassment and death threats. The fear of government-sponsored harassment and murder deepened after the controversial assassinations of Malcolm X in 1965 and King in 1968.

The FBI expanded its counterintelligence program (COINTELPRO) from surveillance and harrassment of Communists to include a massive offensive throughout the 1960s to divide, infiltrate, and essentially break the Black movement. FBI director J. Edgar Hoover described the Panthers, who became the main focus of the government assault, as posing "the greatest threat to the internal security of the country."[17] COINTELPRO used tactics including spying, wiretapping, burglaries, and infiltration to create disruption and paranoia within select radical groups. Other targeted organizations in addition to the Panthers included potential Arab terrorist groups, radical ethnic and student organizations, and suspected Soviet espionage groups such as U.S. Marxist parties.[18]

Racial violence wielded by private hate groups and individuals accompanied the official harassment. King's home was firebombed in 1956; Black churches were burned throughout the South; Blacks were fired from their jobs, evicted from their homes, and in many other ways terrorized so that they would not take up the cause of desegregation, let alone pick up a gun. In desperate reaction to this violence and repression, by 1967 cities throughout the country were ablaze with Black fury.

Cuba as Haven for Exiles

Many Black fighters sought exile in Cuba in response to this climate of harassment, violence, and ongoing threats to personal security, at times at the invitation of Castro himself. The reality of desperate exiles seeking refuge in an allegedly revolutionary state threw into sharp relief the debate between the Guevarist and pro-Soviet camps over the best strategy for national security. The limits to Cuban solidarity were thus tested throughout the decade and beyond by such leaders as Williams and the Black Panther Party's Cleaver, Newton, and Shakur, as well as other Black militants of all persuasions. In order to illustrate the erratic shifts in policy toward the U.S. Black movement springing from the conflict between the two camps over national security and ideology, two political exile experiences will be reviewed, one occuring early in the decade, the other at its close: those of Robert Williams and Eldridge Cleaver.

Robert Williams

Robert Williams, a southern NAACP leader and also an advocate of armed self-defense against white racial violence, was a radical leader of the early 1960s who inspired the Black Panther Party. He had been one of the first travelers to Cuba with the Fair Play for Cuba Committee, an organization established in the spring of 1960 to support the Castro-led revolution and to assist travel between the two countries.[19] Williams was an outspoken opponent of the Bay of Pigs invasion and other hostility against Cuba and soon became a target of FBI aggression. In August 1961 the bureau attempted to crush Williams's burgeoning self-defense organizations in North Carolina, which had been arming themselves in the face of mounting racial attacks.

Williams fled to Cuba in October of that year after a violent clash among white racists, the police, and the Freedom Riders, a direct action group organized by the inter-racial Congress of Racial Equality (CORE).[20] This clash led to an FBI warrant for Williams' s arrest on fabricated kidnapping charges and interstate flight. At the personal invitation of Castro, Williams was able to enter Cuba.[21] This escape led to the first highly publicized relationship between a U.S. Black leader and the Cuban government.

Within months, Williams had established a network for bringing more Black activists to the island via Canada. He also began broadcasting the pro-Castro radio show *Radio Free Dixie,* calling for a repeat of the Sierra Maestra insurrection to be mounted in the American South. He often spoke at public rallies with Castro as well as at private receptions for African delegations to the island.[22] Initially, Cuba's political climate was favorable to Williams's brand of militancy, since the Guevarist approach to security was still considered a viable option. At that time many within the regime, including Castro, were almost literally thumbing their noses at the United States and had not yet accepted their role within the mounting East-West conflict.

Williams was most anxious to discuss the militant tactics outlined in his book *Theory of Urban Warfare* with his new comrades. In it, he asserted that the vanguard Black revolutionaries would carry out an urban guerrilla campaign. However, it was this plan that would soon lead him to discover the disparity between Cuban revolutionary rhetoric and the actual actions many were willing to take on behalf of U.S. Black liberation; it was on this issue that he first clashed with pro-Soviet forces with regard to Cuban security.[23]

As the Cuban political climate grew more conservative over the next few years, members of the increasingly pro-Soviet DGI[24] and the Communist Party became unwilling to entertain a public discussion of Williams's tactics, particularly given the fragility of U.S.-Cuban relations following the missile crisis. When the leadership continually sought to dissuade his plans for a guerrilla *foco* in the southern United States, Williams grew frustrated.

Radio Free Dixie became another bone of contention. According to Cuban official Domingo Amuchastegui, the extremist views that Williams broadcast over Radio Havana could not be tolerated due to the risk of provoking U.S. retaliation.[25] The Cubans also discouraged Williams from drawing international attention to racial tensions in the United States and refused to strongly criticize the U.S. government's racism.[26] The pro-Soviets saw this as both destructive to the long-term solidarity of the U.S. working class and dangerous to Cuban security. With hindsight, it seems Williams would have fared better with the Cubans had he been a peasant in the Andes rather than a city dweller from the United States. To the pro-Moscow Cubans, the correct approach for the Third World was dangerous to attempt in the First World.

Nonetheless, in the early part of the decade Castro was very much in agreement with the Guevarist approach to national security and therefore eschewed the traditional

Communists' advice, instead granting Williams additional assistance in broadcasting his program.[27] Fidel attempted to help him on a number of occasions when the Communist stalwarts were sabotaging his broadcasts or disrupting the printing of his newspaper, the *Crusader.*[28] Castro also offered assistance in publishing Williams's book *Negroes with Guns.* But as the decade progressed, the pro-Soviets erected obstacles between Williams and his sympathizers within the upper echelon of the regime. One Communist Party USA (CPUSA) adviser working in Cuban radio at the time informed Williams, "Just remember, Fidel is way up there at the top and you are way down here at the bottom; and there are a lot of us in between who can mess you up very badly without him ever hearing about it."[29] The "bourgeois Communists" apparently worked in conjunction with the CPUSA to smear Williams and otherwise diminish his influence and reach throughout North America.

By early 1965 the general consensus within the regime was that Williams's inflammatory anti-Washington rhetoric was jeopardizing Cuba's security.[30] Williams came to suspect that certain members of the DGI and the government were actually working with U.S. intelligence to get him thrown out of Cuba and returned to the United States to face his criminal charges. Doing so would remove a major point of stress in U.S.-Cuban relations and could potentially be a move toward a guarantee of Cuban territorial integrity.

In April of that year, Che confided to Williams that the Guevarist security and ideological position was nearly defeated in Cuba. Che vehemently stated his total disagreement with the direction in which the Communist Party was steering the country as well as with its conservative approach to the U.S. Black Movement.[31] Within weeks of that meeting, the Guevarists were permanently removed from power, thus sealing Williams's fate in Cuba as well. The following year, he was not invited to the first Tricontinental Conference, held in Havana and organized by the Party for African, Asian, and American "revolutionaries." He therefore concluded that "as long as Cuba's leaders believed the only way for their nation to survive was to avoid seriously irritating Washington, there was no hope of their giving anything but hollow words of support to the Black liberation movement in America."[32] The revolutionary dynamic that Williams had fallen in love with at the dawn of the decade had been, in his mind, crippled by party elitism and the Cold War orientation toward national security.

As relations with the regime continued to deteriorate, Williams began to make plans for departing the island. He soon came to blows with the Cuban security forces. According to Cleaver, who spoke at length with Williams later in Tanzania, the "bourgeois Communists" closed down Williams's radio program, forbade him to print any more newsletters, and were forcibly moving him out of his apartment. Shots were allegedly exchanged in anger between Williams and the police, but no one was killed.[33] Soon after, three officials loyal to Castro visited Williams and begged him to reconsider his plans to leave. They said they realized that the government had lost some of its pure revolutionary ideals, but that Fidel needed people like Williams to stay and fight for the soul of the revolution. These men maintained that the most serious problem within the leadership at the time was that Castro was increasingly isolated and misinformed by the pro-Moscow advisers around him.[34]

Williams, however, knew that his battle lay elsewhere, in the liberation of his own people. He had also lost faith in Castro's ability to effect radical change, particularly after the purging of Guevara's influence from the regime. Although Williams felt Castro's heart was in armed struggle for liberation, he saw that what a man is willing to do as an individual and what he is able to do as head of state were radically different. Williams concluded that Cuba's degradation into a bureaucratized state necessitated the isolation of its revolutionaries, like Che and Fidel, since the existence of charismatic personalities had always posed a threat to the bureaucrat.[35] Therefore, for Castro to survive as the leader of Cuba, he had been either convinced of, or forced to accept, the pro-Soviet security dictates.

On July 17, 1966, Williams left Cuba for China, a place for which he still harbored revolutionary hopes and from which he expected support for U.S. Black liberation. He soon wrote a letter to Castro that was allegedly blocked from reaching him by Williams's enemies within Cuba; he therefore sent it as an open letter through press channels. In it he thanked Fidel for the Cubans' hospitality and pledged his support for the revolution, but said that he wanted to draw Castro's attention to certain revisionist leaders within the regime who posed a threat to the very survival of the Cuban revolution. He accused Major Manuel Piñeiro Losada, head of the DGI, René Vallejo, Castro's personal aide and physician, and Osmany Cienfuegos, Minister of Construction, of being thieves or worse.[36] This letter was Williams's final attempt to reach a leader he deemed increasingly isolated and misled into allowing reactionary policies to be implemented toward the U.S. Black movement due to misguided security concerns.

Eldridge Cleaver

As Williams's disappointed and frustration-filled departure from Cuba illustrated, security policy at the time of Cleaver's exile was largely under the control of the traditional Communist Party faction. However, these "bourgeois Communists" could not afford to give up the revolutionary facade perpetuated by bold phrases of official international solidarity and support for insurrection due to the domestic security ramifications. Consequently, asylum was granted to the Black Panther leader in late 1968.

Due to the mounting efforts of COINTELPRO to eliminate the Black Panthers and, more urgently, Cleaver's impending return to prison stemming from the April shoot-out with Oakland police, he secretly requested asylum in 1968 through a Cuban representative to the United Nations in New York. Cleaver asked for a special assurance from Castro himself that he would be received as a fugitive under Cleaver's own conditions.[37] Amuchastegui stated that after much debate on the issue of risking retaliation from the United States, the Cuban regime conceded.[38] Cleaver then received word through the Cuban mission in New York that Fidel granted him "safe passage, security, and help." In addition, Castro acknowledged that Cleaver would be in charge of organizing the start-up of a military training facility on an abandoned farm outside Havana that the Cubans had promised the Black Panther Party some time earlier.[39]

Cleaver and the Cubans agreed that his stay would be kept as discreet as possible. The Panther leader understood that if the U.S. government found out that the Cubans were harboring militant fugitives, it would be a good excuse to accuse the regime of meddling in U.S. internal affairs and thus attack the island either overtly or covertly. This was a deep concern for both parties involved and was discussed at length in the planning stages of Cleaver's flight into exile.[40] Following an arduous escape, Cleaver arrived in Havana on Christmas morning 1968.

But the initial relief of Cleaver's escape soon dissolved into ambivalence, frustration, and disillusionment in exile as he came face to face with the pro-Soviet-dominated regime. He was kept under close supervision by Major Piñeiro and Mr. Silva, who, when asked, dodged his questions of an exact date when the training facility could be opened and Panther Party members could begin coming to the island. In addition to these incessant delays in opening the facility, another major point of contention between Cleaver— along with the other exiled Black militants in general—and the Cuban government was the issue of the treatment of airplane hijackers.

"Air piracy," as it was officially branded, had become a chronic security threat for the Cuban leadership throughout the late 1960s and 1970s. From the onset the Cubans were trying to reach an accord with the United States over this issue,[41] which they eventually achieved in 1973. The risks to the Cubans were enormous, since they did not know if these planes were on a mission to attack the island (à la Bay of Pigs), CIA or FBI spies posing as U.S. dissidents, or genuine fighters fleeing the United States for political reasons.

There was justifiably some confusion and frustration for hijackers once they landed in Cuba: thinking they had reached freedom, they were instead greeted by security forces and jailed in the interim. The Cubans maintain, however, that this was standard and necessary procedure. They insist that the idea of Cuba as a welcoming haven for oppressed Black revolutionaries was correct to a point, but this welcome was never intended for those who resorted to air piracy as their means of transport.[42]

Cleaver criticized the regime over this internment process of U.S. hijackers as well the rumored inhumane treatment of imprisoned Cubans. The government in turn accused Cleaver of meddling in Cuba's internal affairs. Eventually his hosts admitted to Cleaver that they could not abide by their agreement to train the Black Panthers for two reasons. First, they had concluded that the Black movement had become too infiltrated by FBI and CIA agents, to the point where they didn't know who they could and could not trust. Training and arming the U.S. movement would pose a great threat to internal security due to the possibility of mistakenly arming undercover counterrevolutionaries, and it also threatened Cuba's national security due to the danger of U.S. intelligence learning of their assistance and thus feeling justified to attack. The second reason they gave was since Guevara's death, the policy of active assistance to liberation struggles had been discontinued. At the time, Cleaver took the Cubans at their word and believed that when they had initially promised the training facility to the Panthers a year prior, they had been genuine.[43] What seems most likely is that the Cuban representatives to the UN maintained a Guevarist approach to the U.S. movement longer than the majority of the leadership on the island did. Therefore, these representatives were still promising revolutionary support as late as 1967 or 1968 to Black militants in the United States, even though this practice had been deemed insupportable by the bulk of the regime in Havana by mid-decade.

In fact, throughout Cleaver's stay in Havana, the government attempted to redirect his revolutionary thinking away from armed struggle, since the pro-Soviets concluded that the conditions did not exist within the United States for it to even be considered. Furthermore, the Cubans understood that public statements from a top Black Panther leader emanating from Havana could have disastrous effects on the safety of the country. Amuchastegui asserted that in the late 1960s they were not willing to risk almost certain retaliation for *any* leader.[44]

The mystery surrounding Cleaver's disappearance from the United States was solved when a Reuter's reporter learned that the Panther leader was in Havana and confronted him at his apartment. Both Cleaver and the Cubans knew that the U.S. government might use the discovery as an excuse to retaliate. Cleaver was concerned for his own safety, however, from two directions: not only was he a fugitive from U.S. law, but given his constant conflicts with the Cuban government and increasing disillusionment in the face of what he saw to be reactionary features in the regime and within Cuban society itself, he no longer felt safe in the care of his Cuban hosts.[45]

With Cleaver's consent, the Cubans arranged for him to temporarily leave the island in May 1969 and seek refuge in Algeria, to which he was escorted by a Cuban diplomat. But by that time Cleaver had concluded—like Williams before him—that real solidarity and support for the U.S. revolution would have to be sought elsewhere. Therefore, immediately upon arrival, Cleaver made arrangements to remain in Africa.[46]

Conclusion

The issue of security—both the Black leaders' individual safety concerns and Cuba's national security—was decided by the outcome of the struggle to set policy that raged between the two Cuban factions throughout the first half of the decade. The traditional Communist Party, or pro-Moscow, faction, which eventually prevailed, sought to move Cuba into the Soviet camp for protection and economic stability. The Guevarists, by contrast, lobbied for spearheading the forceful overthrow of the world capitalist system in order to ultimately safeguard Cuban security without sacrificing its independent revolutionary path.

Addressing Black leaders' personal safety concerns within the fluctuations of Cuban security policy was in many ways a difficult task. Every U.S. Black leader faced a threat to his or her personal safety, as illustrated in the harassment and eventual assassinations of King and Malcolm X. The FBI, in coordination with other enforcement agencies, waged a massive and in many ways illegal counterintelligence effort throughout the decade to crush the Black movement.

Therefore, as desperate exiles fled to Cuba seeking shelter in the allegedly revolutionary and sympathetic state, the debate between the Guevarists and the pro-Soviets over the most effective national security strategy was thrown into sharp relief. The limits to Cuban solidarity were tested throughout the decade and beyond by Black activists such as Robert Williams and Black Panthers Eldridge Cleaver, Huey P. Newton, and Assata Shakur seeking exile.

The sojourns of Williams and Cleaver illustrate the erratic shifts in Cuban policy toward the U.S. movement. Far from the omnipotent and omnipresent leader that he is usually considered, Castro was often perceived by both Williams and Cleaver as being unaware of or misinformed about actual policy actions taken toward U.S. Blacks, as reactionary elements within the regime impeded communication and relations with some militants. Both of these leaders eventually left Cuba, citing a betrayal of revolutionary ideals on the part of powerful Communist Party stalwarts.

Two years before his death, Eldridge Cleaver reflected on the Black Panther Party's relationship with the evolving regime in its nascent years: "Although some of the Cubans certainly believed there could be a U.S. revolution, you have to distinguish between politics and practice. In looking at whether the Cubans are 'revolutionary,' both in their official political statements and their voting record at the United Nations they never waivered from total support of the Black Movement. But in *practice,* that's where problems came in. They would invite African Americans to be there for special occasions, but the problem lay in the kind of actual support we needed to make the revolution here in the Unites States."[47] In the end, this is where the Cuban regime fell short in the minds of many 1960s Black radicals who were desperately seeking that elusive international ally willing to risk all for the revolution in the belly of the beast.

13

"Revolutionary Art Is a Tool for Liberation"

Emory Douglas and Protest Aesthetics at the *Black Panther*

Erika Doss

A poster-size drawing by Emory Douglas titled *Shoot to Kill* (figure 1) occupied the back page of the November 21, 1970 issue of the *Black Panther*, the Black Panther Party's newspaper. The drawing, which featured scenes of black men killing white policemen, was subtitled "Our Minister of Culture, Emory Douglas, Teaches: 'We Have to Begin to Draw Pictures That Will Make People Go Out and Kill Pigs.'"

As the authors of a government report remarked in the mid-1970s, the Black Panthers were "blessed with a theatrical sixth sense that enabled them to gain an audience and project an image [that] frightened America."[1] Recognition of that image is central to an understanding of the Panthers and their politics. Emory Douglas, the primary artist at the *Black Panther* during the party's peak from the late 1960s to the early 1970s, produced hundreds of pictures promoting the Panthers' program of armed militance and community welfare. Challenging long-standing assumptions about race and racism in America, Douglas crafted a protest aesthetic aimed at convincing audiences of black power.

In a 1970 essay in the *Black Panther,* Douglas detailed the central role of visual images in raising revolutionary consciousness: "Revolutionary art gives a physical confrontation with the tyrants, and also strengthens people to continue their vigorous attack. Revolutionary art is a tool for liberation." Insisting, in another newspaper essay, that "all progressive artists take up their paints and brushes in one hand and their gun in the other," Douglas instructed revolutionary artists to paint pictures of "fascist judges, lawyers, generals, pig policeman, firemen, Senators, Congressmen, governors, Presidents, et al., being punished for their criminal acts against the American people and the struggling people of the world. Their bridges, buildings, electric plants, pipelines, all of the Fascist American empire must be blown up in our pictures."[2]

This chapter was published in *New Political Science* 21, no.2 (June 1999), as a revised version of a paper presented at the conference "Toward a History of the 1960s," University of Wisconsin, Madison, April 1993. For an expanded version see Erika Doss, "Imaging the Panthers: Representing Black Power and Masculinity, 1960s–1990s." *Prospects: An Annual of American Studies* 23 (1998), pp. 470–493. The author would especially like to thank Emory Douglas, John Gennari, Rickie Solinger, and Rebecca Yule for their assistance and advice with this essay.

Figure 1   Emory Douglas, *Shoot to Kill,* 1970. Offset collage, *Black Panther,* November 21, 1970. Courtesy The Center for the Study of Political Graphics (CSPG), Los Angeles.

From 1967 to 1973 Douglas matched his rhetorical call to arms with the pictures he produced for the *Black Panther.* Ranging from inflammatory images of resistance and revolution such as *Shoot to Kill* to drawings that focused on inner-city poverty and the need for social and political change (figure 2), Douglas's pictures were highly visible and highly regarded within the party during the Black Power era.

Figure 2   Emory Douglas, *When I Spend More Time . . .* , c. 1971. Back-page drawing, *Black Panther*. Courtesy CSPG, Los Angeles.

The Black Panthers and Visual Imagery

The Panthers counted on media, both their own and that of the mainstream press, to spread their message. Reporters flocked to the Panthers, certainly led by the promise of a good story about American anarchy but perhaps more attracted by the Panthers' own visual presence. With their black berets and leather jackets, their Afros, dark glasses, raised fists, and military drill formation, the Panthers made great visual copy. This was no accident: the Panthers were extraordinarily astute about the appeal and influence of visual imagery as a tool for raising political consciousness. Huey Newton's assertion that "the Black community is basically not a reading community" may be considered an acknowledgment of the central importance of oral expression in African-American culture. But it also suggests an understanding that in the modern age people increasingly gained their information, knowledge, and political and cultural directives from visual sources. As Douglas echoed, "Every revolutionary movement that I've known of has some type of revolutionary art."[3] Indeed, the pictorial, the visual, became an essential component of Panther ideology. Their dramatic redefinition of black identity, and in particular their assault on previously held assumptions of the passivity and powerlessness of black men, garnered the Panthers immediate attention. Their canny attention to visual authority made the Panthers' mode of self-representation *the* image of 1960s radicalism.

Contesting mainstream caricatures of black men, the Panthers also defied middle-class and liberal representations of black masculinity tentatively put in place by the leaders and followers of the civil rights movement. The Panthers projected black power, not egalitarianism. If Martin Luther King Jr. tried to challenge dominant racist stereotypes by claiming black men as citizen-subjects, the Panthers subverted that civil rights image by reconfiguring and romanticizing black men as the very embodiment of revolutionary rage, defiance, and misogyny. "We shall have our manhood," Eldridge Cleaver insisted in *Soul on Ice* (1968), adding, "We shall have it or the earth will be leveled by our attempts to gain it." Angered by the limited field of integration and autonomy that the civil rights movement had achieved, alienated by older, "establishment" patterns of political activism, and incensed by their ongoing status as second-class Americans, the Black Panthers (like other black liberation movements of the 1960s) "sought to clear the ground for the cultural reconstruction of the black subject."[4]

Both civil rights and revolutionary black nationalist movements saw that black subject primarily on masculine terms: the placards carried by striking sanitation workers in Memphis in 1968, for example, asserted "I Am a Man." The Black Panther Party's interest in more aggressive forms of masculinity followed from perceptions of very real threats to America's black men—from the large numbers of black men drafted into the U.S. military during the Vietnam War to blatant forms of domestic oppression. Believing that the civil rights movement had failed to alleviate those threats and as such was physically, psychologically, and socially impotent, the Panthers devised a forceful image of black masculinity that asserted male power in a mostly male sphere.

In so doing, they clearly aimed to recuperate the socially constructed masculine attributes of power, militarism, independence, and control that had been denied subordinated black men since slavery. But by aligning black masculinity with symbols and styles traditionally associated with potent white masculinity, the Panthers also reinscribed the most egregious forms of patriarchal privilege and domination, from machismo and misogyny to violence and aggression.[5] Their heterosexist and homophobic brand of revolutionary black nationalism excluded black women and homosexuals and limited the context of black liberation and black power to conflicts over the definition and manifestation of black masculinity. Rather than reconstructing black masculinity on terms that would have truly disturbed white power, the Panthers aided in codifying the obviously still current cultural demonization of both black male youth and political radicalism.

Affirming the Panthers' demand for a specifically masculinist black power, one of the first writers to depict them titled his 1971 book *A Panther Is a Black Cat*. The Panthers, Reginald Major declared, were soldiers at war in "the jungle which is

America," warriors "moving to bring greatness to the American Experience" by "completing the work begun by the revolution of 1776."[6] Militarism and military metaphors were rampant among the Panthers, not simply because they saw the struggle for black power as a battle against white oppression but because 1960s America was itself thoroughly steeped in military action and rhetoric, overseas and at home. It became Emory Douglas's job to visualize the militance of the Black Panther Party and to articulate an image of black masculine power that meshed with the party's overall ambitions. In May 1967 Douglas took over the layout and visual renderings for the *Black Panther.* Working side by side with Cleaver and Newton, Douglas created a visually dominant newspaper style that one managing editor described as "a tremendous factor" in the *Black Panther's* circulation, which reached over 100,000 weekly by 1969 (fairly high volume for underground newspapers at the time) and was the "most reliable and lucrative source of income for the Party."[7]

Emory Douglas and the *Black Panther*

From the start, Douglas's visual style was direct and angry, its content rooted in years of urban poverty in San Francisco's black slums, its pictorial sensibility nourished in reform-school printing shops and in college art classes. As one author notes, "The story of Emory Douglas's harrowing youth is the story of the breeding of a Black Panther." Born in Grand Rapids, Michigan, in 1943, Douglas moved with his mother to the Bay Area in 1951 after her stormy relationship with his father ended in divorce. While his mother found work operating a concession stand at Juvenile Hall, an arm of San Francisco's Youth Guidance Center, Douglas worked on his "rep" as a brawler and burglar. In 1958, double-charged with truancy and fighting, he wound up at Log Cabin Ranch, a rural facility for juvenile offenders. Douglas spent a year there, assigned in particular the tasks of "taking care of the pigs and keeping the pigpen clean." When he left Log Cabin Ranch, he entered San Francisco's predominantly black Polytechnic High School. After being arrested on burglary charges, Douglas was sentenced to fifteen months at the Youth Training School in Ontario, California, near the men's prison in Chino. His work-study experience there was concentrated in the prison's printing shop, and after his release, Douglas decided to pursue commercial art.[8]

In 1964 Douglas began taking graphic design courses at San Francisco's City College. He also joined the college's Black Students Union and was drawn to political activism. Doing classroom assignments geared at teaching artists how to appeal to the tastes and dollars of mainstream consumers, Douglas made drawings of black consumers: "One of the school projects involved our doing story board drawings for an animated film. I chose to do a 'brother' being denied courtesy and service in a public place until he donned the garb of an African V.I.P. As [the teacher] took a look at what I was doing he suggested that I needed to be more provocative. . . . Ha ha ha ha! The man had no idea how provocative I actually was. The thing was that I hadn't been able up to that time to apply my anger to my drawing and painting."

Tossing aside "aspirations to join the bourgeoisie" of mainstream commercial advertising, Douglas put his aesthetic energies into designing props for the theater workshops that playwright and poet LeRoi Jones (Amira Baraka) gave while teaching at San Francisco State College in the mid-1960s.[9] He also became involved in the Black Panther Party. As he recalled, "I was drawn to it because of its dedication to self-defense. The civil rights movement headed by Dr. King turned me off at that time, for in those days nonviolent protest had no appeal for me. And although the rebellions in Watts, Detroit, and Newark were not well organized they did appeal to my nature. I could identify with them."[10] As a "brother off the block," Douglas found the Panthers' message of aggressive self-reliance and revolutionary action far more persuasive than the principles of pacifism and negotiation at the core of civil rights discourse. The Panthers spoke specifically to the social reality of his urban life. They valorized an image of hard-core, militant, virile, and invincible black manhood already prevalent among the youthful black male underclass, and fused it with a political culture that similarly justified street violence and outlaw behavior.

Joining Huey Newton, Douglas was one of several heavily armed Panthers who, in February 1967, "escorted" Betty Shabazz during the First Annual Malcolm X Grassroots Memorial at Hunter's Point, a predominantly black community in San Francisco. Canny to the PR opportunities inherent in their protection of Malcolm X's widow, Newton's Panthers were eager to shape their first testing of the media waters around claims to Shabazz, despite the fact that she had actually been invited to speak by the Black Panther Party of Northern California. The press played into Newton's hands, producing headlines such as "A Frightening Army" in the *San Francisco Chronicle*.[11] Soon joined by Cleaver, Newton's Panthers went on to become *the* Black Panthers, and the San Francisco group aligned with the Afrocentrism of Maulana Karenga's US (United Slaves) organization. The split was hardly amicable: repeatedly over the next few years, the *Black Panther* featured vicious cartoons and blistering essays blasting the "armchair revolutionaries" of cultural nationalism, for whom black liberation was found in "back to black" clothing, hairstyles, language, and holidays (cf. Kwanzaa) rather than in armed resistance and revolution. Bobby Seale sneered, "I have a natural and I like it, but power for the people doesn't grow out of the sleeve of a dashiki."[12]

Emory Douglas was present, too, at the Panther's next heavily publicized action. On May 2, 1967, Bobby Seale and thirty fully uniformed, fully armed Panthers stormed the California State Capitol in Sacramento to protest the Mulford Bill, an ordinance motivated by Oakland police fears of armed black resistance and aimed at curtailing the Panthers by banning the display of loaded guns in public. Eldridge Cleaver was present as well, as a reporter for *Ramparts*. While Governor Ronald Reagan's handlers quickly hustled him inside the building (he'd been giving a speech to a teenage group of Future Youth Leaders on the capitol lawn), the Panthers made their way toward the state assembly and Seale delivered Executive Mandate No. 1, a lengthy statement condemning not only the pending bill but the "racist California Legislature" and the "racist war of genocide in Vietnam." The journalists and news reporters who had come out in droves to cover the story asked Seale to read it again and he did, twice.[13]

Media coverage of the Panthers "invasion" of Sacramento (and the arrest of over twenty Panthers, including Douglas, on their way back to Oakland) swelled. *U.S. News and World Report* demonized the Panthers as a gang of "armed Negroes" who had swept through capitol corridors crowded with schoolchildren. Photographs showing the Panthers as a disciplined and tough-looking cadre of militant and macho revolutionaries were published in *Life* and *Time* and the *New York Times Magazine*. Angela Davis, then studying in Frankfurt at the Goethe Institute with Theodor Adorno, recalls seeing the image of "leather-jacketed, black-bereted warriors standing with guns at the entrance to the California legislature" in German newspapers. The "appeal" of that image called her back to the United States "into an organizing frenzy in the streets of South Central Los Angeles." But it also, she would later write, came to represent the problematic "masculinist dimensions of black nationalism."[14]

Out on bail after returning from Sacramento, Douglas began full-time work at the *Black Panther*. Breaking away from Baraka, who had become deeply involved with cultural nationalism, Douglas in his earliest newspaper art mostly attacked counterrevolutionary "paper panthers" opposed to armed resistance. One 1967 editorial by Cleaver damning the "scurvy-ness of the NAACP" was accompanied by Douglas's montage of a "bootlickers gallery," which positioned photographs of Martin Luther King Jr., Bayard Rustin, and Roy Wilkins against a crude cartoon of a prostrate black man licking the cowboy boots of President Lyndon Johnson. Douglas's scornful caricatures of the "Old Toms" of the civil rights movement, and his insinuations as to their apparent complicity with mainstream American politics, helped visually prop the aggressive and oppositional tenets of the Black Panther Party. Within a year, however, Douglas (known as "Emory" in the party and at the newspaper, as he signed his drawings with his first name) developed a more refined and brightly colored graphics style of "revolutionary art" that concentrated on "new images of victory" to "get the defeatist attitude out of the people's minds."[15] He also began writing newspaper essays and giving speeches on revolutionary art's centrality to black liberation.

Reproaching the social realism of an earlier generation of black artists, Douglas remarked, "Charles White used to draw various pictures dealing with the social injustices the people suffer but it was civil rights art." White's 1950s images of "mothers scrubbing the floors" were "valid," said Douglas, but they weren't geared toward raising revolutionary consciousness. Dismissing too, many contemporary black artists, especially musicians, Douglas wrote: "What I see Aretha [Franklin] and B. B. King singing about is cultural nationalism from the beginnings of slavery up to now. But it isn't anything that TRANSCENDS COMMUNITIES and creates revolution."[16] The civil rights movement, and the art associated with it, were seen by the Panthers as toothless and soft; the "soul style" sensitivity of cultural nationalism was viewed on similarly derisive terms. In contrast, Douglas crafted a hard and unyielding visual narrative grounded in black resistance and revolution.

The revolutionary artist, by extension, was committed foremost to the revolution. As Black Panther artist Brad Brewer explained in 1970, "The primary thing about a revolutionary artist is that he is a revolutionary first. The question confronting Black people today is not whether or not he or she is 'Black' but whether or not he or she is a revolutionary. With politics guiding the brush, and the gun protecting them both, the potential Black revolutionary artists could rid themselves of their tendencies of cultural nationalism. Because their talents are geared in behalf of preparing for revolution, they aren't involved in dealing in life style but rather [in] offering solutions."[17]

Douglas found aesthetic inspiration for those solutions in "the art coming out of the struggle in Vietnam. Their pictures . . . always express the victorious spirit, a picture of a mother holding her baby—we will fight from one generation to the next!"[18] Sixties-era underground newspapers attentive to international struggle frequently reprinted the well-designed, semiabstract posters produced by OSPAALA (the Organization of Solidarity of the Peoples of Africa, Asia, and Latin America). Many, including the *Black Panther,* subscribed to the Liberation News Service and received twice-weekly mailings of news bulletins, feature articles, and graphics detailing armed revolution around the world. Inspired by propaganda posters from Southeast Asia, Africa, and Cuba picturing heroic sword- or gun-toting peasants—male and female—in indigenous garb, Douglas often pictured Panthers similarly outfitted in cotton pajamas and thongs, draped in bandoliers, carrying rifles.

The fact that few, if any, Black Panthers dressed this way, much less carried Kalishnikovs, didn't matter: this was revolutionary art that transcended the realities of inner-city America in deference to a vision of global black liberation. Women had a place in this revolutionary art, too: Douglas's 1969 cartoon *All Power to the People* depicts a

Figure 3   Emory Douglas, *Revolutionary Art Exhibit,* 1969. Offset print, *Black Panther,* October 10, 1970. Courtesy CSPG, Los Angeles.

black female, machete in tow, hawking copies of the *Black Panther; Revolutionary Art Exhibit* (figure 3; 1969), a poster Douglas designed to advertise a display of his pictures, illustrates a black mother cradling her child, dressed in a cotton shift and head scarf, a rifle slung over her back. But by casting black women within conventional and limited roles, as salesgirls and mothers, for instance, Douglas reinforced the patriarchal conceits that largely dominated the Black Panthers' political image and program.

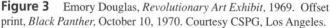

Honing the City College commercial art lessons that had given him "insights into how to appeal to the audience I was trying to reach," Douglas turned Madison Avenue advertising and global agitprop into a form of revolutionary art aimed at empowering the Black Panther Party. Perceiving a key relationship between black liberation and pictures, Douglas stressed the educative and preparative role of revolutionary art, and laid out the precise means by which revolutionary artists were to operate. Rather than forecasting a utopian future to be lived after the revolution, revolutionary artists were instructed to illustrate the ongoing political struggle: "When we say that we want decent housing, we must have pictures that reflect how we're going to get decent housing." Taking their cues from Fanon's advice that the oppressed must destroy their oppressors, revolutionary artists were ordered to "create brand new images of revolutionary action for the entire community" that would convince "the vast majority of black people—who aren't readers but activists—[that] through their observation of our work, they feel they have the right to destroy the enemy."[19]

In a 1968 issue of the *Black Panther,* Douglas listed the images that revolutionary artists should cull to elicit such reactions:

> We draw pictures of our brothers with stoner guns with one bullet going through forty pigs, taking out their intestines along the way. . . . We draw pictures that show Standard Oil in milk bottles launched at Rockefeller with the wicks made of cloth from I. Magnin. . . . This is revolutionary art—pigs lying in alleyways of the colony dead with their eyes gouged out. . . . Pictures that show black people kicking down prison gates—sniping bombers, shooting down helicopters, police, mayors, governors, senators, assemblymen, congressmen, firemen, newsmen, businessmen, Americans.[20]

In each edition of the *Black Panther,* Douglas matched these scenes with quotes and slogans from Panther leaders or from the pages of various revolutionary tracts: "By Any Means Necessary," "In Defense of Self-Defense," "All Power to the People." Concentrating especially on pictures of young, gun-wielding black men, sometimes dressed in Black Panther regalia and sometimes outfitted in military uniforms appropriated from OSPAALA or Liberation News Service images of international freedom fighters, Douglas provided an iconography that clearly supported the Panthers' profoundly militant and masculinist thrust.

If pictures of black men hoisting guns were essential to the Panther's ideological directives, Douglas's most influential images were those of black men fighting pig-policemen. Considered the in-house "expert on the way pigs look and act" because of his pigpen chores at the Log Cabin Ranch reform school, Douglas has been credited with inventing the era's visual symbolization of policemen as fat, mean, uniformed pigs. Linking policemen with pigs actually has much earlier roots: Francis Grose's 1811 *Dictionary of the Vulgar Tongue* has: "Pig, police officer. A China Street pig; a Bow Street officer. Floor the pig and bolt; knock down the officer and run away." Still, if not exactly an innovation of the Black Power movement, Douglas's cartoons helped revitalize a broad national trend of vilifying cops as pigs. His pig pictures were a regular feature in *Black Panther,* and "readers looked forward every week to seeing them."[21] Douglas later extended this anthropomorphic demonization to represent politicians as rats and businessmen as vultures.

The purpose of his caricatures, said Douglas, was "to make the people aware of the character of those who oppressed us" and to provide visual examples that would inspire them to "revolt against the slavemasters" and "kill the pigs." Some cartoons highlighted the badge numbers of policemen "who were harassing blacks in the community." Others were more ideological: one 1969 cartoon featured four hogs swinging from a tree, labeled respectively "AVARICIOUS BUSINESSMEN," "DEMAGOGUE POLITICIANS," "PIG COPS," and "U.S. MILITARY." The text below read: "ON LANDSCAPE ART: 'It is good only when it shows the oppressor hanging from a tree by his mother f—kin neck'" (figure 4).[22]

With their straightforward slogans and images, Douglas's pig pictures recast despised figures of institutional authority in negative symbolic form. The contrast between the clarity of his political cartoons and the "happy" type and obfuscated imagery of the psychedelic styles used in other 1960s-era underground newspapers is obvious. Keyed to revolutionary instruction rather than counterculture euphoria, Douglas's artwork was visual reinforcement for a radical politics of militant black struggle; the pictorial linchpin, as he explained, to a "revolutionary culture that serves the people."[23]

Douglas's Effects on Others

During his years with the *Black Panther,* Douglas shaped a protest aesthetic with which the Black Panther Party aspired to revolutionize the black masses. Along with Fanon's *Wretched of the Earth* and Bakunin's *Catechism of the Revolutionist,* Douglas's pictures of black men fighting pig-policemen, and his heroizing posters of "Bobby" and "Huey," were aimed at generating ideological conviction among the black lumpen. For white leftists who claimed the Panthers as "irresistible allies," and for Panther leaders who found power in pictures, Douglas's art was held in highest esteem. Eldridge Cleaver claimed that "the ideology of the Black Panther Party and the teachings of Huey P. Newton are contained in their purest form in Emory's art." Reginald Major boasted that "Emory, as artist, is more of a vanguard than the Panthers as politicians," and added, "As an artist, he has more effective freedom of expression than Eldridge as a writer, or Hilliard [David Hilliard, Panther Chief of Staff] as an orator. Emory's views on the purposes of revolutionary art have had a decided influence on the politics of the Party." His art had immense visual cachet with black audiences: the Black Student's Union at San Francisco State College adopted his image of a "loin-clothed black man with a gun in one hand and a book in the other as the symbol of their educational aspirations." In homes across America, Douglas's poster-portraits of Panther personalities bedecked living room walls.[24]

The Black Panther Party advanced the visual appeal of Douglas's pictures by often printing ten to twenty thousand copies of posters and circulating them throughout urban black neighborhoods. From "the Christian to the brother on the block, the college student and the high school drop-out, the street walker and the secretary, the pimp and the preacher," revolutionary art, said Douglas, was for everybody. The ghetto, he added, was "the gallery" for the revolutionary artist. "His art is plastered on the walls, in store front windows, on fences, doorways, telephone poles and booths, passing busses, alleyways, gas stations, barber shops, beauty parlors, laundry mats, liquor stores, as well as the huts of the ghetto." Douglas believed in the revolutionary power of art, and often stated that image making and consumption were, in and of themselves, revolutionary praxis. "The people are the masterpieces," he intoned, thus rejecting art-world ideas about aesthetic autonomy and insisting on revolutionary culture's populist (albeit primarily male) and pragmatic underpinnings. "The community," he recalls, "was the museum for our artwork. Some people saw art for the first time when they saw my posters. Some joined the Black Panther Party, some got inspired to make art too."[25]

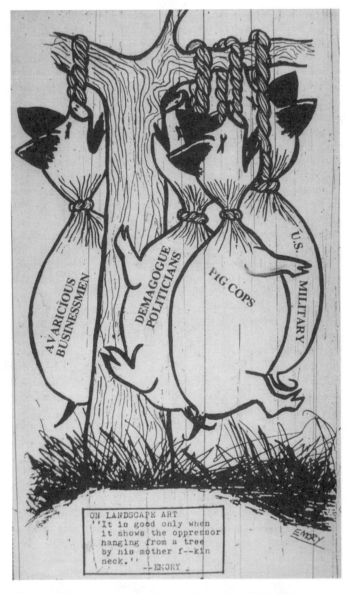

Figure 4   Emory Douglas, *On Landscape Art,* 1969. Offset print, *Black Panther,* January 4, 1969. Courtesy CSPG, Los Angeles.

Some of those inspired were community muralists. Throughout the late 1960s, urban artists painted gigantic Walls of Dignity and Walls of Respect on the sides and facades of inner-city buildings, representing Panthers en masse and Panthers engaged in standoffs and shoot-outs with the police. Other African American artists produced similarly militant and visually compelling prints, posters, and easel paintings focused on black power. Faith Ringgold's *The Flag Is Bleeding* (1967) and David Hammons's

Injustice Case (1970) utilized the American flag's symbolic reference to freedom and justice to point out the duplicity of such imagery: in Ringgold's painting, a black man pledges allegiance to that flag with blood pouring from his heart; in Hammon's body-print, a black man bound and gagged in a courtroom chair (a nod to Bobby Seale's treatment during the 1969 trial of the Chicago 8) looks in anguish and anger at that flag. In *Fred Hampton's Door* (1970), Dana Chandler paid tribute to the chief of the Chicago Panthers, slain when police fired more than ninety rounds of ammunition through his apartment. Painting his picture of Hampton's bullet-ridden door a vivid red, and then shooting at the finished painting and piercing it with bullet holes, Chandler remarked, "I'm not trying to be aesthetically pleasing. I'm trying to be relevant."[26]

Like Douglas, most of these artists aimed at raising revolutionary consciousness by picturing black struggle and liberation primarily on masculinist terms. Others, including sculptors Betye Saar and Elizabeth Catlett, were also inspired by the anger and violence of the Black Power movement's protest aesthetics, but challenged its exclusionary preoccupation with black men. In *The Liberation of Aunt Jemima* (1972) and *Homage to My Young Black Sisters* (1968), Saar and Catlett, respectively, drew on the guns and fists of Panther iconography and raised questions about black power's patriarchal focus: Saar posing a stereotypical Mammy (broom in one hand, rifle in the other) against a Warholesque grid of Aunt Jemima pancake-mix boxes; Catlett paying tribute to the stylized figure of a woman giving the Black Power salute.[27] But their depictions were exceptional: most African-American protest artists of the Black Power era were more engrossed with the threatening image of aggressive black masculinity that the Panthers projected.

Emory Douglas stayed at the *Black Panther* until the newspaper folded in 1979. But his art shifted from inflammatory images of resistance and revolution to the "loves, joys, hopes and dreams of black people in America: the bright side as well as the dark side of life." Abandoning the militant and masculinist underpinnings once central to Panther ideology, Douglas now concentrated on pictures of black families and black children and imaged African-American solidarity. As he explained in 1993, "My art was a reflection of the politics of the party, so when the party changed to community action so did my art, from pigs to kids."[28] Other African-American artists also abandoned the Black Power movement's protest aesthetic: Betye Saar, for example, began to make shrines and altars that reclaimed ethnic and minority histories and religions, and which dealt extensively with her powerful female ancestors. As she explained in 1975, "Now, my messages are more subtle. There is more secretiveness about them because I think this represents the way Black People feel about the movement today. They've got over the violent part and have become more introspective."[29]

Douglas had initially used his protest aesthetic to convince black audiences about the efficacy of a radical black political culture. By the early 1970s, however, that aesthetic was being used in ways that challenged the original meaning and intentionality of revolutionary art. The pig-policeman image that Douglas reinvigorated was appropriated by American cops, who began sporting buttons marked P.I.G.—"Pride, Integrity, Guts." Black Power fists became the design motifs for consumer items ranging from coffee table sculptures to rings. Black men wearing Afros and leather coats were cast as the macho antiheroes of blaxploitation movies like Shaft (1971).[30] Even if such films as Melvin Van Peebles's 1972 movie *Sweet Sweetback's Baadasssss Song* challenged dominant cultural assumptions about black men, they reproduced and strengthened the tropes of a raging, outlaw, heterosexual, and sexist black masculinity that the Panthers had themselves helped set in place only a few years earlier. While liberatory visions of justice and the possibilities of a transformative political culture largely evaporated, the visualization of black patriarchal power that the Black Panther Party promoted in the late 1960s and early 1970s spread.

The impact of the women's movement, the economic changes rendered by deindustrialization, the antiminority actions of current political culture, and the grim statistics regarding unemployment, imprisonment, and average life expectancy for black men in America are all factors that have led many African-American men in the 1990s to glance backward at the Panthers and to resuscitate the last set of images that represented black power and patriarchal control. Likewise, as figures such as Louis Farrakhan aim to generate a new politicized public culture for black Americans, they too draw on the patriarchal dimensions of Black Power, whereby black men assume control of the black family and black life. However much Farrakhan has been credited with rebuking the "pernicious role model" of the Black Panther cum gangsta rapper, the Million Man March clearly aimed at vindicating black manhood by creating "a new black patriarchy."[31]

In the 1990s the Black Panthers remain a potent symbol. Rappers like Paris and the late Tupac Shakur (whose mother, Assata Shakur, was a member of the New York 21) have claimed the Panthers as black heroes; more than a few Public Enemy songs and videos pay homage to Panther attributes (black berets, black leather jackets) and catchphrases ("Power to the People"). As contemporary black men struggle to gain meaning and control in their lives, it is no surprise that the Panthers imaging of black masculine power and authority retains immense appeal. However, as former Panther leader Elaine Brown cautioned in 1992, "a lot of young people look back on the Black Panther Party and they see icons. But icons are a very dangerous thing to create. Icons make mistakes." Critic bell hooks warns, further, that we should all vigilantly reconsider the icons we identify with, lest we continue to perpetuate "the spectacle of contemporary colonization, dehumanization, and disempowerment where the image serves as a murder weapon."[32] Prompting that cultural critique demands revisualizing black experience and radical politics in diverse and egalitarian terms, rather than placing faith in an imaging of black power that the Black Panthers projected in the late 1960s, and which continues to persist in contemporary American culture.

14

White Radicals, Black Panthers, and a Sense of Fulfillment

Stew Albert

The civil rights movement stirred up white middle-class kids who were bored by the conformity and McCarthyism of the 1950s. By 1967 they were hungry for Black friendship. The idea of rebelling without Blacks as beneficiaries seemed like a put-on. The movement's call to follow an ideal no matter the risk stood starkly against the moral compromises and deceits of their parents. The white kids came mostly from leftist and pacifist backgrounds at first, but the Vietnam War and the counterculture opened the social flood gates of one-dimensional America. The ranks of the white movement filled with an absolutely eclectic mixture, which saw children of labor organizers, wealthy capitalists, artists, Mafia dons, CIA founders, welfare recipients, and every imaginable stripe of middle-class and suburban material success and spiritual poverty.

And, as in the days of the Abraham Lincoln Brigade, many of the activists were Jewish. However unreligious, they carried an ancient imperative that commanded them to fight for the poor, the oppressed, and *the stranger.*

In our souls there resounded the words of the ancient rabbi philosopher Hillel, "If you are only for yourself, you are nothing."

The original ideals of the Black-led civil rights movement continued to inspire what was being called a New Left. The movement had put forward values like the loving community and nonmanipulative grassroots democracy as well as personal commitment and putting your body on the line. These concepts, and the deeds that supported them, provided a never-ending inspiration to the mostly white New Left in all its offshoots. The free speech movement, the peace movement, the surrealistic Yippies, and the women's movement were all under its influence.

The possibility of building a friendly relationship with a hot Black organization, in the new era of Black Power and separatism, was delicious. We wouldn't exactly be joining hands in a loving community. The Panthers would remain an all-black outfit. What the Black Panther Party was proposing, in fact, sounded more like a diplomatic pact than brotherhood in a loving community. But this represented the best news white radicals had heard from Black America in quite some time.

It was Eldridge Cleaver who first brought me news of the Black Panthers. We had been friends since he was paroled from San Quentin Prison. He was an editor at *Ramparts* magazine and becoming world-famous as the latest militant Black author. His primary interest, however, remained revolution. Cleaver had already met with representatives of various ideologically based Communist organizations in Berkeley. He concluded that they talked a good game, but the appropriate militant action was missing from their modus operandi. Then he met Huey Newton and Bobby Seale, who carried shotguns and organized patrols of the racist Oakland police. The ex-con enthusiastically volunteered as a general in Newton's army. Huey appointed him Minister of Information.

Cleaver showed up at my pad and wanted to put a large personality poster of Huey seated in a wicker chair, holding a spear and a shotgun, up on my wall. Because Eldridge was so happy with his new friends, I agreed. But when he gave me a bunch of posters for my "associates," I felt unspoken reservations about their corniness. Besides, personality posters were relatively new. Even our new San Francisco rock stars hadn't as yet made use of them. They seemed narcissistic and quasi-cultic, not really ideal food for egalitarian revolutionaries.

The Newton trial made the spear poster chic. Huey developed tremendous support on the full spectrum of the white left, from liberal to pro-Albanian Communist, and he rose to become a controversial folk hero in Black America. Eldridge was the prime mover of the White-Black alliance. He made friends with everybody but retained a Yippie soft spot for Jerry Rubin, Abbie Hoffman, Phil Ochs, and me.

Newton was convicted on a count of manslaughter. His beating the murder one charge with its guaranteed gas chamber was considered a commanding victory. The Panthers could plainly see that multiracial partnerships paid off. Huey's radical lawyer, Charles Garry, was a brilliant ex–Communist Party activist, and absolutely dedicated to his client. He was white, and Free Huey rallies that included many thousands of young white people, in all their cultural and political diversity from graduate students at UC Berkeley to street people off Telegraph Avenue, had certainly served notice on the jury and the Oakland establishment that they wouldn't only be dealing with very angry black people if Newton was convicted of murder.

Cleaver joined Bobby Seale in the Panther leadership while a jailed Newton appealed his conviction. The Party became a national organization with functioning chapters in all major cities. Party unity was maintained by traveling men Eldridge and Seale and a nationally circulating weekly newspaper, filled with Cleaver writing and wild, hilariously mean cartoons by artist Emory Douglas. Emory's militant chutzpah peaked when he portrayed Santa Claus as a mean-looking pig.

Cleaver embodied more than Black anger turned to political militancy. In his ferocious physical presence and his brilliant manipulation of language he represented the accumulation of every American rebel's rage. He rose above race, voicing an anger that included the pent-up fury of young whites rebelling against their own cultural repression. Eldridge was called "The Rage" by Panther members. His style exploded beyond politics into the metaphysical. He seemed to be at war with the cosmos, eternity, and even God. The Minister of Information was fond of quoting John Milton's devil, who would "rather rule in hell than serve in heaven." And Cleaver's fondness for marijuana and Bob Dylan didn't hurt his reputation with white rebels.

Newton would eventually win his appeal and be released on bail. While his lawyers prepared for a second trial, Huey took charge of the Party he had inspired. No longer just a few wild guys with guns who were willing to go the limit, the Black Panther Party had grown into a large organization that served free breakfasts for children, ran health clinics, set up schools, and distributed free chickens to celebrate Newton's birthdays. Huey Newton had a big problem. His deeds and example had inspired the Panther Party, but the jailed Newton had not been its builder. Huey would feel uncomfortable and out of place in the organization that named him its Supreme Commander.

I met Huey Newton in a glass cage. We were on the top floor of the Alameda County Court House jail. It was turning into a going-away party. In addition to the Panther leader and myself, lawyer Charles Garry was present, and so was Debora, the Panther's current white jailhouse flame. Good-bye, Alameda County Court House; tomorrow Huey was going to Vacaville Prison for fifteen years, and there would be no more easy visits.

The jury had found him guilty of manslaughter. This was a compromise verdict between those who wanted the death penalty and jurors who thought Newton deserved a medal. Judge Monroe Friedman gave Newton the maximum sentence and denied appeal bond.

In a tumultuous attempt to urge repentance on the judge, Judy Gumbo, future rabbi Michael Lerner, Debora, and I had picketed Friedman's Oakland synagogue on Yom Kippur. The judge was a no-show. The bored kids left services to come out and cheer us on, but the Temple's elders came very close to calling the police. But I won the day of atonement by asking, "How can you arrest Jews on Yom Kippur?"

And now awaiting transfer to a permanent prison, Huey was in a relaxed mood. "I guess they're going to complain about the candy. I'm not allowed to eat between meals here."

Garry got up. He wanted to know why the guard was shouting through the soundproof window. The glass cage reminded me of a giant gas chamber. For the past year I haven't been able to think about Huey Newton without conjuring up gas chambers.

Garry was back. "It's OK. They were interested in something else."

Huey was calm. He was an amiable host, passing out candy to his guests. He drew flirtatious cartoons and passed them to Debora. She giggled. He giggled. She was recently divorced, Jewish, cerebral, smoldering sexy, and very radical.

Newton seemed gentle, self-assured, with nothing to prove. Not a big man, half the size of Eldridge, but with thick biceps and no obvious demons in his young, almost pretty face.

"I know about that talk," Huey says. "It's completely untrue. Eldridge and I run together. I support what he did in Ann Arbor in relation to Jerry Rubin, picking him as his running mate in the presidential election. If he supports the Yippies, so do I. Fighting back changes the way Blacks think about white radicals. The original bias was to think of long-haired men as being effeminate."

We talked for an hour. And we were all in awe of Huey. It's like meeting a Wizard of Oz who is for real. He's given revolutionary faith back to the old-time progressive labor lawyer Charlie Garry. To Debora he's given pride via a knowing twinkle and many sweet smiles. She knows that so many women would envy her.

And blond Jewish me who made himself tough by pumping iron in his Brooklyn basement. No mama's darling here. Huey has given me special recognition and grace. The strongest and best of men has said I'm the genuine article.

Huey went on about his favorite East Oakland bars. He did his best political organizing in saloons. There was a longing in his voice and the slightest hint of a quiver.

Our hour was up. Good-byes were brief. Huey's guests were now silent in the elevator. Garry had left $25.00 in Newton's commissary. The lawyer's face was gray; a hardness flickered every now and then. The elevator opened into a crowded bustling floor of cops and crooks.

Only on the courthouse steps did Garry speak. "We have got to organize a worldwide Free Huey movement. Otherwise he'll rot in jail for fifteen years. Ronald Reagan will let him rot."

My interview with Huey appeared on the front page of the *Berkeley Barb*. I wasn't just Eldridge Cleaver's best white friend. Now I was the official best white friend of the Black Panther Party. This relationship continued and strengthened after Cleaver went into exile.

I was proud of my status. Diplomacy was now my game. I was the go-between connecting revolutionary Black America to the funkiest edges of rebellious White America. What a bizarre looking-diplomat I was, having been recently described by right-wing crusader Fred Schwartz in his anticommunist publication as "a glassy eyed gargoyle with his hair in calculated disarray."

My relationship with the Panthers took on a matter-of-fact relaxed quality. Genuine affection and friendship developed. Behind the scenes Panther-Yippie association could be funky and very laid-back.

> *Hanging out for afternoon hours in Mrs. Seale's living room. Bobby's mother. Bobby's father lives there, but as a second-class citizen. Doing nothing for hours in the company of Bobby, his brother John, and their body guards. Bobby Seale in the kitchen cooking stew for the guys. Nothing happens but idle chatter. Kidding around. Slow speech. Plastic on the furniture. Not that much different than my mother. Lower middle class. Bobby's mother is real friendly, but she's off to see some church ladies. Seale looks in from the kitchen. He boasts about the recipe. He can cook for a hundred. Five or six guys, no matter how much they eat, are no problem. Ordinariness, the Panther without glamour or myth.*

Eldridge called our house the hippie palace. He would drop in at night, bringing along Panthers and friends. We would sit around a giant water pipe inhaling large doses of marijuana and sake. Eldridge loved telling pointless stories, and we would all collapse into ferocious gales of laughter.

"When I was a Muslim I believed the chicken evolved from the snake. I don't remember why. I never ate chicken. Other Muslims wouldn't eat pork but I got to a point where I couldn't even look at a chicken." And Eldridge would start laughing and maybe fall off his chair. We would all roll around on the floor. I thought that one of these times we wouldn't be able to stop. We might go on forever, lifetime citizens of a laughing utopia.

When the newly formed Peace and Freedom Party nominated Cleaver as its presidential candidate, Eldridge insisted that Yippie Jerry Rubin be his running mate. Jerry was at that exact moment—the summer of 1968—making headlines in Chicago by running a pig for president. This was way too weird for the P. and F. faithful—they refused to nominate *scum*—and so Cleaver rebelled against his own supporters. He proclaimed Jerry his vice no matter what and invited Rubin to campaign with him.

The Peace and Freedom Party was the product of an attempt by white radicals to create a viable third party. Although strongest in California, it had many chapters around the country. Its mass appeal was to broad sections of the white left, the cadre who went door to door obtaining signatures to put the party on the ballot. And the party's platform was radically reformist without quite being openly revolutionary.

While Peace and Freedom membership was extremely diverse, the party's prime movers tended to be of an ideological bent that in some cases leaned to Leon Trotsky and in others Mao Tse-Tung. The ideologues kept their purity intact by aligning their organization with the Black Panther Party and its program.

Initially, Eldridge felt reluctant to break ranks with some of his closest white backers from among the ideologically inclined. Weeks before the summer 1968 Ann Arbor gathering, Cleaver had suggested Jerry as a running mate, but when his idea picked up no support from the Marxists and Maoists, he seemed to have dropped the idea.

Judy and I had taken a brief leave from the Chicago Yippie wars with Mayor Richard Daley and Lyndon Johnson in order to attend the Peace and Freedom national convention taking place in nearby Ann Arbor. Eldridge wanted to take some time out. "Hey man, why don't you and Gumbo and I check out some weed?"

I thought it was about letting us off easy about who would be his running mate. But Eldridge didn't say much. He complained; everyone was down on Jerry, especially the Maoist Bob Avakian.

And I said, "Look, I understand, no hard feelings, Pigasus is our candidate anyway." And Eldridge joked about how people might like Pigasus because he was a real pig, the only candidate they could eat, and then he said, "Oh well, fucken Avakian can eat me, let's go nominate Jerry for running mate."

Word spread like napalm. Eldridge was going to nominate Jerry Rubin as his vice presidential running mate on the Peace and Freedom Party ticket. Most of the delegates at the Ann Arbor convention believed jolly Jerry was by now a destroyed dope fiend, and that only on his better days.

Cleaver went directly to his caucus, taking Judy and me with him. The caucus members were the Panthers' day-and-night allies in the Peace and Freedom organization. These were among his special white people.

"Eldridge, you never discussed Rubin with us."

"Eldridge, you told us Rubin was lying when he said you wanted him."

The voices reflected absolute shock. Words came haltingly. They worshiped Cleaver. And some would die for him. But for them supporting Jerry Rubin was worse than death.

Bob Avakian took the floor. He was my chief rival for the title of Eldridge Cleaver's Best White Friend. A photo of Bob pointing a gun had recently appeared in the Panthers' newspaper. This son of a superior court judge declared he would "kill any pig who gets in my way." Avakian was once a young liberal, but under Cleaver's tutelage he had quickly changed. Now the short, pudgy revolutionary was earning notoriety for picking fistfights with mean cops. His father's prominence afforded him only partial protection against getting his ass kicked. He detested Jerry, who happened to be the son of a truck driver and a Teamster Union official.

"I knew Jerry Rubin in the Vietnam Day Committee." Avakian spoke with a trembling voice. "I knew him when he was a revolutionary. When he used his talents for a progressive purpose. But now Jerry is a clown. He has abandoned politics for drugs and being a fool. Eldridge, you demean yourself by supporting him."

Eldridge radiated fury. How dare this rich fat little punk oppose him?

I took a shot at cajoling persuasion. "Jerry is still political. Right now he is in Chicago preparing for what will be a bloody week. He could get killed. We all could. He isn't in Chicago to smoke dope or run naked in the streets." Maybe I lied a little bit. "He's in Chicago protesting the war."

I wasn't changing any one's mind. "Rubin is scum, all Yippies are scum," was the dominant response.

"That's what Mayor Daley calls us. Hey, why don't you come to Chicago and say that, you lousy bastard," I replied.

Now everyone was screaming, whistling, and denouncing Jerry Rubin. Eldridge asked for calm. "I remember when they called the Panthers scum. Now you call the Yippies scum. The government doesn't think Jerry is apolitical. They subpoenaed him before HUAC."

Avakian, bursting at his seams, responded with damaged fury and hysterical indignation. "Eldridge, better men than Rubin have been called before HUAC."

"Maybe better men have, Bob, but you aren't one of them."

Tears streaming from his round face, my former rival fled the room. I thought he might return with his gun.

My long-standing and well-known friendship with Eldridge brought many rewards. No matter what anybody on the left thought of me and my politics, my having Cleaver's private phone number demanded respect. Eldridge introduced me to Bobby Seale and David Hilliard, and if I was Eldridge's friend, I was their friend. I brought Seale into People's Park, which he happily endorsed as "righteous socialism" and declared that he would encourage Panthers to "come around and help in this progressive construction."

Overnight I realized my mother's worst nightmare and became the Black Panther's best white pal. This wasn't exactly worthy of headlines in the *Hadassah Newsletter* about another Jewish boy making good.

Cleaver, Judy, Jerry Rubin and I sealed our friendship by writing and publishing a Panther-Yippie pact in the *Berkeley Barb*. It proved to be a controversial call for blending the Black and white countercultural revolutions. Eldridge even gave my girlfriend, Judy Clavir, her great nickname "Gumbo."

"Gumbo is a stew, dig it."

Huey Newton came out of prison in charismatic flamboyance, ripping off his shirt, showing off his muscles, and offering to train Black soldiers for the Vietcong. But he soon started disappointing some of his strongest white and Black admirers. His public speeches were very abstract and philosophical, and spoken in an annoyingly high-pitched voice. If the audience got bored or asked hostile questions, he would lose his temper, flex his muscles, and declare, "You can kiss my Black ass." What's more, Huey was living in a luxury apartment and accepting the title Supreme Commander. When that was met with some derision, he switched to Supreme Servant. That humble compromise only made matters worse.

In the midst of growing mass movement disillusionment with our leading icon, I had a two-hour phone conversation with Huey. He wanted to get to know me better since I was a long-time white friend of the Panthers, and he hadn't seen me since our jailhouse going-away party.

In private conversation Huey was neither arrogant nor abstract nor high-pitched; he was painfully honest and down-to-earth about his unhappiness. As I remember our talk, he said, "I don't know about the Panthers. I don't know the members, the other chapters, around the country—are they right for the Party? I didn't recruit them. I didn't build them. Are they or this organization any good?

"People expect me to work miracles, but I might leave the Party. I might go back to college and get a Ph.D. I can do what I want. The Party doesn't own me. I don't know them."

And for two hours he repeated varieties of these words, and I felt what I never thought I would feel for this brave and brilliant man. I felt sorry for him.

In 1972 Jerry Rubin and I introduced Huey and Panther leader Elaine Brown to our new friends Yoko Ono and John Lennon. The get-together took place in Ono and Lennon's Bank Street apartment in Greenwich Village.

It was a polite, good-humored meeting, and it went for an hour at the most. Nothing momentous was said, and no commitments asked for or made.

Later I heard that Elaine was impressed by the scars on Lennon's face: "He looks like he's been in a few good fights."

But the big news was that Huey sent John a letter saying that he thought the words of Lennon's beautiful song "Imagine" spelled out the essence of the Black Panther's, and his, new intercommunal philosophy.

The Beatle was very proud of the Panther's words and put the letter up on the wall. And I was left with the almost impossible task of explaining the meaning of intercommunalism to its latest converts.

During the Chicago conspiracy trial (1969–70) Judy and I traveled first to Paris and then to Algiers. In Paris we linked up with Ellen Wright, the Jewish widow of the great Black novelist Richard Wright, and then the three of us headed on to Algeria and a visit with Eldridge and Kathleen Cleaver. Wright had an electric typewriter that some French writers had purchased for Cleaver, and my Yippie mission was to talk the Panther into writing an introduction to Jerry Rubin's new book. I brought a manuscript of *Do-It* with me and hoped that Cleaver would use his new typewriter to say something friendly about the Yippies for Rubin's first book.

Our visit was a success. Eldridge wrote a splendid introduction to *Do-It*. It was warmly reminiscent about the dinner party that was his first meeting with us in Berkeley, and of the roads we had all traveled since. He predicted great things for himself and our gang: "Thinking back to that evening in Stew's pad in Berkeley, I remember the huge poster of W. C. Fields on the ceiling, and the poster of Che on the wall, with his farseeing eyes, staring fiercely and fearlessly into the revolutionary future and at the death he surprised with his heroic welcome. None of us knew, that night, what the future would be, except that we all knew that we would be trying. And we have tried. And we will continue to try. And we will have successes that will surprise us."

Honestly speaking, our collective future was to be filled with nightmarish political and personal failures. The Panthers collapsed in an FBI-encouraged bloody civil war that set Newton and Cleaver against each other. Yippie Abbie Hoffman was busted for coke dealing, and Yippie Jerry Rubin became a businessman and a pyramid schemer. Judy and I retreated to an isolated Catskill cabin, where we were monitored day and night by the FBI.

But personal friendships have persisted. Bobby Seale and David Hilliard roasted me at my fiftieth-birthday party in Berkeley. The last time I saw Eldridge was at Jerry Rubin's funeral, where we poured earth on Jerry's casket and then embraced. Kathleen recently attended a party honoring the college graduation of our daughter Jessica.

Unbelievably, Eldridge, Jerry, Huey, and Abbie and Anita Hoffman and Phil Ochs are now dead. But in the deepest part of my soul great memories live on about a time when we, Black and White, fulfilled each other's best dreams by joining in an outlaw's alliance dedicated to completely remaking and repairing the world.

PART FOUR

Continuing the Resistance

15

Shadow of a Clue

Errol Anthony Henderson

The black liberation movement has taught its students that success must be measured by both the struggle's ability to transform society and its ability to transform those who engage in it. Hugh Pearson's *Shadow of the Panther* critically examines the Black Panther Party's most noted figure and cofounder, Huey P. Newton.[1] Pearson maintains that, on the whole, Newton failed to transform himself from criminal to crusader. One reviewer noted that if Pearson's assessment of Newton was accurate, then the BPP leader was little more than an intelligent, drug-addicted sociopath.[2] Relying on interviews with former Panthers Landon Williams, Mary Kennedy, Sheba Haven, and a handful of BPP supporters and detractors, Pearson's 422-page volume focuses on the criminality that the BPP, primarily Newton, was never quite able to distance itself from. In it Pearson catalogs the failures, the betrayals, the murders, rapes, robberies, and extortions, occurring within the BPP as it developed into the most recognized organization of the Black Power movement. Pearson gives far less significance to the free clinics, free breakfast programs, food giveaways, schools, ambulance service, voter registration, community patrols, and other social programs. His account also underplays the significance of Hoover's counter intelligence program (COINTELPRO), which targeted many black organizations of that era with covert police actions to disrupt and destroy them.

Pearson rejects the tendency for "messiah-making" within the black community that grants deceased leaders a "martyr's immunity against criticism" and severely limits our ability to learn from their mistakes. Since constructive criticism of leadership is necessary to push the movement forward, failure to provide it leaves supporters ill equipped to build progressively on previous work. For example, it is a disservice to the Nation of Islam (NoI) to fail to acknowledge and condemn the adultery of Elijah Muhammad by today suggesting that his secretaries somehow—unknown to everyone else, including his devoted wife, Clara Muhammad—were his wives. Likewise, it would be a mistake for us not to learn from the successes and failures of leaders such as Malcolm X, Queen Mother Moore, or Huey P. Newton. At the same time, however, criticism should respect and appreciate the meaningful contributions that push the legitimate struggle for black liberation forward. Therefore, Pearson's critical assessment is timely, necessary, and deserving of careful review.

This chapter is revised from "The Lumpenproletariat as Vanguard?" *Journal of Black Studies* 28, no. 2 (1997): 171–99.

The Historical Roots and Antecedents of the BPP

To his credit, Pearson sought to provide a historical context for the emergence of the BPP. He roots radicalism in black Oakland with the earlier struggles of the Sleeping Car Porters under the leadership of A. Philip Randolph. He grounds Newton's radicalism in the grassroots activism of the civil rights movement, for example: he discusses how the BPP adopted the black panther symbol from SNCC's initiative in the Lowndes County Freedom Organization; he also asserts that the BPP embraced certain practices of the Deacons for Defense and Justice and the Community Alert Patrol (CAP) in Los Angeles.[3] While grounding the BPP historically is necessary, it is evident that Pearson has little grounding in the history of the era. For example, he incorrectly attributes the founding of the CAP to Roger "Crook" Wilkins, and confuses Robert Williams's armed NAACP chapter in Monroe, North Carolina, with the Deacons for Defense, which emerged in Bogaloosa, Louisiana.

Pearson's assessment of the impact of Malcolm X, Frantz Fanon, and Mao Tse-Tung's philosophies on the BPP, however, is correct. He also correctly notes the historical tendency for blacks victimized by the system to victimize others and rationalize their criminality as the pursuit of black liberation. This victim/villain dichotomy, which the author believes to be at the heart of black struggle since the Brown case, is the template for Pearson's analysis of Newton and the BPP.

The Victim/Villain Dichotomy

According to Pearson, the victim/villain dichotomy was evident in the Montgomery bus boycott, where E. D. Nixon rejected a "would-be Rosa Parks" named Claudette Colvin. Prior to the infamous incident with Parks, Colvin refused to give up her seat on a Montgomery bus, but she was not supported in the same manner as the seamstress when she was arrested. Pearson suggests that this was due to the fact that Colvin was an unsuitable "victim" for the civil rights leadership because she was pregnant and unmarried.[4] The dichotomy was also evident, for Pearson, in the conflict within the NAACP when Robert Williams, the leader of the chapter in Monroe, North Carolina, used guns to defend the black community from white supremacist mobs. Unwilling to countenance Williams's use of armed self-defense, the national leadership suspended him. At issue was the black bourgeoisie's image of a respectable victim that could be promoted as the focus of protest, evocative today of debates concerning the "deserving" versus the "undeserving" poor, which largely reflect the elitist, sexist, and often assimilationist orientation of the upper classes.

While Pearson seems to appreciate the dialectic between activism and criminality in an unjust society (many in the civil rights movement were, in light of racist laws, technically criminals), he does not fully appreciate the fusion and transformation of the two (activism and criminality) that Malcolm X represented, and his impact on the black activists of the 1960s.[5] This process was even more dramatic for the black lumpenproletariat elements that the BPP was attracting and, following Fanon, promoting as the vanguard of the black revolution.[6] For Pearson, Newton's most telling failure was his inability to transform himself along the lines of Malcolm X, and this failure, for Pearson, was not only personal but represented the collective failure of the Black Power movement. However, only if we reduce the BPP to Newton and then reduce Newton to his criminal behavior while ignoring all else can this claim be substantiated. Although such a view is clearly ahistorical and inaccurate, Pearson seems to endorse it.

Pearson finds successful cases of former Panthers who transformed their lives from their previous criminal behavior, such as Landon Williams and Flores "Fly" Forbes. Their will to survive and transform themselves, he believes, was largely absent from other Panthers, including Newton.[7] But Pearson's sweeping censure is not supported by a thorough analysis of Newton and members of the BPP from across the country, and his review of the Oakland Panthers (the national headquarters) does not license wholesale condemnation of BPP members. Further, even in regard to Newton, Pearson's assessment is inadequate.

While Pearson understands that the transformation process, which he suggests Panthers did not manifest, depends on a "will to survive and transform," he ignores these characteristics in Newton. Pearson should be reminded that Newton had a strong will and drive to better himself; after all, Dr. Huey P. Newton did successfully complete a Ph.D. program at the University of California, Santa Cruz. More importantly, Pearson misunderstands the nature and extent of Newton's addiction—something of which David Hilliard, the former Panther Chief of Staff and recovering addict who introduced Newton to crack cocaine, is keenly aware.[8] The nature and extent of Newton's addiction should be understood within the context of whether he had the will to survive and transform himself. This would require a deeper analysis than Pearson provided, which would allow us to appreciate what led to Newton's addiction without ignoring his responsibility for his actions.

Hilliard suggests that Newton's addiction began with his response to the assassination of George Jackson—an event that traumatized Newton.[9] The isolation of Newton in the penthouse (orchestrated by Hilliard and Elaine Brown) not only angered the rank and file but furthered Newton's alienation and incipient paranoia, ensuring a situation in which his descent into alcohol and drug abuse accelerated. Pearson's simplistic victim/villain dichotomy does not allow him to distinguish the subtle gray areas between the black and white of Newton's life. Thus restricted, Pearson takes for granted that there are no lessons to be learned from Newton's descent. Newton's was not a singular fall, but it was only the more tragic in light of his awesome potential. Moreover, it is a route taken by so many of those same urban blacks that the BPP successfully transformed. Clearly, Newton tried to adapt to changing political and personal realities (for which he was harshly criticized), but such attempts should not be dismissed because they were ultimately unsuccessful. His personal failures were rooted in his personal choices, his drug addiction, his paranoia (exacerbated by COINTELPRO), political repression, and finally, his failure to create and maintain a supportive environment in which members could adequately assist in his (and others') transformation. The important question that Pearson does not ask, is whether Newton's effort was insufficient in light of greater force from an outside party, or whether Newton simply gave up and became the hollow shell that Tyrone Robinson killed on August 22, 1989. The answers to these questions should be informed by the study of those who have journeyed this path and transformed themselves while remaining in the movement, such as Safiya Bukhari, Akinsanya Kambon, and Marian Stampps. Pearson's marginal association with— and knowledge of—movement activists precludes his full examination of the context of Newton's experiences. This is merely one of the many shortcomings of Pearson's work.

Criticism of the Criticism: The First Negation

Pearson's narrative, insightful at times, suffers from both substantive and technical problems. The footnote style he utilizes has no numbers in the text, though footnote references were numbered in the endnotes. The larger issue is the substantive mistakes Pearson makes in his historiography. Though he attempts to provide a historical backdrop to his narrative, his chronology of "Premier Negro Leaders"—an annoying phrase he utilizes throughout the text—shows glaring errors of fact. These "Premier Negro Leaders," in Pearson's view, are oedipally slain and succeeded by the next "Premier Negro Leader" under criteria and for reasons seemingly known only to Pearson. This role during the twentieth century passed from Booker T. Washington to W.E.B. Du Bois, from Du Bois to A. Philip Randolph, from Randolph to Adam Clayton Powell, from Powell to Martin Luther King, from King to Stokely Carmichael, and apparently from Carmichael to Newton.[10] Pearson was not able to situate Marcus Garvey, Malcolm X, or organizational leadership such as the National Association of Colored Women, SNCC, and the NAACP in his historiography, opting instead for a "great man" model of history. Though he mentions Ella Baker and Fannie Lou Hamer, he does not develop them or their importance. Bypassing the role of the Communist and Socialist Parties, even though his "Premier Negro Leader" Randolph was a member of the latter, he does not offer an analysis of the contradictions in the nationalist-Marxist power struggle that could have informed his analysis of the BPP and the role of the white left in its development and its later factioning.[11] He also fails to connect the sexism of the black church to the sexism throughout the civil rights and Black Power movements. This failure to acknowledge the persistence of sexism in the church leaves nationalists as the whipping boy of Marxists, who assert the virtual equivalence of nationalism and sexism. The white left continues to use this argument to draw attention away from its own long history of sexism and racism. Pearson fails to engage this very important discourse because he largely ignores the agency of women in his treatment of the BPP and the wider black liberation struggle.

Pearson also reports as fact some very contentious assertions, including the disputed police account of George Jackson's assassination. He even suggests that the rapacious COINTELPRO checked itself whenever activist lives were at risk—which is clearly at odds with what is known of the COINTELPRO.[12] He insists that upon expelling Bobby Seale from the BPP, Newton bullwhipped and raped him—an assertion Seale has publicly denied.[13] He accepts the BPP caricature of Maulana Karenga's Us organization by calling it United Slaves (US) instead of the actual name, Us (as opposed to "them").[14] In addition, he incorrectly credits the seminal use of the appellation *black* over *Negro* to Carmichael and Willie Ricks, ignoring the public proclamations of Malcolm X, who constantly referred to "blacks" as opposed to " Negroes."[15] It was Malcolm's more than anyone else's use of the term *black* that led to SNCC, the BPP, and a whole generation of black youth accepting it.

Pearson also seems to be unfamiliar with some basic aspects of BPP history. For example, he does not mention the transformation of party chapters into the National Committees to Combat Fascism—a signal event in BPP history. He does correctly attribute to Fred Hampton the "Rainbow Coalition" program that was later appropriated by Jesse Jackson. He reminds us that Bobby Hutton probably would not have died in the manner he did if Eldridge had not orchestrated a "jackanape" attack on the police that resulted in the shoot-out and murder of Hutton on April 6, 1968. However, Pearson does not focus his analytic lens on the enduring and deadly conflicts like that between Us and the BPP. The prominence of this episode involving Karenga and former Panthers still lingers, second only to the culpability of the NoI in the assassination of Malcolm X, as the most divisive unresolved conflict within the Black Power movement. His woefully incomplete internal analysis of the BPP leaves the reader bereft of the context necessary to fully evaluate the BPP's actions. Further, it leaves one unprepared to apply the lessons of the BPP to the present conditions facing blacks in America. Such limitations lead one to question Pearson's intentions in critiquing the BPP, which appear to be an attack on the very idea of black activism—especially black nationalist mobilization in the United States.

The Glorification of the "Lumpen" and Its Impact on the Victim/Villain Dichotomy

Pearson does admit that "strong BPP chapters . . . which contained dynamic leaders such as Michael Tabor and Dhoruba Moore" existed in New York as well as in Fred Hampton's Chicago. However, as Robinson notes, this appears as an afterthought.[16] Pearson's central concern and focus seems to have been detailing the salacious allegations and rumors about Newton and the Oakland BPP, while leaving the FBI relatively unscathed with respect to their often vicious treatment of the activists. Generally, Robinson is correct that in his attempt to document Newton's criminality, Pearson seeks to indict, by implication, the BPP as a whole. He goes so far as labeling the BPP as "little more than a temporary media phenomenon."[17] He is upset that "radical Left and the Left-liberal media continued to play a major role in elevating the rudest, most outlaw element of black America as the true keepers of the flame in all it means to be black."[18] He maintains that the destructive repercussions of this process of glorifying "lumpenism" are visited upon the present generation. In this assessment, Pearson is partially correct; however, the impact of glorified lumpenism is hardly the result of the BPP alone.

The reality is that the black urban centers today have become war zones where dope dealers and gang leaders are respected, and the gun is often the final arbiter of conflict. Notwithstanding the impact of larger politico-economic forces that have given rise to urban violence (not to mention the criminality of the perpetrators themselves), one could argue that it is the absence of the Black Power activists that has allowed the same streets they once patrolled to become the "stomping grounds" of the worst elements of the black community. Nonetheless, while popular media, especially hip-hop, has generated a new interest in the black liberation struggle among the youth, its more prominent impact has been its glorification of criminality and sexism in the black community.[19] The recent writings of former Panthers also have had an impact on this phenomenon—whether intended or not. The present proliferation of Panther exposés can be labeled "The Growth Industry of Panther Revisionism; or, When Radical Chic Meets the Statute of Limitations." Here we find Panthers such as Elaine Brown, fresh from her Paris home, descending upon the movement and offering her analysis after a decade and a half. (We are reminded of Julius Nyerere's instruction to black intellectuals: "We have to be part of the society which we are changing; we have to work from within it, and not try to descend like ancient gods, do something, and disappear again."[20]) David Hilliard emerges from his recently discovered sobriety to offer a difficult-to-read overview of the party and his relationship with Newton. Both authors settle no pressing issues, and show an incredible facility for incriminating others while remaining exculpate themselves. Further, they both, especially Brown, were put on whirlwind tours by their publishers, sometimes presented as among current black leadership—a designation that neither merits by present activity. While we may respect their earlier work, just as Newton had descended from leadership, so have these two. Their experience gives them much to comment on, but their exposés seem largely gratuitous and deftly ambiguous. In any case, the writing of books after twenty years of absence from struggle does not qualify a person for the mantle of leadership.

Further, Pearson admonishes the popular press for promoting former Los Angeles gang member Cody Scott (Sanyika Shakur) in a manner ominously similar to the marketing of Eldridge Cleaver. *Atlantic Monthly Press's* Morgan Entrekin's elevation of Scott as a "primary voice of the black experience" is, for Pearson, another case of promoting "defiant posturing over substance." He also argues that Leon Bing's book about L.A. gangs, *Do or Die,* rests subliminally on a "threat of rape" foundation similar to Cleaver's *Soul on Ice.*[21] The gangster-Panther relationship actually deserves a broader treatment than Pearson supplies, as it has been evident since the inception of the BPP.

For example, Alprentice "Bunchy" Carter was a BPP leader in L.A. as well as a leader of the Slausons, a dominant territorial gang in South Central. As youths, Danifu (Raymond Scott), along with Irving Hakim and Crip founder Raymond Washington, were politicized by L.A. BPP members, primarily John Huggins and Bunchy Carter, in an attempt similar to that undertaken in Chicago by Fred Hampton with Jeff Fort's Blackstone Rangers and Hispanic gangs. It appears that Raymond Washington had wanted to become a BPP member but was too young. He nonetheless put superficial aspects of Panther philosophy (CRIP is an acronym for Continuing Revolution In Progress), style (cripping), and fashion (the BPP powder blue shirt as the Crip blue rag) into his early organization.[22] However, the BPP was not simply transferring imagery to gangs. BPP member Akinsanya Kambon worked to organize gang truces across California from the early 1970s. It is ironic that it was a gang member, Tyrone Robinson, allegedly trying to "make rank" in the Black Guerrilla Family (BGF), who killed Newton.[23] Is this the slaying of the father that Pearson emphasizes in his evolution of "Premier Negro Leaders"? Does this represent the passing of the torch from the Panthers to the urban gangs? What are the lessons that the destruction of Huey Newton and the BPP teaches us? Pearson's glaring failure to adequately address these issues weakens his analysis.

The Need for Our Own Referents: Learning the Correct Lessons from History

Pearson is correct that the BPP's downfall cannot simply be attributed to COINTELPRO—though it stands as a principal agent of its destruction. While inserting its own operatives in the volatile organization, COINTELPRO capitalized on internal weaknesses and contradictions. We are reminded of one of the major lessons of Amilcar Cabral: "In the general framework of the daily struggle this battle against ourselves—no matter what difficulties the enemy may create—remains the most difficult of all. . . . I am convinced that any national or social revolution which is not based on the knowledge of this reality runs great risk of failure.[24] This is a more eloquent statement of the maxim that the personal is political. Cabral insisted that culture played a key role in the resolution of these contradictions.

The BPP did not fully appreciate the necessity for cultural transformation in the movement. Instead, they promoted a "revolutionary culture" that was amorphous and often self-serving, rooted in a Machiavellian rationalization of Malcolm's "by any means necessary" dictum whereby members simply legitimized their lumpen activities by asserting that these were somehow "revolutionary" while labeling those who decried these activities as "counterrevolutionary." This approach facilitated the sexual exploitation of women, the character assassination of rivals, the misuse of BPP funds by the national leadership, and the justification of internecine violence within both the BPP itself and the

Black Power movement as a whole. This glorified lumpenism was so expansive that Hilliard reports that Newton required that BPP members watch *The Godfather,*[25] as he began to argue for a "progressive capitalism."[26] Allegedly the Panther nightclub the Lamp Post even became, among other things, a front for prostitution and funding source for Newton's and the Central Committee's personal indulgences.

Clearly, there is no such thing as a revolutionary culture, per se. Cultures are only revolutionary in opposition to some other culture. The fact that people are engaged in revolution does not suggest that they possess a revolutionary culture—at least not in any developmental sense. For example, Pol Pot led a revolution in Kampuchea, and the product was killing fields and millions of deaths, but not the creation of a meaningful revolutionary culture. The BPP's condemnation of cultural nationalism actually reflected its antipathy toward the Us organization (exacerbated by COINTELPRO and the gang conflict of Los Angeles). But Pearson did not explore the roots of the Us/Panther conflict, so such issues are not raised.

The BPP, owing to disjointed Maoist borrowings, the influence of white leftists, and the personal battles with Karenga and Us, largely ignored the challenge of cultural transformation. This owed, in part, to their conflating of popular culture with national culture and their consideration of the latter in a very superficial way. Though the BPP maintained a Minister of Culture (Emory Douglas), leaders attacked cultural nationalism as an ideology and an approach to revolutionary struggle. The negation of the transformative power of cultural practice, especially in the area of ethics and social conduct, aggravated the BPP's vulnerability to outside manipulation and control. Ironically, they did not appreciate how the transformation they sought through the provision of survival programs was ultimately a cultural transformation rooted less in Marx and more in Malcolm. This misunderstanding allowed Newton to evoke Papa Doc Duvalier as a prime example of the vacuity and inappropriateness of cultural or "pork chop" nationalism.[27] The Oakland BPP, unlike the New York BPP members—whom Hilliard labeled cultural nationalists[28]–also misunderstood the basic Pan-African (and American) nature of black culture and were ultimately unable to successfully channel it for the party's own ends.[29]

Moreover, none of the successful revolutions that the BPP evoked were explicable unless one appreciated the role by which leaders utilized their indigenous culture as a means of mobilization and transformation. Such revolutionaries did not await a "revolutionary" culture; instead they grounded themselves in their national heritage and evoked the best of it, and the best of it was in opposition to the status quo of their (neo)colonial oppressors—especially in the areas of values, views, and ethics, the latticework for the struggle that Cabral argues. This insight led Cabral to conclude that within culture is found the seed of opposition that leads to the fashioning of the liberation movement. The wars of national liberation that the BPP celebrated (in Vietnam, China, Algeria, Cuba) centered on a nationalistic base from which even Marxist-Leninist revolutionaries directed their efforts and derived their commitment. Successful revolutionary leaders appreciated that insofar as an important aspect of struggle is to capture the hearts and minds of the people, a revolution that attacks the cultural hegemony of their oppressors forms the basis of the larger political-military struggle for national self-determination. Without it, the masses, suffering under the cultural hegemony of their colonizers, will be unconvinced of their capacity to liberate themselves.

In its rejection of the revolutionary role of cultural transformation, the BPP was distancing itself not only from revolutionary practice but from the core of the black liberation movement itself, of which "cultural nationalism actually provided much of its thrust and dynamic."[30] This was notable in the writings of the father of what became known as "revolutionary black nationalism," Malcolm X. In his 1964 "Statement of the Basic Aims and

Objectives of the Organization of Afro-American Unity," he wrote, "We must launch a cultural revolution to unbrainwash an entire people." Further, Malcolm insists that "armed with the knowledge of the past, we can with confidence charter a course for our future. Culture is an indispensable weapon in the freedom struggle. We must take hold of it and forge the future with the past."[31] While seemingly aware of these precepts,[32] too often the BPP operated as if it was oblivious to them. Further, the heavy rhetoric of the times made a meaningful discussion of these issues problematic at best and "counterrevolutionary" at worst. A misreading of Maoism and the influence of the white left (many of whom would later become some of the most trenchant critics of the BPP) led the BPP to embrace a "cultureless leftism" that even led them to reject the teaching of Black studies.[33]

The transformative power of the BPP was not in taking up the gun—blacks had a long history of armed resistance up to that time. The transformative power, on the individual level, was to be found in the provision of the community with patrols and development (survival) programs in a context of political education and activism. It was the Oakland leadership, the security elements, exiles, and many members of the underground, largely out of touch with the day-to-day grounding and operation of these programs, who lacked the opportunity to be transformed by this reorienting of values in the community. It was the service to the community that transformed peoples of all classes from college students to gang members. As these projects, especially in California, came to be extortionist plans and strong-arming attempts, they lost their capacity to transform folk in a constructive way. In fact, they further legitimized the unprincipled lumpen activities of the BPP and reduced its capacity to substantively transform its members and the larger community.

The survival programs taught through practice the ethics of love, caring, diligence, reciprocity, community, creativity, responsibility, and struggle—all of these representative of the best aspects of a truly African-American culture. These "poor people's programs" provided a cultural reorientation for participants, allowing for the political transformation envisioned by the BPP. The cultural reorientation was toward the best in African-American culture. Because of the opposition between this national culture and the dominant white supremacist culture, the result was a very revolutionary *process,* as opposed to the revolutionary *act* of organizationally picking up the gun for a political objective. This cultural (largely ethical) transformation provided the resin for subsequent political activity.

The BPP's attempt to organize the most disorganized group in the United States, the lumpenproletariat, on a program that drew from Mao, Fanon, and Guevera, was impressive, although it was sure to flounder given the myriad sources it drew upon from outside the United States; the people required examples more consistent with their own experiences. Newton seemed to understand this when he wrote "The Correct Handling of a Revolution" (May 18, 1967) and later attempted to expand his analysis based on Panther experiences in his "Intercommunalism." But few Panthers (and few academics) understood Newton's later formulations, so they dismissed them. This was due in part to Newton's shortcomings as a public speaker, but also to the rejection of his thesis by the white left, who could accept, and even glamorize, Newton's thuggery but not his theory. Hilliard points out that leftists "like us picking up guns and shooting it out with the pigs. But they don't want us as theoretical leaders."[34] They didn't want theorizing but only thuggery. In similar fashion, Pearson reduces Newton's paradigm, ultimately a Ph.D. dissertation, to a paragraph.[35]

The foreign nature of the neo-Marxist models and their inapplicability to the condition of African-Americans was exacerbated by BPP members' lack of familiarity with black history and political science. Former Panther, BLA member, and revolutionary exile Assata Shakur concurs that "the basic problem stemmed from the fact that the BPP had no systematic approach to political education. They were reading the Red Book but didn't know who Harriet Tubman, Marcus Garvey, and Nat Turner were. They talked about intercommunalism but still really believed that the Civil War was fought to free the slaves. A whole lot of them barely understood any kind of history, Black, African or otherwise. . . . That was the main reason many Party members, in my opinion, underestimated the need to unite with other Black organizations and to struggle around various community issues."[36] This failure to unite with progressive elements in the black community was underscored by the BPP's alliances with groups outside of the black community—primarily the antiwar movement. However, the antiwar movement had no coherent ideology nor much stomach for revolution. The white left seemed less intent on revolt and more on keeping its followers out of Vietnam. Not surprisingly, BPP alliances with these leftists dried up as the war wound down.

Further, the antagonistic language of Marxism-Leninism, vanguardism, and the cult of personality allowed for purges and excommunication in a manner unforeseen in the black community. The Panther use of the bullwhip for punishment, and the introduction of some of its most esoteric and confusing precepts—including the wholesale attack on spirituality—was so foreign and far removed from black culture that it was sure to engender community disenchantment with the Panthers. Pearson does not examine these influences fully, and without such an undertaking the BPP story hovers outside history.

Criticism of the Source: The Second Negation

Pearson's difficulties are apparently rooted in his limited exposure to the BPP, his reliance on three BPP insiders—"those who would never forgive Huey for what he did to the party"—and the fact that it was easiest for him "to gain the cooperation of nonblacks who had been affiliated with Newton and the party."[37]

Pearson's attempts to discern the internal workings of the BPP would be difficult, considering the history of betrayal, infiltration, harassment, and imprisonment to which its members have been subjected. Nonetheless, the issue of Pearson's historical grounding and knowledge of the subject that could have allayed the fears of members needs to be addressed. Having said that, the author's suggestion that his original intent in writing this book was to promote positive male Panthers seems rather incredible. In fact, it begs the question of the author's grounding in BPP history that he would focus on Newton—a Jekyll and Hyde individual at best—rather than, for instance, Fred Hampton, Geronimo ji Jaga, Sundiata Acoli, Akinsanya Kambon, or a litany of others.

However, the burden of historical grounding is not Pearson's alone. Surviving Panthers (and movement activists, more generally) have a clear responsibility to educate the generations that follow them and not sacrifice those generations to their paranoia. Unless there is a disclosure by the 1960s activists to the present generation of the methods, means, and opportunities that underlay COINTELPRO, then both the present and future generations of activists will suffer from this lack of information. The police need send no new informants; most in the struggle are not even clear on who the old ones were, or what to do when they are discovered. The past generation was good at many things, but discovering infiltrators, and handling informants—much less counterintelligence—were hardly their strong points. In fact, we could argue that we were better at isolating, bad-jacketing, and killing innocents than ferreting out the villains from among them. I think the deaths of Malcolm X, Sandra Pratt, Fred Hampton, Michael Baynam, Mark Clark, Sam Napier, Fred Bennett, Alex Rackley, James Carr, and many others attest to this. Nonetheless, the present generation should know what happened—from the BPP (and the NAIM)[38] perspective—if the struggle is to continue. Therefore, what Pearson sets out to do, in its best light, is a useful undertaking, and one that serious students and practitioners of black liberation need to carry out effectively.

Pearson's Basic Failure

Pearson's basic failure lies in his attempt to deny the value of the movement by pointing out (correctly) some of the worst aspects of Huey P. Newton and the BPP. Although he understands that the experience of other chapters across the country, particularly those in New York and Chicago, was different, he is upset by what he discovers about the Oakland BPP. However, lacking a history of struggle in the movement and the hard lessons learned from that struggle to reassure him, he ultimately becomes disillusioned. Vested in a great-man model of history, Pearson is left rudderless by Newton's apparent "irredeemability." Thus, by extension, Newton and the black liberation struggle are nullified. Pearson's conclusion is sure to win praise from many who neither countenance nor fathom the motivation of blacks who militantly pursue their right of self-determination.

On a more personal level, Pearson fails to understand both the transformative power of the BPP and the limitations of that power that led not only to Newton's failure to be transformed but to his descent into an abyss of drugs and destruction. More telling is Pearson's apparent antagonism for the Black Power movement, which led him to focus primarily on Newton's personal failures. Understanding Newton's personal failures will provide some contribution to our understanding of the BPP; however, such analysis is woefully incomplete. What is needed is a work that would situate Newton in context while offering a way forward for the struggle that Newton and the BPP joined and expanded in meaningful ways.

Instead of such an undertaking, Pearson moves from attacking Newton's personal failures to indicting the BPP as a whole (the vast majority of whose members were not criminals of any sort). Had he chosen instead to make a more thorough analysis, he probably would have reached the conclusion that activists should reject formations that promote messianic leaders and cults of personality in organizations that have a paramilitary element. These factors lead to the arbitrary use of power to silence dissent. Further, the violence and criminality of followers in such organizations are often sanctioned by "divine right" (as in the NoI) or rationalized in the name of the revolution (as in the BPP). These processes led to the assassination of Malcolm X by members of the NoI and the murders of James Carr, Fred Bennett, Sam Napier, Michael Baynam, and others within the BPP. These critiques of the Black Power movement are relevant and have implications for the present struggle, but unlike Pearson's analysis they are informed by the history of black struggle and do not denigrate the movement as a whole. *The Shadow of the Panther* leaves the reader without a synthesis of the divergent tendencies clashing within the Black Power movement and projects Pearson's own inability to synthesize trends in the Black Power movement as the movement's inability to provide a compass for present mobilization. The author simply fails to appreciate both the context and the implications of the Black Power movement and the BPP on important issues within the black community today.

Conclusion: The Negation of the Negation

In sum, Pearson teaches a "catechism of impossibilities": those who resist—especially those who rise up in the name of Black Power—are doomed. But Black Power cannot be simply reduced to Huey P. Newton and the BPP. Newton's life and the BPP, at their best, are massive positive contributions to the cause of freedom, dignity, and black liberation. At their worst, they reflect a personal and collective failure to study and learn the lessons of black liberation and the enormous personal and social costs that such a struggle entails. Newton's life is set on a destructive path due to his actions, not because of some inherent deficiency in the black liberation struggle. Huey Newton died a crackhead's death, and that should not be glamorized or rationalized as a "plot" of COINTELPRO. It was a testament to the work left undone that Newton's death was neither. Pearson attacks Newton for his failures but is blind to the redemptive quality of the struggle itself—ultimately a liberating process; for what would Huey Newton have been in life were it not for the black liberation struggle?

The burdens that Newton placed on himself and others and those to which he eventually succumbed are rooted in larger failures of policy that were endemic in the BPP program and the context of political repression in the United States. Most fundamentally, the BPP confused an historic moment of incredible reform in the United States with an opportunity to wage revolution in the name of a multiracial proletariat that did not exist in any meaningful way. They misconstrued the interests of white leftists, who were more intent on avoiding war than on waging revolution; thus they confused an antiwar movement with a revolutionary struggle to bring down the government. These shortcomings reflected their utilization of a revolutionary compass grafted from foreign struggles that was not oriented to the demands of the United States political economy. Further, by ultimately eschewing black nationalism for intercommunalism, they dislodged themselves from the very basis of their support in the black community. With respect to these issues and their impact on Huey Newton, the BPP, and the black liberation struggle in general, Pearson doesn't appear to have a shadow of a clue.

While a full discussion of the BPP's strategies and tactics is beyond the scope of this essay, the legacy of the BPP makes it clear that no class or group has an innate quality that ordains them as the "vanguard." Instead, we should build in our everyday practices, relationships, and institutions the nurturing and positive values and interests that is the stuff of successful liberation struggles. Finally, we must ensure that present and future generations learn from the rich history of struggle of which the BPP and Huey P. Newton have played a significant part. This struggle includes successes and failures, and quite a bit of "in-betweens." We should be critical in our assessment of the BPP, Newton, and all of our social movements. Such acts of criticism, born from grounding in the movement and continued dedicated practice in it, are both virtuous and necessary. We are still waiting for such a constructive and critical analysis of the Black Power movement, the Black Panther Party, and Huey P. Newton.[39]

16

Rediscovering the Black Panther Party

Victor Wallis

The Black Panther Party, despite its short life span, has much to tell us about the conditions for a revolutionary politics in the United States. Brought to prominence by direct confrontations with police in Oakland, California, but inspired from the outset by a larger vision, the BPP quickly built up a wide following. In so doing, however, it set off the loudest possible alarms in the nation's power centers. The result was an official repressive campaign of unprecedented ferocity, which destroyed the party within a few years and inflicted a long-term setback not just on its own constituency but on the whole of the U.S. Left.

Now, a full generation later, the Left appears to be recovering its vitality. Given the dramatic changes that have occurred in the interim (both within and outside the United States), new openings for activism have appeared. Struggles that had previously been carried on separately—whether across social groups or across national borders—are now increasingly seen to require coordinated responses and a common framework of analysis.[1] Most importantly, however, the Left is taking on a new generation of activists, who need urgently to understand the successes and failures of their predecessors.

So far as the Panther experience is concerned, there is no better place to start than with Lee Lew-Lee's remarkable film *All Power to the People: The Black Panther Party and Beyond.*[2] Made in the aftermath of the 1992 Los Angeles uprising (which Lew-Lee witnessed as a cameraman for network news), the film maintains a good balance between historical framing, firsthand narrative by Panther veterans (with an American Indian Movement subtext), and commentary on repression featuring prominent FBI and CIA whistleblowers. These qualities have earned the film prime-time TV exposure abroad as well as numerous awards at home. Characteristically, however, the U.S. media oligarchy has kept it off the air where it matters most.

What the networks fear now differs little from what the government feared thirty years ago. It's not that one can't find elsewhere the information given in this film, but film brings it to life, compresses it, and makes it accessible to people at every level of familiarity with the issues raised. The film is clearly sympathetic to the Panthers (Lew-Lee is himself a former Panther), but what is more important is that it provides a major part of the framework needed to understand the Party's vulnerability. This is a necessary first step in defining the Panthers' legacy, and it makes the subsequent steps a bit easier.

Why is such a process of definition important—and a matter of legitimate concern—to those who, like myself, are not a part of the Panther constituency? My own view is, in the first place, that the overriding issue is how to build an authentic popular movement, and that the only viable approach to the subdivisions of such a movement is the old slogan "All for one, and one for all!" The "one" originally meant any individual, but it can just as easily be a constituency defined by any particular form of oppression; the slogan itself, in turn, is one of reciprocal support rather than of domination or control. Second, in the specific setting of a country in which the working class has been racially divided, it is clear that no popular movement can make headway—against the priorities of capital and on behalf of real human needs—unless it is resolutely multiracial. Third, the Panthers themselves have a distinctive importance in this regard, not only because of their strong roots in their own community, but also because of their consistent advocacy of collaboration across racial lines.

Although Lew-Lee's film skirts the ideological debates on such matters, it dramatizes the moral force of a unified response to injustice, suggesting at the same time that it was this very prospect that most alarmed the defenders of privilege. Malcolm X is thus shown, in the sequence preceding his assassination (1965), concluding a public lecture with the words, "I, for one, will join in with anyone, I don't care what color you are, as long as you want to change this miserable condition." Gunshots are then heard before the scene shifts, after which we hear commentaries (from Herman Ferguson and Philip Agee) suggesting a link between Malcolm's death and U.S. counterintelligence.

Martin Luther King's death, just three years later, appears in a similar context, despite the different path by which King arrived at his "dangerous" posture. He is shown denouncing the Vietnam War and, in a TV soundbite, affirming the need for a "revolution of values" while giving unexpected vibrancy to John F. Kennedy's dictum about peaceful and violent revolution (viz., that those who make the former impossible make the latter "inevitable"). Commentaries on King's death (most notably, that of ex-FBI agent Wesley Swearingen) do not even mention the alleged hit man but instead focus squarely on J. Edgar Hoover's long-standing vendetta against King.[3]

Former BPP Chairman Bobby Seale, earlier in the film, cited Malcolm X, with his call for "not Integration but Freedom," as the party's major precursor. Just as Malcolm's message, however, was more universal than was acknowledged by his detractors, so King's was more radical than portrayed by those who accepted his posthumous sanctification. Although the two leaders never linked up organizationally, they nonetheless became the twin targets of official repression. This very fact constitutes an important backdrop to the campaign against the Panthers. While official rationalizations for the campaign stressed the Panthers' armed challenges to police authority, the disruption of the Party left no dimension of its work untouched. Even the program of free breakfasts for school children came under attack, as the FBI pressured churches to deny it space.[4]

In the film, the repression is omnipresent, reaching a climax in the carefully planned assassination (in 1969) of Chicago BPP leader Fred Hampton. Hampton, at 21, was already a particularly vital player in the larger movement, in view of his unique role in politicizing neighborhood gangs and in building multiracial alliances. Kathleen Cleaver, in an interview, cites him as the originator of the Rainbow Coalition that would later be taken up first in Boston (around Mel King) and then nationally (around Jesse Jackson). Hampton had a distinctive ability to articulate theory and strategy in popular language;[5] he is here shown, at an outdoor rally, speaking words that define his mission as one of revolutionary scope: "Racism is an excuse used for capitalism."

Both the details of Hampton's murder and the larger pattern of COINTELPRO repression have already been extensively documented.[6] The film can offer only the most fleeting glimpses of the relevant paper trail, but it provides stark testimony from Panther activists (including, among others, Dhoruba Bin Wahad, Mumia Abu-Jamal, and George

Edwards) about the suspicions, splits, frame-ups, and killings that were thus orchestrated. The general pattern of police harassment is unremitting, and many of the charges were made to stick, mostly on the basis of fabricated evidence and many resulting in long prison sentences (invariably longer than for "nonpolitical" defendants convicted of similar offenses). For authoritative information on this type of practice, however, the written word is a more useful medium than film.[7]

Of singular interest in Lew-Lee's film, nonetheless, are comments from George Edwards, citing the opinion of ex-CIA officer John Stockwell to the effect that BPP cofounder Huey Newton was, possibly as early as 1971, subject to manipulation by CIA-type "psychological operations." Apart from additional references to highhandedness and drug involvement on Newton's part, we also see some particularly telling shots of a rather dazed-looking Newton—hands quivering, eyes glistening, and with a continuous smile—saying that "the people are not interested in socialism at this time" (around 1974) but that if they were ever to express such an interest "democratically," the Panthers would be the first to support them!

From its specific focus on the destruction of the Panthers, the film turns to a wider look at the government's repressive mechanisms and activities, encompassing the assault on the American Indian Movement (AIM), the development of the Federal Emergency Manpower Agency (FEMA), and the onset of the "drug war." The campaign against AIM parallels the one against the Panthers; the fraudulent conviction of Leonard Peltier,[8] here criticized by former U.S. attorney general Ramsey Clark, is among its offshoots. FEMA, with its concentration camps, and the drug war, are touched on only briefly. We get a flashed page of Gary Webb's investigative series on the Los Angeles drug market, while Philip Agee comments on federal complicity in a process that led, as he puts it, to the depoliticization of "a whole generation of young black males."[9]

Following a brief tribute, in the form of a photo gallery, to current U.S. political prisoners and prisoners of war, the film's leading interviewees and its director invite us to reflect. This would ideally be the conversation of a live audience, but the issues I would pose for discussion are these: 1) Are there any important dimensions of the story that are missing from the film? 2) Is there anything about the Panthers' own origins and/or conduct that might have facilitated the government's repressive agenda? 3) Which ideas and practices of the Panthers remain of permanent value?

As to missing dimensions, I think first of language. The popular Panther rhetoric of the period is gone, not only from the retrospective interviews but even from most of the archival selections. "Pig" appears in passing only once, although it is a concept that was so widely used that both Huey Newton and Bobby Seale gave public rationales for it at the time.[10] Language that was strong to some but offensive to many was, for better or worse, endemic. Newton wrote at one point, "We had all sorts of profanity in our paper and every other word which dropped from our lips was profane."[11] A second missing dimension is the prison struggles. There is no mention, for example, of George Jackson, a Field Marshal of the BPP, whose prison writings made him one of the best-known revolutionaries of that period. Third, no attention is given to ideological differences between the Panthers and other sectors of the Black Liberation movement.

The upshot of these omissions is to make the Panthers appear somewhat less controversial now than they were in their own time. Insofar as this film is meant to be introductory in character, the effect may be intended and may even be justified. But it does not absolve us from having to take the next steps. In fact, a greater awareness of the problematic dimensions of the Panthers may eventually give us a fuller appreciation of their qualities.

The Panthers' vulnerability is a huge topic, and I cannot hope to do it justice here. In some ways, much like the larger Left movement that they helped shape, the Panthers came on the scene in response to an emergency.[12] Although Malcolm X had sounded the tocsin, the urban black populations were still largely without any grassroots political expression. The Panthers were the first to respond at a level that began to address the real problems. Should they be blamed for not coming into being with a fully developed democratic organization? In any event, their language reflected a certain bravado and masculinism—sometimes spilling over into an easy acceptance of violence—which undoubtedly made disruption somewhat easier than it might otherwise have been.[13] Another expression of the same problem, discernible in the film though not emphasized by it, is the way in which Seale, even while criticizing Newton's power plays, nonetheless describes all the countermeasures in terms of his own personal actions.

The larger vulnerability reflected in all this has everything to do with the Panthers' meteoric rise to prominence, in an implacably hostile official environment. The BPP was hastily grafted onto the chaotic conditions of an oppressed community. Party and community alike were affected, moreover, by the highly competitive, super-individualistic ethos of the dominant culture. Although many of the Party's cadre were well aware of this problem, and fought persistently against its effects, the organization as a whole, once it had attained the national spotlight, was never granted a moment's respite to recover its balance. Battered relentlessly by every state institution, the Panthers spent much of their energy in futile conflicts far removed from the implementation of their political program. This could not but have a disorienting effect, with sometimes tragic results.[14]

But whatever the Panthers' weaknesses or failings, they left an enduring positive legacy. This is seen most clearly in the steps they took to organize and educate their communities. They popularized the demand for community control of police and drew similarly wide support for their free breakfast program. In addition, they established free clinics and encouraged independent popular education. Beyond all this, as an autonomous grassroots organization, they never had any fear of being "controlled, or partly controlled, by whites," and thus were able, as Eldridge Cleaver put it, "to sit down with whites and hammer out solutions to our common problems without trembling in our boots about whether or not we might get taken over in the process."[15] The resulting openness allowed the Panthers to keep their focus on capitalism as the people's principal enemy.

The underlying insight, the metaphoric violence, and the closeness to the people are fused in Fred Hampton's extraordinary spoken parable of political education:

> . . . [T]heory's cool, but theory with no practice ain't shit. . . .
>
> What are we doing? The Breakfast for Children program. We are running it in a socialistic manner. . . . People are gonna take our program and tell us to go on to a higher level. . . . What'd the pig say? He say, "Nigger—you like communism?" "No sir, I'm scared of it." "You like socialism?" "No sir, I'm scared of it." "You like the breakfast for children program?" "Yes sir, I'd die for it." Pig said, "Nigger, that program is a socialistic program." "I don't give a fuck if it's Communism. You put your hands on that program motherfucker and I'll blow your motherfucking brains out."[16]

17

Tracking Down the Empirical Legacy of the Black Panther Party; or, Notes on the Perils of Pursuing the Panthers

Claudia Dahlerus and Christian A. Davenport

All we wanted was to find out what the Black Panthers said, did, and what happened to them. We didn't want to conduct surveys or interviews (at least not initially). All we wanted were the written records: i.e., the police, FBI, and Black Panther files, newspaper reports, pamphlets, and so forth. We knew the task would be difficult, and we knew much of the information we sought would not be readily available. But never, never did we expect that the journey would be so arduous, nor would we have guessed who and what would stand in the way of our pursuit of information. The naïveté of youth, a faith in the myth that those that seek shall find, or a penchant for sleuthing (like Poirot, Columbo, or Barbara Neely's Blanche)—all of these things clouded our understanding of what would transpire.

In the thirty years since the Panthers first emerged, things have been lost, misplaced, hidden, or simply forgotten.[1] There are stories that people want to tell (and they deserve to be told), as well as opinions that must be interjected—seemingly everything but a clearly identifiable historical record. Obviously, many people and institutions were helpful in finding different pieces of the puzzle (resources that are invaluable to this sort of research). Generally, however, these people and institutions were few and far between. Maybe it was just us and how the various organizations/individuals responded to us. It's likely some people we interacted with were not that accustomed to dealing with six-foot-tall, shaven-headed, African-American males, or five-foot-five, long-haired, white females, both with postsecondary degrees, an acute interest in contention, and possessing both impatience and laptops.

Then again, maybe it wasn't us. It is difficult to tell; discussions about the quest for political-historical information collected for quantitative purposes are rare.[2] Very often we do not discuss our individual information-gathering experiences from a particular project unless we are within our own circle of intellectual acquaintance. This is problematic, for it sends others invariably back down the same paths—again and again. In an effort to make other scholars aware of the many hurdles we encountered, we offer our reflections.

The following essay identifies the pitfalls confronted by two scholars trying to obtain and code (content analyze) the Black Panther Party's newspaper, the *Black Panther,* four Bay Area newspapers *(the Bay Guardian, Berkeley Barb, Oakland Tribune,* and *Sun Reporter),* and the *New York Times,* as well as police department and court records from around the Bay Area, including Oakland, Berkeley, San Francisco, and Alameda County. We have highlighted the pitfalls because we feel they are most useful for future researchers to anticipate and overcome. To protect the innocent, the not-so-innocent, and ourselves from both, we generally relay these experiences as abstracted principles for investigating contentious social movement organizations. Sometimes, however, names will be named. Regardless, we will attempt to be as true to the experiences and as straightforward as possible.

Three categories are specifically addressed within this chapter. The first section, "Big Brother," includes those experiences that were generally expected regarding the police/intelligence community and the various limitations that they imposed on those investigating "militant" or "conflictual" social movements. Second, we present "A Tribe Called Quest," which concerns different aspects of the research effort, such as the tedious expenses of conducting archival analyses and the difficulties in acquiring adequate student assistance. Third, and last, we discuss "Non-Strictly Business."[5] This section addresses many of the interpersonal dynamics that scholars will confront when they attempt to conduct this type of research, across different political and social institutions, different races, different classes of people, and different regions of the country.

Big Brother

The first formidable, but expected, obstruction to overcome was the various restrictions put forward by different agents of the state. For example, one encounters resistance in the course of trying to gather information about their actions, what they are monitoring, and why they are doing it. Attempt to use the Freedom of Information or Public Records Acts (California Public Records Act specifically; see appendix A)[3] to obtain information, however, and you will find yourself in a bureaucratic labyrinth, the likes of which no minotaur or seasoned researcher could escape. Although the nuances of accessing information are well addressed by Ann Mari Buitrago and Leon Immerman, FOIA Inc., Richard O. Curry, and Eve Pell, the reality is far more devastating on the mind and morale of the researcher.[4] Indeed, we are reminded of Parenti's comment, "power is always more [effective] when cooptive, covert, and manipulative than when nakedly brutish."[5] In analysis, as in many things, Huxley trumps Orwell.

The police and court agencies effectively exercise power through their control over access to information, thus reducing the various public records acts to little more than the window dressing of democracy. For example, in trying to obtain police records from the Oakland Police Department and San Francisco courts for certain members of the Black Panther Party, first we had to locate the appropriate department within the police and court institutions. Apart from being informed that "this is not public information," more often than not we were sent on the proverbial wild-goose chase, being bounced from one office or institutional jurisdiction to another, only to learn that (a) the police/courts no longer have this information (section 1.1); (b) it is kept off-site and you must provide ridiculously detailed information about the individual's records for which you are inquiring[6] (section 2); (c) some exorbitant amount of money is required before they will even process your request; and (d) the various departments have their own idiosyncratic rules as to how many records you could request at one time (appendices B and C). Paranoid? Call or write the twenty-one police organizations listed in appendix B and ask about accessing everything on the Black Panther Party for 1968. The responses are comparable.

Statue of Limitations (Ain't Got It)

Second, you will likely hear that there is a statue of limitations. Note that we did not use the correct term, *statute,* for this implies that the obstacle is less concrete than it actually is. The limitations we confronted seemed much more final in nature. Reminding us of something that one of our grandmothers used to say, when asked about a file or newspaper, they would simply reply, "We ain't got it;" they were destroyed five years ago (as in the case of Berkeley PD) or ten years ago (in the case of the San Francisco PD). You might also hear something like, "We used to have it, but it was given to someone, somewhere, some time ago." When pushed to give up such information, however, they seem unable to recall whether such a transaction took place. What can you do in response to this? Nothing. Again, you return to the beginning and try to figure out where else you saw the information.

This identifies another problem for us: what is listed in archives is not always genuine. The lesson seems straightforward enough, and you would think that you would remember this, but one has to constantly update who has what, altering what is provided on faxes, websites, and within the pages of old books. For example, UC–Berkeley listed its volume/issue information on the *Black Panther* newspaper out of sequence with the corresponding dates on the papers themselves: for example, April 1968 had an earlier volume/issue number than March 1968. Additionally, the list of holdings at Stanford University included several issues that were not physically in their collection.[7]

Indeed, when studying the BPP, one is repeatedly forced to travel to different locations and search through the documents oneself (in our case, Oakland, San Francisco, Berkeley, East Lansing, New York, Houston, Los Angeles). This is great for gaining an understanding of what exists, but it is simultaneously exhausting, costly, and oftentimes simply disenchanting.

The lesson is simple: don't believe the long-distance, holding-the-list hype. Acquaint yourself with the library/archival staff and draw upon your relatives and friends (if money for the project has not yet been procured) to "eyeball" the information themselves. You should draw on all available sources of help—from middle school students to senior citizens. But assistants over sixty-five, as we discovered in one case, may significantly slow down your progress (as you wait for *One Life to Live* to get boring and the time for research once again to resume).

Filed Away, Far Away (Ain't Gonna Be Gettin' It Any Time Soon)

Among the array of sophisticated skills and qualities demanded for conducting archival/field research on the BPP, patience and persistence must be included. For example, two of the libraries that hold significant archival collections on the BPP house either most or all the materials at some remote facility that is fairly close but off-limits to non–library personnel. The real test of patience came when filing a request, which had to be done in person and which could take as little as one day and as much as three. You could only receive one item at a time, and since you never really knew what was going to be in the collection, you might find, as we did on several occasions, that much of the material listed in the archives is in fact irrelevant to what you believed the collection contained. Add to that the limited hours of access to many archival departments, and one is overwhelmed with yet more obstacles to laying hands on the data. The whole process consequently involves a significant amount of time, deflated hope, and of course, cost.[8] Suggestion: every university should have a program where undergraduates/high school students are assigned to different holdings of these documents (social protest collections), and each must write a research report detailing their contents as well as the research methods they used to acquire the documents.

The time it takes to receive the requested material may be one hurdle, but one is further disenchanted after all the time spent leafing through the material only to find the relevance to the information you seek is marginal at best. Unfortunately, librarians' descriptions are sometimes misleading —or shall we say geared toward objectives other than those pursued by us. What you think and hope you are getting may prove an anticlimactic event when you set eyes on the much-anticipated archival material. Note: It is unwise to communicate one's dissatisfaction to the library staff. It appears that not too much effort or resources are devoted to African-American collections, and thus the institutions are quite interested in finding out who is using it and how one could use this information. Pick your battles carefully. It is particularly disheartening to come across library staff responsible for overseeing the BPP holdings who know nothing about social movements, repression, Black Liberation, Civil Rights, or African Americans. They are merely gatekeepers of the documents, very often unaware of the wealth of history they oversee.

On more than one occasion it struck us as odd that much of the information about the BPP was stored, monitored, and serviced by apolitical, middle-class white staff within institutions that had been somewhat antagonistic to BPP activity on their campuses when they were around. This type of oversight is analogous to yet another form of institutional control over information. In fact, through archives (and the people who manage these collections), we have simply traded one manner of political control (the more overt and repressive kind) for a more benign version, albeit one affecting access to and subsequent research on movements like the Black Panthers.

Names, Birthdays, and Other Inaccessibles
(Ain't Gonna Get It Without Sump'n First)

Quite frequently we would come up against a problem that seemed to be unresolvable. Many police-related organizations would stipulate that they could not release particular files (arrest reports specifically) unless we could provide individuals' birth dates, social security numbers, and specific dates of the reports in question. The logic here is that there might be several individuals with the same name who have reports on file. Rather than release information not pertinent to the request (preventing violations of privacy) and as a way to decrease the cost for the police department for going into these records, they cite privacy laws and refuse to open any records at all.

This is problematic in the case of investigating the Black Panther Party because there are really no formal lists of members to consult. No comprehensive membership list for the BPP exists, at least nothing in the public domain. To further complicate matters, numerous individuals changed their names, adopting a more African-sounding or revolutionary one. Frequently, we did not know these people's "legal" (or "slave") names. Moreover, there is little likelihood of us coming up with the birth dates or social security numbers for thousands of folk who came, were active, quit, were arrested, went into exile, or just moved on to another location and another struggle.

Obviously, this does not apply to every BPP member: Huey P. Newton's birthday is remembered by millions of people the world over because every year he was in jail there was a huge rally to celebrate his birth, accompanied by shouts of "Free Huey." Oakland Police Department had very little trouble handing over this file. Most of the arrests were published in other locales as well. This logic might also apply to members of the central committee (such as Bobby Seale, Eldridge and Kathleen Cleaver, David Hilliard, or

Elaine Brown), whose lives were examined by newspapers and their faces posted on Wanted signs from Compton to Crown Heights.

For the majority of the membership, however, the lack of access to public exposure kills off any comprehensive investigation of the subject. From the police records, we are limited to discussing repression directed against the BPP in terms of a few high-profile arrests or, supplemented with newspapers, documenting a few well-covered protests and shoot-outs. From FBI records we are limited to a few inflammatory statements by Director Hoover and other agents or a few useless memos about cartoons or letters being sent to different BPP members. There is no discussion of police raids, planting of evidence, disregarding police protocol, harassment arrests, and so forth—activities that many believe to have taken place and that have been identified within numerous sources. Of course, one might always consult the Black Panther newspaper, which contains a wealth of information about repressive as well as dissident activity, providing specific dates, relevant actors, and so forth. This brings up another problem, however, discussed below.

A Tribe Called Quest

The second series of obstacles concern aspects of conducting the research itself. These include experiences from the pursuit of information. Some were expected, as in the case of Big Brother. Others we would not have anticipated under any circumstances.

Costs

Back in the 1960s and 1970s there was a much less public and less widely discussed revolution taking place in the United States—a behavioral revolution. In an effort to better understand and document political dissent, several scholars began collecting large amounts of data about this type of political activity.[9] This effort has continued into the present.[10]

Just as much as the social one, this intellectual revolution required large amounts of capital. Everything costs, from taking time to browse through materials in the library, to copying documents, to travel for archival work. In fact, let us briefly detail what had to be done to scan in every issue of the Black Panther newspaper from 1967 to 1973 as well as code numerous newspapers for events involving the BPP.

What may appear as a fairly straightforward task of events-based data collection for a mere seven-year time period is in fact a project unto itself. More often than not we encountered dead ends when trying to locate our primary data source–the Black Panther newspaper. Identifying the disparate locations of libraries and collectors that might own the BPP newspaper required persistence, patience, and money. Numerous hours and dollars were spent on long-distance telephone calls to libraries and collectors who might own the newspaper. But the charges did not stop once you hung up the phone. Faxed requests for information were often required from libraries in order to make our case as to why we needed access and explain why we must scan in the newspapers, as opposed to simply looking at them or relying on microfilm.

Despite increasing sophistication of maintaining holdings records on-line, many of the libraries contacted did not necessarily have accurate lists of their archival material (they had some; they just never took the time to see which ones). Often the only way to verify the holdings was to first call and perhaps speak to someone with considerable institutional memory and knowledge, or travel to the library itself. On several occasions inconsistencies plagued library records as to which specific dates they had in their collection. Question marks and "incomplete" were a common sight on many of the library records. This was especially true about all the issues from 1967 (first year of publication) into the first half of 1968 (when publication becomes more stable). It still remains a mystery how many issues were actually published for this time period (any assistance here would be much appreciated).

Adding to the complexity of this project, we needed the original hard copies of the newspaper because we were scanning in the material to save as files that would then become the primary data set for the project. When completed, this will be similar to a BPP on-line dataset, which could be searched like Lexis-Nexis.[11]

Unfortunately, many libraries, in the interest of consolidating space, have the newspaper available only on microfilm. In those rare instances when we finally managed to locate libraries or individuals who possessed an ample run of the newspaper in hard-copy format (which we visually verified by going through their collection), we then had to maneuver through another set of potential roadblocks. Often, we had to first get permission to scan the material, while assuring them the scanner would in no way damage the newspapers. Occasionally, in the case of individual collectors, we would have to offer them a little something "for their troubles" before the conversation/negotiation could continue. Amounts would never be discussed. One individual suggested that we recommend an amount and that insulting him would only result in our not getting access (we left).

One year later, we can easily estimate that the amount of time spent on locating newspapers in hard-copy form far exceeds the time spent actually scanning and coding it. However, in that time we were able to slowly piece together locations for the newspaper, while learning which locations were more inclined to assist us in our endeavor, and those that were not.

Table 1 shows the budget for the project. As you can see, by far the largest expense went for coders/scanners. These employees were labeled under three different categories, which designate various types of work: (1) contract workers—these individuals are contracted by us (off and on campus) to work for a specified period of time and for one lump sum payment after they have completed the assignment; (2) hourly employees—these individuals are paid bimonthly, by the hour, and work for long periods of time; and, (3) work study—these individuals represent those that work during the summertime and are subsidized by the federal government to work on different projects on campus.

The expenses alone might explain why so little data collection takes place with regard to African-American social movements (Aldon Morris, Herbert Haines and Doug McAdam aside).[12] We were only looking at one social movement over six years, however. Consider the effort of Ted Robert Gurr,[13] who examined 115 polities from 1955 to 1970 in one study; or Charles Tilly,[14] who in one study examined approximately 97 departments (political jurisdictions) in France over sixty years. Consider what it would take to identify and code for various characteristics (size, objective, organizational structure, strategies, location, degree of violence, success) all African-American social movement activity: slave rebellions, guerrilla warfare undertaken by Maroons, "Back to Africa" movements, Black secessionist movements, civil rights activity from the founding through the present, Black liberation activity, Black trade union activism, and so on. The amount is staggering (albeit clearly worthwhile). There is nothing even approaching this level of comprehension about the political activity of one ethnic group over time (see Susan Olzak,[15] the Feierabend et al. study, or even the Minorities at Risk dataset compiled by Gurr for worthwhile, yet partial attempts).

The neglect of African-American social movement/dissident behavior may also be explained by the fact that the discipline of political science has left the subject to the

Table 1   *Budget for Project (Title: Rhetoric under the Gun, NSF# SBR-9617900)*

Expense	Cost
Contracted workers (scanners and coders)	$5,845.50
Hourly employees (coders)	$6,072.00
Work-study (coders)	$2,511.60
Worker's compensation	$110.85
Postage	$3.80
Federal Express	$84.13
Copying	$1,282.13
Scanner	$283.62
Supplies	$285.60
Travel	$5,711.18
Total	$22,190.41

sociologists. Unfortunately, the number of sociologists interested in African-American social movements, and who are empirically oriented in their research methods, are quite limited. Another explanation for the neglect may be that many political scientists are trained in the art of political-historical approaches and look askance at coding events and doing regression analyses. It is possible that if African-American scholars or those interested in African-American sociopolitical history carried out research in this area, they would perhaps begin to study the subject more thoroughly and actually investigate it differently from how it is currently being practiced.

In addition to the costs identified above, the difficulties posed by the rules of other institutions and whims of individuals, political science operates by its own set of rules governing data collection that impose another type of cost. One primary issue, and often a source of considerable contention among scholars, is that of replication, i.e., replicating the overall data collection and research effort.

Adhering to the ideal of data replicability refers to the expectation that other scholars ought to be able to follow the same methods the original researcher used to collect and test the data. By definition, this places considerable responsibility on us as scientific investigators to ensure that we document the entire process of our data collection process. In detailing how we located and gained access to the data, we pave the way for future scholars to collect the same information, albeit with less costs in time, money, and effort. In short, replication lends to the scientific integrity of the work we conduct and the results we obtain. As Gary King et al. note, "replicability means that scholars who use unpublished or private records should endeavor to ensure that future scholars will have access to the material on similar terms; taking advantage of privileged access without seeking access for others precludes replication and calls into question the scientific quality of the work."[16]

In the case of our investigative effort on the BPP, however, it is difficult to imagine the same type of access enjoyed by us being provided to other scholars. Imagine telling a former party activist, one that perhaps no longer relishes recounting his or her days in the party or one that has "no love" for white folks, that he or she must expect to be available to other inquiring social scientists in order to ensure replicability. More likely, demanding such access for others will result in us being precluded from obtaining the information we seek in the first place.

Do fear, mistrust, or a healthy suspicion due to past repression and racism felt by the individuals we speak to invalidate our research effort? How can one deal with the problems of replicability placing the problems of accessing data within the context of a society highly divided in terms of race, class, and gender? In order to replicate our work properly, do you think King et al. considered the fact that the researchers would have to be a six-foot African-American male with a Ph.D. and a white female interested in women's collective action? Is research invalidated that, initially undertaken by white males at Michigan or Stanford, for example, cannot be replicated by other ethnic groups/genders because of the institutional/personal biases of those who might provide assistance or because of differential access to technological/economic resources? These questions merit further investigation.

Cash Rules Everything around Me: Grants and Playing the Mainstream

One of the authors of this piece, Christian Davenport, was awarded a grant from the National Science Foundation to facilitate the data collection effort. "How was this accomplished?" I am frequently asked. Well, to begin I have not pigeonholed myself in one particular topic, thus my vita has not really paid any exclusive attention to African-American issues. My work has concentrated on investigating specific hypotheses/theories with various datasets. The placement of these publications within "major" journals has been decent (many of the reviewers of the grant highlighted this, suggesting that I had deserved the chance to investigate the subject).[17] In my opinion, the successful grant attempt was based, in part, on this *hidden* interest in African-American life.

Additionally, when one looks at the grant (provided at my website: http://www.bsos. umd.edu/cidcm/projects/rip/rip.html), it doesn't really discuss the Black Panthers. The "pitch" is principally one about different arguments within social science; the exercise is one of hypotheses-testing, not in finding out about the BPP per se. Indeed, except for a brief comment in the introduction, the BPP is not discussed until the end of the proposal.

Is this trickery? No. With previously rejected grant proposals submitted to other funding agencies, I came across the difficulties of investigating the Black Panther Party and contentious/marginalized groups in general. "Why would anyone care about this?" I was asked. "Why is this important?" I made the additional mistake of identifying the Black Panther newspaper (exclusively) as a source for information about what happened, to which I got the response, "The author knows that the source is problematic and that another one should be selected." In other words, the source was pro-BPP, an independent news agency that did not rely on the police for all their information, and they are not easily found at a library near you. This could not possibly be trusted as an objective source of information.

Of course, this was discouraging (and quite enraging). You learn to adjust your strategy and resubmit elsewhere. I could not simply explain to the potential financial source that there is simply no good, reliable data on African-American social movements worthy of investigating the questions that I am interested in. I could not say that reliance on biographies and the *New York Times* provide only a biased, narrow vision of reality, and to have another data source (even one covering a small number of years) would add significantly to the "marketplace of ideas." Nor could I say, I disagree, it *is* important. Granting institutions do not function in this manner, and—until Magic Johnson gets bumped from late night, runs into someone like Cornell West who convinces him that it is worthwhile, and then gets Michael Jordan, Halle Berry, Oprah, Tiger, and Denzel to talk about it (and maybe commissions Maya Angelou to write a poem, Whitney to come out of semiretirement to belt one out, and resurrect Basquiat to paint something)—we need to get the money for our research where we can and how we can.

Archival Coding

A cost that we did not expect, in terms of time and patience, was that of hiring and keeping research assistants. Upon initially hearing about the project of investigating the BPP, people were always very positive and inquisitive, eager to participate in something exciting and racy like the BPP. People would willingly give us their numbers, tell us appropriate times to call them at home, and even recommend some other people that we should contact.

Before we could even begin our data collection, however, we had to sort through the myriad of interested and not so interested, responsible and not so responsible, and seemingly hardworking people interested in signing on to work on the project. We spent considerable time explaining to people what they would be doing, for how long, and how much they would be compensated—the bottom-line rules, regardless of the subject matter.

One part of the interview process proved particularly useful in at least teasing out who did and did not possess the skills needed to do the coding. Everyone was given a pretest using one of the Bay Area newspapers we were coding. Although one cannot assess the range of skills of someone from one indicator (in this case the pretest), it was almost always a reliable predictor of a coder's understanding and skill level. This part of the interview also gave the potential research assistants a taste of what they would be doing, and allowed them to decide whether or not they would be willing to do it fifteen to twenty hours a week. For many, this piqued their interest in the project.

Despite a seeming interest in studying a social movement like the Black Panthers, several drawbacks arose. One common problem was the commitment level of people hired to assist in the research. Several of the coders tended to romanticize their contributions to the research effort, and were somewhat disappointed after realizing they would be sitting at a microfilm machine for hours on end, or scanning newspaper after newspaper in a remote location of the library with no windows, where archival material is housed.

After about a week or two, we would usually hear something like; "Brother/sister, I'm down with the study and all . . . I truly respect what you're doing, but damn the library is boring, the chairs are uncomfortable, the microfiche print is small, Ewing scored 48 last night, and I got another gig that is offering more money" (we paid between $8 and $10 an hour). How can one compete with this? Neil Postman, in a book titled *Amusing Ourselves to Death,* argues that the dominant mode of communication (currently the television) militates against discipline, focus, coherence, tedium, and even thought itself. We would hate to believe that he was correct, but observing the number of individuals who expressed interest and disappeared or the number who started and dropped off, this does lend some credence to his point.

Then there are the coders who are *too* interested in the subject matter and who do not mind contributing their own theoretical two cents' worth. A few individuals, later dropping out of the project, were more interested in developing the "grand theory" about who and what the BPP was. While we generally encouraged these efforts, we reminded individuals that they were being paid for a specific activity and that theoretical developments could be undertaken after work had been completed. In many cases, this message was not taken well.

In fact, one coder who worked on the project did so only briefly because of this. This research assistant, an outspoken social activist and Black Man (capitals in the original), serves as one example of such an obstacle we encountered in the course of the coding. One of the authors in charge of the hiring, training, and general oversight of the project had the most interactions with this individual, and in retrospect realized the potential hazard of hiring research assistants with their own political and social agendas. Unfortunately, the person hired to do coding was not content with this assignment alone; he wanted to help generate theories with the principal investigator of the project, and contribute something to the cause of political and social justice. There was no contribution to be made in the library.

Another obstacle encountered during the data collection/coding phase came down to issues of gender, age, and perhaps race.[18] First off, the thought on many people's minds whom we interviewed for possible employment was sometimes apparent—Why would a youngish, white woman be interested in studying the Black Panther party; is it out of some sense of white liberal guilt? Aside from insinuations such as these, there was the more prevalent and ongoing problem of working with males who invariably seemed to have a difficult time being trained, supervised, and having to take instructions from a woman.

Such experiences delayed the project of data collection several times throughout the year. For example, another assistant hired to do some scanning of the BPP newspaper was outright insulting to one author upon being queried when he would have the scanning completed. Not only did his apparent problem with having to take instructions from a woman impede our scanning timeline, but his attitude is likely symptomatic of many experiences other female scholars have or will encounter in the course of their own fieldwork. It is probably no coincidence that the final core of coders who remained on the project for the long haul were women.

We observed some interesting comparisons between using undergraduate and graduate students for the coding. Many scholars often rely almost exclusively on the research assistance of graduate students for coding and other methods of data collection. Because our project involved the coding of several daily newspapers for the seven-year time frame, it necessitated that we extend our pool of coders to include both graduate as well as undergraduate research assistants. One might assume that the skills and quality of work, effort, and commitment of graduate research assistance surpasses that of undergraduates, yet this was not always the case. The youthful exuberance an exceptional undergraduate brought to the project outstripped the occasional "seasoned" work ethic of an unmotivated graduate student.

At some level we expected the waxing and waning of effort level put forth by some of our coders. However, we experienced significantly more difficulty with the graduate students working on the project than with our undergraduates.[19] At one point midway through our data collection phase, we had just recruited two additional students (graduates) to help with coding of the Bay Area newspapers. One of the authors of this piece who was in charge of the supervision for the coding made an impromptu trip out to the research site (in the midst of the semester's teaching responsibilities and approaching Ph.D. exams) in order to set up and train these newest coders. All indications pointed toward their genuine interest and commitment to work on the project, yet no sooner had I landed in California than both of the graduate students who pledged to work on the project ended up bailing out.

One plausible explanation for the problems we encountered in working with graduate students is that they may more easily overextend themselves in an effort to participate in all types of research that seem relevant to their specific academic pursuits. But after speaking with their own particular graduate advisers, they are often talked out of committing to someone else's research and told instead to focus on their own coursework or the work of their supervisor.

Ultimately, we cannot really know whether there is a benefit to using undergraduates versus graduate students on research projects. Both types of assistance have their positive and negative points. We have found that graduates can be less attentive to detail, instead being more interested in just completing the work, while undergraduate students want to impress and thus pay more attention to detail, sometimes to a fault. What we did learn is that it is costly to go through subsequent coders, both in terms of time and money. The more people you hire, whether initially or as replacements along the way, the more the startup costs in terms of training, paying yet another person (who you hope will not abandon the project after two weeks), and of course spending time filling out employment paperwork. As anyone who has carried out field research knows, paying research assistants is not as easy as handing them cash or a personal check. With the prestige and luxury of carrying out grant-funded research comes the equally abundant amount of bureaucratic red tape that pays for the research assistants as well as all other costs incurred.

Non-Strictly Business

This final section addresses the problems that emerge when interacting with individuals. We chose to call this section "Non-Strictly Business"[20] because these relationships seemed to deviate entirely from what was either expected or, frequently, desired.

Memory of Limitations

Invariably, we would come across somebody who wanted to tell us something about the Black Panthers. Many of these discussions were helpful in filling in the gaps between the documents we consulted. Others seemed to miss how the documents filled the gaps in some of their own thinking. On this point, Milan Kundera once wrote, "Try to reconstruct a dialogue from your own life, the dialogue of a quarrel or a dialogue of love. The most precious, the most important situations are utterly gone. Their abstract sense remains (I took this point of view, he took that one, I was aggressive, he was defensive), perhaps a detail or two, but the acousticovisual concreteness of the situation in all its continuity is lost . . . so we can neither hold on to it in our memory nor reconstruct it through imagination."[21]

We mention this not to depress anyone about life lost or the worthlessness of talking to people about events long past. Rather, this is mentioned because the limitations and strengths of the written as well as the oral record seem to mirror one another in ways that made us think about the importance of using both and the problem of relying upon any one of them exclusively as we attempt to understand what has happened. Simply, our methodological biases act as much as a formidable barrier to research as "Big Brother."

Navigating the Factions

Several times in the research effort we came across what we call a factional affiliation problem. One individual, knowing that we had been talking to another member, began our conversation noting, "Oh you so and so's boy/girl?" This would be followed by a grueling interrogation to see what we believed to be the "true essence" of the BPP, and occasionally we would be prompted to say something negative about the faction that our interrogator accused us of sympathizing with. If you fall too easily for this one, however, then you still won't get information, for some people seemed to believe that you could just as easily turn against them.

This affiliation issue was especially problematic because information is already scarce. The right conversation could put you on the path to yet undiscovered documents, or to someone well positioned to have access to information. Consider further the divisions: at one point, there was a Cleaver faction, a Newton faction, a West Coast faction, and an East Coast faction. In fact, one could argue that each chapter (prior to consolidation and relocation back to Oakland) displayed similarities as well as differences.

To engage with different parts of the BPP therefore is to engage somewhat different realities that wish to clarify their positions and guarantee their dissemination. Coming into one realm from another, the interloper must be checked out, cleansed of other thoughts, and brought into the fold. Ironically, this process is akin to the debriefing done by government surveillance agencies like the FBI and CIA.

It should be clear that none of this is said with any harshness or lack of understanding. We both approached individuals affiliated with the BPP with respect for what they had done and sacrificed. At the same time, it is clear that individuals affiliated with the organization were at war with society (in some cases), the state, and themselves. Additionally, it was clear that interacting with them is sometimes akin to interacting with war victims or those suffering from post-traumatic stress syndrome. The desire to tell their story, the distrust of those seeking to understand, the persecution of others considered as challengers —all of this makes sense when viewed in context.

What we learned from those who told their stories is that the telling of such events can bring up unpleasant experiences but can also serve as a cathartic function where those individuals are able to purge the built-up memories that may haunt their daily lives. Both aspects benefited our research, although, as will be discussed below, it required patience and delicacy in our interactions with those actually involved in the war.

Antiempiricism and Afrocentric Research

One person contacted for information about police contacts thought it amusing that we were having so much trouble getting information from the police about arrests and COINTELPRO activity. The individual commented that he had been given the "grand tour" of Oakland Police Department on a related project regarding the BPP. He even went into great detail about seeing old film footage and touching old police uniforms/nightsticks.

All we could say to this was, "That was nice, but did you get access to actual arrest reports so that we could identify when someone was arrested, where they were arrested, what they were arrested for, what their bail was, and so forth"? The response was, "No, I did not—why would I want this information?" To which we replied, "So that we could better understand what happened, its sequence, scope, severity, and so forth." The conversation was over.

This experience was by no means unique. Many individuals suggested that what we were conducting was "European" or, alternatively, "Negro" research. What did this mean? Well, it appeared to refer to the process of going through records to reassemble, as best as one could, what took place and examine it with empirical methodologies.

The limitation was difficult to overcome (especially when the individual on the accusing side controlled access to some of the information) because once confronted, it could not be surpassed. No amount of discussion would be sufficient to prove the merit of collecting the information, and no answer seemed acceptable to the question; "What are you going to do with it *if* you get it?" Indeed, the only way that the subject could be circumvented was by invoking a healthy dose of self-flagellation/criticism or (time permitting) a lengthy discussion about the African origins of mathematics and logic. Once this had taken place, with a nod or a knowing glance the ledgers would be opened, and we would be allowed to pass into the "cave of wonders."[22]

Now, we obviously cannot generalize from these experiences. It may just as well be the case that investigation of any social movement, involving communication with the activists themselves, might elicit such responses. Clearly the adversarial nature of activism sometimes militates against the objectives of scientific inquiry. This having been said, the obstacle merits identification.

My Life Was My Own and F That Time

There were a few moments when the most insurmountable of obstacles would be thrown up. While engaged in a conversation that appeared to start off pleasantly enough, for no apparent reason we would be cut off, and it would then be suggested that we leave. Sometimes the person would add that they did not wish to go back to that time or that they had changed their mind (the degree of hostility appeared to vary significantly). When we tried to figure out what happened, reconstruction of the conversations never appeared to shed any light. There appeared to be no patterns whatsoever. Often serendipitous experiences were few and far between.

There Are 8 Million Stories about the BPP (and You Are Going to Hear Every Damn One of 'Em)

On the opposite end of the communication spectrum from those who promptly ended conversations were those people who would just not stop talking. In these cases, the interview far exceeded what was expected (or desired), much of the information was not germane to what we thought we wanted to know, and there was absolutely no delicate way of ending such an interview. The opinion on this issue is quite complex. Michel-Rolph Trouillot[23] argues that

> *history reveals itself only through the production (telling, distribution) of specific narratives. . . . We cannot exclude in advance any of the actors who participate in the production of history or any of the sites where that production may occur. Next to professional historians we discover artisans of different kinds, unpaid or unrecognized field laborers who augment, deflect, or reorganize the work of the professionals as politicians, students, fiction writers, filmmakers, and participating members of the public. In so doing, we gain a more complex view of academic history itself, since we do not consider professional historians the sole participants in its production.*

Simultaneously, he also suggests that not all narratives are given the same weight. Some are promoted and advanced while others are silenced. "Silences enter the process of historical production at four critical moments: the moment of fact creation (the making of sources); the moment of fact assembly (the making of archives); the moment of fact retrieval (the making of narratives); and the moment of retrospective significance (the making of history in the final instance)."[24]

Listening to the silenced voices of history thus provides us with new understandings about what has transpired (beyond where perhaps we were prepared to go), and listening further restores power to the silenced. Much of what we learned during these conversations/interactions was less about the BPP than humanity and the power of history. Of course, the complexities of the research hit all at once—we are not paid to hear stories that are irrelevant to the grant but instead to gather information about what happened, which leads directly to a publishable article. Confronted with a silenced participant in history, or, in Kundera's words, someone who has just recalled what rendered them alive, how could one not listen? The silences of history speak volumes and demand to be heard. If we do not even have the patience to sit through the whole story, beginning to end, we might undermine the integrity of the very research enterprise we are engaged in. How can we understand the Black Panther Party without taking in the context of everything that took place?

A Little Help from Some Friends

Although this chapter was prompted in an effort to communicate some of the pitfalls of researching a historically marginalized, radical African-American organization, it is impossible to end without mentioning the importance of "underground railroad" conductors or the kindness of strangers, as well as the strange.

In investigating this type of subject, you feel as if you are on the underground railroad trying to get somewhere that you know is better than where you are—call it the truth. Along the path you meet individuals who throw up hurdles. Along the path you also meet individuals who assist in your journey. "Look at this book," they say; "Call this person," "Go to this store," "Try these documents"—the list is endless. One cannot count on these connections, and therefore this can be viewed as something of a limitation, for it can seriously impede the research effort. In a sense, coming across such invaluable people with their vast historical knowledge and insight is simply luck—serendipity.

As scholars caught up in the pursuit of information that many are reluctant to share, we may or may not be lucky enough to discover someone willing to tell what he or she knows and contribute to our journey back through a tumultuous history. When such people do come along, however, they quickly and profoundly become crucial to our research endeavor. We wish to say thank you (and "much props") to those of you who offered these moments of wisdom, insight, and strength.

Concluding Remarks

We suppose that the best way to conclude is with the statement that we got the data we needed. Despite problems, we have scanned and coded every newspaper that we set out to. It may not have come easily, but we did get it, and when ready, we will distribute it for those who wish to conduct investigations into BPP rhetoric, actions, and interactions with different police agencies.

It is worthwhile to state that our research effort has reminded us about the tedium of the enterprise, the day-to-day trials and tribulations of life on a quest. Additionally, we have been reminded about the pristine nature of available datasets on political dissent in particular but also other data in general. Dial a number or click a website address, data is delivered to us. Yet with such technological conveniences comes the implicit realization that more accessible data is not always the most revealing in terms of mapping out contentious politics.

While such data are being downloaded into our systems, we must contemplate the myriad decisions that have been made, the things that were never even considered, the shortcuts, the unresolvable difficulties, the costs, the effort, and the convenience of it all. For at the same time that the data comes into our lives, improving our capacity to examine and replicate, it also silences other realities, other perceptions—those that did not have the resources, the time, or the wherewithal to transcend the above-identified problems.

Now, we do not advocate throwing the baby out with the bathwater. If we cannot get "good" data, we are not suggesting that we leave the data business alone. Rather, we suggest a different approach. Maybe we should accept the defeatist attitude inherent within the phrase "God bless the child that's got its own" and alter it, adding to the end: "and can distribute it widely, pushing out all others to establish monopolization, domination, and hegemony." The wake-up call suggested here is much clearer than that heard at the end of Spike Lee's film *School Daze* or even that heard at the end of Haile Gerima's film *Sankofa*. Simply, we need to collect our own data now, store it, and distribute it for others to use and examine. Otherwise all that was fought for will be in vain—hidden off-site in tombs like in *Raiders of the Lost Ark*, recast as in *Panther,* or ignored, as in the film *The Drop Squad.*

Let us begin to systematize our legacies, for that is the only way social science recognizes history—systematically.[25] Let us continue to examine what lessons they hold. If we do not undertake this battle for history on the quantitative front, complementing it with the realm of qualitative research, then we have lost an important battle in the war for our hearts and our minds.

In essence, we must speak all the languages of political science, lest our stories and history be ignored. The language of quantitative facts and figures is one of the keys exposing the historical contributions of African-American social movements like the Black Panthers, and it provides one of the keys for more comprehensively investigating the theories about contentious politics that exist, which are normally tested without considering these types of social movements.[26]

Turning one's back on such intellectual constraints may be morally rewarding and principled action in theory, but you also risk sacrificing the telling of stories like that of the BPP. Do we really want their complex history, and ones like it, to be relayed within the confines of the entertainment industry and packaged for mass consumption and short attention spans? Do the contributions and sacrifices of the BPP deserve to be reduced to one simple story? No. It is equally necessary to understand and explain this important piece of African-American history in a manner worthy of its legacy.

18

Remembering King's Assassination

Kathleen Neal Cleaver

The year 2000's celebration of Martin Luther King Jr.'s birthday fell on January 17, the same day that two Black Panther leaders were assassinated on UCLA's campus thirty years ago. Millions were inspired by King's eloquent vision of America without racism, exploitation, or militarism, and they justly mourn his death but rarely discover the connection between his killing and that of revolutionaries like John Huggins and Alprentice Carter, who died on January 17, 1969. The link between these assassinations, however, lies in the covert world of the counterintelligence programs that the FBI and other agencies mounted deliberately to disrupt, discredit, and destroy the black freedom movement.

Despite the recognition decades ago by the House Committee on Assassinations, and the December 1999 jury verdict rendered in Memphis finding a conspiracy responsible for his death, the shadowy manipulations that ended with King's brutal killing on April 4, 1968, have long remained hidden. And the startling murders on the UCLA campus have been forgotten by all but the families and colleagues of those who died.

Back in 1969 when the murders occurred, Wesley Swearingen was an FBI agent on the Los Angeles "racial squad." After retiring, he published a firsthand account of his experiences entitled *FBI Secrets*. In this book he reveals that shortly after being reassigned to Los Angeles, he discovered that Nick Galt, a fellow agent on the squad, had arranged for "informants" placed within Ron Karenga's Us organization to kill Alprentice Carter, the Panther's Los Angeles Minister of Defense, and John Huggins, the Minister of Information. Swearingen described how he later verified that Larry and George Stiner, the two men eventually convicted of the murders, were in fact FBI informants. Within a few years, the Stiner brothers "escaped" from San Quentin prison, where they were serving life sentences, but the agents responsible for planning the murders of Carter and Huggins were never charged. Interviewed in the 1996 documentary *All Power to the People,* Swearingen said he found it remarkable that so many FBI "informants," like William O'Neal within the Chicago Black Panther Party or George Sams, who infiltrated the New Haven chapter, were involved in killing people.

I vividly remember the day I learned of the murders. Carter, whom everyone knew then as "Bunchy," had been a witness at my marriage to Eldridge Cleaver right after Christmas in 1967. He and my husband, both from Los Angeles, met in Soledad prison in an African history class and became best friends. Before joining the Black Panther Party, John Huggins had served in the military and attended Lincoln University. Alprentice Carter had been a feared leader of the Slauson gang, but committed his life to the Black Panther Party after his release from prison. Both John and Bunchy were talented, fearless young men whose lives were needlessly destroyed by government-financed corruption, deceit, and lawlessness. The news of Bunchy's death felt like a dagger in my heart, although his parole officer had warned him to expect to be killed. Just weeks before, his close friend Frank Diggs, a Black Panther captain, was found lying dead in an alley; his brother Arthur had been killed a few months earlier, and the summer before three Panthers had been murdered in a shoot-out with the Los Angeles police.

As early as 1968, Los Angeles police and FBI agents collaborated in their cold-blooded attempt to provoke outright warfare between Us and the Black Panthers. The tactics included planting provocateurs within each organization, sending forged letters to the different leaders, and drive-by shootings. Following J. Edgar Hoover's directive that all offices should submit imaginative and hard-hitting COINTELPRO (counterintelligence) measures aimed at crippling the Black Panther Party, the special agent in charge of Los Angeles sent Hoover a two page memorandum dated November 29, 1968. The memorandum described the following "operation under consideration":

> *The Los Angeles office is currently preparing an anonymous letter for Bureau approval which will be sent to the Los Angeles Black Panther Party (BPP) supposedly from a member of the "US" organization in which it will be stated that the youth group of the "US" organization is aware of the BPP "contract" to kill RON KARENGA, leader of "US," and they, "US" members, in retaliation, have made plans to ambush leaders of the BPP in Los Angeles.*

Under the heading "developments of counterintelligence interest," the memorandum describes the continuing friction between the BPP and "US," with (name blacked out), another "US" member, slated to be killed, and states that Black Panther leaders believe that (name blacked out) is an "US" infiltrator. The Los Angeles special agent ended his memorandum to the FBI director with the notation that his office would "utilize every technique to capitalize on this development," and hinder the Black Panther Party's effort to lead the black nationalist movement.

Hundreds of Panthers and other young men and women committed to black liberation were arrested, tried, and convicted on charges trumped up by FBI-police collaboration in cities implementing COINTELPRO operations. Although the program was exposed during the 1972 hearings held by the U.S. Senate's Select Committee on Intelligence Activities ("the Church Committee"), and COINTELPRO was purportedly disbanded, no federal agents have ever been punished for the crimes they committed. Unfortunately, it took nineteen years for Dhoruba Bin Wahad, one of the leaders of the New York chapter of the Black Panther Party, to win his release by proving that the charges against him were false, and Geronimo ji Jaga, who succeeded Alprentice Carter as Defense Minister in Los Angeles, spent over twenty-six years in California prisons, including eight years in solitary confinement, before winning his release from a conviction on false murder charges. Others, like Romaine Fitzgerald, framed for murdering a policeman in 1970, remain behind bars, still paying for the crimes of COINTELPRO.

The government has covered up the truth for too long. As we stand on the threshold of a new century, the commemoration of King's birthday marks a fitting moment to launch a coordinated demand for the full-scale, impartial investigation of all federal and state counterintelligence operations targeted against the black movement. The documentary evidence produced within such an investigation may finally allow those unfairly targeted, prosecuted, imprisoned, or assassinated to receive their due respect. Anything less allows injustice to continue to triumph, and secures the victory of all those who worked to destroy Martin Luther King.

19

Lockdown at Angola
The Case of the Angola 3

Scott Fleming

Introduction: The Louisiana State Penitentiary at Angola

Known as "The Farm," the Louisiana State Penitentiary at Angola is the largest prison in the United States. Around three-quarters of its inmates are African American. According to the Academy Award–nominated documentary *The Farm,* 85 percent of the inmates who are sent to Angola will die there.

Angola is an 18,000-acre complex of antebellum plantations that the state of Louisiana purchased and converted into a prison around the turn of the century. The penitentiary is called Angola because most of its former slaves came from the African country of the same name. Angola still operates on the plantation model. Prisoners perform backbreaking labor, harvesting cotton, soybeans, and other crops from dawn to dusk.

In the early 1970s, Angola was known as the most brutal prison in the United States, with stabbings an almost-daily occurrence. Armed "inmate guards" patrolled the prison, and they frequently used their state-issued rifles to settle scores with other inmates, sometimes at the behest of Angola officials. On one occasion, a prisoner died after five men were locked together in a sweltering isolation cell, without food or water, during the hottest days of summer. Dozens of bodies are rumored to be buried in the swampland where Angola borders the Mississippi River.

Among the men who have been left to die at Angola are Albert Woodfox, Herman Wallace, and Robert King Wilkerson. Of the world's political prisoners, few have been held in solitary confinement for as long as they have: twenty-nine years. All three men initially arrived at Angola with sentences for robbery and a dedication to political activism. Their activism led them to found a chapter of the Black Panther Party at Angola, but it also quickly made them targets of the all-white prison administration. In 1972 and 1973, in an effort to put a stop to their organizing, prison officials concocted murder charges against Woodfox, Wallace, and Wilkerson, and placed all of them on permanent lockdown. Relying on the testimony of prison snitches and arguing their cases to all-white juries, Angola officials won convictions against the three men, all of whom received sentences of life without parole.

For more information, visit the Angola 3 website, www.prisonactivist.org/angola, or e-mail scott@prisonactivist.org.

The Formation of the Black Panther Party at Angola

In 1971 Woodfox and Wallace organized the Black Panther Party at Angola. Woodfox had joined the Party in New York, where he had fled after a daring 1969 escape from the courthouse in New Orleans. After spending time imprisoned under an assumed name in New York, where he helped organize several rebellions in the New York City correctional system, Woodfox, along with his newfound politics, was extradited back to Louisiana. Wallace became a Panther while he was incarcerated at the New Orleans Parish Prison with the political prisoners known as the New Orleans Panther 12. When they were shipped off to Angola, Woodfox and Wallace took the Black Panther Party with them.

The Angola Panthers not only challenged the prison administration but also organized to end aspects of the inmate social order that hindered prisoner unity and played into the hands of the guards. The Panthers risked their lives to protect younger and weaker inmates from the rape, prostitution, and sex slavery that pervaded prison life. As Woodfox puts it, "It wasn't much help to go to the security because most of the security people were condoning that type of activity. They would benefit from it because they would get money or favors for allowing rapes to happen. Some of the guards themselves would be involved in the rapes."

The Panthers worked to mend the schism between black and white prisoners that the prison officials manipulated to their advantage, a difficult feat considering that the prisoner housing, dining halls, and worksites were still racially segregated, with privileged living arrangements and work assignments going to white prisoners. The BPP also exposed the widespread corruption of the people who ran Angola, many of whom came from families that had lived on state land and had worked at the prison for several generations. Guards often diverted food, grown by the prisoners for their own consumption, to their own families and friends or sold it in town.

The administration of the prison responded to the rise of the Panthers by filling its isolation units with activist prisoners. The associate warden of the prison, Hayden Dees, testified in court proceedings to the need to keep "a certain type of militant or revolutionary inmate, maybe even a Communist type," on permanent lockdown.

Indeed, Woodfox and Wallace believe they were targeted for prosecution and long-term lockdown because of their organizing. "I think the fact that they were never able to break my spirit or Herman Wallace's spirit, the fact that they could not shake our political beliefs or convictions, contributed to the reason why we were held in CCR [Closed Cell Restricted, or solitary confinement]," Woodfox says.

The Murder of Brent Miller and the Convictions of Woodfox and Wallace

The April 17, 1972, killing of Officer Brent Miller took place in the context of this politically and racially charged atmosphere. Just the day before, on April 16, a wooden guard shack had been firebombed, and the guard inside was burned.

On the morning of April 17 there was a "buck," or work stoppage, in the kitchen, where inmate workers were protesting their punishing sixteen-hour shifts. Inmates arrived at breakfast, only to be told to return to their dormitories until food could be served. Within a short time, the buck had been resolved, and the inmates were ordered back to the dining hall. During the inmates' second trip to breakfast, the Pine 1 dormitory was emptied of all but a few inmates and a guard, Brent Miller. By the end of breakfast, Miller lay dead in a pool of his own blood, thirty-two stab wounds in his body.

Only one inmate, a man named Hezekiah Brown, claimed to have witnessed the killing. According to the prison's field security captain, Hilton Butler, "Hezekiah was one you could put words in his mouth." Two days after the murder, however, Brown was awakened sometime after midnight and confronted by high-ranking members of the Angola administration, who told him they could place him at the scene of the murder, which took place near his bed. According to his later testimony, the institutional files of Woodfox and Wallace were placed before him. Terrified that he would be charged with the murder if he did not provide information, Brown pointed to the files of Woodfox and Wallace and accused them of the murder. He also named inmate Chester Jackson, and, at some later point, added Gilbert Montegut as well. Today, two former Angola wardens, C. Murray Henderson and Hilton Butler, have now admitted that Brown was pressured into naming him by Angola security chief Hayden Dees. Over the years, Woodfox and Wallace have obtained documentation proving that prison officials bribed Brown into giving statements against Woodfox, Wallace, Jackson, and Montegut.

Woodfox, alone, was tried and convicted by an all-white jury. Later, Wallace and Montegut were tried together. On the second day of their trial, Chester Jackson walked into court after the lunch break and sat down at the prosecution table, announcing that he had struck a deal with the state and was going to confess to the crime and testify against Wallace and Montegut. After being allowed only a half-hour to regroup, defense attorney Charles Garretson cross-examined Jackson, his own client. Despite his obvious conflicts of interest, Garretson was forced to proceed.

Wallace was convicted, but Montegut, who had an alibi, was acquitted; even Angola's then-warden, C. Murray Henderson, acknowledges in his book, *Dying to Tell,* that Montegut was framed by Associate Warden Dees. In exchange for testifying against Wallace and Montegut, Jackson was allowed to plead guilty to a charge of manslaughter.

For the next two decades, Woodfox and Wallace, from their isolation cells, struggled to continue their activism. Over the years, they have helped hundreds of inmates with their legal cases. Until inmate-to-inmate mail was recently banned, they even helped inmates at a nearby women's prison with their legal work. In 1998, while Woodfox was away from Angola awaiting trial, Wallace got nearly every inmate on Louisiana's death row to sign a petition in support of Mumia Abu-Jamal.

The Case of Robert King Wilkerson

Like Herman Wallace, Robert King Wilkerson was recruited into the Black Panther Party in the Orleans Parish Prison. He arrived at Angola in April 1972, days after Officer Miller was killed. Angola officials placed him directly into solitary confinement. It seems most likely that he was placed on lockdown because of his reputation as an activist prisoner. The authorities, however, gave him a different reason: they told him that he was assigned to segregation because he was "under investigation," although they would not tell him what they were investigating. Some nineteen years later, perhaps by accident, the classification board told him that he was being investigated for the Miller killing, even though he was not yet at Angola when the murder took place. For the past twenty-eight years, Angola's classification committee has reviewed Wilkerson's placement in CCR every few months. Each time, they have told him that his continued confinement in isolation is justified by the fact that he is "under investigation."

Wilkerson's original sentence for armed robbery and escape expired years ago; he would be a free man if Angola officials hadn't concocted charges that could keep him in solitary confinement until he dies. On June 10, 1973, a fight broke out on CCR's B Tier (where Wilkerson lived) between two inmates, Grady Brewer and August Kelly. Both men produced knives; August Kelly was stabbed to death. Eleven of the tier's fourteen inmates had been out of their cells at the time of the fight, which took place amid a scene of mass confusion. All eleven inmates were indicted for the murder. Charges against nine were later dropped, but indictments against Wilkerson and Brewer remained.

When the case proceeded to trial, Brewer acted disruptively. The judge responded by shackling both defendants and having their mouths taped shut in front of the jury. Wilkerson and Brewer were both convicted, entirely on the basis of two inmates' testimony. In 1974 the Louisiana Supreme Court reversed Wilkerson's conviction, ruling that it had been improper for the trial judge to gag Wilkerson in response to Brewer's outbursts.

Wilkerson was tried again in 1975. Just as before, Wilkerson was tried in St. Francisville, the closest town to Angola, and a place where most of the jury pool is composed of prison employees, their families, and their friends. This time, one of the state's inmate witnesses refused to testify. Brewer, Wilkerson's erstwhile codefendant, took the stand and testified that he alone had stabbed Kelly, in an act of self-defense (Kelly was known to have killed at least two other inmates). Nevertheless, on the basis of one inmate's testimony, and in the face of compelling exculpatory evidence, the jury reconvicted Wilkerson. Once again, he received a sentence of natural life, meaning life without the possibility of parole.

In the years since, the case against Wilkerson has further evaporated. Both inmates who originally testified against him have recanted their testimony. One, Charles Lawrence, signed an affidavit swearing that his testimony against Wilkerson was false and "given under circumstances of extreme duress." He further swore that his trial testimony was prepared by former Angola warden Richard H. Butler, and that officials told him that if he did not testify he would be tried for the murder and would be given the death penalty.

The other inmate, William Riley, signed an affidavit, "being in full awareness of the penalty for perjury," in which he admitted his trial testimony was false. Riley swore that he had been in the shower when Kelly was killed, meaning he had not been in a position to witness the crime.

Finally, Wilkerson's codefendant, Grady Brewer, has added to his trial testimony an affidavit in which he swears that he killed August Kelly in self-defense, and that "Robert King Wilkerson had nothing to do with the death of August Kelly and he was not involved in the murder."

Thus far, the total collapse of the state's case against Robert King Wilkerson has not resulted in his freedom. In 1994 the U.S. Court of Appeals granted Wilkerson another new trial because African Americans and women had unconstitutionally been excluded from the grand jury that indicted him. Only months later, however, the court voted to re-hear the case, and they reversed their previous decision, taking away his new trial. The court did not deny that Wilkerson's grand jury had been comprised exclusively of white men; it merely ruled that the technicalities of habeas corpus law provided the court with an excuse for not even considering his claims. In December 2000, the U.S. Court of Appeals ruled for the second time that Robert King Wilkerson's conviction was obtained unconstitutionally. It remains to be seen whether the technical rules of habeas corpus— the rules the politicians say are intended to "streamline" and "speed up" the appeals process—will once again be used as an excuse to prevent Wilkerson from going free.

Woodfox's Conviction Is Reversed

In 1992, a Louisiana court agreed that Woodfox's original conviction had been obtained in violation of the U.S. Constitution because his lawyer had failed to challenge the grand jury that had indicted him, which was also illegally impaneled through a process that excluded African Americans and women. The court granted Woodfox a new trial.

Because Woodfox's original sentence, fifty years for armed robbery, was about to expire, the state convened a new grand jury to reindict him for Miller's murder. One of the members of the new grand jury was Anne Butler, who happened to be the wife of C. Murray Henderson, the warden who had presided over the original investigation of the Miller murder. Together, Butler and Henderson had authored *Dying to Tell,* a book that chronicles Henderson's tenure as warden. The book's opening chapter, entitled "Racist Pigs Who Hold Us Captive," is about the Miller case, and it argues that Woodfox and Wallace committed the murder.

During later court proceedings, the district attorney testified that he allowed Butler to use her book to make a presentation to other grand jurors about the Miller murder. Butler herself testified that she passed her book around, and some of the other grand jurors may have read from it before deciding to indict Woodfox.

Despite Woodfox's objections to the existence of a prejudiced, interest-conflicted grand juror, Judge Bruce Bennett refused to quash the indictment, ruling that, "There's nothing wrong with a grand juror having some knowledge of a case, even if they happened to have written a book about the case."

(As a result of a bizarre turn of events a few miles outside Angola, Warden Henderson himself is now in prison. In January 1999, Henderson, aged seventy-eight, was sentenced to fifty years for the nonfatal shooting of his wife, author and grand juror Anne Butler.)

Woodfox's Retrial

After several years of legal wrangling over evidentiary and other issues, Woodfox's trial finally began on December 7, 1998. Because of the notoriety of the case in West Feliciana Parish, where Angola is situated, the court granted Woodfox a change of venue. Unfortunately, it quickly became apparent that there was no chance of the trial taking place in neutral territory, as the proceedings were moved to the small town of Amite, about an hour east of Baton Rouge. It just so happens that much of Brent Miller's family lives near Amite, and Miller's body is buried there. The area is known as a hotbed of Ku Klux Klan activity.

When the trial opened, the courtroom was packed with Woodfox's supporters. During the trial, his family was flanked by former Black Panthers from Louisiana and California, local community activists, members of New Orleans' Crescent Wrench anarchist collective, Ashaki Pratt (wife of Geronimo), Luis Talamantez of the San Quentin 6, and representatives of Baltimore anarchist Black Cross.

When jury selection was complete, Woodfox faced a panel of ten whites and two African Americans. In the first two days of trial, the prosecution began presenting its case. Woodfox and his supporters were elated as the state's evidence seemed to disintegrate.

First, the prosecutor, Assistant Attorney General Julie Cullen, called an inmate named Leonard "Specs" Turner to testify. Cullen expected Turner, to whom even guards referred, under oath, as a "snitch," to testify that he had seen Woodfox at the scene of the crime. When Cullen questioned him, however, Turner said he had seen nothing and had no information implicating Woodfox in the murder.

Over the defense's motion for a mistrial, the judge allowed Cullen to introduce an unsigned, undated statement, in a guard's handwriting, in which Turner allegedly said that he saw Woodfox and Wallace participate in the murder. Warden Henderson, straight from lockup himself, appeared in court and testified that he had never heard of the statement, even though, if it were legitimate, it would have represented the first break in the Brent Miller murder investigation. Henderson, rather, said that he had met with Turner two nights after the murder (and the night before Turner was scheduled to be paroled) and told him that, "If you don't give me some information . . . I'm gonna call the parole board and see that you do the rest of your eight years, flat." In response, Turner said that he didn't know who had killed Miller. Despite Turner's testimony that he had no information about the crime, Judge Bennett allowed Cullen to introduce the statement to the jury.

To add to the embarrassment of Turner's testimony, the state's forensic investigators were forced to acknowledge that they acted with either gross incompetence or blatant misconduct. At issue was their handling of a bloody fingerprint found at the scene of the crime. Investigators found what they admit was an identifiable bloody fingerprint near Miller's body, but when they discovered that it didn't match any of their chosen defendants, they never bothered to try to find out whom the print belonged to. If the print had been left there by an inmate, finding out who left it would not have been difficult, since officials had every inmate's fingerprints on file. The state, however, made no effort to trace the print.

In an attempt to muddle the issue for the jury, the prosecution called another fingerprint expert to testify that what the state had always admitted was a bloody fingerprint might really be an unidentifiable palmprint. Cullen did not notify the court or the defense about the existence of this witness until less than an hour before she called her to testify, in violation of court rules that require attorneys to give opposing counsel fair notice of witness testimony. Cullen told the judge that she had come up with the palmprint theory thirty minutes before the witness was called, but on cross-examination the witness admitted to the defense that she had informed Cullen of the theory nearly two years earlier, in April 1997. The defense moved for a mistrial on the basis of prosecutorial misconduct, but the court denied the motion.

Near the close of its case, the prosecution presented the testimony of its star "eyewitness," Hezekiah Brown. Since Brown is now dead, his 1973 testimony was read to the jury. Brown testified that on the morning of the murder he and Miller were alone in Pine 1 dormitory, but his version of events contradicted the physical evidence in several crucial respects.

As Miller sat on Brown's bed, he testified, Woodfox, Wallace, Jackson, and Montegut entered the room. He claimed that Woodfox grabbed Miller around the neck, pressed his body against Miller's, and began stabbing him in the back. Somehow, Miller ended up on the floor some distance away, and the other three men joined in the stabbing. In the end, Miller had been stabbed thirty-two times, and his wounds were gushing with blood. Curiously, however, the state never found any blood on the bed where Brown said that Woodfox began stabbing Miller. In fact, the unruffled bed bore no signs of any struggle.

The final nail in the coffin of Hezekiah Brown's credibility is the fact that prison officials paid him for his testimony. At Woodfox's 1973 trial, Brown unequivocally denied that he had been promised anything in exchange for his testimony: "Nobody promised me nothing," he testified. Prison records later obtained by Woodfox tell an entirely different story.

An April 7, 1978, letter written by Angola warden Frank C. Blackburn to Secretary of Corrections C. Paul Phelps confirms that Warden Henderson agreed to pay Brown "one (1) carton of cigarettes per week," as part of a "commitment made to him in the past with respect to his testimony in the Brent Miller murder case." In his reply, Phelps agreed that the cigarette ration should be disbursed, because "Warden Henderson made the original agreement with Brown."

For a man like Hezekiah Brown, however, a weekly carton of cigarettes was small change compared to the promise of an early release. Only a few years before the Miller killing, Brown had been sentenced to death for aggravated rape. In 1971 that sentence had been commuted to a sentence of life without parole. On February 15, 1974, only a month after Wallace had been convicted and sentenced to life without parole, Warden Henderson began writing letters in an attempt to secure immediate release for Brown. Over the next few years, Henderson intervened with a judge, the director of corrections, and the Board of Pardons, pleading Brown's case. He always cited Brown's service in the Miller case (in which "a white officer was killed by three black militants," he wrote) as the prime reason that release was justified. Other documents show that Henderson was joined in his crusade for Brown's freedom by the associate warden, the district attorney, the deputy sheriff, and several Angola guards. In 1986 Henderson's efforts bore fruit: Brown was granted clemency and released from Angola.

In addition to free cigarettes and clemency, there is compelling evidence that Brown was paid in cash. Prison records show that he entered Angola in 1971 with no money. Warden Henderson testified that Brown "didn't have any money at all, and he didn't earn any money at Angola. He had no relatives, or anybody that came to see him." Upon release in 1986, however, Brown had $931.24. And, according to a 1974 article in a New Orleans newspaper called the *Courier,* Brown testified at Wallace's trial while wearing a new gold watch.

To divert the jury's attention from its compromised witnesses and lack of physical evidence, the prosecution dredged up information about Woodfox's Panther past and used it as evidence that he was guilty of the murder. Before the trial, prosecutor Cullen had termed Miller's death a "hate crime" and "a racially-motivated Black Panther murder." In the courtroom, using tactics eerily similar to those enlisted against Mumia Abu-Jamal (Mumia's prosecutors told the jury in his case that they should sentence him to death because he agreed with Mao Tse-Tung's maxim that "political power grows out of the barrel of a gun"), Cullen introduced letters she said Woodfox wrote over twenty years ago, in which he allegedly spelled America "AMERIKKKA" and denounced the "white racist pigs" and "fascists" who ran Angola. To Cullen, this furthered her theory that the Black Panther Party was a racist organization dedicated to killing white people. Refusing to acknowledge the Panthers' history of establishing children's breakfast programs, publishing an important community newspaper, and inventing the practice of "copwatching," Cullen attempted to persuade the jury that Woodfox's membership in the organization constituted evidence that he was a murderer.

At the close of the trial, Albert Woodfox took the stand on his own behalf. All of his supporters agreed that he was calm, sincere, and incredibly convincing. On cross-examination, Cullen repeatedly attempted to bully or trick him into making incriminating statements, but he stood firm. In deflecting one such question, Woodfox testified that he did not kill Brent Miller and told Cullen, truthfully, "You know I didn't kill Brent Miller because you know I passed a lie detector test." During a posttrial interview with Pacifica Radio, one of the jurors said that the jury was turned off by that statement, because polygraph evidence is inadmissible in court, and she felt that Woodfox was deliberately breaking the rules by trying to communicate such important information to the jury.

On the final day of trial, over a dozen uniformed police and prison guards, along with several parish sheriffs, packed the courtroom. After closing arguments, the jury deliberated for only about five hours. In spite of the overwhelming lack of physical evidence, the fully compromised credibility of the state's witnesses, and Woodfox's truthful polygraph examination and convincing testimony, the jury came back with a guilty verdict. After waiting two months, Woodfox was finally sentenced on February 23, 1999, to natural life—meaning life without possibility of probation, parole, or suspension of sentence.

Conclusion

In the two years since Albert Woodfox was returned to Angola, the campaign to free the Angola 3 has continually expanded. A solid community organizing effort is now underway in New Orleans and elsewhere. Benefit concerts in New Orleans have attracted hundreds of people, a significant development considering the Angola 3 case was mostly unknown just two years ago. The American Civil Liberties Union has entered the fray, filing a civil rights lawsuit that seeks to have the Angola 3's twenty-nine-year stay in solitary confinement declared cruel and unusual punishment.

A legal team has also been assembled to challenge the men's criminal convictions, although it is sorely underfunded. Herman Wallace is in the state courts, pursuing the first meaningful and comprehensive appeal he has ever had. Albert Woodfox is in the Louisiana Supreme Court, still in the beginning stages of appealing his 1998 reconviction. And Robert King Wilkerson is working to convince the courts that the procedural intricacies of habeas corpus law should not be invoked to prevent the invalidation of his conviction, a conviction that the U.S. Court of Appeals has now twice ruled was obtained unconstitutionally.

If the state of Louisiana has its way, Albert Woodfox, Robert King Wilkerson, and Herman Wallace will die in their isolation cells at Angola. Only through outside support—political, legal, and financial—will these courageous and principled men ever taste freedom again.

Notes

1 Repression Breeds Resistance: The Black Liberation Army and the Radical Legacy of the Black Panther Party

Akinyele Omowale Umoja

1. Angela D. LeBlanc-Ernest, "'The Most Qualified Person to Handle the Job': Black Panther Party Women, 1966–1982," *The Black Panther Party Reconsidered*, ed. Charles E. Jones (Baltimore: Black Classic Press, 1998), 305; Ollie Johnson, "Explaining the Demise of the Black Panther Party: The Role of Internal Factors" in Jones, *Black Panther Party,* 407; Kathleen Neal Cleaver, "Back to Africa: The Evolution of the International Section of the Black Panther Party (1969-1972)", in Jones, *The Black Panther Party Reconsidered,* 239.
2. Charles Hopkins, "The Deradicalization of the Black Panther Party, 1967–1973," (Ph.D. diss., University of North Carolina, Chapel Hill, 1978).
3. Kit Kim Holder, "The History of the Black Panther Party, 1966–1971: A Curriculum Tool for Afrikan-American Studies" (Ph.D. diss., University of Massachusetts, 1990), 317.
4. Dhoruba Bin Wahad, "War Within: Prison Interview," in *Still Black, Still Strong: Survivors of the War against Black Revolutionaries,* ed. Jim Fletcher, Tanaquil Jones, and Sylvère Lotringer (New York: Semiotext[e], 1993), 13; Jalil Muntaqim, *On the Black Liberation Army* (Montreal: Anarchist Black Cross, 1997), 4; Sundiata Acoli, 15 August 1983 testimony in *United States v. Sekou Odinga et al.,* in *Sundiata Acoli's Brinks Trial Testimony,* a pamphlet published by the Paterson (New Jersey) Black Anarchist Collective, 21.
5. Geronimo ji Jaga, interview with author, September 14, 1998, Morgan City, La.
6. Assata Shakur, *Assata: An Autobiography* (Chicago: Lawrence Hill, 1987), 241.
7. "Reconsidering Panther History: The Untold Story," in Jones, *The Black Panther Party Reconsidered,* 1–2.
8. For examples of these, see Robert Daley, *Target Blue: An Insider's View of the N.Y.P.D.* (New York: Delacorte Press, 1973); and John Castellucci, *The Big Dance: The Untold Story of Kathy Boudin and the Terrorist Family That Committed the Brinks Robbery Murders* (New York: Dodd, Mead, 1986). Daley was the prosecutor in trials involving Panthers and BLA members. Castellucci, a reporter for the *Rockland Journal-News,* a local newspaper in upstate New York, covered the trials of BLA members and other revolutionaries in the early 1980s.
9. Counterinsurgency campaigns against the BLA were often coordinated by the FBI and local law enforcement. The FBI's use of the media in counter-insurgency campaigns is well documented. For information see Kenneth O'Reilly, *"Racial Matters": The FBI's Secret File on Black America* (New York: Free Press, 1989), 198–99, 207, 215, 275. Also see Evelyn Williams, *Inadmissible Evidence: The Story*

of the African-American Trial Lawyer Who Defended the Black Liberation Army (New York: Lawrence Hill, 1993), 122. Williams, the attorney for BLA member Assata Shakur and other black revolutionaries, describes the *New York Daily News* as the "primary media agents" for the FBI's counterinsurgency efforts against the BLA in New York area trials. In the 1970s the *Daily News* often published prosecution-oriented features concerning the BLA.

10. Theodore G. Vincent, *Voices of the Black Nation* (Trenton, N.J.: Africa World Press, 1991), 123
11. For more information, see Akinyele Umoja, "Eye for an Eye: the Role of Armed Resistance in the Mississippi Freedom Movement" (Ph.D. diss., Emory University, 1996).
12. Ibid., 202–4.
13. Robert Brisbane, *Black Activism: Racial Revolution in the United States, 1954–1970.* (Valley Forge, Pa: Hudson Press, 1974), 182.
14. Robert Williams, quoted in Robert Carl Cohen, *Black Crusader: A Biography of Robert Franklin Williams* (Secaucus, N.J.: Lyle Stuart, 1972), 271–72. "USA: The Potential of a Minority Revolt" originally appeared in the May-June issue of Williams's newsletter the *Crusader.*
15. Maxwell C. Stanford, "Revolutionary Action Movement (RAM): A Case Study of an Urban Revolutionary Movement in Western Capitalist Society" (master's thesis, Atlanta University, 1986), 99.
16. Ibid., 67–68.
17. Brisbane, *Black Activism,* 182.
18. Revolutionary Action Movement, "On Organization of Black Ghetto Youth" in *Riots, Civil, and Criminal Disorders: Hearings before the Permanent Subcommittee Investigations of the Committee on Government Operations,* U.S. Senate, 91st Cong., 1st sess., 1969, 4221–24.
19. Ibid.
20. Huey Newton, "The Correct Handling of a Revolution," in *The Black Panthers Speak,* ed. Philip S. Foner (New York: Da Capo Press, 1995), 41–42.
21. Ji Jaga, interview.
22. Louis G. Heath, *Off the Pigs! The History and Literature of the Black Panther Party* (Metuchen, N.J.: Scarecrow Press, 1976), 46; "Rules of the Black Panther Party," in Foner, *Black Panthers Speak,* 5.
23. Geronimo ji Jaga, "A Soldier's Story," interview by Bakari Kitwana, *Source,* February 1998, 132.
24. Ibid.; ji Jaga interview with author; Earl Anthony, *Picking Up the Gun: A Report on the Black Panthers* (New York: Dial Press, 1970), 66-67.
25. Ji Jaga, interview with author.
26. Ji Jaga, interview with author; ji Jaga "A Soldier's Story," 132; David Hilliard and Lewis Cole, *This Side of Glory: The Autobiography of David Hilliard and the Story of the Black Panther Party* (Boston: Little, Brown 1993), 218.
27. Johnson, "Demise," 391–93.
28. Ji Jaga, "A Soldier's Story," 132.
29. Testimony of Detective Sgt. Thomas J. Courtney, in U.S. Senate, *Riots, Civil, and Criminal Disorders,* 4237.
30. J. Edgar Hoover quoted in Ward Churchill and Jim Vander Wall, *Agents of Repression: The FBI's Secret Wars against the Black Panther Party and the American Indian Movement* (Boston: South End Press, 1988), 77.
31. Frank Donner, "Chronology of the Black Panther Party," in Fletcher, Jones, and Lotringer, *Still Black,* 229–33.
32. Frank Donner, *Protectors of Privilege: Red Squads and Police Repression in Urban America* (Berkeley and Los Angeles: University of California Press, 1990), 180.
33. Donner, "Chronology of the Black Panther Party," 233; Cleaver, *"Back to Africa,"* 237.
34. Craig Williams, "Reflections of Geronimo: The Essence of a Panther," *Black Panther,* August 29, 1970, 14.

35. Huey Newton, quoted in Holder, "History," 257. One exception to this was Elaine Brown, who moved up the ranks of the BPP to the inner circle of the national leadership.

36. Hilliard and Cole, *Glory,* 299–300; 304–12; ji Jaga, interview with author; Churchill and Vander Wall, *Agents of Repression,* 87.

37. Holder, "History", 55–56.

38. O'Reilly, *"Racial Matters,"* 320.

39. Geronimo Pratt (ji Jaga), "The New Urban Guerrilla," in *Humanity, Freedom, Peace* (Los Angeles: Revolutionary Peoples Communication, 1972), 26.

40. Huey Newton, "On the Expulsion of Geronimo from the Black Panther Party," *Black Panther,* 23 January 1971, 7.

41. "Open Letter to Weather Underground from Panther 21," *East Village Other* 8 (January 19, 1971): 3.

42. Ibid., 20.

43. Rod Such, "Newton Expels Panthers," *Guardian,* 20, no. 21 (February 1971): 4; E. Tani and Kae Sera, *False Nationalism, False Internationalism* (Chicago: Seeds beneath the Snow 1985), 209; Akinyele Omowale Umoja, "Set Our Warriors Free: The Legacy of the Black Panther Party and Political Prisoners," in Jones, *The Black Panther Party Reconsidered,* 421–22.

44. FBI memorandum quoted in Huey P. Newton, *War against the Panthers: A Study of Repression in America* (New York: Harlem River Press, 1996), 67–68.

45. Holder, "History," 275–77; "A Call to Dissolve the Central Committee," *Right On! Black Community News Service,* April 3, 1971, 3.

46. Newton, *War against the Panthers,* 65–71.

47. Cleaver, *"Back to Africa,"* 236–239.

48. Jack A. Smith, "Panther Rift Aired in Algiers," *Guardian* 23, no. 29 (17 April 1971): 3.

49. Ibid.; Walter "Toure" Pope Political Cadre of the Afro-American Liberation Army, "Writ No. 2: On the Hooligan Right Wing Newton Clique and the Flunkeys," in *Humanity, Freedom, Peace,* 22–23.

50. Huey Newton, "On the Defection of Eldridge Cleaver from the Black Panther Party and the Defection of the Black Community," in Foner, *Black Panthers Speak,* 272–78.

51. George Jackson, *Blood in My Eye* (Baltimore: Black Classic Press, 1990), 11–72; Hilliard and Cole, *Glory,* 379–80.

52. Johnson, "Demise," 407.

53. Hopkins, "Deradicalization," 231.

54. Acoli, *Brinks Trial Testimony,* 21.

55. Ibid., 10.

56. Kes Kesu Men Maa Hill, *Notes of a Surviving Black Panther: A Call for Historical Clarity, Emphasis, and Application* (New York: Pan-African Nationalist Press, 1992), 71; Dhoruba Bin Wahad, interviewed by Bill Weinberg, "Dhoruba Bin Wahad: Former Panther, Free at Last," *High Times,* 241 (September 1995): <http://www.hightimes.com/ht/mag/959/dhoruba.html> [Accessed January 12, 1999]; Shakur, *Assata,* 162–72; Clayborne Carson, *In Struggle: SNCC and the Black Awakening of the 1960s* (Cambridge: Harvard University Press, 1995), 298.

57. Williams, "Reflections of Geronimo," 74.

58. Ibid.

59. "By Any Means Necessary: Writings of the Black Liberation Army" *Breakthrough: The Political Journal of the Prairie Fire Organizing Committee* 2, no. 2 (fall 1978): 50; United States Justice Department-LEAA (Law Enforcement Assistance Act) document, quoted in Muntaqim, *Black Liberation Army,* 5.

60. "By Any Means Necessary," 50; Muntaqim, *Black Liberation Army,* 5.

61. Muntaqim, *Black Liberation Army,* 6.

62. J. Edgar Hoover, quoted in O'Reilly, *"Racial Matters,"* 321.

63. FBI memorandum quoted in ibid., 321.

64. "One Panther killed, another imprisoned," *Guardian* 25, no. 31 (May 16, 1973): 17.

65. Michael Kaufman, "Seized Woman Called Black Militants' Soul," *New York Times,* May 3, 1973, 47.
66. Lennox Hinds, "Foreword," in Shakur, *Assata,* xi.
67. Michael Kaufman, "Slaying of One of the Last Black Liberation Army Leaders Still at Large Ended a 7-Month Manhunt," *New York Times,* November 14, 1973, L-10; Williams, "Reflections of Geronimo," 109; Owadi, "The Saga Of Twyman Myers," *New Afrikan Freedom Fighters* 1, no. 1 (June 1982): 8.
68. Kaufman, "Slaying."
69. BLA communiqué titled "Looking Back," quoted in "By Any Means Necessary," 56–57. "Woody" and "Kimu" are Woody Changa Olugbala Green and Anthony Kimu Olugbala White. Both of these men were members of the Olugbala tribe, a unit of the BLA. Green and White were killed in January 1973 in a shootout with police in Brooklyn, New York.
70. Black Liberation Army Coordinating Committee, "Message to the Black Movement: A Political Statement from the Black Underground Coordinating Committee: the Black Liberation Army," reprinted in *Dragon-Fire,* (newsletter of the National Committee for the Defense of Political Prisoners), 1, no. 4 (December 1976): 11–13, 17; Muntaqim, *Black Liberation Army,* 13.
71. Muntaqim, *Black Liberation Army,* 13.
72. Kwame Afoh, Chokwe Lumumba, Imari Obadele, and Ahmed Obafemi, *A Brief History of Black Struggle in America* (Baton Rouge, La.: House of Songhay, 1991), 36–37. Consistent with contemporary written alphabets of indigenous African languages, members of the black nationalist movement often spell "Afrika" with a "k."
73. Ahmed Obafemi, interview with author, December 20, 1996, Birmingham, Ala.; Chokwe Lumumba, interview with author, December 22, 1996, Jackson, Miss.
74. Masai Ehehosi, interview with author, December 28, 1996, Chicago; Safiya Bukari, "Coming of Age: Notes from a New Afrikan Revolutionary," *Afrikan Prisoner of War Journal* 7 (1988): 12; Afoh et al., *Brief History,* 42.
75. Huey Newton, "Let Us Hold High the Banner of Intercommunalism," *Black Panther,* January 23, 1971, B-G.
76. Holder, "History," 273.
77. Shakur, *Assata,* 225–26.
78. Williams, *Inadmissible Evidence,* 171.
79. "To: The Black Community and the Black Movement, Special Communiqué (Joanne Chesimard), From: Coordinating Committee, B.L.A., Subject Freeing of Sister Assata Shakur on 2 November 79," *Breakthrough: Political Journal of the Prairie Fire Organizing Committee* 4, no. 1 (winter 1980): 12.
80. Assata Shakur, "Statement from Assata Shakur" *Breakthrough: Political Journal of the Prairie Fire Organizing Committee* 4, no. 1 (winter 1980): 13–15.
81. Reverend Herbert Daughtry, "Run Hard Sister, Run Hard," *Amsterdam News,* December 1, 1979, 17.
82. The Black Community, "Peace to Assata Shakur," *Amsterdam News,* January 5, 1980, 5.
83. Hill, *Surviving Panther,* 72; "A Chronology of Key Events, 1979–1982," *New Afrikan Freedom Fighter,* March 1983, 6; Williams, *Inadmissible Evidence,* 176.
84 . "A Chronology of Key Events", 6; Williams, *Inadmissible Evidence,* 176.
85. Williams, *Inadmissible Evidence,* 177.
86. "Chronology of Key Events," 6.
87. Assata Shakur, *From Somewhere in the World: Assata Shakur Speaks to the New Afrikan Nation* (New York: New Afrikan Womens Organization, 1980), 10.
88. Ibid., 12.
89. "Chronology of Key Events," 6.
90. Williams, *Inadmissible Evidence,* 179.
91. "Chronology of Key Events," 6; Castellucci, *Big Dance,* 3–21.
92. Williams, *Inadmissible Evidence,* 178–79; "Chronology of Key Events," 6; Castellucci, *Big Dance,* 237; "BLA Trial," *Death to the Klan: Newspaper of the John Brown Anti-Committee* 4 (fall 1984): 8–9.

93. "Chronology of Key Events," 6–7.

94. "Fulani Is Free!," *New Afrikan: Organ of the Provisional Government of the Republic of New Afrika,* 9, no. 3 (December 1983): 5; Fulani Sunni Ali, "Black People, My People! My Name is Fulani-Ali," *Arm the Spirit: A Revolutionary Prisoners Newspaper* 14 (fall 1982): 6.

95. Silvia Baraldini, "Silvia Baraldini: Italian National Political Prisoner," in *Can't Jail the Spirit: Political Prisoners in U.S.* (Chicago: Editorial El Coqui, 1988), 143–44; .

96. "Marilyn Buck," in *Can't Jail the Spirit,* 151–53.

97. Black Liberation Army communiqué, "On Strategic Alliance of the Armed Military Forces of the Revolutionary Nationalist and Anti-Imperialist Movement," in Imari Abubakari Obadele, *America the Nation-State: The Politics of The United States from a State-Building Perspective.* (Baton Rouge: Malcolm Generation, 1998), 423–24.

98. Acoli, *Brinks Trial Testimony,* 30.

99. BLA communiqué, "Strategic Alliance," 423.

100. "Inside the Brinks Story: A War of National Liberation Disclosed," *New Afrikan: Organ of the Provisional Government of the Republic of New Afrika* 9, no. 3 (December 1983): 6.

101. "Freedom Fighters: Profiles of Struggle," *New Afrikan Freedom Fighter* 2, no. 1 (March 1983): 8. This article profiles BLA soldiers Sekou Odinga and Kuwasi Balagoon and RATF members Judy Clark and David Gilbert. It is an indication of the varied political perspectives in this armed alliance.

102. BLA communiqué, "Strategic Alliance," 423.

103. Afoh et al., *Brief History,* 43; "Sekou Odinga: I Am a Muslim and a New Afrikan Freedom Fighter," *New Afrikan: Organ of the Provisional Government of the Republic of New Afrika* 9, no. 3 (December 1983): 4.

104. Umoja, "Set Our Warriors Free," 429–31; "Memorandum from Dr. Mutulu Shakur to Judge Charles Haight," November 26, 1987; *United States of America v. Mutulu Shakur* (defendant), United States District Court Southern District of New York, Affidavit 3 sss 82 Cr. 312 (CSH).

105. "In US-Brinks' Trial New Afrika Wins!" *New Afrikan: Organ of the Provisional Government of the Republic of New Afrika,* 9, no. 3 (December 1983): 3.

106. "Marilyn Buck," 153; Chokwe Lumumba, interview with author, November 22, 1998, Jackson, Miss.

107. "Sekou Odinga," 8; Castellucci, *Big Dance,* xiv, 71. According to Castellucci, Odinga rented a safehouse in Pittsburgh in January 1974. If this is true, one can assume he was in the United States in 1973.

108. Sekou Odinga, Hanif Shabazz Bey, Mutulu Shakur, Kojo, Jalil Muntaqim, Jihad Mumit, Sundiata Acoli, and Geronimo ji Jaga,"Statement in Support of Consolidation from New Afrikan POWs and Political Prisoners in Lewisburg, New York, and California Prisons: Toward the Objective of Building a National Liberation Front," *Jericho Movement* (commemorative newspaper for March 27, 1998, march in Washington, D.C.), 3. This statement was originally drafted by New Afrikan political prisoners and BLA members in the federal prison in Lewisburg, Pennsylvania, and endorsed by political prisoners in other locations. Its initial circulation was in November 1993.

109. "Kansas City Summit: NALF Work Summation," in founding documents of New Afrikan Liberation Front (August 1994).

110. Jalil Muntaqim, "From Jericho to New Jerusalem," in *Jericho Movement,* 4.

2 Global Solidarity: The Black Panther Party in the International Arena

Michael L. Clemons and Charles E. Jones

1. Hanes Walton Jr., *Invisible Politics: Black Political Behavior* (Albany: State University of New York Press, 1985), 269.

2. See Wilson J. Moses, *Classical Black Nationalism: From the American Revolution to Marcus Garvey* (New York: New York University Press, 1996); Waldo E. Martin Jr., *The Mind of Frederick Douglass* (Chapel Hill, N.C.: University of North Carolina Press, 1984), 114–16; Alfreda Duster, ed., *Crusade for Justice: The Autobiography of Ida B. Wells* (Chicago: University of Chicago Press, 1991); Manning Marable, *W. E. DuBois: Black Radical Democrat* (Boston: Twayne Publishers, 1986), 99–107; Louise D. Hutchinson, *Anna J. Cooper: A Voice from the South* (Washington, D.C.: Smithsonian Institution Press, 1998), 112–13; Clayborne Carson, *In Struggle: SNCC and the Black Awakening of the 1960s* (Cambridge: Harvard University Press, 1981), 268–86.

3. Karin L. Stanford, *Beyond the Boundaries: Reverend Jesse Jackson in the International Affairs* (New York: State University of New York Press, 1997), 93–100.

4. Charles E. Jones and Judson L. Jeffries, "'Don't Believe the Hype': Debunking the Panther Mythology," in *The Black Panther Party Reconsidered,* ed. Charles E. Jones (Baltimore: Black Classic Press, 1998), 37.

5. George Katsiaficas, *The Imagination of the New Left: A Global Analysis of 1968* (Boston: South End Press, 1987), 13.

6. Ibid., 23–27.

7. Ibid., 7.

8. Ibid., 10.

9. Ibid., 29.

10. Ibid., 10.

11. Ibid., 23–27.

12. Ibid., 6.

13. Ibid., 21.

14. Ibid., 20.

15. Philip S. Foner, ed., *The Black Panthers Speak* (New York: Da Capo Press, 1995), xxxvii; "Men Accused of Plot," *London Times,* November 27, 1968; Deborah Bernstein, "Conflict and Protest in Israeli Society: The Case of the Black Panthers of Israel," *Youth and Society* 14 (1984): 129–51; "Revolutionary People's Communication Network: International News (Bermuda)," *Right On!* September 1971, 13. On the Australian BPP: "Black Panthers Form Party," *Washington Post,* January 19, 1972. On the Dalit Panthers in India: Runoko Rashidi, "Dalits: The Black Untouchables of India," in *African Presence in Early Asia,* ed. Ivan Van Sertima and Runoko Rashidi (New Brunswick, N.J.: Transaction Books, 1988), 246; Arjun Dangle, ed., *Poisoned Bread: Translations from Modern MaRath: Dalit Literature* (Bombay: Orient Longman, 1992); Gail Omvedt, *Dalits and the Democratic Revolution: Dr. Ambedkar and the Dalit Movement in Colonial India* (New Delhi: Sage, 1994).

16. Huey P. Newton and Bobby Seale adopted the name and symbol of the Black Panther from an independent black political party formed in Lowndes County Alabama by the late Kwame Turé (Stokely Carmichael) and other activists of the Student Nonviolent Coordinating Committee. While we do not discuss domestic organizations within the United States, there were also significant emulators of the BPP in the United States. The Brown Berets, Young Lords, Young Patriots, White Panthers, and later the Grey Panthers all directly modeled themselves on the BPP.

17. Rashidi, "Dalits," 241.

18. Ibid., 246.

19. Bernstein, "Conflict and Protest," 130.

20. John Pilger, *A Secret Country* (New York: Alfred Knopf, 1989), 50.

21. "Black Panthers Form Party."

22. Brother Mitchell, interview by Charles E. Jones, July 24, 1993, Detroit. Brother Mitchell, who requested anonymity, was a member of the Black Panther Movement from 1970 to 1972.

23. See "Kill Police Order Alleged in Black Panther Case," *London Times,* August 13, 1968; "Revolutionary People's Communication Network," 13; and the pamphlet *Abbey*

Wood Chapter—White Panthers, (London: White Panther Party U.K., 1971), located in the special collection of the Tamiment Library, New York University, in folder titled "White Panther Party, U.K."

24. Bernstein, "Conflict and Protest" 140.
25. "Revolutionary People's Communication Network," 18.
26. "Executive Mandate No. 1: May 2, 1967," in Huey Newton, *To Die for the People, The Writings of Huey P. Newton* (New York: Writers and Readers, 1995), 12.
27. "Revolutionary People's Communication Network," 13.
28. "Black Panthers Form Party."
29. Bernstein, "Conflict and Protest," 138.
30. Andrew Billen, "Interview: Andrew Billen Talks to Darcus Howe," *Observer Magazine,* November 21, 1993, 8.
31. Althea Jones, "Announcement of the National Conference on the Rights of Black People, May 22–23 1971," April 23, 1971. This letter and program of the conference are located in the special collection on the BPP at the Archives of Labor History and Urban Affairs, Wayne State University, Detroit, Michigan.
32. See "Revolutionary People's Communication Network," 13; Bernstein, "Conflict and Protest" 133–138.
33. Bernstein, "Conflict and Protest," 135. Brother Mitchell reported that between 1970 and 1972 the Black Panther Movement had a small core membership base.
34. See Bernstein, "Conflict and Protest," 135; and the position paper authored by four members of the Black Panther Movement, Tshaka Beckles, Eddie Lecointe, Althea Jones Lecointe, and Lloyd Vidale, "Position Paper on Recent Events in the Black Workers Movement," November 29, 1973. We wish to thank Professor Hashim Gilbril, of Clark Atlanta University, for sharing this document with us.
35. Arie Bober, ed., *The Other Israel: The Radical Case against Zionism* (New York: Anchor Books, 1972), 27.
36. Kathleen Neal Cleaver, "Back to Africa: The Evolution of the International Section of the Black Panther Party (1969–1972)," in Jones, *The Black Panther Party Reconsidered,* 216.
37. Huey P. Newton, "Speech Delivered at Boston College: November 18, 1970," in Newton, *To Die for the People,* 32. Also see Floyd W. Hayes III and Francis A. Kiene III, "'All Power to the People': The Political Thought of Huey P. Newton and the Black Panther Party," in Jones, *The Black Panther Party Reconsidered,* 157–76; and Jimmy Mori, "The Ideological Development of the Black Panther Party," *Cornell Journal of Social Relations* 12 (1977): 137–55.
38. Huey P. Newton, *Revolutionary Suicide* (New York: Writers and Readers, 1995), 192–93.
39. Ibid., 111. See also Eldridge Cleaver, interview by Charles E. Jones, Virginia Beach, Virginia, March 24, 1995.
40 Bobby Seale, *Seize the Time: The Story of the Black Panther and Huey P. Newton* (Baltimore: Black Classic Press, 1991), 26.
41. Frantz Fanon, *The Wretched of the Earth* (New York: Grove Press, 1968), 37; also see Robert C. Smith, "Fanon and the Concept of Colonial Violence," *Black World* 22 (1973): 23–32.
42. Fanon, *Wretched,* 103.
43. Seale, *Seize the Time,* 30.
44. *Black Panther,* January 16, 1971, 10.
45. Eldridge Cleaver, *On the Ideology of the Black Panther Party* (June 1970, pamphlet), 3.
46. Bobby Seale, "Explains Panther Politics: An Interview," in Foner, *Black Panthers Speak,* 86.
47. *Panther Bullet* (Richmond, California, branch of the Black Panther Party), no.1 (January 1969). This document is located in the special collection on the Black Panther Party at the University Research Library, University of California at Los Angeles.
48. Eldridge Cleaver, *Soul on Fire* (Waco, Texas: Word Books, 1978), 90.

49. Newton, *To Die for the People,* 25.
50. Ibid., 26.
51. Cleaver, *On the Ideology of the Black Panther Party,*1.
52. Kathleen Cleaver, *On the Vanguard Role of the Black Urban Lumpen Proletariat* (London: Grass-Roots, 1975); Eldridge Cleaver, "On Lumpen Ideology," *Black Scholar* 3 (1972): 2–10.
53. Henry Winston, "Crisis of the Black Panther Party," in *Strategy for a Black Agenda: A Critique of New Theories of Liberation in the United States and Africa* (New York: International Publishers, 1973), 207–235; also see Jones and Jeffries, "Don't Believe the Hype," 43–47. See Chris Booker, "Lumpenization: A Critical Error of the Black Panther Party," in Jones, *Black Panther Party,* 337–62, for a fuller discussion of the lumpen interpretation of the BPP.
54. Cleaver, *Soul on Fire,* 111.
55. Ibid., 112.
56. *Black Panther,* June 27, 1970, 8. Also see Dae-Sook Suh, *Kim Il Sung: The North Korean Leader* (New York: Columbia University Press, 1988).
57. G. Louis Heath, ed., *Off the Pigs! The History and Literature of the Black Panther Party* (Metuchen, N.J.: Scarecrow Press, 1976), 149; Newton, *Revolutionary Suicide,* 70
58. Peter C. Sederberg, *Fires Within: Political Violence and Revolution Change* (New York: Harper Collins, 1994), p. 283.
59. Ibid.
60. Ernesto Guevara, *Guerrilla Warfare* (New York: Praser, 1970), 4. Also see Regis Debray, *Revolution in the Revolution? Armed Struggle and Political Struggle in Latin America* (New York: Monthly Review Press, 1967).
61. Newton, *To Die for the People,* 201.
62. Connie Matthews, "The Struggle Is a World Struggle," in *Black Panthers Speak,* Foner, 158.
63. For the offer made by Newton and the Vietnamese response, see George Katsiaficas ed., *Vietnam Documents: American and Vietnamese Views of the War,* (Armonk, N.Y.: Sharpe, 1992).
64. Eldridge Cleaver, "To My Black Brothers in Vietnam." This flyer is located in the special collection of the Tamiment Library, New York University, folder titled "Black Panther Party."
65. For a detailed discussion of this intraparty strife, see Ollie Johnson, "Explaining the Demise of the Black Panther Party: The Role of Internal Factors," in Jones, *Black Panther Party,* 399–403.
66. See Winston A. Grady Willis, "The Black Panther Party: State Repression and Political Prisoners," in Jones, 363–90; Nelson Blackstock, *Cointelpro: The FBI's Secret War on Political Freedom,* (New York: Anchor Foundations, 1975); and Ward Churchill and Jim Vander Wall, *Agents of Repression: The FBI's Secret Wars against the Black Panther Party and the American Indian Movement* (Boston: South End Press, 1988).
67. Kathleen Rout, *Eldridge Cleaver* (Boston: Twayne, 1991), 63. Eldridge Cleaver credited the late Kwame Turé (Stokely Carmichael) for the demonstration in Tanzania.
68. Earl Anthony, *Picking Up the Gun: A Report on the Black Panthers* (New York: Dial Press, 1970), 140; Newton, *Revolutionary Suicide,* 193; Heath, *Off the Pigs!* 60.
69. The Church League of America, *The Black Panthers in Action* (Wheaton, Ill.: Church League of America, 1969), 17; Michael Newton, *Bitter Grain: Huey Newton and the Black Panther Party* (Los Angeles: Holloway, 1980), 116–17; "Weekend of Solidarity with the Cuban Revolution," *Black Panther,* July 24, 1977, 13. Assata Shakur and William Brent are among other BPP members who still live in exile in Cuba. See William Lee Brent, *Long Time Gone: A Black Panther's True-Life Story of His Hijacking and Twenty-five Years in Cuba* (New York: Times Books, 1996); Roberta Alexander, "All Power to the Sanya Liberation League," *Black Panther,* October 11, 1969, 8.

70. Cleaver, *Lumpen Proletariat,* 222–24.

71. Ibid., 226.

72. See Elaine Brown, summary report of the "Anti-Imperialist Delegation, 1970," series 2, box 4, folder 12, Newton Foundation Records, Stanford University.

73. "Cleaver and Black Panther Group Attend Hanoi Observance," *New York Times,* August 19, 1970, 13.

74. For a firsthand insight account of the Panther delegation to the Peoples' Republic of the Congo, see Cleaver, *Lumpen Proletariat,* 240–44; and Eldridge Cleaver, *Revolution in the Congo* (London): Revolutionary Peoples' Communications Network, 1971.

75. Newton, *Revolutionary Suicide,* 322.

76. "Program by Category of the Black Panther Party Delegation in the Peoples' Republic of China and People Assigned to report to Specific Categories," series 2, box 12, folder 2, Newton Foundation Records, Stanford University; and Audrea Jones, interview by Charles E. Jones, Rahway, N.J., June 14, 1997.

77. Cleaver, *Lumpen Proletariat,* 225–26; See also Kit Kim Holder, "The History of the Black Panther Party, 1966–1972: A Curriculum Tool for Afrikan-American Studies" (Ph.D. diss., University of Massachusetts, 1990), 170; Heath, *Off the Pigs!* 189.

78. See "Letter from the Black Panther Party Solidarity Committee in the Scandinavi to the Law Offices of Garry, Dreyfus, McTernan and Brotsky," September 14, 1969, series 2, box 10, folder 5, Newton Foundation Records, Stanford University; "23 Arrested in Danish Class," *London Times,* June 2, 1970, 3; Heath, *Off the Pigs!* 189; "British Solidarity with the Movement to Free Bobby Seale," *Black Panther,* April 25, 1970, 16.

79. Foner, *Black Panthers Speak,*128–30 and 154–59; Church League of America, *Black Panthers in Action,*12; "In the Spirit of Revolutionary Intercommunal Solidarity," Inner Party Memorandum no.13, series 1, box 4, folder 10, Newton Foundation Records, Stanford University.

80. "Irish Give Key to City to Panthers as Symbol," *New York Times,* March 30, 1970, 31. Eldridge Cleaver credited the late Kwame Turé (Stokely Carmichael) for cultivating the support of Kwame Nkrumah and Sekou Toure. See Rout, *Cleaver* 63; *Here and Now for Bobby Seale: Essays by Jean Genet* (Committee to Defend Panthers, 1970); and Robert Sandarg, "Jean Genet and the Black Panther Party," *Journal of Black Studies* 16 (1986): 269–82.

81. Holder, "History," 164; also see Cleaver, *Lumpen Proletariat,* 226–30.

82. The author, Michael Newton, who is not related to the party's cofounder, claimed that "nothing of any real consequence would be done in Algeria." See Newton, *Bitter Grain,* 118.

83. Rout, *Cleaver,*110.

84. See Cleaver, *Lumpen Proletariat,* 245–49; Cleaver, *Soul on Fire,* 155–61; "Panther Office Raided in Algeria: Why?" *Right On!* August 1972; "Black Panther Villa in Algeria Sealed Off after Raid by Police," *New York Times,* August 12, 1972, 6; "Panthers Appear to Have Left Algeria," *New York Times,* March 28, 1973, 24.

85. James C. McKinley Jr., "A Black Panther's Mellow Exile: Farming in Africa," *New York Times,* November 23, 1997, 3; and *Black Panther in Exile: The Story of Pete O'Neal,* documentary produced Media Genesis, 1989.

86. Huey P. Newton, "CBS Morning News Transcript," July 4, 1977, 2; Jack Slater, "Huey Newton Speaks Out," *Los Angeles Times,* August 25, 1977, 1; 12–15; Lionel Martin, "Huey Newton Returns to U.S. to Face Charges," *Washington Post,* June 25, 1977, 1, 17.

87. Akinyele Omowale Umoja, "Set Our Warriors Free: The Legacy of the Black Panther Party and Political Prisoners," in Jones, *The Black Panther Party Reconsidered,* 425; Assata Shakur, *Assata Speaks: Message to the New Afrikan Nation* (Stone Mountain, Ga.: Universal Truth, n.d.); "Assata on Religion," *Michigan Citizen* (Highland Park, Mich.), July 18–24, 1993, B8; Charles Brooks, "CBC Betrayal of Assata: Anger and Outrage in the Black Nation," *Nationtime: The Voice of the New Afrikan Liberation Front,* winter 1998, 5.

3 A Life in the Party: An Historical and Retrospective Examination of the Projections and Legacies of the Black Panther Party

Mumia Abu-Jamal

1. Huey P. Newton, *To Die for the People: The Writings of Huey P. Newton* (New York: Writers and Readers, 1995), 90–91.
2. Hugh Pearson, *The Shadow of the Panther: Huey Newton and the Price of Black Power in America* (Reading, Mass.: Addison-Wesley, 1994), 118; Charles E. Jones, ed., *The Black Panther Party Reconsidered* (Baltimore: Black Classic Press, 1998), 4.
3. Carl G. Gustavson, *A Preface to History* (New York: McGraw Hill, 1955), 123–24.
4. Pearson, *Shadow of the Panther*, 179.
5. Tracye Matthews, "'No One Ever Asks, What a Man's Place in the Revolution Is': Gender and the Politics of the Black Panther Party, 1966–1971," in Jones, *The Black Panther Party Reconsidered*, 291.
6. Pearson, *Shadow of the Panther*, 179.
7. Angela D. LeBlanc, "'The Most Qualified Person to Handle the Job': Black Panther Party Women, 1966–1982," in Jones, *The Black Panther Party Reconsidered*, 307–8.
8. Regina Jennings, "Why I Joined the Party: An Africana Womanist Reflection," in Jones, *The Black Panther Party Reconsidered*, 262–63.
9. Elaine Brown, *A Taste of Power: A Black Woman's Story* (New York: Anchor, 1992), 368–70.
10. LeBlanc, "Most Qualified Person," 310.
11. Eric Foner, *Reconstruction: America's Unfinished Revolution, 1863–1877* (New York: Harper, 1988), 98–99; LeBlanc, "Most Qualified Person," 314.
12. Kathleen Neal Cleaver, "Back to Africa: The Evolution of the International Section of the Black Panther Party (1969–1972)" in Jones, *The Black Panther Party Reconsidered*, 236.
13. David Hilliard and Lewis Cole, *This Side of Glory: The Autobiography of David Hilliard and the Story of the Black Panther Party* (Boston: Little, Brown, 1993), 168.
14. Huey P. Newton, *Revolutionary Suicide* (New York: Writers and Readers, 1995), 71.
15. Bobby Seale, *Seize the Time: The Story of the Black Panther Party and Huey P. Newton* (New York: Vintage, 1970), 54–56.
16. Jonina M. Abron, "'Serving the People': The Survival Programs of the Black Panther Party," in Jones, *The Black Panther Party Reconsidered*, 186.
17. Charles E. Jones and Judson L. Jeffries, "'Don't Believe the Hype': Debunking the Panther Mythology," in Jones, *The Black Panther Party Reconsidered*, 29.
18. Ibid., 27.
19. Memo from San Francisco field office to FBI HQ, dated 5/15/70. See ibid., 29.
20. Abron, "'Serving the People,'" 182.
21. Huey P. Newton, *War against the Panthers: A Study of Repression in America* (New York: Harlem River Press, 1996), 16, 55.
22. Jones and Jeffries, "'Don't Believe the Hype,'" 37.
23. Huey P. Newton, *To Die for the People*, 31.
24. Huey P. Newton and Erik Erikson, *In Search of Common Ground: Conversations with Erik H. Erikson and Huey P. Newton* (New York: Norton, 1973), 29–30.
25. Hilliard and Cole, *Glory*, 11; Newton, *To Die for the People*, 31.
26. The writer participated in this collective.
27. LeBlanc, "Most Qualified Person," 326. Njeri's son, Fred Hampton Jr., is considered an APSP political prisoner who is serving a term of fourteen years in Statesville Prison, Joliet, Ill.
28. Jones, *The Black Panther Party Reconsidered*, 6.
29. Ibid.
30. Ibid.

4 Mobilizing for Mumia Abu-Jamal in Paris

Kathleen Neal Cleaver

1. "Cleaver Seeks Political Asylum in France," *New York Times* April 4, 1973.
2. During the summer of 1995 numerous human rights and anti-racist organizations, opponents of the death penalty, and a prisoner support group united in a collective to prevent Mumia Abu-Jamal from being executed in the United States. They solicited support from internationally known French intellectuals, occupied the Paris office of American Express, and mounted demonstrations outside the American Embassy. In addition, they collected thousands of signatures on petitions to the Governor of Pennsylvania demanding that Mumia not be executed. See generally Chemin Anne, "Des associations réclament la grâce d'un condamné a mort aux Etats-Unis," *Le Monde,* July 27, 1995.
3. Gerard Le Puill, "Le Pavé de Paris décline le droit des femmes au féminin," *L'Humanité* (Paris), November 27, 1995.
4. William Drozdiak, "French Strikes Cripple Nation, Reforms," *Washington Post,* November 29, 1995; Thomas Kamm and Douglas Laviv, "French Stand Tough against Strikers to Prove Readiness for Monetary Union," *Wall Street Journal,* November 30, 1995. See generally Raghu Krishnan, "The First Revolt against Globalization," *Monthly Review,* 48, no. 1 (May 1, 1996).
5. Christopher Burns, "Spirit of 1968 Lives On at Student Rebellion's Birthplace," *Associated Press,* May 8, 1993; Julie Street, "Talking about a Revolution," *Independent* (London), December 17, 1995.
6. "Czechoslovakia Invaded by Russians and Four Other Warsaw Pact Forces," *New York Times,* August 21, 1968; "Russians Seize Dubcek and Six Colleagues," *New York Times,* August 22, 1968.
7. See, e.g., "Fighting Intense in Saigon Region," *New York Times,* August 29, 1968.
8. See Kathleen Cleaver, "On Eldridge Cleaver," *Ramparts,* June 1969; Elizabeth Mehren, "Witness to History: Kathleen Neal Cleaver," *Los Angeles Times,* July 19, 1995.
9. Malcolm Gladwell, "Abu-Jamal's Bitter Philadelphia Story," *Washington Post* August 23, 1995. According to an October 24, 1969, FBI memorandum, "Wesley Cook [Mumia's previous name], Negro Male, age 15, has been affiliated with the BPP in Philadelphia since 5/1/69. . . . Currently Cook is enrolled in the eleventh grade of Benjamin Franklin High School" (SAC Philadelphia to Military Intelligence Philadelphia, Naval Investigative Philadelphia, Office of Special Investigation Philadelphia, and Secret Service Philadelphia, October 24, 1996, U.S. Dept. of Justice, Federal Bureau of Investigation [hereinafter FBI] field office no. 157-3937).
10. Amnesty International, *The Case Of Mumia Abu-Jamal: A Death Sentence Based On Politics* (Amnesty International Fact Sheet, 1995): "Amnesty International is deeply concerned that reference to Mumia Abu-Jamal's purported political beliefs and statements made as a teenager—which had no direct bearing on the case—may have unjustly swayed the jury in its sentencing decision. The prosecutor indeed explicitly suggested that the remarks made by Abu-Jamal in the 12-year-old newspaper interview (which included a quotation from Mao Tse Tung that 'political power grows out of the barrel of a gun') 'might ring a bell as to whether or not you are an executioner or endorse such actions.' Given that Mumia Abu-Jamal had no prior convictions for any offense, or any history of involvement in politically motivated violence, such a line of questioning in our view was highly prejudicial." See also Linda Grant, "A Lawful Lynching: Black Panther Mumia Abu-Jamal," *Guardian* (London), July 22, 1995; "Call from Death Row," Africa News Service, February 14, 1997.

11. "Vie sauve pour Mumia Abu-Jamal," *L'Humanité,* July 17, 1995; see Sonya M. Haynes, "Ridge Signs Abu-Jamal Death Warrant," *New Pittsburgh Courier,* June 7, 1995; Reginald W. Major, "Mumia Death Warrant Signed Three Weeks after Big Lie," *Sun Reporter,* June 8, 1995.

12. See Françoise Germain-Robin, "Le Nom de Mumia Abu-Jamal résonné à Paris," *L'Humanité,* August 10, 1995, reporting that thousands of people gathered in the Place de la Concorde to protest the execution of Mumia Abu-Jamal; Jacques Derrida, "Pour Mumia Abu Jamal," *Le Monde,* August 8, 1995. See also Scott Kraft, "U.S. Inmate Has a Hold on Europe's Power Elite," *Los Angeles Times,* September 6, 1996.

13. Following the end of World War II, the demagogic senator Joseph McCarthy rose to prominence for his flamboyant anticommunist witch hunts, investigations, and prosecutions. The paranoia unleashed against so-called Communists ruined the careers of artists, entertainers, academics, and government officials, and threw a pall over organizations and individuals holding radical political views that lasted until the early 1960s. See generally Fred J. Cook, *The Nightmare Decade* (New York: Random House, 1971); Robert Griffith, *The Politics of Fear* (Lexington: University Press of Kentucky, 1970).

14. See Jill Smolowe, "Mumia on Their Mind," *Time,* August 7, 1995.

15. See Michel Muller, "Sabo: la loi, l'ordre et la piqûre," *L'Humanité,* August 1, 1995; Michel Muller, "Rapports truqués et faux témoins," *L'Humanité,* August 2, 1995.

16. See *International Political Prisoners Unite to Save Mumia Abu-Jamal: Art and Writings against the Death Penalty,* proposal for the art project initiated by 67 imprisoned men and women (1994), on file with author.

17. Alberto Rodriquez, Jihad Mumia, Tim Blunk, "Free Mumia Abu-Jamal," open letter (September 1994), on file with author.

18. See "Death Row Inmate Sues NPR for Refusing to Air His Commentaries," *Public Broadcasting Report,* April 5, 1995; Sam Husseni, "The Broken Promise of Public Radio," *Humanist,* September 1, 1994.

19. See William Drozdiak, "Pennsylvania Death Row Prisoner Captivates Europeans," *Washington Post,* August 4, 1995, A1; Farhan Haq, "Pending Execution Sparks International Outcry," Inter Press Service, August 3, 1995.

20. See Alexander Cockburn, "Lynching Mumia," *Nation,* 260, no. 25 (June 26, 1995): 911; Rupert Cornwell, "Abu Jamal Supporters Worldwide Plead with US State to Retry Case," *Irish Times,* August 2, 1995; Gregg Zoroya, "Journalist's Death Sentence Has People Judging the Judge," *Los Angeles Times,* September 13, 1995.

21. See "Mumia Abu-Jamal Files Appeal in Pennsylvania Supreme Court," *Sun Reporter,* February 22, 1996.

22. Smolowe, "Mumia on Their Mind"; Cockburn, "Lynching Mumia."

23. See Tawanda D. Williams, "Abu-Jamal Supporters Decry New-Trial Ruling in Oakland Rally," *Pittsburgh Post Gazette,* September 17, 1995, A29.

24. The *Philadelphia Inquirer* reported that the FOP meeting entertained "hours of speeches praising Sabo's decision." See Acel Moore, "The Blueprint Exists to Overhaul Our Racist Criminal-Justice System," *Philadelphia Inquirer,* August 17, 1995.

25. Since the Supreme Court upheld new capital punishment laws in 1976, 393 people have been put to death, and 3,300 more are on death row (David J. Garrow, "Two Death Penalty Cases, One Dilemma," *New York Times,* June 17, 1997).

26. See Donald Shockley, review of George Jackson's *Soledad Brother: The Prison Letters of George Jackson, Commonweal,* March 26, 1997, 65–67 (book review). See "Soledad 3 On Trial," *Black Panther,* April 6, 1970; "George Jackson Speaks from Prison," *Black Panther,* October 17, 1970.

27. "Prisons: San Quentin Massacre," *Newsweek,* August 30, 1971; "George Jackson Lives!" *Black Panther,* August 28, 1971 (issue dedicated to George Jackson); "Jackson Family Demands U.N. Investigation of George Jackson Death," *Black Panther,* September 18, 1971.

28. André Benedetto, a well-known activist-playwright working out of his own theater in

southern France, was the first European dramatist to write a play on Mumia's case. At Julia Wright's request, he worked on his *Theatrical Attempt to Clarify the Case of Mumia Abu-Jamal* throughout the summer of 1995. The world premiere of his play took place at the Paris opening of the *Art against the Death Penalty* show. The play has also been translated into Italian.

29. MRAP is an acronym for Mouvement contre le racisme et pour amitié entre les peuples, or Movement against Racism and for Friendship among Peoples.
30. Suzannne Lowery, "Politicians' Wives Pursue La Glorie Paris Life," *Daily Telegraph* (London), February 22, 1996, 13. The article described Marie-Claire Mendès-France as "one of France's most remarkable political wives of the last generation".
31. Marie-Claire Mendès-France, statement in support of Mumia Abu-Jamal, Paris, November 27, 1995, on file with Leonard Weinglass, Esq.
32. See "Lettre de Georges Marchais à Jacques Chirac," *L'Humanité,* August 4, 1995, Marchais' letter to Jacques Chirac urging the President to take political action on behalf of Mumia Abu-Jamal; "Une Declaration de Georges Marchais: Notre responsibilité," *L'Humanité,* September, 14, 1995.
33. See James Morrison, "A World: Embassy Row," *Washington Times,* August 8, 1995; "France Urges Mercy for Controversial Death Row Prisoner in US," Agence France-Presse, August 7, 1995.
34. See Kathleen Neal Cleaver, "Back to Africa: The Evolution of the International Section of the Black Panther Party," in *The Black Panther Party Reconsidered,* ed. Charles E. Jones (Baltimore: Black Classic Press, 1998), 211, 231.
35. President Clinton signed the $30 billion crime bill, the Effective Death Penalty and Public Safety Act of 1996, Pub. L. No.104-132, 110 Stat. 1214. See generally Jeffrey Rosen, "Shell Game: Unconstitutional, Politically Motivated Effective Death Penalty and Public Safety Act of 1996," *New Republic,* May 13, 1996, explaining that this bill "greatly increase[s] the possibility that ordinary defendants can be convicted or executed after a state trial that has been tainted with constitutional or factual errors."
36. Data from the Pennsylvania Department of Corrections and the U.S. Department of Justice reveal that in Philadelphia alone eighty African Americans for every ten white persons are sent to death row. The figure far surpasses those of the southern United States, where seven African Americans are on death row for every ten white death row inmates. See *Death Penalty Newsletter* (Amnesty International) 3, no. 3 (summer 1997).
37. Mumia published his prison writings to critical acclaim as *Mumia Abu-Jamal, Live from Death Row* (Reading, MA: Addison-Wesley, 1995).
38. See generally Edward J. Boyer, "New Attorney Denied for Pratt at Parole Hearing: Prisons: Kathleen Cleaver Won't Be Able to Represent the Convicted Black Panther at Session Wednesday," *Los Angeles Times,* August 23, 1994.
39. Amnesty International is concerned about both the fairness of Mumia's trial and the evidence on which he was convicted. The specific issues Amnesty cites include (1) "concern about the jury selection process which related in an overwhelmingly white jury in an area where a significant minority of the population was black," (2) "questions about the reliability of the identification evidence and possible pressure on witnesses," (3) "the withholding of evidence that might have been helpful to the defense," (4) "doubts about the veracity of a purported 'confession' made by Abu-Jamal after his arrest," (5) "the competence of Mumia's trial counsel," and (6) "the lack of adequate funding afforded to the defense to investigate its case." Amnesty's letter-writing campaign on behalf of Mumia asks that letters be sent to Pennsylvania Governor Tom Ridge urging that he "immediately halt the execution of Mumia Abu-Jamal" (*The Case of Mumia Abu-Jamal,* Amnesty International Fact Sheet, 1995).
40. John Donne, "Devotions upon Emergent Occasions, Meditation XVII" in *The Complete Poetry and Selected Prose of John Donne,* ed. Charles M. Coffin (New York: Random House, 1952).
41. See Marc Kaufman et al., "Convicted Killer Now a Symbol," *York Daily Record,* August 21, 1995.

42. Memorandum from Special Agent in Charge (SAC) Philadelphia to FBI Director, January 1, 1970, FBI file no. 157-3937-60/157-15510, Report of SA [deleted] 10/24/69 at Philadelphia, "Wesley Cook, aka RM-BPP."

43. "Kathleen Cleaver for Assemblywoman; 18th District, San Francisco, California," *Black Panther,* May 18, 1968.

44. Bobby Seale, "Revolutionary Action on Campus and Community," *Black Panther,* January 10, 1970.

45. An April 30, 1970, FBI memo,"Wesley Cook, aka RM-BPP," reported that "it is to be noted that Cook is a juvenile and does not have an arrest record." The memorandum also enclosed a photograph of Mumia taken a year earlier to be sent to the San Francisco FBI office, SAC Philadelphia to Director, April 30, 1970, FBI File no. 157-3937-75; A subsequent FBI memo dated July 21, 1970 reports that "fifth source advised that Wesley Cook was presently in Juvenile Hall as he was arrested at Tenth and Washington Streets, Oakland, California, for improper identification and crossing against a red light. Cook was selling BPP newspapers at the time of his arrest." SAC Letter July 21, 1970, Bureau File No. 157-3937-101.

46. "The first edition of the RPCN [Revolutionary People's Communications Network] biweekly newspaper *Babylon,* dated 11/1-14/71, has just been published, and its list of correspondents includes the name 'Mumia' of Philadelphia." SAC Philadelphia to director, November 12, 1971, FBI file no. 157-3937-80.

47. U.S. Senate Select Committee to Study Governmental Operations with Respect to Intelligence Activities, *Final Report,* bk. 3; "The Panthers: Their Decline—and Fall?" *Newsweek,* March 22, 1971. See generally Ward Churchill and Jim Vander Wall, *Agents of Repression: The FBI's Secret Wars against the Black Panther Party and the American Indian Movement* (Boston: South End Press, 1988).

48. "Subject [Mumia] is being placed in Category II of Administrative Index (ADEX)" the FBI special agent justified the placement by explaining that Mumia "has now actively aligned himself with the Cleaver Faction of the Black Panther Party" (SAC Philadelphia to Director, December 9, 1971, FBI file no. 157-3937-18). See also Gladwell, "Bitter Philadelphia Story." Mumia was deleted from ADEX in March of 1973, although sources "continued to report periodically on COOK and, although he has not displayed a propensity for violence, he has continued to associate himself with individuals and organizations engaged in Extremist activities" (SAC Philadelphia to Director, April 4, 1974, FBI file no. 157-3937-259).

49. Mumia was called the "Voice of the Voiceless" for his extensive and uncompromising coverage of police brutality and disadvantaged and unpopular groups such as MOVE ("Political Prisoners Here," *Harrisburg Patriot,* February 23, 1990). He was called an "eloquent activist not afraid to raise his voice" by the *Philadelphia Inquirer* and named one of "81 people to watch in 1981" by *Philadelphia Magazine.* He won a Peabody Award for a series on radio station WHYY on the pope's visit to Philadelphia (T. T. Nhu, "Inmate's Voice Heard on Radio," *Cincinnati Enquirer,* June 11, 1994; Terry Bisson, "A Journalist's Last Deadline," *Newsday,* June 22, 1995.) Mumia was also the president of the Philadelphia Association of Black Journalists (Todd Burroughs, "Abu-Jamal Juggles Roles of Writer and Activist: Career of Condemned Reporter Sheds Light on Black Journalism," *Philadelphia Tribune,* March 5, 1996).

50. Mumia continues to work as a journalist while in prison and still writes and speaks out about MOVE and other oppressed groups. See Mumia Abu-Jamal, "COINTEL-PRO Continues: The Bari Bombing," *Michigan Citizen,* May 18, 1996; Abu-Jamal, "Barring None," *Essence,* November 1, 1996. His writings have been carried by several major publications, ("A Hole in the Soul," *Chicago Tribune,* June 16, 1996; Mumia Abu-Jamal, "Parole Denied for Geronimo—Again!," *Michigan Citizen,* June 8, 1996). Additionally the *Yale Law Journal* published his article "Teetering on the Brink: Between Death and Life," *Yale Law Journal* 100 (1991): 993. Abu Jamal's work has also been translated and published abroad, "Voici le texte de la préface du livre du journaliste noir americain condamné a mort: 'En Direct du couloir de la

mort, ici Mumia Abu-Jamal,'" *L'Humanité,* trans. Michel Muller, August 9, 1995.
51. Nhu, "Inmate's Voice."
52. See generally Holly Sklar, *Chaos or Community: Seeking Solutions not Scapegoats for Bad Economics* (Boston: South End Press, 1995); "Slicing the Cake (Economic Inequalities)," *Economist,* November 5, 1994, which reports that for forty years after 1930 the gap between rich and poor in America narrowed, but since the end of the 1960s it has been widening and is greater now than at any time since the creation of the modern welfare state; see also "Among Hills and Hollows: The South," *Economist,* April 13, 1996, which discusses the racial disparities in Southern poverty.
53. Stephen Moore Dean Stansel, "Put an End to Corporate Welfare," *USA Today,* September 1, 1995; Dante Ramos, "The War against the Poor" (book review), *Washington Monthly,* December 1, 1995; Howard Gleckman, "Welfare Cuts: Now, It's Corporate America's Turn," *Business Week,* April 10, 1995.
54. See "Scapegoating and Slander: Blaming the Poor for Poverty," *Economist,* July 17, 1996.
55. For a thoughtful discussion of the politics and significance of death penalty litigation, see Austin Sarat, "Representation and Capital Punishment: Bearing Witness and Writing History in the Struggle against Capital Punishment," *Yale Journal of Law and Humanities* 451 (1996); Stephen B. Bright, "The Electric Chair and the Chain Gang: Choices and Challenges for America's Future," *Notre Dame Law Review* 71 (1996): 845.
56. See Leonard Weinglass, *Race for Justice* (Monroe, ME: Common Courage Press, 1995), 17, 147. *Race for Justice* compiles legal documents concerning the Abu-Jamal case, including the Memorandum in Support of Petition for Post-Conviction relief, Petition for Post-Conviction relief, the Motion for Recusal of the Honorable Albert F. Sabo, and exhibits and information about the campaign to save Mumia's life. See also Kathy Deacon, "In Sabo's Court: Jamal Wins a Stay as the Legal Farce Continues," *Village Voice,* August 15, 1995.
57. Weinglass, *Race for Justice,* 17, 55–58, 146–47.
58. Ibid., 56.
59. Ibid., 17–19, 20, 67–74, 112–15, 119–20, 165–67, 179–81 (1995). Mumia's trial attorney has subsequently acknowledged his inadequate defense. In an affidavit Mr. Jackson stated, "I did not prepare Mr. Jamal for the eventuality [i.e., the death penalty phase], investigate possible mitigating factors or review any aspect of his life or character that merited special consideration, specifically I never counseled Mr. Jamal on what were his available mitigating circumstances, the burden of proof involved, and how each factor could be established through documentary and testamentary evidence. In fact, I did not meet with Mr. Jamal between the time the jury returned the guilty verdict Friday Afternoon of July 2nd and the next morning just before the penalty phase was to begin." See also "Lawyer Admits Poor Defense of Abu-Jamal," *Baltimore Evening Sun,* July 28, 1995.
60. Weinglass, *Race for Justice,* 17–18, 57–67, 74–89, 162–64, 167–71.
61. Ibid., 30, 38, 41, 147–48.
62. Ibid., 30–32, 38–41.
63. *Commonwealth of PA v. Mumia Abu-Jamal a/k/a Wesley Cook,* Post Conviction Relief Appeal Brief to the Pennsylvania Supreme Court, Brief for the Appellant, Appeal from Order of the Court of Common Pleas, Philadelphia County January Sessions, 1982, nos. 1357–1358, 54–55.
64. The saga continues into the present. At a hearing in 1997 Veronica Jones, a prosecution witness against Mumia, recanted her trial testimony and revealed that the police had pressured her to lie in 1982. Immediately after she testified at the hearing, the police arrested her on bad check charges and reinstated prosecution on a fourteen-year-old charge of prostitution (Dina Wisenberg Brin, "Witness Recants Story in Murder: Woman Arrested during Hearing for Abu-Jamal Trial," *Pittsburgh Post-*

Gazette, October 3, 1996; David Kinney, "Lawyer for Abu-Jamal Witness Says Old Charges Are Intimidation: The Witness Was Arrested on the Stand after Changing Testimony in the Murder Case," *York Daily Record,* October 4, 1996). Additionally Pamela Jenkins, a close friend of another prosecution witness, gave a sworn statement that the prosecution witness, Cynthia White, was being pressured by the police to testify against Mumia (Dinah Wisenberg Brin, "Ex-Prostitute Supports Abu-Jamal Case—Woman, 31, Claims That Police Threatened the Life of a Witness," *Harrisburg Patriot,* March 11, 1997; "Judge Bars Recantation of Witness Who Helped Convict Abu-Jamal," Associated Press, November 1, 1996; Christopher Hitchens, "Death and the Maidens," *Nation,* April 14, 1997, 8). See also Weinglass, *Race for Justice,* 30–32, 39, 42, 53–54.

More recently, the validity of Pamela Jenkins's recollections of Cynthia White's statement has been questioned by the prosecution, who claim that Cynthia White died in 1992—before Pamela Jenkins says she spoke with her. Judge Sabo allowed testimony from New Jersey officials who claim that White died in 1991, and excluded defense witnesses who claim to have seen White within the past two years ("Ex-FBI-Informant to Testify Philly Police Coerced Key Witness in Abu-Jamal Trial," *Harrisburg Patriot,* June 10, 1997; "Woman's Status Key to Murder Appeal: Is Cynthia White Dead or Alive?" *Harrisburg Patriot,* July 1, 1997).

65. Weinglass, *Race for Justice,* 34, 146.
66. Ibid., 32–34, 145–46.
67. Ibid., 146.
68. Ibid.
69. Terry Bisson, "A Journalist's Last Deadline?" *Newsday,* June 22, 1995. See also Gladwell, "Bitter Philadelphia Story": explaining that "The animosity between Frank Rizzo's police department and Abu-Jamal and other black activists became highly personal. When the Black Panthers were at their height, Rizzo made them a kind of public challenge, as if the police and the Panthers were combatants on a playground. 'We'd be glad to meet them on their own terms,' Rizzo said. 'Just let them tell us when and where.'" FBI files from as early as 1969, when Mumia was fifteen years old record Mumia as calling Rizzo a "pig" as well as speaking "the usual trash about the oppressor" ([deleted] to [deleted], August 11, 1969, FBI file no., 157-3937-5). See generally "Rizzo's Reign of Terror," *Black Panther,* May 29, 1971; Gene Gilmore, "The Night Stick Candidate," *Nation,* October 25, 1971. As police commissioner, Rizzo was closely associated with his nightstick. In response to the federal lawsuit filed by the Justice Department alleging police brutality in the Philadelphia police department, Rizzo responded, "It's very easy to break some of these nightsticks nowadays" (William Lowther, "Nightstick Justice in Rizzo's Town," *MacLean's,* August 27, 1979).
70. See "A Police Force that 'Shocks the Conscience,'" *U.S. News and World Report,* August 27, 1979. The Justice Department stated that the Philadelphia police department's curtailment of the rights of individual citizens was "arbitrary, unreasonable and shocking to the conscience." Rizzo and his department were charged with shooting nonviolent suspects, abusing handcuffed prisoners, stopping pedestrians and motorists without probable cause, and conducting illegal searches. The Justice Department also reported that Philadelphia's police department shot approximately 75 people per year ("Nightstick Control," *New Republic,* August 25, 1979; "Philadelphia: Brotherly Excess?" *Newsweek,* August 27, 1979). The Justice Department's suit was not particularly successful in halting police brutality or corruption. Recently scores of arrests in Philadelphia were reviewed and overturned because of the numerous guilty pleas of officers who had been involved in the arrests (Don Terry, "Victimized by Criminals in Blue: A Police Scandal Shakes Philadelphia to the Core," *Star Tribune,* August 29, 1995; see Rupert Cornwell, "FBI Investigates 100,000 Philadelphia Arrests," *Independent* [London], September 2, 1995; Elizabeth Gleick, "The Crooked Blue Line," *Time,* September 1, 1995).

71. See notes 46 and 47.
72. "Chronology of Events in FBI's Investigation of Police Corruption," *Philadelphia Inquirer,* February 2, 1985. The investigation focused on the Sixth District, where the shooting occurred; see "Twenty-two Are Notified They Are Targets in U.S. Probe of Police," *Philadelphia Inquirer ,* October 3, 1983.
73. Captain Giordano, who back in 1981 was one of the officers who allegedly heard Mumia "confess," pleaded guilty to charges of tax evasion in connection with payoffs he had received; see "Ex-Inspector Tells of Police Cheating, Roofers Payoffs," *Philadelphia Inquirer,* May 22, 1986.
74. See Kraft, "U.S. Inmate Has a Hold on Europe's Power Elite," *Supra,* note 12.
75. *See,* e.g., "Mandela Letter Supports Abu-Jamal," *Pittsburgh Post-Gazette,* August 15, 1995; Paul Resch, "Governor Flooded by International Mail Supporting Abu-Jamal," September 3, 1995.
76. Cardinal Anthony J. Bevilacqua, archbishop of Philadelphia, issued a statement "strongly" urging Governor Tom Ridge and judicial leaders "not to allow the imposition of the death penalty" on Abu-Jamal or four other prisoners for whom execution dates had been set. The statement continues, "In the coming weeks, the Commonwealth of Pennsylvania plans to proceed with the capital punishment of several convicted criminals, I must make my voice heard and the voice of the whole church, including that of Pope John Paul II, heard. . . . While the church believes that those found guilty must face punishment, it also is keenly aware of the many modern methods within our penal system to punish guilty persons without taking life." Marc Kaufman, "Rendell, Once DA, Appalled at Abu-Jamal Celebrity Status," *Harrisburg Evening News,* July 25, 1995.
77. Formerly known as Upper Volta, this landlocked nation obtained independence from France in 1960. In 1987 the military leader Thomas Sankara christened the country "Burkina Faso," a name that translates roughly as "Land of Upright Men." See *Africa,* in *2 Worldmark Encyclopedia of Nations* 32 (1988).
78. Librarie La Point du Jour was the headquarters for the Comité de Soutien aux Prisonniers Politiques aux Etats-Unis (Support Committee for Political Prisoners in the United States) and a frequent gathering place for other radical organizations.
79. See William Drozdiak, "Strike Showdown Nears in France; Juppé Presses Reforms as Unions Set Protests," *Washington Post,* December 6, 1995; Rose Marie Burke, "French Debate: How Much Pain for Reform Gain?" *USA Today,* December 8, 1995.
80. See "France Braces for New Strike Wave: Railroad Workers Keep Up Pressure on Juppé" *International Herald Tribune,* November 28, 1995.
81. Ben MacIntyre, "Strikers Challenge Juppé with Biggest Show of Strength," *Times of London,* December 13, 1995; "Turn-Out at Protests Put at Between 600,000 and Two Million," *Agence France-Presse,* December 16, 1995.
82. William Drozdiak, "Chirac Dissolves New French Government," *Washington Post,* November 8, 1995.
83. See "A Victim and a Monster: Socialist Party," *Economist,* November 25, 1995; Paul Hockenos, "Making Hate Safe Again in Europe: Right Cultural Revolutionaries," *Nation,* September 19, 1994.
84. See Francoise Germain-Robin, "Le Nom de Mumia," *Supra,* note 12.
85. Burns, "Spirit of 1968"; Street, "Talking about a Revolution."
86. "Cleaver's Wife Barred by Bonn and France," *International Herald Tribune,* November 25, 1970.
87. Ibid.
88. See also "Frankfurt Police See Arson Linked to Panther Rally," *International Herald Tribune,* November 30, 1970. See "Frankfurt Police"; "Germany: Panthers in Frankfurt," *Newsweek,* July 19, 1971; Tyon Reney, "Kathleen Cleaver Denied Freedom of Speech in West Germany," *Black Panther,* December 13, 1971.
89. "Americans Held in Shooting of German Guard," *International Herald Tribune,* November 23, 1970.
90. See generally "Cleaver Returning after Seven-Year Exile," *New York Times,*

November 18, 1975; "Cleaver Seized on Return Here After Seven-Year Exile," *New York Times,* November 19, 1975.

91. *Land and Freedom: A Story for the Spanish Revolution* (Parallax Pictures, Mesidor Films and Road Movies, 1995).

92. George Orwell, *Homage to Catalonia* (London: Secher and Warburg, 1959), 50, 51.

93. "Abu-Jamal Execution Postponed: 'Hangman' Judge Holding Hearings to Decide on New Trial," *Washington Times,* August 8, 1995; "Interview with Leonard Weinglass," *Progressive,* May 1, 1996.

94. Adam Bell, "Mumia, Inc.," *Sunday Patriot-News Harrisburg,* August 20, 1995.

6   "To Disrupt, Discredit and Destroy": The FBI's Secret War against the Black Panther Party

Ward Churchill

1. "Evidence and Intimidation of Fascist Crimes by U.S.A.," *Black Panther,* February 21, 1970.

2. See generally, Akinyele Omowale Umoja, "Set Our Warriors Free: The Legacy of the Black Panther Party and Political Prisoners," in *The Black Panther Party Reconsidered,* ed. Charles E. Jones (Baltimore: Black Classic Press, 1998), 417–42.

3. Safiya Bukhari-Alston, "We Too Are Veterans: Post-Traumatic Stress Disorders and the Black Panther Party," *Black Panther,* February 1991.

4. Citizens Research and Investigation Committee and Louis Tackwood, *The Glass House Tapes: The Story of an Agent Provocateur and the New Police-Intelligence Complex* (New York: Avon, 1973); Jo Durden-Smith, *Who Killed George Jackson? Fantasies, Paranoia and the Revolution* (New York: Alfred A. Knopf, 1976).

5. William Kunstler, "Writers of the Purple Rage," *Nation,* no. 227 (December 30, 1978).

6. Ollie A. Johnson, "Explaining the Demise of the Black Panther Party: The Role of Internal Factors," in Jones, *Black Panther Party,* 391–414.

7. Ward Churchill and Jim Vander Wall, *The COINTELPRO Papers: Documents from the FBI's Secret Wars against Dissent in the United States* (Boston: South End Press, 1990).

8. U.S. Senate Select Committee to Study Government Operations with Respect to Intelligence Activities, *Hearings on Intelligence Activities, vol. 6: The Federal Bureau of Investigation,* 94th Cong., 1st sess., 1975, 30, 605.

9. Robert Justin Goldstein, *Political Repression in Modern America, 1870 to the Present* (Cambridge/New York: Two Continents/Schenkman, 1978).

10. Isaac Balbus, *The Dialectic of Legal Repression* (New York: Russell Sage Foundation, 1973).

11. Diane Gordon, *The Justice Juggernaut: Fighting Street Crime, Controlling Citizens* (New Brunswick, N.J.: Rutgers University Press, 1990); Elihu Rosenblatt, ed., *Criminal Injustice: Confronting the Prison Crisis* (Boston: South End Press, 1996).

12. On creation of the bureau's "gang-busters" mythology, see Richard Gid Powers, *G-Men: Hoover's FBI in Popular Culture* (Carbondale: Southern Illinois University Press, 1983).

13. Richard Gid Powers, *Secrecy and Power: The Life of J. Edgar Hoover* (New York: Free Press, 1987), 5–35.

14. Fred J. Cook, *The FBI Nobody Knows* (New York: Macmillan, 1964), 57.

15. Robert A. Hill, "The Foremost Radical of His Race: Marcus Garvey and the Red Scare, 1918–1920," *Prologue,* no. 16 (winter 1984); Robert A. Hill and Barbara Blair, eds., *Marcus Garvey: Life and Lessons* (Berkeley and Los Angeles: University of California Press, 1987).

16. Emory J. Tolbert, "Federal Surveillance of Marcus Garvey and the UNIA," *Journal of*

Ethnic Studies 14, no. 4, (winter 1987): 27.

17. Hoover's Oct. 11, 1919, memo summarizing the results of the first investigation, and recommending that it be continued, is reproduced in Churchill and Vander Wall, *COINTELPRO Papers,* 12.

18. Tolbert, "Federal Surveillance," 27–31; informant report is reproduced in Churchill and Vander Wall, *COINTELPRO Papers,* 13. Also see Theodore Kornweibel Jr., *Seeing Red: Federal Campaigns against Black Militancy, 1919–1925* (Bloomington: Indiana University Press, 1998), 19–35.

19. Ted Vincent, *Black Power and the Garvey Movement* (Oakland, Calif. Nizga, 1987), 203.

20. Quoted in Hill, "Foremost Radical," 229.

21. The first quote is taken from an Airtel dated March 4, 1968, and addressed from Hoover to all field offices; reproduced in Churchill and Vander Wall, *COINTELPRO Papers,* 108–11 (quote at 110). The rest will be found in U.S. Department of Justice, *Investigative Activities of the Department of Justice,* 66th Cong., 1st sess., 1919, S. Doc. 153, 162–63, 187.

22. Kenneth O'Reilly, *"Racial Matters": The FBI's Secret Files on Black America, 1960–1972* (New York: Free Press, 1989), 19.

23. Ibid., 14.

24. The statement, which appears in U.S. Department of Justice, *Investigative Activities,* 163, was made in 1919, a year in which seventy-six documented lynchings of African Americans occurred.

25. Quoted in David Garrow, *The FBI and Martin Luther King, Jr.: From "Solo" to Memphis* (New York: Penguin, 1981), 160.

26. David Caute, *The Great Fear: The Anti-Communist Purge under Truman and Eisenhower* (New York: Simon and Schuster, 1978).

27. Athan Theoharis, *Spying on Americans: Political Surveillance from Hoover to the Huston Plan* (Philadelphia: Temple University Press, 1978), 136; U.S. Senate Select Committee to Study Government Operations with Respect to Intelligence Activities, *Final Report: Intelligence Activities and the Rights of Americans, Book II,* 94th Cong., 2d sess., 1975, 66.

28. O'Reilly, *"Racial Matters,"* 18.

29. Michael Belknap, *Cold War Political Justice: The Smith Act, the Communist Party, and American Civil Liberties* (Westport, Conn.: Greenwood Press, 1977); William Tanner and Robert Griffith, "Legislative Politics and 'McCarthyism': The Internal Security Act of 1950," in *The Specter: Original Essays on the Cold War and the Origins of McCarthyism* , eds. Robert Griffith and Athan Theoharis (New York: New Viewpoints, 1974), 174–89.

30. Quoted in Theoharis, *Spying on Americans,* 136.

31. Ibid. I say COINTELPRO-CPUSA served as a "laboratory" because the party was known by the bureau to be essentially moribund before the program was initiated; William C. Sullivan with Bill Brown, *The Bureau: My Thirty Years in Hoover's FBI* (New York: W. W. Norton, 1975), 266.

32. *Hearings on Intelligence Activities,* 821–26.

33. Ibid., 88–89, 170–72, 186–88, 486–94, 535–38, 766–84.

34. Memos concerning Operation Hoodwink are reproduced in Churchill and Vander Wall, *COINTELPRO Papers,* 42, 44–45.

35. Quoted in Sanford J. Ungar, *FBI: An Uncensored Look behind the Walls* (Boston: Little, Brown, 1975), 120.

36. As with other COINTELPROs, this one was lodged under William C. Sullivan's Domestic Intelligence Division (Division Five). More specifically, it was administered by Sullivan's head of Racial Intelligence, George C. Moore. Moore placed Theron D. Rushing in charge of coordinating the counterintelligence initiative itself; *Hearings on Intelligence Activities,* 383–85; U.S. Senate Select Committee to Study Government Operations with Respect to Intelligence Operations, *Supplementary Detailed Staff*

Reports on Intelligence Operations and the Rights of Americans, Book III , 94th Cong., 2d sess., 1976, 20–21.

37. *Hearings on Intelligence Activities,* 386–92.
38. Ward Churchill and Jim Vander Wall, *Agents of Repression: The FBI's Secret Wars against the Black Panther Party and the American Indian Movement* (Boston: South End Press, 1988), 45–47.
39. A Janurary 22, 1969, memo in which Hoover appears to credit the bureau with the assassination of Malcolm X is reproduced in Churchill and Vander Wall, *COINTELPRO Papers,* 102. Also see Clayborne Carson, *Malcolm X: The FBI File* (New York: Carroll and Graf, 1991); George Breitman, Herman Porter, and Baxter Smith, *The Assassination of Malcolm X,* 2d ed. (New York: Pathfinder, 1991).
40. Garrow, *FBI and Martin Luther King;* Sullivan with Brown, *The Bureau,* 133; O'Reilly, *"Racial Matters,"* 366; Imari Abubakari Obadele, *Free the Land! The True Story of the RNA in Mississippi* (Washington, D.C.: House of Songhay, 1984); Maulana Karenga, *Roots of the US/Panther Conflict* (San Diego: Kawaida, 1976).
41. *Hearings on Intelligence Activities,* 601.
42. *Intelligence Activities and the Rights of Americans,* 301, 632.
43. The FBI admitted, for example, that it engaged in a total of 238 "surreptitious entries"—i.e., burglaries—against fourteen targets between 1942 and 1966 for purposes of gathering political intelligence. In truth, restricting the time frame to just the years 1952 through 1957, there had been more than 500 such "black bag jobs" conducted in Chicago alone; M. Wesley Swearingen, *FBI Secrets: An Agent's Exposé* (Boston: South End Press, 1995), 165.
44. Former attorneys general Katzenbach and Clark, for example, testified before the Senate Select Committee on December 3, 1975, that they'd either never seen or not understood Hoover's memoranda briefing them on "COINTELPRO-White Hate Groups"; *Hearings on Intelligence Activities,* 202, 206–7, 213–18, 221, 224, 231–35, 240–47, 513–27.
45. *Staff Reports,* 188.
46. O'Reilly, *"Racial Matters,"* 291.
47. John Gerassi, ed., *The Coming of the New International: A Revolutionary Anthology* (New York: World, 1971); Paul Joseph, *Cracks in the Empire: State Politics in the Vietnam War* (Boston: South End Press, 1981); Carl Oglesby, ed., *The New Left Reader* (New York: Grove Press, 1969).
48. George Katsiaficas, *The Imagination of the New Left: A Global Analysis of 1968* (Boston: South End Press, 1987).
49. Stokely Carmichael and Charles V. Hamilton, *Black Power: The Politics of Liberation in America* (New York: Vintage, 1967).
50. Barbara Joye, "Young Lords," in *The Movement toward a New America: The Beginnings of a Long Revolution,* ed. Marshall Goodman (Philadelphia/New York: Pilgrim Press/Alfred A. Knopf, 1970), 238–41; Carlos Muñoz Jr., *Youth, Identity, Power: The Chicano Movement* (New York: Verso, 1989); Paul Chaat Smith and Robert Allen Warrior, *Like a Hurricane: The American Indian Movement from Alcatraz to Wounded Knee* (New York: New Press, 1996).
51. James Miller, *"Democracy Is in the Streets": From Port Huron to the Siege of Chicago* (New York: Simon and Schuster, 1987).
52. Ron Jacobs, *The Way the Wind Blew: A History of the Weather Underground* (London: Verso, 1997).
53. Nancy Zaroulis and Gerald Sullivan, *Who Spoke Up? American Protest against the War in Vietnam, 1963–1975* (Garden City, N.Y.: Doubleday, 1984), 263–73.
54. Theodore Roszak, *The Making of a Counterculture: Reflections on the Technological Society and Its Youthful Opposition* (New York: Doubleday, 1969). On efforts to politicize this disenchanted mass, see Abbie Hoffman, *Revolution for the Hell of It* (New York: Dial, 1968); *Woodstock Nation: A Talk Rock Album* (New York:

Vintage, 1969).
55. William L. O'Neill, *Coming Apart: An Informal History of America in the 1960s* (Chicago: Quadrangle, 1971).
56. On the founding of the Black Panther Party for Self-Defense, as it was originally called, see Huey P. Newton, *Revolutionary Suicide* 1972; reprint, (New York: Readers and Writers, 1995) 110–13.
57. Nikhil Pal Singh, "The Black Panthers and the 'Undeveloped Country' of the Left," in Jones, *Black Panthers Reconsidered,* 57–108.
58. "The Panther Program," in Bobby Seale, *Seize the Time: The Story of the Black Panther Party and Huey P. Newton* (New York: Random House, 1970), 59–68. For emulations by other groups see, e.g., "Young Lords Party 13 Point Program and Platform," in Philip S. Foner, ed., *The Black Panthers Speak* (Philadelphia: J. B. Lippincott, 1970), 235–37.
59. Gene Marine, *The Black Panthers* (New York: New American Library, 1969); Edward M. Keating, *Free Huey! The True Story of the Trial of Huey P. Newton for Murder* (Berkeley, Calif.: Ramparts Press, 1971).
60. Singh, "Undeveloped Country," 64.
61. *Intelligence Activities and the Rights of Americans,* 187.
62. *Staff Reports,* 528–31.
63. Clayborne Carson, *In Struggle: SNCC and the Black Awakening of the 1960s* (Cambridge, Mass: Harvard University Press, 1981), 284.
64. Goldstein, *Political Repression,* 451–52; *Staff Reports,* 214–15.
65. According to retired FBI agent Arthur Murtagh, many of the worst COIN-TELPRO actions were never recorded in writing; *Hearings on Intelligence Activities,* 1044.
67. *Staff Reports,* 187.
68. "Panther Supporters: Many Black Americans Voice Strong Backing for Defiant Militants," *Wall Street Journal,* January 13, 1970.
69. *Staff Reports,* 35–36, 218–20.
70. "How the FBI Used the Media against the Panthers," *Revolutionary Worker,* September 19, 1980.
71. Frank J. Donner, *The Age of Surveillance: The Aims and Methods of America's Political Intelligence System* (New York: Vintage, 1981), 239–40
72. "FBI Used the media," 20.
73. Donner, *Age of Surveillance,* 238. Also see Kathleen Cleaver, "How TV Wrecked the Black Panthers," *Channels,* November/December, 1982.
74. Interviewees were selected by the FBI on the basis that they "not have the ability to stand up to a professional newsman." The result, as the Miami SAC bragged, was that they displayed an "inability to articulate" and thus conveyed what he called "a simpering and stupid appearance"; quoted in Donner, *Age of Surveillance,* 239.
75. The special, titled *Fear of the Secret Dark,* first aired on October 9, 1969; Carson, *Malcolm X File,* 162.
76. Quoted in Donner, *Age of Surveillance,* 239
77. "Hughie [*sic*] Newton" and, by extension, the BPP were also on the Nixon Administration's "Enemies List," incorporated into the 1970 Huston plan for "screwing" political opponents by a variety of extralegal means, including placement of disinformation in the media; Senate Committee, *Staff Reports,* 923–28.
78. For an excellent selection of FBI-facilitated or -produced anti-Panther materials, see Norman Hill, ed., *The Black Panther Menace: America's Neo-Nazis* (New York: Popular Library, 1971).
79. "FBI Used Media," 20; Chip Berlet, "Journalists and G-Men," *Chicago Reader,* January 12, 1978.
80. "FBI Used media," 20.
81. Ibid.
82. Ibid.

83. Ibid. For the most comprehensive selection of false statements advanced in this media blitz, all of them attributed directly to police sources, see Roy Wilkins and Ramsey Clark, *Search and Destroy: A Report of the Commission of Inquiry into the Black Panthers and the Police* (New York: Metropolitan Applied Research Center, 1973).

84. Plaintiff's Brief, *Iberia Hampton et al. v. Edward Hanrahan et al.* (Nos. 70C-1384, Cons [N. Dist., Ill., 1975]), 56.

85. Ibid., 56–58.

86. Wilkins and Clark, *Search and Destroy,* 47.

87. Quoted in Foner, *Black Panthers Speak,* 264.

88. *Hampton, v. Hanrahan,* 58–59.

89. Report of Dr. David Spain, independent pathologist, quoted in Wilkins and Clark, *Search and Destroy,* 149. Also see Alfred Allan Lewis with Herbert Leon MacDonell, "The Black Panther Shoot-out/In," in *The Evidence Never Lies: The Casebook of a Modern Sherlock Holmes* (New York: Laurel, 1984), 95.

90. "The Panthers and the Law," *New York Times,* May 18, 1970.

91. The result, Hoover said, would be to "help cripple the BPP"; Senate Committee, *Staff Reports,* 214.

92. David Hilliard and Lewis Cole, *This Side of Glory: The Autobiography of David Hilliard and the Story of the Black Panther Party* (Boston: Little, Brown, 1993), 154.

93. Quoted in Foner, *Black Panthers Speak,* xxviii.

94. The "Eight Points of Attention" and even more pointed "Rules of the Black Panther Party" will be found in Jones, *Black Panther Party,* 476–78.

95. Memo, FBIHQ to Chicago and seven other field offices, May 15, 1970.

96. Memo, SAC San Diego to Dir., FBI, August 18, 1970; quoted in *Staff Reports,* 214–15.

97. Ibid., 215. The latter proposal was definitely implemented in several variations; see, e.g., the "Minutemen" death-threat postcard reproduced in Churchill and Vander Wall, *COINTELPRO Papers,* 227.

98. Memo, SAC New York to FBIHQ and San Francisco field office, October 11, 1969; quoted in *Staff Reports,* 214.

99. Memo, SAC San Francisco to FBIHQ, May 22, 1970; quoted in *Staff Reports,* 214.

100. Memo, FBIHQ to SACs, 39 cities, November 11, 1970; quoted in *Staff Reports,* 216.

101. Memo, G. C. Moore to W. C. Sullivan, June 26, 1970; quoted in *Staff Reports,* 216–17. The idea was dropped when the Chicago field office pointed out that disclosure of FBI involvement in encouraging such a conflict might serve to bring the NoI and BPP closer together.

102. Memo, FBIHQ to San Francisco and eight other field offices, January 23, 1970; quoted in *Staff Reports,* 218.

103. Memo, SAC San Francisco to FBIHQ, May 26, 1969; quoted in *Staff Reports,* 217–18.

104. Memo, SAC San Francisco to FBIHQ, March 18, 1970; quoted in *Staff Reports,* 218. The "antisemitism" ploy was used frequently, because the bureau appears to have believed that Jews were disproportionately represented among the white New Leftists supporting the Panthers, as well as the party's more liberal financial backers; representative documents are reproduced in Churchill and Vander Wall, *COINTELPRO Papers,* 136–37, 162–63.

105. Memo, SAC Chicago to FBIHQ, February 10, 1969; quoted in *Staff Reports,* 217.

106. Memo, FBIHQ to Chicago field office, February 20, 1969; quoted in *Staff Reports,* 217–18.

107. As even the *Wall Street Journal* noted at the time, "blacks support the Panthers because they admire[the] less-publicized activities of the Party such as its free-breakfast programs for ghetto youngsters, its free medical program and its war on narcotics use among black youth"; quoted in Foner, *Black Panthers Speak,* xiii. For a more complete list of the BPP survival programs, see Table I in Charles E. Jones and Judson L. Jeffries, "'Don't Believe the Hype': Debunking the Panther Mythology," in Jones, *The Black Panther Party Reconsidered,* 30.

108. Memo, FBIHQ to SAC San Francisco and 39 field offices, May 10, 1969.
109. Memo, SAC San Francisco to Hoover, May 14, 1969.
110. Memo, Dir., FBI, to SAC San Francisco, May 27, 1969.
111. Ibid.
112. Reginald Major, *A Panther Is a Black Cat: A Study In-Depth of the Black Panther Party—Its Origins, Its Goals, Its Struggle for Survival* (New York: William Morrow, 1971) 86–87. For a broader survey of the tactics employed, see Charles E. Jones, "The Political Repression of the Black Panther Party, 1966–1971: The Case of the Oakland Bay Area," *Journal of Black Studies,* no. 18 (1988).
113. Memo, FBIHQ to SAC San Francisco, July 30, 1969; quoted in *Staff Reports,* 210.
114. Major, *Black Cat,* 87.
115. Memo, SAC, San Francisco to, FBIHQ, November 30, 1970; quoted in *Staff Reports,* 210.
116. See Erika Doss, "'Revolutionary Art as a Tool of Liberation': Emory Douglas and Protest Aesthetics at *The Black Panther,*" Chapter 13 of this book; Major, *Black Cat,* 87.
117. This account was confirmed by former Party Communications Secretary and Central Committee member Kathleen Cleaver during testimony before the Senate Select Committee on Intelligence Activities on April 8, 1976; quoted in *Staff Reports,* 210.
118. Seale, *Seize the Time,* 383–90.
119. U.S. Senate, Committee on Government Operations, Permanent Subcommittee on Investigations, *Hearings on Riots, Civil and Criminal Disorders,* pts. 1–25, 90th Cong., 1st sess.–91st Cong., 2d sess., 1967–70.
120. On the Powells, see Hugh Pearson's *Shadow of the Panther: Huey Newton and the Price of Black Power in America* (Reading, Mass: Addison-Wesley, 1994). Readers should be warned that Pearson's is a biased and inaccurate account, taking whatever was said by any police informant at face value while discounting virtually everything accruing from Panther sources as "myth."
121. "Panthers Denounce 'Agents and Fools,'" *Oakland Tribune,* January 3, 1969; "Angry Denial of Ex-Panthers' Story," *San Francisco Chronicle,* June 19, 1969.
122. Airtel, SAC San Francisco to FBIHQ, February 4, 1974. In an echo of Hoover's campaign against Marcus Garvey, the SAC therefore recommended continuing, intensifying and expanding the investigation; quoted in Huey P. Newton, *War against the Panthers: A Study of Repression in America* (New York: Harlem River Press, 1996), 46.
123. U.S. News and World Reports, *Communism and the New Left* (New York: Macmillan, 1970), 105. The book is self-evidently a product of the FBI's Mass Media Program (see note 75).
124. During his 1970 testimony before the House Subcommittee on Appropriations concerning the bureau's annual budget, J. Edgar Hoover claimed that five policemen had been killed by Panthers by the first of that year; quoted in Peter Zimroth, *Perversions of Justice: The Prosecution and Acquittal of the Panther 21* (New York: Viking, 1974), 41, 43. For rebuttal, see Michael Newton, *Bitter Grain: Huey Newton and the Black Panther Party* (Los Angeles: Holloway House, 1991), 98–99.
125. Agents sometimes impersonated "concerned parishioners" in their telephone calls; memo, SAC San Diego to FBIHQ, August 29, 1969; quoted in *Staff Reports,* 210–11.
126. Whether a copy of the famous coloring book was among the items sent is unknown. However, the severity and abruptness of the bishop's reaction suggests that it was; *Staff Reports,* 210.
127. Memo, SAC San Diego to FBIHQ, October 6, 1969; quoted in *Staff Reports,* 211.
128. Memo, SAC New Haven to FBIHQ, November 12, 1969; quoted in *Staff Reports,* 211.
129. Lowell Bergman and David Weir, "Revolution on Ice: How the Black Panthers Lost the FBI's War of Dirty Tricks," *Rolling Stone,* September 9, 1976, 47.
130. *Hampton v. Hanrahan* 11–12, 17; Steve D. McCutchen, "Selections from a Panther Diary," in Jones, *The Black Panther Party Reconsidered,* 126. Jimmy Slater, a member of the Cleveland BPP chapter from 1968–72, recalls that the free clinic there was "blown up" in 1969. He attributes the attack to COINTELPRO; Charles E. Jones,

"'Talkin' the Talk and Walkin' the Walk': An Interview with Panther Jimmy Slater," in Jones, *The Black Panther Party Reconsidered,* 148.

131. "SNCC, Panthers Announce Merger," *National Guardian,* February 24, 1968.

132. Seale, *Seize the Time,* 221.

133. Two members of SNCC's steering committee were working for the FBI during this period; Carson, *In Struggle,* 293 (citing a memo from SAC Atlanta to FBIHQ, March 10, 1969). At least one, Earl Anthony, was involved on the Panther side (see n. 165).

134. C. Gerald Fraser, "SNCC in Decline After 8 Years in Lead: Pace-Setters in Civil Rights Displaced by Black Panthers," *New York Times,* October 7, 1968. The article is referenced as evidence of "a successful counterintelligence initiative" in a memo from Hoover to the SAC, Washington, D.C., October 24, 1968. According to both Forman and Sellers, the alleged torture never occurred; James Forman, *The Making of Black Revolutionaries* (New York: Macmillan, 1972) 537–8; Cleveland Sellers with Robert Terrell, *The River of No Return: The Autobiography of a Black Militant and the Life and Death of SNCC* (New York: William Morrow, 1973), 203. Anthony reported to Robert O'Connor and Ron Kizenski, agents in the Los Angeles field office's Racial Matters Squad, from more or less the moment he joined the chapter in late 1967. He himself recounts this in his autobiographical *Spitting in the Wind: The True Story behind the Violent Legacy of the Black Panther Party* (Malibu, Calif.: Roundtable, 1990), 38. At 48–49, he gives his version of the Cleaver/Forman incident, which conforms almost perfectly with that appearing in the 1968 *New York Times* article.

135. The FBI, which had among other things been phoning Forman up in the middle of the night with anonymous "Panther death threats," credits itself for inducing his "paranoid" state; memo, SAC New York to FBIHQ, August 7, 1968. Instructively, the document is filed among those pertaining to COINTELPRO-BPP rather than those concerning SNCC in the FBI reading room in Washington, D.C. Credit is also taken for the split between SNCC and the BPP; memo, SAC New York to FBIHQ, September 9, 1968.

136. "Carmichael Is Expelled by SNCC in Dispute," *Washington Post,* August 22, 1968; "S.N.C.C. Breaks Ties with Carmichael," *Washington Post,* August 23, 1968.

137. On Cardoza being an infiltrator, see Sullivan with Brown, *Bureau,* 133.

138. An excerpt from this document, dated July 10, 1968, is reproduced in *COINTELPRO Papers,* 128.

139. Memo, SAC New York to FBIHQ, September 5, 1968. Earl Anthony repeats the allegation that Carmichael was targeted for assassination, adding in Forman and Rap Brown for good measure; *Spitting in the Wind,* 48. There is no evidence at all to support the contention.

140. "Carmichael Quits Panthers," *Los Angeles Times,* July 4, 1969.

141. Memo, G. C. Moore to W. C. Sullivan, October 10, 1968; quoted verbatim in Churchill and Vander Wall, *Agents of Repression,* 44.

142. Angela D. LeBlanc-Ernest, "'The Most Qualified Person for the Job': Black Panther Party Women, 1966–1982," and Chris Booker, "Lumpenization: A Critical Error of the Black Panther Party," in Jones, *The Black Panther Party Reconsidered,* 308, 351.

143. Memo, SAC Atlanta to FBIHQ, March 10, 1969; Sellers with Terrell, *River of No Return,* 250.

144. Memo, SAC Atlanta to FBIHQ, August 1, 1969; Forman, *Black Revolutionaries,* 550. There was further fallout from this occurrence. After leaving SNCC, Forman became an officer in the League of Revolutionary Black Workers, a Detroit organization seeking to radicalize the United Auto Workers Union. In this capacity, he was positioned to derail potential coalitions between the Panthers and the league; James A. Geschwender, *Class, Race and Worker Insurgency: The League of Revolutionary Black Workers* (New York: Cambridge University Press, 1977), esp. 142.

145. For reasons never clarified, the FBI initially identified Brown as being one of the two dead men; "Mystery and Distrust over Bombings Grow," *National Observer,* March 23, 1970; "Charlotte Featherstone Reveals Doubts, Fears," *Chicago Defender,* May 14, 1970.

146. Memo, SAC New York to FBIHQ, December 11, 1973.

147. Based in part upon his interpretation of and effort to adapt Fanon to the U.S. context, Huey Newton had from the outset taken recruitment of the criminalized black inner-city underclass as a high priority for the Party; see, e.g., the chapter entitled "The Brothers on the Block" in *Revolutionary Suicide,* 75–78. Eldridge Cleaver then subjected the idea to a considerable honing and development, most explicitly in his essay "On Lumpen Ideology," *Black Scholar,* no. 3, (1972).

148. Memo, SAC Chicago to FBIHQ, December 16, 1968; quoted in *Staff Reports,* 195. Also see *Hampton v. Hanrahan,* 19. For background on the P. Stone Nation, see R. T. Sale, *The Blackstone Rangers: A Reporter's Account of Time Spent with Blackstone Rangers on Chicago's South Side* (New York: Random House, 1971).

149. Winston A. Grady-Willis, "The Black Panther Party: State Repression and Political Prisoners," and Johnson, "Demise of the Party," both in Jones, *The Black Panther Party Reconsidered;* see 372, 391.

150. Memo, Chicago field office to FBIHQ, December 12, 1968; noted in *Staff Reports,* 195.

151. Memo, Chicago field office to FBIHQ, December 16, 1968; quoted in *Staff Reports,* 195–96.

152. Memo, Chicago field office to FBIHQ, January 10, 1969; quoted in *Staff Reports,* 197.

153. Memo, SAC Chicago to FBIHQ, January 13, 1969; quoted in *Staff Reports,* 197.

154. Ibid.

155. Ibid. This segment of the document is reproduced in Churchill and Vander Wall, *COINTELPRO Papers,* 138. It should be noted that the Stoetzal had earlier requested and received specific information on Jeff Fort's propensity for violence from the Chicago Police Gang Intelligence Unit. Moreover, he was informed that the GIU had "linked the [P. Stone] and rival gangs to approximately 290 killings from 1965–69"; ibid., 195; memo, Chicago field office to FBIHQ, December 12, 1969; noted in *Staff Reports,* 195.

156. Memo, Hoover to SAC Chicago, January 30, 1969; noted in *Staff Reports,* 198.

157. *Staff Reports,* 187–223; quote at 198.

158. Ibid. Johnson approved each phase of the operation. In 1976 he was subpoenaed by the plaintiffs in the *Hampton* case to testify as to its underlying intent. On the stand, he claimed to believe that a "hit" meant "something nonviolent in nature." Bob Greene, "Laundered Box Score? No Hits, No Guns, No Terror," *Chicago Sun-Times,* February 12, 1976.

159. Memo, SAC Chicago to FBIHQ, January 28, 1969; quoted in *Staff Reports,* 198.

160. Patricia King, "A Snitch's Tale: The Killer Gang: An Informant Tells about Life in El Rukn," *Newsweek,* November 6, 1989.

161. Memo, G. C. Moore to W. C. Sullivan, December 12, 1968; quoted in *Staff Reports,* 208. A November 28, 1968, memo from the SAC Los Angeles to Hoover, outlining a plan to disrupt the PFP's relations with the BPP, is reproduced in Churchill and Vander Wall, *COINTELPRO Papers,* 132. Also see Marine, *Panthers,* 106–22.

162. *Staff Reports,* 208.

163. Memo, FBIHQ to SAC San Francisco, March 5, 1970; quoted in *Staff Reports,* 209.

164. Memo, SAC Los Angeles to FBIHQ, September 24, 1969; quoted in *Staff Reports,* 208.

165. Memo, SAC Los Angeles to FBIHQ, July 25, 1969; quoted in *Staff Reports,* 208.

166. Memo, SAC San Francisco to FBIHQ, July 28, 1969; quoted in *Staff Reports,* 208.

167. *Staff Reports,* 208; Frank Donner, *Protectors of Privilege: Red Squads and Police Repression in Urban America* (Berkeley: and Los Angeles University of California Press, 1990), 262–63.

168. Swearingen, *FBI Secrets,* 116.

169. Memo, FBIHQ to SAC Los Angeles, June 25, 1970; quoted in *Staff Reports,* 209. The document is reproduced in Swearingen, *FBI Secrets,* 128–29.

170. Swearingen, *FBI Secrets,* 127.

171. Memo, SAC Los Angeles to FBIHQ, September 10, 1970.

172. Memo, SAC San Diego to FBIHQ, February 3, 1970; noted in *Staff Reports,* 209;

Donner, *Protectors of Privilege*, 263–64; Eric Cummins, *The Rise and Fall of California's Radical Prison Movement* (Stanford, Calif.: Stanford University Press, 1994), 254.

173. *Staff Reports*, 208–9.

174. David Richards, *Played Out: The Jean Seberg Story* (New York: Playboy, 1981), 238; Gid Powers, *Secrecy and Power*, 587. Relevant documents are reproduced in Swearingen, *FBI Secrets*, 122–25.

175. Memo, SAC Los Angeles to FBIHQ, June 3, 1970; noted in *Staff Reports*, 209.

176. Joyce Haber, "Miss A Rates as Expectant Mother," *Los Angeles Times*, May 19, 1970.

177. O'Reilly, *"Racial Matters,"* 330; *"Newsweek* Blamed for Death," *Washington Post*, August 28, 1970.

178. O'Reilly, *"Racial Matters"*, 331–32; Richards, *Played Out*, 374, 378.

179. Seale, *Seize the Time*, 19–23.

180. *Staff Reports*, 188–89.

181. Memo, G. C. Moore to W. C. Sullivan, November 5, 1968; quoted in *Staff Reports*, 189–90.

182. Quoted in Newton, *War against the Panthers*, 79. A November 29, 1968, memo from the SAC Los Angeles to Hoover, outlining a plan to employ such tactics in sparking "an 'US' and BPP vendetta," is reproduced in Churchill and Vander Wall, *COINTELPRO Papers*, 132.

183. Newton, *War against the Panthers*, 79. Also see Ernest Volman, "Othello," *Penthouse*, April, 1979.

184. In 1975 Perry provided two affidavits on these matters in connection with *Black Panther Party v. Levi*, Civ. No. 76-2205 (U.S. Dist., D.C., 1976); Newton, *War against the Panthers*, 101–2.

185. Swearingen, *FBI Secrets* 82–83. Perry's version seems somewhat more accurate and complete, in that it accounts for the third gunman, Claude Hubert. The Stiner brothers were tried and convicted of participating in the killings of Carter and Huggins in 1970. Sentenced to life imprisonment, they "escaped" in 1974 and were never recaptured; Newton, *War against the Panthers*, 78–81; Donner, *Age of Surveillance*, 222. Claude Hubert was never even questioned on the matter. Perry contends this was because he was immediately whisked away to New York and eventually relocated to a foreign country. In 1978, L.A. Police Lieutenant Dan Cooke admitted his investigators had been aware for years that Hubert was residing in Guyana; "Assassin of B.P.P. Members Reported in Guyana," *Black Panther*, December 29, 1978.

186. Memo, SAC San Diego to FBIHQ, February 20, 1969; quoted in *Staff Reports*, 190.

187. *Staff Reports*, 193; quoting a memo from SAC, San Diego, January 23, 1969. Sample cartoons are reproduced in Churchill and Vander Wall, *COINTELPRO Papers*, 131, and *Agents of Repression*, 43, 80.

188. Memo, FBIHQ to SACs, San Diego, Los Angeles, and San Francisco, January 29, 1969; quoted in *Staff Reports*, 193–94.

189. Memo, SAC San Diego to FBIHQ, April 10, 1969; quoted in *Staff Reports*, 191.

190. Butler reported both to Held and to Detectives Ray Callahan and Daniel P. Mahoney of the LAPD's Criminal Conspiracy Section (CCS); Swearingen, *FBI Secrets*, 84.

191. Ibid., 83. Stark no doubt confused Holt with being a real Panther.

192. Ibid., 84. The killing is referenced in a self-congratulatory memo sent by the SAC San Diego to FBIHQ on June 5, 1969. In the same document, San Diego also credits its COINTELPRO initiatives for having escalated the general pattern of hostility between US and the BPP "from mere harassment [to the] beating of various individuals"; quoted in *Staff Reports*, 192.

193. Memo, SAC San Diego to FBIHQ, June 13, 1969; quoted in *Staff Reports*, 192.

194. Memo, FBIHQ to San Diego field office, June 17, 1969; noted in *Staff Reports*, 192.

195. Memo, SAC San Diego to FBIHQ, June 6, 1969; noted in *Staff Reports*, 192.

196. Memo, SAC San Diego to FBIHQ, August 20, 1969; noted in *Staff Reports*, 192.

197. Swearingen, *FBI Secrets,* 84.
198. Volman, "Othello," 159–61.
199. Memo, SAC San Diego to FBIHQ, September 18, 1969; quoted in *Staff Reports,* 192–93.
200. Ibid.
201. Memo, SAC San Diego to FBIHQ, September 3, 1969; quoted in *Staff Reports,* 193.
202. Memo, SAC Newark to FBIHQ, October 2, 1969; excerpt reproduced in Churchill and Vander Wall, *COINTELPRO Papers,* 134.
203. The cartoon is reproduced in *COINTELPRO Papers,* 134. For Baraka's view of the operation, see his *Autobiography of LeRoi Jones* (New York: Freundlich Books, 1984), 250–84.
204. Memo, FBIHQ to SAC San Diego, January 29, 1970; quoted in *Staff Reports,* 193–94.
205. Memo, SAC Los Angeles to FBIHQ, May 26, 1970; quoted in *Staff Reports,* 194.
206. Ibid. The violence between the two organizations thereupon subsided.
207. One could make a strong case that the prototype for the FBI's style of utilizing "informants" in the political sphere was the Pinkertons' insertion of the provocateur James "McKenna" (McParlan) into the Molly Maguires in 1874; Kevin Kenny, *Making Sense of the Molly Maguires* (New York: Oxford University Press, 1998), 199–200, 231–33.
208. For distinctions, see Gary T. Marx, "Some Thoughts on a Neglected Category of Social Movement Participant: The Agent Provocateur and Informant," *American Journal of Sociology,* no. 80 (September 1974).
209. *Staff Reports,* 228, 252–55, 518; *Hearings on Intelligence Activities,* 17.
210. The plan was dubbed "BLACPRO"; O'Reilly, *"Racial Matters,"* 334, quoting memo, Hoover to SAC Baltimore, and fourteen other field offices, July 16, 1970.
211. On the number of infiltrators, see *Hampton v. Hanrahan,* 12. On expenditures, see Volkman, "Othello," 158.
212. Tackwood reported to Callahan and Mahoney in CCS, as well as agents Held and Richard H. Bloesser in the Los Angeles COINTELPRO section; Citizens Research Committee and Tackwood, *Glass House Tapes.* On CCS, see Donner, *Protectors of Privilege,* 245–89.
213. On Eggleston, see Murray Kempton, *The Briar Patch: The People of the State of New York v. Lumumba Shakur, et al.* (New York: E. P. Dutton, 1973), 55. On Thomas, see Goldstein, *Political Repression,* 527.
214. Grady-Willis, "State Repression," 368. On BOSS, see Donner, *Protectors of Privilege,* 155–96.
215. Donner, *Protectors of Privilege,* 182.
216. The estimate is arrived at by assuming an average of three police operatives per chapter—a total of 129—and adding the 67 federal operatives, to arrive at a total of 195. This is balanced against a Party membership that had declined to approximately 2,000 by mid-1970.
217. Seale, quoted in Foner, *Black Panthers Speak,* xxvi.
218. On O'Neal, see Robert McClory, "Agent Provocateur," *Chicago,* February 1979. On White, see Donner, *Protectors of Privilege,* 183. On Smith, see Lee Richardson, "Ex-FBI Agent Exposes Use of Informants to Destroy the BPP," *Freedom* 18, no. 5, (January 1985). On Dubonnet, see Newton, *Bitter Grain,* 175.
219. *Hampton v. Hanrahan,* 9, 13.
220. The best reconstruction of what actually occurred will be found in Don Freed, *Agony in New Haven: The Trial of Bobby Seale, Ericka Huggins, and the Black Panther Party* (New York: Simon and Schuster, 1973).
221. In addition to the named individuals, those charged were Lonnie McLucas, Frances Carter, George Edwards, Margaret Hudgins, Loretta Luckes, Rose Smith, and Rory Hithe.
222. Major, *Black Cat,* 101
223. Pardoned in 1974, Sams was immediately placed in the FBI's Witness Protection

Program under a new identity. Three years later, he was reimprisoned for another violent offense; "Parole Court Jails Pardoned Killer," *Hartford Courant*, April 30, 1977. Kimbro entered a guilty plea, not to Rackley's murder, but to having helped dispose of the body. McLucas was convicted of complicity for not having intervened to prevent the torture-slaying; Freed, *Agony in New Haven*, 331.

224. "Charges Dropped in the Seale Case," *New York Times*, May 25, 1971; "Ex-Chief Says New Haven Police Had No Evidence against Seale," *New York Times*, April 4, 1972.

225. Freed, *Agony in New Haven*, 27–28.

226. Pearson, *Shadow of the Panther*, 194.

227. Donner, *Age of Surveillance*, 230–31.

228. The list of targets was rapidly expanded to encompass twenty-two defendants; Kathleen Neal Cleaver, "Back to Africa: The Evolution of the International Section of the Black Panther Party (1969–1972)," in Jones, *The Black Panther Party Reconsidered*, 228–29.

229. A skeleton, discovered in a local park, was originally identified as that of a white man, aged 30. Cause of death was listed as "drug overdose." After being handled by the FBI lab in Washington, however, the bones mysteriously became those of Anderson, a black man, aged 20, killed by a shotgun blast. Either way, direct involvement of the U.S. attorney general in such a case is atypical, to say the least; Donner, *Age of Surveillance*, 230.

230. "Police Admit Paying Witnesses in Panther Slaying Case," *Washington Post*, June 18, 1971; "Key State Witness's Testimony Stricken in Turco Trial," *Baltimore Sun*, June 23, 1971; "The Turco Case: Kebe Withdrawn, Testimony Stricken from Record," *Baltimore Afro-American*, June 26, 1971.

231. "State's Attorney Blasts Panther Indictments," *Baltimore Afro-American*, May 25, 1971.

232. Fred Bennett was apparently executed at a "Panther training center" in the Santa Cruz Mountains at some point in early January 1971; "Shattered Body of Panther Found," *San Francisco Chronicle*, April 21, 1971. Jimmie Carr was shot to death in front of his San Jose home on the morning of April 6, 1972. Lloyd Mims and Richard Rodriguez, members of the LA Panthers and Brown Berets, respectively, were tried and convicted of the murder, but their motives remained ambiguous; Durden-Smith, *George Jackson*, 122–25.

233. Memo, SAC San Diego to FBIHQ, February 19, 1969; quoted in *Staff Reports*, 221.

234. Quoted in Johnson, "Demise of the Party," 402.

235. Charles R. Garry, "The Persecution of the Black Panther Party: The Old Rules Do Not Apply," in Foner, *Black Panthers Speak*, 257.

236. Ibid., 257–58.

237. Donner, *Protectors of Privilege*, 301.

238. *Hampton v. Hanrahan*, 10–11, citing tr. at 4954–67, 6921–32.

239. Ibid., 11.

240. "As George Sams traveled around the country, spending large amounts of money, certain things began to happen to the Panthers. Each city he visited was thereafter subjected to predawn raids by combinations of city, state and federal police. But Sams was never caught; he always managed to leave before the raids were made," Freed, *Agony in New Haven*, 24–25.

241. *Hampton v. Hanrahan*, 18.

242. In the second incident, a group of Vice Lords, infuriated that FBI infiltrator O'Neal had accused one of their leaders of being a "police agent," had fired into the Panther office. Police then assaulted the Panthers, Ibid., 8, 18.

243. Freed, *Agony in New Haven*, 65, 279.

244. Zimroth, *Perversions of Justice*, 84.

245. The raiders came equipped with an armored personnel carrier, helicopters, dynamite, and an array of automatic weapons. Durden-Smith, *George Jackson*, 134–35; "What Really Happened in Los Angeles," *Black Panther*, December 20, 1969. Photographs of

damage done to both the interior and exterior of the BPP's main office in Los Angeles during the assault appear in *Agents of Repression*, 83.

246. "63 Verdicts End Panther Trial," *Los Angeles Tribune,* December 24, 1971.

247. Donner, *Protectors of Privilege,* 214.

248. "N. Philadelphia Fortress Raided: 7 Arrested, Arms Seized," *Philadelphia Inquirer,* March 12, 1970.

249. Donner, *Protectors of Privilege,* 214–15.

250. "Panther Conference Opens with Court Victories," *New York Times,* September 6, 1970.

251. "Bernard McCormick, "The War of the Cops," *New York Times Magazine,* October 8, 1970; Lenora E. Berson, "'The Toughest Cop in America' Campaigns for Mayor," *New York Times Magazine,* May 16, 1971.

252. Donner, *Protectors of Privilege,* 215.

253. Huey P. Newton, "To the Revolutionary People's Constitutional Convention: September 5, 1970," in *To Die for the People,* 156–62.

254. Donner, *Protectors of Privilege,* 216.

255. Zimroth, *Perversions of Justice,* 84.

256. There had also been two smaller raids of the Indianapolis office in June, sixteen Panthers arrested, and charges subsequently dropped. Newton, *Bitter Grain,* 127.

257. On April 26, 1969, the Des Moines headquarters was destroyed by a dynamite blast. State police, who seem to have been waiting nearby, immediately arrested several local leaders for blowing up their own office, but charges were shortly dropped. Newton, *Bitter Grain,* 126–27.

258. Zimroth, *Perversions of Justice,* 84.

259. Newton, *Bitter Grain,* 156.

260. The fusillade fired by fifty police officers during the second raid, ostensibly in response to Panther gunfire, wounded two Panthers. None of the Panthers was arrested for their supposed assault, however, and even Police Chief Anthony Bosch later expressed doubts as to whether his men's cover story was accurate. The pretext for the raid was to arrest a Panther named John McClellan for killing a police officer, William Miscannon. McClellan was subsequently tried and acquitted; Newton. *Bitter Grain,* 139–40.

261. Twelve Panthers were charged with conspiring and attempting to murder police after a raid on September 15. In August 1971, a jury spent less than thirty minutes acquitting them. Two BPP offices in New Orleans were then mysteriously burned to the ground by "party or parties unknown." Newton, *Bitter Grain,* 130–32.

262. Fifteen Panthers were charged with murder as a result of this exchange. Of these, twelve were acquitted outright, and three convicted only of assault. Newton, *Bitter Grain,* 138–39.

263. Memo, SAC San Diego to FBIHQ, Feb. 27, 1969; quoted in *Staff Reports,* 220–21.

264. Memo, SAC San Diego to FBIHQ, Dec. 3, 1969; quoted in *Staff Reports,* 221.

265. Hilliard, *Glory,* 364–66.

266. Goldstein, *Repression,* 468; Garry, "Persecution," 259.

267. Later, in court, Chicago SAC Marlin Johnson testified that he understood the word *impel* as meaning "to restrain." *Hampton v. Hanrahan,* 9, citing tr. at 4277–83 (also see n. 187).

268. Ibid., 9, citing tr. at 29186–90, 28324–26, 21896–907.

269. Bruce later testified, and O'Neil corroborated, that Bruce had declined because "robberies were against Party policy." Ibid., 9.

270. Ibid., 13.

271. Ibid., 10, 14.

272. By far the most comprehensive treatment of the Panther 3 case is Paul Chevigny's book-length analysis *Cops and Rebels: A Study of Provocation* (New York: Curtis Books, 1972). Also see "Ex-Panthers Acquitted of Conspiracy to Murder," *New York Times,* September 27, 1970; "Police, FBI Infiltrators Stir Trouble for Panthers," *Civil Liberties,* December 1970; and Chevigny's "Red Squads: The Verdict Is Entrapment," *Village Voice,* February 11, 1971.

273. Jon R. Waltz, "Staked Out for Slaughter," *Nation,* July 5, 1971.

274. Newton, *Bitter Grain*, 125.
275. Quoted in Zimroth, *Perversions of Justice*, 43.
276. Jason Epstein, *The Great Conspiracy Trial* (New York: Random House, 1970), 50–52.
277. On the nature of Seale's "participation" in the Chicago confrontations, see John Schultz, *Motion Will Be Denied: A New Report on the Chicago Conspiracy Trial* (New York: Morrow, 1972), 40. For the official "police riot" finding, see Daniel Walker et al., *Rights in Conflict: The Violent Confrontation between Demonstrators and Police during the Democratic Convention* (New York: Bantam, 1968).
278. Epstein, *Conspiracy Trial*, 423, 430.; Tom Hayden, *Reunion: A Memoir* (New York: Collier, 1988), 452, 458–59. Also see *The "Trial" of Bobby Seale* (New York: Priam Books, 1970).
279. Those arrested on the morning of April 2 were Lumumba Shakur (Anthony Coston), Afeni Shakur, Ali Bey Hassan (John Casson), Cetewayo (Michael Tabor), Richard Dhoruba Moore, Jamal (Eddie Joseph), Abayama Katara (Alex McKeiver), Baba Odinga (Walter Johnson), Joan Bird, and Robert Collier. Clark Squire, Lonnie Epps, and Curtis Powell turned themselves in the same afternoon. Kuwasi Balagoon (Donald Weems) and Richard Harris were already in jail in Newark on robbery charges, later dropped, and shortly extradited. On April 3 police arrested Lee Berry at the Manhattan VA hospital, where he was being treated for epilepsy, and whisked him off to jail. Lee Roper and Kwando Kinshasa (William King) left New York for Columbus, Ohio, where they were arrested by the FBI in November. Sekou Odinga (Nathaniel Burns), Mshina (Thomas Berry), and Larry Mack evaded arrest altogether by joining Eldridge Cleaver's International Section in Algeria. Kempton, *Briar Patch*, 10–12.
280. Zimroth, *Perversions of Justice*, 26, 27–28.
281. Ibid., 34–35.
282. Ibid., 30–31, 98.
283. "Black Panther Defense Finishes Cross-Examining of Infiltrator," *New York Times*, December 23, 1970. Also see Donner, *Protectors of Privilege*, 186–87.
284. Ibid., 189–90.
285. Ibid., 190. Also see "Panther Defense Presses Witness," *New York Times*, February 12, 1971; "Agent Is Queried at Panther Trial," *New York Times*, March 2, 1971. Still another BOSS infiltrator, Carlos Ashbrook, fared even worse; see "Another Fake Panther on the Grill," *New York Post*, March 25, 191.
286. Newton, *Bitter Grain*, 189–90; Donner, *Protectors of Privilege*, 191. For a juror's-eye view of the trial, see Edwin Kennebeck, *Juror Number Four: The Trial of 13 Black Panthers as Seen from the Jury Box* (New York: W. W. Norton, 1973).
287. Goldstein, *Political Repression*, 487–93.
288. For background, see Dhoruba Bin Wahad, "War Within," in *Still Black, Still Strong: Survivors of the U.S. War against Black Revolutionaries*, Jim Fletcher, Tanaquil Jones, and Sylvère Lotringer, (New York: Semiotext[e], 1993), 9–56.
289. The witness, Pauline Joseph, had initially come forward to offer testimony that Bin Wahad was *not* the shooter. She was then held incommunicado by BOSS and the bureau for a period of two years before taking the stand, testifying to the exact opposite during the second trial. Timothy Clifford, "Convicted Activist Claims Evidence was Concealed," *New York Newsday*, April 19, 1988; "Ex-Panther Says Evidence Was Concealed," *New York Times*, April 7, 1981.
290. William Kunstler, "The Continuing Ordeal of Dhoruba Al-Mujahid Bin Wahad," *City Sun*, March 28, 1990; Robert J. Boyle, "COINTELPRO: The 19-Year Ordeal of Dhoruba Bin-Wahad," *Covert Action/Information Bulletin*, no. 36 (1990); Grady-Willis, "State Repression," 380–82.
291. Swearingen, *FBI Secrets*, 85. For background on this proceeding, and on the Pratt case more generally, see Brian Glick, *G's Life and Times, 1967–1972* (San Francisco: Geronimo Pratt Defense Committee, 1979); Reginald W. Major and Marcia D. Davis, "Prisoner of War," *Emerge*, June 1994; Tackwood et al., *Glass House Tapes*, 213–14, 237.
292. Swearingen, *FBI Secrets*, 84–87; Johnnie L. Cochran with Tim Rutten, *Journey to*

Justice (New York: One World, 1996), 137.

293. Swearingen, *FBI Secrets*, 86–87; Grady-Willis, "State Repression," 378. Also see Amnesty International, *Proposal for a Commission of Inquiry into the Effect of Domestic Intelligence Activities on Criminal Trials in the United States of America* (New York: Amnesty International, 1980).

294. *60 Minutes* broadcast, November 25, 1987.

295. Edward J. Boyer, "Pratt Strides to Freedom," *Los Angeles Times,* June 11, 1997.

296. "Rice-Poindexter Case," *Black Panther,* fall 1991; Cory Zurowsky, "2867 Ohio Street," *Buffalo Chip* 2, no. 2 (June 1997).

297. *Rice v. Wolff,* 388 F. Supp. 185 (U.S. Dist. for Neb., 1974); *Rice v. Wolff,* 513 F.2d 1280 (1974); *Stone v. Powell,* 428 U.S. 465 (1976).

298. Don Walton, "NAACP seeks hearing for 2 jailed in killing," *Lincoln Journal Star,* March 20, 1997; Leslie Boellstorf, "Rice Loses Hearing: Inmate's Lawyers Allege Impropriety," *Omaha World Herald,* December 13, 1997; Francis Mendenhall, "Maybe No 'Criminal,'" *Omaha World Herald,* June 19, 1997; Nan Graf, "Miscarriage of Justice: The Mondo We Langa/Ed Poindexter Case," *Nebraska Report,* July/August 1997.

299. Memo, ASAC Omaha to FBIHQ, March 17, 1970; cited in Graf, "Miscarriage."

300. Quoted in Zurowsky, "Ohio Street."

301. Quoted in Leon Scatterfield, "Anti-Government Rant (circa 1970): Rice-Poindexter Revisited," *Lincoln Journal Star,* June 30, 1997.

302. Newton, *Bitter Grain,* 99.

303. Umoja, "Warriors," 426; Paul Shoates, "Update on Political Prisoners: Marshall Eddie Conway," *Black Panther,* fall 1991.

304. Donner, *Protectors of Privilege,* 180.

305. For process analysis, see Balbus, *Dialectics of Legal Repression;* Otto Kircheimer, *Political Justice: The Use of Legal Procedure for Political Ends* (Princeton, N.J.: Princeton University Press, 1969).

306. Garry, "Persecution," 259.

307. Ibid.

308. *Hampton v. Hanrahan,* 14–17, 59, 24–27 citing tr. at 24943, 24831–34, 26055, 23993–94, 29653, 9422–23, 5026, 5032. Also see Wilkins and Clark, *Search and Destroy,* 32.

309. *Hampton v. Hanrahan,* 22–27, 31; citing tr. at 22841–42, 6910–50, 22440, 6824, 22429–32, 22422–26, 22433–36, 9430, 25304. The floor plan itself is reproduced in Churchill and Vander Wall, *Agents of Repression,* 70.

310. This is according to the subsequent testimonies of both Gorman and Davis, quoted in *Hampton v. Hanrahan,* at 42–43. Gorman said he "stitched" the wall, firing through it and into Hampton's bedroom from left to right.

311. *Hampton v. Hanrahan,* 43–44, citing tr. at 16876–78, 16994, 16457. Also see Wilkins and Clark, *Search and Destroy,* 140–42; Akua Njeri, *My Life With the Black Panther Party* (Oakland, Calif.: Burning Spear, 1991), 38.

312. *Hampton v. Hanrahan,* 41–42, 35–36, citing tr. at 21212–398, 15642–44, 14118–19, 29763. Also see Wilkins and Clark, *Search and Destroy,* 158–77, 140–43.

313. Memo, SAC Chicago to FBIHQ, December 3, 1969; teletype, SAC Chicago to FBIHQ, December 4, 1969 (marked "Most Urgent"); quoted in *Hampton v. Hanrahan,* 34, 52. At trial, Piper again described the raid as a "success"; tr. at 9529.

314. Memo, SAC Chicago to FBIHQ, December 11, 1969; quoted in *Hampton v. Hanrahan,* 65, 68.

315. *Hampton v. Hanrahan,* 37, 35, 45–46; citing tr. at 15648–51, 33842–55, 33970, 17783, 29203–5.

316. Ibid., 78–79, 80–81, citing tr. at 27980, 5339, 27780–86, 27789, 28036.

317. Ibid., 67, 69.

318. For samples of Johnson's postretirement perjuries, see n. 159.

319. Ward Churchill, "COINTELPRO as a Family Business: The Strange Case of the FBI's

Two Richard Helds," *Z Magazine,* March 1989.

320. S. K. Levin, "Black Panthers Get Bittersweet Revenge," *Colorado Daily,* November 10, 1982.

321. *Hampton v. Hanrahan,* 35, citing tr. at 29203–5, 29687, 24599–600.

322. Durden-Smith, *George Jackson,* 136.

323. Memo, SAC Los Angeles to director, FBI, December 8, 1969; memo, W. C. Sullivan to G. C. Moore, December 17, 1969. Also see Durden-Smith, *George Jackson,* 134–35.

324. It is a matter of record that before settling on the Tennis Court murder case, both the FBI and CCS actively considered using infiltrator Julius C. Butler as a "witness" in developing a case against Geronimo Pratt in the Diggs slaying (Pratt supposedly confessed this killing to him, too); Glick, *G's Life and Times,* 97–98. Also see Fletcher, Jones, and Lotringer, *Still Black,* 228.

325. The twenty-eight-year-old Morris's case is almost identical to Diggs's, other than that it seems to have triggered no police "investigation" at all; "Fallen Comrades," *Black Panther,* spring 1991.

326. Ibid.

327. Newton, *Bitter Grain,* 125.

328. Ibid., 93–94.

329. Glick, *G's Life and Times,* 75–76; Fletcher, Jones, and Lotringer, *Black/Proud,* 232–33.

330. "Fallen Comrades," *Black Panther,* summer 1991; also see Kirkpatrick Sale, *SDS* (New York: Random House, 1973), 641.

331. Interview with Dhoruba Bin Wahad, Boulder, Colorado, March 1993 (tape on file).

332. In an attempt to cope, a three-month probationary period was announced for all new members in January 1969; Louis Heath, ed., *Off the Pigs! The History and Literature of the Black Panther Party* (Metuchen, N.J.: Scarecrow Press, 1976), 92. Eventually, recruitment was suspended altogether, and Newton "sent a message from jail that people who were not doing any work should be expelled from the Party"; Seale, *Seize the Time,* 369.

333. See, e.g., Huey P. Newton, *To Die for the People,* 44–75; Hilliard and Cole, *Glory,* esp. 326–27, 363–64; Elaine Brown, *A Taste of Power: A Black Woman's Story* (New York: Pantheon, 1992), 248, 276–77.

334. For use of the term "Afro-American Liberation Army," see the collection of materials written by Geronimo Pratt and assembled under the title, *Peace, Humanity, Freedom* (New York: Revolutionary People's Communication Network, 1971).

335. By all accounts, Newton maintained the "Squad," a handpicked unit devoted to both internal enforcement and the external projection of Party muscle, as a core element of his operation; see, e.g., Akinyele Omowale Umoja, "Repression Breeds Resistance: The Black Liberation Army and the Radical Legacy of the Black Panther Party," *New Political Science,* 21, no. 2, (June 1999): 143. More symbolically, he carefully cultivated a close association with George Jackson's mostly fictional "People's Army"; Durden-Smith, *George Jackson,* 243, 259.

336. John Castellucci, *The Big Dance: The Untold Story of Kathy Boudin and the Terrorist Family that Committed the Brinks Robbery Murders* (New York: Dodd, Mead, 1986) 53–55, 71–76.

337. Memo, FBIHQ to SAC Newark and two other field offices, September 18, 1969; cited in *Staff Reports,* 200–201.

338. The text of this letter appears verbatim in Churchill and Vander Wall, *COINTELPRO Papers,* 151.

339. Memo, FBIHQ to Legat, Paris, and SAC San Francisco, April 10, 1970; cited in *Staff Reports,* 201.

340. Ibid.

341. An FBI-monitored telephone conference was conducted between Cleaver, Matthews, Elbert "Big Man" Howard, and Roosevelt "June" Hilliard for this purpose on May 7, 1970; memo, SAC San Francisco to FBIHQ, May 8, 1970; quoted in *Staff Reports,* 201.

As a result, the top levels of FBI leadership elected to intensify the bureau's efforts to foment a split; memo, G. C. Moore to W. C. Sullivan, May 14, 1970; reproduced in Churchill and Vander Wall, *COINTELPRO Papers*, 149.

342. Hilliard was literally the only senior member of the Party hierarchy available to take charge by mid-1969, everyone else being either in prison (e.g., Newton), in jail pending trial (e.g., Seale) or exiled (e.g., the Cleavers). A plan was afoot to draft Fred Hampton into a position of national leadership, perhaps as a replacement for Hilliard, when he was assassinated; *Hampton v. Hanrahan*, 21.

343. Cleaver, "Back to Africa," 236.

344. Keating, *Free Huey!*, 63; Brown, *Power*, 243, 258.

345. Johnson, "Demise," 401–2, 406.

346. "Let Us Hold High the Banner of Intercommunalism and the Invincible Thoughts of Huey P. Newton, Minister of Defense and Supreme Commander of the Black Panther Party," *Black Panther*, Jan. 23, 1971. Also see Brown, *Power*, 257; Hilliard and Cole, *Glory*, 318.

347. Memo, SAC Philadelphia to FBIHQ, August 13, 1970; quoted in *Staff Reports*, 202.

348. Memo, G. C. Moore to SAC Philadelphia, August 19, 1970; cited in *Staff Reports*, 202.

349. Memo, SAC Los Angeles to FBIHQ, December 3, 1970; quoted in *Staff Reports*, 203.

350. Memo, FBIHQ to SAC, San Francisco, December 16, 1970; cited in *Staff Reports*, 203.

351. Memo, FBIHQ to SAC, San Francisco, January 6, 1970; quoted in *Staff Reports*, 203–4.

352. "On the Purge of Geronimo from the Black Panther Party," *Black Panther*, January 23, 1971. Also see John Roemer, "The Framing of Geronimo Pratt," *San Francisco Weekly*, February 12, 1992.

353. Lane's body was discovered on January 13; memo, SAC Los Angeles to FBIHQ, January 14, 1971. Also see "Panther Factions Blamed in Killing," *San Francisco Sunday Examiner and Chronicle*, Nov. 14, 1971; Glick, *G's Life and Times*, 63–64.

354. Memo, FBIHQ to Boston and three other field offices, January 28, 1971; quoted in Newton, *War against the Panthers*, 99.

355. "An Open Letter to the Weather Underground from the Panther 21," *East Village Other*, January 19, 1971; "A Call to Dissolve the Central Committee," *Right On!* April 3, 1971.

356. "Enemies of the People," *Black Panther*, February 13, 1971; Rod Such, "Newton Expels Panthers," *Guardian*, 20, no. 21 (February 1971).

357. Memo, FBIHQ to SAC Boston and three other field offices, January 28, 1971; quoted in *Staff Reports*, 205.

358. Newton, *War against the Panthers*, 68; citing memo, FBIHQ to 29 field offices, February 2, 1971; memo, FBIHQ to SAC San Francisco, February 19, 1970. On Bennett, see n. 260. It should be noted, however, that Fred Bennett was closely associated with Geronimo Pratt, which makes it entirely possible that his murder occurred for factional reasons rather than as a result of suspicions that he was a police infiltrator. As Pratt observed in 1972, "The killing of Fred Bennett . . . was a heavy loss"; quoted in Durden-Smith, *George Jackson*, 144.

359. Memo, FBIHQ to SAC, San Francisco, February 10 1971; cited in *Staff Reports*, 205.

360. The apartment was *not* underwritten with Party funds. Rather, it had been rented by Hollywood producer Bert Schneider. The FBI managed to create a contrary appearance via Ed Montgomery, its mouthpiece at the *San Francisco Chronicle;* Brown, *Power*, 264. In a February 25, 1971, report to FBIHQ on its recent COINTELPRO "successes," the San Francisco field office took credit not only for planting the Montgomery article but for sending copies to "all BPP offices across the United States and to three BPP contacts in Europe"; quoted in Newton, *War against the Panthers* (book version) 62.

361. Memo, FBIHQ to SAC San Francisco, February 19, 1971; cited in *Staff Reports*, 205.

362. Earl Caldwell, "The Panthers: Dead or Regrouping?" *New York Times*, March 1, 1971.

363. Johnson, "Demise," 402.

364. Cleaver, "Back to Africa," 238.

365. "Death Here Tied to Panther Feud," *New York Times,* March 10, 1971; "New York Slaying Tied to Panther Split," *San Francisco Chronicle,* March 10, 1971. Also see Grady-Willis, "State Repression," 376.

366. See Donald Cox, "The Split in the Party," Chapter 7 in this book.

367. Memo, FBIHQ to San Francisco and Chicago field offices, March 25, 1971; quoted in *Staff Reports,* 207.

368. Approved on March 25, the letter had been submitted for consideration in a memo from the SAC San Francisco to FBIHQ, on March 16, 1971; quoted in *Staff Reports,* 207.

369. "Whatever Happened to the United Black Panthers?" *U.S. News and World Report,* May 3, 1971.

370. Arrests were made as far away as Michigan, but the only charges filed were against seven New York Panthers and a white supporter. "The case dragged on for months through a series of mistrials, finally ending when four members of the spin-off Black Liberation Army pled guilty to manslaughter"; Newton, *Bitter Grain,* 207. Among the four were Dhoruba Moore and Jamal Joseph; Zimroth, *Perversions of Justice,* 31; Hilliard and Cole, *Glory,* 326.

371. Cleaver, "Back to Africa," 239.

372. Heike Kleffner, "The Black Panthers: Interviews with Geronimo ji Jaga Pratt and Mumia Abu Jamal," *Race and Class* 35, no. 1 (1993). Also see n. 317.

373. Newton, *Bitter Grain,* 199.

374. Local chapter nuclei were retained only in Chicago and Winston-Salem, North Carolina; Johnson, "Demise," 404–5, 410n4, 413n58.

375. Ibid., 405, 410n4.

376. Herman Bell, "The BPP and Political Prisoners," *Black Panther,* February 1991, 11.

377. Quoted from Chris Bratton's and Annie Goldson's excellent documentary film, *Framing the Panthers in Black and White: Dhoruba Bin Wahad, the Black Panther Party and the FBI's Counterintelligence Program* (New York: Pressa, 1990).

378. For the best overview of these findings, see Morton Halperin, Jerry Berman, Robert Borosage, and Christine Marwick, *The Lawless State: The Crimes of U.S. Intelligence Agencies* (New York: Penguin, 1976).

379. Nicholas Horrock, "Gray and Two Ex-FBI Aides Indicted in Conspiracy in Search for Radicals," *New York Times,* April 11, 1978; Tony Poveda, *Lawlessness and Reform: The FBI in Transition* (Pacific Grove, Calif.: Brooks/Cole, 1990), 83.

380. Eve Pell, *The Big Chill* (Boston: Beacon Press), 193–94.

381. Interview with Geronimo ji Jaga, People's International Tribunal for Justice for Mumia Abu-Jamal, Philadelphia, December 6, 1997 (tape on file).

382. This assessment of the weight carried by Held in the Pratt case is based on interviews with appeals attorney Stuart Hanlon (San Francisco; April 1987) and former agent M. Wesley Swearingen, who worked in the Los Angeles COINTELPRO Section during the crucial period (Santa Fe, N.M.; October 1994).

383. Documents demonstrating Held's involvement in the Peltier case are reproduced in Churchill and Vander Wall, *Agents of Repression* 268, 269.

384. Augusto Delgado, "La invasión del viernes 30," *Claridad,* September 12, 1985; Candida Cotto, "Madrugada del 30 augusto," *Claridad,* September 12, 1985; Juan Mari Bras, "El escirro Richard Held," *Claridad,* September 13, 1985; Manuelo Coss, "Delicuente al servicio del FBI," *Claridad,* September 20, 1985.

385. In 1993 Held retired from the FBI. He now serves as head of security for the Visa Corp.; Ward Churchill, "The FBI Targets Judi Bari: A Case Study in Domestic Counterinsurgency," *Covert Action Quarterly,* no. 47, (winter 1993–94).

386. In the wake of the Felt/Miller convictions, the FBI Agents Association, an exceedingly potent lobby, went to work to ensure that none of its members would again be subject to prosecution for comparable criminal activity; Donald Kessler, *The FBI* (New York: Pocket Books, 1993), 344.

387. Senator Jeremiah Denton, March 25, 1983; quoted in Pell, *Big Chill,* 194.

388. Pell, *Big Chill,* 200. Also see "The Executive Order," *Covert Action Information Bulletin,* no. 16 (March 1982). The CIA had of course been involved in such activities for a considerable period; "CIA Reportedly Recruited Blacks for Surveillance of Panthers," *New York Times,* March 17, 1978; Newton, *War against the Panthers,* 90–92, 106–7; Grady-Willis, "State Repression," 369.

389. Quoted in Pell, *Big Chill,* 201.

390. See generally, Craig Uchida and David Weisburg, eds., *Police Innovation and Control of the Police* (New York: Springer-Verlag, 1993).

391. Bin Wahad, "War Within," 49–50. Also see Michael Dewar, *Weapons and Equipment of Counter-Terrorism* (London: Arms and Armour Press, 1988); Ward Churchill, "To Serve and Protect? The Social Context of Michael Dewar's *Weapons and Equipment of Counter-Terrorism," New Studies on the Left,* 14, nos. 1–2 (winter–spring 1989).

392. The decision to create a fully national counterintelligence/counterinsurgency apparatus, and to coordinate it with comparable establishments in several other countries (notably West Germany and Great Britain), can be dated from an international "counterterrorism" conference hosted by the FBI in San Juan, Puerto Rico, from August 28–September 1, 1978; "Secret Counter-Insurgency Conference Held in Puerto Rico," *SI: Research Papers,* October 1982.

393. Diana Reynolds, "FEMA and the NSC: The Rise of the National Security State," *Covert Action Information Bulletin,* no. 33, (1990).

394. See, e.g., Margot Harry, *"Attention, MOVE! This Is America!"* (Chicago: Banner Press, 1987); Ross Gelbspan, *Break-ins, Death Threats and the FBI: The Covert War Against the Central America Movement* (Boston: South End Press, 1991); Stuart A. Wright, ed., *Armageddon in Waco: Critical Perspectives on the Branch Davidian Conflict* (Chicago: University of Chicago Press, 1995).

395. The dating is a bit nebulous, but is most commonly begun with Reagan's 1986 signing of a National Security Directive expanding the role of U.S. military forces ostensibly combating drug suppliers in Latin America. Actually, the preliminaries had commenced as early as 1982; Elaine Shannon, *Desperadoes: Latin Drug Lords, U.S. Lawmen, and the War America Can't Win* (New York: Viking, 1988), 85, 362.

396. See, e.g., Alfred W. McCoy, *The Politics of Heroin: CIA Complicity in the Global Drug Trade* (Chicago: Lawrence Hill, 1991); Peter Dale Scott and Jonathan Marshall, *Cocaine Politics: Drugs, Armies, and the CIA in Central America* (Berkeley: University of California Press, 1991); Clarence Lusane, *Pipe Dreams: Racism and the War on Drugs* (Boston: South End Press, 1991). Also see Sam Meddis, "Drug Arrest Rate is Higher for Blacks," *USA Today,* Dec. 20, 1989. James Austin and Aaron M. Davis, *The Impact of the War on Drugs* (San Francisco: National Council on Crime and Delinquency, 1989).

397. Marc Mauer, "Americans behind Bars: Comparative Rates of Incarceration," in *Cages of Steel: The Politics of Imprisonment in the United States,* ed. Ward Churchill and J.J. Vander Wall, (Washington, D.C.: Maisonneuve Press, 1992), 25–26.

398. Mauer, "Americans behind Bars," 24, 26.

399. For further data and insights into this trend, see Daniel Burton-Rose, Dan Pens, and Paul Wright, eds., *The Celling of America: An Inside Look at the Prison Industry* (Monroe, Me.: Common Courage Press, 1998), esp. the section entitled "Money and Warm Bodies: The Prison-Industrial Complex in the United States" (102–67).

400. Steve Whitman, "The Crime of Black Imprisonment," *Chicago Tribune,* May 28, 1967.

401. Martin Carnoy, *Faded Dreams: The Politics and Economics of Race in America* (Cambridge, UK: Cambridge University Press, 1994).

402. See, e.g., Catherine Caufield, *Masters of Illusion: The World Bank and the Poverty of Nations* (New York: Henry Holt, 1996); William Greider, *One World, Ready or Not: The Manic Logic of Global Capitalism* (New York: Simon and Schuster, 1997).

403. Contributions to this "discourse" over the past thirty years have been legion. The linchpin of contemporary articulation will probably be found, however, in Gene Sharp's

Social Power and Political Freedom (Boston: Porter Sargent, 1980). Also see Sharp's 3-volume *Politics of Nonviolent Action* (Boston: Porter Sargent, 1973).

404. For critique, see Ward Churchill with Mike Ryan, *Pacifism as Pathology: Observations on the Role of Armed Struggle in North America* (Winnipeg: Arbiter Ring, 1998).

405. Ollie Johnson discusses this and related issues in "Demise." Probably most constructively, he brings perspectives offered by the late C. W. Cassinelli to bear on the BPP's "Newton cult" phenomenon; C. W. Cassinelli, "The Law of Oligarchy," *American Political Science Review*, no. 47, (1953). Of related interest is the "élite theory" expounded by Robert Michels in his *Political Parties: A Sociological Study of the Oligarchical Tendencies of Modern Democracy* (New York: Free Press, 1962).

406. Chris Booker offers a valuable, although by no means completely satisfying, analysis of the very question in his essay "Lumpenization." Other especially useful readings in this connection include those cited in n. 147, as well as David G. Epstein, "A Revolutionary Lumpen Proletariat?" *Monthly Review*, December 1969; Clarence J. Mumford, "The Fallacy of Lumpen Ideology", *Black Scholar*, no. 4 (1973); and Kathleen Cleaver, *On the Vanguard Role of the Black Urban Lumpen Proletariat* (London: Grass/Roots, 1975).

407. A superb recent analysis of these matters is offered by Dhoruba Bin Wahad in his "Toward Rethinking Self-Defense in a Racist Culture: Black Survival in a United States in Transition," in Fletcher, Jones, and Lotringer, *Still Black/Still Strong*, 57–76. Also see Clarence Lusane, "To Fight for the People: The Black Panther Party and Black Politics in the 1990s," in Jones, *Black Panthers Reconsidered*, 443–63.

408. As is readily evident in Robert Justin Goldstein's monumental study, *Political Repression in Modern America*, the same sorts of violently repressive techniques have been employed to a greater or lesser extent against every potentially effective movement in the United States for more than a century, irrespective of the targets' adherence to nonviolent principles.

409. See, e.g., the argument developed by Joy James in *Resisting State Violence: Radicalism, Gender and Race in U.S. Culture* (Minneapolis: University of Minnesota Press, 1996).

410. The segment entitled "Prospects for the Future" in Brian Glick's *War at Home: Covert Action Against U.S. Activists and What We Can Do About It* (Boston: South End Press, 1989), while inadequate, represents a start in this regard.

7   The Split in the Party

Donald Cox

1. The Harlem Panther office was on Seventh Avenue between 121st and 122nd. On March 8, Spider went to investigate a report that Panthers from the Newton faction were selling papers on the corner of 125th Street. When he arrived, he was shot in the back of the head.

2. The relationship between Huey and myself and our knowledge of each other was such that in no way can Robert Webb's assassination be attributed to COINTELPRO's efforts to destroy the BPP. The murder of Spider was naked vengeance.

3. When North Philly burned in the 1964 insurrection, the Seidlers lost two stores. They were the only whites that returned and rebuilt after the disturbances. Miriam said, "Don't run away from Blacks. . . . Stay there in the neighborhood and make it work."

4. Elaine Brown, *A Taste of Power*, (New York: Pantheon, 1992), 5. As Brown said in August 1974, announcing to an assembly that she was the new head of the gang after Newton's flight to Cuba to avoid prosecution for the murder of a seventeen-year-old girl: "I have control over all the guns and all the money of this party. There will be no external or internal opposition I will not resist and put down. I will deal resolutely with

anyone or anything that stands in the way."

5. *Black Panther,* January 23, 1971. Geronimo was accused of plotting to assassinate Newton and Hilliard.

6. Sam was the first person I met that had a real natural natural. Sam was with us from the beginning in San Francisco, and he turned us onto the Socialist Workers' Party office, where we found all the literature available at the time on Malcolm X, including the album *Ballots or Bullets,* which became an organizing tool.

7. Elaine Brown (*A Taste of Power,* 266) says that the assassination of Sam "was the beginning of a frightening, internecine battle as our troops, Huey's party, responded." This is a feeble attempt to revise history. Dates of events are clear evidence of who responded to whom. Sam's death was the last, not the first.

8. David Hilliard and Lewis Cole, *This Side of Glory* (Boston: Little, Brown, 1993), 325–26.

9 Black Fighting Formations: Their Strengths, Weaknesses, and Potentialities

Russell Shoats

1. Sun Tzu, *The Art of War* (New York: Oxford University Press, 1984); Karl von Clausewitz, *On War* (New York: Viking Press, 1983).

2. National Advisory Commission on Civil Disorders, *Report of the National Advisory Commission on Civil Disorders* (Washington, D.C.: Government Printing Office, 1968), 19–21.

3. Maxwell C. Stanford (Akbar Muhammad Ahmad), "Revolutionary Action Movement (RAM): A Case Study of an Urban Revolutionary Movement in Western Capitalist Society," (master's thesis, Atlanta University, 1986).

4. George Jackson, *Blood in My Eye* (Baltimore: Black Classic Press, 1990).

5. Gregory Armstrong, *"The Dragon Has Come"* (New York: Harper & Row, 1974); and Paul Liberatore, *The Road to Hell: The True Story of George Jackson, Stephen Bingham, and the San Quentin Massacre* (New York: Atlantic Monthly Press, 1996).

6. Imari Abubakari Obadele (Milton Henry), *Free the Land! The True Story of the Trials of the RNA-11 in Mississippi and the Continuing Struggle to Establish an Independent Black Nation in Five States in the Deep South* (Washington, D.C.: House of Songhay, 1984).

7. Eric Mann, *Comrade George: An Investigation into the Official Story of His Assassination, His Work for the People, and Their Response to His Death* (Cambridge, Mass.: Hovey Street Press, 1972).

10 Organization and Movement: The Case of the Black Panther Party and the Revolutionary People's Constitutional Convention of 1970

George Katsiaficas

1. In *Bitter Grain, the Story of the Black Panther Party* (Los Angeles: Holloway House 1980), author Michael Newton maintains that the event analyzed in this essay never took place (157).

2. I develop this concept in relation to the autonomous movement (or *Autonomen*) in Europe to indicate that seemingly spontaneous crowd behavior can have a great underlying intelligence. See *The Subversion of Politics: European Social Movements*

and the Decolonization of Everyday Life (Atlantic Highlands, N.J.: Humanities Press, 1997).

3. For more discussion, see the introduction to this volume.

4. Checking a dozen of the most important histories of the 1960s in the United States, I found that ten did not even mention the RPCC, and the other two contained only brief references to it. To the best of my knowledge, this is the first attempt to deal with it even in an essay. Charles Jones, one of the preeminent historians of the BPP, points out that leaders' autobiographies and analyses of events are more common in Panther historiography than are rank-and-file accounts or longitudinal studies. The paucity of material about the RPCC indicates the extent to which it is a forgotten case even among movement events. See Jones, "Reconsidering Panther History: The Untold Story," in *The Black Panther Party Reconsidered,* ed. Charles E. Jones, (Baltimore: Black Classic Press, 1998), 9–10.

5. See Joseph A. Califano Jr., *The Student Revolution: A Global Confrontation* (New York: W. W. Norton, 1970), 64.

6. *New York Times,* January 2, 1971.

7. *The Imagination of the New Left: A Global Analysis of 1968* (Boston: South End Press, 1987; new printing, 1998).

8. This process is described in Bobby Seale, *Seize the Time!* (1970; reprint, Baltimore: Black Classic Press, 1991).

9. Ibid., 62.

10. See the *Black Panther,* August 15, 1970, 19, for one example.

11. See particularly Tracye Matthews, "'No One Ever Asks, What a Man's Place in the Revolution Is': Gender and the Politics of the Black Panther Party, 1966–1971," in Jones, *Black Panther Party,* 267–304. The entire section on gender dynamics in Jones's book is excellent. Also see Kathleen Cleaver's article, chapter 8 in this volume.

12. David Hilliard and Lewis Cole, *This Side of Glory: The Autobiography of David Hilliard and the Story of the Black Panther Party* (Boston: Little, Brown, 1993), 312.

13. Russell Shoats, unpublished memoir.

14. Manning Marable, *Race, Reform and Rebellion: The Second Reconstruction in Black America* (Jackson: University Press of Mississippi, 1971), 110.

15. Hilliard and Cole, *Glory,* 313.

16. *Black Panther,* September 19 and October 31, 1970.

17. G. Louis Heath, ed., *Off the Pigs! The History and Literature of the Black Panther Party,* (Metuchen, N.J.: Scarecrow Press, 1976), 186–87.

18. "Newton, at Panther Parley, Urges Socialist System," *New York Times,* September 6, 1970, 40; Paul Delaney, "Panthers Weigh New Constitution," *New York Times,* September 7, 1970, 13.

19. *Washington Post,* November 27, 1970, C10.

20. *New York Times,* September 6, 1970, 40.

21. Kit Kim Holder, "The History of the Black Panther Party, 1966–1972" (Ph.D. diss., University of Massachusetts, 1990), 131.

22. I call this phenomenon the "eros effect." See my book *The Imagination of the New Left: A Global Analysis of 1968* (Boston: South End Press, 1987). Also see my exchange with Staughton Lynd in *Journal of American History,* June 1990, 375–77. Lynd originally asserted that "as a resident of the Kent-Lordstown area for more than ten years, I have yet to meet a participant in either happening who felt that the events at Kent caused those at Lordstown." After reading the exchange, Tom Grace, one of the students involved at Kent State, sent me a leaflet from Lordstown that he had saved for twenty years that proved impetus for the actions there did, in fact, come at least in part from the shootings at Kent State.

23. Shoats, memoir, C. That the armed struggle was endorsed by the BPP–including Huey Newton–can be ascertained by their reaction to Jonathan Jackson's taking over a courtroom in Marin, California, on August 7, 1970, an action that cost many lives. The rela-

tion and articulation of these levels of struggle remains an unresolved problematic facing radical movements. For discussion, see Katsiaficas, *Imagination of the New Left,* 182.

24. *Black Panther,* August 22, 1970, August 29, 1970, 11.
25. *Black Panther,* September 19, 1970, 11.
26. "Not to Believe in a New World after Philadelphia Is a Dereliction of the Human Spirit," unsigned article, *Black Panther,* September 26, 1970, 17.
27. Holder, "History," 131.
28. See his "Letter to the National Liberation Front of South Vietnam (with Reply)" in *Vietnam Documents: American and Vietnamese Views of the War,* George Katsiaficas, ed. (Armonk, N.Y.: Sharpe, 1992), 133–36.
29. *Black Panther,* August 21, 1970, 5.
30. Holder, "History," 132.
31. "Huey's Message to the Revolutionary People's Constitutional Convention Plenary Session September 5, 1970 Philadelphia, PA." Document in my collection.
32. Hilliard and Cole, *Glory,* 313.
33. Ibid., 314.
34. "Not to Believe in a New World" 19.
35. Ibid., 20.
36. See point 2 of the workshop on the Family and the Rights of Children, in the appendices, for one example.
37. "The People and the People Alone Were the Motive Power in the Making of the History of the People's Revolutionary Constitutional Convention Plenary Session!" *Black Panther,* September 12, 1970, 3.
38. Nikhil Pal Singh, "The Black Panthers and the 'Undeveloped Country' of the Left," in Jones, *Black Panther Party,* 87.
39. See Douglas Amy, *Real Choices/New Voices: The Case for Proportional Representation Elections in the United States* (New York: Columbia University Press, 1993).
40. Laurie Asseo, "Study Ties Drug War, Rise in Jailed Women," *Boston Globe,* November 18, 1999, p. A18.
41. Chris Bangert, "Marijuana: The Hemp of the Past and the 'Drug' of the Present," unpublished paper, Brewster, Mass., 1999.
42. Enforced at a cost of billions of dollars per year and tens of thousands of perpetrators of victimless crimes in jail, the present drug policy includes decades of evidence of the CIA's involvement with both the heroin trade in Southeast Asia and the cocaine trade in Central America as well as existence of a Contra-connected crack pipeline to Watts (South Central Los Angeles), first reported in the pages of the *San Jose Mercury-News.* As a result of the continual generation of mega-profits based on certain drugs' illegal status (witness the price of oregano or baking soda in any supermarket), control of the drug trade by the "government within the government" is a major source of funds for covert operations hidden from public and congressional oversight. To understand these dynamics, one could begin with Leslie Cockburn, *Out of Control: The Story of the Reagan Administration's Secret War in Nicaragua, the Illegal Arms Pipeline, and the Contra Drug Connection* (New York: Atlantic Monthly Press, 1987). Also see Alfred McCoy, *The Politics of Heroin: CIA Complicity in the Global Drug Trade* (New York: Lawrence Hill, 1991).
43. For more information on these groups, see Katsiaficas, *Subversion of Politics.*
44. Indeed, if the press continued to report spontaneously generated popular acts of rebellion as they did in the 1960s—and there is considerable evidence the media do not—a strong argument could be made that with the advent of television and satellites, the international impact of uprisings, general strikes, insurrections, massive occupations of public space—all the weapons in the arsenals of popular movements—would be their most notable effect.
45. Floyd W. Hayes III and Francis A. Kiene III, "'All Power to the People': The Political Thought of Huey P. Newton and the Black Panther Party," in Jones, *Black Panther*

Party, 157–73.

46. See the *Black Panther,* June 13, 1970, 14. Cleaver insists the RPCC was "actually implementation of Point 10 of the Black Panther Party platform and program."

47. Hilliard and Cole, *Glory,* 308.

48. Ibid., 317.

49. Ivan C. Brandon, "Panthers Seek Site for Talks: Negotiations with Howard Broken Off," *Washington Post,* November 27, 1970, C1.

50. Ibid.

51. Elaine Brown, *A Taste of Power: A Black Woman's Story* (New York: Anchor, 1992), 351.

11   The Influence of the Black Panther Party (USA) on the Vanguard Party of the Bahamas, 1972-1987

John T. McCartney

1. Mary Frances Berry and John Blassingame, *Long Memory: The Black Experience in America* (New York: Oxford University Press, 1982), 461.

2. For an excellent commentary on the status of blacks in the urban centers, especially in the North, see Kenneth B. Clark, "Racial Progress and Retreat: A Personal Memoir," in Herbert Hill and James E. Jones Jr., eds., *Race in America: The Struggle for Equality* (Madison: University of Wisconsin Press, 1993), 3–18.

3. Estimates of the racial makeup of the Bahamas range from 10 percent White vs. 90 percent Black, the figure used most often in conventional Bahamian society, to Thomas D. Anderson's estimate: 10 percent white, 10 percent mixed, and 80 percent Black, which he bases on American Central Intelligence Agency (CIA) estimates. (See Thomas D. Anderson, *Geopolitics of the Caribbean* (New York: Praeger, 1984), 45. Since race is not used as an official category in Bahamian governmental records, there is little official literature on the demography of race, even though the Bahamas has a higher percentage of Whites in its population than any other nation in the English-speaking Caribbean. The 1980 U.S. Census lists African Americans at 11.7 percent of the population, and they constituted the largest ethnic minority at the time. It is now believed, although it has to be confirmed by new census data, that America's Hispanic population equals the African American.

4. For a very good discussion of the practices of White minority politics in the Bahamas, see Colin Hughes, *Race and Color in the Bahamas* (New York: St. Martin's, 1981), especially chapters 3 and 4.

5. For a detailed account of the racism and manipulations of the Bay Street Boys, see Hartley Cecil Saunders, *The Other Bahamas* (Nassau: Nassau Guardian, 1991).

6. For an excellent personal account of the PLP's founding, see Sir Henry Taylor, Kt.J.P., *My Political Memoirs* (Nassau, privately printed, n.d.).

7. Frederick Douglass, *Life and Times of Frederick Douglass* (New York: Collier, 1962), 353.

8. The Vanguard Nationalist and Socialist Party of the Bahamas, *The Struggle for Freedom in the Bahamas* (Nassau: Vanguard, 1980), 21.

9. See the speech entitled "On the Relevance of the Church" in Huey P. Newton, *To Die for the People* (New York: Vintage, 1972), 65.

10. Ibid., 67.

11. See the section entitled "Huey Newton Talks to the Movement about the Black Panther Party, Cultural Nationalism, SNCC, Liberals and White Revolutionaries," in *The Black Panthers Speak,* ed. Philip S. Foner (New York: Lippincott, 1970), 57.

12. For an excellent review of the ferment and change in the Caribbean region in the 1970s and 1980s, see Anthony Payne and Paul Sutton, eds., *Modern Caribbean Politics* (Baltimore: Johns Hopkins, 1993), especially 1–27.

13. For a good discussion of the achievements and limits of the Cuban model during this

period, see Jean Pierre-Beuvais, "Achievements and Contradictions of the Cuban Workers State," in *Crisis in the Caribbean,* ed. Fitzroy Ambursley and Robin Cohen (New York: Monthly Review Press, 1983), 47–71.

14. For a discussion of the limits of the Puerto Rican model in Jamaica, see Michael Manley, *Jamaica: Struggle in the Periphery* (London: Third World Media-Oxford University Press, 1982), especially 25–38.

15. Clive Thomas, "State Capitalism in Guyana: An Assessment of Burnham's Cooperative Socialist Republic" in Ambursley and Cohen, *Crisis in the Caribbean,* 32.

16. See table 1, which is an abbreviated version of the Vanguard Party's Ten Point Program.

17. Huey P. Newton, speech, "To the Revolutionary Peoples Convention," Sept. 8, 1970, in Newton, *To Die for the People,* 159.

18. "To the National Liberation Front of South Vietnam," in ibid., 181.

19. Amy Jacques-Garvey, ed., *Philosophy and Opinions of Marcus Garvey* (New York: Atheneum, 1969), 36.

20. For another example of the interconnectedness of the struggles against racism, colonialism, and imperialism, see Amilcar Cabral's interview, "Connecting the Struggles: An Informal Talk with Black Americans," in *Return to the Source: Selected Speeches by Amilcar Cabral* (New York: Monthly Review Press, 1973), 75–92.

12 Cuba, the Black Panther Party, and the U.S. Black Movement in the 1960s: Issues of Security

Ruth Reitan

1. Eldridge Cleaver, interview with the author, Miami, January 20 and February 11, 1996.

2. For a full elaboration of this argument, see Ruth Reitan, "Issues of Security," in *The Rise and Decline of an Alliance: Cuba and African American Leaders in the 1960s* (East Lansing: Michigan State University Press, 1999).

3. Ricardo Rojo, *My Friend Che* (New York: Grove Press, 1968), 94.

4. Domingo Amuchastegui (formerly an official in the Cuban Ministry of Foreign Affairs, Intelligence, and the head of the Department of Organization vis-à-vis the Tricontinental organizations during the 1960s and 1970s), interview with the author, Miami, March 23, 1995.

5. Robert Carl Cohen, *Black Crusader: A Biography of Robert Franklin Williams* (Secaucus, N.J.: Lyle Stuart, 1972), 314.

6. Amuchastegui, interview.

7. The Black Panther Party for Self-Defense, "The Black Panther," in *Black Nationalism in America,* ed. John Bracey Jr. et al., (Indianapolis: Bobbs-Merrill, 1970), 526–27.

8. Amuchastegui, interview.

9. This theory of struggle called for cells of guerrilla fighters based in the countryside practicing revolutionary insurrection and working among the masses.

10. Cleaver, interview; and Rojo, *My Friend Che,* 94.

11. Rojo, *My Friend Che,* 85.

12. Ibid., 86.

13. Ibid., 165.

14. Carlos Moore, *Castro, the Blacks, and Africa* (Los Angeles: Center for Afro-American Studies, University of California, 1988), 4.

15. Ward Churchill and Jim Vander Wall, *The COINTELPRO Papers: Documents from the FBI's Secret Wars against Dissent in the United States* (Boston: South End Press, 1990), 95–96, 102–3.

16. See ibid., 105–230.

17. In JoNina M. Abron, "The Legacy of the Black Panther Party," *Black Scholar,*

November–December 1968, 33.

18. Seymour M. Hersh, "Alien-Radical Tie Disputed by C.I.A." *New York Times,* May 25, 1973.

19. Moore, *Castro,* 60.

20. CORE was the first group to directly challenge segregation laws and customs in inter-state transportation in the South in May 1961. John Hope Franklin, *From Slavery to Freedom* (New York: Alfred A. Knopf, 1967), 627.

21. Cohen, *Black Crusader,* 225.

22. Moore, *Castro,* 121–22.

23. Cohen, *Black Crusader,* 225.

24. The Cuban intelligence and security apparatus.

25. Amuchastegui, interview.

26. Ibid., and Cohen, *Black Crusader,* 208.

27. Cohen, *Black Crusader,* 210.

28. Ibid., 223–25.

29. Ibid., 302.

30. Cleaver, interview; and Amuchastegui, interview.

31. Cohen, *Black Crusader,* 292.

32. Ibid., 314.

33. Cleaver, interview.

34. Cohen, *Black Crusader,* 313.

35. Ibid., 315.

36. Ibid., 320.

37. Cleaver, interview.

38. Amuchastegui, interview.

39. Cleaver, interview.

40. Ibid.

41. Amuchastegui, interview.

42. Ibid.

43. Cleaver, interview.

44. Amuchastegui, interview.

45. Cleaver, interview.

46. For details of Cleaver's exile in Algeria and his establishment of the Black Panther Party International headquarters, see Kathleen Neal Cleaver, "Back to Africa: The Evolution of the International Section of the Black Panther Party (1969–1972)", in *The Black Panther Party Reconsidered,* ed. Charles E. Jones (Baltimore: Black Classic Press, 1998).

47. Cleaver, interview.

13 Revolutionary Art Is a Tool for Liberation: Emory Douglas and Protest Aesthetics at the *Black Panther*

Erika Doss

1. G. Louis Heath, *Off the Pigs! The History and Literature of the Black Panther Party* (Metuchen, N.J.: Scarecrow Press, 1976), 214.

2. "On Revolutionary Art," *Black Panther,* January 24, 1970, 5; Lawrence Alloway, "Art," *Nation* 211, no. 12 (October 19, 1970), 382.

3. Newton quoted in Brad Brewer, "Revolutionary Art," *Black Panther,* October, 24, 1970, 17; Douglas quoted in "Revolutionary Art: A Tool for Liberation," taken from a speech delivered at Malcolm X College (Chicago) at the First Revolutionary Artist Conference, June 8, 1970, and reprinted in *Black Panther,* July 4, 1970, 12–13. For an extended analysis of the role of the media in shaping and directing radical politics, see

Todd Gitlin, *The Whole World is Watching: Mass Media in the Making and Unmaking of the New Left* (Berkeley and Los Angeles: University of California Press, 1980).

4. Eldridge Cleaver, "Initial Reactions on the Assassination of Malcolm X," in *Soul on Ice* (New York: McGraw Hill, 1968), 61; Kobena Mercer, *Welcome to the Jungle: New Positions in Black Cultural Studies* (New York: Routledge, 1994), 139. See also William L. Van Deburg, *Black Camelot: African-American Culture Heroes In Their Times, 1960–1980* (Chicago: University of Chicago Press, 1997), 78–81.

5. See, for example, bell hooks, *Black Looks: Race and Representation* (Boston: South End Press, 1992), 87–113; Herman Gray, "Black Masculinity and Visual Culture," in Thelma Golden, ed, *Black Male: Representations of Masculinity in Contemporary Black Art* (New York: Whitney Museum of American Art, 1994), 175–80; and Mercer, *Welcome to the Jungle,* 141–54.

6. Reginald Major, *A Panther is a Black Cat* (New York: William Morrow, 1971), 280–82.

7. Frank Jones, "Talent for the Revolution," *Black Panther,* March 16, 1969, 9; Robert H. Brisbane, *Black Activism: Racial Revolution in the United States, 1954–1970* (Valley Forge, Pa.: Hudson Press, 1974), 218.

8. Elton C. Fax, "Emory Douglas," in *Black Artists of the New Generation* (New York: Dodd, Mead, 1977), 257–78.

9. Fax, "Emory Douglas," 270; and Phineas Israeli, "Emory Grinds Down the Pigs," *Black Panther,* November 22, 1969, 6, reprinted from *Berkeley Tribe* (n.d.).

10. Fax, "Emory Douglas," 273.

11. Hugh Pearson, *The Shadow of the Panther: Huey Newton and the Price of Black Power in America* (New York: Addison-Wesley, 1994), 120–26; Major, *Black Cat,* 70–72, and Mario Van Peebles, Ula Y. Taylor, and J. Tarika Lewis, *Panther: A Pictorial History of the Black Panthers and the Story Behind the Film* (New York: New Market Press, 1995), 31–32.

12. On cultural nationalism see William L. Van Deburg, *New Day in Babylon: The Black Power Movement and American Culture, 1965–1975* (Chicago: University of Chicago Press, 1992), 170–91.

13. The full text of Executive Mandate No. 1, written by Huey Newton, is reprinted in Major, *Black Cat,* 289–90.

14. On media coverage of the Panthers see, for example, Abe Peck, *Uncovering the Sixties, The Life and Times of the Underground Press* (New York: Pantheon, 1985), 65; Peebles, Taylor, and Lewis, *Panther,* 39; and Angela Davis, "Black Nationalism: The Sixties and the Nineties," in *Black Popular Culture: A Project by Michele Wallace,* ed. Gina Dent, Dia Center for the Arts, Discussions in Contemporary Culture, no. 8 (Seattle: Bay Press, 1992), 319.

15. Israeli, "Emory Grinds Down the Pigs," 6.

16. Ibid.

17. Brewer, "Revolutionary Art," 17.

18. Douglas, quoted in Israeli, "Emory Grinds Down the Pigs," 6.

19. Fax, "Emory Douglas," 274, Douglas, "Revolutionary Art," 13; Emory Douglas, "Revolutionary Art/Black Liberation," *Black Panther,* May 18, 1968, 20.

20. Douglas, "Revolutionary Art/Black Liberation," 20.

21. Fax, "Emory Douglas," 276–77. On the etymology of policemen as pigs, see Philip Howard, *The State of the Language* (New York: Oxford University Press, 1985), 28.

22. Fax, "Emory Douglas," 277; Douglas, "On Revolutionary Art," 5, and quoted from author interview, April 27, 1993. In another version of the cartoon, Douglas labeled the four hogs "Dean of Rusk," "Mad McNamara," "L.B.J.," and "R.F.K."; see *Black Panther,* March 16, 1968, 10.

23. Douglas, "On Revolutionary Culture," in *New Black Voices: An Anthology of Contemporary Afro-American Literature* ed. Abraham Chapman, (New York: New American Library, 1972), 489–90.

24. Todd Gitlin discusses radical left attraction to the Panthers in *The Sixties: Years of*

Hope, Days of Rage (New York: Bantam, 1987), 350–51; Cleaver quoted in "Eldridge on Weathermen," *Black Panther,* November 22, 1969, 5, reprinted from *Berkeley Tribe* (no date given); Major, *Black Cat,* 139, 140, 142.

25. Douglas, "On Revolutionary Art," 5; Douglas, author interview, April 27, 1993. See also Fax, "Emory Douglas," 276–77.

26. Alan Barnett, *Community Murals: The People's Art* (Philadelphia: Art Alliance Press, 1984); Albert Boime, "Waving the Red Flag and Reconstituting Old Glory," *Smithsonian Studies in American Art* 4, no.2 (spring 1990): 3–25; Samella S. Lewis and Ruth G. Waddy, *Black Artists on Art,* vol. 1 (Los Angeles: Contemporary Crafts Publishers, 1969), 39–42; Fax, "Dana Chandler," in *Black Artists of the New Generation,* 345–61; and Elsa Honig Fine, *The Afro-American Artist: A Search for Identity* (New York: Holt, Rinehart and Winston, 1973), 203–4.

27. Lucy Lippard, *Mixed Blessings: New Art in a Multicultural America* (New York: Pantheon, 1990), 234; Elizabeth Catlett, "The Role of the Black Artist," *Black Scholar,* June 1975, 10–14.

28. Douglas, quoted in *Black Panther,* January 18, 1972; Douglas, author interview, April 27, 1993.

29. Saar, quoted in a 1975 interview with Benny Andrews, "Jemimas, Mysticism, and Mojos: The Art of Betye Saar," *Encore American and Worldwide News,* March 17, 1975, as noted in *Betye Saar* (Los Angeles: The Museum of Contemporary Art, 1984), 23, 41.

30. An illustration of Black Power–era merchandise is seen in Van Deburg, *New Day in Babylon,* 14.

31. See Nicholas von Hoffman, "Pop Goes the Gangsta, Farrakhan's Message Routs a Pernicious Role Model," *Washington Post,* November 12, 1995, C1, C4; and Donna Franklin, "Black Herstory," *New York Times,* October 18, 1995, A19.

32. Brown quoted in Pearson, *Shadow of the Panther,* 336; hooks, *Black Looks,* 7.

15   Shadow of a Clue

Errol Anthony Henderson

1. Hugh Pearson, *The Shadow of the Panther: Huey Newton and the Price of Black Power in America* (Reading, Mass.: Addison-Wesley, 1994).

2. Lori Robinson, "A Panther Caged by His Own Demons," *Emerge,* June, 1994, 66.

3. Pearson, *Shadow of the Panther,* 108, 109.

4. Ibid., 23.

5. Ibid., 30–32.

6. The lumpen proletariat consisted of the vagabonds, ex-convicts, ex-slaves, swindlers, pickpockets, beggars, and so on that Louis Bonaparte used during his power struggle. Karl Marx, in *The Eighteenth Brumaire of Louis Bonaparte* (1852; reprint, New York: International Publishers, 1969), saw them as "scum" and he did not consider them revolutionary (76–77). By contrast, Frantz Fanon, in *The Wretched of the Earth* (New York: Grove, 1968), 136–37, drawing on the experience of revolutionary Algeria, insisted that the lumpen proletariat is essential to the success of the revolution.

7. Pearson, *Shadow of the Panther,* 335.

8. David Hilliard and Lewis Cole, *This Side of Glory* (Boston: Little, Brown 1993), 407–8.

9. Ibid., 353.

10. Pearson, *Shadow of the Panther,* 13–108.

11. See Harold Cruse, *The Crisis of the Negro Intellectual* (New York: William Morrow, 1968).

12. See Ward Churchill and Jim Vander Wall, *Agents of Repression: The FBI's Secret Wars against the Black Panther Party and the American Indian Movement* (Boston:

South End Press, 1988).

13. Pearson, *Shadow of the Panther,* 264.
14. Ibid., 151.
15. See Malcolm X with Alex Haley, *The Autobiography of Malcolm X* (New York: Grove Press, 1964).
16. Robinson, "Panther Caged."
17. Pearson, *Shadow of the Panther,* 347.
18. Ibid., 339.
19. Errol Henderson, "Black Nationalism and Rap Music," *Journal of Black Studies* 26, no. 3 (1996): 308–39.
20. Julius Nyerere, *Freedom and Development.* (New York: Oxford University Press, 1974), 25.
21. Pearson, *Shadow of the Panther,* 339.
22. The author is indebted to Akinsanya Kambon for the discussion of Scott, Washington, and Hakim.
23. The BGF is allegedly the remnant of the organization developed by former BPP field marshal George Jackson, which operates primarily (though not exclusively) behind the walls of California prisons. A rift developed between the BGF and Huey Newton in the early 1970s as Huey began to opt more for reform and the BGF advocated a much more militant stance.
24. Cited in Basil Davidson, *The Liberation of Guinea* (New York: Penguin, 1971), 74.
25. Hilliard and Cole, *Glory,* 338–39.
26. Huey Newton, "Black Capitalism Reanalyzed," *Black Panther,* June 5, 1971, 9.
27. Cited in Philip S. Foner, ed., *The Black Panthers Speak* (New York: J. B. Lippincott, 1970), 50.
28. Hilliard and Cole, *Glory,* 168.
29. See Errol Henderson, *Afrocentrism and World Politics* (Westport, Conn.: Praeger, 1995).
30. William Van Deburg, *New Day in Babylon* (Chicago: University of Chicago, 1992), 176.
31. Malcolm X, "Malcolm X Founds the Organization of Afro-American Unity [Statement of Basic Aims of the Organization of Afro-American Unity]," In *Black Protest Thought in the Twentieth Century,* ed. A. Meier, E. Rudwick, and F. Broderick (1964; reprint, New York: Macmillan, 1971), 419–20.
32. See Eldridge Cleaver, "Culture and Revolution: Their Synthesis in Africa," in *Pan Africanism,* ed. R. Chrisman and N. Hare (New York: Bobbs-Merrill, 1974), 75–79.
33. Foner, *Black Panthers Speak,* 124–27.
34. Hilliard and Cole, *Glory,* 319.
35. Pearson, *Shadow of the Panther,* 234–35. Also, see John McCartney, *Black Power Ideologies* (Philadelphia, PA: Temple University Press, 1992), 136–50, noting Newton's contribution to black political theory (e.g., Huey Newton, *War Against the Panthers: A Study of Repression in America* [New York: Harlem River Press, 1980]).
36. Assata Shakur, *Assata: An Autobiography* (Chicago: Lawrence Hill, 1987), 221.
37. Pearson, *Shadow of the Panther,* 344.
38. NAIM—New Afrikan Independence Movement—includes the RNA, New Afrikan People's Organization, the BLA, and other ancillary organizations that support the liberation of the "New Afrikan" nation in the United States (see Chokwe Lumumba, *The Roots of the New Afrikan Independence Movement* [Jackson, Miss.: New Afrikan Productions, 1992]).
39. Works in that direction include Shakur, *Assata;* and Sundiata Acoli, *Sunviews* (Newark, N.J.: Creative Images, 1983).

16   Rediscovering the Black Panther Party

Victor Wallis

1. For a more detailed discussion of this evolution, see my articles "Keeping the Faith: The U.S. Left, 1968–1998," *Monthly Review* 50, September 1998, 4; and "The U.S. Left Since 1968: Decline or Growth?" *New Political Science* 21, September 1999, 3.
2. *All Power to the People,* a two-hour documentary completed in 1996, is available on videotape from Electronic News Group, P.O. Box 86208, Los Angeles, CA 90086-0208.
3. For documentation on the role of U.S. government agencies in the King assassination, see William F. Pepper, *Orders to Kill: The Truth Behind the Murder of Martin Luther King* (New York: Carroll & Graf, 1995).
4. Winston A. Grady-Willis, "The Black Panther Party: State Repression and Political Prisoners," in *The Black Panther Party Reconsidered,* ed. Charles E. Jones (Baltimore: Black Classic Press, 1998), 374.
5. See for example Hampton's 27 April 1969 speech, in Philip S. Foner (ed.), *The Black Panthers Speak* (New York: Da Capo Press, 1995 [1970]), 138–144.
6. See Ward Churchill's chapter in this book, most of the research for which was detailed in his earlier work (with Jim Vander Wall), *Agents of Repression: The FBI's Secret Wars against the Black Panther Party and the American Indian Movement* (Boston: South End Press, 1988). Both Churchill and Vander Wall are interviewed in Lew-Lee's film.
7. See Grady-Willis, "The Black Panther Party: State Repression and Political Prisoners"; also *Cages of Steel: The Politics of Imprisonment in the United States,* ed. Churchill and Vander Wall (Washington, DC: Maisonneuve Press, 1992). For current information, see www.thejerichomovement.com.
8. See Jim Vander Wall, "A Warrior Caged: The Continuing Struggle of Leonard Peltier," in *Cages of Steel,* 244–269.
9. The CIA's long-delayed acknowledgment of its role in this process was reported in the *New York Times,* 17 July 1998, A1. For background, see Alexander Cockburn and Jeffrey St. Clair, *Whiteout: The CIA, Drugs and the Press* (London: Verso: 1998).
10. *The Black Panthers Speak,* 61, 82.
11. Ibid., 277.
12. The "emergency" dimension of the New Left is a theme of my previously cited 1998 article; the Panthers' influence on the wider movement is discussed in my 1999 article, p. 369.
13. Chris Booker, "Lumpenization: A Critical Error of the Black Panther Party," in Jones, *The Black Panther Party Reconsidered.*
14. Right-wing and mainstream critics, following the lead of David Horowitz, have built up a cottage industry of decontextualized horror stories about certain Panthers or former Panthers. I would not wish to question the severity of some of the cases they describe, but I do question the critics' sense of proportion. They routinely disregard, on the one hand, the many ways in which state repression set the tone for people's interaction and, on the other, the numerous examples of BPP members who, despite enormous imposed hardships (especially in prison), have maintained their integrity.
15. Eldridge Cleaver, "An Open Letter to Stokely Carmichael," in *The Black Panthers Speak,* 105.
16. *The Black Panthers Speak,* 139.

17 Tracking Down the Empirical Legacy of the Black Panther Party; or, Notes on the Perils of Pursuing the Panthers

Claudia Dahlerus and Christian A. Davenport

1. Often "conveniently" forgotten or misplaced, in the case of law enforcement agencies.
2. For useful commentaries on qualitative research see John Van Maanen, *Tales of the Field: On Writing Ethnography* (Chicago: University of Chicago Press, 1988); and William Shaffir and Robert Stebbins, eds., *Experiencing Fieldwork: An Inside View of Qualitative Research* (Newbury Park, Calif.: Sage, 1991).
3. Appendices and tables may be obtained by writing the authors at: Center for Comparative Politics, Department of Political Science, University of Colorado-Boulder, Campus Box 333, Boulder, CO 80309.
4. Ann Mari Buitrago and Leon Immerman, *Are You Now or Have You Ever Been in the FBI Files?* (New York: Grove Press, 1981); FOIA Inc., *Freedom of Information Act* (New York: FOIA Inc., 1988); Richard O. Curry, ed., *Freedom at Risk: Secrecy, Censorship and Repression in the 1980's* (Philadelphia: Temple University Press, 1988); Eve Pell, *The Big Chill: How the Reagan Administration, Corporate America, and Religious Conservatism Are Subverting Free Speech and the Public's Right to Know* (Boston: Beacon Press, 1984).
5. Michael Parenti, *Inventing Reality: The Politics of News Media* (New York: St. Martin's Press, 1993), 24.
6. Yet we would not be making the inquiry if we knew everything to begin with.
7. This might be attributed to their somewhat outdated (or antiquated) card catalog system, which had a significant amount of information written on each card, accompanied by crossed-out and ambiguous writing.
8. We mention cost particularly because when visiting various libraries in the course of our field research, we operated under very tight time and budgetary constraints. Simply, we did not have the luxury to spend weeks on end at each library, waiting and sifting through their often eclectic collections of "BPP" or social protest material.
9. Rudolph Rummel, "Dimensions of Conflict Behavior within and between Nations," *General Systems Yearbook* 8 (1963): 1–50; Charles Tilly, *Study of Urbanization and Political Upheaval in France: Codebook for Intensive Sample of Disturbances* (Boston: Joint Center for Urban Studies of the Massachusetts Institute of Technology and Harvard University); Ted Gurr and Associates, *Comparative Studies of Political Conflict and Change: Cross National Datasets (Civil Strife Events, Conflict Magnitudes, Conflict and Society, Polity Persistence and Change)* (Ann Arbor, Mich.: Inter-University Consortium for Political and Social Research, 1978); Arthur Banks, *Cross-Polity Time-Series Data* (Cambridge: MIT Press, 1971); Ivo Feierabend, Rosalind Feierabend, and Betty Nesvold, *Systemic Conditions of Political Aggression* (Ann Arbor, Mich.: Inter-University Consortium for Political and Social Research, 1975); Charles Taylor and Michael Hudson, *World Handbook of Political and Social Indicators,* 2d ed. (New Haven, Conn.: Yale University Press, 1972).
10. Charles Taylor and Michael Hudson, *World Handbook of Political and Social Indicators,* 3d ed. (New Haven: Yale University Press, 1983); Doug Bond and Joe Bond, *Protocol for the Assessment of Nonviolent Direct Action* (codebook for dataset); Ron Francisco (codebook for dataset, available from http://lark.cc.ukans.edu/~ronfran/data/index.html); Will Moore and Ronny Lindstrom, *The Violent Intranational Conflict Data Project* (codebook for dataset, available from http://garnet.acns.fsu/edu/~whmoore/).
11. Please consult the website for updates and more information: http://www.bsos.umd.edu/cidcm/projects/rip/proj1.htm
12. Aldon Morris, "Black Southern Student Sit-In Movement: An Analysis of Internal

Organization," *American Sociological Review 45* (1981): 744–67; Herbert Haines, "Black Radicalization and the Funding of Civil Rights, 1957–1970," *Social Problems* 32 (1984/1985): 31–43; Doug McAdam, *Political Process and the Development of Black Insurgency, 1930–1970* (Chicago: University of Chicago Press, 1982).

13. Ted Robert Gurr, *Comparative Studies of Political Conflict and Change: Cross National Datasets* (Ann Arbor, Michigan: Inter-University Consortium for Political and Social Reseach, 1978).

14. Charles Tilly, *From Mobilization to Revolution* (Reading, Mass.: Addison-Wesley Publishing Company, 1978).

15. Susan Olzak, *The Dynamics of Ethnic Competition and Conflict* (Stanford, Stanford University Press, 1992).

16. Gary King, Robert Keohane and Sidney Verba, *Designing Social Inquiry* (Princeton, N.J.: Princeton University Press, 1994), 27.

17. Whether social science should be practiced in this manner is beside the point; the issue is how best to maximize the likelihood that one can obtain funding for research.

18. I say "perhaps" only because race seemed to be an issue at certain points throughout my work with the coders. To ignore it as such would be indulging in naïveté, yet placing too much emphasis on race as a factor is to be oversensitive. Either extreme impedes the overall objective, which is to collect information.

19. We do not mean to undervalue the skills and contributions of graduate research assistants. Comparatively, one expects to see more dedication, understanding, and simple mature responsibility in terms of the work they perform for the project because of their own professional pursuits in graduate school. In fact, it is this last that might make graduates less devoted to their research duties for other faculty.

20. An inversion of the title of a record album by EPMD.

21. Milan Kundera, *Testaments Betrayed: An Essay in Nine Parts* (New York: HarperCollins, 1995), 128–29.

22. Or, to invoke Plato's metaphor of knowledge, we were out of the cave of fictional reality and into the world of forms and understanding.

23. Michel-Rolph Trouillot, *Silencing the Past: Power and the Production of History* (Boston: Beacon Press, 1995), 25.

24. Ibid., 26.

25. Many view this as the curse of rational scientism, and a by-product of Eurocentric enlightenment thinking.

26. This intellectual agenda setting is analogous to Peter Bachrach and Morton S. Baratz's second dimension of power—that of setting political agendas which decide what issues are worthy of discussion, and who may participate in such discourses, See Bachrach and Baratz, *Power and Poverty* (New York: Oxford University Press, 1970); and John Gaventa, *Power and Powerlessness* (Illinois: University of Illinois Press, 1982), 4–14.

Appendices

October 1966 Black Panther Party Platform and Program

What We Want, What We Believe

1. *We want freedom. We want power to determine the destiny of our Black Community.* We believe that black people will not be free until we are able to determine our destiny.

2. *We want full employment for our people.* We believe that the federal government is responsible and obligated to give every man employment or a guaranteed income. We believe that if the white American businessmen will not give full employment, then the means of production should be taken from the businessmen and placed in the community so that the people of the community can organize and employ all of its people and give a high standard of living.

3. *We want an end to the robbery by the white man of our Black Community.* We believe that this racist government has robbed us and now we are demanding the overdue debt of forty acres and two mules. Forty acres and two mules was promised 100 years ago as restitution for slave labor and mass murder of black people. We will accept the payment in currency which will be distributed to our many communities. The Germans are now aiding Jews in Israel for the genocide of the Jewish people. The Germans murdered six million Jews. The American racist has taken part in the slaughter of over fifty million black people; therefore, we feel that this is a modest demand that we make.

4. *We want decent housing, fit for shelter of human beings.* We believe that if the white landlords will not give decent housing to our black community, then the housing and the land should be made into cooperatives so that our community, with government aid, can build and make decent housing for its people.

5. *We want education for our people that exposes the true nature of this decadent American society. We want education that teaches us our true history and our role in the present-day society.* We believe in an educational system that will give to our people a knowledge of self. If a man does not have knowledge of himself and his position in society and the world, then he has little chance to relate to anything else.

6. *We want all black men to be exempt from military service.* We believe that Black people should not be forced to fight in the military service to defend a racist government that does not protect us. We will not fight and kill other people of color in the world who, like black people, are being victimized by the white racist government of America. We will protect ourselves from the force and violence of the racist police and the racist military, by whatever means necessary.

7. *We want an immediate end to POLICE BRUTALITY and MURDER of black people.* We believe we can end police brutality in our black community by organizing black self-defense

groups that are dedicated to defending our black community from racist police oppression and brutality. The Second Amendment to the Constitution of the United States gives a right to bear arms. We therefore believe that all black people should arm themselves for self-defense.

8. *We want freedom for all black men held in federal, state, county and city prisons and jails.* We believe that all black people should be released from the many jails and prisons because they have not received a fair and impartial trial.

9. *We want all black people when brought to trial to be tried in court by a jury of their peer group or people from their black communities, as defined by the Constitution of the United States.* We believe that the courts should follow the United States Constitution so that black people will receive fair trials. The 14th Amendment to the U.S. Constitution gives a man a right to be tried by his peer group. A peer is a person from a similar economic, social, religious, geographical, environmental, historical and racial background. To do this the court will be forced to select a jury from the black community from which the black defendant came. We have been, and are being tried by all-white juries that have no understanding of the "average reasoning man" of the black community.

10. *We want land, bread, housing, education, clothing, justice and peace. And as our major political objective, a United Nations-supervised plebiscite to be held throughout the black colony in which only black colonial subjects will be allowed to participate, for the purpose of determining the will of black people as to their national destiny.* When, in the course of human events, it becomes necessary for one people to dissolve the political bands which have connected them with another, and to assume, among the powers of the earth, the separate and equal station to which the laws of nature and nature's God entitle them, a decent respect to the opinions of mankind requires that they should declare the causes which impel them to the separation.

We hold these truths to be self-evident, that all men are created equal; that they are endowed by their Creator with certain unalienable rights; that among these are life, liberty, and the pursuit of happiness. *That, to secure these rights, governments are instituted among men, deriving their just powers from the consent of the governed; that, whenever any form of government becomes destructive of these ends, it is the right of the people to alter or to abolish it, and to institute a new government, laying its foundation on such principles, and organizing its powers in such form, as to them shall seem most likely to effect their safety and happiness.* Prudence, indeed, will dictate that governments long established should not be changed for light and transient causes; and, accordingly, all experience hath shown, that mankind are more disposed to suffer, while evils are sufferable, than to right themselves by abolishing the forms to which they are accustomed. *But, when a long train of abuses and usurpations, pursuing invariably the same object, evinces a design to reduce them under absolute despotism, it is their right, it is their duty, to throw off such government, and to provide new guards for their future security.*

Rules of the Black Panther Party (Central Headquarters, Oakland, California)

Every member of the BLACK PANTHER PARTY throughout this country of racist America must abide by these rules as functional members of this party. CENTRAL COMMITTEE members, CENTRAL STAFFS, and LOCAL STAFFS, including all captains subordinate to either national, state, and local leadership of the BLACK PANTHER PARTY will enforce these rules. Length of suspension or other disciplinary action necessary for violation of these rules will depend on national decisions by national, state or state area, and local communities and staffs where said rule or rules of the BLACK PANTHER PARTY WERE VIOLATED.

Every member of the party must know these verbatim by heart. And apply them daily. Each member must report any violation of these rules to their leadership or they are counter-revolutionary and are also subjected to suspension by the BLACK PANTHER PARTY.

The Rules:

1. No party member can have narcotics or weed in his possession while doing party work.
2. Any party member found shooting narcotics will be expelled from this party.
3. No party member can be DRUNK while doing daily party work.
4. No party member will violate rules relating to office work, general meetings of the BLACK PANTHER PARTY, and meetings of the BLACK PANTHER PARTY ANYWHERE.
5. No party member will USE, POINT, or FIRE a weapon of any kind unnecessarily or accidentally at anyone.
6. No party member can join any other army force other than the BLACK LIBERATION ARMY.
7. No party member can have a weapon in his possession while DRUNK or loaded off narcotics or weed.
8. No party member will commit any crimes against other party members or BLACK people at all, and cannot steal or take from the people, not even a needle or a piece of thread.
9. When arrested BLACK PANTHER MEMBERS will give only name, address, and will sign nothing. Legal first aid must be understood by all Party members.
10. The Ten-Point Program and platform of the BLACK PANTHER PARTY must be known and understood by each Party member.
11. Party Communications must be National and Local.
12. The 10-10-10 program should be known by all members and also understood by all members.
13. All Finance officers will operate under the jurisdiction of the Ministry of Finance.
14. Each person will submit a report of daily work.
15. Each Sub-Section Leaders, Section Leaders, and Lieutenants, Captains must submit Daily reports of work.
16. All Panthers must learn to operate and service weapons correctly.
17. All Leadership personnel who expel a member must submit this information to the Editor of the Newspaper, so that it will be published in the paper and will be known by all chapters and branches.
18. Political Education Classes are mandatory for general membership.
19. Only office personnel assigned to respective offices each day should be there. All others are to sell papers and do Political work out in the community, including Captains, Section Leaders, etc.
20. COMMUNICATIONS—all chapters must submit weekly reports in writing to the National Headquarters.
21. All Branches must implement First Aid and/or Medical Cadres.
22. All Chapters, Branches, and components of the BLACK PANTHER PARTY must submit a monthly Financial Report to the Ministry of Finance, and also the Central Committee.

23. Everyone in a leadership position must read no less than two hours per day to keep abreast of the changing political situation.
24. No chapter or branch shall accept grants, poverty funds, money or any other aid from any government agency without contacting the National Headquarters.
25. All chapters must adhere to the policy and the ideology laid down by the CENTRAL COMMITTEE of the BLACK PANTHER PARTY.
26. All Branches must submit weekly reports in writing to their respective Chapters.

Eight Points of Attention

1. Speak politely.
2. Pay fairly for what you buy.
3. Return everything you borrow.
4. Pay for anything you damage.
5. Do not hit or swear at people.
6. Do not damage property or crops of the poor, oppressed masses.
7. Do not take liberties with women.
8. If we ever have to take captives do not ill-treat them.

Three Main Rules of Discipline

1. Obey orders in all your actions
2. Do not take a single needle or a piece of thread from the poor and oppressed masses.
3. Turn in everything captured from the attacking enemy.

Why the Free Breakfast?

The Free Breakfast for Children is just one of the programs being carried out by the Black Panther Party that can be attributed to Huey P. Newton. Huey P. Newton, organizer and Minister of Defense of the Black Panther Party says that the Party must go forth to meet the basic desires and needs of the people. Huey says the members of the Party are oxen to be ridden by the people.

How is the Party ridden by the people? Panthers working the breakfast program get out of bed at approximately 6:00 A.M. every school day. They set tables, clean facilities, cook and prepare the food, they direct traffic to see that the children cross the streets safely. After a day's breakfast has been completed, the Panthers attend to the constant task of procuring food from the merchants who do business in the community, to see that the program is constantly supplied with the necessary food. Why a Breakfast for Children Program? The answers to this question need be answered for only those who belong to the upper or so-called middle class. The majority of all Black, Mexican-American, Orientals and poor Whites know from their American experience that it is impossible to obtain and sustain any education when one has to attend school hungry.

Huey P. Newton knew that these conditions existed and that the American school system has not seen fit to alleviate them. Validity has been added to Huey's knowledge by the fact that the Free Breakfast program has spread like wild fire across the United States wherever Black Panther Chapters and Branches exist.

The Free Breakfast for Children program is a socialistic program, designed to serve the people. All institutions in a society should be designed to serve the masses, not just a "chosen few." In America this program is revolutionary. In capitalist America any program that is absolutely free is considered bad business. The Black Panther Party is a vanguard organization and a vanguard organization educates by example. The Black Panther Party is educating the people to the fact they have a right to the best that modern technology and human knowledge can produce. "The world belongs to all the people."

For too long our children have gone hungry (*The Black Panther,* October 4, 1969).

Revolutionary Peoples' Constitutional Convention September 1970, Philadelphia Workshop Reports

Workshop on Internationalism and Relations with Liberation Struggles around the World

The Revolutionary Peoples' Constitutional Convention supports the demand of the Chinese people for the liberation of Taiwan. We demand the liberation of Okinawa and the Pacific Territories occupied by U.S. and European imperialist countries. The Revolutionary Peoples' Constitutional Convention supports the struggles and endorses the government of the provisional revolutionary government of South Vietnam, the royal government of National Union of Cambodia, and the Pathet Lao (Huey P. Newton, Minister of Defense, Black Panther Party).

In order to insure our international constitution, we, the people of Babylon, declare an international bill of rights: that all people are guaranteed the right to life, liberty and the pursuit of happiness, that all people of the world be free from dehumanization and intervention in their internal affairs by a foreign power. Therefore, if fascist actions in the world attempt to achieve imperialist goals, they will be in violation of the law and dealt with as criminals.

We are in full support with the struggle of the Palestinian people for liberation of Palestine from Zionist colonialism, and their goals of creating a democratic state where all Palestinians, Jews, Christians and Moslems are equal.

We propose solidarity with the liberation struggle of the Puerto Rican people, who now exist as a colony of the United States and have many groups who are fighting for liberation, such as C.A.L. (Armed Commandos for Liberation), M.I.R.A. and the Young Lords Party.

We propose that, whereas the universities in the United States are used by the imperialist system to provide the knowledge that that system uses to perpetrate the exploitation of the Third World and repression against national liberation struggles, we propose that the universities and their resources be turned over to use for, by, and of the peoples of the world so that they may implement their vision of a new socialist world.

1. The United States is an international federation of bandits and we denounce its rights to nationhood.
2. We should provoke the destruction of all racists and fascists in capitalistic countries and the world over. We should not rest until all of them are wiped off the face of the earth.

Mimeographed originals in the collection of George Katsiaficas.

3. We support all liberation struggles throughout the world and we oppose all reactionary struggles throughout the world.
4. Our constitution will guarantee the right of all people to travel and communicate with all peoples throughout the world.
5. We stand resolute in our unrelenting convictions to destroy Pig Amerikka.
6. Wherever the word "men" appears it should be replaced with the word "people" to express solidarity with the self-determination of woman and to do away with all remnants of male supremacy, once and for all.
7. We propose that we declare a just peoples' war against capitalism and remain in that state until capitalism is abolished from the face of the Earth.
8. We should have an organization or army to defend the kidnapping and terror of pigs as a means of freeing political prisoners of war.
9. We oppose such organizations as NATO and SEATO and all lackeys of U.S. imperialism.
10. We demand immediate withdrawal of all American forces around the world.
11. Reparations should be made to oppressed people throughout the world, and we pledge ourselves to take the wealth of this country and make it available as reparations.
12. We will not allow or accept this country going into other countries and utilizing their wealth.
13. We will administer all foreign aid given by the U.S. by an international body composed of representatives from revolutionary people.
14. We will use our more advanced revolutionary brothers and sisters to better the struggle.
15. We demand an end to the genocide caused by sterilization programs in different forms—nationally and international.

All Power to the People

Self-Determination of Street People

What We Want

We want an immediate end to the crimes of pimping, prostitution, number rackets, gambling, dope pushing, fencing, loan sharking, sexism, rape, theft, pick pockets, bribery, extortion, union corruption, etc., committed on the people by organized crime syndicates which work hand in hand with the pig power structure and those lackeys within our communities who refuse to deal with these problems.
1. Creation of investigative councils run by the people.
2. Encourage informers to turn over information to these councils.
3. Remove by force those elements which have been exposed.
4. Confiscation or destruction of property controlled by organized crime syndicates.
5. The encouragement of all progressive forces and elements to change corruption in government and enforce revolutionary justice.

Education

All people will be provided with the kind of schooling they desire and need. All levels of schooling will be provided free by the government. Schooling must be non-compulsory.

The community will control the schools, education, curriculum, and educators. Education must be part and parcel of the political realities of the time. Education must always serve the people by teaching the true nature of this decadent society.

Dope

We recognize that hard drugs (smack, speed, etc.) are counterrevolutionary, sapping the strength of the people in their struggle. This problem must be dealt with on two levels. The seller of hard drugs must be eradicated from the community by any means necessary. The user must be helped to rid himself of addiction by the people. We urge setting up of a People's Rehabilitation Center by the people.

We recognize that psychedelic drugs (acid, mescaline, grass) are important in developing the revolutionary consciousness of the people. However, after the revolutionary consciousness has been achieved, these drugs may become a burden. No revolutionary action should be attempted while under the influence of any drug. We urge that these drugs be made legal. Or rather that they should not be illegal, that is, there should be no law made against them.

Land

We hold that private property is theft.

We demand the use of parks, streets, rural areas, and unused land to carry on our revolutionary struggle for survival. We will seize the land we need by any means necessary. Streets and urban parks must be liberated to be used for people's needs such as: 1) mass meetings, 2) concerts and recreation, 3) sleeping area, and other everyday activities.

Rural land and large state parks must be liberated to be used for: military training in the techniques of self defense and urban guerilla warfare in order to fight a war of liberation, and land to be used for farming and other productive needs.

Grievance

All private rural land has been stolen from the people. It originally belonged to the people. It is being used for capitalistic goals and is being destroyed ecologically.

Food, Housing, Clothing, Health

We demand the right for all people to have free food, housing, free clothing, free medical care and all other rights established by the Revolutionary People's Constitutional Convention.

Recognizing our responsibility as revolutionary street people in this period of transition

1. We call for free de-centralized medical care and the availability of medical information (curative and preventive) for all the people in the neighborhood to meet the daily situations in a revolutionary manner.
2. We call for the establishment of free inter-relative community food cooperatives to collect, exchange, store, distribute and provide food and cooking facilities for the community needs.

3. We demand community control of the means of production of clothing and adequate sharing and distributing of clothing to meet the needs of the people.
4. We demand the replacement of deteriorated housing with the construction of adequate low-income housing which is available for those people whose housing is replaced and the control of community removal programs by the people in those communities.

Finally, we call for the formation of Revolutionary People's Community Councils to be responsible for the implementation of all collective needs of the community.

Workshop on the Self Determination of Women

- We recognize the right of all women to be free.
- As women, we recognize that our struggle is against a racist, capitalist, sexist system that oppresses all minority people.
- This capitalistic country is run by a small ruling class who use the ideas and practices of chauvinism and racism to divide, control and oppress the masses of people for their own greedy gains and profit.
- We want equal status in a society that does not exploit or murder other people.
- We will fight for a socialist system that guarantees full, creative, non-exploitative life for all human beings.
- We will not be free until all oppressed people are free.

Family

Whereas in a capitalist culture, the institution of the family has been used as an economic tool or instrument, not serving the needs of the people. We declare that we will not relate to the private ownership of people. We encourage and support the continued growth of communal households and communal relationships and other alternatives to the patriarchal family.

We call for socialization of housework and child care with the sharing of work by men and women.

Women must have the right to decide when and if we want to have children. There should be free and safe birth control, including abortion, available upon demand. There should be no forced sterilization or mandatory birth control programs which are now used as genocide against third world sisters and against poor people.

Every woman has the right to decide whether she will be homosexual, heterosexual or bisexual.

Employment

Whereas women in a class society have been continuously exploited, through their work, both in their home and outside their home, we call for:

1. Guaranteed full, equal and non-exploitative employment, controlled collectively by the working people.
2. Guaranteed adequate income for all. This would entail the sharing of necessary, non-creative tasks and the maximum utilization of revolutionary technology to eliminate these tasks.

3. An end to the sexism which forces women into the lowest paying service jobs and the racism that insures that third world women will be the lowest paid of all.
4. Guaranteed paid maternity leave.

Education

Whereas women historically have been deprived of education, or only partially educated and mis-educated in those areas deemed appropriate for us by those ruling powers who would benefit by our ignorance; we call for:

1. The right to determine our own goals.
2. The end of sex roles regarding training or skills.
3. Self-knowledge: the history of women, our relation to society and the knowledge of our bodies.
4. Guaranteed technological and professional training and in the interim, special programs should be set up in every field in which women have been denied equality, such as child care.
5. Men to be trained in those areas in which they have been denied equality, such as child care.
6. Control of non-authoritarian education by the people it serves in the language and cultural style of the people.

Services

Whereas the services provided for the people have been inadequate, unavailable or too expensive, administered in a racist and sexist manner, we declare that:

1. All services—health care, housing, food, clothing, transportation and education—should be controlled by the people: and should be free.
2. Services for women should be controlled by the women of the community which they serve.

Media

The mass media is not permitted to exploit women's bodies in order to sell or promote products. Women must be treated with respect and dignity at all times by the peoples' media. The peoples' media will work to eliminate sexist terminology: he, man, mankind; when we mean person, people, humanity.

Self-Defense

Whereas the struggle of the people must be borne equally by all the people fighting for their liberation, we declare that women have the right to bear arms. Women should be fully trained and educated in the art of self-defense and the defense of the peoples' nation. We recognize that it is our duty to defend all oppressed people.

Women in Our Own Right

Whereas we do not believe that any person is the property of any other person, we declare that women have the right to bear their own surnames, not names determined by their husbands or fathers. We demand that all organizations, ranging from health insurance to social security to banks, deal with women in our own right as people, rather than as the property of men.

Equal Participation in Govenment

Whereas all revolutionary people must share equally in the decisions which effect them, we are dedicated to the national salvation of all humanity.

All Power to the People

Statement of Demands from the Male Representatives of National Gay Liberation

We demand:

1. The right to be gay anytime, anyplace.
2. The right to free physiological change and modification of sex upon demand.
3. The right of free dress and adornment.
4. That all modes of human sexual self-expression deserve protection of the law and social sanction.
5. Every child's right to develop in a non-sexist, non-possessive atmosphere, which is the responsibility of all people to create.
6. That a free educational system present the entire range of human sexuality, without advocating any form or style . . . that sex roles and sex determined skills not be fostered by the schools.
7. That language be modified so that no gender takes priority.
8. That the judicial system be run by the people through people's courts and that all people be tried by members of their peer group.
9. That gays be represented in all governmental and community institutions.
10. That organized religions be condemned for aiding in the genocide of gay people, and enjoined from teaching hatred and superstition.
11. That psychiatry and psychology be enjoined from advocating a preference for any form of sexuality, and the enforcement of that preference by shock treatment, brainwashing, imprisonment, etc.
12. The abolition of the nuclear family because it perpetuates the false categories of homosexuality and heterosexuality.
13. The immediate release and reparations for gay political prisoners from prisons and mental institutions; the support of gay political prisoners by all other political prisoners.
14. That gays determine the destiny of their own communities.
15. That all people share equally the labor and products of society, regardless of sex or sexual orientation.
16. That technology be used to liberate all peoples of the world from drudgery.
17. The full participation of gays in the Peoples' Revolutionary Army.
18. Finally, the end of domination of one person by another.

Gay Power to Gay People

All Power to the People

Seize the Time

Workshop: The Family and the Rights of Children

1. The discussion was not truly representative of all oppressed groups, since, for example, there were no children present.
2. Some people felt that the traditional family was so oppressive that it must be abolished and replaced by a different family grouping. Others felt that there were positive things in the traditional family that should be perpetuated in the new world. It was also pointed out that we can't predict what the traditional family might be like under socialism.
3. It was agreed that children are not possessions and are not to be treated as possessions by parents, collectives or the state.
4. General agreement was that children are entitled to the broadest possible education.
5. Children are entitled to be brought up to have the greatest trust, confidence and sense of sharing with the other people in their society.
6. The responsibility for creating those conditions that would enable a child to be a whole human being rests with all of us.
7. We agreed that children's feelings and viewpoints should be respected.
8. It was agreed that children have the right to be breast fed.
9. A child must be reared to be sexually free and have his choices respected.
10. Children are essential to adults as teachers because children naturally resist oppression.
11. Children must be loved in a truly revolutionary manner. Children are people.

All Power to the People

Control and Use of the Legal System and Political Prisoners of War

The present judicial system in the United States is nothing more than an instrument and tool of class rule, representing the will of the racist ruling class, made into a law for everyone. The laws themselves and the procedural aspects such as bail, cater to the customs and mores of the ruling class.

At this time, in the transitional stage prior to the post revolutionary society, the call for peoples' revolutionary tribunes will be made. The function of these tribunals will be as the peoples' tribunals for revolutionaries who might be at the same time, on trial in the existing legal system of the ruling class. These tribunals will be decentralized and arise out of the area where the incidents or alleged crimes themselves took place.

While the struggle is still being waged, the people must learn to manipulate and utilize the existing court system, through political trials, in order to develop a revolutionary political consciousness and illustrate the true nature of this corrupt legal system before the people.

The courts should serve the people and in this racist society that can only be done by a jury of one's peers. Understanding of the laws is a matter of interpretation which directly reflects one's social, economic and racial background. So if one is to be judged, he must be judged by a jury of his peers instead of by those with the standards and ideas of the racist ruling class.

If we are to talk of creating a legal system that has its foundation in man's human nature, we must talk of transforming the entire society. Therefore it becomes necessary to define for ourselves what is criminal.

Therefore:

Principles are the foundation by which the will of the people is insured. And if we are to talk of legality, criminals and crime, we must first talk of the ultimate crime. That is the crime of exploitation of man by man and the legal system that endorses and upholds it.

Since exploitation deprives people of the necessities of life and the fruits of their labor, it is the supreme crime and the exploiters are the supreme criminals.

We feel that all of the natural resources of the earth belongs to, and any exploitation, usurpation of man's labors and of the natural resources of the earth is an attack on man's survival and a crime. Any lack of action that denies human beings their right to exist are crimes against the people. Therefore, if the people are to control their destiny and thereby assure their own survival, then we must have a legal system that insures the abolishment of all forms of exploitation.

We recognize the armed body of the state, the fascist police force, is the protector and perpetrator of criminal acts and crimes. Not because the police per se are criminal by nature or criminal men, but because the function of the police and the armed forces in a capitalist society is criminal by nature. So we feel that the police should come from the community in which they live and that there should be no distinction between the people and the police because of their function.

Every man was born and therefore he has a right to live, a right to share in the wealth. If he is denied the right to work then he is denied the right to live. If he can't work, he deserves a high standard of living, regardless of his education or skill. It should be up to the administrators of the economic system to design a program for providing work or a livelihood for the people. To deny him this is to deny him life.

Because the present constitution in words guarantees us the right to live, in practice we are denied this most basic human right, we list the following guidelines as essential to our continued survival and prosperity:

1. All juries must consist of one's peers.
2. All courts should be peoples' courts.
3. All decisions of the people should be implemented in a collective manner by the people.
4. No judge, no policeman, no advocate should serve more than one year in any position of administrative trust without being reviewed by the people.

These guidelines, we, the people feel, are the best pre-requisites needed to insure a just and humane system.

Rights of Oppressed People and Political Prisoners

1. Because of the genocidal acts of the government of the United States, against the people of this country and the world:

Oppressed people (any class, ethnic group or social group that has its rights restricted by any means by any other group) have an absolute right and responsibility to defend themselves by any means necessary and effective against all forms of aggression, whether this aggression be by a direct act of violence or by the violation of their human rights, among which are the rights to food, clothing, shelter, adequate medical care, education and the inalienable right to self determination.

2. The people have not only the right to self-defense by any means necessary, but also the right to organize against all oppression and exploitation, to alter or abolish all existing legal structures, and to reorganize the society for the benefit of all the people.

3. Because the legal system of the U.S. exists to serve the ruling class and facilitate oppression and exploitation of the people, those people that are held in jails and prisons have not necessarily been incarcerated for crimes against the people; that therefore all prisoners be returned to their communities for trial by the peoples' court under a revolutionary process.

4. That all charges be dropped against the peoples' leaders so that they can return to leadership of their communities from jail and from exile because they have not committed any crimes against the people . . . . Bobby Seale, the Conn. 9, N.Y. 21, L.A. 18, Angela Davis, Soledad Brothers, Ahmed Evans, Martin Sostre. We say that while held, all political prisoners of war must be treated under international agreements regarding humane treatment.

Control and Use of the Educational System

1. Liberation schools set up for pre-school age children.
2. Entering school with a political consciousness.
3. Community control of schools:
   a. Parents controlling curriculum.
   b. Community elected board officers.
   c. Power to hire and fire teachers belongs to community elected board.
4. Intellectual and cultural education shall be available to all persons:
   a. Education will deal with the means of survival of the various portions of society.
   b. Education for students will deal with the student as an individual.
   c. The working of the system or political education should be taught for constant political consciousness.
   d. Schools and institutions will be free and make advanced study available to any person.
   e. The schools will encourage all persons to expand and realize their creative aspirations. It will especially encourage study in socialist society, human survival, and the truth and workings of the present society.

Students' Rights

1. Students in any school will have the right of freedom of speech, dress and assembly.
2. Student government should be controlled by the students:
   a. No rules set up for who runs for office, ex., grades, conduct, politics, participation in other activities.
   b. Student controlled press (paper), student board to decide what goes in paper and what does not go into it.
   c. Freedom to assembly whenever problems arise that the students feel should be solved collectively on a face to face basis.

d. Student activities not mandatory.

e. Assemblies left to student decision in accordance with what they feel should be solved relevant to those things that directly relate to them.

f. No guards in schools for any reason. Community and students will deal with all problems, major and minor.

g. Students decide their courses according to what they want and think they need. No set curriculum. Courses will be fit to students, not students to the courses.

h. New grading system established.

We the people believe that education should serve the people. It should expose the true nature of this society. Education should assist in teaching us our socialist ideas, and stand as a basis for our socialist practice.

The power of education should and will belong in the hands of the people. We believe that education plays a major role in this system of programming. So we the people must generate and seize this tool of the power structure and turn it into a weapon to be used against it.

All Power to the People

Workshop: Control and Use of Military and Police

Proposals on the Military

1. National defense shall be provided by a system of peoples' militia, trained in guerilla warfare, on a voluntary basis and consisting of both men and women.

2. The U.S. shall not maintain a standing army, since historically a standing army has been used for offensive actions against the people of the United States and around the world.

3. No genocidal weapons shall be manufactured or used.

4. All presently existing offensive equipment and installations shall be made inoperable and unserviceable for its original purpose.

5. The people shall be educated and informed on the action of the militia, and all records shall be open to the public.

6. The government shall be prohibited from sending any personnel, funds, or equipment to any nation for military or police purposes. It should also be prohibited from spending more than 10% of the national budget for any military or police purposes. This can be overridden by a majority vote in a national referendum.

7. No person shall serve full-time in the militia; those serving in the militia shall be paid a fair wage.

8. Militia members shall be governed by the laws of the community in which they serve (or governed by the laws of the nation??).

9. National defense shall be provided by a system of peoples' militias.

10. There shall be no conscription for any armed forces.

11. No peoples' militias shall be stationed outside national boundaries.

12. Government people and military personnel should be defined as one and the same, and not as separate entities in or of the power structure.

13. The people shall have the right to bear arms.

a. No citizen shall be prohibited the possession, control or purchase of small arms without the due process of law.

b. Free programs shall be set up in the training and use of small arms.

Organization, Use of, and Control of the Police

1. The police force shall be a rotating volunteer non-professional body coordinated by the Police Control Board from a (weekly) list of volunteers from each community section. The Police Control Board, its policies, as well as the police leadership, shall be chosen by direct popular majority vote of the community.
2. There shall not be set up, or permitted to exist, a national body of police, or secret body of police, nor shall un-uniformed police be permitted to exist.
3. Any citizen can bring charges against any member or officer of the police force before the Control Board, and the Control Board shall have the power to relieve that member or officer of the police force of his or her duty.
4. Community Police Councils may set up working relations and exchange information with police forces in other communities.
5. The purpose of the people's police force shall be to serve and protect the community.
6. No person can serve on both the police force and the Control Board at the same time.
7. Any member of the Control Board can be removed by direct, popular vote of the people.
8. Funds for community police and for the community's Control Board shall be provided for by national government under direction of the local Control Board.

Health

Health care is a right, not a privilege. We say that comprehensive medical care should not be sold as a commodity by a class of exploiters, interested in profit only. We recognize this profit motive is the outgrowth of a capitalist system which thrives on the exploitation of people and divides them on racist, sexist and class lines. Our solution is to make all aspects of health care meet the demands of all people through prevention, education and community control of health services.

1. Prevention (health checkups).
   a. Nutrition (educating people with regard to eating the right diets).
   b. Maternal and child care to put an end to:
      1. genocide.
      2. experimentation in the hospitals of oppressed people.
      3. experimentation in the public school system as a so-called mental health program.
      4. exploitation of children's behavior; children are given tranquilizers and put in a category as threats to the capitalist system.
   c. Senior citizens services (the right to be able to work as long as they can function).
   d. Regular examinations for all people.
   e. Better detection facilities (more emphasis should be placed on diseases that are more prevalent in minority group areas, e.g. sickle cell anemia).

    f. Medical teams should be sent out into the communities to seek out diseases and illnesses.

2. Education.
    a. Health education of the masses (symptoms of diseases in the home, first aid in the home).
    b. Training and retraining of present health workers.
    c. Ending professionalism (titles, etc.).
    d. Open admissions to all who want medical training.

3. Community control.
    a. Right of self determination to have children (not to be told by the capitalist system how many to have).
    b. Right to adequate economic means.
    c. Community boards should run all medical institutions.

4. Mental health.

We consider mental health to include both physical and mental well being. We recognize that much of the mental illness in our society is caused by the oppression of the capitalist system where psychiatry is used as a tool of fascism. It has also been used against homosexuals.

We are opposed to the medical industrial complex of medicine. We believe in socialized medicine. Inherent in this concept is prevention and free comprehensive, community controlled medicine. The only way to socialize medicine is through revolution.

Revolutionary Art

The workshop on the Revolutionary Arts and Artists hereby submit the following declaration to the Plenary Session of the Revolutionary People's Constitutional Convention:

We recognize:

1. That all people are born with a creative potential and that the society must guarantee that every person has the opportunity to develop and express that potential.
2. That art is a creative expression of a people's culture or way of life.
3. We recognize the right of every people's culture to its form of expression and that those forms of expressions should be preserved, encouraged and developed.
4. We recognize that art should be related to the interest, needs and aspirations of the people.

About the Authors

Mumia Abu-Jamal is an award-winning journalist, activist, and author who has been on Pennsylvania's death row since 1982 after having been convicted, under highly dubious conditions, of the December 1981 killing of a Philadelphia police officer. Prior to that event, he had gained prominence for his investigative reporting, particularly on issues of police misconduct. A member of the Black Panther Party when he was a high school student, he was subsequently president of the Philadelphia chapter of the National Association of Black Journalists. He holds a B.A. from Goddard College and an M.A. from California State University, Dominguez Hills. His essays, which cover a wide range of topics, have been collected in three books, which have sold more than 100,000 copies in seven languages: *Live from Death Row* (1995), *Death Blossoms* (1997), and *All Things Censored* (2000).

Stew Albert is an original Yippie, former editor of the *Berkeley Tribe,* onetime candidate for sheriff of Alameda County, former inmate of the Alameda County Jail, and an early white supporter and friend of the Black Panther Party and Black Panthers. He was an unindicted coconspirator in the Chicago 8 trial. He was a close associate of Jerry Rubin, Abbie Hoffman, Eldridge Cleaver, and Bobby Seale. Some of his life and times are portrayed in an upcoming Hollywood movie, *Steal This Movie.* Stew and his wife, Judy, coauthored *The Sixties Papers,* a widely used anthology of 1960s writings. He writes about the Black Panthers and many 1960s topics in his memoir, *Who the Hell Is Stew Albert?*, which is to be published by Red Hen Press in 2001. <stewa@aol.com>

Ward Churchill is professor and associate chair of the Department of Ethnic Studies at the University of Colorado, Boulder. The author, editor, or coauthor of seventeen books, he has been a member of the leadership council of the American Indian Movement (AIM) of Colorado since 1981. In 1969 he participated in the Rainbow Coalition established by Fred Hampton in Chicago and shared a house downstate with Mark Clark.

Kathleen Neal Cleaver worked full-time with the Student Nonviolent Coordinating Committee (SNCC), and afterward became the Communications Secretary of the Black Panther Party. Returning to the United States after sharing years of exile with her former husband Eldridge Cleaver, she subsequently earned both a B.A. and a J.D. from Yale University during the 1980s. As an assistant professor of law at Emory University, she served on Georgia's Supreme Court Commission on Racial and Ethnic Bias and became a board member of the Southern Center for Human Rights. She devoted many years to the defense of Geronimo ji Jaga (Pratt), a former Black Panther Party leader who won his habeas corpus petition in 1997 after being imprisoned for twenty-seven years as a result of being framed on murder charges. Cleaver, who has been a visiting professor at Benjamin N. Cardozo School of Law in New York, and at the History Department and African American Studies Program at Yale, has taught legal ethics, torts, and a legal history seminar entitled "The American Law of Slavery and Anti-Slavery." She is a member of the editorial board of *New Political Science,* and her writing has appeared in numerous magazines and newspapers, including *Ramparts,* the *Black Panther,* the *Village Voice,* the *Boston Globe,* and *Transition,* and she has contributed scholarly essays to the books *Critical Race Feminism, Critical White Studies,* and *The Black Panther Party Reconsidered.* She is completing *Memories of Love and War,* a memoir forthcoming from Random House.

Michael L. Clemons is an associate professor of political science and director of the Institute for the Study of Race and Ethnicity at Old Dominion University (Norfolk, Virginia). His research interests include African-American political mobilization and development. His publications have appeared in the *Review of Black Political Economy, Southeastern Political Review,* and the *Journal of Black Studies.* He has also published several book chapters. <mclemons@odu.edu>

Donald Cox, who was managing a printing company and active in CORE (Congress of Racial Equality) in San Francisco, joined the BPP during 1968. Designated a Field Marshal and assigned to the Central Committee, Cox coordinated the Eastern Region of the Black Panther Party following the wave of mass arrests that rocked the Party during 1969. In 1970 he was secretly indicted for conspiracy to commit murder in Baltimore. Leaving the country clandestinely as soon as he discovered the charges against him, Cox joined the staff of the International Section of the Black Panther Party in Algeria. He has remained exiled, and currently lives in southern France, where he writes, conducts historical research, and grows lavender for the local perfume industry. <ivoire@wanadoo.fr>

Claudia Dahlerus is a research associate with the Center for Comparative Politics at the University of Colorado, Boulder. She is currently finishing her dissertation, entitled *Contentious Consolidations: Assessing State Repression against Political Challenges during Democratization.* Her research interests include comparative human rights and examining how repression varies according to challenges from specific dissident populations. Other interests are democratization, the measurement/analysis of human rights, and contentious political behavior (i.e. protest movements and repression). In addition, she recently organized a special panel talk on women's political activism titled "'Sisters Doin' It for Themselves': Mobilizing Women's Communities." She also is project coordinator for data collection and supervised a twenty-member team of coders for two National Science Foundation projects. <dahlerus@sobek.Colorado.EDU>

Christian A. Davenport is an associate professor of political science at the University of Maryland at College Park as well as a senior fellow and director of research at the Center for International Development and Conflict Management. His primary research interests include human rights violations, social movements, measurement, and racism. He is the author of numerous articles appearing in the *American Political Science Review,* the *American Journal of Political Science,* the *Journal of Politics, Political Research Quarterly, Social Science Quarterly,* the *Journal of Conflict Resolution, Electoral*

Studies, the *Journal of Political and Military Sociology,* and the *Monthly Review* (among others). One edited volume has recently been published, *Paths to State Repression: Human Rights Violations and Contentious Politics,* and he is currently working on a book entitled *The Rashomon Effect in the Social Sciences: The News Media, State Repression, and the Importance of Perspective.* <cdavenport@cidcm.umd.edu>

Erika Doss teaches art history and directs the American Studies Program at the University of Colorado, Boulder. She is the author of several books and numerous articles on American and contemporary art, including most recently *Elvis Culture: Fans, Faith and Image.* <doss@spot.Colorado.EDU>

Scott Fleming, a criminal defense attorney from Oakland, California, represents the Angola 3. He graduated from UC Berkeley's Boalt Hall School of Law and is the director of the National Lawyers Guild Prison Law Project. <scott@prisonactivist.org>

Errol Anthony Henderson is a community activist in Detroit, who earned his Ph.D. in political science at the University of Michigan and is associate professor of political science at Wayne State University, where he teaches world politics. He is the author of *Afrocentrism and World Politics* and publications in *International Studies Quarterly, Journal of Politics, Journal of Conflict Resolution, Journal of Peace Research, World Affairs, Peace & Change,* and the *Journal of Black Studies.* <e.henderson@wayne.edu>

Geronimo ji Jaga, formerly Elmer "Geronimo" Pratt, arrived on the UCLA campus in 1968 on the GI Bill, a decorated Vietnam vet. Recruited into the Black Panther Party, he became the defense minister for the Los Angeles chapter upon Alprentice Carter's 1969 assassination at UCLA, and was soon targeted by the Los Angeles police and FBI for "neutralization." Framed on murder charges, ji Jaga won his release in 1997 on a habeas petition after twenty-seven years in California prisons. A seasoned human rights advocate, ji Jaga now devotes himself to securing the release of political prisoners left behind the walls. <ekpe@petronet.net>

Charles E. Jones is an associate professor and the founding chair of the Department of African American Studies at Georgia State University in Atlanta, Georgia. He previously taught at Old Dominion University, where he served as the director of the Institute for the Study of Minority Issues and associate professor of political science. He has published articles in the *Journal of Black Studies, Legislative Studies Quarterly, Southeastern Political Review, Phylon,* the *Western Journal of Black Studies, Review of Black Political Economy,* and the *National Political Science Review.* A member of the editorial board of *New Political Science,* Professor Jones is the editor of *The Black Panther Party Reconsidered* and is co-authoring a manuscript with Judson L. Jeffries tentatively entitled *Vanguard of the People: An Analytic History of the Black Panther Party, 1966–1982.* <aadcej@panther.Gsu.EDU>

George Katsiaficas is editor of *New Political Science,* author of *The Imagination of the New Left: A Global Analysis of 1968,* and a longtime activist. His book *The Subversion of Politics: European Social Movements and the Decolonization of Everyday Life* won the 1998 Michael Harrington award. With Rodolfo D. Torres, he edited *Latino Social Movements: Historical and Theoretical Perspectives.* He teaches at Chonnam National University in Korea and is working on a study of Korean social movements. <katsiaficas@wit.edu>

Dr. John T. McCartney taught at Purdue University from 1970 to 1979. From 1979 to 1986, he was chairman of the Vanguard Party in the Bahamas, and he is the author of the book *Black Power Ideologies*. He has taught in the Department of Black Government and Law at Lafayette College since 1986, and has been chairman of the department since the fall of 1998. He is the recipient of numerous teaching awards. <panovecr@lafayette.edu>

Ruth Reitan has a master of arts degree in international studies and is the author of *The Rise and Decline of an Alliance: Cuba and African American Leaders in the 1960s.* <r_reitan@bellsouth.net>

Russell (Maroon) Shoats is currently a prisoner in the "control unit" of the Waynesburg Pennsylvania State Institution. He was a founding member of the Black Unity Council, a group that merged with the Philadelphia chapter of the Black Panther Party in 1969. Since his conviction in 1972 for the 1970 assault on a Philadelphia police station in response to the unjustified killing of an African-American youth, he has twice escaped. Shoats has been imprisoned in the "hole" for seventeen years. He remains a committed New Afrikan Freedom Fighter.

Akinyele Omowale Umoja is an assistant professor of African-American studies at Georgia State University. Umoja's primary research focuses on African-American political and cultural resistance movements. He is currently completing a manuscript entitled *Eye for an Eye: the Role of Armed Resistance in the Mississippi Freedom Movement.*

Victor Wallis teaches in the General Education Department at the Berklee College of Music. He previously taught for many years in Indiana, where he was active in support of prisoners' rights struggles. He is on the editorial board of *New Political Science.* <ZENDIVE@aol.com>

Index